MW00823773

Dance, Somatics and Spiritualities

Dance, Somatics and Spiritualities
Contemporary Sacred Narratives

Edited by Amanda Williamson, Glenna Batson,
Sarah Whatley and Rebecca Weber

intellect Bristol, UK / Chicago, USA

First published in the UK in 2014 by
Intellect, The Mill, Parnall Road, Fishponds, Bristol, BS16 3JG, UK

First published in the USA in 2014 by
Intellect, The University of Chicago Press, 1427 E. 60th Street,
Chicago, IL 60637, USA

A catalogue record for this book is available from the
British Library.

Cover designer: Holly Rose
Cover image: Top left – Meredith Haggerty and Kayoko Arakawa,
    photograph by Teri Koenig; top middle – Ju/'hoan Bushman
    dancers, photograph by Patrick Hill; Top right – Amanda Williamson,
    photograph by Scott Closson; Middle – Jill Green, photograph
    by Talani Torres; Bottom left – Julie Rothschild, photograph by
    Julie Rothschild; Bottom right – Rebecca Weber, photograph
    by Weston Aenchbacher.
Copy-editing: MPS Technologies
Production managers: Jessica Mitchell and Tim Elameer
Typesetting: Contentra Technologies

Print ISBN: 978-1-78320-178-5
ePDF ISBN: 978-1-78320-289-8
ePUB ISBN: 978-1-78320-290-4

Printed and bound by TJ International Ltd, Padstow, Cornwall

In memory of Jill Hayes (24.9.1959 – 27.2.2014)

moonshine, root and rock, wildflower

Contents

Acknowledgements

The creation and inception of this international anthology took a long time. We would like to extend our thanks and gratitude to Intellect, and to all the authors and peer reviewers involved in this project—there were many times when we had to wait for each other to revise, or consolidate ideas. This extensive teamwork involved patience and endurance—thank you—to all of you—for your perseverance and creative visions.

Thanks from Amanda Williamson to Scott Closson, Tala Olive Closson and Rafferty Stewart for their love, support and guidance throughout this project. A special thanks to Jill Hayes and Chichester University.

This anthology grew simultaneously with the development of *The Journal of Dance, Movement and Spiritualities* (Intellect), and the existing *Journal of Dance and Somatic Practices* (Intellect).

The book was sponsored by Mary Abrams, Director of Moving Body Resources (MBR), New York.

Preface

Don Hanlon Johnson

1. Graffiti

After spending some two years sifting through the many texts that comprise this volume, finding a path through them, wondering, inspired, I ask: what am I left with that moves me to keep my fingers moving on this keyboard? What needs to be written here?

Strangely, what comes are not the more obvious themes of this book, but something easily forgotten, like our breathing, yet terribly relevant, shaping the whole project. It is the physicality of a community of gifted, experienced, bodily aware scholars with much to contribute to a broken world moving fingers across keyboards. Like the physicality in other gestures and activities of life, this too deserves an inquiry into the traces of keyboarding haunting our thinking and words.

Making texts by keyboarding is radically different from putting chisel to stone, quill to parchment, brush to vellum, stick to bar of soap, pen to paper, spray can to concrete. Unlike those more fleshy ways of communicating, the typewriter and the computer create the illusion that one writing is something like a Cartesian ghost sending messages to its host machine through an ether. And yet paradoxically, writing in these chapters is about the body and its movements. Because we spend a good portion of our time exploring the wilds of the body in lively movement and quiet perception, keyboarding can seem pale, ghostly, and hard to coordinate with the heft of what is learned directly.

I think of the Russian poet Irina Radushinskaya who wrote what she called the soap poems in the gulag. Arrested with her husband for her activities in *samizdat*, separated from him and taken to Siberia in the final days before *perestroika*, she used old match-sticks to scratch out poems on her allotment of soap, keeping the scrawls until she had memorized them, then washing them away. When she was finally liberated, she wrote them all down.

I will cross the land—
in a convoy…
commit it all—

to memory—they won't take it away!
How we breathe—
each breath outside law.
What we stay alive by—
until tomorrow.

(Radushinskaya 1987: 27)

That image of her on those bone-chilling days of hunger and weariness in the camp, struggling to get down the words to anchor and make sense of her experiences, is a symbol for the difficulties in giving words to what is not commonly expressed and the crucial importance of doing so. She stands as a sober reminder to us, raised in warm classrooms and libraries, sitting at our iMacs, with dictionaries and spellchecks, cursing the inadequacies of language to express our precious experiences.

Anne Carson is a poet and classics scholar. Like the dancer-scholars in this volume, her work demands that she bridge the gap between the dense world of poetry and the abstract realms of the academy.

I have struggled since the beginning to drive my thought out into the landscape of science and fact where other people converse logically and exchange judgments—but I go blind out there. So writing involves some dashing back and forth between that darkening landscape where facticity is strewn and a windowless room cleared of everything I do not know. It is the clearing that takes time. It is the clearing that is a mystery.

(Carson 1999: vii)

She turns to the ancient Greek poet Simonides of Keos and the German poet Paul Celan as special examples of people who have maneuvered across that gap. Simonides was constrained by what he could chisel on a stone slab of a defined shape. Paul Celan had already shaped himself as a poet in the language of those who murdered his family. After that tragic event and the others of the Holocaust, he could not but wrestle with that vocabulary and syntax as he continued to create the tortured language of his poems.

Unlike us easily gliding across the keys in our comfortable rooms, spewing forth words as easily as breaths, they were confronted each moment by the shapes and volumes of what they were writing. Like Chinese calligraphers and Benedictine scribes, they had to pay as much attention to the formation of each word and phrase as a dancer does to the flow of movements. As those ancient writers crossed the gap between direct experience and the page, it would be hard for them not to notice the movements of the body itself in the writing and thinking. Not so with the ease at which our keyboards appear to transmit our thoughts directly onto the screen.

In the chapters that follow, you find a document crafted by people like Radushinskaya and Carson who, with most of their lives embedded in the dense world of intense experience are faced with the need to communicate out of their enormous treasures of insights, not simply moving to the winds or the music but to the demands of a keyboard. The crossover

Figure 1: Me, dog and ancient sequoia. Photographer: Barbara Holifield.

is unimaginably demanding and fraught with challenges that endanger doing justice to the depths of experiential knowledge one has worked so hard to achieve.

In this volume, we are dealing with the emergence of the voices of 'the' body, or 'our' bodies, of blood pulsing, of muscular strength and weakness, of air's flowing through and around us, of touch and being touched, voices that had been silenced by the European Enlightenment which enshrined a disembodied reason, divorced from what was argued to be the deceptive, seductive, confusing voices of a *corpus* or a *res extensa*. That imagined metaphysical rupture also divorced direct experience from language and concept, so that the model of academic achievement was high abstraction. The 'body's' wisdom hovers in the same realm as the wisdom of women, tribal peoples, marginalized populations, and children. Intricate words and syntaxes have been eviscerated by the dominant abstractions of power. Many of us have suffered the language abuses of the abstract academic conventions. Susan Griffin compares these conventions to the dissociated language of the Pentagon (Griffin

1992: 62). The Argentinian scholar Maria Julia Carozzi calls them a systemic language of denial (Carozzi 2005: 25). You will find in these pages much wrestling with language crossing back and forth between the verbal and nonverbal doing the careful archaeological sifting to find the articulations buried under centuries of repression.

Ray Schwartz commenting on his difficulties of locating the body-appropriate words writes in his chapter of how one particular Somatics community, that of Moshe Feldenkrais, works systematically with the recovery of language in service of bodily intelligence:

> When I began my Feldenkrais training, I was struck by the way words were used in such a precise way. As part of the methodology of 'Awareness through Movement™,' the teacher does not demonstrate the movements contained in the lesson. Rather, he describes them with precise and specific language. A good teacher can be very exacting in his descriptions and the students are able to find their own relationship to the instructions. In this way, the students are not modelling the actions of something outside of themselves but are invited to engage with their own patterns and habits as a way of knowing themselves better. In learning this method, I became fascinated with the subtext implied in the words chosen to describe things. To say 'move your body,' or 'lift your arm' was to emphasize the body as an object, something passive, without its own intelligence, that we controlled and which was subject to the whims of a separate entity in the pilot's seat.
>
> Master teachers in the training often made statements like 'feel the contact with the floor,' 'observe the self rising and falling,' or 'lift the arm' rather than 'lift your arm.' As subtle a difference as it is, these language choices seemed to me to be an attempt to amend the Cartesian split, to reunify body, mind and spirit in to a single integer—a self—which could describe the integrated whole that we are energetically activating when we enter into somatic processes. In my own work, I often use the term 'self' rather than 'body.' I find it slightly more expansive and thus slightly more available to contain the wholeness with which I wish to engage.
>
> (this volume: 318)

It is not words that betray our deeper experiences, but banal words, ready-made words, truisms, slogans, ethereal generalized words. The poet, literary novelist, songwriter, spoken word hip-hopper: words for them are juicy, powerful, moving, earthy, leading us to an even more complex experience of reality rather than washing out its colours.

Under the radar of intellectual history, slipping through the cracks of peer review has been a slowly emerging revolution in thinking and writing about thinking to which these authors contribute. In contrast to the old spectator model of the quiet scholar, putting aside all the restlessnesses of everyday life in his quiet study or lab and thinking great thoughts, we have here a new (and older) model of thinking arising from movement itself. As we dance, we penetrate more deeply into the meaning of things and we come together in a sharing of the new revelations and generate more profound communal knowledge. Hillel Schwartz named it the 'new kinaesthetics of torque,' (Schwartz 1992: 75). He argued that, contrary to the popular complaint, the contemporary image of the body is not edging more and more towards the mechanical but towards the sensually twisting, turning, reaching, stretching, inquiring organism that began to emerge during the great movement and dance revolutions of the late 19th and 20th century—revolutions in which these dancer-writers have taken a major part. Up to that period, the ideal in the West was embodied in classical dance with its upwards-soaring emphasis, minimal contact of foot and ground, rigid gender roles, and hierarchy: exact mirrors of the enlightenment notion of reason.

A very different kind of experience is revealed in what Anne Carson refers to as that dashing back and forth between the imaginative world of direct experience to the abstract world of academic language. That dashing is actually where one gets a particularly vivid experience of the process of thinking itself and the ways in which that process is not well accepted or even articulated in the academic and scientific world.

Susan Leigh Foster, another dance-scholar, coined the phrase 'ambulant scholarship' to articulate a different approach to intellectual activity emerging from thinkers who are also experienced movers:

> As a body in motion, the writing-and-written body puts into motion the bodies of all those who would observe it. It demands a scholarship that detects and records movements of the writer as well as the written about, and it places at the center of investigation the changing positions of these two groups of bodies and the co-motion that orchestrates as it differentiates their identities. This ambulant form of scholarship thus acknowledges an object of study that is always in the making and also always vanishing. It claims for the body, in anxious anticipation of this decade's collapse of the real and the simulated into a global 'informatics of domination,' an intense physicality and a reflexive generativity.
>
> (Foster 1995: 16)

These dancer-scholars are thinking differently because they are deliberately thinking *out of* their lives of conscious movement, allowing words to come from it, fresh words and concepts. Kimerer LaMothe makes this a central point of her chapter, whose title alludes to the Nietzschean challenge she poses to exclusively sedentary intellectuals: 'Can They Dance?':

> We need to cultivate a sensory awareness of the movements making us that will guide us in creating and becoming patterns of sensation and response that honor the sources of our living… It is not something our minds can claim for us; it is a strength and sensitivity our bodily selves *receive* when our thinking bends to attend to the movements we are making and how they are making us.
>
> (this volume: 147)

LaMothe, a farmer, tellingly uses the word 'cultivate,' a series of actions sustained over the long seasons, a word which figures largely in the critique the late Japanese philosopher Yuasa Yasuo makes against the dominant Western model of reason:

> What might we discover to be the philosophical uniqueness of Eastern thought? One revealing characteristic is that personal 'cultivation' is presupposed in the philosophical

foundation of Eastern theories. To put it simply, true knowledge cannot be obtained simply by means of theoretical thinking, but only through 'bodily recognition or realization,' that is, through the utilization of one's total mind and body. Simply stated, this is to 'learn with the body,' not the brain. Cultivation is a practice that attempts, so to speak, to achieve true knowledge by means of one's total mind and body.

(Yuasa 1987: 25)

LaMothe's phrase—'our thinking bends...'—suggests the unique kind of wisdom gained by those engaged in growing things, people used to bending towards the earth, the humus, humble, not uprightly arrogant.

In a similar vein, Helen Poynor writes:

My approach facilitates a kinesthetic encounter with the natural environment: the moving human being is engaged with it in a responsive exchange. This is an encounter between the physicality of the body and the materiality of the landscape: a meeting of rock, earth, water and wind with bone, muscle, blood and breath. The environment becomes the teacher, different elements and changing weather elicit different experiences of the body and different movement qualities. I use the term 'natural' to indicate an environment in which elements such as cliffs, sea, rock, earth and trees predominate rather than man-made structures, while acknowledging that such elements are frequently subject to human influence.

(this volume: 213)

Eugene Gendlin argues that a common mistake which hinders our moving from experience into language is the assumption that the function of words is to mirror or photograph what is 'inside' the mind or in experience. If that were the case, it is evident that our experiences are infinitely more interesting than dull photographs of them in abstract language. But if you look at the way we actually feel a need for words, it is because they move us forward; they do things in the very way that gestures do. We speak and write because we bump up against problems that stump us and we need help. The words carry us further into getting it. Or we feel we've found something important that, if communicated, will enrich our being together. In mainstream academic culture, words, like the body itself, have been etherealized. And yet they, like our bodies, are things: material, sonic, audible, visible realities that are affecting changes in our experience just like these lattice-like lines in front of you now (Gendlin 1992: 342).

The solution Gendlin proposes—the heart of his widely used method 'focusing'—is to slow down the rush to verbalize, settling more deeply into our experience waiting for words to come, just as, in many movement disciplines, we wait for movements to come instead of making up gestures. The evidence that our language is in fact coming from experience instead of being pasted onto it is in the felt sense of resolution when the 'right' words are found: the sigh of relief, the 'ahas' marking a shift in experience.

Making sense of these things requires the enormously difficult task of recovering language from its dissociated heights in academic/scientific jargon or from its debased commercial uses, back to its guttural origins in breathing, gesturing, moaning, only through long journeys gathering words that mean and matter, that link blood to ink.

2. The Experiential Treeline

One of the most dangerous chasms to cross is the abyss between the lush fields of experience and the high-altitude tundras of spiritual language. Amanda Williamson's work in this volume with Martha Eddy, Rebecca Weber, Glenna Batson and Sarah Whatley, along with her earlier work, provide an authoritative and comprehensive map of the territory. I add only this:

A. A reflection on the process itself of leaping across the gap between experiences and verbal expressions about spirituality.
B. Remarks on the relation between the incipient spiritualities of these communities of movement and those of pre-colonial tribal communities and of post-colonial primal movements like butoh and Continuum.

A. Leaping

Too often, those moving from intense and profound personal experiences into 'spiritual' language make the Christopher Columbus mistake of proclaiming that they have found a new world, not knowing it has already been found, inhabited, and highly civilized for millennia before they took sight of it. The dangers here are apparent everywhere: look at the popes, ayatollahs, chief rabbis, gurus new and old—men in costumes (a very small percentage of women) telling everyone else what they should do and think because they each lay claim to spiritual authority. The divisions among these tenacious claims continue to tear apart our world, with vast ideologically committed populations claiming authority over other populations with differently held, equally tenacious counter-beliefs, all in the name of spiritual values.

The writers in this volume are experts in preparing for the leap. They call their students into the minutely specific intricacies of our earthly being: cells, lungs, arteries, spinal and seminal fluids, bones and muscles: humus, soil, earth, humility. Those evocations slow one down so that old ready-made phrases fall away in the face of more vital new words and thoughts that bloom forth in the silence.

This passage from the late Charlotte Selver, a pioneer in the practice of Sensory Awareness, is typical of the way many in this community have discovered links between transcendent experiences achieved in simple bodily processes like sensing and traditional modes of describing spirituality:

> What people call 'mystic'—the experiences one has, for instance in breathing, in balance, or whatever it is, in contact with another person—this can be very clearly experienced and yet experienced as a wonder, too. In other words, I feel it would be marvelous if one could work to pin-point certain very clear revelations, which come out of experience and which in themselves are astonishing. The revelations can come from the very smallest experience. For instance, eating.
>
> (Selver 1977: 17)

But it is not so easy to distinguish between the kinds of fervour associated with intense devotion to a formal religion with its exclusive claims to absolute truth, and what is meant here by 'spirituality.' Many scholars have attempted to extricate themselves from these confusions by moving into a universalism that abstracts from the particularity of our yearning bodies. The work of these scholars is important in placing the body at the core of spirituality.

One of the formative experiences of my understanding of the relation between language, thought, and the spiritual occurred during a long summer half a century ago when I stumbled upon a little known yet widespread tradition in the writings of Christian, Jewish, and Muslim mystic theologians: the *via negativa*. As a Jesuit philosophy student I was working my way through the complete works of Thomas Aquinas in Latin. As I struggled my way through the medieval syntax and scholastic formalisms, I eventually found my way to the climax of his long treatises on so-called 'proofs' for the existence of God, where to my shock he argued that the peak of human reasoning is to arrive at the humbling understanding that anything we assert about God cannot be true precisely because God is what absolutely transcends anything we can say. On the one hand, this line of reasoning seemed strange because it countered all I had been taught; on the other, it made perfect sense in its giving full acknowledgement to the utter transcendence of mystical experience, of which I had had glimpses in my meditation practice, over rational explanations.

Pursuing Aquinas's arguments, I would go on to find that there has always been an undercurrent of what had been named the *via negativa*, the negative path, in Christian, Islamic, Judaic, and Vedic mystical theologies: long intricate arguments for the nature of divinity are allowed to cascade to where they eventually curl back on themselves and crash, knowingly, on the shores of the infinite. This medieval tradition presages what Eugene Gendlin would later articulate: that language cannot capture reality like a camera taking a scene. Its function is to carry us ever further towards the real. In this case, the intricacies of these complex theological exercises took their authors to that brink where they were overwhelmed by the majesty of the vastness that encompasses us all, impossible to capture, but susceptible of experiential awe, joyous song and dance.

In terms of this volume and our subcommunity, it is important to recognize that there is a crucial difference between the *via negativa* and just saying words cannot do justice to direct experience. The former creates a knife-edge of discernment that keeps one from claiming 'spiritual authority,' mitigating any urges towards mystical megalomania by creating what might be called a metaphysical humility. It showed dramatically in the last years of Aquinas's life. One day after saying mass, he turned to his server and said that after the experiences he had there, his writings seemed like straw. For the remaining two years of his life, he did not return to writing, and died leaving his major work unfinished.

The luminous and liberating realizations of the *via negativa*, the results of a life of struggling with language, gives a context not only for understanding the struggles of these authors but of a widespread movement throughout the world to recover or, perhaps better, create a shared spirituality purged of the viruses that have contaminated what has gone before: sexism, authoritarianism, dissociation from the body, disrespect for non-human realities, dogmatisms. The struggle is for a shared love for what is given us: the earth, air, water, animals, plants, hearts and brains and genitals. This movement has to work hard like salmon going upstream to their breeding pools, climbing against the tenacious forces of regression: the Taliban, Christian and Hindu fundamentalists, scientific dogmatists, Artificial Intelligence transcendentalists, and a host of others who would consider our earth and bodies but moments in a more important life.

B. The Archaic

In their chapter, Hillary and Bradford Keeney write of their work among the *Ju/'hoansi* Bushmen, who embody what must be among the closest similarities to the consciousness possessed by our ancestors at our evolutionary origins. In the Keeney's account, the dances are aimed at the evocation of what they call *n/om* (life force, spirit, *duende*). They make this telling observation about the enormous amount of literature about the Bushmen:

> Though the Bushmen were arguably studied more than any other culture in anthropology, their healing dance epistemology has evaded scholars' attempts to pin it down…
>
> Their most valued form of experience, knowledge and teaching is somatically held. More specifically, the movements and sensations of their body in relationship and interaction with others constitute their way of knowing and being. They are a dancing culture. They know through dance and what they dance includes their arms and legs, as well as their ideas, emotions and laughter. Their world moves, like the changing seasons, and they move with it, valuing the constant movement and change more than any particular frozen moment.
>
> (this volume: 361–2)

This passage—'They are a dancing culture. They know through dance and what they dance includes their arms and legs, as well as their ideas…'—cuts right to the core notion that makes it so difficult for Western intellectuals to grasp what these dancing scholars are working to express.

Jill Hayes joins an old world of wisdom teaching when she writes of the profound difference it makes to open oneself to the world of spirit in dealing with a life-threatening illness:

> I felt that it was vital to feel and express the suffering I had been carrying in my womb as well as to access the stream of healthy life which I sensed in subtle movements inside my body. I felt that this womb-suffering was mine, but that it was more than just mine alone. In my suffering, I felt the suffering of my grandmother who had died young of this same cancer. I felt the suffering of the Earth too, in the attacks on her body and the attempts to control her wild creativity. It seemed to me that I had been a part of a pattern of neglect and control in my loss of relationship with my own body and with my own creativity. I believed that by way of the body I would awaken creativity again. I wanted to breathe life into every cell of my body (just as Sophia does) to reawaken my capacity to sense and feel my inner life, and I hoped that this somatic awareness would rejoin me with a greater swell of creativity. Through my body, I could be in active relationship with the delicate hidden life of organic forms all around me.
>
> (this volume: 65–66)

Her essay is so important in addressing the topic of how moving in depth, into and through suffering, opens one's heart to the world, finding the compassion that so many spiritual traditions have made the ultimate goal of their works.

Celeste Snowber expresses how all these themes intertwine:

> The body, through dance, becomes the place where the invisible and visible meet and physicality and spirituality are intertwined. This is not a spirituality for the mind, but a space which opens all that is within the heart and soul, hidden in the recesses of the body. It is a place where mystery dwells, and the life force, however one articulates it, can be in communion with flesh. When the body is spoken of, too often it is referred to as a disembodied text and an object, rather than the lived body, which has sweat, tears, moans, sighs and has the capacity for both paradox and deep joy. This chapter weaves the call to have a poetic and sensuous language, which honours embodied knowing as a place to articulate a visceral knowledge and wisdom.
>
> (this volume: 117)

As I look back over my own now fairly long sweep of history, it seems that what I might call the axis of spiritual dialogue has shifted from east/west to north/south. Certainly I don't mean this in any rigorous literal sense: there is undoubtedly a strong multidirectional spiritual geography. But it is striking to me how many young people are turning towards the spiritual practices of first nations peoples in the Americas, the Amazon basin, Australia and Africa. The dancing, drumming, chanting described by the Keeneys is emerging as prominent a mode of spiritual practice as quiet sitting meditation. This turn towards archaic cultures seems to me to reflect our growing communal realization of the central role of earth and its creatures in the evolution of our consciousness, now that its very existence is threatened. This movement into the archaic is also reflected in such postmodern practices as butoh and Continuum. Although these arise from a radically contemporary sensibility, they share with the ancient practices an orientation to the most basic movements of the organism, pulsing, twisting, waving like seaweeds in the surf.

Mind, knowing, intellect, reason: these are not something apart from the realm of movement; they emerge from it, are conditioned by it, nurtured by it. The rough edges in Western thought, the places where intellectuals stumble, find their origins in the culture's tragic leaving behind the rich pre-verbal world into which we are born.

Jayne Stevens ends her heart-rendingly beautiful account of the work of Akram Khan's with this quote from him that cuts to the soul of this volume:

There is just 'us', or 'we' left behind, a collection of artists, of different disciplines, different languages, different cultures, different education, but we are all in the same room, in silence, and all our passionate gestures and fierce negotiations, have come to a standstill, and with it, a sense that we all want a single 'truth', that this journey together has to end up giving birth to our creation [...] that somehow, we as individuals, are like small jigsaw pieces, but together, we form a single, but powerful and larger fuller picture.

(Khan 2011a)

References

Carson, A. (1999), *The Economy of the Unlost*, Princeton, NJ: Princeton University Press.

Carozzi, M. J. (2005), 'Talking minds: The scholastic construction of intercorporeal discourse', *Body & Society*, 11, pp. 25–34.

Foster, S. L. (1995), 'Choreographing History', in S. L. Foster (ed.), *Choreographing History*, Bloomington, IN: Indiana University, pp. 3–19.

Gendlin, E. (1992), 'The primacy of the body, not the primacy of perception: How the body knows the situation and philosophy', *Man and World*, 25:3–4, pp. 341–353, www.focusing.org.

Griffin, S. (1992), *A Chorus of Stones: The Private Life of War*, New York, NY: Doubleday.

Radushinskaya, I. (1987), *Beyond the Limit* (trans. F. Brent and C. Avins), Chicago, IL: Northwestern University Press, lines from 'For Tanya Osipova and Vanya Kovalev', p. 27.

Schwartz, H. (1992), 'Torque: The new kinaesthetic', in J. Crary and S. Kwinter (eds), *Incorporations*, New York, NY: Zone Press, pp. 71–126.

Selver, C. (1977), 'Interview with Ilana Rubenfeld', *Somatics*, 1:2, pp. 17–20.

Yuasa, Y. (1987), *The Body: Towards an Eastern Mind-Body Theory* (trans. T. Kasulis and N. Shigenori), Albany, NY: SUNY Press.

Introduction

Amanda Williamson, Glenna Batson and Sarah Whatley

This anthology is dedicated to the challenging and provocative subject of 'spiritualities' within the broad domain of 'Somatic Movement Dance Education' (SMDE)—we use the aforementioned term to encompass and delineate a broad and varied international field defined by the integration of somatic movement techniques, and/or the application of somatic principles into Dance and Movement Studies. SMDE arises from a heterogeneous compendium of body-mind disciplines derived from diverse cross-cultural and philosophical sources dating back to the turn of the 20th century that have informed all levels of dance education, praxis and performance. At their core, these disciplines pose a radical view of embodiment by placing perceptual awareness through movement at the centre of dismembering dualism. While the discourse of somatic practices in relation to dance and body-based practices has steadily grown over the last three decades, research into spiritualities within this context remains in its infancy. Our aim therefore is to redress the marginalization of this important topic by opening dialogue in a subject that has eluded wider academic debate. To this end, we bring together in one volume a collection of innovative writings by those committed to the present-day study of spiritualities in SMDE. As the first resource in this field that captures the scope of the topic, we offer the reader a rich collection of chapters from prominent academic authors and movement practitioners from the United Kingdom, the United States and Canada.

Words like 'spirit' and 'spirituality' appear frequently in articles and books within the field of SMDE. While the field is thus clearly body-mind-spirit-centric, paradoxically, the term 'spirituality' remains under-theorized. This publication then, opens a new door, offering innovative research approaches to a subject that rarely finds a place other than at the periphery of university dance curricula and independent training programmes. While spirituality in the broader field of dance 'has retained a degree of centrality in non-Western scholarship, it has struggled to find high-profile platforms for debate and discussion in Western contexts' (Williamson and Hayes 2012: 3). Thus, spiritual experience in Dance Education 'is perhaps one of the most enchanting, yet elusive elements of pedagogical practice—fraught with definitional, conceptual and methodological problems, it is often easier to leave the subject alone' (Williamson 2012: 3). Many authors in this anthology have similarly noted that the subject of spirituality has remained sidelined within the dominant discourses of Dance Studies. Indeed, while 'the study of spirituality and non-Western dance forms is widely appreciated, scant attention is paid to contemporary experiences of spirituality in Western educational dance/movement contexts' (2012: 3). Spirituality often is considered beyond 'the realms of rationality, materiality, logic and reason—the ineffable by definition is inexpressible and thus beyond words' (Williamson 2010: 38). We hope that this collection will therefore address the need for intelligent conversation and discourse to ground the ephemeral, fleeting and elusive nature of spirituality.

By adopting the term 'spiritualities', we are acknowledging the spiritual diversity, heterogeneity, eclecticism, plurality and syncretistic expressions inherent within this anthology. In acknowledging that '[t]he diversification of spirituality globally is central and pivotal to this growing research area,' (Williamson and Hayes 2012: 3) we bring together writings that are purposefully inclusive of different faith orientations and personal spiritual expressions. Each author explores his or her topic with personal voice. Each enquiry, in turn, reflects wider dimensions of the Euro-American holistic spiritual landscape—extensively typified by poly-variant expressions, often religiously non-traditional and oriented towards embodied practices.

Hence, the plural 'spiritualities' in the title of this anthology seeks to push the limitations of the singular 'spirituality'—a term often used in Dance Studies without critique or investigation. Additionally the singular has a monocultural, Eurocentric and androcentric connotation and overtone. In contrast, the plural seeks to embrace, reflect and engage with a dimension of Dance Studies that is spiritually diverse and fluid and evidently marked by global exchange. Thus the plural acknowledges the cross-cultural, intercultural and multicultural discourses that shape the continued growth of Dance Studies internationally. This statement is not without its problems, for some theorists may still view the plural through a Eurocentric lens—a spiritual heritage imposed on world cultures that do not possess equivalent dualities such as matter/spirit and heavenly/earthly. However, the plural endeavours to embrace cognate terms in other cultures, recognizing that the term 'spirituality' has gained cross-cultural and intercultural currency and is extensively articulated beyond the dualistic constraints and androcentric roots of Christianity. It is also commonly expressed and experienced through immanental, rather than transcendental practices. Finally, it may be linked to external socio-cultural/political pursuits, and is poly-variant in its global expressions, vicissitudes and fusions. Thus, it continues to fluidly mutate while travelling across cultural boundaries. The plural, for some, may serve to agitate and dismantle the sexist, dualistic and imperialist power of the religious meta-narrative by acknowledging a multiplicity of viewpoints and spiritual histories, inviting voices of difference. Perhaps for others, the plural 'spiritualities' encapsulates and augments a postmodern milieu: the impossibility of spiritual or religious truth; the partiality of truth; the deconstruction of the religious metanarrative; and the consequent spiritual freedoms to imagine, create, choose, synthesize, explore, debate and question (Williamson and Hayes 2014: 14)

Mapping the Field: Sketching the Landscape

As noted above, we use the term 'Somatic Movement Dance Education' to encapsulate a diverse educative field defined by the integration of somatic movement techniques, and/or the application of somatic principles into Dance and Movement Studies. Within university contexts, one can observe distinctive areas—such as, the application and integration of a particular somatic technique: Ideokinesis, Body-Mind Centering®, Laban Bartenieff

Movement Fundamentals, Skinner Releasing Technique, Feldenkrais and the Alexander Technique (Brodie and Lobel 2004, 2006; Fortin and Girard 2005). Further applications can be found in the integration of shared somatic principles into dance pedagogy (Batson and Schwartz 2007), such as 'the four fundamental principles found in somatic disciplines': 'sensing the environment', 'connection to breath', 'connection to ground' and somatically conscious movement 'initiations' (Brodie and Lobel 2004: 80–87). Other applications also share somatic principles, such as deepening improvisational movement strategies underpinned by 'deep-body listening', 'attentive connection with body-self', 'attentive connections to others', 'depth-support-in-movement', 'sensory comfort and pleasure' and 'attentive connection to the imagination' (Williamson 2010). Also of interest are the application of Jungian and post-Jungian theories into dance and movement, such as Authentic Movement; and the application of somatic principles to dance and movement within the realms of expressive arts and transpersonal psychologies. Many pedagogies are underscored by eco-somatic principles and approaches (Bauer 2008; Enghauser 2007). Of these themes and practices, many are the subject of the chapters that follow. The authors in this compendium address what might be seen as more obvious links between contemporary spirituality and somatic movement exploration. Searching for embodied wholeness, health, vitality, balance, integration and connection, for example, are aspects of the holistic spirituality paradigm—a paradigm simultaneously embraced and explored within the field of SMDE.

In the studio and lecture theatre, however, the word 'spirituality' may elicit a range of responses. These responses span a spectrum from those who celebrate and embrace the word with enthusiasm and curiosity, to those who are highly skeptical and critical. In academic contexts, the word can evoke joy and interest, or provoke acute discomfort. Essential to initiating a serious approach to studying spirituality is first to recognize that the word is potentially problematic and controversial. Most notably, the word is at once rooted in traditional connotations, yet applied widely in non-traditional venues and contexts. On the one hand, contemporary spirituality implies inclusivity, encompassing a wide variety of religious practices and secular activities cross-culturally (King 2009). On the other hand, the origin of the word largely is Christian. While loosened from its patriarchal construction and framework considerably, the word 'spirituality' is nonetheless historically associated with a male-centred, heterosexist and imperialist religion (Plaskow and Christ 1989; Christ and Plaskow 1992; Daly 1973). The topic of the body within spirituality still suffers from centuries of codified religious suppression, Cartesian dualism, and Puritanism. Theological terms such as 'sacred', 'soul' and 'divinity' remain lodged in conceptions of socio-cultural repression and ideological disassociation of body, mind and spirit. Even though the word extends beyond the boundaries of institutionalized Christianity, its male-centred dualistic roots denigrate the body, flesh, nature, women and immanence. This atmosphere persistently causes tension and disquiet in the lecture theatre and particularly in Dance Studies—a subject often dedicated to the body as an integral resource for and site of sacrality and intelligence and, in some genres, redemptive mystery. To use Mary Daly's words, the 'patriarchal possession' of the body may put people off engaging in the subject of spirituality, significantly and with ease (1973). Notably, these patriarchal associations are particularly uncomfortable after the arrival of feminist spirituality, which advanced post-patriarchal, socio-spiritual values (Daly 1973; Plaskow and Christ 1989).

Historically the word is associated with socio-cultural abuses, such as the exclusion and subordination of women. It therefore is naturally subject to scrutiny and suspicion in a field where women's voices are strong, and where the fleshy body is so visible and central in academic discourse. However, even though dualistic gendered religious symbols are somewhat entrenched in our shared Western consciousness, it is also clear that spirituality today has gained cultural currency beyond patriarchal orders of the divine. Spirituality that challenges ingrained dichotomies by holistically embracing body, nature, femininity, sexuality and immanent sacredness clearly offers the antithesis to Western patriarchy (Tacey 2001). New forms of spirituality, particularly holistic or New Age, 'compensates our established religious traditions by forcing us to attend to what has been repressed or ignored by Western religion' (Tacey; preface). Many theological terms have been extensively contemporized and re-formed, yet the body still lacks a voice in the development of emergent and alternative holistic spiritualities in the West. Enter the *moving* body into the intellectual arena, and the conceptual paradoxes between the secular and the sacred loom even larger. Hence this anthology gives voice to body, and particularly the moving body, expressing a collective, deep commitment to embodied spirituality, spiritual democracy and freedom.

Somatic Movement Dance Education as a Site for Spirituality

While spiritual dimensions are embedded in SMDE pedagogy, many of these are uncharted. Little is known about exactly how the spiritual informs educational pedagogy. Confusion arises because the field is not informed or shaped by specific religious traditions. Rather, it is often inspired and informed by principles found in Eastern embodied/bodied traditions (Eddy 2002). Consequently, a great deal of spiritual eclecticism characterizes the field. Wide-ranging principles drawn from diverse spiritual and cultural sources shape and inspire practice. The field is also open 'to non-institutionalized spirituality, and is supportive of self-spirituality and syncretistic spirituality (the formation and expression of personal sacred narratives in movement, dialogue and pedagogy—the mixing and blending of sacred narratives from diverse sources)' (Williamson 2010). The anthology therefore is marked by eclecticism, suggesting a high degree of personal experimentation.

Readers may be struck by the differing methodological approaches developed by the authors. That lies in part because Somatics (and contemporary dance) are reflective of a resurgent interest in embodied and self-spirituality; a counter-revolutionary movement against materialism and mechanistic science and its fragmentation of lived experience. Nonetheless, shared commonalities exist throughout. Many authors draw attention to the internal/external, personal/communal, private/public aspects of spirituality, and in doing so reveal the field's commitment to developing spiritualities that extend beyond the subjective realms of the individual. Subjective (deeply personal) approaches to spirituality are balanced by socially active, politically engaged and communal spiritualities. Socio-spiritual similarities, in particular, are driven by the enduring themes of questioning and dismembering authority and hierarchy. Democracy, freedom and anti-authoritarianism are clear themes across the field. Spirituality 'is [thus] free from the imposition of fixed sacred narratives, of external and intellectually abstracted religious and spiritual ideals' (Williamson 2010: 47). Moreover, many of the chapters point to a relationship (either explicitly or implicitly) with spiritualities associated with the growth of the New Age movement and holistic spirituality. These are varied, but evidently engage in many New Age spiritual themes extensively researched by Paul Heelas (1999) and David Tacey (2001, 2004). Practice, for example, is often shaped by the appreciation of non-Western/pre-modern cultures; eco-literate and earth-centred political commitments/activisms; the application of Eastern principles (particularly breath awareness, cyclical movement forms and meditative/contemplative practices); electric, hybrid and syncretistic spirituality; a commitment to a subjective bodily spirituality (sensuous, sensual, emotional and affective experiences); and the search for unity and connectivity. In addition, one can view broad themes of spirituality in this anthology that bear direct relevance to progressive spirituality, particularly how 'Nature, within progressive spirituality, is typically seen as sacred, as a site of divine life and activity' (Lynch 2007: 53).

Various strands of somatic movement exploration likewise spiritualize or sacralize nature. These are biocentric and eco-literate in trajectory. They seek greater union and communication with the life force within. As well, these explorations seek deeper sensory unification with others, nature and the cosmos; and sacralize the inner self as a site of inspired, inspired intelligence—a valid, close, intimate source of knowledge (Williamson 2010). Notably, SMDE is fundamentally biocentric in its approach to the body and ecology—many somatic movement dance modalities are underpinned by an eco-literacy that works to establish a balanced and healthy relationship with other life-forms and ecologies. The field thus resonates with deep ecology through variant eco-somatic approaches, which 'sees humanity as simply one part of the greater "web of life"' (Capra, in Lynch 2007: 36). Notably, '[i]n its more spiritual forms, deep ecology recognizes the importance of mystical states of consciousness in which the individual person achieves a sense of their deeper unity with all that is' (Lynch 2007: 36–37). In particular, the writings in the anthology coalesce around select themes—unity and depth of connection among them.

Background and Choosing Our Authors

Questions that have informed the development of the anthology include:

- Why are issues of spirituality and religion absent or marginalized in the evolution of somatic theory and practice?
- Why have these issues likewise been sidelined within dance education?

- In what ways can the 'spiritual' and the 'sacred' find a place at the somatic table without either body or knowledge sacrificing somatic authenticity and empowerment?
- Where is spirituality most visible in practice and how can it be theoretically realized/explicated on the academic page?
- Why is it important to theorize spirituality within SMDE for students and facilitators?
- How does theory help concretize *praxis* to ensure an enduring and rigorous discourse?

Taken together, the chapters in the anthology aim to bring more clarity and academic visibility to the largely uncharted and often academically under-represented subject of spirituality; more specifically it aims to clarify how a broad range of embodied sacred narratives are informing pedagogy, as well as educational and therapeutic practice. We invited authors who are world-renowned as practitioners and/or writers, or who are offering what we believe are important contributions to this field of research. Many have been at the forefront of the Somatics movement, having reached prominence through their innovative training and teaching programmes, through influential publications or through a combination of both. The rationale for our choice of contributors is two-fold. First we have drawn together a group of highly influential figures. Although many often work alone, they have established themselves as significant authorities within their respective fields. Secondly, our choice of authors reflects the continuous historical exchange between somatic movement training programmes that operate beyond the constraints of institutionalized academia and those that operate within. Importantly, the pioneering development of somatic movement training programmes developing beyond the strictures of conventional academia have often been the fertile and highly innovative ground to which institutionalized Dance Studies has turned for sustenance and advancement (of many aspects of embodied knowledge—sensory awareness, easeful movement articulation and the metaphorical, symbolic and poetic language of the body). Hence, this anthology includes contributions from authors and practitioners leading non-institutionalized programmes, as well as those teaching within higher education. Representing these different contexts provides the international breadth and scope illustrative of the on-going dialogue and exchange between worlds—worlds that are becoming increasingly integrative. We acknowledge, however, that there are many other scholars and practitioners who might have plenty to add to this subject; the scope of the anthology is representative of current themes, yet not complete. We nonetheless have sourced writings that provide the reader with a comprehensive range of viewpoints and propositions, which collectively forges a new path, and which we hope will encourage other scholars to follow and build upon.

Structuring the Book

With the advent and growth of SMDE internationally (particularly throughout the last three decades), the topic of spirituality merits new attention. However, renewed attention brings forward the paradoxes, arguments and debates, as well as intellectual curiosity.

A central paradox that appears to belie the field is—the field is secular in some quarters, yet intensively spiritual in others. The authors thus do not write with a unified methodological, theoretical or artistic approach. Some authors approach the subject with ease, guided by a clearly confirmed belief structure underpinning their work. Others are more sceptical and questioning of their enquiry. Such richness of theoretical and pedagogical ideas presented us with interesting challenges and questions about how to structure these diverse approaches to the subject, while maintaining clarity and coherence. Accordingly, the anthology does not advocate a singular viewpoint, or a one-track academic vision with regards to the subject of spiritualities and pedagogy, but rather is a lively, assorted (spirited and colourful) collection of works, made distinctive by its differing approaches. Consequently, we present a book that is comprehensive, in its spiritual pluralism and methodological diversity.

Importantly, the trajectory of this anthology is neither historical nor sociological; rather, it reconnoiters ideas of the spiritual primarily through the creative lens of practice-based research (reflection on practice and the production of insightful ideas largely emergent through embodied practice). The authors employ a wide range of disciplinary approaches and methodologies, but all are immersed or interlaced with practice. The sincere and rigorous quality of the research and reflection demonstrates the potential of researching about spirituality through the body and through practice, rather than considering the subject from a disembodied intellectual place. Methodologies include: philosophical critique, case study, auto-ethnography, qualitative studio research and 'ethnographic tales', postpositivist interview methods, conventional interviews, contemplative conversational meditations, arts-based methodologies of embodied enquiry and autobiographical enquiry, pedagogical analysis and reflection and performance research. Chapters are wide-ranging, covering topics from embryological development exploring our earliest relational structures, to alchemy and the meditative movement practices rooted in C. G. Jung's active imagination, to meditations on language, spirit, magic and somatic practice. Other themes explore how shamanic traditions are informing specific training programmes, to the archetypal story of Sophia according to ancient Gnostic visions, to how the mindfulness of Zen Meditation supports and develops somatic movement research. The writing ranges from critiques of Deleuze and Guattari, Jane Bennett, and David Abram, through to unearthing the progressive spiritual values underpinning performance, to the anthropological study of the healing dance of the Ju/'hoansi Bushmen (San) of southern Africa.

The book is divided into three parts. While the themes in each part certainly overlap, each has a discrete trajectory. Part I, "Moving Spiritualities", contains six chapters, offering many accounts of spiritual experiences underpinned by somatic methodologies, such as varied and derivative meditative practices rooted in C. G. Jung and the application of active imagination to movement and dance. Other themes embrace ecological earth-centred approaches to spirituality, dance and movement (a deep moving spiritual immanence developed through eco-somatic literacy and resonance). These authors foreground the *moving, feeling, reflecting body* as integral to spiritual and transformational processes.

Part II, "Reflections on the Intersections of Spiritualities and Pedagogy", is very different in its academic orientation and includes nine chapters that together provide interesting insights into the intersection of spiritualities and pedagogy. Notably, this section does not deal with Jungian and post-Jungian themes, but rather critiques and reflects upon a broad range of pedagogies. Voices of difference express secularized or explicitly sacred pedagogies. Methodologies include postpositivist interview methods, conventional interviews, contemplative conversational meditations, philosophical appraisal and pedagogical analysis and reflection.

Part III, "Cultural Immersions and Performance Excursions", includes five chapters, which are broad in their subject orientations. These chapters reflect on the field of dance and movement studies by considering diverse ways to approach spirituality. The authors write from a cross-cultural perspective. Some of the chapters address spirituality through accessing rituals from other cultures and reflect on whether it is possible for non-Western imports to revitalize spirituality within Western dance pedagogy without misappropriation. These methods are drawn directly (or are adapted mainly from) cultural anthropology. These are sensitively poised narratives with rich (thick) description through case study designs, participant (performer and audience) observation and interviews, immersion with journaling and witnessing, archival and historical analysis and critique within contemporary cultures.

In incorporating these many approaches, explorations and reflections, this three-part anthology offers multiple research avenues for advancing the field of spirituality through dance, Somatics and embodiment. We invite readers to join in the moving narratives, where the *felt lives* of moving bodies dance across the academic page.

References

Bauer, S. (2008), 'Body and earth as one: Strengthening our connection to the natural source with Ecosomatics', *Conscious Dancer,* Spring, pp. 8–9.

Batson, G. and Schwartz, R. (2007), 'Revisiting the value of somatic education in dance training through an inquiry into practice schedules', *Journal of Dance Education*, 7:2, pp. 47–55.

Brodie, J. and Lobel, E. (2004), 'Integrating fundamental principles underlying somatic practices into dance technique class', *Journal of Dance Education*, 4:3, pp. 80–87.

——— (2006), 'Somatics in dance—dance in Somatics', *Journal of Dance Education*, 6:3, pp. 69–71.

Christ, C. and Plaskow, J. (eds) (1992), *Womenspirit Rising: A Feminist Reader in Religion*, New York, NY: HarperCollins.

Daly, M. (1973), *Beyond God the Father: Towards a Philosophy of Women's Liberation*, Boston, MA: Beacon Press.

Eddy, M. (2002), 'Somatic practices and dance: Global influences', *Dance Research Journal*, 34:2, pp. 46–62.

Enghauser, R. (2007), 'The quest for an ecosomatic approach to dance pedagogy', *Journal of Dance Education*, 7:3, pp. 80–90.

Fortin, S. and Ginard, F. (2005), 'Dancer's application of the Alexander Technique', *Journal of Dance Education*, 5: 4, pp. 125–31.

Heelas, P. (1999), *The New Age Movement*, London, UK: Blackwell.

Heelas, P. and Woodhead, L. (2005), *The Spiritual Revolution: Why Religion is Giving Way to Spirituality*, Oxford, UK: Blackwell.

King, U. (2009), *The Search for Spirituality: Our Global Quest for Meaning and Fulfilment*, London, UK: Canterbury Press Norwich.

Lynch, G. (2007), *The New Spirituality: An Introduction to Progressive Belief in the Twenty-First Century*, New York, NY: I.B. Tauris.

Plaskow, J. and Christ, C. (eds) (1989), *Weaving the Visions: New Patterns in Feminist Spirituality*, New York, NY: Harper & Row.

Tacey, D. (2001), *Jung and the New Age*, East Sussex, UK: Brunner-Routledge.

——— (2004), *The Spirituality Revolution: The Emergence of Contemporary Spirituality*, London, UK: Routledge.

Williamson, A. (2009), 'Formative support and connection: Somatic movement dance education in community and client practice', *Journal of Dance & Somatic Practices*, 1:1, pp. 29–45.

——— (2010), 'Reflections and theoretical approaches to the study of spiritualities within the field of somatic movement dance education', *Journal of Dance & Somatic Practices*, 2:1, pp. 35–61.

Williamson, A. and Hayes, J. (2012), 'Dance, movement and spiritualities', *Journal of Dance & Somatic Practices*, 4:1, pp. 3–9.

Williamson, A. and Hayes, J. (2013), *The Journal of Dance, Movement and Spiritualities,* 1:1, p. 14.

Part I

Moving Spiritualities

Amanda Williamson

To research organic life, I need to use an organic method; a method that stays close to the felt sense of life unfolding, growing, expanding, blossoming, dwindling, shrinking, dying and dissolving.

(Hayes, this volume: 67)

The topic of spirituality occupies a fascinating, yet complicated space in Western dance history. On the one hand, dance is rooted in the ancient sacred, but on the other, the Dance Studies curriculums we know today developed within our modern secular education system. While modern dance rejected materialism and affirmed intuition, feeling and the immaterial realm as a source of spiritual knowledge, dance in higher education is nonetheless institutionalized within the non-religious, materialist and cultural materialist discourses on which much of our higher education system is built. Subsequently one can view how spirituality in dance has tended to retain its centrality in non-Western scholarship, but struggled to find high profile platforms for debate and discussion in Western contexts. Classical and folk traditions from both Western and non-Western contexts are rooted in spirituality and provide a rich source for enquiry into the numinous in dance, and non-Western dance forms have long been the rich ground to which Western theatrical dance has turned for artistic and spiritual inspiration. Such influences and sacred roots allow a certain degree of visibility for the study of spirituality in dance in higher education, yet it is rare to find university dance departments that offer the study of spiritualties in contemporary contexts and Western cultures. While our higher education system is secular, one cannot help but notice the presence and expression of variant spiritualities in Dance Studies internationally—and particularly within the field of Somatic Movement Dance Education (SMDE). The advent and growth of variant somatic movement/dance modalities, with their unique co-extensive emphasis on the *felt* internal (deep interiority) and connective external (socio-communal/ecological/political) life of the body, sets forth major challenges in higher education. These modalities potentially disrupt our secular university contexts, through explorations into breath/spirit, the imagination, symbol, myth, metaphor, touch, ecosomatics, and multi-sensory and intuitive experiences. The academic and artistic centralization of the sensory body acquiring 'other' forms of embodied knowledge in dance departments, plays a major role in not only opposing the male-centred dualistic roots of higher education, but also the secular roots of the modern education system.

Part I, written by six women with highly influential careers, explores a spirituality of the moving body. Within this section we depart company from positivist, discriminatory analytic methods, which often deny the legitimacy of intuition and the artistic expression

Phenomenology

of *felt sensation* as research tools. Authors use research methods that are not predicated on distance and separation, but rather closeness, participation and relatedness. These authors are personally involved with the source of investigation—for research into spirituality, Somatics and movement often requires listening into and documenting the subtleties of bodied *felt life* (rich in sensory consciousness and connections).

A unique offering from the somatic movement/dance community, when studying spirituality academically, is the principle of being intimately immersed in the focus of study—to life energy, to breath, to heart, to cell. These Somatic research approaches challenge dichotomous perceptions, particularly the ingrained antithesis between spirituality and materiality—spirit and body. Throughout Part I, many questions arise both explicitly and indirectly—particularly, what are the meeting points between embodied somatic practice and spirituality, and how can they be analysed and theorized without diminishing the *felt-life* of the moving body? How can we theorize practice without smothering sensation? How can we intelligently write about subjective *deeply felt* spiritual processes of, for example, *being and cellular presence*? Equally important, how can we write about practice making sure comprehensible intelligent ideas are offered (useful theories and methods that enhance and elucidate international practice), avoiding the enduring idea that depth of embodied spiritual experience cannot be adequately articulated in words, and thus remains hidden in the realms of the nonverbal?

Within Part I, two bodies of water meet—the language of the interior sensate moving body (rich in delicate, often fleeting images, symbols, metaphors and poetry), and the academic word (often seeking to express clearly through theoretical frameworks and rational meaning-making systems). Rather like a muddy estuary, it is sometimes a place of unease—a murky place—yet a place where unusual life-forms and discoveries are made. This tension—this enduring problematic—drives those innovative methodologies and theoretical frameworks so unique and particular to Somatic Movement Dance Studies. Language, ideas, and the development of practice emerges through slow-time intimacy with the *felt-senses*. Emergent research of this nature differs from the abstractions of disembodied, calculative and dichotomous thinking.

A central theme in this section is the questioning of androcentrism—not through an explicit critique of male-centred religious power, but rather through reading about women who participate in their spirituality with a strong sense of agency and self-authority. These voices challenge patriarchy through an embodied self-authority that agitates and disrupts androcentric values. Thus, the relationship between SMDE and earth-centred feminist spirituality is felt—particularly in those voices that reflect on the dominance of patriarchal dualism—the extradition and belittling of body and earth (reflected in the current ecological crisis). Notably, all the authors in this section are women. Here lies an open concern for developing (through practice) a non-hierarchical, participatory, eco-literate relationship with both body and nature. Body and nature are centralized and sacralized (given extra special attention)—cared for academically, bringing living cellular presence onto the academic page.

In seeking to express the somatic spiritual experience in movement, it is not surprising that some authors turn to Carl Jung's theories and the application of active imagination to dance and movement studies. The application of active imagination provides a spiritual practice that respects subjectivity. Part of this practice is attending to symbols, sensations and feelings emerging from within the moving body—thus a mover immersed in Jungian discourse is the author of her/his own spiritual experience. This subjective turn—of sensing, *feeling into*, and making meaning from one's own embodied experience underpins self-authority in moving spirituality. Embodied empirical research that embraces epistemologies of subjectivity offers fresh and multiple perceptions of spirit and spirituality, challenging exclusive, objectified, and distant models of religious knowledge.

Many of the chapters in Part 1 highlight healing through embodied movement, spirituality and health. Diverse, yet interrelated themes are introduced, from embryological development exploring our earliest relational structures, to alchemy and the meditative movement practices rooted in C. G. Jung's active imagination. Other themes range from 'relational imaginal sensing' and the archetypal story of Sophia according to ancient Gnostic visions, to philosophical critiques of Deleuze and Guattari, Jane Bennett, and David Abram. Similarly a range of theories and methodologies are employed—philosophical critique, miniature case study, auto-ethnography, practice-based research, and arts-based methodologies of embodied and autobiographical enquiry.

Linda Hartley offers an immanental model of spirituality rooted in embryology and somatic movement exploration, in Chapter 1 'Embodiment of Spirit: From Embryology to Authentic Movement as Embodied Relational Spiritual Practice.' Hartley notes she has developed two primary interests during her career—Somatic Movement Education and embodied spiritual practice. She offers an exploration of these two kindred areas, discovering how they interface through the exploration of embryology as embodiment of spirit. Drawing on Ken Wilber's theories, Hartley reflects on 'how experience in the pre-personal, pre-egoic realms of early life and the transpersonal, trans-egoic realms of mature spiritual experience interface' (this volume: 11). She further relates these theories to the embodiment practices of Body-Mind Centering® and Authentic Movement, offering an insightful and moving account of how the spiritual can be *felt, sensed* and theoretically located in practice.

Linda Hartley, Tina Stromsted, Jill Hayes and Daria Halprin offer chapters inflected and shaped by C. G. Jung and the application of active imagination to movement and dance—or derivative non-stylized movement forms that value the imagination-in-movement as a source for spiritual transformation and development. Thus, these chapters speak of alchemy, elemental resonance, transformation, archetype, symbol, myth, metaphor, anatomy and psyche—a bodily descent into the unconscious, supported by somatic movement processes of bodily and communal support, such as breathing and compassionate witnessing. These authors clearly illustrate a sensorial *moving* engagement with body-life-processes, and the potential for transformation initiated through a deep descent into the moving imagination. At times, we are invited into the heart of suffering—but equally invited to perceive suffering as containing the seeds for personal growth.

Tina Stromsted in Chapter 2, 'The Alchemy of Authentic Movement: Awakening Spirit in the Body', focuses on the embodied transformative process as it's experienced through the practice of Authentic Movement—'a therapeutic and body/mind meditative practice with roots in C. G. Jung's active imagination approach' (this volume: 37). Stromsted shares sophisticated research, examining the relationship between modern psychotherapy, Carl Jung's theories, Authentic Movement and alchemy, intricately weaving and melding alchemical theory with Authentic Movement. Within this chapter, Stromsted challenges traditional 'cognitive therapeutic approaches [that] prioritize mental insight over embodied experience and the spiritual dimensions of the healing process' (this volume: 37). Stromsted explores how healing takes place within the moving body, and the body's essential role, and *moving* centrality, in supporting transformational process. The author exquisitely highlights that it is not just that we have a body during a spiritual process (taken along for the ride), but rather that the moving body is the substance, intimately involved in the transformational process.

Sharing similarities with Stromsted's chapter, Jill Hayes, in Chapter 3, 'Dancing in the Spirit of Sophia', openly shares her experience of illness with cancer and her recovery aided by somatic movement exploration. Hayes writes that she 'wanted to breathe life into every cell of [her] body to reawaken [her] capacity to sense and feel [her] inner life' (this volume: 66). She describes how she descended into her body to be with (to meet) her illness on an intimate sensorial and imagistic level—inherent in her moving journey is her trust in the intuitive sense of the ebb and flow of creative and destructive energies in the living cosmos. Hayes immersed herself in somatic movement processes that helped her to feel 'a greater swell of creativity,' aiding her recovery (this volume: 66). She employs what she terms in her practice 'relational imaginal sensing,' and the archetypal story of Sophia according to ancient Gnostic visions, in order to find companionship and inspiration on her movement journey (this volume: 70).

Echoing many of the authors above, Daria Halprin, in Chapter 4, 'Body Ensouled, Enacted and Entranced: Movement/Dance as Transformative Art,' correlates spiritual experience with transformative experience. She draws on her heuristic research in meditation practice, as an artist/dancer, therapist and teacher of the past 35 years, sharing a multi-step practice/process. Halprin examines the complex relationship between, and inter-dependence of, physical sensation and kinesthetic expression, feelings and emotions, thoughts, memories and the imagination. She reflects on how her approach to movement does not remove the mover from daily life concerns (or from the pain of life). 'Like clay for the sculptor, dance shapes the mover in ways that express the full spectrum of who we are on all levels of our being: physical, emotional and mental' (Halprin, this volume: 93). Thus her movement model engages with a spirituality that creatively responds to the trials and tribulations of life. Within this model we are invited to examine ways in which movement reflects and engages with many aspects of life, body and psyche, supporting newfound health, synthesis and creativity. This is a model of deep sensory interiority, supported by careful communal and facilitator witnessing—a delicately crafted personal and collective transformative process.

Running throughout all the chapters (and much of the anthology), but particularly explicit in these last two chapters is an ecologically aware spirituality that finds companionship with, and may complement deep ecology. We encounter a spirituality that initially emerges from the body (a *felt sense* and connection with the natural world), but extends beyond the realms of the personal, cultivating an active participatory, non-hierarchal and resonate relationship with the earth and ecological systems. Celeste Snowber, in Chapter 5, 'Dancing on the Breath of Limbs: Embodied Inquiry as a Place of Opening,' offers a chapter rooted in arts-based research, using methodologies of embodied and autobiographical enquiry—notably, such methodologies allow for the delicacies and subtleties of embodied experience a voice. Snowber shares her personal movement practice, 'writing from the body' (this volume: 117)—a practice where 'language becomes a physical extension of the body' (this volume: 117). She explores somatically emergent language—language that grows out of the body, resonating with the living world—listening for, sensing into, for example, breath and bone—words that 'become utterances of the belly' (this volume: 117). Snowber clearly illuminates a central pedagogical method within the field of SMDE—that is, listening 'to the pulses of the human heart through sound, gesture, eyes, belly, touch, skin and bones,' and seeking through this intimate *felt sense*, words and poetry that support the creative expression of depth of human feeling and life-force mystery (this volume: 117).

Reflecting Snowber's love of place, body and earth, Kimerer LaMothe, in Chapter 6, '"Can They Dance?": Towards a Philosophy of Bodily Becoming,' introduces 'a local, living philosophy that privileges bodily movement as the source and *telos* of human life' (this volume: 133). Critiquing the work of Deleuze and Guattari, Jane Bennett, and David Abram, LaMothe makes the case that we need to dance—'for the sake of our well-being as creatures on this planet.' LaMothe's work complements and supports the advancement of work taking place in deep ecology. She provides a unique philosophical paradigm that explores what it means to be relational creatures through movement and sensory awareness. Distinctive to this chapter is the manner in which LaMothe shifts between acute academic philosophical critique and her own sensory movement exploration, bringing bodily presence into the heart of the philosophical argument.

Chapter 1

Embodiment of Spirit: From Embryology to Authentic Movement as Embodied Relational Spiritual Practice

Linda Hartley

Throughout four decades of study and professional practice as educator and therapist, my two primary interests—somatic movement exploration and embodied spiritual practice—have woven together in both implicit and explicit ways. A foundation of my somatic work has been the study of infant movement development, as taught by Bonnie Bainbridge Cohen in the somatic movement practice of Body-Mind Centering® (Cohen 1993; Hartley 1995). I continue to be fascinated by the way that re-embodying early movement patterns can give support and clarity to posture, movement expression, emotional life and the psychological development of a sense of self, as well as essential grounding and inspiration for spiritual opening and creative work.

My interest has led me to explore more deeply our earliest origins in embryological development, and it is here that I sense most directly the interface of the somatic and the spiritual. Ken Wilber has written about the pre-trans axis, showing how experience in the pre-personal, pre-egoic realms of early life and the transpersonal, trans-egoic realms of mature spiritual experience interface, and can lead, one into the other (1980: 49–57). I see this connection most clearly in the unfolding development of the embryo, from conception into human form; I have come to understand this embryological process as the embodiment of spirit.

Another foundation of my practice is the discipline of Authentic Movement, as developed by Janet Adler (Pallaro 1999, 2007; Adler 2002). In this discipline, material emerging from the unconscious—pre-personal, personal, transpersonal and collective—is embodied in movement, gesture, stillness and sound in the presence of a witness who attends to her own experience in the presence of the one moving. Both engage in a direct experience of the moment that is both individual and shared. Sometimes moments of clarity and resonance—a unitive state—enable a shared experience of the sacred, of the divine, of the spiritual or transpersonal (Adler 2002: 209).

In this chapter, I would like to weave a path between these two areas of study and practice—the experiential study of embryology as embodiment of spirit and Authentic Movement as embodied relational spiritual practice. I will refer to a map, informed by Buddhist principles, of Source, Being and Self, developed by Maura and Franklin Sills, to give context (Sills 2009). In my paraphrasing of their map, Source is the pure and universal consciousness, out of which we differentiate into individual Being. Being is pure presence and awareness, which becomes inevitably obscured as we meet the environment that we are conceived in, born into and nurtured by. Self develops as patterns of need, feeling, behaviour,

Figure 1: Embodying the gestures of the embryo: folding and unfolding. Mover: Aki Omori. Photographer: Christian Kipp.

perception, attitude and thought form our individual character, our unique way of meeting and responding to relational others and the world as we grow. Self represents the functional unity of psyche and soma (Reich 1970: 241–42).

In this model, there is always health and wellness at the level of Being: though it may often be obscured, it is always present and available to us. In this state of pure awareness and presence, we are no longer fragmented and disconnected. Self manifests our wounds, the ways we lose touch with Being, but Being is always present, a profound resource we can return to and through which we can connect to Source. Sometimes embodying early movement processes—perhaps present before later disruptions and trauma severed our innate wholeness—offers direct access to feelings of integration and well-being, and to our core sense of Being and Source.

Embodiment Practice

Describing the embodiment practice of Body-Mind Centering®, which she has been evolving since the 1970s, Bonnie Bainbridge Cohen writes:

The process of embodiment is a being process, not a doing process, not a thinking process. It is an awareness process in which the guide and the witness dissolve into cellular consciousness. Visualization and somatization provide steps to full embodiment, helping us return to preconsciousness with a conscious mind.

Embodiment is automatic presence, clarity and knowing [...], the cells' awareness of themselves [...]. It is a direct experience; there are no intermediary steps or translations.
(2008: 157)

This work needs to be experienced; it cannot be understood through a solely cognitive approach, as embodiment is about states of awareness and presence that are experienced beneath and beyond the cognitive processing of higher brain centres. Just as in the practice of meditation, if we settle for a moment into spaciousness of mind, a place of pure awareness and presence—of Being—beyond the chattering mind, and if we have also anchored ourselves in our physical being through mindfulness of body sensation, then we become in that moment fully aware, present and embodied. Immanent spirituality, as distinct from transcendence, can be touched.

Embodiment practice enables intimate explorations into the extraordinary processes of human anatomy, physiology and development. We learn to perceive from the cells of our body—not the mind looking at the cells, but mind being fully centred in the body, in the cells themselves, and perceiving from there, the cells knowing themselves. We can learn to perceive from the cells of different tissues in the body and to experience the different qualities of awareness, perception, touch, feeling and movement that each tissue evokes.

In exploring, as adults, the process of infant movement development, we embody movement patterns and principles of sensory-motor integration that underlie our phylogenetic (species) and ontogenetic (individual) evolution (Cohen 1993; Hartley 1995; Aposhyan 1999; Brooks 2001; Stokes 2002). By embodying these movements fully, from initiation, through the sequencing of an action, to its completion, we re-establish core support, strength and ease of movement. Our nervous system recognizes the basic neurological patterns that are the foundations of all adult movement potentials, and will choose the pathways that offer the greatest ease of organization, connectivity and flow once they have been embodied. Our inner self will choose health when supported to do so. Through this practice, movement is re-patterned for greatest efficiency and grace. We may also gain insight, through embodying early movement processes, about the psycho-emotional dimension of those experiences. A direct knowledge of embryological, fetal, perinatal and infant states of being and feeling can be accessed.

It is important that we bring conscious awareness to these explorations, or we may regress to a preconscious, pre-egoic state that cannot be integrated into consciousness. With conscious awareness, we open the pre-trans axis, a potential flow of experiencing that links spiritual qualities such as joy, wonder, wisdom, love and deep connectedness with insight about our early pre-egoic development. As in the discipline of Authentic Movement, we seek to maintain the presence of an internal witness as we enter the realms of the pre-personal or transpersonal, so that these altered states of consciousness can be encountered safely and integrated into consciousness.

The 'Gestures' of the Embryo

In the experiential study of embryology, Cohen describes how it is 'the place of space' which we embody (2008: 166). For example, the notochord, precursor to the spine, disperses as the vertebral spine develops, but we can connect to the sense of space between spine and digestive tract to contact the location of the embryonic notochord. Moving from this space has a distinctly different quality from movement initiated with awareness centred in the spine or digestive tract.

The embryonic structures no longer exist in physical form; yet the relative place and shape in the body that they once occupied can be contacted. As we move from this place and sense of spatial structure, we may come to 'know' something of the experience of the embryo at that stage of development through our embodied cellular consciousness. Moving through the changing forms of the growing embryo, we may discover something about the meaning of becoming a human being.

Embryologist Jaap van der Wal talks of the speech of the embryo as being a sequence of gestures that the embryo makes as it grows (2005). Development involves the expression of polarities that emerge in sequence and whose integration leads to a new level of form and function; integration of all polarities gives the human embryo its uniqueness. He describes how development is movement, an extraordinary dance that invites spirit to enter into matter. By entering into the forms and movement gestures of the embryo, embodying them, we can discover what the gesture is communicating. He writes:

> If you open your heart and try to put yourself into the position of the embryo and join in experiencing the gestures of growing that are taking place there, all at once the embryo will tell you a very profound story. It will tell you the story of becoming a HUMAN BEING, of the struggle of the person and his [or her] spirit to come to light through the tough resistance of cells, genes, tissue. A human being performs so much work and lives so intensely while being an embryo!
>
> (van der Wal 2011; original emphasis)

He encourages us to look at the gestures of the embryo from a phenomenological viewpoint, rather than observing and analysing behaviour as science generally does. The latter gives explanations, but the former invites a journey deep into ourselves to address questions as to 'why.' It invites discovery of sense and meaning:

> If you don't enter the marvellous world of the embryo with the detached and cold contemplation of the onlooker, but you open your heart and your soul and join in to EXPERIENCE what's happening there, you will be able to discover behind the facts nothing less than the activity of SPIRIT.
>
> (van der Wal 2011; original emphasis)

With this invitation, I would like to offer a description of some of the gestures the embryo makes as it comes into form, and a glimpse into the meanings they may suggest. I also propose that the embodiment practices of Body-Mind Centering® and Authentic Movement are ideal vehicles through which to explore the embryological journey.

An Embryological Journey: The Dance of Conception—Masculine and Feminine Polarities

The two that are polar opposites belong together. The egg (ovum) and sperm cell are both extreme in their form and function, and will move towards death if they do not come together in conception. With conception the opposite occurs—a new life begins (van der Wal 2005: 3).

The ovum has been present in a woman's body since she was a fetus in her own mother's body—we each began life in the womb of our grandmother. The ovum carries our ancient history and connection to our maternal lineage. It is the largest cell in the body, with a large cytoplasmic body, spherical, not very mobile, but stable; its movement tends to be rotational. In contrast, sperm cells are short-lived, active, mobile, small and lean; they have virtually no cytoplasmic body, just a nucleus and tail, and their movement is quick and linear.

By imagining ourselves into these forms and movement qualities, we may experience the very different energies that these two original cells contribute to our fundamental sense of being; the archetypes of masculine and feminine are at the root of all that we will become.

The dance of conception takes about 24 hours. The hundreds of sperm cells that have reached the ovum, against all odds and through great adversity—the original heroic journey—swim around the large egg cell and set her in motion, spinning slowly on her axis. However, only one sperm will penetrate the zona pellucida, a membrane that surrounds the ovum. Only one sperm will be 'invited' through the ovum's membrane; the membranes then fuse and the sperm's body is incorporated into the cytoplasm of the egg, all of this initiated through mutual chemical processes (Grossinger 2000: 103). The first experience of relationship, of opening to 'other,' has taken place. The next will occur about a week later with implantation into the uterine wall.

The process of conception, and the actual fusion of the two cells' nuclei, strikingly resembles a sensual courtship dance, culminating in the act of love-making itself. Barry Werth writes, 'the egg's protoplasm starts to shimmy, violently. The nuclei of sperm and egg sidle towards each other, enlarge and shed their protective membranes' (Tsiaras and Werth 2002: 50). Within twelve hours, the nuclei merge and the maternal and paternal chromosomes attach to form a full set of 46; they will soon begin the process of differentiation into the trillions of cells that make up the unique individual being that the zygote will become.

Cleavage: Many Differentiating Out of One

A single-celled being has been born. It has an inside that is separated from the outside by a double-layered membrane. Communication happens between the inside and the outside through the process of cellular breathing or internal respiration. The polarities of inside and outside are integrated by fluids passing through this defining membrane, enabling nourishment and energy to be absorbed, and supporting a new level of existence to emerge—a new life. The subtle pulsation of expansion and contraction of the cell is the first movement the new being makes, and it continues to be the fundamental motion of life throughout the whole life cycle. Our health depends on the integrity of our cell membranes and their ability to mediate between the internal cellular environment and the external fluid environment in which they live.

The first cell division, or cleavage, takes place about 30 hours after fertilization, forming a pre-embryo consisting of two virtually identical cells. What is happening during this long time of apparent inactivity? A pause while the decision to incarnate is made? A time for soul or spirit to enter matter, to inspire it into growth? We can but speculate, but when we embody the dance of conception, then take time to feel this spacious moment, a little of the mystery of the process of new life beginning may be glimpsed.

Two days after conception, cell division occurs again, and then regularly every ten to twelve hours, until the one cell has become a sphere of individual cells, all similar but

Figure 2: Embodying the gestures of the embryo: opening and receiving. Mover: Charlotte Darbyshire. Photographer: Christian Kipp.

beginning to differentiate. Then something remarkable occurs: some of the cells migrate around the inner surface of the zona pellucida, to form a softer protective membrane (trophoblast) made up of cells that are part of the self-structure of the pre-embryo. The remaining cells form an inner cell mass that will become the embryo itself (Grossinger 2000: 149; Martini 2001: 1069). At this point, we are both body and containing membrane, the one held and the one who is holding. I feel this has profound implications, offering a template for wholeness and self-integrity.

From now on, these two structures will follow entirely different lines of development. The outer membrane will interface with the mother's body, the womb-home, thus embodying relationship. The securing of nourishment through the placenta and of protection through further development of the membrane will both be served by this outer layer. The inner cell mass, called the embryonic disc, will grow into a human embryo.

Implantation—Self and Other: Coming into Relationship

After several days floating in the womb, as if in space (Nilsson 1990: 62), the blastocyst must implant, or come into relationship with the maternal environment, to survive. Implantation is the process of embedding into the uterine wall, finding a home within which to develop. At this point, another extraordinary event occurs: 'the blastocyst hatches from the zona pellucida, which allows it to expand and release the cells on its surface to interact with the outside' (Tsiaras and Werth 2002: 57).

You can feel this moment by imagining you are wearing a tight bodysuit to create a feeling of constriction in your whole body, then imagine you take off the suit and feel the expansion and release that this enables. You may be able to feel the sense of expansion in the cells themselves as they are released. Feel how different it is to relate to someone with this sense of constriction and then with the feeling of release. Sometimes we retreat back into our

Figure 3: Embodying the gestures of the embryo: reaching out and connecting. Mover: Gaelin Little. Photographer: Christian Kipp.

protective membrane and inhibit the flow of connection with the world; at other times we bravely, fearfully, lovingly or joyfully open and expand to meet it.

After hatching, the blastocyst backs into the endometrium wall, burrowing deep within the maternal tissue until completely embedded. It will continue its journey hidden and protected within the wall of the uterus.

During hatching and implantation, the embryonic roots of our experience of attachment to another are imprinted; the first expression of the relational style we will develop might be intimated at this stage, as the first and most intimate connection with mother's body is forged. The source of attitudes, feelings and beliefs, which will later be gathered into this relational pattern, may be discerned in the way that hatching and implantation are experienced.

Placentation—Bonding and Defence

Once embedded within the womb, the placenta begins to form. Cells on the outer membrane of the blastocyst interact with the uterine wall to form an organ of shared cells and vessels. The blastocyst's cells also form a tough membrane called the *chorion* that will surround and protect the embryo and fetus throughout gestation, and separate the embryo's cells from those of the mother within the placenta (Martini 2001: 1072–75). Again, we see how the pre-embryo secures its own self-integrity in the process of coming into relationship. The placenta embodies the two primary functions of bonding and defence; the embryo secures its nourishment through both reaching out to connect and through establishing a membranous boundary to protect itself.

The umbilical cord forms and, through the movement of blood through umbilical arteries and veins, the embryo and fetus experience the movement towards and away from self, claims Frances Mott (1959). He describes this as a potential experience of self and loss of self, of life and death, of aggression and invasiveness as it senses itself moving towards the placenta, or vulnerability and emptiness as blood flows away from self, or power and fullness as the inflow nourishes (Mott 1959: 37–40). We each experience our first embryonic relationship in unique ways.

As the umbilical cord lengthens, the embryo will make another significant gesture: it will spiral around to face the placenta-mother, and spend the rest of the gestation facing her. If we embody this gesture in relation to another we may experience the profound moment of turning to face the other for the first time. We might also discover the twirling motions of many a dance form: from rock-and-roll to ballroom to country-dance.

The Folding and Unfolding of Form

Meanwhile, safe within its protective membranes, the embryonic disc is emerging into form through a process of folding and unfolding, a kind of origami of cells, fluids and tissues that will culminate, at eight weeks, in a perfectly formed human fetus. Forms emerge and dissolve, shape-shift, transform, open out and fold in.

Two layers of cells form, to give a front and a back; the nutritional yolk sac grows out of the front layer, and the protective amniotic sac out of the back layer (Martini 2001: 1073). Now we have a front and a back, supported by two large fluid-filled cushions, and integrated by a subtle flow of fluids between them that causes a rhythmic movement of opening and closing, extension and flexion. This supports the fundamental life rhythm of opening out towards the world, and returning into oneself. The two sacs are like the precursors, or the archetypes, of the nurturing Mother and protective Father. They are formed from and are part of the embryo, not external to it; the archetypal Mother and Father are part of us from the very beginning.

The development of the primitive streak along the length of the disc now gives a central axis with a top and a bottom; the embryo begins to organize around a vertical axis. Already, at just twelve days old, we have emerged out of an undifferentiated cell mass into a verticality that intimates our orientation throughout life to the above and below, to heaven and earth. The primitive streak orients the development of the notochord (pre-spine) and later the spine itself.

A third layer of cells begins to form, and cells from all three layers engage in a stunningly complex dance as they endlessly differentiate, flow and stream into their own specific locations to form the different tissues of the body. This miracle of shape-shifting organization continues until all of the organs and tissues of the embryo have formed. If we could see the flows and streamings, the turns and spirals, involutions and evolutions of the cells and fluids as they organize into form and function, we might glimpse patterns that are familiar to us. We might recognize the elegant spatial tapestries that are the dances that tribes and cultures have created since the beginnings of human society, rituals that bonded communities in a shared experience of life, growth, love, war and sometimes death. The forms of tribal, sacred, folk and social dances echo the emerging into form of the embryo (Menzam 2002: 177).

As mentioned in the introduction, we can 'embody the place of space' (Cohen 2008: 166)—the place in the body where embryological structures once were; they no longer exist in material form, but an energetic trace of their former presence can still be felt and continue to inform us. As our dance progresses—from that of the containment, fullness and spherical organization of the original one-cell, where all dimensions are equal, and only inside and outside are differentiated, to the dance of verticality, where we integrate heaven and earth along with all the dimensions of the body in space and in relationship—we are in the process of becoming a human being. I would like to mark a few significant landmarks on this continuing journey.

Embodying Ground and Spirit

As we observe the folding and unfolding of the embryo's development, we see a bringing in of what was outside, an internalizing and personalizing of what was external and in touch with the universal. I imagine this as the drawing in, the embodying, of spirit.

The very first form the embryonic heart takes is a simple tubular structure, and it is located at the very top of the embryo, sitting as if on the forehead. Only a membrane separates it from the embryonic brain. During the second week, the heart folds into the centre of the body, and from its outward and upward facing position it now becomes deeply embedded within the body. The embryo folds around it into a deep C-curve. Later, the arm buds will rest softly over it, as if in prayer or contemplation.

Next the brain and spinal cord involute. The skin and nervous system share a common origin in the layer of germinal cells that form the back of the embryo. Some of these cells fold in, along the length of the back surface, then break away from the skin layer to form an internal tube along the length of the embryo, which will become brain and spinal cord. As Deane Juhan says, 'Depending upon how you look at it, the skin is the outer surface of the brain, or the brain is the deepest layer of the skin. Skin and innermost core spring from the same mother tissue' (Juhan 1987: 35).

And finally the intestines, which up until about nine weeks of gestation have lived partly outside of the body within the umbilical cord, spiral in to become fully enclosed inside. The ribcage and eyes, which have both been open until this time, also close. It is as if the embryo now turns inward to focus on the task of growth and preparation for life; it has become a perfectly formed and self-contained fetus, buried deep within the uterine wall for the remainder of the gestation.

It is curious that these three major organs—representing crucial organs of the head, heart and belly centres, and reflecting our mental, emotional and physical life—begin life interfacing with what is outside, other and ultimately universal. Then each turns inwards, as if gathering within something of that which is outside. I imagine a quiet turning inwards to embrace, reflect and integrate—a time to hold, nurture and incarnate the essence of what was glimpsed in that first outward facing moment. First we open out into the universe; then we look in and draw within us something of spirit.

The fetus now elongates out of its tightly folded C-shape and takes on a gesture of verticality, sitting with softly crossed legs, arms folded loosely over its heart, attached to and facing mother via its umbilical cord. The human fetus is thought to be the only mammalian fetus that returns to this gesture of verticality and maintains it throughout most of the gestation time. Does this uniquely human gesture signify an orientation towards spirit, an emphasis on the heaven-to-earth axis of verticality? Van der Wal claims:

The morphogenesis of the human being is typified by stretching and becoming upright, accompanied by the unfolding and polarizing of arms and legs, head and pelvis; all of this is necessary in order to stand straight and maintain that upright position into adulthood. Standing upright is more than just an anatomical gesture, it is also a spiritual gesture.

(van der Wal 2005: 41)

Frank Lake, one of the pioneers into pre- and perinatal development, has named the archetypal experience of the womb as the womb of spirit, the place where spirit incarnate is held and nurtured (Lake 1979; Sills 2009: 119). The following story (author unknown), which I first heard from Jaap van der Wal, speaks delicately and imaginatively to this idea.

An Unimaginable Existence—Is There Life After Birth?
A conversation between twins in the womb (from van der Wal 2011)

Once upon a time, twin boys were conceived in the womb. Seconds, minutes and hours passed as the two dormant lives developed. The spark of life flowed until it fanned the fire with the formation of their embryonic brains. With their simple brains came feeling, and with feeling came perception—a perception of surroundings, of each other, of self.

Weeks passed into months, and with the advent of each new month, they noticed a change in each other and each began to see changes in themselves. 'We are changing,' said the one, 'What can it mean?'

'It means,' replied the other, 'that we are drawing near to birth.'

An unsettling chill crept over the two, and they both feared for they knew that birth meant leaving all of their world behind.

'What do you think? Mightn't there be a life after birth?' asked the one.

'Yes, I think so. Our existence here is just meant to grow and develop in order to prepare ourselves for the life after birth so that we will be strong enough for what we will meet.'

'How can there be life after birth?' cried the one, 'How would it look?'

'Well, I do not know that exactly. But at least it will surely be much brighter than it is here. And maybe we will walk around and feed ourselves with our mouth.'

'What nonsense! How can that be, walking around? That is impossible. And eating with your mouth, what an extraordinary idea! We have the umbilical cord that nourishes us, don't we? And walking around will also be impaired by that cord; even now it is much too short.'

'Yet, I think it exists. Everything will just be a little bit different from the circumstances here.'

'Have you ever talked to one who has been born? Has anyone ever re-entered the womb after birth? NO! With birth our lives will end. And life in here is just dark and tormenting. That is all.' He fell into despair, and in his despair he moaned, 'If the purpose of conception and all our growth is that it ends in birth, then truly our life is absurd.'

'Though I do not exactly know how life after birth will look, surely we will meet our mother then and she will take care of us,' said the one.

'Mother? You believe in the existence of a mother?'

'But there is a mother,' protested the other. 'Who else gave us nourishment and our world?'

'We get our own nourishment, and our world has always been here. And if there is a mother, where is she? Have you ever seen her? Does she ever talk to you? NO! We invented the mother because it satisfied a need in us. It made us feel secure and happy.'

'No, she is here, all around us. We live by her and in her. Without her we could not even exist!'

'Nonsense. I never have noticed anything of "a mother." So she does not exist at all.'

'Yet, sometimes, when we are quiet, you may hear her sing for us. Or feel how she caresses our world.'

Relationship as Crucible for the Development of Consciousness

For the embryo, fetus and infant, there can be no life and growth without relationship, that connection to the other who holds and nurtures through the raw vulnerability of coming into existence. We are first held within the crucible of the womb of spirit: our first home offers a container for our growing psyche-soma, and a facilitating environment for the embodiment of spirit when mother can perceive, witness and welcome the unique being and spirit that is her child.

The experience of being held within another's awareness enables the sense of an authentic, embodied self to grow. Being witnessed and attended to by another enables the infant and child, and also the embryo and fetus, to feel its own existence, and even more than this, to discover meaning in that existence. William Segal writes:

Attention is the quintessential medium to reveal man's [or woman's] dormant energies to himself [or herself]. Whenever one witnesses the state of the body, the interplay of thought and feeling, there is an intimation, however slight, of another current of energy. Through the simple act of attending, one initiates a new alignment of forces. [...] Opening to the force of attention evokes a sense of wholeness and equilibrium.

(Segal 1987, opening to the *Force of Attention*)

Lynne McTaggart brings together various sources of scientific research to describe what she calls the Zero Point Field—the 'space' of the universe: an infinite, chaotic, unformed energy. She describes how our perception, attention and intention create a wave-like potential that stabilizes this random energy into form. Hence, our presence and attention bring form, order and meaning to the random, chaotic, potential source of energy that is the Zero Point Field. She writes, 'By the act of observation and intention [...], a living system of greater coherence could exchange information and create or restore coherence in a disordered, random or chaotic system' (McTaggart 2001: 138–39).

Developmental psychologists also understand how 'good enough' attending by primary carers enables the infant to thrive and develop a healthy sense of self; the quality of relationship enables healthy growth. Winnicott's 'good enough mother' is one who sees her child for who he or she is—not as an extension of herself or a container for her own projections, needs and aspirations, but as a unique Being with his or her own connection to life and Source. She responds empathically, in an accepting, caring and compassionate way, not reacting out of her own sense of chaos, disorder or futility. In this way, her attention can help her child to develop a sense of self with integrity, coherence and meaning. The mother who has herself been witnessed with enough clarity and compassionate attention will be able to offer this to her child.

Inadequate attention and unclear witnessing of the infant hinder healthy development; wholeness, coherence, psychological integrity and meaning remain beyond its reach unless it has been held well enough within a 'facilitating environment,' one which witnesses, mirrors and responds empathically to the infant's feelings, needs and very being (Winnicott 1965; Stern 1985). This is the relational crucible so essential to healthy psychological and somatic growth. There are now many wonderful studies within the fields of developmental psychology, neuroscience and attachment theory that bear out this truth (Gerhardt 2004; Cozolino 2006). And of course, it is the lack of clear and compassionate holding in early life that brings us, as adults, to seek greater coherence and meaning in our lives through various psychological, spiritual and embodiment practices.

Authentic Movement as Embodied Relational Spiritual Practice

The Discipline of Authentic Movement is one such practice; it offers a creative and sacred space within which to explore the crucible of relationship through embodied practice. The practice of Authentic Movement was originated by Mary Starks Whitehouse (Pallaro 1999a); dance movement therapy, Jungian depth psychology and spirituality all influenced Whitehouse's work. Janet Adler, a former student of Whitehouse, has been developing and deepening Authentic Movement as a mystical discipline for several decades. Her orientation away from its therapeutic roots and towards the spiritual was triggered by her own initiation into the mysteries (Adler 1995). Her evolution of Authentic Movement offers forms and rituals to contain a process that embraces personal, transpersonal and creative dimensions. She has also deepened an understanding of the relationship between mover and witness (Adler 2002).

The dyadic structure of one mover and one witness is the ground form of the practice; it reflects both the mother-child dyad, and that of the therapist and client. In long-term work, psychological issues can be addressed through the encounter, in movement, with material arising from the unconscious; the containment offered by the witness enables this material to be processed and integrated within the crucible of the relationship (Chodorow 1991; Adler 1999a: 121–31).

Through her attentive and embodied presence, the witness holds a safe space, a sacred circle, within which the mover can enter deeply into her inner world. This space reflects the 'womb of spirit', the first embrace within which we were held and witnessed. Now it is the attention of the external witness and the mover's own internal witness that form the containing membranes within which the mover embodies gesture and form, seeking growth and meaning within her experiences.

Held by the witness's compassionate presence, the mover turns her attention inward to focus on internal and self-generated impulses. They may come as subtle internal shiftings or impulses to move, bodily sensations or external sense impressions, powerful emotions or just the fleeting trace of a feeling, and images or stories. She attends to, and allows herself to be moved by, these impulses. Whitehouse describes:

> The open waiting, which is also a kind of listening to the body, an emptiness in which something can happen. You wait until you feel a change—the body sinks or begins to tip, the head slowly lowers or rolls to one side. As you feel it begin, you follow where it leads, like following a pathway that opens up before you as you step.
>
> (1999b: 53)

By keeping attention focused on the impulses that arise, moment by moment, the mover stays present to her direct experience, keeping it grounded in her physicality as she tracks movement and sensation. When we are present to bodily sensation, we can be nowhere but in the present moment, here and now. Like many forms of meditation practice, Authentic Movement offers a discipline for cultivating mindful presence and embodied awareness, a necessary foundation for immanent, or embodied, spirituality.

The tracking of movement, sensation, feeling and image, which both mover and witness practise, also reflects the Buddhist understanding of the creation of self out of pristine awareness through the unfolding of the five *skandhas*. This ancient psychology describes how we are drawn away from direct experience and pure mind through a cascade of emotional and mental reactions to the experience of pure awareness and presence (Hartley 2011). As we separate our awareness from direct experience, we become entangled in a web of longing, fear and hatred, and live through our projections, judgements and interpretations, rather than the felt sense of life and spirit flowing through us. Authentic Movement offers a path, a bridge back into the present moment and authentic embodied experiencing. I suggest that this discipline also enables us to approximate the immediacy of embodied experience of the embryo and fetus, before the entanglements of emotion, thought and judgement developed.

Just as the mover attends to her direct experience, so too does the witness as she sits at the edge of the space, noticing what is evoked in her in the presence of the one moving. She does not seek to analyse or interpret the movement, but learns to take ownership of her own experience. In this way, she begins to clear a space within herself to see the mover clearly, not through the haze of her own projections, interpretations and judgements. She allows the mover to be 'the expert of her own experience' (Adler 1993, from personal teaching notes), as she takes ownership of her own.

At the end of the movement time, they each share their experiences, describing the movements, sensations, feelings and images that arose. Seeking to be true to themselves, they come into a relationship that holds compassion, acceptance, authenticity and clarity at its heart. Sometimes difference is clarified, and the mover can experience her own sense of self more clearly as mover's and witness's experiences differ. At other times, their experiences converge and a moment of attunement, of shared understanding and connection, can be felt. Both can be healing for the mover, and revealing for the witness.

Most importantly, the mover can feel that the detailed and heartful attention that the witness pays to her is a gift. Being witnessed in this way gives significance and meaning to each experience, brings order to chaos and fragmentation, and coherence to random or dissociated states, as McTaggart suggests (2001). The mover may not have received the gift of clear and compassionate witnessing in early life, so her inner world may be distorted by self-criticism, false perceptions and harsh judgements; relationship to herself, to other people, and to her spiritual Source may be compromised, limited, misguided or even impossible with any degree of authenticity and safety. 'Presence is a loving act,' states Adler (2000, from personal teaching notes). A loving, witnessing presence is the gift that can help a consciousness, which is disordered, chaotic, out of balance, or lacking a sense of meaning, return to balance, integrity, coherence and fulfilment. Like the twin in our story, the mover may sense the attentive embrace of the witness as an invitation for spirit to awaken and meaning to be restored.

Levels of Consciousness

In Authentic Movement practice, movement can originate from any level of consciousness; we enter the movement in a state of open receptivity, like the embryo surrendering to the forces of life operating from deep within and around it. At the most conscious level, I feel that I am the originator of my movement: 'I move.' Movement from deeper levels of unconsciousness evokes the feeling of 'being moved.' Whitehouse describes how we seek a place where both feelings integrate so that we can surrender to, and be moved by, deeper impulses from the unconscious, yet also stay in conscious relationship to them. She describes how a 'balance between action and non-action allows individuals to live from a different awareness. [...] Then something new is created' (Whitehouse 1999c, in Pallaro 1999: 83). This third position enables us to transcend polarities and integrate a higher level of functioning (Chodorow 1999, in Pallaro 1999: 236). We see this transcendent function at work throughout the embryological journey, where, at each stage, the integration of polarities enables a new form of life to emerge (Jung 1916: 90).

An impulse to move may originate in the personal unconscious, carrying material from our personal history that is unique to us. Such movements are often highly idiosyncratic, and the witness must attend carefully to her somatic and felt responses in order to stay close to the mover's experience. Sometimes we see movements that remind us of the gestures of the embryo or fetus, or early infant movement patterns, and we know the mover is accessing early preconscious material (Menzam 2002).

At times, a movement emerges that has its source in the transpersonal, archetypal or collective levels of the unconscious. Gestures, postures and movement patterns may arise that are recognizable because they are expressions of a shared history, culture and mythology. We may see movements reminiscent of ancient yoga postures, traditional dance sequences, archetypal and mythical figures, such as the old hag, the warrior, the wind-goddess, the grieving woman or the shaman.

Trauma and the Transpersonal

Just as transpersonal material can be recognized as originating from a source beyond ordinary consciousness, so can material with traumatic associations. Adler writes that, 'Sometimes, a specific gateway into the numinous is experienced within the exact same movement pattern that held the most significant childhood trauma' (Adler 1999b: 185).

Over a period of time, a mover may explore a series of movements with a common theme. A development can be felt as material is explored from many perspectives. Piece by piece, the charge of the trauma can be integrated within the compassionate holding of the witness's attention. Then, at some point, when the trauma has been integrated well enough, the same movement or gesture opens into an experience of the numinous, or transpersonal. Such shifts may bring a sense of resolution, a release of energy or a new perspective. A moment such as this may be experienced as a unitive state, as the witness resonates with and shares in the mover's experience of the numinous.

I have also witnessed the reverse process in movers who have needed to connect to the transpersonal first, in order to approach traumatic material gradually. Here the gesture that carries the numinous content also contains the trauma until the mover's ego and internal witness are strong enough for her to begin to approach the difficult material. She must be able to stay present to, and track, her embodied experience in order to do this safely.

In both cases, we see the activation of Wilber's pre-trans axis. We often see such linkings in relation to very early pre- and perinatal processes, where the openness and vulnerability of the embryo, fetus and infant leave them particularly permeable to the unformed realms, in both their chaotic and divine aspects.

The Collective Body—Embodiment of a Shared Process

Practice within the collective body is another aspect of Authentic Movement that Adler has researched. As the internal witnesses of individual movers develop, they each become readied to take on the role of witness for others; the longing to be seen clearly evolves into the longing to see another clearly. In seeing another clearly, we also come to see ourselves with more clarity. Adler writes:

> No matter how well and objectively one can witness oneself, that self-witnessing is transformed only after truly seeing another as she is. It is as though there is now a reversal. In the same way that being seen by another originally enabled me to see myself as I am, in a further sweep of the spiral, seeing another as she is—loving her—enables me to see myself as I am.
>
> (Adler 1999c, in Pallaro 1999: 154)

Now there is a collective of movers and witnesses, and a form called the 'long circle' developed to hold a fluid exchange of roles as movers become witnesses, and witnesses take their experience back into the circle to become movers. As well as each one expressing her own personal story, we begin to witness the evolution of collective stories: each individual mover and witness takes her place in the larger story even as she expresses her personal truth. The collective body practice allows us to explore our sense of belonging, to understand the place we hold as individuals within the wider collective of community, and also humanity as a whole (Adler 2002: 91; Hartley 2004: 67).

We can imagine the embryo in the womb feeling itself to be at one with, an integral part of, the womb-universe. In the collective body, we may again experience this sense of mystical participation, but now with a depth of conscious awareness of self and other as being both separate and profoundly interconnected.

Development of Witness Consciousness

Through being witnessed over a period of time, in a way that is accepting and compassionate enough, the mover 'internalizes' the witness: her own internal witness—a centre of clear, non-judgemental awareness—develops, which enables her to hold herself and the material that arises. Moving within the compassionate gaze of the external witness, while her own internal witness is also active, a new kind of conscious relating can develop. It develops in the interface between the internal witness of the mover and the external witness. I liken it to a psychological and energetic reflection of the membranes that formed in the first days of embryonic life: an inner protective, containing membrane, formed out of the embryo's self-structure (the internal witness), interfacing with an outer protective membrane formed from the maternal tissue (external witness). The two touch, but are also distinct. In Authentic Movement, this meeting occurs again between the internal witnesses of both mover and witness; now, the membraneous boundaries are made up of the stuff of energetic presence and conscious awareness. The boundaries that were once made of highly perceptive cells have been internalized as the witness consciousness.

Three Realms of Relating

Adler has identified three types of relationship between mover and witness (Adler 1993, from personal teaching notes). This is not a hierarchy; within a single movement session, there can be a fluid shifting between all three. The first she calls empathic relating or witnessing; here the witness feels with the mover. She has internalized the mover to some extent and resonates with her experience at an emotional and somatic level; she may also intuit or 'know' the mover's images, associations or meaning when she is keenly empathic. The witness feels the sadness the mover feels; she resonates with the sensation of weight settling through the bones, something that the mover is also experiencing. The witness must stay alert if she is not to become merged with the mover and lose track of her own embodied presence.

In the second realm, compassionate witnessing, the mover feels something in relation to the mover. If the mover is experiencing fear, the witness may sense a surge of protective feelings rise within her. She may notice her body wishing to move towards the mover and touch her gently, even as the mover is withdrawing into herself. In this realm, the witness is clearly aware of her separateness, but also her deeply human connection to the mover.

In the third realm, unitive presence, or clear seeing, the witness has 'cleared the density of her personal history' (Adler 2000, from personal teaching notes) to the extent that, in this moment, she sees the mover clearly. Such moments come 'by grace'; they cannot be created, just as a moment of connection to Source in meditation practice cannot be contrived. But we slowly and painstakingly prepare the ground through long years of practice into the ownership of projections, judgements and interpretations, so that we can be open to such moments—to a shared experience of something beyond the ordinary.

In these moments, movers and witnesses both report an altered sense of space, time, body boundaries or other elements of ordinary reality. This often comes as a sense of expansion, dissolution or timelessness. It can be differentiated from a dissociated state by the ability to stay present to movement, sensation and spatial awareness. The discipline of tracking movement and sensation, being able to witness them even while surrendering to an uncensored flow of movement, is essential to encountering such altered states safely. Without the ability to stay present to, and grounded in, somatic experience, altered states of consciousness can indeed become dissociative or, at best, remain unintegrated.

However, when a unitive state occurs between mover and witness, or between two movers, the experience can be grounded in the body and in relationship, and both can be inspired, deepened, renewed and changed. Both are transported beyond the bounds of normal perception, opened to an awareness of the transpersonal, of that which is greater than the limited sense we have of ourselves. To experience the opening to Source or spirit, in a fully embodied way and within the crucible of relationship, is indeed a precious gift.

Perhaps this is a coming full circle, another turn of the spiral where, now in full consciousness, we remember the first dance of relationship of egg and sperm—the shared experience which invited spirit to embody and initiate new life and consciousness.

I would like to end by describing a personal experience that occurred during an Authentic Movement retreat led by Janet Adler. It took place in her studio in the hills of California, and is an account of a subjectively experienced and embodied, shared movement process.

The Angel and the Stone Bowl

The following excerpts are from my personal journal, written during a retreat with Janet Adler in Sebastopol, California. (Hartley 2003)

First Encounter

I am standing with my back to the long wall, touching, leaning slightly where the back of my head, shoulders and pelvis meet the surface of wood and glass. I feel the presence of an Angel behind me, a little to my right. I am taken aback at how tall and how extraordinarily powerful I feel this presence to be, and I feel surprised. I am not sure if Angels really exist for me! Yet this feels real, his presence bringing my whole being to attention. I cannot turn to look.

The Stone Bowl

The noise and activity in the room has disturbed me, and I seek refuge in the small space of the corner of the room, squeezed in behind the carved stone bowl. I feel calm here, and profoundly present. I am sitting cross-legged, occupying a liminal space between moving and witnessing, and I feel safe.

My hands touch the cool surface of the bowl, tracing the tiny indentations of the artist's chisel. I enjoy the surprise of its rough-hewn quality, its quiet presence, the ancient stillness of stone beneath the detailed marks of the human hand at work. My hands slip over into the empty space contained within the bowl. They sink deeper and deeper into the emptiness, my fingertips diving in slowly, fearlessly. Now there is nothing but emptiness. I feel the forms of my body begin to dissolve. The stone bowl deepens and widens, becomes translucent; there is nothing but emptiness and my fingers slowly diving deeper and deeper. The space feels infinite and the journey endless.

My eyes open slightly, allowing in the dissolving forms of the bowl, and of my own hands. Then another mover, dressed in white, appears. She faces me, tall, bowing towards me over the rim of the bowl; she reaches her hands towards mine, reaching into the depths of the bowl. We share the emptiness for a moment; we share eternity for a moment. Our fingers barely touch, a light fleeting contact. Then she leaves, as quietly as she came. I know her as an Angel.

Third Encounter

I have been moving on the floor. I feel like a very young child as I reach my right hand slowly upwards above my head. My forefinger is pointing, stretched upwards as my other fingers tuck softy around my thumb. At this exact moment, another forefinger enters exactly the same place in the space, pointing downwards. It touches the tip of my finger. I feel a current of energy run through us. The image of Blake's painting of God reaching down from heaven springs into my imagination. I let it go in order to stay present to the exquisiteness of this moment. I am kneeling, and I lean gently into the side of her upright body, feeling grateful for such a miraculous and delicate moment of connection.

Later, as we share our experiences, I recognize my 'white angel' from the bowl as the one whose fingertip met mine in the very centre of the circle. I feel blessed and in the presence of the sacred.

Concluding Words

In this chapter, I have outlined some key elements of embryological development as a dance of movement, gesture, changing form and integration of polarities. Following the invitation of embryologist Jaap van der Wal to re-embody the gestures of the embryo, our experience may inform us of the process by which spirit incarnates during this earliest phase of life.

We saw how, at the end of the first week after conception, the pre-embryo divides into an inner cell mass and an outer membrane, which forms a container within which the embryo will grow. I have suggested that the embodiment practice of Body-Mind Centering® is an excellent vehicle through which to enquire into the experience of the embryo itself and the meaning of the gestures it makes. We can also explore the early imprinting of attachment styles through an embodied study of the development of the membranes, placenta and umbilical cord, which form the interface between embryo and mother.

I also suggest that Authentic Movement offers a practice within which we can embody early development, and deepen awareness to the experience of Self, Being and Source through surrendering to the open and receptive state of the embryo. I have likened the interface of the embryo's containing membranes with the maternal tissue to the interface of consciousness that develops in Authentic Movement practice between the awareness of the external witness and the internal witness of the mover.

In moments of clear seeing and unitive presence, mover and witness may share an experience of a transpersonal or spiritual nature. I have likened this to an embodied relational spiritual practice. Such moments are reminiscent of the embryological dance of matter-with-spirit, which brought new consciousness to life within the embrace of clear and compassionate relationship.

References

Adler, J. (1993), from personal teaching notes.

—— (1995), *Arching Backwards*, Rochester, VT: Inner Traditions.

—— (1999a), 'Integrity of body and psyche', in P. Pallaro (ed.), *Authentic Movement*, London, UK: Jessica Kingsley Publishers, pp. 121–31.

—— (1999b), 'Body and soul', in P. Pallaro (ed.), *Authentic Movement*, London, UK: Jessica Kingsley Publishers, pp. 160–89.

—— (1999c), 'Who is the witness', in P. Pallaro (ed.), *Authentic Movement*, London, UK: Jessica Kingsley Publishers, pp. 141–59.

—— (2000), from personal teaching notes.

—— (2002), *Offering from the Conscious Body*, Rochester, VT: Inner Traditions.

—— (2003), from personal teaching notes.

Aposhyan, S. (1999), *Natural Intelligence*, Baltimore, MD: Williams & Wilkins.

Bainbridge Cohen, B. (1993), *Thinking, Feeling, and Action*, Northampton, MA: Contact Editions.

—— (2008), *Thinking, Feeling, and Action*, 2nd ed., Northampton, MA: Contact Editions.

Brooks, A. (2001), 'From conception to crawling', Body-Mind.net, http:// www.body-mind.net. December 2001.

Chodorow, J. (1991), *Dance Therapy and Depth Psychology*, London, UK: Routledge.

—— (1999), 'Dance therapy and the transcendent function', in P. Pallaro (ed.), *Authentic Movement*, London, UK: Jessica Kingsley Publishers, pp. 236–52.

Cozolino, L. (2006), *The Neuroscience of Human Relationships*, New York, NY: W W Norton & Co.

Gerhardt, S. (2004), *Why Love Matters*, London, UK: Routledge.

Grossinger, R. (2000), *Embryogenesis*, Berkeley, CA: North Atlantic Books.

Hartley, L. (1995), *Wisdom of the Body Moving*, Berkeley, CA: North Atlantic Books.

—— (2003), Personal writing from a retreat with Janet Adler. Sebastopol, CA.

—— (2004), *Somatic Psychology: Body, Mind and Meaning*, London: Whurr/Wiley.

—— (2011), 'An enquiry into direct experience: Authentic Movement and the five skandhas', http://www.authenticmovementjournal.com. Accessed 11 October 2011.

Juhan, D. (1987), *Job's Body*, Barrytown, NY: Station Hill Press.

Jung, C. (1916), 'The transcendent function', in C. Jung (ed.), *The Collected Works of C.G. Jung*, 2nd ed., vol. 8, Princeton, NJ: Princeton University Press, p. 90.

Lake, F. (1979), 'Studies in constricted confusion: Exploration of a pre- and perinatal paradigm', Oxford, UK: Clinical Theology Association, http://www.bridgepastoral.org.uk. Accessed 21 August 2013.

Martini, F. (2001), *Fundamentals of Anatomy & Physiology,* 5th ed., Upper Saddle River, NJ: Prentice Hall.

McTaggart, L. (2001), *The Field: The Quest for the Secret Force of the Universe*, London, UK: Harper Collins.

Menzam, C. (2002), 'Dancing our birth: Prenatal and birth themes and symbols in dance, movement, art, dreams, language, myth, ritual, play, and psychotherapy', Unpublished thesis (Ph.D.), Cincinnati, OH: Union Institute Graduate College.

Mott, F. (1959), *The Nature of the Self*, London, UK: Allan Wingate.

Nilsson, L. (1990), *A Child Is Born*, New York, NY: Bantam Doubleday Dell Publishing Group.

Pallaro, P. (ed.) (1999), *Authentic Movement*, vol. 1, London, UK: Jessica Kingsley Publishers.

——— (ed.) (2007), *Authentic Movement*, vol. 2, London, UK: Jessica Kingsley Publishers.

Reich, W. (1970), *The Function of the Orgasm*, New York, Meridian.

Segal, W. (1987), *The Structure of Man,* Attleboro, VT Green River Press, Still Publishers.

Sills, F. (2009), *Being and Becoming*, Berkeley, CA: North Atlantic Books.

Stern, D. (1985), *The Interpersonal World of the Infant*, New York, NY: Basic Books, Harper Collins.

Stokes, B. (2002), *Amazing Babies*, Toronto, ON: Move Alive Media.

Tsiaras, A. and Werth, B. (2002), *From Conception to Birth*, London, UK: Vermilion, Random House.

van der Wal, J. (2005), 'Dynamic morphology and embryology', edited teaching manual, originally published in G. van der Bie and M. Huber (eds) (2003), *Foundations of Anthroposophical Medicine—A Training Manual*, Edinburgh, UK: Floris Books.

——— (2011), 'An unimaginable existence: Is there life after birth?', http://www.embryo.nl. Accessed 1 October 2011.

Whitehouse, M. S. (1999a), 'C. G. Jung and dance therapy', in P. Pallaro (ed.), *Authentic Movement*, London, UK: Jessica Kingsley Publishers, pp. 73–101.

——— (1999b), 'Physical movement and personality', in P. Pallaro (ed.), *Authentic Movement*, London, UK: Jessica Kingsley Publishers, pp. 51–57.

Wilber, K. (1980), *The Atman Project: A Transpersonal View of Human Development*, Wheaton, IL: The Theosophical Publishing House.

Winnicott, D. W. (1965), *The Maturational Environment and the Facilitating Environment*, London, UK: The Hogarth Press.

Chapter 2

The Alchemy of Authentic Movement: Awakening Spirit in the Body

Tina Stromsted

What makes alchemy so valuable for psychotherapy is that its images concretize the experiences of transformation that one undergoes in psychotherapy [...] Alchemy provides a kind of anatomy of individuation.

(Edinger 1985: 2)

In today's Western world, many traditionally verbal, cognitive therapeutic approaches prioritize mental insight over embodied experience and the spiritual dimensions of the healing process. Yet genuine healing involves more than verbalization: true insight emerges from experiencing feelings in the body, which, when held and responded to within a conscious, empathic relationship, can become further integrated within the individual and brought into the community.

Modern psychotherapy is similar to alchemy in that it has the capacity to transform the unwanted, uncomfortable material of everyday life into something meaningful, thus helping us find the 'gold' in the shadow. Alchemy, the forerunner of modern chemistry, was practised by mystics who sought to make gold from base elements. Psychotherapy takes unconscious matter and brings it into the light, supporting healing and development at deeper levels of complexity and wholeness. Familiarizing ourselves with alchemy's basic elements can illuminate our understanding of *embodied* transformative processes (experienced spontaneously through the practice of Authentic Movement, a therapeutic and body/mind meditative practice with roots in C. G. Jung's active imagination approach). Both practices bring awareness to what we least value: base matter, known as *prima materia* by the alchemists and as unconscious, 'shadow', qualities by Jung. In fact, some analysts equate the body—with its implicit processes, unmetabolized affects and unknown interior landscapes—with the unconscious (Conger 1988; Wyman-McGinty 1998). Providing a timeless 'map' of the stages in the transformative/individuation process, alchemical practice uses the 'dross' of unwanted material to generate new life. Such a map can help orient people in their therapeutic work, particularly when they are immersed in unconscious material that may provoke feelings of anxiety, impatience or dissolution. Without understanding these as natural parts of the healing process, the individual may abandon his or her efforts.

Authentic Movement practice can help people inhabit themselves and bring them back into contact with their instinctual wisdom and sense of self. Alchemy, too, is a practice that balances the material/embodied dimension with the spiritual dimension: its practitioners underwent profound development, accessing mystical states that enlarged their worldview while maintaining their connection with the foundations of natural life. In fact, as distinguished from the aims of the Christian Church of their day, which sought to diminish

Figure 1: 'The Peacock' in the alchemical flask whose appearance provided assurance of the colour to emerge after a period of darkness and confusion. © *The British Library Board*, Harley 3469, f.28.

the powers of nature and made bodily instincts sinful, the alchemists' aim was to study nature and to learn from its profoundly transformative capacities.

Cultural Contexts

Pre-dating the all-powerful, paternal God of Genesis who is said to have created the world from 'the Word,' there existed many thousands of years of Mother Goddess cultures, in which nature was seen as the sacred ground from which all of life emerged (Gadon 1989: 2). Nature and spirit were not divided, but rather the sacred was experienced as *immanent* in matter. The Greeks introduced the idea of the 'separate body,' stemming from a philosophy that elevated the abstract, cognitive intelligence of the mind over the passions of the body, while venerating 'perfection' of the body through competitive sports. Later, in the Judeo-Christian tradition, the body was named as the repository and transmitter of sin. 'The belief that the body must be controlled, mortified, made to suffer for its desires and in general brought into a relationship of subjection to the mind is very deeply engrained in the Christian psyche,' says Jungian analysts Anne Baring and Jules Cashford (Baring and Cashford, 1991: 529). Dance, long practised as a kind of devotion, came to be viewed with suspicion. In many parts of the world it was prohibited, and took with it the people's connection to the rhythms, social mores, and embodied spiritual values that gave them a direct experience of the order of the cosmos (Grauer 1993). In the West, the feminine, the body and a participatory sense of connection to the sacred in nature have come to be devalued, suppressed and/or used for private gain (Stromsted 1994/95: 19; 2009: 7).

The alchemists were working to bring some of the lost feminine consciousness associated with the earlier goddess traditions to the new solar, masculine, reason-oriented traditions that followed during the Bronze Age. It was this imbalance that the alchemists were instinctively working to remedy through the transformation of the opposites in their flasks, and within themselves. The culmination of the process came to be known as the 'sacred marriage' of the king and queen, Sol and Luna, sun and moon—the masculine and feminine aspects of our nature—resulting in the 'divine child,' a higher level of consciousness that transcended the splitting of spirit and matter, both within the individual and in the world.

Even today, the 'Unholy Trinity' of the Body, the Feminine and the Shadow (described by Jung (1951) and analyst Joan Chodorow (1983)) are perceived as underdeveloped aspects of culture. The feminist movement, a rising concern for the ecosphere, the study of interpersonal neurobiology, and increasing attention to embodiment practices such as yoga and mindfulness meditation in the West serve as evidence that these elements are making their way towards greater consciousness. That said, long-held traditions are deeply embedded in the collective psyche, and today's industrialized culture continues to emphasize logic, efficiency, acquisitiveness and competition at the expense of feeling and genuine relationship—with oneself, with others, with the community and with nature. 'Doing' is valued over 'being,' the conscious over the unconscious, light over dark and performance over authenticity and integrity. The body suffers in such a climate, leaving the spirit 'homeless.' Given thousands of years of diminishment of the feminine and the body, for women in particular the body may become the measuring stick for a sense of self-worth. Anxious embodiment is evident in eating disorders, epidemic obesity, self-harm and the abuse of mood-altering drugs; efforts to achieve perfection include dramatically rising trends in plastic surgery, breast implants, liposuction, botox injections and chronic dieting, even among teenage girls (Stromsted 1994/95; Orbach 2009; Martin 2008). To become 'embodied' in this climate is to swim upstream against the current of societal images, messages and rewards that, once internalized, can wreak havoc on our natural sense of wholeness. The psychological consequences can include neurotic repression (submerged forbidden, rejected or despised aspects of the self); underdevelopment (exacerbated by insufficient early nurturing); and dissociation (unmetabolized, unbearable experiences) causing the brain's reflective centres to go off-line, leaving the individual detached from her bodily experience and from empathic relationship to others (Levine 1997; Kalsched 1996, 2010; Schore 2003, 2009; Schore and Schore 2012; Ogden et al. 2006; Bromberg 2011).

Healing the split between body and spirit is a transformative process that goes beyond conscious control and social and cultural ideology: genuine healing requires access to and acknowledgement of compensatory material in the unconscious. In contemporary Western culture, however, the means of access to embodied experience is limited. Untethered from the senses and emotions, spiritual practice can leave practitioners vulnerable to dogma. On the other hand, on the somatic end of the spectrum, bodily practices that overemphasize the concrete, material dimension, with little awareness of spiritual aspects, run the risk of becoming too mechanical. As fads catch on, even yoga—one of the oldest continuous spiritual practices created to develop mind/body/spirit unity—may be reduced to a method for sculpting perfect abs. When either spiritual or bodily perspectives become too one-sided, opportunities are missed for accessing what is emerging from the unconscious, integrating body, brain, psyche and spirit.

Authentic Movement

Movement, to be experienced, has to be found in the body, not put on like a dress or a coat. There is that in us which has moved from the very beginning; it is that which can liberate us.

(Whitehouse 1963: 53)

Authentic Movement, or embodied active imagination, is a simple yet powerful meditative and therapeutic approach that bridges body and psyche through expressive movement. In essence, the individual is invited to move from within, while being witnessed with sensitivity and presence. The process is initiated by closing one's eyes, waiting, and then moving in response to felt bodily sensations, movement impulses, emotions and images. By turning to the embodied self with an attitude of curiosity and open attention, the mover allows himself or herself to be guided by what arises spontaneously. In the process, the mover also learns to experience the 'difference between movement that is directed by the ego ("I am moving") and movement that comes from the unconscious ("I am *being* moved")' (Chodorow 1991: 28; Whitehouse 1958: 43). By closing his or her eyes, the mover eliminates external visual data. This allows enhanced access to more primary stimuli, such as sound, touch, smell, inner images, emotions and memories. Personal associations, preverbal experience, wounds seeking healing and reintegration, 'unfinished business' from one's daily life, numinous experience and mythic journeys may arise.

Through sensitive tracking, the witness, who sits to the side of the space, holds and contains the experience of the mover, so that the mover may descend to the depths he or she is drawn to by the psyche. Essential to the practice is having already developed a strong enough ego position to be able to contain and navigate the upwelling of material from the unconscious (Stromsted 1994/95; Stromsted and Haze 2007: 58). Following the movement, the mover may draw, write or work with clay, bringing further form to what has arisen from the body. Then he or she speaks with the witness, gradually finding words to express heretofore nonverbal, implicit experiences. Tending to the verbal aspect of the process is important for conscious integration, as the mover's safety in exploring vulnerable, emergent material is protected through the witness's capacity to simply describe specific movements that he or she has seen, without judgement or projection, supporting conscious integration. The witness also reflects back ways that the mover's journey touched him or her (in the form of sensations, feelings, images, memories and so forth), feedback that develops embodied resonance and empathy.

Just as the early alchemists sought balance, harmony and transformation—the gold in matter, the eternal in the temporal—Authentic Movement practice offers a pathway to discovering the inherent healing power of the Self as it seeks expression through the cellular intelligence of the body. For clinicians new to working at a body level, the practice can enhance elements essential to the healing relationship: the creation of a safe container, observational and listening skills, the use of non-judgemental language, the identification of projections, boundary-making, affective attunement, the development of embodied consciousness and the somatic underpinnings of the transference and countertransference dynamics within the intersubjective relationship.

Alchemy: Early Beginnings

The self has its roots in the body, indeed in the body's chemical elements.
(Jung 1953b: para 242)

Various sources have pointed to alchemy having its origins in ancient Egypt, but it may actually belong to a lost tradition that goes back to the dawn of civilization (von Franz 1980). Alchemy, the forerunner of modern chemistry, is most often understood as a primitive scientific attempt to create elemental gold, but in fact it had more to do with seeking 'inner gold' through engaging the elemental makeup of matter—the wisdom of nature—in order to reveal her secrets and evoke spiritual experience. The physical aspect of alchemical practice involved heating materials in a hermetically sealed flask in order to 'cook' them down to their most essential components.

This brought about change not only in the physical materials in terms of colour and consistency, but in the consciousness of the alchemist attending the process. 'Dissolve and coagulate' was an often-used phrase to refer to the art. Jungian analyst Edward Edinger compares the process to the development in the individual that occurs in psychotherapy:

> One [alchemical] text says, 'Bodies cannot be changed except by reduction into their first matter' (Kelly). This procedure corresponds to what takes place in psychotherapy. The fixed, static aspects of the personality allow for no change. They are established and sure of their rightness. For transformation to proceed, these fixed aspects must first be dissolved or reduced to *prima materia*. This is done by the analytic process, which examines the products of the unconscious and puts the established ego attitudes into question.
>
> (Edinger 1985: 47–48)

Those who practised alchemy as a literal or acquisitive process—who could not 'hold the tension between the opposites,' of spirit and concrete matter—were considered charlatans. Partly responsible for the demise of the alchemical art during the 18th century, they were known as 'puffers,' as they erroneously thought that keeping their flasks at maximum heat by continually puffing away with their bellows would produce gold more quickly (Somers 2004: 171). Perhaps this is where we find ourselves today, suffering from the spirit/matter split, as exemplified by the get-rich-quick schemes of corporate moguls, healers who promise miracle cures during a few sessions of treatment, or the quick fix of an over-reliance on pharmaceuticals. Similarly, the word 'chemistry,' which appeared for the first time in the 17th century and is derived from the same root as 'alchemy,' has come to be associated with the objective, material aspect of the alchemist's work, rather than the esoteric mystical aspect.

The word 'alchemy' is derived from the Arabic phrase *Al-Khemia*, meaning 'the land of Khem,' an Egyptian term for the fertile black soil of the Nile River delta (Hauck 1999). What was placed in the flask was not worthless dirt, but rather 'fertile soil' that became the catalyst for rich growth. This *prima materia* was subjected to processes including the four different elements—fire, water, earth and air—containing the qualities of warmth, wetness, dryness and coolness (von Franz 1980: 152). Edinger notes that, psychologically, this 'corresponds to the creation of the ego out of the undifferentiated unconscious by the process of discriminating the four functions: thinking, feeling, sensation and intuition' (1985: 10). Jung summarized the alchemical process in four main stages, each characterized by a colour: (1) *nigredo, calcinatio*: the blackening; (2) *albedo, solutio*: the whitening; (3) *citrinitas, coagulatio, fixatio*: the yellowing (preliminary yellow-gold) and (4) *rubedo, sublimatio, coniunctio*: the reddening (the eternal red-gold). Procedures such as heating, liquefying, cooling and distilling a substance were intended to undo the rigidity of a particular element, promoting mutability and further refinement. This undoing paved the way for the *coniunctio*, the eventual union of opposites at a higher level. The result was known as the 'elixir' or the 'Philosopher's Stone,' encompassing both the process and the end product. It was thought to lead to the symbolic birth of new life through the 'divine child' and new consciousness (Edinger 1985: 9, 14). With this further distillation came a transformation of the instincts, an awareness of the divinity in matter, and the capacity to extract spiritual purpose and meaning from the concrete reality of everyday life (Somers 2004: 138). At this stage, one perceives with new eyes; primitive reactions, acquisitiveness and lust are replaced by love as the redeeming agent.

Professor emeritus of philosophy and religion David Ulansey has observed that, 'the alchemical tradition has within it the record of the human imagination's effort at experiments to transform itself' (Conference presentation 1995). Psychologically speaking, the potential for the sacred is embedded in the ordinary: from the lump of coal comes the diamond; gold can be generated from the dross or *'prima materia'* of daily life. Within the context of psychotherapy, this could be said to parallel the initial lack of value the client places on his 'shadow' material (or his relationship to his unconscious). This includes aspects of himself that his ego rejects, projects onto others or would like to improve. The prescription for the development of the Self—the intelligent, creative life force and central guiding principle— lies within the wound, the very place where the ego is least likely to look for it.

C. G. Jung and the Transcendent Function

Having already immersed himself in the study of myth, religion and fairy tales, with their timeless images depicting the dynamics of the psyche, Jung realized that though their symbols had originated in the unconscious experience of individuals, these stories had since been worked upon by tradition through countless retellings. In such collective stories, selective changes are made, and 'what fits or coincides with what is already known is handed on, while other details tend to get dropped, because they seem strange and one does not know how to deal with them' (von Franz 1980: 16). In contrast, in the study of alchemy, Jung found 'an astonishing amount of material from the unconscious, produced in a situation where the conscious mind did not follow a definite programme, but only searched' (von Franz 1980: 22). It was this openness to the uprising of unconscious material, including odd details, mysteries and contradictions, that made a confrontation with the ego's more fixed, conditioned qualities possible. In Jung's view,

> [e]motional dysfunction is most often a problem of psychological one-sidedness, usually initiated by an over-evaluation of the viewpoint of the conscious ego. As a natural compensation, an equally strong counter position automatically forms in the unconscious. The most likely result is an inner condition of tension, conflict and discord.
>
> (Chodorow 1997: 4)

The concept of the 'transcendent function' arose out of Jung's attempt to understand the innate, dynamic process that serves to unite opposite positions within the psyche, 'drawing polarized energies into a common channel' (Chodorow 1997: 4; Jung 1916).[1] So, too, the alchemical Opus was characterized by the coming together of opposites at increasing levels of development. The opposites, said Jung, cannot be reconciled until they are made conscious (Somers 2004: 85). Drawings and wood engravings of alchemical practice from the late 13th century depict opposites—like Sun and Moon, eagle and serpent, gold and silver, masculine and feminine and king and queen—moving from an initially unconscious, undifferentiated 'merged' state (lacking the adequate development and boundaries required for a separate sense of self), through a coming apart or *mortificatio*, and finally towards a transformed state of essence or 'gold.' The coniunctio or 'sacred marriage' that resulted was the goal of the Opus: a coming together of the opposites in a fuller, more refined and more conscious union that can be likened to Jung's concept of the transcendent function, in which 'either/ or' choices become 'both/and' (Jung 1916).

Jungian analyst Joan Chodorow, one of the pioneers of Authentic Movement, describes such a 'transcendent' experience in the development of containment:

> For years I fostered cathartic release over suppression as if they were the only choices. But gradually, the image of containment became clear as a third option. To contain the affect is not to suppress or deny it. And it's not to get rid of it through a cathartic purge. To contain is to feel deeply what is in us, bear the terrible discomfort, and find a way to express it symbolically. Symbolic expression holds the tension of the opposites [...] the therapeutic relationship is at once container and process [...] the alchemical temenos.
>
> (1991: 37)

Jung's work was the first to indicate the ways in which alchemy can be relevant to contemporary therapeutic practice: as a means of accessing the unconscious; as a model for the further development of consciousness/individuation; as a process of healing and transformation, accessing the vital essence or animating spirit in matter; and as a way of contextualizing the transformational process within the myths and cultural traditions across cultures. Perhaps most importantly, alchemy's emphasis on the harmonious marriage of opposites makes it a useful lens through which to view the contemporary problems of the mind/body/spirit split.

Building a Conscious Container

> *When there has been a radical split, a somatic container must be prepared to receive the psychic labor. There must be a greeting of the spirit, a chalice to receive the wine.*
>
> (Woodman 1982: 69)

The container or 'cooking' vessel for the substances to be transformed in the alchemical process held an important place in the minds of early practitioners. Kleopatra, an Alexandrian alchemist, compared the work of alchemy to the creation of a foetus in a womb. Her contemporary, Maria Prophetissa (or Maria the Jewess), a famous early alchemist, saw the alchemical container as a Hermetic vessel which 'must be completely round, in imitation of the spherical cosmos, so that the influence of the stars may contribute to the success of the operation' (Jung 1953a: para 338). She and those who followed also envisioned the alchemical retort as a kind of matrix or uterus from which the *filius philosophorum*, the miraculous stone, was to be born. It was therefore required to be not only round but also egg-shaped (Jung 1953a: para 338).

Warmth, presence, and a quality of focused attention were also essential elements. Throughout the phases of *calcinatio* (dismemberment of the old form through heating up/cooking), *solutio* (liquefying/washing/moistening), *coagulatio* (solidifying, coming into new form), *sublimatio* (distilling and raising up to a higher level of consciousness), and *coniunctio* (the 'sacred marriage' that unites the more fully developed opposites toward wholeness) the alchemists worked with the flame under the vessel, 'titrating' the heat to achieve the ideal temperatures and exposure times. Contemporary trauma theory has adopted this term from the practices of chemistry, medicine and homeopathy, where the client must 'titrate the affects into a window of tolerance'—in other words, she must work with regulating the level of emotional 'heat' in her system ('affect regulation'). She must neither be so 'hot' that she moves into hyperarousal (the activation of the sympathetic nervous system that accompanies high stress), nor so 'cold' that she drops into 'hypoarousal' and dissociation ('the inability to integrate bodily, emotional and relational-contextual information') (Carroll 2005: 25). Once that happens, the therapy relationship breaks down, because the client is no longer truly 'in' her body. Freud famously posited that 'the ego is first and foremost a bodily ego' ([1923] 1961: 26); Jungian analyst James Hillman adds that 'the body is the vessel in which the transformation process takes place' (Hillman 1976: 146).

The body needs the time and right circumstances to grow strong enough to hold and support authentic feeling, experience and expression, eventually becoming its own conscious container as it develops within the context of the healing relationship. This requires just the right amount of attunement and warmth in the therapeutic relationship—for without this, the unconscious, and the animating soul spark within it, remains repressed or disassociated, unable to find the right environment in which to emerge, take root and find a home in the body.

From a psychological perspective, we might understand the alchemical retort as the 'holding environment' that British paediatrician and psychoanalyst D. W. Winnicott describes as central to enabling the client to soften the adaptive, defensive 'false self' (the socially mannered persona that has been constructed to survive in a challenging, abusive or neglectful environment) (Winnicott 1965). Alchemically, this is equivalent to the process of descent (including regression), death and rebirth that are essential elements of depth analysis. So, too, in the practice of Authentic Movement: without a sense of being safely 'held' by a witness who can sustain conscious awareness of the embodied self and contain any critical judgments that might arise, the mover cannot relax her vigilance—her 'inner self-care system' comprised of early object relations (Kalsched 1996)—enough to open to her unconscious material. The witness helps to hold and metabolize affects and images that the mover is not yet able to hold for herself, until the ego is strong enough (a process described as the development of an 'internal witness') (Adler 1987: 183). The client/mover has an opportunity to summon the 'wounded healer'—the deeper healing powers of the Self—inside of himself or herself, which, in turn, acts upon the therapist/witness, in a truly intersubjective healing relationship.

Dark Night of the Soul: Descent, Depression and Dissolution in the Alchemical Process

As in countless myths, Authentic Movement practitioners and clients in depth-oriented analysis rediscover what the early alchemists learned: that transmutation of the human body and spirit requires the practitioner to go through many ordeals in a death and rebirth process. For women, experiences of descent and return are often depicted in stories like those of Psyche and Eros, or Demeter and Persephone, illustrating the feminine individuation journey. For women and men alike, sometimes the descent can be initiated by difficult events like divorce, the death of a loved one, or the loss of a valued job or home. At other times, powerful impacts to the body—such as illness, accidents, pregnancy or menopause—can bring about a descent experience. Here the individual enters the nigredo, encountering mortificatio: the dark, dismembering, initial phase of the journey. This is often accompanied by confusion, a loss of orientation, disintegration of one's old internal sense of self, and depression and despair (Somers 2004: 75). To make matters worse, our culture often views depression as a sign of weakness or craziness, rather than as a time to 'be with' one's own internal darkness, the Al-Khemia or fertile soil, which can be deeply nourishing.

Surrender plays a major role here, as the ego's fixed attitudes begin to soften, cook (*calcinatio*) and liquefy (*solutio*); this represents a necessary humbling of the defences that have kept identity in a familiar, protected position. It involves genuine suffering, as distinguished from neurotic pain. Jungian author Helen Luke makes a vital distinction between these two kinds of suffering, describing 'a neurotic state of meaningless depression' that is 'totally unproductive,' in contrast to the piercing kind of suffering that is 'the essential condition of every step on the way to what C. G. Jung has called individuation' (Luke 1995: 56). Neurotic suffering involves a passive collapse into self-pity, a leaden depression, rather than 'carrying the weight in full consciousness.' Luke further distinguishes between the two:

Deeply ingrained in the infantile psyche is the conscious or unconscious assumption that the cure for depression is to replace it with pleasant, happy feelings, whereas the only valid cure for any kind of depression lies in the acceptance of real suffering. To climb out of it any other way is simply a palliative, laying the foundations for the next depression. Nothing whatever has happened to the soul. The roots of all our neuroses lie here, in the conflict between the longing for growth and freedom and our incapacity or refusal to pay the price in suffering of the kind which challenges the supremacy of the ego's demands.

(Luke 1995: 57)

The Christian story provides an example of this kind of conscious suffering: pinned to the cross, Jesus contemplated his experience without fleeing from it through the false pride of matrydom.

In this case, dissolution represents not a collapse, but an active process of holding an awareness of one's pain, allowing it to deepen through experiences that press one towards growth. For this, a *temenos* is needed, and with compassionate support for the feelings and images that arise, the seeds of new life can begin to grow in the darkness. Inchoate, unnameable or unbearable sensations in the body can then become transformed into imagery or verbalization, and genuine mourning and healing can occur (Bloch 2010: 268). Through the process, the client learns to do this for himself, and also gains a capacity for empathy and compassion for the internal darkness of others - a quality of embodied resonance that is consciously held. Compassion means 'suffering with,' as 'every time a person exchanges neurotic depression for real suffering, he or she is sharing to some small degree in the carrying of the suffering of mankind, in bearing a tiny part of the darkness of the world. Such a one is released from his small personal concern into a sense of meaning' (Luke 1995: 59). As Jungian analyst Marion Woodman puts it, 'because of the anguish in my own soul I have been totally in communication with the anguish in others. Until your heart breaks open, you don't know what love is about' (personal communication, February, 1998.) Through the process, authentic feeling, love and an acknowledgement of the objective situation replace neurotic guilt, the fog of self-pity, or the distress of living with unmetabolized, unsymbolized somatic states, unnamable pain locked in the body.

A mythical example of this descent and return is contained in our earliest recorded story, the ancient Sumerian myth of the Goddess Inanna, queen of heaven and earth. Inanna descends to the underworld to attend her brother-in-law's funeral and comfort her dark sister, Erishkagel. While there, Inanna is killed by her sister's dark gaze and hung on a meat hook to rot. Inanna's maidservant Ninshubar enlists the aid of Enki (god of wisdom, creation, water and crafts), who sends his spirit helpers to rescue her, returning her to the upper world of the living, where she revives (Perera 1981). This legend precedes Christ's crucifixion and resurrection story by centuries, providing one of the earliest known blueprints for individuation: the soul's journey through the cycles of death and rebirth, broken-heartedness and healing, rupture and repair that are required to live a whole and conscious life.

During her descent into the underworld, Queen Inanna is stopped at each of the seven gates guarded by Erishkagel's manservants, who require her to give up her jewels, her fine clothes and her crown. Psychologically, we can understand this process as one of opening to the unconscious, allowing the body and personality to be stripped of their outer garb, including costuming and signs of earthly rank and status. This trajectory requires Inanna to drop down further and further, until she is naked and vulnerable, falling towards the dark, creative void to which all forms must return and out of which all new life emerges

(Stromsted 1994/95: 26; Ashton 2007). Through a process of witnessing and empathic mirroring of the dark sister's anguished cries, the spiritual helpers secure Inanna's release from her death state (Perera 1981).

Like Inanna, we generally have an 'outer' reason or crisis for beginning this search, but from the perspective of our solar, rational consciousness, we cannot fathom that we must suffer a kind of death in order to recollect our dark sister—or for men, the dark or wounded hero in stories such as the Holy Grail and the Egyptian myth of Osiris. This 'sibling' represents our shadow side, without which we can never be fully human, nor experience compassion for others who suffer within our community. What we have forgotten and need to relearn is how to surrender to this descent process, trusting that something rich and good can come from it (Stromsted 1994/95: 24, 26).

This is also a deeply somatic process, understood as a descent into the lower, darker regions of the body, accessing implicit memories, instinctive energies, and the 'gut wisdom' that is rooted there. This marks a potent shift from a lifestyle directed by the ego and the head, to one that is guided by the deeper wisdom of the Self, a cellular intelligence that is fundamental to all forms of life. In the myth, Inanna is humbled and enriched by her experiences in the underworld and remerges in the upper world as queen of heaven and earth, having integrated light and dark, or spirit and body/earth (Meador 2000).

In the practice of Authentic Movement, the level of safety and awareness enables movers and witnesses alike to discover the light in dense matter—consciousness in the leaden body (which often initially feels stiff or 'depressed,' heavy, defended, brick-like or armoured, often constricted by psychological complexes or frozen with dissociated affects, lacking vitality and the light of consciousness). As pioneering Authentic Movement teacher Janet Adler states:

> The evolutionary process that we are each living, as clients, therapists, artists, seekers, is about the transformative power of suffering [...] Much of the work in authentic movement is difficult, painful, redundant and frustrating. It involves hiding, risking, premature insight and paralysis, as well as reward. When it works, as when a piece of art works, the clarity and simplicity—the gift of wholeness—is stunning.
>
> (Adler 1987: 158)

Adler underscores the point that difficulty and paralysis are not only to be tolerated, but are often precursors to growth, as illustrated in the case vignettes noted later in this chapter.

Natural movement, rooted in the deep, instinctual parts of the brain, can engage the more recently developed neocortical brain in a more robust dialogue, promoting further development and integration within and between the two major hemispheres. Insight, then, does not necessarily depend upon cognitive understanding, and this is why the descent process is so crucial to progress. Zen masters, for example, use koans: riddles that, while unbalancing the intellect, may suddenly trigger *satori,* or enlightenment (Suzuki 2007: 80). Authentic Movement practitioners similarly follow bodily cues to access the wisdom of the body. This process finds reflection in the alchemical theme of the differentiation and integration of the opposites.

In the alchemical Opus, the King, representing the old patriarchal ruling principle—'the deficient values and belief systems that currently rule our culture' (Baring 2003)—struggles to find new ways to relate to the dragon, who personifies the reptilian and mammalian brain, the repository of our most ancient instincts. British Jungian analyst Anne Baring suggests that it is unwise to try to conquer the dragon: 'The solar hero has been trying to kill the dragon for the last 4000 years, with very poor results' (Baring, 1995; Baring 2013). It is important to understand that, in alchemy, progress occurs not by way of striving for perfection on a 'higher plane' via 'spiritual bypass' (a denial of difficult emotional experiences; Stromsted 1994/95: 26), but rather by association with death, illness and descent—paradoxically both confronting and collaborating with the dragon of the *prima materia* in all of its manifestations, instead of trying to overcome it through repression (Baring 1995) or debilitating dissociation.

In making the journey into the underworld and encountering the great dragon or serpent who personifies it, the hero assimilates and transforms the mighty powers of the instincts and thereby gains the 'treasure'—the strength and wisdom of the instincts and the ability to heal (Baring 2003). We descend, and our old ego attitudes and identifications are ripped away; we feel lost, left to wander in the wasteland, wondering if anything of value is happening. In the process, we regain contact with a deeper instinctual wisdom which can guide us from within. Through dismemberment, death and rebirth we are transformed and find meaning in our experiences. Suffering an ordeal and gaining a level of mastery can then lead to the capacities of a 'wounded healer,' one who can recognize a range of feelings and tend to the stuckness, pain and suffering of another with compassion, having been through a similar process oneself.

Baring's story also points to the central importance of love in the process of healing and transformation. Referring to the imagined fairy tale she recounted, she says that it was in placing his hand over the wounded heart of the dragon that the King was able to awaken his own heart, experience his own pain and, through loving the dragon, heal not only the dragon, but also himself and his entire kingdom (an image of the larger Self, in the Jungian sense; Baring 1995). The image of the dragon appears both at the beginning and the end of the alchemical Opus, representing 'the half-human, half-animal semi-conscious state, the chaos of natural impulses, the unconscious entanglement with the instincts that is the inevitable result of the slow creation of consciousness from the matrix of nature' (Baring 2003).

Alchemy and Contemporary Therapeutic Practice

The symbols of the self arise in the depths of the body.

(Jung 1940: para 291)

Though both men and women engage in Authentic Movement as a meditative practice and a source for creative work, women's experience of menstrual cycles, giving birth, nursing and other processes can bring them closer to the cycles of nature as they are experienced within their own bodies. The contemporary challenge of reintegrating mind, body and spirit poses a particular problem for women, who have been more closely associated with the body in a culture which is remarkably alienated from it.

Here I will explore some of the elements that often draw women to this approach in a healing context, illustrated with two examples. Some come to the sessions with a strong desire for movement that they cannot quite articulate, not knowing the source of their longing, but sensing that their lives are out of balance in some essential way. Others experience the spirit/body split in specific symptoms such as eating disorders, a lack of connection to their instinctual ground or to their sexuality (which has often been denigrated or abused), or a sense of being unmothered by women who did not have access to their own deep feminine natures. These women may suffer from a wide range of painful difficulties, including distorted body image, poor sense of self, low self-esteem, depression, physical injuries, autoimmune disorders, chronic infections or body inflammations and uterine and breast cancer. Among other things, these symptoms represent a call from the ravaged body to be honoured, cherished and understood in a new way.

Paradoxically, in attending to our bodies in the current cultural context, we may benefit from drawing on ancient and indigenous sources. For example, when a woman has struggled with an inner 'negative mother' complex (including a harsh inner critic that diminishes or drives her), she may seek nourishment through a still deeper source in the underground streams of the 'archetypal mother'—the eternal, fertile cycles of nature. Through contacting the flow of life force both in her own body and in the natural world around her, she can access the resources needed for her healing and wholeness.

Bringing further awareness to the *quality* of one's interpersonal relationships is essential to the process as well, as a felt lack of mothering is a common source of difficulty in embodiment. Our own mothers (and mothers for generations before them) have struggled for equality in ways that often *distanced* them from their bodies; as a result there are few female role models who know how to pass this birthright of healthy embodiment on to their daughters. We can conceptualize the protected, fertile and transmuting aspects of the alchemical process as a kind of symbolic replacement of that flawed, literal parentage: the 'cooking' that goes on in the context of open, conscious, compassionate attending is also a kind of parental nurturing. Over the years I have come to see Authentic Movement as a 'safe enough' container, a kind of uterus from which the client/mover may be reborn, in the presence of an outer witness or 'good enough' mother figure, from the 'symbolic mother' of her own unconscious. This in turn roots her in the instinctual ground of all of nature, the Great Mother. My practice has made it clear to me that containment—psychic, physical, emotional and spiritual—is necessary in order for deep transformation to unfold. In this 'cocoon,' the melting of old defences, including the body stiffening that reflected them and held them in place, can begin to soften. At the deepest level, a dismemberment of the individual's previous sense of self can occur—through processes of *solutio* and *coagulatio*—resulting in the death of an old dispensation and the reintegration of a sense of self within the context of human relatedness.

Psychotherapist Pamela Sorensen's description of the mother/infant dyad provides a helpful framework for understanding the witness/mover dyad, particularly when preverbal material is being explored. The three essential elements in this process are observation, clarification and emotional resonance:

> The first element and the basis for all the others is observation itself. This is fundamental to maternal mental work and the foundation of the containing process […] When mother is uninterested or unobservant, we are worried, for we know that somehow keen observation is not only necessary for keeping the baby alive, but also the foundation of a loving relationship.
>
> (1995: 3)

Contemporary research in pre- and perinatal psychology, interpersonal neuroscience, attachment theory and polyvagal theory (among others) confirm that the mother's sensitive witnessing presence—her attuned, responsive interactions—form the underpinnings of a sense of self, human relatedness and embodied consciousness in the developing infant (Schore 2009; Schore and Schore 2012; Cozolino 2006; Siegel and Hartzell 2004; Wilkinson 2010; Bromberg 2011; Porges 2011).

Cassie: Containment and Rebirth

By way of example, Cassie, a psychotherapist who studied at our Authentic Movement Institute (Berkeley, California, 1992–2004) and longed to experience more genuine intimacy with herself and others, risked the emergence of a helpless, mute part of herself, which she came to call her 'stone child.' As her defences began to soften in the safety of the witness circle, she was able to allow a deeper generative process to unfold. An example of the work's power is illustrated in her writing about her movement and subsequent drawing experience:

> My stone child is here again. She is so terrified. I am so ashamed. I don't want anyone else to see her. I try to keep her hidden. She wraps herself around my heart turning it stone cold. She darts forward when I least want to see her. I feel her pain. I mark her presence in this circle again. She steps forward into the light. The ice around my heart begins to melt. A new person is here. Will she see my stone child with compassion or will she be repulsed? This pain is almost unbearable. I cannot look. I am terrified. I do not want to see the rejection I imagine is there.

Here we can see an experience of Authentic Movement in the context of alchemical metaphors. Beginning with the cold stone of the *prima materia* in the *nigredo* (dark, initial, painful) phase, Cassie fears that these underdeveloped shadow parts of herself—which were shamed or remained unseen in childhood and were thus relegated to her body/somatic unconscious—will also be shunned by the witness as she emerges from her experience.

In the process of daring to stay with her genuine feelings, a *solutio* (moistening/washing) experience begins:

Cold tears spill out of my eyes. My throat tightens and breath becomes shallow. I struggle to stay beside her ... I draw my feelings—the colour and shape of a stone appears on the paper, empty inside. I am not empty, but my feelings are a tangled, matted mess. I cannot name them. I choose a colour and make a mark inside the stone shape. It looks like a yolk sac. Another colour and different gesture and a tiny fluke-like worm appears, attaching itself to the yolk sac. Out of the yolk sac a snake appears, uncoils and strikes out.

As her tears fall, they give rise to new life in the yolk sack of the egg, the emergence of new form—coagulatio. Thus we see the importance for the mover of bearing the excruciating feelings within the alchemical container, as well as the essential healing power of being seen for who we are by a compassionate witness, for which Cassie dares to hope as she emerges from her shell, into life:

Compassion explodes into the empty place, dances throughout this stone container that has become uterus. There is a quickening. My stone child waits. Will she be welcomed? Will she find a place in the circle this time? There are other eggs waiting outside to be fertilized. What will become of them? She is placed in the circle. She will be seen by many eyes, by how many hearts?

(Stromsted and Haze 2007: 59)

Cassie ultimately moved away from damaged or absent parenting into the more primal, archetypal dimension of her experience, reflected in eternal images of incubation and birth. She found a loving ground of being from which to draw resources for healthy growth, while being safely held by a circle of empathic witnesses. Myths, fairy tales, creation stories and dreams similarly offer guidance when new ground is emerging from the undifferentiated waters, following the melting of old structure in the *solutio* phase. These ancient, universal resources provide wisdom that springs from a deeper source than the superego's injunctions (Jung 1947: para 403–04)—the 'shoulds' and black-and-white 'rights and wrongs' that the child navigated in the world of his or her parents, the infant's first gods.

Gail: Recovering the Ravaged Body

Illness can force a person to bring awareness to aspects of the self that are underdeveloped or out of balance, which might otherwise be disregarded or undervalued. The following is an illustration of a woman recovering from breast cancer who came into a new relationship with her body, following the trauma of surgery. It reveals another element that is essential for women in the transformative process: the development of a healthy relationship to the inner masculine, or *animus*, as Jung called it. This involves developing a capacity for discernment and for cutting through a tangle of feelings that could otherwise be crippling.

Gail participated in a research project that studied the efficacy of Authentic Movement in the recovery process (Dibbell-Hope 1989, 1992). All of the women in the group had had mastectomies, and though they had volunteered for the project, they nevertheless felt some resistance to the process, saying things like, 'Why should I go back into my body? It betrayed me!' (personal communication, 1989). Over time, however, enough safety grew in the group, together with enough trust in the process that each woman was willing to close her eyes and listen attentively to her body's responses. Many remembered being on the surgery table under anaesthesia and described themselves as having been 'out of their bodies' (personal communication, 1989). Each was 'held' in this frightening and painful experience by her witness. As the trauma was worked through, allowing each mover to stay in her body as this experience became consciously felt, many regained access to earlier memories of sensuality and a zest for life they had known before becoming identified with their illness. Most were surprised to discover that when they 'blocked the difficult feelings,' they 'didn't get the positive ones either' (personal communication, 1989). A kind of renewal came about as each began to 're-inhabit' her body, gaining a more accurate and accepting post-surgery body-image and recovering a sense of pleasure in life. A slim, athletic woman in her thirties, Gail reported:

> I curl up from the ground and stand tall in the middle of the circle, my right hand over the place my right breast used to be, my left arm raised first toward the heavens and then extended out in front of me toward my witness. Later, I shared how ashamed I have been of my 'flat, deformed side.' During my movement, however, I experienced my right as my 'masculine side' and my left breast as my 'feminine side,' realizing how both have served me so well and how much more integrated I feel in my life now.
>
> (personal communication, 1989)

Within the supportive container of the group, Gail was able to enter the *nigredo* and soften to her feelings in *solutio*, as she grieved the loss of her breast and reconnected with her love for her body and for her children. The embodied experience of the *coniunctio*—a palpable sense of her masculine and feminine energies coming together within her—brought her a new sense of self. For mover and witness alike, the women's grief at the loss of their breasts became collectively palpable in this group; through the spontaneous enactment that Authentic Movement fosters, fear, alienation and shame were replaced by a sense of empowerment, respect, care, and a new appreciation for the attuned relating and body wisdom that lead them through these changes (Stromsted 2009: 203; Stromsted 2007: 139–40).

The Future of Alchemy and Authentic Movement

The therapeutic field is increasingly concerned with the foundations of healthy development and the treatment of interpersonal trauma, integrating a number of disciplines such as neuroscience, attachment theory, infant observation, trauma work and others. Yet only recently has the embodied dimension of experience been valued and further developed within traditional, verbal psychotherapeutic models. Contemporary neurological research shows us that early trauma is stored in the preverbal right brain and in the body, so it is to these that we must turn if healing is to be effective (Schore 2003, 2009; Schore and Schore 2012; Wilkinson 2010).

Alchemy plays a role in this work, because it teaches us to respect the concepts of balance and metaphor: the true key is neither in language nor in the body alone, but in letting the body speak through symbols and stories, together with sensations, emotions and natural movement. Those in the Body Psychotherapy/Somatics field do not always use imaginal/archetypal/ creative elements in ways that engage both implicit and symbolic processing, but instead often remain focused on the literal body ('matter'). Similarly, Jungians and other primarily verbally oriented psychotherapists often privilege words, dreams and imagination, and overlook the cries of the body, not knowing how to decipher its language, nor how to work with it. In this way, we once again risk 'puffery' in splitting the body/psyche/spirit connection, missing subtle, non-verbal cues and intuitions, and denying the existence of correspondences, synchronicities and invisible influences in nature.

In an effort to gain a better understanding of human development and the healing impact of the therapeutic relationship, our times have also seen an increasing emphasis on 'intersubjective psychotherapy', working relationally in the bi-personal, co-created energetic/co-transference field. This work seeks to address and repair the patient's (and perhaps also the therapist's) early relational wounds—and yet this too may leave out the body and the imaginal/archetypal elements: the creative, self-healing energies of our inner wellsprings. Jung described the alchemical process as a process of individuation—a movement from the unconscious towards integrative consciousness, from identification with the aims of the ego towards the Self—through which the practitioner becomes more whole. Alchemy provides a framework for understanding the evolving relationship between body, brain, psyche, spirit and attuned relationship in the transformative process, and Authentic Movement provides a pathway for facilitating this process. Jung anticipated the necessity for such integrative, embodied practices when he said,

> If we can reconcile ourselves to the mysterious truth that the spirit is the life of the body seen from within, and the body the outward manifestation of the life of the spirit—the two being really one—then we can understand why the striving to transcend the present level of consciousness through acceptance of the unconscious must give the body its due.
>
> (Jung 1928: para 195)

Jung warned that, 'The fate of the world hangs by a thin thread, and that thread is the psyche of man' (1971: 14). Here, the personal and the global come together, as the less one knows about one's complexes (splinter psyches and their attendant, bundled affects stored in the body), the

Figure 2: Dame Nature, whose clear footprints the alchemist seeks to follow. Copyright © Adam McLean 1999.

more one is likely to project them onto others and the environment, distorting one's ways of perceiving, thinking and behaving. By contrast, a more evolved awareness of one's self makes possible a more sensitive and nuanced relationship with one's environment—interpersonally, politically and ecologically. The body plays a central role in this; for with a more vital, felt sense of one's own embodied experience, one cannot help but resonate with the life force that animates all living beings. Instead of fleeing to spirit when the feelings there are too uncomfortable to bear, passing them from generation to generation through unconscious trauma patterns, one can find a spiritual home in the body. Embodied consciousness is essential not only to self-development and the evolution of therapeutic practice, but to the health and well-being of our world. In the body lies the gold, suspended in a dark matrix, waiting to be witnessed and cherished; only then can its fragments coalesce into a vibrant wholeness.

Acknowledgements

My deep appreciation to the individuals who gave permission to include their embodied experiences in this chapter. I have used fictitious names to protect their identities.

References

Adler, J. (1987), '"Who is the witness?" A description of Authentic Movement', in P. Pallaro (ed.), *Authentic Movement: Essays by Mary Starks Whitehouse, Janet Adler, and Joan Chodorow*, London, UK: Jessica Kingsley Publishers, pp. 141–59.

Ashton, P. (2007), *From the Brink: Experiences of the Void from a Depth Psychology Perspective*, London: Karnac Books Ltd.

Baring, A. and Cashford, J. (1991), *The Myth of the Goddess: Evolution of an Image*, London, UK: Penguin Books Ltd.

——— (1995), presenter; 'The sacred marriage: Alchemy at the edge of history', conference sponsored by the California Institute of Integral Studies, San Francisco CA, 12–14 May.

——— (2003), 'Seminar 11: The great work of alchemy—base metal into gold: The process of the soul's transformation', http://www.annebaring.com/anbar08_seminar11.htm. Accessed 1 January 2011.

——— (2013), *The Dream of the Cosmos: A Quest for the Soul: Who Are We and Why Are We Here*, Wimborne, Dorset, UK: Archive Publishing.

Bloch, S. (2010), 'Mercy: The unbearable in Eigen's writings and John Tavener's *Prayer of the Heart*', in P. Ashton and S. Bloch (eds), *Music and Psyche: Contemporary Psychoanalytic Explorations*, New Orleans, LA: Spring Journal Books, pp. 261–82.

Bromberg, P. M. (2011), *The Shadow of the Tsunami and the Growth of the Relational Mind*, New York, NY: Taylor & Francis.

Carroll, R. (2005), 'Neuroscience and the "law of the self": The autonomic nervous system updated, re-mapped and in relationship', in N. Totton (ed.), *New Dimensions in Body Psychotherapy*, Berkshire, UK: Open University Press, pp. 13–29.

Chodorow, J. (1977), 'Dance therapy and the transcendent function', in P. Pallaro (ed.), *Authentic Movement: Essays by Mary Starks Whitehouse, Janet Adler, & Joan Chodorow*, London, UK: Jessica Kingsley Publishers, pp. 236–52.

——— (1983), 'Dance therapy and the unholy trinity: Feminine, body, shadow', Keynote speaker at the *18th Annual Conference of the American Dance Therapy Association: The Healing Power of Dance Therapy*, Asilomar Conference Center, 21–24 October, Pacific Grove, CA.

——— (1991), *Dance Therapy and Depth Psychology: The Moving Imagination*, New York, NY: Routledge.

———— (ed.) (1997), *Jung on Active Imagination*, London, UK: Routledge.

Conger, J. (1988), *Jung and Reich: The Body as Shadow*, Berkeley, CA: North Atlantic Books.

Cozolino, L. (2006), *The Neuroscience of Human Relationships: Attachment and the Developing Social Brain*, New York, NY: W. W. Norton & Company Ltd.

Dibbell-Hope, S. (dir.) (1989), 'Moving toward health: A study of the use of dance-movement therapy in the psychological adaptation to breast cancer, research jointly sponsored by the American Dance Therapy Association and the American Cancer Foundation', unpublished doctoral dissertation, The California School of Professional Psychology, Berkeley/Alameda, CA.

———— (dir.) ([1992] 2014), *Moving Toward Health*, video and DVD. Available from sandydh@sonic.net.

Edinger, E. (1985), *Anatomy of the Psyche: Alchemical Symbolism in Psychotherapy*, La Salle, IL: Open Court Publishing Company.

Freud, S. ([1923] 1961), 'The ego and the id', in J. Strachey (ed.), *The Standard Edition of the Complete Psychological Works of Sigmund Freud*, London, UK: Hogarth Press, pp. 3–66.

Gadon, E. W. (1989), *The Once & Future Goddess*, San Francisco: Harper & Row Publishers.

Grauer, R. (ex. prod.), (1993), *Dancing: An Eight-part Series on the Pleasure, Power, and Art of Movement,* PBS television series produced by Thirteen/WNET in association with RM arts and BBC-TV.

Hauck, D. W. (1999), *The Emerald Tablet: Alchemy for Personal Transformation*, New York, NY: Penguin Putnam Inc.

Hillman, J. (1976), *Suicide and the Soul*, Zurich: Spring Publications.

Jung, C. G. (1916), 'The transcendent function', in C. G. Jung (ed.), *Collected Works 8, 2nd ed.*, Princeton, NJ: Princeton University Press, pp. 67–91.

———— (1928), 'The spiritual problems of modern man', in *Collected Works 10*, Princeton, NJ: Princeton University Press, pp. 74–96.

———— (1940), 'The psychology of the child archetype', *Collected Works 9.1*, Princeton, NJ: Princeton University Press, pp. 151–81.

———— (1946), 'The psychology of the transference', *Collected Works 16*, Princeton, NJ: Princeton University Press, pp. 163–232, 1970.

———— (1947), 'On the nature of the psyche', *Collected Works 8*, Princeton, NJ: Princeton University Press, pp. 159–234.

———— (1951), 'Background to the psychology of Christian alchemical symbolism', *Collected Works 9(2)*, New York, NY: Bollingen Series, Pantheon Books, pp. 173–183.

———— (1953a), 'Psychology and alchemy', *Collected Works 12*, New York, NY: Bollingen Series, Pantheon Books.

———— (1953b), 'The spirit mercurius; part 1', *Collected Works 13*, Princeton, NJ: Princeton University Press, pp. 193–98.

———— (1971), *Psychological reflections*, London, UK: Routledge & Kegan Paul.

Kalsched, D. (1996), *The Inner World of Trauma: Archetypal Defenses of the Personal Spirit*, New York, NY: Routledge.

———— (2010), 'Working with trauma in analysis', in M. Stein (ed.), *Jungian Psychoanalysis: Working with the Spirit of C. G. Jung*, Chicago, IL: Open Court Publishing Company, pp. 281–95.

Levine, P. (1997), *Waking the Tiger: Healing Trauma*, Berkeley, CA: North Atlantic Books.

Luke, H. (1995), *The Way of Women: Awakening the Perennial Feminine*, New York, NY: Doubleday.

Martin, C. (2008), *Perfect Girls, Starving Daughters: How the Quest for Perfection is Harming Young Women*, New York, NY: Penguin Group Inc.

Meador, B. d. S. (2000), *Inanna: Lady of Largest Heart*, Austin, Texas: University of Texas Press.

Ogden, P., Minton, K., Pain, C. and Siegel, D. (2006), *Trauma and the Body: A Sensorimotor Approach to Psychotherapy*, New York, NY: W. W. Norton & Company.

Orbach, S. (2009), *Bodies*, New York, NY: Picador Press.

Perera, S. B. (1981), *Descent to the Goddess: A Way of Initiation for Women*, Toronto, ON: Inner City Books.

Porges, S. W. (2011), *The Polyvagal Theory: Neurophysiological Foundations of Emotions, Attachment, Communication, and Self-Regulation*, New York, NY: Norton and Company.

Schore, A. N. (2003), *Affect Regulation and the Repair of the Self*, New York: Norton and Company.

———— (2009), 'Right-brain affect regulation: An essential mechanism of development, trauma, dissociation, and psychotherapy', in D. Fosha, M. Solomon and D. Siegel, (eds), *The Healing Power of Emotion: Integrating Relationships, Body and Mind: A Dialogue Among Scientists and Clinicians*, New York, NY: WW Norton, pp. 112–44.

Schore, A. N. and Schore, J. R. (2012), 'Modern attachment theory: The central role of affect regulation in development and treatment', in A. N. Schore, *The Science of the Art of Psychotherapy*, New York: W.W. Norton & Company, pp. 27–51.

Siegel, D. and Hartzell, M. (2004), *Parenting From the Inside Out*, New York, NY: Jeremy P. Tarcher/Penguin.

Somers, B. (2004), *The Fires of Alchemy: A Transpersonal Viewpoint*, Lincolnshire, UK: Archive Publishing.

Sorensen, P. (1995), 'Thoughts on the containing process from the perspective of infant/mother relations', *Melanie Klein and Object Relations*, 13:2, pp. 1–15.

Stromsted, T. (1994/1995), 'Re-inhabiting the Female Body', *Somatics: Journal of the Bodily Arts & Sciences*, X(1), pp. 18–27.

———— (2007), 'Embodied imagination: Form grows from emptiness', in P. Ashton (ed.), *Evocations of Absence: Interdisciplinary Encounters with Void States*, New Orleans, LA: Spring Journal Books.

———— (2009), 'Authentic Movement: A dance with the divine', *Body, Movement and Dance in Psychotherapy*, 4:3, pp. 201–13.

Stromsted, T. and Haze, N. (2007), 'The road in: Elements of the study and practice of Authentic Movement', in P. Pallaro (ed.), *Authentic Movement: Moving the Body, Moving the Self, Being Moved: A Collection of Essays, Volume II*, Philadelphia, PA: Jessica Kingsley Publishers, pp. 56–68.

Suzuki, S. (2007), *Zen Mind, Beginner's Mind*, Boston, MA: Shambhala Publications, Inc.

Ulansey, D. (1995), presenter, 'The sacred marriage: Alchemy at the edge of history', conference sponsored by the California Institute of Integral Studies, San Francisco CA, 12–14 May.

Von Franz, M. L. (1980), *Alchemy: An Introduction to the Symbolism and the Psychology*, Toronto, ON: Inner City Books.

Whitehouse, M. S. (1958), 'The Tao of the body', in P. Pallaro (ed.), *Authentic Movement: Essays by Mary Starks Whitehouse, Janet Adler, and Joan Chodorow*, Philadelphia, PA: Jessica Kingsley Publishers, pp. 41–50.

——— (1963), 'Physical movement and personality', in P. Pallaro (ed.), (1999), *Authentic Movement: Essays by Mary Starks Whitehouse, Janet Adler, and Joan Chodorow*, Philadelphia, PA: Jessica Kingsley Publishers, pp. 51–57.

Wilkinson, M. (2010), *Changing Minds in Therapy: Emotion, Attachment, Trauma, and Neurobiology*, New York, NY: W. W. Norton & Company, Inc.

Winnicott, D. W. (1965), *The Maturational Process and the Facilitating Environment: Studies in the Theory of Emotional Development*, New York, NY: International UP Inc.

Woodman, M. (1982), *Addiction to Perfection: The Still Unravished Bride*, Toronto: Inner City Books.

Wyman-McGinty, W. (1998), 'The body in analysis: Authentic Movement and witnessing in Analytic Practice', *Journal of Analytical Psychology*, 43, pp. 239–60.

Note

1   For an illuminating discussion of this process highlighting the embodied dimension, see Chodorow (1977).

Chapter 3

Dancing in the Spirit of Sophia

Jill Hayes

Part One: Inspiration

Introduction

Inspiration for my struggle with illness came from the story of Sophia, who desires to be mortal and who chooses to fall from the infinity of space to the time-bounded earth. Sophia's story illustrates my perceived destiny: my living with an eternal process in a time-bound body. Inspired by the story of Sophia carrying life into matter, I let breath awaken all my cells, so that life springs up inside them, creating movement and image. I can say that the breath of Sophia inspires my dance, and that she is with me as I dance my mortal life.

Sophia's Story and the Link with My Own

'Ever faithful' Sophia is, according to ancient Gnostic visions, a spirit born of the One Silence,[1] who flies down to the earth and becomes 'soul of the world' (Sardello 2004: 22).[2] Feeling love for the earth, Sophia turns her gaze away from ethereal realms and descends, her attention caught by the strange quality of earthly presence. She seeks union with the earth and feels love in her embrace of the earth. This loving union of Sophia and the earth reflects my own feeling of being on the earth, where I sense a spiritual connection to all living things through the physicality of my body.

Gnosticism suggested that the source of all life could be perceived directly through embodied meditation, instating the body as receptor of images from the source. Story was sensed as symbolic manifestation of essential energetic being. Many versions of Sophia's story exist, but the ones that touch me most introduce her as an emanation of the One Silence, who breathes life into the earth and who, through this breath, restores a connection with the One Silence. The themes in these versions of Sophia's story that move me are her love of the earth, her compassion for human vulnerability and her longing to reconcile her divinity with her humanness. In this last aspect, there is always conflict: Sophia never forgets her spiritual home, so her sense of exile on earth is ever present—and yet her sense of belonging to the earth is also heartfelt, so her allegiance is torn. Thus the state of exile in Sophia's story is woven with paradox. While exiled from purely spiritual being, she refuses to be exiled from her body; in fact to be exiled from her body would be her final exile from spirit.

Figure 1: Mover: Jill Hayes. Photographer: Paul Wilson.

Her body is her only remaining link to spirit. It is through her body that she perceives spirit. Spirit passes through her form, through her blood, her tissues and her bones. Sophia, soul of the world, becomes a symbol for physical connection with spirit.

Sophia's story is an evocation in images of the dropping of spirit into the body of the earth, into the bones of the mountains, into the blood of the rivers, into the flesh of the soil. It is also an evocation of spirit descending into each living creature's body, into my own crystal bones, my own red rivers of blood, my own clay flesh. For me, her story symbolizes the moment of spiritual conception in matter—the planting and awakening of spiritual life in the body. This is a moment that has been deeply felt by human beings since ancient times.

To find my way back to Sophia has been my yearning since falling ill with cancer of the womb and having a hysterectomy in 2009. The Greek derivation of 'hysteric' is 'suffering in the womb' (Skeat 1978: 253), and it felt significant to me that my womb—a place that I perceive as sheltering the birth of spirit in body, a quintessential centre of creativity—was suffering and dying. I was in a time of my life when I was working hard, giving little time for my own creativity. My own movement practice had been virtually erased in favour of empathic movement in which I felt the sufferings of others, without acknowledging my own. My movement had become jagged and harassed, confined by time. In this suffering of my womb, I felt darkness, a feeling that seemed to echo Sophia's perception of the earth as a dark chaos emanating from her own womb (Martin 2010: 33). Becoming aware of this, Sophia chooses to breathe life into the darkness, animating expressive forms. This animation of darkness is a process that I have activated in myself by breathing into the suffering of my body, releasing movements, emotions and images from pain. This somatic/visual way of engaging with my body is meaningful to me. It helps me to be inside my living, changing body, and I feel like I am awake to the life inside me. During my illness, I felt this inside life as a pattern of energy with a tendency towards destruction of creativity as well as a healthy eternal flow pulsing through my body.

Sophia provided me with a template for being present with my human emotions and sensations as well as sensing spirit in my body. She forms a bridge between human suffering and spiritual freedom. Experiencing her body as both separate and confluent with an eternal stream of life, she cultivates the body as ground of human emotions as well as the channel of spirit.

I wondered if I had unconsciously abandoned my body and my heart (my physical/affective responses to my human existence), and in doing so, lost my relationship with nature and dissolved my sense of connection with the delicate flow of life all around me. I wondered if perhaps the roots of my illness lay in the neglect of these aspects of my life.

Thus, I felt that it was vital to feel and express the suffering I had been carrying in my womb as well as to access the stream of healthy life that I sensed in subtle movements inside my body. I felt that this womb-suffering was mine, but that it was more than just mine alone. In my suffering, I felt the suffering of my grandmother who had died young of this same cancer. I felt the suffering of the Earth too, in the attacks on her body and the attempts to control her wild creativity. It seemed to me that I had been a part of a pattern of neglect and control in my loss of relationship with my own body and with my own creativity. I believed that by way of the body I would awaken creativity again. I wanted to breathe life into every cell of my body (just as Sophia does) to reawaken my capacity to sense and feel my inner life, and I hoped that this somatic awareness would rejoin me with a greater swell of creativity. Through my body, I could be in active relationship with the delicate hidden life of organic forms all around me.

I felt drawn to begin my reconnection with the cells of my body through somatic practice influenced by Authentic Movement (Hayes 2007). I wondered what emotions and images would emerge when I entered freely into this process of embodiment.[3] From previous experience (Hayes 2007), I looked forward to creative exchange and growth via a particular form of performance exchange, in which a heightened state of awareness of the cells is cultivated by performer and witnesses alike. I wondered how this process of connectivity would unfold. I felt the weight of my own cancer as both emotional and physical heaviness and I felt the weight of my grandmother's cancer in my own (Romanyshyn 2007). I knew that it was time to listen to my (her) body and to be listened to by other empathic bodies.

Listening to Sensation and Image as Method of Research

Human perception of three-dimensional images arising from forms or felt sensations of nature was a common reality in the past (Harper 2002). Abram suggests that this ability to perceive images in nature was due to a sensuous affinity with nature—the ability to be in sentient relationship with nature (1996: 262–63). He claims that this sense of relationship has been lost, and with it, the ability to see images of the animate world. These images were perceived as manifestations of spirits, who could show the way to the divine (Harper 2002).

Therefore, perhaps the re-enchantment of everyday life is dependent on an ability to sense the energy in nature and an ability to imagine forms emanating from this energy—ultimately to be in an energetic and imagined relationship with nature (Moore 1996: 299). Abram argues that the door to the numinous was locked a long time ago when the gods of intellect and reason took hold of the human mind. Language became dissociated from the sensuous qualities of the natural phenomenon (Abram 1996: 73–92), and so drove a wedge between the word and the presence of the thing itself. In this way, by becoming the users of disembodied words, we became disembodied ourselves and could no longer be in an embodied relationship, losing an essential connection with the numinous in the physical world.

If Abram is right, I need to re-establish the living body as the central method of research in my enquiry into perceptions of the numinous. I need to put my faith in the living body as perceiver of spirit. This conceptualization of the body overturns centuries of rational enquiry and challenges the notion that the human intellect is the only lens by which to examine ourselves in the world. While phenomenological enquiry seeks to magnify the processes of human consciousness, somatic enquiry seeks by way of the body to expose intelligence other than that of the human mind (Reeve 2011). In order to reawaken my connection to spirit, and to perceive the movement of the numinous, I need to develop my interior sense of movement. If I can perceive subtle expansions and contractions inside me, I attune myself to feel subtle movement in the natural world. Inner awareness of movement potential encourages its free evolution and develops movement synergy with organic life outside of my own body.

Thus, in this chapter, I use my own internal sensory experience of movement and the image landscape that emerges during the movement process as a touchstone for reflection on myself in the world. The subjective first-person pronoun is therefore adopted throughout. I can say nothing about the body with integrity if I am not embedded in my own sensory experience. Autoethnography (Etherington 2004) is thus appropriately selected as a valid methodology for exploration of personal experiences of sensing the numinous. Description of empirical subjective awareness of invisible sensations and images gives detailed form to subtle manifestations. By paying close attention to the particulars of my sensed experience, I find I have much to say about the movement of life inside my body.

To research organic life, I need to use an organic method; a method that stays close to the felt sense of life unfolding, growing, expanding, blossoming, dwindling, shrinking, dying and dissolving. Organic enquiry needs to cultivate an ability to stay with emerging organic forms; it is deeply somatic, resonating with the force that drives the growth. Transpersonal organic research has been described as 'grounded in responsibility, and reverence, and awe for the world and all her inhabitants as well as for the mysteries of creativity' (Clements et al. 1998: 117). The words that affect me here are 'reverence,' 'awe' and 'mystery,' because they clinch something vital in experiences of spirituality. Researching spirituality parts company from rational research, because it bows to the experience of not being in control, to a sense of being 'dependent' and 'enchanted' (Moore 1996). When I research spirituality, it is no longer appropriate to make a research plan because my intellect, which makes the plan, limits my vision and amputates my reach towards that which is explicable. Numinous experience startles me as vital and meaningful, while at the same time denying me access to this meaning. As Moore writes, 'Once, people knew of nature's reticence to be seen and known fully' (1996: 300).

If nature will not yield to human intellect, I need to find another research method that does not depend upon my human mind. I need to develop a research forum, which does not require the focus of research to be defined and positioned according to human consciousness. I need to cultivate a research attitude in which I simply anticipate a deeper relationship with the focus of enquiry. I suggest that I need to reawaken the presence of a sensibility that has been deadened in the methodologies that dominate contemporary Western research. This sensibility, which is rooted in the body (Abram 1996), I will call 'soul,' personified by Sophia. It is the sensibility towards a most fragile and delicate inner life, which hovers on the surface of the felt sense. The 'I' that perceives this fragile life is not my ability to reason. It is an awareness that is in relationship with emotion and imagination.

Experiencing research as an organic process, I seek to 'till the soil' I am rooted in to find this fragile inner life. Like Sophia, I do not stay up in the stars, but come down to the earth of my own experience and sense myself as 'stone' (Rilke 1902). In dancing, my body is the soil and my 'tilling' akin to the processes of 'concentration,' 'meditation,' 'picture-making' and 'contemplation,' described by Sardello (2004: 29). The emerging danced narrative (Etherington 2004) is the craft on which I leave the shore of the known universe.

In this chapter, the story of Sophia is a dynamic visual backdrop to my autobiographical movement experience. Dancing stories of felt experience is a dynamic narrative method that has been used in organic enquiry to externalize and therapeutically change patterns of life through performance relationship (Hayes 2007). In embodied story, I discover, as Abram writes, 'a mode of awareness that precedes and underlies the literate intellect' which 'strives to be faithful not to the written record but to the sensuous world itself, and to the other bodies or beings that surround us' (1996: 265). Through embodied performance, I expose my experience to the creative responses of my audience, which can optimally result in my giving up fixed patterns and moving more freely.[4]

In dancing stories, I suggest that I am making my felt sense visible in three dimensional dynamic shapes, externalizing the internal, and so manifesting the sensibility that I am calling 'soul.' This sensibility arrives from an interrelationship between myself and my environment, born through physical resonance. Abram, using the term 'mind', rather than 'soul,' states:

> The human mind is not some otherworldly essence that comes to house itself inside our physiology. Rather it is instilled and provoked by the sensorial field itself, induced by the tensions and participations between the human body and the animate earth. The invisible shapes of smells, rhythms of cricketsong, and the movement of shadows all, in a sense, provide the subtle body of our thoughts.
>
> (Abram 1996: 262)

Abram's vision of mind is similar to my vision of soul; a sensibility that is intimately and delicately woven with the faint whispers and tracings of the numinous in the animate world.

Resonances with Other Writers and Practitioners

In this chapter, my reflections on soul and spirit resonate with the writing, the experiences and the art of others. There is an affinity with the contemplations on the nature and experience of soul offered by Post-Jungians James Hillman, Thomas Moore, Robert Sardello and Robert Romanyshyn. I also feel connected to the writings of David Abram, who draws upon his own felt sense of an animate world, Merleau Ponty's theories of flesh (as cited in Abram 1996: 68) and an anthropological awareness of historical human relationship with the natural world. The Taoist perspective of Authentic Movement founder Mary Starks Whitehouse is present in my work in its surrender to the energy of nature and in its engagement with polarities. The participatory, environmental dance movement art of Anna Halprin always inspires me to give up control in favour of surrender to creativity beyond my own intellect (Hayes 2011). The writings of the poets Rainer Maria Rilke (1875–1926), David Herbert Lawrence (1885–1930) and contemporary Post-Jungian poet Noel Cobb (1938–) feel to me like faithful echoes of sensed spirituality and resonate with my own felt sense of the animate world. In particular, I explore Lawrence's (1991) concept of 'wounds to the deep emotional self' as wounds to the soul and I draw deeply from the well of his works, which are a song to the splendours of living and the fullness of life. I quote Noel Cobb's (2006) poem 'Why Rumi Stayed Awake' to provide a bright glimpse of soul hidden beneath the external forms of the world. All these perspectives are brought together in my reflections upon the expressive body as a moving metaphor awakening soul.

A Reconceptualization of 'Soul Journey'

In archetypal psychology, the purpose of the 'soul journey' was 'individuation' (Jung 1981a), a process whereby the protagonist fulfilled his/her unique potential through transformation and rejoined the divine. Transformation was alchemically imagined as purification of base metal into gold, with blackening and suffering an inherent part of the process. While sensing the pull of a journey involving growth and change, I firstly feel this as a physical journey into the cells of my body, rather than an imagined symbolic journey separate from my embodied experience. In dwelling with the sensations in my cells, I seem to awaken emotions about my 'little' life as well as to feel a deep pulse of life that is beyond my human emotion. Sensation and emotion often stir movement, from which images are born. These moving images carry life themes as well as solutions from the organic pulse of life. Thus, 'soul journey' is re-conceived as finding the core of my existence through experiencing it first physically, then emotionally and symbolically.

Sophia in My Dance; From Sensation to Image and Reconnection with Spirit

Sophia's story is a symbolic backdrop echoing my own physical experience. Her story resonates with my own, and the qualities that she possesses feel helpful to me in my quest to release my creative body from the felt oppression of a rational, linear, dried-out life. Because her trust in the physical is so strong, she inspires me to trust my own body in discovering my inner experience. Her loyalty to the Earth guides me to stay with my own body and emotions, and her patience in listening for a pulse of life helps me to stay still and listen for the inner impulses of life inside me and around me. Thus Sophia is a kindred spirit in my movement journey to soul. Her sense of loss in exile echoes my own loss of flow, just as her openness to spirit reflects my own felt connection with an ancient flow of life (Abram 1996: 261). Sophia feels to me like my shadow and my inspiration in my quest for soul.

I find that Sophia is often present in spirit in my dance, which I experience as a process of material/spiritual and temporal/eternal entwinement. Dancing feels to me like an echo of Sophia's experience of falling to earth. In dancing, my human expressive body helps me to feel the sorrow and the beauty in human life, as well as to feel dissolved in a bigger tide.

Embodiment (Hayes 2007) helps me to give birth to images, which I experience as taking me across a threshold. I leave the temporal world for a moment to find an eternal, mythic, storied entelechy, unfolding itself in pictures.[5] Embodied imagination takes me into an imaginal or archetypal stream of life (Hillman 1991: 24–27). As I cross from the temporal to the imaginal, I enter a symbolic stream of challenges, deaths and transformations from a mythic 'waterfall.' An imaginal form indicates something other than an image produced by a self-contained mechanical imaginative faculty in a human brain; it suggests a spiritual image-presence arising from the heart of the living form. I experience embodiment as a way of attuning my body to inner sensations inside myself and all organic forms around me—it is this attunement that initiates the flow of images from the sensory field.

Sardello invites us to consider Sophia's gift of soul to the world, which he names as the gift of internal or psychic life (2004: 22). Post-Jungians Moore (1996) and Cobb (2006) bring this animate life to our attention. They evoke a world where 'each rose bush' is perceived as 'a giant ear' (Cobb 2006: 87). In their writings, I find a special sensibility to the pulsing and breathing of life in nature as more than a finite physical expression. Their descriptions indicate a deeper psychic life in the core of all pulsation and breath, such as when Cobb states, 'a ball of bones and bright feathers holds a whole world' (2006: 87).

The emphasis that these authors give to the pulsations of the world as doorway into soul fills me with inspiration for sensing, moving and dancing as my own methods of contacting and joining with the psychic presence of the world, the interior sensibility or soul. It is a kind of dancing that listens to and appreciates the imaginal presences arising inside the physical forms of the natural world. Sardello offers the concept of 'imaginal sensing' as the physical sensation of archetypal image (2004: 37). As a development of this concept, I offer 'relational imaginal sensing' as a joint practice through which imaginal forms arise. I am suggesting, echoing Voss that imaginal forms are kissed into life through attunement (2006: 206). Moore writes:

> Life is full of cracks, windows and doorways that allow us to glimpse the eternal that lies hidden beneath the surfaces of the temporal. These glimpses may be momentary epiphanies, rare sensations of awe that come along unexpectedly.
>
> (1996: 299)

'Sensations of awe' as a 'doorway' into the eternal world are often present in dance and movement. In the moment when the Body 'is moved,' there is commonly a felt sensation of being moved from somewhere other than the thinking directive brain, and a felt emanation of image arising inside the movement (Whitehouse 1958). I am suggesting that this experience is one in which the numen is speaking through the receptive and expressive human dancing body. Numen is translated as 'the presiding power or spirit' in the Oxford English Dictionary (as cited in Moore 1996: 298). It is as if the story of Sophia is told over and over again, endlessly in our human dancing as she constantly descends to the earth of our bodies and fills us with spirit.

It is because such experiences of awe are so inexplicably meaningful in our lives that they call us to them. They ask us to pay them attention. We may gasp with a sharp physical intake of breath, or our hearts may well up with emotion; whatever our aweful response, it can never be quite fully explained. Spirit remains unknowable and yet calls us to know it. Moore refers to Otto's (1958) concept of 'creatureliness' as 'an awareness that comes upon us when we have a momentary sensation of divinity' (Moore 1996: 299). Moore elaborates:

The recognition that the world is infinitely more vast and mysterious than we can imagine when we regard it only scientifically and that a voice, music or some other kind of utterance emerges from it, providing an opportunity for us to be related to it and profoundly affected by it.

(1996: 299)

From a rational perspective, human spirituality forms part of the divine process of consciousness, familiarly cited in many theologies as explanation for the creation of the world. In order to know itself, the power that created the world needed to see itself, and so this is why the word was made flesh. As individual human beings become conscious of the creative power inside all things, the dynamic cycle is complete; both the visible and the invisible are realized, resting in completeness (Meher 1970).

Dancing in the spirit of Sophia offers a different perspective, because sensations of spirit are woven with emotions arising from earthbound experience. Cerebral considerations of spirit can feel like a denial of this earthbound experience, while dancing may feel like a way of honouring it and still opening to spirit. Sophia does not experience her earthly journey with rational clarity, disembodied; she feels the suffering in her body and her journey is full of conflict, patterned with both darkness and light (Perera 1981). Her journey is marked with confusions as well as moments of lucidity and peace, with twists and turns, with disappointments and moments of dizzy joy, with death as well as life (Bolen 2007). Sophia brings us to the labyrinth of our own experience. She invites us to experience our deep and innermost lives as they are, keenly feeling our losses.

And yet as soul, she invites us to move into a different relationship with our own wounds as they throb in our bodies; she invites us to release their images through feeling them. In this way, we may come to experience them on a symbolic level, scraping away at the meaning they hold for our innermost layer of being, our creative core, which joins us to the source. Crites writes about this meeting of the sacred with the mundane: 'Sometimes the tracks cross, causing a burst of light like a comet entering our atmosphere. Such a luminous moment, in which sacred, mundane and personal are inseparably conjoined, we call symbolic in a special sense' (1971: 305).

Thus I perceive Sophia as representing two different yet interrelated ways of finding connections between earth and spirit. First, by feeling the deep rhythms of our bodies, we dissolve our boundaries and unite with spirit. Second, by feeling sensations and emotions arising from our separate lives and releasing images, we cultivate the quality of soul, which in its internal sensibility lies close to spirit.[6] To develop our potential for sensing, feeling and image-birthing, we need to open up to the 'sense streams' (Williamson 2009) in animate life, both visible and invisible (Abram 1996) and to the 'image streams' (Crites 1971) which commonly lie dormant inside and between the forms of the world.

To blend with these streams of sensation and image, we need to dissolve in some way our rational perspectives, which I perceive as preventing connection with the spiritual. If we can move beyond these perspectives, we enter a different reality, invisible to the temporal eye but that can be sensed by the meditative body and seen by the dreaming eye (Winterson 1996). Attunement to our felt sense encourages inner awareness of sensation as well as sensibility to invisible energies beyond the confines of our own skin (Gendlin 1981; Abram 1996). This quality of physical sensibility encourages archetypal vision (Chodorow 1991), creating processes of moving imagination (Chodorow 1991) and moving the dreambody (Mindell 1995). From a Jungian perspective, we enter the collective unconscious accessed through a process of active imagination through which a person welcomes and learns from the image as a living presence (Boznak 2009: 11).

Sophia's choice and intention to feel her life on earth is similar to a process that Keats (1819: 3–4) and Hillman (1991: 114) have called 'soul making.' Keats writes to his brother and sister: 'I say "Soul making", Soul as distinguished from an Intelligence—There may be Intelligences or sparks of the divinity in millions—but they are not Souls till they acquire identities, till each one is personally itself' (Keats 1819: 3–4).

Here is an affinity with Jung's concept of individuation (Jung 1990). Keats and Jung both seem to value the process of transformation in the individual in order to 'make soul.' I compare this process of transformation to the organic flow of sensation, emotion and image as I dance. As they arise in me, they are deeply felt and expressed, and I am able to move on from them. In this flow, I am constantly changing, but each feeling provides the ground from which the next feeling springs, so that there is a sense of sustainment, of continuity, of coherence. This seems to me like the process which Keats describes later in his letter:

I began by seeing how [humankind] was formed by circumstances—and what are circumstances?—but touchstones of his heart? And what are touchstones?—but proovings of his heart? And what are proovings of his heart but fortifiers or alterers of his nature? And what is his altered nature but his Soul?—and what was his Soul before it came into the world and had these proovings and alterations and perfectionings?—An intelligence— without Identity—and how is this Identity to be made? Through the medium of the Heart? And how is the heart to become this Medium but in a world of Circumstances?

(Keats 1819: 4–5)

Keats' sense of human struggle as spiritual journey, like Jung's (1990) alchemical visions of transformation of the soul, suggest that reconnection of the human heart with its spiritual source is forged through suffering and self-awareness. While troubled by the hierarchical concept of perfectioning, which is common to many religions and philosophies, I find in Keats a love of humanity—the same love that Sophia showed when she came down to earth and became soul. For Jung, too, it is the heart which feels the sufferings of the soul, and it is soul rather than spirit which lies at the centre of his archetypal psychology (Hillman 1983).

When I dance, I move and make a soul journey, which involves me in proving (discovering the existence of) my hidden emotions. To find these emotions, I need to loosen my grasp on the temporal, automatic, repetitive patterns of my life; I need to cross the threshold into a deeper pattern of my being (Rilke 1923). By making a space for sensing, feeling and image-birthing, I discover my organic responses to life, which brings me nearer to spirit. In letting go of my fear of exposure, I refresh my relationship with spirit as organic creativity, allowing it to interweave with my life pattern, making it more dynamic and fluid.

Sardello (2004) suggests a structure for crossing the threshold, which I elaborate here because I consider it helpful in understanding how dance can become a process of soul making. Sardello (2004) makes a metaphoric connection between the 'elements' of air, fire, water and earth and the human processes of concentration (air), meditation (fire), picture making (water) and contemplation (earth) as a four-stage method of experiencing the fragile inner life (soul) that provides a connection to the numinous. In dance, the first two 'elements' involve cultivation of embodiment and the second two involve sensing and feeling the imaginal.

Sardello (2004) writes about silence beckoning soul. It is only when I am silent, and I make a silence in and around myself, that the inner journey can begin. As I have stated before, 'An essential starting point for the body's experience of spirit is the silent sensing of breath and blood in the stillness of the present moment' (Hayes 2007: 8).

In the discipline of Authentic Movement, the mover is not only silent but also in darkness. Eyes close to the temporal world, and an inner dark space is entered outside of time, where images arise as in a dream. Sometimes images seem to manifest identifiable fears and anxieties (Freud 1908) and sometimes they are deeply mysterious (Jung 1977).

Concentration (stilling thought and focusing on breath and sensation) invites embodiment; the dancer descends into their living body, aided by breath. Attention to breath brings awareness of air passing through the body, and so an awareness of connection woven in the breath to all living things. As air feeds the cells of the body, they are awakened; they feel.

Sardello (2004) links meditation to fire. It is as if, in the silence of focusing on breath and body, something bursts into flame. From an ancient fire, imaginal forms come dancing up into awareness. These forms only arrive in mind when awareness is altered. In meditation, the frontal lobe is no longer in command, allowing imaginal beings to arise through the archaic mind.

However, dancing with the imaginal can sometimes be a frightening and disorientating experience. Bosnak writes about Wild Mercury, the crazed god of the divide between the temporal and the imaginal worlds, as a dangerous being capable of great savagery and destruction (1993: 215–26). He notes Jung's Eranus lecture in 1942 (as cited in Bosnak

1993: 219), when he took as his material 'The Spirit in the Bottle,' the Grimm's fairy tale. Here, the great and powerful Mercury must be sealed in a bottle before he can ensilver the world. This story advocates the creation of a hermetic vessel that can hold the potentially volatile images emerging in a meditative state. It is a challenge to engage with them and survive, to swallow their poison and yet live (Bosnak 1993: 215).

In dancing, the 'element' of water is present in the flow of images through the living body. To avoid being pulled under or possessed by the imaginal forms, development of emotional strength is required. Filtration of image-toxicity and absorption of image-essence are dependent on both emotional vulnerability and emotional resilience. To be affected creatively by the image, there must be both permeability and responsiveness. Thus the emotions of the dancer must be heard and cradled so that he or she can feel brave and strong against any aggressive and malign intention sensed in the image itself. When the heart feels strong it can listen to its innate response to the poison without being destroyed by it. It can clasp its response as a talisman as well as the next creative moment in the dance.

'Active imagination' is Jung's term for active engagement with the image as intelligent (Chodorow 1997: 6). The first premise that Jung gave for this process was the concept of the image as imaginal, as symbolic of an eternal truth, which was a truth shared by all humankind, an elemental and existential truth. Thus, the images that come into awareness through dream, myth and story are not perceived simply as telling about events that have happened to us alone, but as telling about the archetypal journey of all of us born into time. This journey is represented over and over again in the myths and legends about humans meeting challenges that shake their bodies and pierce their hearts.

An important concept in these stories and legends is the developing psychic awareness of the characters. They tell of the mindful changes in the heart of the person who is developing soul. This is a journey that may grind the person down, leave the person lying on the ground, desperate and alone and longing for return to what was lost (Romanyshyn 2007: 226). Research can also become a soul journey in which imaginal images provide a doorway into psychic awareness. Romanyshyn describes the alchemical hermeneutic method of research, which he defines as a branch of imaginal enquiry (2007: 222–26). He indicates that it is 'almost opposite in its spirit to the tradition of philosophical hermeneutics,' in that it does not come to the image with a historical knowledge-based template for explanation of meaning, but rather lingers heartfully with the image to find out what it has to say about unconscious levels of psychic experience—an organic communion and listening (Romanyshyn 2007: 223). The image is always appreciated as something more than itself, as a metaphor containing opposites and therefore confusions, which reflects John Keats' notion of 'negative capability [...] of being in un-certainties, Mysteries, doubts, without any irritable reaching after fact and reason' (1817).

In dancing, I can engage psychically, imaginatively, emotionally and bodily with the image, and I can be affected by its psychic potency, which may indeed ultimately affect my physical health (Harris 2001). Yet the focus of the engagement is psychic or soulful; the journey takes place on a symbolic level, not a temporal one (poison is metaphorically imbibed rather than actually drunk). Embodying metaphor activates the symbolic in kinesthetically felt movement. In this way, the image comes alive and has a voice in the human temporal dimension. Relationship between the eternal and the temporal is cultivated.

Thus I move between the time-bound and the timeless, feeling at the heart of my experience the presence of 'being' shining through my being (Romanyshyn 2007: 227). I feel like my story is linked to the story of Sophia, which is a human story of both longing for return to eternal spirit and loyalty to time-bound joy and sorrow. The tension of longing for the presence of both somehow creates an energy that binds them together like the double helix of our DNA, like the density and the lightness woven in the dancing body.

Dancing in the spirit of Sophia, soul of the world, has connections with butoh, which Viala (1998) describes as 'Shades of Darkness' and Fraleigh (1999) evokes as a mysterious process in which one body becomes the body of everyone. This unites with Romanyshyn's vision of 'research with soul in mind' in its emphasis upon the collective calling through the individual channel, which might be aligned with the eternal calling through the temporal (2007). Thus, in the dance, soul calls the dancer to embody and move the unrealized forms as messages from an eternal collective memory. Lawrence writes, 'I am ill because of the wounds to the soul, to the deep emotional self,' indicating that his illness is his—he feels it—but that it has a deeper source in the wounding of the soul as an emotional presence that is greater than the individual (1991: 76). Lawrence's sense of betrayal of this presence is echoed in my longing to give back to Sophia her place in our lives—in other words, to listen to her mythic voice inside our hearts.

In awakening myself into Sophia's story, I need to find a way into the storied heart of my own experience. I need to loosen my body and shake loose the ties of my reason and logic. I need to open myself up to the inexplicable, to the sense streams (Williamson 2009) and image streams (Crites 1971) that pulse in the waters of my living body. From the embodied silence, a movement image that takes form though me emerges as an embodied dynamic image that releases emotion and tells me about my deeper psychic life (Hayes 2011). The creation of a watery world in which to freely move and imagine is essential for the emergence of soul. Sardello's (2004) sequence of concentration to meditation to picture-making offers a useful method for creating the watery world in which movement propelled by relational imaginal sensing can evolve, inviting deep change and growth (Halprin 2003).

What is it like in this watery world of soul? What are the qualities of soul/Sophia? Lawrence links the soul to the 'deep emotional self,' and I suggest that this correspondence is also present in Sophia's story (1991: 76). Sophia loves humanity so much that she chooses ephemeral life rather than a chance for eternity. Experiencing love, she chooses the condition of mortality. It is as if, through the experience of a truly human emotion, she is brought home to loss. Influenced by her heart in love and aware of the inevitable pain of death, she makes a choice to be human, to live a life in which emotion will be felt. As soul of the world, she reminds us of our human feeling and seeks to make us aware of our joys and our losses. Holding opposites in her nature (she is visible and invisible, eternal and temporal) she forms the bridge of Soul between the two. As human soul, she contains opposing emotions (love and hate, curiosity and fear). She is a symbol of the conflicts felt in the human heart. Jungian analyst Tuby reflects upon individuation as 'a slow process of growing self-awareness' in which polarities 'become conscious' and 'are painfully suffered,' and may then miraculously give birth to a 'third' healing symbol, referred to by Jung as the 'transcendent function' (as cited in Pearson 1996: 34).

Seen with archetypal psychological vision, images or pictures arrive on a watery consciousness, enhanced through flowing body movement in dancing, as messengers from an ancient source (Romanyshyn 2007). Particularly in creative psychotherapy, art is perceived as a vessel in which to cross between the temporal and the eternal. As vessel, art might serve as a hermetic flask, carefully containing the volatile substances of our feelings and emotions, or it might be conceived as a boat helping us across the river from one world to another. This river might be The River Styx, and we cross to the underworld to be initiated into darkness. While the underworld may be construed as the realm of death, it might equally be construed as the dark and difficult emotional aspects of our lives, and therefore a necessary destination for psyche to find soul (Perera 1981; Bolen 2007). Psyche enters the underworld to become conscious of her fatal flaw: the wish to deny her mortality. Her link to Sophia becomes apparent: Sophia embraces mortality, while Psyche struggles against it. While in opposition, their soul stories are the same—the expanding emotional awareness of their human nature and existence, and with it, a developing ability to contain opposites.

Going underground is also a metaphor for entering the body. The archetypal journey under the ground might therefore represent a journey into the felt sense of the body, moving into Sardello's (2004) fourth stage of developing soul: 'contemplation.' Dekker says, 'The value of physical movement and enactment [...] is in the bringing through of emotions into the body, where they can flow and be "earthed"' (1996: 41). This is Sophia's story. She comes to earth, which is both our planet and the earth of her body. She becomes human, and because of her humanity, she now senses her body and feels her emotions.

From the perspective of body psychotherapy, the body is the ground in which our emotions are planted. But it has also been referred to as 'holy ground,' as in Conger:

When we withdraw from the body as if it were beneath us, we lose our groundedness in Spirit. We don't believe in the body, in its beauty and its meaning down to the very edges of its form. What pleasure it is to study the body without judgement, to develop a sense of the body as holy ground. If we could see the body as spiritual manifestation, we would not be at war with its aging.

(1994: 70)

Conger's concept of the body as 'holy ground' suggests that body memory might act on different levels. On an energetic level, remembering may be a felt physical resonance with nature and other living beings. On a personal level, remembering may be the opening of wounds of the heart, the loss of self, friends, family and lovers. And on a mythic level (as in Sophia's story) it may be felt as the awakening of the deeper loss of an eternal home. It may be that all these levels intertwine: that by deeply feeling and sensing loss of loved ones, and by deeply energetically sensing our vibrational connection with all living forms, we grow back into relationship with the presence from which we are parted.

Part Two: Expression

Introduction

The story of Sophia encouraged me to make a dance about experiencing my own pain. Sophia falls to earth through choice and now it was my choice to fall into my feeling body, to be present with my embodied experience of life and death and to let my body move creatively in response. Inspired by Sophia's story, I wanted to let my body express the pain I felt in separation and death. In this expression, I discovered a new impulse for life as my body reached out from the black cloth anchoring me to the earth.

Sophia in Embodied Performance

I felt profoundly moved and inspired when I watched Anna Halprin's film *Returning Home* (Wilson 2003), in which she sits under the roots of an ancient tree and reflects on her relationship to it. Her naked body is whitened and there are tree roots growing out of her hair, entwining her with the tree above. She reflects upon the beauty of her aging body corresponding with all forms aging in nature. She enjoys the sensation of the mud that moulds her to the ground on which she sits. In this moment of witnessing, I am flown to my own childhood and the adult times in my life when I have been sensuously present in my natural environments: bound to the elements, melded with the aromatic turf of mountains, pulled in by the power in the sea, released by the shoots of birdsong in the wind, and expanded by the orange force in the fire. Halprin lives her 'life art' process by making art in nature, by using her senses as starting points for her art (Halprin 1995).

Halprin has also used embodied performance as a method of healing from cancer. She describes her healing dance at the beginning of her book, *Returning to Health with Dance, Movement and Imagery*. It is a dance in which she fully awakens and expresses the harsh feelings of rage and anger that trouble her life (Halprin 2002: 10). Once she has stepped into the mud of her dark life, she is able to envision the healing element of water, flowing through her 'out to the endless vastness of the sea' (Halprin 2002: 11). In this dance, I find the presence of soul and spirit, awareness of human emotions and of connection to life beyond human form.

Figure 2: Mover: Jill Hayes. Photographer: Paul Wilson.

I feel Halprin's story when I descend into my body and dance. I am aware of the presence of those people, mythical and actual, who have danced their lives before me (Pinkola Estes 1992). They become symbols of soul, the bridge between the temporal and the eternal. In soulful dancing, the sensuous awareness of my body and my environment fill me with a heightened sense of the flow of energy through all organic life forms (Abram 1996). It feels to me that, from this heightened somatic awareness, I open a channel for imaginal forms to come to life inside my body, bursting into dynamic shapes from this sea of sensation. As I embrace the imaginal forms, as I let them into my body and become them, my emotions shift and flow, and I am able to trust that in their release new forms and feelings will arise.

Tuby looks at the derivation of the word 'symbol' and reminds us that it derives from the Greek word 'symbolon,' which means 'that which has been thrown' (1996: 34). She continues:

covenant

> It was used to designate the two halves of an object which two parties broke between them as a pledge to prove their identity when they met at a later date. The symbol was thus originally a tally referring to the missing piece of an object.

> (1996: 34)

This is what it feels like when I am dancing; like I am finding missing pieces.

As illustration of 'Dancing in the Spirit of Sophia,' I offer a miniature autobiographical case reflection. This takes the form of an embodied performance in which dance was employed as a healing art (Halprin 2002). This practice of embodied performance has evolved from the teachings and writings of the people I have mentioned above (and many others not named) and is applied in the professional contexts of dance movement psychotherapy and community arts. An essential healing dynamic interaction in this type of performance is the relationship between witnesses (audience) and performer. It is qualitatively different to the entertainer-entertained/active-passive model of performance. Requiring the active participation of both mover and witness, embodied performance defines this participation in a somatic way. Therefore, the witnesses are asked to notice the sensations of their bodies, as well as emotions, images and thoughts; and to begin to reflect upon the interconnections taking place between these different levels of awareness (Halprin 2003). They are then asked to make a performance response themselves, first through their bodies, then through image or word. In this way, a somatic relationship between performer and witness is developed and the wisdom of the intuitive body is shared for mutual benefit. The flow of spirit in the body is being called upon to respond to the performance, as well as the particular kinesthetic, emotional and imaginative abilities of the individual witness.

I share with you now my soul life in a dance that was born from a deeply sensed process of moving before and during performance. In this process, I was led by my body. The images that arose in my mind felt like they were propelled by my movement. These images were experienced as symbolic. I felt that they told me something about my soul life of which I was not fully aware before I began moving. Here is a section from my performance 'rebirth,' with reflections interwoven:

I lean upon a huge ball covered in pink silk and, in this moment of sinking into and pushing away the ball which holds me, I remember my mother, my grandmother and the earth. In the moment of separation, there is grief and holding on; life does not let me stay, but I want to so much. As I wash myself in red velvet, I feel the blood which covers me. I feel it dripping from my body as my womb is cut, and I am strangely born again from this severing. I feel the two strands of life in opposition: the loss of my womb and the birth of myself. From this death/birth a 'third' symbol emerges (Tuby 1996: 34): the black silk of pain taking me back into the labyrinth of my experience of cancer. I summon all my courage and will to fight while I long for a return to my youth and my innocence and my fertility. I struggle on, and I raise my fist to the air in my defiance of the illness which is bringing me down. Incomprehensibly, at the same time, I am staying with the black silk which covers me now. I feel its presence; I wrap myself up in it. From this place of being in the black death of my life, in the corner of my eye, I glimpse the tiny form of a little goddess on a shelf, carved roughly from a white stone. I hold the little stone figure and I stroke her and I feel connected to this rock of the Earth and of my body. Somehow, the little white stone becomes my heart and I begin to move like a small round pebble rolling and swirling in the tides.

Tuby writes, 'Active imagination is like dreaming awake, except that for this inner theatre to have a cathartic effect, it is necessary for the ego to participate, to be involved' (1996: 36). By first letting the metaphors arrive inside my body, then letting them alter through my movement, I find that there are both intensification and release of emotion, as well as the clearing of space in which new metaphors arrive on the sands of my body, washed free of emotional debris. I experienced sorrow as I rocked with the ball. I experienced desperation, defiance and resignation as I struggled in the black silk. I experienced sorrow and love as I stroked the small white stone. In dancing, I awaken the life of soul. I let it expand and grow.

From a 'locked in' place, my expressive body began to breathe during performance. I realized that the cause of my illness was just this: the imprisonment of my body and my creativity, and that these two imprisonments were interwoven. I realized that my movement had been increasingly held back, energetically restrained, and that flow, moving towards life (Halprin 1995), had been frozen. Now in performance devoted to soul, I began to let my body speak of its need to move more fluidly, and in this flowing movement, my feelings about my losses were being released and symbols emerged to hold and guide me to the centre of my labyrinth, showing me what I was feeling and what I needed to do to feel peace.

My witnesses' performance responses were equally life-releasing. One witness freely sounded through her moving body, like the expanding, echoing howl of a wolf. Another became an animal bounding around, feeding and digesting. And then another began tearing papers into little pieces and rearranging them into new shapes. In these responses, I was nourished by free flowing creative energy, which I received both as a personal creative response and energetic manifestation of spirit. I felt like a creative stream of energy passed through me from these performances, increasing the force of life in my body.

In awakening the creative life of body and image, I felt that I was revitalizing and ensouling my life. In freeing my body, I was freeing the subtleties of my 'deep emotional self' (Lawrence 1991: 76). From this kinesthetic and emotional release, ancient stories as old as human life were also freed. The images that surfaced were certainly meaningful in my little life, but they were also clearly archetypal. Mother as earth and rock are ancient symbols shared by humankind (Jung 1981b). My feeling of mother in blood and in stone created awareness of my need for softness, for compassion and for love.

In contrast, by freezing movement and image, I had stunted the growth of soul and contributed to the formation of an unconscious shadow (Conger 2005). This shadow has been conceived as a destructive life-obliterating force (Bly 1988), directed towards self and other people. By dancing freely, unbounded by thought, the shadow is released, and with it the forces that threaten our very existence. In dancing the shadow, a new relationship with the darkness in human life is made. Instead of an invisible dictatorship of anger, fear and sorrow, emotions are danced out and transformed in creative flowing movement.

The dancing figures that populate my movement sometimes resemble the pantheistic and animistic universes of ancient mythologies and religions. They conjure in me the vitality present in these narratives. Perhaps, as Jung (1981a) suggests, I am becoming conscious of my ancient roots, my primordial blueprint, when I dance—a contemporary evocation of symbolic life. The vitalizing of my images feels like a necessary journey if I am to find the core of my being. And from this place at the heart of my life, I experience a return to the fluid, the eternal, the elemental.

Closing Reflections on Dancing in the Spirit of Sophia

In many religions, spirit is considered superior to and 'other than' body, and escape from body is perceived as means of finding spirit. In contrast, in this chapter, I have suggested the opposite. Rather than escaping from body, I feel that it is by dwelling in body that spirit may be found. I feel, like Abram (1996) that return to spirit happens through sensed connection, so my body becomes my spiritual touchstone; it is a 'bodyspirit' (Hayes 2007: 2).

Dancing in the spirit of Sophia brings soul into the dance through emotional presence. Instead of 'rising above' my emotions and detaching from them, I engage with them and give them physical expression. Emotions are my immediate human responses to my experiences of connection and loss; they tell a story of my raw human relationship to spirit.

As I dance with physical and emotional presence, I invite spirit to become image. As I anchor my awareness in bodyspirit and emotion, images emerge from the felt sense of my being, and I experience them as soul, in some way bringing me back into alignment with spirit.

Jung envisioned the body as 'ancestral soil,' saying, 'You turn outward and drift away, and try to conquer other lands because you are exiled from your own soil' (Jung 1939, cited in Jarrett 1998: 373). It is possible that in returning to my body I reconnect with an ancient source of life (spirit), that by turning inward and anchoring awareness in my body, emanations of spirit may be sensed, and soulful emotional responses to this may be felt, while soulful imaginal forms, like shooting stars spanning the space between spirit and my human life, take flight.

References

Abram, D. (1996), *The Spell of the Sensuous*, New York, NY: Vintage Books.

Bly, R. (1988), *A Little Book on the Human Shadow*, W. Booth (ed.), New York, NY: HarperCollins.

——— (1991), *Iron John*, Shaftesbury, Dorset, UK: Element Books Ltd.

Bolen, J. S. (2007), *Close to the Bone: Life Threatening Illness as a Soul Journey*, Canada: Conari Press.

Bosnak, R. (1993), *A Little Course in Dreams: A Basic Handbook of Jungian Dreamwork*, Boston, MA: Shambhala.

——— (2009), *Embodiment: Creative Imagination in Medicine, Art and Travel*, Hove, UK: Routledge.

Chodorow, J. (1991), *Dance Therapy and Depth Psychology: The Moving Imagination*, London, UK: Routledge.

Chodorow, J. (1997), *Jung on Active Imagination*, New Jersey, Princeton, NJ: Princeton University Press.

Clements, J., Ettling, D., Jenett, D. and Shields, L. (1998), 'Organic research: Feminine spirituality meets transpersonal research', in W. Braud and R. Anderson (eds.), *Transpersonal Research Methods for the Social Sciences: Honoring Human Experience*, London, UK: Sage, pp. 114–27.

Cobb, N. (2006), 'Why Rumi stayed awake', *Falling Out of the Skin into the Soul: A Divan for Scheherazade*, Oxford, UK: Godstow Press, p. 87.

Conger, J. (1994), *The Body in Recovery: Somatic Psychotherapy and the Self*, Berkeley, CA: North Atlantic Books.

——— (2005), *Jung & Reich: The Body as Shadow*, Berkeley, CA: North Atlantic Books.

Crites, S. (1971), 'The narrative quality of experience', *Journal of the American Academy of Religion*, 39, pp. 291–311.

Dekker, K. (1996), 'Why oblique and why Jung?', in J. Pearson (ed.), *Discovering the Self through Dance and Movement: The Sesame Approach*, London, UK: Jessica Kingsley Publishers, pp. 39–45.

Etherington, K. (2004), *Becoming a Reflective Practitioner: Using Our Selves in Research*, London, UK: Jessica Kingsley Publishers.

Fraleigh, S. (1999), *Dancing into the Darkness: Butoh, Zen and Japan*, London, UK: Dance Books.

Freud, S. (1908), 'Creative writers and day-dreaming', in A. Dickson (ed.), *Freud: Art and Literature*, vol. 14, London, UK: Penguin, pp. 129–42.

Gendlin, E. (1981), *Focusing*, New York, NY: Bantam.

Halprin, A. (1995), *Moving toward Life*, Hanover, NH: Wesleyan University Press.

—— (2002), *Returning to Health with Dance, Movement and Imagery*, Mendocino, CA: LifeRhythm.

Halprin, D. (2003), *The Expressive Body in Life, Art and Therapy*, London, UK: Jessica Kingsley Publishers.

Harper, P. (2002), *The Philosopher's Secret Fire: A History of the Imagination*, London, UK: Penguin.

Harris, J. (2001), *Jung and Yoga: the Psyche Body Connection*, Toronto, ON: Inner City Books.

Hayes, J. (2007), *Performing the Dreams of Your Body: Plays of Animation and Compassion*, Chichester, UK: Archive Publishing.

—— (2011), 'Moving the metaphor: An act of surrender', *Body, Movement and Dance in Psychotherapy*, London, UK: Routledge, pp. 117–27.

Hillman, J. (1983), *Loose Ends: Primary Papers in Archetypal Psychology*, Dallas, TX: Spring Publications.

—— (1991), *A Blue Fire*, New York, NY: HarperCollins Publishers.

Jung, C. G. (1934–1939 [1998]), *Jung's Seminar on Nietzsche's Zarathustra*, J. Jarrett (ed.), vols. 1 and 2, Bollingen Series XCIX (abridged edition), Princeton, NJ: Princeton University Press.

—— (1969), 'Answer to Job', *Psychology and Religion: West and East, The Collected Works of C. G. Jung*, vol. 11 (trans. R. F. C. Hull), London, UK: Routledge & Kegan Paul, pp. 355–470.

—— (1977), 'Healing the split', *The Symbolic Life*, The Collected Works of C. G. Jung, vol. 18 (trans. R. F. C. Hull), London, UK: Routledge & Kegan Paul, pp. 253–64.

—— (1981a), 'The transformation of libido', *Symbols of Transformation*, The Collected Works of C. G. Jung, vol. 5 (trans. R. F. C. Hull), London, UK: Routledge and Kegan Paul Ltd., pp. 142–70.

—— (1981b), 'Symbols of the mother and of rebirth', *Symbols of Transformation, The Collected Works of C. G. Jung*, vol. 5 (trans. R. F. C. Hull), London, UK: Routledge & Kegan Paul, pp. 207–73.

—— (1990), *Memories, Dreams, Reflections*. London, UK: Fontana.

Keats, John (1817), 'Letter Sunday 21 December 1817', http://en.wikipedia.org/wiki/negative_capability. Accessed 28 May 2011.

—— (1819), 'Letter Sunday 14 February–Monday 3 May 1819', http://www.mrbauld.com/keatsva.html. Accessed 26 May 2011.

Lawrence, D. H. (1991), 'Healing', in R. Bly (ed.), *Iron John*, Shaftesbury, Dorset: Element Books Ltd., p. 76.

Martin, S. (2010), *The Gnostics: The First Christian Heretics*, Harpenden, Herts: Pocket Essentials.

Meher, B. (1970), *God Speaks: The Theme of Creation and Its Purpose*, New York, NY: Dodd, Mead & Co.

Mindell, A. (1995), 'Moving the dreambody: Movement work in process-oriented psychology', *Contact Quarterly*, winter/spring, pp. 56–62.

Moore, T. (1996), *The Re-Enchantment of Everyday Life*, New York, NY: HarperCollins Publishers.

Otto, R. (1958), 'The feeling of it', *The Idea of the Holy* (trans. John W. Harvey), London, UK: Oxford University Press, p. 12.

Perera, S. B. (1981), *Descent of the Goddess: A Way of Initiation For Women*, Toronto, ON: Inner City Books.

Pinkola Estes, C. (1992), *Women Who Run with the Wolves: Contacting the Power of the Wild Woman*, London, UK: Rider.

Reeve, S. (2011), *Nine Ways of Seeing a Body*, Axminster, UK: Triarchy Press.

Rilke, R. M. (1902 [1995]), 'Evening', in S. Mitchell (ed. and trans.), *Ahead of All Parting: The Selected Poetry and Prose of Rainer Maria Rilke*, New York, NY: Random House Inc., p. 17.

—— (1923 [1995]), 'The sonnets to Orpheus', in S. Mitchell (ed. and trans.), *Ahead of All Parting: The Selected Poetry and Prose of Rainer Maria Rilke*, New York, NY: Random House, p. 503.

Romanyshyn, R. (2007), *The Wounded Researcher: Research with Soul in Mind*, New Orleans, LA: Spring Journal Books.

Sardello, R. (2004), *Facing the World with Soul: The Reimagination of Modern Life*, Great Barrington, MA: Lindisfarne Press.

Skeat, W. (1978), *A Concise Etymological Dictionary of the English Language*, Oxford, UK: Oxford University Press.

Tuby, M. (1996), 'Jung and the symbol: Resolution of conflicting opposites', in J. Pearson (ed.), *Discovering the Self through Drama and Movement*, London, UK: Jessica Kingsley Publishers.

Viala, J. (1988), *Butoh: Shades of Darkness*, Tokyo, Japan: Shufunotomo.

Voss, A. (2006), 'The secret life of statues', in N. Campion and P. Curry (eds.), *Sky and Psyche: The Relationship between Cosmos and Consciousness*, Edinburgh, UK: Floris Books, pp. 201–29.

Whitehouse, M. S. (1958 [1999]), 'The tao of the body', in P. Pallaro (ed.), *Authentic Movement: Essays by Mary Starks Whitehouse, Janet Adler and Joan Chodorow*, London, UK: Jessica Kingsley Publishers.

Williamson, A. (2009), 'Formative support and connection: Somatic movement and dance education in community and client practice', *Journal of Dance & Somatic Practices*, 1:1, pp. 29–45.

Wilson, A. A. (dir.) (2003), *Returning Home*, USA: Open Eye Pictures. DVD.

Winterson, J. (1996), *Art Objects: Essays on Ecstasy and Effrontery*, London, UK: Vintage.

Notes

1   The One Silence is defined in many Gnostic texts as the One Source or Potential from which all life emanates (Martin 2010).

2   The concept of a world soul, as opposed to an individual soul, lies at the heart of Gnostic philosophy. It denotes an emanation of spirit flowing inside and through all organic life, connecting all living forms (Martin 2010).

3   Embodiment involves release of the cells of the body from the control of human thought. It expands the potential for sensation, emotion and image-creation, which resides in the whole body. It is therefore a process in which the mover is encouraged to stop thinking about the body and to start sensing the body, to become aware of the life of the body. The breath is important in embodiment, stirring the life in the cells, animating them.

4   Negative inter-relational processes may be connected to fear and lack of clarity concerning shared creative role and healing intention.

5   'Entelechy' suggests destiny, or an unfolding of events which have not been set in motion by human decision. Here, I am suggesting that images may arise from deeply dwelling in sensory experience, and that these images comprise an alternative stream of life to the one which we intend in our temporal existence.

6   Spirit may be described as an impulse of life, born spontaneously from a pregnant void, bursting like fire into flame. Soul may be described as the first ripple of being, felt in body, emotion and image.

Chapter 4

Body Ensouled, Enacted and Entranced: Movement/Dance as Transformative Art

Daria Halprin

The day after, I find you again
Still dancing inside the costume of your skin,
Still finding the steps of your feet in the rhythm of your breath.

I watch you shifting with each inhale and exhale,
Between reflected pools of sunlight and shadow on the floor.
I feel you, still breathing and so alive in the aftermath of the storm.

Rain drops glistening on your heart,
Tree branches fallen across your rib bones.
Lungs held tenderly between stones.

Breaking through the silent empty space
Breath, you trace each birth and death
As you come and go, rise and fall.

And in the path of your dance
Is left behind

Something so utterly profound
And so utterly simple,

That even God falls in love
With us again.

by Daria Halprin

Origins

My life as a dancer began in early childhood. It was when I danced that I felt most connected to everything in my internal and external life, to what could be seen and what could not.

Movement evoked a particular sense of, and creative play with, the myths and metaphors of my life, bringing me into contact with a vast human narrative. I danced to feel and express

Figure 1: Mover: Cindy Davis in Pods by Lesley Ehrenfeld, Halprin Studio.
Photographer: Rick Chapman.

Figure 2: Tamalpa Institute training students in session with Daria Halprin, 2012.
Photographer: Laurence Demont.

what was beautiful in life, to survive what was destructive, unknowingly walking a path of movement/dance as art, medicine and meditation.

As a young adult, I became interested in psychology, drawn to it by my own demons and difficulties. Later, bridging my history as a dancer with my studies of psychology, I became a movement teacher and therapist.

In 1975, I started defining an approach to work with others based on the ways in which I myself had experienced dance as a healing medicine and transformative medium. My interest was in how movement/dance could be applied to our personal, interpersonal and group issues, and to a process of restoration. The central principle of my work was based on the application of metaphors in order to use movement/dance to process unconscious and conflicted material into higher degrees of consciousness and creative expression.

This heuristic research has been conducted in the Tamalpa Institute studio with students from diverse backgrounds and cultures, through private practice and with students of somatic movement and expressive arts therapy at various universities.

In these contexts, I have experienced how dance is a moving bridge upon which we are able to cross from an individual to a collective story, transmuting and elevating the mundane and grievous to the extraordinary and uplifting. It has an expressive and a reflective capacity, revealing what we know and what has not been fully realized. It can be a medicine and a meditation, an expression of self, of community, of the shared human experiences and needs that transcend differences, and can connect us to an expanded sense of humanity. For both the witness who observes and for the dancer who is authentically connected with her feelings and story, dance/movement can bring us into direct sensory and emotional contact with our most human and collective narratives. When we dance, we inhabit our bodies in non-ordinary ways, we are lifted out of our small proprietary selves and narratives. We dance to connect to others, to celebrate, to express our suffering, to heal our pains, to get in touch with ourselves and to connect with an enlarged sense of ourselves beyond personality or patterned ways of being. Such a dance experience opens us to another realm of experience, to what we might call a felt sense of the divine, the sacred or the holy.

Dance has been linked with religious rites, healing and spiritual traditions throughout time. It has kept a sense of spirit alive for individuals and communities in celebration and crisis. The ways in which the shaman, the spiritual teacher, the therapist, the educator and the artist utilize dance as a transformative medium share the same intrinsic principles. It is the medium that interconnects body, mind and spirit, reflecting and transcending personality, history and culture (Dissanayake 1992).

Some approaches to transformative experience seem to ask us to remove ourselves from daily life concerns. There is an implication that by ascending to something above or outside ourselves we will connect with a spiritual source. I propose that by becoming more embodied, we gain greater and more meaningful access to transformative experiences of self, others, the world and the infinite source. The dance I am suggesting has us go inward and downward as a way through, forward, up or beyond. The metaphors that animate this journey are the body as home, instrument and temple. Rumi gives us the image of the body as a guest house, reminding us to welcome all who arrive (Barks and Moyne 1995: 109). Movement is the body's language. It is our way to enter into the house, meet with all that we contain—cleanse, restore, tune, play and transmute.

Movement is intrinsic to whom we are as human beings, and dance is movement made conscious. When explored and shaped with intention, it is an individual and collective medium that expresses and transforms all the material of our lives. Movement/dance can also be a way to experience and sustain our connection to things larger than ourselves, to enlarge ourselves beyond mundane, ordinary life and beyond what restricts our sense of self and other. Like clay for the sculptor, dance shapes the mover in ways that express the full spectrum of who we are on all levels of our being: physical, emotional and mental. In this dynamic interplay, transformative experiences are evoked (Halprin 2003: 104–110). Dance as a transformative medium serves as spirit's muse and guardian, providing inspiration, refuge and a sense of deep interconnection which keeps us moving with life and all of its circumstances.

In this chapter, I will consider how movement/dance transforms our sense of self, other and world through a multi-step process that I have evolved over many years of working with people around the world. The movement/dance that I am suggesting gives full expression to our stories without binding us to disabling histories and ways of defining ourselves. It uplifts without bypassing, transforms without discounting and brings us strongly into contact with our embodied experiences. The anatomy of the body and the psyche reflect each other (Dychtwald 1977). Movement expresses and reveals metaphors and meaning beyond our intentions or conscious awareness. It acts as a mirror reflecting the breaks that need mending, discordances seeking harmony and the potentialities that await us patiently. It connects feeling to image and makes spirit visible, ensouling, enacting and entrancing the body.

With the phrase 'movement/dance,' I wish to connote the significant relationship to dance when non-stylized movement is made conscious with the intention of creative expression. Non-stylized movement offers the mover and her witness an opportunity for a physical, emotional and spiritual expression unconstrained by set conventions of dance or the body.

Body and Breath

Breath and body are inextricably linked. Ancient people commonly linked the breath to a life force and to spirit. The Hebrew Bible refers to God breathing the breath of life into clay to make Adam a living soul. 'Spirit,' 'Qi,' 'Prana' and 'Psyche' are related to the concept of breath. In everything we do, sense, feel and think, breath is present, sometimes as an active partner and sometimes as a silent one. We are involved in a constant breathing dance, whether we know it or not. Making the breath/body partnership conscious changes our very state of being and is one of the foundational steps for encountering the transformative power of dance/movement.

Figure 3: Tamalpa Institute training students in session with Daria Halprin, 2012. Photographer: Laurence Demont.

Mabel Ellsworth Todd stated:

The diaphragm and its associates, both nervous and muscular, reach into the deepest recesses of the individual. [Breath] is tied up with every living function, from the psychic to the structural, and within its nervous mechanism sends out ramifications to the remotest points of the sphere of living. Like the equator, it is the dividing line of the two great halves of being: the conscious and the unconscious, the voluntary and the involuntary, the skeletal and the visceral. Through the deeper study of the unconscious we unlock more of its mystery.

(Todd 1937: 217)

In addition to being the essential force sustaining life, breath is central to the healthy functioning of our body/mind. Breathing relaxes muscles, stimulates brain function through oxygenation, boosts lymphatic stimulation, increases blood flow and feeds the neuro-pathways. The oscillations of breathing create ripple effect movements in key body parts, most notably the ribcage, but as importantly, all along the spine, which connects with all the other major body parts. It plays a significant role in our ability to vocalize, and to move with flow, ease and tone.

Breath and breathing patterns have a profound impact on physiological function, mental states and on issues related to emotional containment and expression. Breath sets up internal cues and adaptive responses, allowing us to shift out of cultural and habitual patterns and defences (Feldenkrais 1985: 71). It is our breathing that creates a natural self-regulatory motion. Breathing, along with heartbeat and pulse, are the central, repeating daily dances of life.

When we are connected with the actual sensory experience of our breath, we become more aware of all our bodily sensations, with the qualities and possibilities inherent in each movement. Breath softens our body armour, giving us more access to our feelings and mental states (Reich 1968: 57–72). Breath releases tension, keeping the doors and windows open so that things can move more easily in and out of our body/mind.

The capacity to stay somatically connected to our breath helps us develop the ability to ground emotion, thought and imagination in the here and now and let our awareness shift and change. Our breathing movement is one of the best medicines we have for being with reality, for letting go and for opening up to new impressions. Breath, when connected to feeling, emotion, imagination and associative thinking, helps bridge body, mind and spirit. Connecting with our breathing brings more awareness, more presence, more attention and more expression in the body.

Being Here and Now

When our sense of breath, body and movement deepens, so does our capacity to become aware and fully present in the here and now. In fact, it is only with awareness in this here-and-now state that anything can be transformed. Movement with awareness is itself

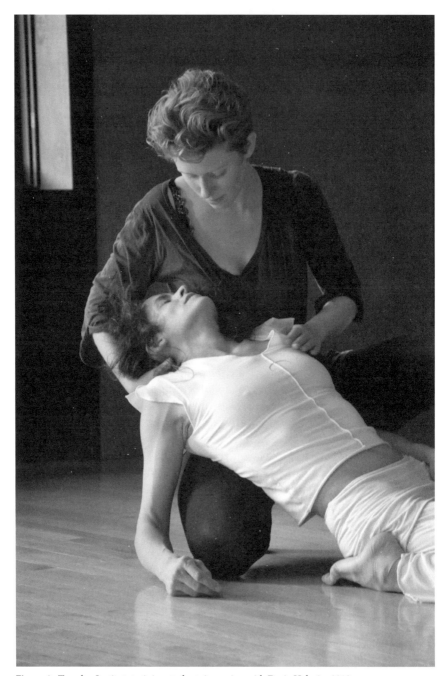

Figure 4: Tamalpa Institute training students in session with Daria Halprin, 2012.
Photographer: Laurence Demont.

a vehicle and a path that allows us to enter into an experience of the present moment. In his formulation of Gestalt therapy, one of the early and significant body-centred therapies of the 20th century, Fritz Perls developed a method of embodiment through creative enactment, having movers work with their historical material and memories in the present tense in movement and role play. He said that awareness itself was curative (Perls 1973: 16). Here, I am speaking of curing a sickness of the soul, and of resolving our past so as to live more fully, and more responsibly, in the present. Such a process places the body and mind in a dialogue that helps tend to the split between the authentic and defended self. This is a dialogue human beings undertake by being embodied, in movement, with awareness in the here and now.

There is a dynamic paradox at play, a constant gravitational pull towards the past, that makes the awareness of the present moment particularly important and challenging. All the imprints of our lives are housed in our bodies—in our organs, skeletal structure, nervous system, blood and muscles. Alexander Lowen went so far as to say that 'a person's body is his past' (1965: 34). This keeps us limited by old somatic and psychological patterns and behaviours.

Our body postures, our way of moving, our behaviour and the choices we make are a reflection of our past. However, while the past remains alive in the memory bank of the body and psyche, body and movement also have the potential to unlock an organic and creative process that brings us more fully into the present, facilitating insight, healing and change (Feldenkrais 1985).

Movement evokes, reveals and channels feeling, emotion, memories, images and story. In consciously expressive movement, we can meet all our life material, giving us a way to break the impasse between past and present. We can play with our material, grapple with it, confront it, shape and re-shape it. When we move with awareness, and when we move with the intention to express, release and transform our experiences and perceptions, then movement will change us. This is its inherent nature.

With an understanding of the ways in which physical anatomy and psychological anatomy reflect one another, we can use movement as a medicine, resource and transforming agent— as a means to identify, open up and re-pattern ourselves so as to foster optimal expression and support new ways of experiencing and being.

In laughter or in tears, in the lightening upbeat or the enlightening downbeat, staying connected to breath, body, emotion and images and moving with whatever comes up gives us a way to enact and untangle the past, experience ourselves in the present and create new possibilities for the future. Each dance has its own rhythm and pacing, wisdom and mystery, burning questions, challenges and resources. Like gardening, dance is a way to dig and plant, fertilize, weed, harvest, cook, compost and recycle. Experience and transformation, like movement, unfold, develop and change in nonlinear phases, cycles and seasons. Such a perspective—which allows for flux—requires the ability to stay in the here and now. The creation of a dance that has meaning, which touches and transforms, becomes a way of being with exactly what is.

Personal Mythology and the Alchemy of Change

Every dance is born of the personality and gives back to the personality. It brings form, integration and enrichment.

(H'Doubler 1940: 167)

Personal mythology refers to the way in which we give meaning to, understand and tell our life story. It encompasses the archetypal dimensions while taking into account the particular imprints of family and culture. Becoming aware of living mythically connects the individual to a larger human narrative. It invites a relationship with the collective psyche and with the ever-present possibility of an evolving narrative (Hillman 1976: 125–127). Movement/dance becomes interwoven with our transformative journey through personal myth making.

Archetypal psychologist James Hillman suggests an approach that would have us mythologize our lives rather than focus on our pathologies (Hillman 1989: 121). At the same time, he admonishes us not to sweep illness, in whatever form it appears, under the proverbial rug. Dance offers up a remedy here in a duet between that which ails us and the creative call to live vitally and well. Crafting and enacting the myths and metaphors of our lives in movement elucidates the conflict and dynamic tension we feel between the two. Like rubbing sticks together, dance produces sparks for honest enactment. Rather than leading us away from our lives and the world as it is, movement/dance leads us further into it. In creative encounter and engagement, we come upon insight and change—and the possibility of re-mything our lives.

The dance/movement process that takes on physical, emotional and imaginative power turns us toward myth and metaphor. We dance the emotions we feel; we dance our significant relationships, the wounds in our families, our patterned ways of reacting. Additionally, in dance, we find new myths to move. Here, the metaphor of movement/dance as medicine will help illuminate our path. Movement/dance as medicine asks for a rewiring, a return to health defined by the ability to live artfully with a changing reality. Using an approach that treats the whole person as opposed to merely the symptoms, the homeopathic remedy mirrors the very quality of the illness itself, bringing up to the surface what needs to be cleansed or released. Transformative movement/dance, like homeopathy, mirrors what resides in the mover, bringing up to the surface what is dormant, festering, obstructing or inhibiting full creative expression.

The craft involves a careful encounter, one that does not slap easy solutions, too-quick harmonies, or fix-it band-aids on our compelling challenges and wounds. If there is anger, it is the anger that must be danced; if there is grief, then the tears, the wails and the inconsolable demands must move. We remain diligent in releasing concepts and beliefs of bettering, fixing, healing and resolving. Instead, we let the myth reveal and express itself as fully as possible, trusting that change will appear when we are ready. Specific themes and questions motivate our movement explorations. We dance with the pain we carry, for the healing and change we desire, for the connection to something divine. We dance for our individual needs, and for our relations with others. Dance becomes an intrinsic part of our self-inquiry, catalysing a reflective process that opens our life material in ways that are creative, engaging and productive. Dance functions like a mirror for our life experiences, for our ways of going about things and for the always-present transformational potential.

An interesting aspect of dance is that it allows us to create a healthy distance between our sense of self-identity and the story or emotion in the dance. This ability to distance without disassociating is the very thing that makes dance transformative. There is an arising, a shaping, a choice, a witnessing and a release into the dance. The process of dance itself becomes a metaphor for how we relate to our life experiences, the stories that shape our identity and the healing for which we long. Dance can express what is, what has been and what could be.

Jerome Bruner observed that, 'when the myths no longer fit the internal plights of those who require them, the transition to newly created myths may take the form of a chaotic voyage into the interior, the certitudes of externalization replaced by the anguish of the internal voyage' (1959: 286). Dance accompanies us on that voyage, not only as muse but also as a healing balm; the wounding and its requisite mythic journey become sacred. It lets us relive old situations in new, productive ways. Dance changes the dancer, and the dancer changes the dance.

This is not a movement/dance form that would have us remain within the conscription of the same routine or style. This dance would have us explore variation while moving with the real material of our lives. It asks us to relive, remember and reshape in the here and now. Such a dance approach encourages attitudes that unlock us from fixed stories and old myths. We are explorers who encounter, confront, play with, release and recycle; we are choreographers of change, using all available resources (Halprin 2003: 122–127).

Six Phases of Transformation in Dance/Movement

Movement/dance as an alchemical process requires an approach and a map that turns the *prima materia* of our old myths, shadows and crisis into higher states of consciousness and expression. If it is to be transformative, the right conditions, practices and care must be taken. To channel the energy and guide the direction of the mover and her process, one of the maps I use takes us along a pathway that includes six phases.

First Phase

Naming—The themes, situations, emotions, history and challenges to be explored are identified.

Second Phase

Encountering—Participants enter the material to be enacted in the following ways: movement situations, vocalization, spoken word dialogues, painting, storytelling, performative acts and rituals.

Third Phase

Tending—Explorations are challenged and supported. Mirroring, intensifying, adding, dropping and the blending of elements are considered and facilitated. Confrontations need to be developed, held and guided so that physical states, feelings, images and memories are expressed and expelled.

Fourth Phase

Emerging and transforming—The material opens up, new movements and impressions arrive, other directions are taken and feelings and images change in response to the cumulative proceeding cycles.

Fifth Phase

Harvesting—Participants reflect upon and digest what occurred. They consider what was old, what was new and what were the challenges and resources—what was learned.

Sixth Phase

Transporting—Participants examine how to apply insights and transformations to their everyday life situations. New narratives, myths and their enactments are considered. What has been discovered in the dance and in the studio serves as a reflective model.

Transporting is perhaps the most challenging phase of the work, to recapture what we are able to move and feel and imagine in the studio, and carry it into our lives in meaningful and practical ways. Questions are posed to stimulate imaginative and metaphoric thinking. What I am looking for in this kind of embodied inquiry is to make applications from the transformative movement experience to life circumstances. I ask the mover how the dance is connected to things in her life, if she can envision moving differently, and if there is a new narrative or myth to explore.

Witnessing and Being Seen

Students often report the positive impact that witnessing and being witnessed has on them. Common statements include the following: 'I have never felt so seen and understood'; 'my partner gave me feedback that made me more aware of what I was doing and thinking'; 'hearing and watching my partner mirror back to me increased my appreciation for what I was doing' and 'my partner gave me new resources that I would never have considered myself.'

Figure 5: Tamalpa Institute training students in session with Daria Halprin, 2012. Photographer: Laurence Demont.

The manner of witnessing that allows for this transformation is based first and foremost on empathy. It requires cultivating an approach and skills grounded in certain attitudes and intentions. Witnesses must:

- see and hear the other and the other's work.
- feel how you are touched or provoked.
- let your imagination be stimulated.
- pay attention to what myths get triggered by the movement and own your perceptions.
- communicate from these attitudes and approaches using wording such as, 'I see, hear and notice ... ', 'I feel ... ', 'I imagine ... ', 'What is triggered or evoked for me is ... ' and 'A resource to try out would be ... '.
- remain free of goals, outcomes and directives.
- offer resources.

By going to the aesthetic experience to consider how the mover and the observer have been touched, the empathic attitude—the 'I' and 'thou'—is given and received as a respectful tending (Buber 1970). Empathic witnessing refrains from interpreting, criticizing and analysing. The orientation is towards generating resources together in an equal and collaborative exchange. Criteria that might suggest right way/wrong way, success/failure or even thinking in terms of self-improvement are set aside. Instead, qualities like opening, challenging, supporting, understanding, questioning, searching and exploring are emphasized.

Partnering with witnesses intensifies our experience. This exchange can help both mover and witness gain the mental flexibility to move beyond attachment to particular circumstances or beliefs and engage in a collaboration that embraces a sense of the unknown and infinite. With a witness, one person may initially freeze up, and another may become more alive, alert or outwardly focused. Developing trust and authenticity becomes part of the encounter. To bear witness is to hold space for the other, to sense, feel and imagine with, not for or against (Halprin 2003: 116–118). It is to tend to the shared space in between, to the dancing together—a call and response that weaves the threads of interconnection.

The act of joining and collaborating with another in this creative and reflective dialogue is itself a way of making myth, metaphor and meaning with each other. Dance/movement as empathic medium serves as the language and bridge between witness and enactor (Arnheim 1966: 53).

The value and potency of being witnessed while moving is a teaching, a revelation and a healing in itself. It provides an empathic mirror for the mover that can generate a deep sense of acceptance accompanied by significant insights. With practice, witnessing and being witnessed teach us how to be more present, authentic and empathic with ourselves and with others.

Spirit of Place

The body provides an internal space and container for sensation, feeling and image to be evoked in movement. The studio provides an external stage and a sacred space that sets what happens in it apart from everyday life, ordinary concerns and states of being. As we

Figure 6: Tamalpa Institute training students in session with Daria Halprin, 2012.
Photographer: Laurence Demont.

cross over the threshold from street to studio, we are symbolically entering into another world. The studio itself ritualizes our transition and, when we use the geography of the space intentionally, shifts our experience with everything that happens inside its walls.

We invest the studio with metaphoric significance, giving it its own symbolic resonance that acts upon our imaginations and frames our mythic journey, inspiring and provoking us as we dance to become more than our everyday, habitual selves. The liminal space of studio architecture and symbolism elevates even an everyday movement like walking into a dance. The studio becomes the space in which to receive and to activate. It is a blank canvas upon which impressions appear, disappear, reappear and change form. The studio is the place of practice, where the practitioner stays open to all that arises.

The moment the mover steps through the door of the studio, she does so with the awareness and attitude that she is stepping in to her practice; to utilize her creativity and the art of movement/dance; to shift her perception and her experience; to expand her consciousness; to bring new breath, new presence, new range of motion on all levels, including mind, to her life as a soloist and with others. She enters the studio as choreographer/alchemist. She responds to the sacred geometry of the studio space.

The architecture of the space symbolizes and joins the myths and metaphors being explored. Studio is empty space. It can be a place where things are constructed: altars, installation pieces and everyday objects used as art pieces. Walls and floors are invested with the dancers' imagination and become surfaces upon which to lean, push against, fall into, rise up from, leap and lunge on, run from or towards, circle and spiral around. The studio acts as a childhood home, the place where anything new is possible, the interior space of mind or heart. Windows can be imagined as portals for looking out into the world beyond the literal, for reaching toward things on the other side or far away or doorways as space for entrance and departure dances. Marcel Duchamp reframed postmodernist viewpoints concerning the life/art bridge with his definition of 'object d'arte' as being that object at which the artist points. In this same sense, every pedestrian movement and every object in the studio is infused as a resource for the dance enactment, because it is in the sacred space of the studio. Set apart from the business of life, the studio is a soulful place to go to be energized, a place where everything can be contained, symbolized, enacted and transformed.

Nature as Studio

The quality of living with nature [...] has affected me spiritually as well as physically. It has formed the basis of my design philosophy. I learned not to copy the forms of nature, but to understand the processes by which natural forms arise.

(Lawrence Halprin, 1992; private journal entry
in conversation on the art of environment)

The natural environment is a source of inspiration that brings a sense of spirituality and the sacred to people in a variety of ways. For my father, landscape and environmental

Figure 7: Tamalpa Institute training students in session with Daria Halprin, 2012. Photographer: Laurence Demont.

designer Lawrence Halprin, it was a place for him to find inspiration for his work in the visual experience of nature—in the movement, organic principles and processes of the landscape. He had no interest in mimicry. What he challenged himself to do was to adapt and re-translate so that in any environment, including the heart of urban living, the spiritual qualities that he found in nature could be reinvented and re-experienced in the midst of everyday life. It has been my interest to interact with nature as a metaphoric process, for psychological and transcendent experience as well as for creativity (Halprin, L. 1969: 48).

Looking to translate a spiritual relationship with nature in the creative matter of movement/ dance, I approach the natural landscape as if it is the outdoor studio, a place to move in and through, informing and transforming our movement and our personal mythology. Outer nature becomes a macrocosm for inner nature, a clear mirror that reflects body and psyche in an altogether unique way. When we dance in nature, she mirrors, partners and teaches us.

Natural elements of the environment act upon us and move us differently; they take us to new places in our bodies, emotions and imaginations. We act with nature, using its elements as poetic metaphors for elements in our lives and in our dances. Trees inform us about grounding, rooting into the earth with branches extended. Rivers show us about flow, undercurrents and what happens to movement as it encounters large rocks. Ocean acts as a metaphor for stories in our lives, becoming the untamable waters of life, sometimes calm and other times crashing.

As movers in a natural environment, we are not tourists, simply observing the view, remaining outside or above it. Instead, we enter into it, literally: we engage physically with its physicality (Halprin 2003: 96). It becomes our dance partner as we invest and are invested by what we see, hear, sense, feel and imagine. We throw stones into water as a dance ritual for letting things go. We mirror the movement of tree branches being swayed by the wind, letting the movement itself open us up to something unknown, unplanned. We dig in earth and it becomes a dance of burials, or grappling with something. We climb a hill on all fours, pull ourselves up through plants or over rocks as a dance enactment that tells its own story through the physical encounter between dancer and hill.

Story of a Dance

Thirty students from all over the world have gathered in the Tamalpa Institute studio to explore the living arts of our individual and collective body mythologies. It is a beautiful setting, an indoor studio and outdoor dance deck. Nestled in a redwood grove with the San Francisco skyline on one side, and Mt. Tamalpais on the other, the site suggests thresholds and intersections between nature and urban life.

Figure 8: Tamalpa Institute training students in session with Daria Halprin, 2012. Photographer: Laurence Demont.

106

Students are in a full-time, three-month training programme. Each week, we study a different body part through somatic experience, movement expression, the creative arts and connection with nature. The training takes participants deeply into psychological themes and issues, performance rituals, interpersonal and group communication. This week, the terrain is the head, and the theme for the day is masking and unmasking.

Students begin with breath awareness, tracking small movements generated by deep breathing. Palms of the hands are placed on belly and ribcage, then support the weight of the head as it moves in various ways. Once the somatic focus is established and I call out movement resources, the head is to lead: dropping forward, lifting up, dropping backwards, turning left and right, rotating. Once the expressive movement is developed, I call for the movers to begin noticing and responding to the feelings, images, memories and stories that are being evoked by the movement.

As I observe, several key impressions become visible: intense focus, quality of presence seen in body tone, body part articulation, use of space, sound of breath and overall body responsiveness to the movement itself. The high state of somatic presence expands to include a high state of emotional presence as the expression of feeling emerges in each person's movement. Without specific intention, direction or interaction between people, it looks as if a collaborative, choreographed group dance is unfolding. A palatable quality of animated suspension fills the room. I begin to actually feel myself inside a transforming experience. Inspired by what is unfolding, I call to half of the group to watch as the others continue. I call out to the movers to face those witnessing and at times to intentionally turn away from them, to work with facial expressions that emerge from the body postures, movement gestures, feelings and images that arise. The new spatial setting between movers and witnesses creates a sense of group ritual.

Facial expressions, postures and whole body movements span the entire range of human emotion and condition: anger, sadness, joy, shyness, confusion, fear, courage—we see the critic, the clown, the bully, the victim, the child, the elder and the faces of grief and of compassion all appear in front of us. As this group ritual unfolds, movers and witnesses alike begin to weep. Something very deep and beyond words is being evoked in all of us. An archetypal human struggle and triumph is being enacted. I feel a shift in the air, a quality of luminous suspension.

The beautiful and persistent call of a hawk circling over the studio calls to us. The light in the room shifts from light to dark and back again as clouds pass over the sun. There is a strong quality of unspoken group awareness to all that is present: each movement; the sound of breath; the hawk; changes in light; the gorgeous, raw, at times tortured, at times ecstatic, always vulnerable facial expressions; the accompanying body postures and gestures. I ring a bell. The movers and witnesses change places wordlessly. This seamless shift of roles and physical place between witnesses and movers is a powerful metaphor in the moment and within the dance, as if we are enacting our own ability in life to shift between the two experiences. The masking and unmasking rite continues.

Following the explorations of head masking and unmasking, we travel from indoor studio to outdoor studio in the natural environment. It provides a way to get out of our thinking heads and into our feeling senses, to let the environment change us and to enter into the sacred space of nature for our final act.

We move through three distinct parts of the outdoor environment, each leading into the next: outdoor dance deck, stairs melding into a dirt path, path leading into a redwood grove.

Inspired by the head and the masking and unmasking work we have done, we pass through each area of the outdoors, pausing for ten minutes on the deck to look, connect with and respond in movement to the natural elements. The directions given are to look, listen, smell and touch, then to begin to move around the site, making physical contact, moving in relationship to something that is observed in the landscape.

We enter onto the path and walk out into the woods in silence, paying attention to what we see, smell, hear, feel and imagine. Our task, once we arrive at the redwood grove, is to find a place to move in with the old head stuff, and another place to move in for new resources. We are to create a trail between the two and travel back and forth, moving with the elements along the pathway, as well as in our two chosen sites. We may cross paths with other movers, and we may make sounds.

We take 30 minutes to explore. At the sound of a bell, we travel to each dancer's site to witness the environmental piece that each dancer creates. When all are complete, at a second ringing of the bell, we walk together in silence along the path back to the redwood deck and into the studio. We bring something from our spots in the natural environment with us. Back in the studio, together we create an installation piece—an altar—made up of our found objects from the outdoors.

Participants write poetic odes inspired by the environment, and what we would like to transport back into our lives from this experience. I guide the movers into a standing circle around the environmental altar. With our eyes closed, the unified sound of our breathing is audible, spontaneously becoming a humming song.

Each dancer does a solo, a moving and speaking response using the altar that has become part of the indoor studio dance landscape. A series of mask/unmask images are painted, artefacts left behind to mark and keep the dance experience alive. The painted images connect with individual stories from the lives of each group member, and a life/art dialogue is catalysed. Paintings generate further dramatic enactments in a scene that blends dance with theatre.

The following questions lead into life/art dialogues between people and journal writing for further self-reflection:

- Do you find any correlations between masking and unmasking and how you experience yourself physically, emotionally or mentally in the ways that you relate to yourself and to the world at large?
- How do you mask and unmask yourself in your life—in family, significant relationships, at work?
- What new resources would you like to use as you continue exploring the theme of masking and unmasking in your life?

By posing such questions, we create a bridge between our movement experience and our life experience (Halprin 2003: 149–152). In dialogue, we discover that we share similar responses. Students speak of feeling pure emotion, unattached to any particular content or story, immense waves of compassion for themselves, for people, times, situations in their lives, whom they imagine as they move and for each other as they witness. Qualities like acceptance, forgiveness, deep physical/emotional/mental interconnectedness, release and healing experiences of the past are named. People describe feeling as if they were participating in a sacred rite, both totally personal to each individual while being archetypal, as if the dance is for, about and belonging to all of humanity. We feel transformed by it.

Structuring the Experience

As a teacher, or a kind of choreographer for the experience, I did not go about composing the score with the outcome of a transformative/spiritual experience in mind. The students were not expecting it. The body part, movement structure and theme did not seem to suggest in an obvious or indicative way how deeply touched our spirits would be. However, I did consciously work with an approach and key ingredients that facilitate transformative movement experience. I followed three phases:

1. *Evocation:* Developing connection with physical sensation, emerging feelings and images through heightened awareness, focus, attention, staying present and expression of the here-and-now experience.
2. *Invocation:* Choosing themes and shaping explorations so as to invest the movement with metaphors connected to life material and archetypal meaning.
3. *Convocation:* Setting the space in a way that is designed for the collective experience and for shared activities, with the intention to witness, be witnessed and interact.

Transformation is facilitated by creating an environment where mythic and transcendent themes can be danced, explored and witnessed. *Evocation* by deepening physical awareness and movements, *invocation* through thematic explorations and metaphors and *convocation* through proper setting of the space and all the beings in it, forge that path towards transformation.

Evocation for the dancers in our masking and unmasking piece began with a shift of consciousness away from every day to a deepening of somatic awareness through breath and body sense. A sense of deep connection with the body was foundational, followed by a detailed focus on particular body parts. Body parts and their particular expressive movements became keys to an *invocation* of feelings, images and narrative. The stabilizing baseline of breath and body sense established a point of return, a pause and a physical expression that accompanied the potent emotional responses, vivid images and associated stories and memories from the life experiences of the dancers.

Furthering the invocation was the way in which the dancers were encouraged to stay in the here and now through movement enactment inclusive of situations, memories, personal and archetypal mythologies of the past. In the here and now experience, old material, emotions and imprints were released and an awareness of new possibilities organically arose. Altogether, the layering of this series of building blocks in phases allowed the dancers to encounter themselves and each other at multiple levels, thereby expanding the movement material and the dancers' experiences of it.

The repeatable repertoire of movement that developed became a kind of movement mantra and a unifying element for this dance ritual. Individual responses were encouraged while the individual dancer was freed from thinking ahead or preconceiving outcomes. The coaching voice of the facilitator offered resources that played a significant part, reinforcing each phase, and helping to establish a collective consciousness that allowed for the experience of *convocation* to emerge organically. The key elements that catalysed the dance depended upon each dancer's embodied and interconnected relationship with self on all three levels: physical, emotional and mental. Bringing the dance from the inner sanctum of the studio to the sanctuary of the natural world facilitated an opening to the fourth dimension—a sense of sacred, liminal space and connection with spirit. This individual and group journey transported us into a liminal space where entrancement waited and took us into her arms. By investing dance with authentic feeling, we engaged in soul work, making sacred what was expressed in the dance.

In Her Own Words

The following transcript is from the journal of a student describing her exploration on the mask/unmask theme. It provides a more specific view into the six phases.

Naming

Mask of composure: I feel calm and serene. I feel my breath fill me and slowly, easily, release with a lingering exhalation. I feel my spine long, with my sternum and the crown of my head lifting in alignment. I imagine walking calmly through calamity, with a poised posture, relaxed and self-assured. With this mask, this posture, this persona, I am capable and I am also cold (every part of this mask is blue) and removed. I am uncovering how this mask has been a resource for me, as well as a coping mechanism. What is beneath the mask of composure? It is the idea, the fear, of being seen as a fraud.

Encountering

The fraud: In sound and movement I express all the emotions behind my mask: gurgling, babbling and breathy incoherent ramblings are accompanied by sloppy syncopated movements with shrugged shoulders, floppy arms and loose, wiggly hip joints. I slowly pause and come to stillness.

Tending, Emerging and Transforming

My witness asks me, 'What does the fraud have to say?' I stay with the stillness, imagining the fraud, evoking the emotion behind what it has to say. As I explore on the outside dance deck, the fraud pleads a loud resounding question 'HELLO?' And it echoes over the trees and down the valley, bouncing along the hillsides. I imagine the chorus of echoes whispering, 'Does anybody hear me? Does anybody see me? Hello ...?'

Emerging and Transforming

Now I pause for a moment. I imagine unmasking the fraud and I imagine the beginner's mind beneath. Inspired by this idea, I create another drawing, as I begin shaping a new myth to explore, move and practice.

Harvesting

This is a victim character: The fraud is an attempt to hide my fear of not knowing, my fear of getting it 'wrong,' my fear of being unworthy in comparison to others. The fraud shuts down, and denies the ability to experiment and make mistakes in the learning process and in personal relationships. This inhibits my learning and growing in an effort not to get hurt. It also perpetuates an unhealthy cycle of seeking assurance from others ('Poor me, tell me I am not a Fraud!') thereby holding onto the fear, and the idea that something outside of myself will fulfil me. When that external assurance falls short, I experience a growing insecurity, resulting in my developed pattern of recoiling. This new awareness can influence how I may approach staying open to learning, and experiment with new patterns and ways to let go, or unmask.

Transporting

I wonder how I can embody the patience to be a beginner, with permission to experiment, to meander, to stumble, to play, to practice, to make mistakes, to ask questions, to seek supervision and to be aware of what is harvested inherently in the environment.

In his essay, 'Is Beauty the Making One of Opposites?', Eli Siegel describes an 'aesthetic oneness of opposites' between the world, art and self, in which each 'explains' the other

(1955: 282–83). Movement/dance can provide us with such a dialogue; one in which body, emotion, mind/imagination, personal and collective themes or issues find connection with the other. Such an aesthetic oneness links transformative experience with creativity and embodiment. It gives us a way to sanctify our experience of living with the many personal and collective challenges we face. Movement/dance becomes a sacred path when it supports such a journey.

Conclusion

In this chapter, I have considered the relevance of movement/dance as a healing art applied to transformative experience, linking a particular process centred in body and movement and working with personal and collective life themes and metaphors of participants. A map of the process demonstrates three key stages: evocation, invocation and convocation, using six phases to guide the mover with her/his emergent material. While this template can be articulated and used successfully in different situations, the experience is always unique.

There is a deep and important connection between the physical and emotional experience of the mover. As we descend into the materials of our psyches, movement/ dance can be a medicine that heals and elevates our challenges to higher states of consciousness, facilitating a personal and collective experience of our universal struggles and shared humanity.

From the personal body, to group enactment, myth and ritual, to the studio and nature as liminal space, my work is one illustration of how movement/dance can be transformative.

To dance with life and not against it, to move responsively instead of reactively, this is a way to make spirit visible in the world.

In closing, I offer a meditation and a prayer in movement:

I stand, aware, focused and present in my body.
I am connected with my breath, and let it move me.
I am present and soft with all of my sensations, feelings and images.
I witness myself here and now.
I remember who I have been.
I feel who I am now.
I imagine who I am becoming.
I feel all of the wounds I have received here in this place.
I remember all of the ways in which I have sanctified those wounds, here in this place.
I imagine my body as my studio.
I feel the world, with everything and everyone in it, as my home and my family.
I know my soul and my life as the ultimate dance metaphor.
I know my dance as the way to make peace with it all.

Acknowledgements

Students have granted Daria Halprin permission to use their images and text.

References

Arnheim, R. (1966), *Toward a Psychology of Art*, Berkeley, CA: University of California Press.

Barks, C. and Moyne, J. (1995), *The Essential Rumi*, San Francisco, CA: Harper.

Bruner, J. (1959), 'Myth and Identity', in Murray, Henry A. (ed.), *Myth and Mythmaking*, Cambridge, MA: Daedalus Journal Publishing, 88:2, Spring, pp. 349–58.

Buber, M. (1970), *I and Thou*, New York, NY: Touchstone: Simon & Schuster.

Dissanayake, E. (1992), *Homo Aestheticus: Where Art Comes From and Why*, Seattle, WA: University of Washington Press.

Dychtwald, K. (1977), *Body/Mind*, New York, NY: Philip Tarcher.

Feldenkrais, M. (1985), *The Potent Self*, New York, NY: Harper & Row.

Halprin, L. (1969), *The RSVP Cycles, Creative Processes in the Human Environment*, New York, NY: George Brazilier, Inc.

Halprin, D. (2003), *The Expressive Body in Life, Art & Therapy: Working with Movement, Metaphor and Meaning*, London, UK: Jessica Kingsley Press.

H'Doubler, M. (1940), *Dance, A Creative Art Experience: Madison, WI: The University of Wisconsin Press*.

Hillman, J. (1976), *Revisioning Psychology*, San Francisco, CA: Harper Perennial.

—— (1989), *A Blue Fire*, San Francisco, CA: Harper Perennial.

Lowen, A. (1965), *Bioenergetics*, New York, NY: Coward, McCann & Geoghegan, Inc.

Perls, F. (1973), *The Gestalt Approach & Eye Witness to Therapy*, New York, NY: Bantam Books.

Reich, W. (1968), *Character Analysis*, New York, NY: Farrar, Straus & Giroux.

Siegel, E. (1955), 'Is Beauty the Making One of Opposites?', *Journal of Aesthetics & Art Criticism*, 14:2, pp. 282–83.

Todd, M. (1937), *The Thinking Body*, New York, NY: Dance Horizons, Inc.

Chapter 5

Dancing on the Breath of Limbs: Embodied Inquiry
as a Place of Opening

Celeste Snowber

Introduction

This chapter explores embodied inquiry as a place where the body is an opening to the inner life and an expression of the sensuous and the sacred. In particular, I focus on the connections between the body, dance and an intimate connection to the natural world. The body, through dance, becomes the place where the invisible and visible meet and physicality and spirituality are intertwined. This is not a spirituality for the mind, but a space which opens all that is within the heart and soul, hidden in the recesses of the body. It is a place where mystery dwells, and the life force, however one articulates it, can be in communion with flesh. When the body is spoken of, too often it is referred to as a disembodied text and an object, rather than the lived body, which has sweat, tears, moans, sighs and has the capacity for both paradox and deep joy. This chapter weaves the call to have a poetic and sensuous language, which honours embodied knowing as a place to articulate a visceral knowledge and wisdom. As a dancer, poet, educator and scholar, my task is to bring all of these aspects together in a place of inquiry and language that is both expressive and poetic.

I incorporate what I call 'writing from the body,' where our tissues dance and language becomes a physical extension of the body and where, in turn, the relationship between dance and language is played out. Inhabiting the body fully allows for language to return to breath and bone, where words become utterances of the belly. Or as Helene Cixous has said, 'Writing is not arriving; most of the time it's not arriving. One must go on foot with the body' (Cixous 1993: 65). Just as dance is an avenue to hear and listen to the pulses of the human heart through sound, gesture, eyes, belly, touch, skin and bones, so does writing become a place to dance. I write with the senses, and in particular a connection to visceral knowing. I integrate a variety of arts-based research methods, including poetic inquiry, and performative ways of writing, which allow for a more visceral way of expression. I am thankful for the ongoing way the fields of arts-based research has allowed for alternative ways of writing, which honour embodied and poetic forms (Barone and Eisner 1997; Diamond and Mullen 1999; Fels and Belavieu 2008; Knowles and Cole 2008; Neilson et al., 2001; Leavy 2008; Leggo 2001; Snowber 2002; Bagley and Cancienne 2002; Bresler 2004; Irwin and de Cosson 2004; Pendergast, Leggo and Sameshima 2009, Richmond and Snowber, 2009, 2011).

My teaching, writing and researching over the years have explored the body and sensual knowing as a place from which to live, write and teach (Snowber 2002, 2004, 2005, 2007, 2011). This chapter will include writing that celebrates words that dance and will be peppered by poetry that arises out of the body and the connection to the natural world.

Figure 1: Mover: Celeste Snowber. Photographer: Gary Bandzmer.

The life force that breathes through all, whether it is through creation, humanity, movement, words or the great mystery is investigated as a space to infuse the marrow of our lives. In particular, this chapter reveals one dancer's journey in integrating the poetic and dance in site-specific places within the natural world. The relationship between dancer and creation is explored, where the ocean, trees, wind and earth become a lover and expression of the sacred. This work pushes the boundaries of how an embodied and expressive relationship to the natural world shifts the understanding of ourselves.

> *ocean bears my feet*
> *how can they not move to the pulse*
> *within and without*

The dance between the inner landscape and outer landscape becomes a place of home, belonging and possibility. The connection to the body and dance is an opening to what lies within the heart, soul and creativity. The body becomes the teacher and the sensuous and sacred are transformed to a place where the depths are honoured.

The Wisdom of the Body

The body has long been a source of knowledge, wisdom and insight located through the movement of limbs, torsos, bellies and breath. As dancers, this is understood from a deep visceral place. However, human beings are all given the gift of a body or body-soul, and—as I have said many times—we do not only have bodies, but are bodies. The delicious movement running through our veins opens us to the flow and pulsing life force, which is central to all of life. One can call it many things: the divine, the beloved, God, sacred, mystery, essence, spirit, eros, and so on—but no word can completely proclaim what the body deeply knows. I personally feel most comfortable referring to the divine as the beloved, but I invite you to rename the divine in what resonates with you as a reader. As a dancer who works in a site-specific context, it is in response to the beauty, textures and rhythm of creation where I am catapulted into a wider love and captivated by awe.

The body has a pronouncement all to itself, which is felt in the lived experience of fingers and toes, shoulders and hips, through the heart of veins and on the breath of limbs. This is truly the wisdom of the body.

> *morning light peels back*
> *beloved vibrates within*
> *the skin of time dances*

We all know this in our body memory: the flutter in the chest, the stomach turning, the energy of excitement in our throat, the expanse in our pelvis. The body responds when we encounter another human being, animal or creation. We are an embodied people, and the body continues to respond with a remarkable vocabulary as we move through the world. Unfortunately, spaces where the body can have its voice and wisdom are not always celebrated in Western culture. Inner body wisdom is often more poignant than is given credit for, and the exclamation of the body is sometimes relegated to sports in many cultures. Grief too, has become an endangered species in Western culture, and yet the wise body knows, when words are not enough; it is truly the body where lament takes voice. It has been through dance where I have been able to articulate loss and grief, particularly the loss of loved ones. This too is a form of body prayer and listening, allowing the loss to transform to a place of acceptance (Snowber 2004). The belly knows the place of lament, and finds form for the formless.

Even dance can get away from the fundamental truth that is hidden in the body. In the pursuit of perfection, it can be forgotten that the body is what roots us in the earth, and places us to the ground. Form is important, but what is beneath the layers of form, the animating force of life taken in expression through the cells, is what truly gives form to the inner voice. It is the feet that hold the pulse of the soil, the skin that feels the wind, and the sternum that opens to sky and knows expanse. Even the voice is inextricably linked to breath. Language is oral, and writing needs to return back to the organic connection of blood to ink.

sternum to blue sky
even my cells burst with you
windward is my home

Dance, in its many forms, expresses the variety of the body's knowing, but all people are given dance as a birthright, whether one is trained or not. No mother can deny the dance of the child in the womb. Human beings were created to dance and move. Dance is a birthright. But even more, the ability to connect to the inner geography of our lives and the divine is also a birthright. Dance holds the possibility for an invitation and response to the divine within and without.

Creation Dances: Writing and the Body

Creation moves in a dance alongside us as human beings. The breathing, pulsing, gentle and harsh influx of weather is always moving and changing our planet and our lives. As part of my own artistic practice, I have been integrating dance and site-specific work in creation for many years. It is important to note that for me, artistic practice and spiritual practice are inextricably linked. Both call one to deeply listen, release and ask to come to a contemplative practice—daily, weekly, regularly as a place for the sacred to take shape. Site-specific work connecting dance and poetry first arose out of my daily walks around the Port Moody Burrard Inlet, outside Vancouver, British Columbia, Canada, where the ocean meets land in an inlet of water. Here, streams of fresh water from the mountains flow into the sea—a riparian zone, where fresh and salt water collide. This is the geographic area

Figure 2: Mover: Celeste Snowber. Photographer: Gary Bandzmer.

where I raised my children, and I walked the curves of the inlet every day with my dog for decades. Early on, I had to make a choice when raising three young sons, and having a full teaching/academic life, to either walk or have my meditation practice. Dancing was never optional, one always had to dance, even if in the kitchen! I have always been a both/and woman and chose to combine my walking and contemplation; it is in the depths of physicality that I release to the workings of the inner life. As years passed, this became my spiritual practice, and Creation spoke to me in my solar plexus. Herons, eagles, cedar and winding paths where land and sea collided were my teachers; my lesson was to listen. The land unfolded each season in undeniable beauty; even in rain, snow and inclement weather, the outer landscape became a place to nurture the inner landscape within.

> *live in your nature*
> *eagle is not a salmon*
> *show up for your life*

This walking eventually transformed to hearing the syllables and sentences that formed poems, and my walking could not be contained, for creation became a partner in dances arising within me. My body was embraced at the edge of sea and I entered the earth as a libation. The geography of the inner life beckons me through the visible paths of the natural landscape and I listen, stop, move and dance. Walking and dancing became my litany; the invitation to see and hear again for the first time.

First Sight

first sight
doe opens eyes
gentle break
into spring sky

seeing for the
very first time
as daily ritual
primavera
begs fresh
through the 101
shades of green

to walk the path
as if it is the
first glance
each smell and sound
texture and hue
dances into
a chorus of alleluias

what do insight
and sight have
to do with each
other?

repetition and rhythm
of sight drawn from the
eye to the heart.

I walk the same
inlet path every
day for a decade
of delight.

return to virgin
embrace of natural
world –
an invitation to
inner world.

I now create site-specific performances that explore the connection to inner and outer landscapes, and invite others on this contemplative walk, which includes dance and poetry. Arising out of the embrace of the natural world, my cathedral has been formed in the canopy of creation—not surprising, as I had spent a few decades being a liturgical dance artist and pioneering embodied prayer in Christian circles (Snowber 1995, 2004). I have come to know that no church or structure can contain the magnificent wonder of expressing from the inside out and the outside in.

Breaking and Opening of Forms

I have thought for many years that 'love breaks forms.' We experience love deeply in one form or another, whether that is a parent, spouse, lover or particular form of faith or spiritual practice. As life goes on, people leave for natural or unnatural reasons, and our journeys take different shapes. We would not be growing if we did not have the capacity and openness to change, shift, contract and release into new beginnings. It is much like a dance, and as movers, we know the alchemy of shifting and changing. My particular journey led me to a conversion experience in my early twenties and to an experiential connection to Christ. My immediate response was that I needed to dance this joy that was running through my veins and flesh. That eventually led to many years of integrating dance and faith in a variety of worship settings: seminaries, theological graduate schools, conferences, liturgical and sacred dance settings. Eventually God jumped out of the box that I was in, and spirit could not be contained in any form—and neither could I! Most importantly, I found a theology of suffering (or joy for that matter) did not exist that could embody my visceral connection to the sacred or the world. As time went on, the essence of my spirituality remained the same: a deep connection to spirit, but it has ushered me into doing site-specific work in the natural world. All the time, my dance has been both a response and a listening. I respond to the connection of the wider love running through my cells, and I listen to see how my body needs to move in order to express the interior and exterior life. I share a small piece of my autobiographical narrative to emphasize that love is at the root of the breath in the limbs. It is the beginning breath, which has been given: a deep gift, and one where I am called back to gratitude. I am still connected deeply to the mystics of many faiths, and am beckoned on the journey to surrender, to release and receive what is given through and in the body. And in this place, I touch soul. Body and soul continually connect in a duet of paradox of wonder.

Site-Specific Dance: A Dancer's Journey in the Natural World

No one would deny the incredible spiritual, physical and emotional benefits of interacting with the physical world. The outer landscape of creation holds wonders that animate our hearts through connecting our somatic understanding—whether that is walking, hiking, kayaking, swimming or just playing outside. It has been my practice for many years now to listen to the pulse of the natural world through my creative body, and particularly through dance. Here, the wind teaches me where to move my limbs, and the rocks near the sea ask me to be held by their grounded structure. The trees send my limbs into height, and the earth calls me to touch it with all my skin. This is not just integrating the earth as a stage, but interacting with it as a place to deeply listen to the earth through the flesh. From earth I came, and to earth I will return.

Dance opens us up to the ability to be totally 'wide awake,' as noted by philosopher Maxine Greene (1995). This wide-awakeness is a visceral aliveness, a cellular knowing—an embrace of what is seen and unseen. Knowledge is held in my fingers, feet, pelvis and chest. A deep listening to and through the body opens up the place for magic—the magic of being keenly alive, and the magic of the possibilities of being deeply woven into all of creation. One morning while dancing on the inlet path, I experienced this magic. The following poem encapsulates my experience:

Caught bear/bare dancing

You came back
but this time I was dancing
under the canopy of branches
knurled, twirled, knotted
air breaking between sky

sucked into flesh
I reach, extend, lift
ripple movements
lightly, sensuously
where time stops.

I dance in the morning light
feet crunching leaves
through echoes of sound
in one sideways turn

you are there
you are here

a captive audience
watching me in your
strong black gaze.
my eyes meet your stare
and I am launched to awe.

A few seconds
stretch deep
what does a black bear
think when encountering a
woman caught bare
in dance
on the inlet path?

No human would dare
stand and watch
they know I am a different creature
but you black of bear are
a creature of dance yourself
close to the earth
scent to the ground.

I leave terrified with my black lab
afraid of bear's power
coming to see it is also bear
power within where I take fright

Forever changed in a glance
you were watching the whole time
so close you came and I have
not left amazement

and the morning after
I dare not return
yet.

The Dance of Physicality and Spirituality

I was caught 'bare' dancing, but dance opens up a place of vulnerability. I cannot hide in this place, and I am invited into the paradox of being human, in all its complexity, beauty, fragility and strength. Here, many of our voices catch fire and they glow with the ability to express the nuances of what is the 'lived curriculum,' what takes place in the margins of life. And in the margins, there is the centre. Dance has the capacity to connect to the inner life, no matter what spirituality one is grounded in. I now define 'spirituality,' as much as one can, as the place one connects to the inside, the other, the natural world, ourselves and to the numinous. Spirituality is a huge area, but for the purposes of this chapter, I am emphasizing the ability to connect; dance in particular is a space where we can bring all of our humanity to the space of communion with ourselves, the natural world, and the numinous.

Embodied Inquiry: The Listening Breath of Dance

> *morning light peels back*
> *beloved vibrates within*
> *the skin of time dances*

Dance-making often has a life of its own, and the dancer or artist's task is to listen to where the work is going. As a dancer, scholar and poet, I often marvel that a favourite chapter in a book I have written is the one I did not intend to write, or that the most exciting part of a dance is what arises in the midst of dancing. I often say I am a recovering choreographer, as I have fallen in love with improvisation and continue to see a huge relationship between improvising, listening and being awakened to surprise. Madeleine L'Engle echoes the idea of the artist serving the art in her classic work, *Walking on Water: Reflections on Art and Faith*, stating, 'Inspiration far more often comes during the work than before it, because the largest part of the job of the artist is to listen to the work, and to go where it tells him [or her] to go' (L'Engle 1980: 149). Deep listening to self, other, art and the natural world inform both the practice of mentoring and art-making.

As you and I listen in the process of creating, we listen to our own lives, the whispers and proclamations, the nuances and bold feelings. As I have explored the connection to mentoring, I find that listening in art-making and listening to the pulse of what is happening in a student's life is a sacred act, one that must take form in the soil of mindfulness and loving kindness (Snowber 2005: 397). Every interaction is an invitation to listen, and an act of deep attentiveness. This is an attentiveness that is both body-full and mindful.

> *body signature*
> *my belly moves to pulse of earth*
> *listen to the land*

Dance and raw movement have the capacity to break open the gates and touch the terrain of the emotional life. Many educators and dancers have understood this connection and emphasized the place of dance and its ability for transformation (Cancienne and Snowber 2003; Collins 1992; Halprin 1995, 2000; Hawkins 1991; Levy 1988; Winton-Henry and Porter 1997, 2004). A key ingredient to integrating dance in transformative work is the act and art of deep listening. The body invites one to let loose the spirit within, and listen and hear inwardly. Spirituality is not confined to one aspect of humanness. It includes searching and groping, praying and worshipping, emptying and filling, rejoicing and lamenting. There are times one needs to listen for the ecstatic presence within and dance the extension of joy, and there are times when one needs to listen to lament, which is embodied in the contraction of grief. Many kinds of embodied activity become a place of inquiry—a place of listening to one's life. Dance, movement and improvisation are obvious places for listening through the body, but kayaking, horseback riding, making love, tai chi or walking can be just as significant for a bodily approach to listening and expressing through our bodies. Ultimately, it is always the connection between mind, body and heart where there is a living flow connecting all of who we are.

As I finish this chapter, I am in the midst of preparing for a site-specific performance, 'Tidal Poems and Dances,' on Galiano Island, British Columbia—a small island in the Gulf Islands off the coast of Vancouver.[1]

I go each day this week, dedicated to preparing for this performance. The performance is preparing me to be swayed once again by the seascape of wind-bent trees, rocks and broken shells, winding paths and stone. I listen at nature's feet. I begin a walk on the forest trail, hugging the sea at Montague Harbour. Arbutus trees the colour of burnt sienna, salal, barnacles, seaweed, old driftwood and broken shells line this ancient shore. This is a shore once inhabited by First Nations people, and now few people populate it alongside herons, eagles and seals.

My feet touch ground and I enter my walking ritual, stopping and reading poetry that arose out of the many times I have walked this trail over twenty years, and other times dancing in between driftwood and sea. One particular piece of wood, an old large tree, lies down, appears as an abstract sculpture and calls to me. Even as large as it is, it continues to move location in seasons. I dance around it, my body touching its barnacle-encrusted surface, and feel at home here. The essence of its nature stays the same, but location changes. Words are born from my mouth, half formed poems as my limbs and torso dance about the centrality of change in my life and the importance of essence, even though change is constant. Life continues to shift with many losses and changes, but as I dance amidst the changing shore, I am beckoned to listen for the wisdom within. I am reminded and rebodied to what matters, and ultimately the ability to be deeply alive is the biggest gift. Here, dance becomes a place of inquiry, a sacred space to archive the knowledge and wisdom within my own embodied understanding. I come to deep peace with the changes in my life and treasure what I can often take for granted.

> *driftwood is the unsung lace*
> *air has carved its curves*
> *gravity of grace*

I am always interested in what I do not know more than what I do know, and it is movement that evokes my unknowing. There are times I do not recognize the wisdom or patterns in my own life, which makes sense. It is only as I improvisationally dance, where words and movements arise, does the internal beauty take shape. I take courage from Joan Halifax (1999), anthropologist and author, who expands an alternative to this paradigm. She speaks of initiation as a place to 'plunge inward.' She says, 'Initiation takes us into the unknown and is grounded in not-knowing' (Halifax 1999: 10). A sense of unknowing is central to the art of dance-making, improvisation and creative movement, if not all artistic and spiritual practice. One must suspend what one thinks, and allow the body-mind to speak and truly think on the feet and with the feet. It is going to the edge of the cliff and really seeing that you can fly. The act of improvisation within dance-making becomes an embodied ritual that leads us into not-knowing and ultimately into knowing (Snowber 2002: 25). Dancing outside, I have the privilege to be partnered by creation—the wind, waves, trees, ocean and weather become an ensemble. In this ensemble dance, I am invited both inward and outward at the same time. In this place, I am given comfort as creation dances with me and the raw elements support my inquiry. I, in turn, hope that I give back to creation. This is not rehearsing, but an embodied inquiry in the canvas of the earth—a place to listen, discover and uncover what needs to be born in the heart and body anew. It is interesting that in the word 're(hear)sing' is both 'ear' and 'hear.' I am beckoned back to hear the sounds within the sounds, to listen deeply and find the movements within the movements, to wonder.

Conclusion

This chapter has travelled in many places, and has given a glimpse of the possibilities of integrating dance in the natural world and the relationship between the inner and outer landscapes. It is my hope that I have left a fragrance of the possibilities of returning words and dance to breath, and breath to words and dance. This interplay between the poetic, dance, nature and our own autobiographical stories is a place for ongoing curiosity and investigation. I invite you as a reader to explore your own inquiry through the gift of movement and let creation sing into your life, and in this place, may dance take wings. I leave you with a bodypsalm for the earth. Bodypsalms are poetic forms rooted in the body, which I have been writing. They are a callback to remind us what it means to be living as fully embodied people on this planet.[2] I end with this bodypsalm for the earth, as it arises out of the connection of our bodies and creation, and is my invitation to you.

Bodypsalm for the Earth

The earth is shaking within its core
and our cores in turn are shaken
now is the season to wake up
from the inside out
proclaim the interconnection
to all living beings -
neighbors near and far
sun, stars, sea, plants and plankton

and most of all
the fertile earth
which both gives and takes away
May we return to humility
where humus, humans and humor are born
and taste the mystery and beauty
beneath our feet and bellies
May our limbs stretch to the sky
our soles/souls kiss the ground
and may hope soak
our minds and bodies
through changes of weather
both of the heart and land
May we bear grace in our bones
and be rebodied to the truth -
our flesh is the earth
and the earth is our flesh
May compassion arise from our well
as we return to the fire of love
which has the capacity
to hold more than we know.

References

Bagley, C. and Cancienne, M. (eds) (2002), *Dancing the Data,* NY: Peter Lang.

Barone, T. E. and Eisner, E. W. (1997), 'Arts-based educational research', in R. M. Jaeger (ed.), *Complementary Methods for Research in Education*, Washington, DC: American Educational Research Association, pp. 73–103.

Bresler, L. (ed.) (2004), *Knowing Bodies, Moving Minds: Towards Embodied Teaching and Learning*, Dordrecht, UK: Kluwer Academic Publishers.

Cancienne, M. B. and Snowber, C. (2003), 'Writing rhythm: Movement as method', *Qualitative Inquiry*, 9:2, pp. 237–53.

Cixous, H. (1993), *Three Steps on the Ladder of Writing*, New York, NY: Columbia University Press.

Collins, S. (1992), *Stillpoint: The Dance of Selfcaring, Selfhealing*, Fort Worth, TX: TLC Productions.

Diamond, C. T. P. and Mullen, C. A. (eds) (1999), *The Post-Modern Educator: Arts Based Inquiries and Teacher Development*, New York, NY: Peter Lang.

Fels, L. and Belliveau, G. (2008), *Exploring Curriculum: Performative Inquiry, Role Drama and Learning*, Vancouver, BC: Pacific Education Press.

Greene, M. (1995), *Releasing the Imagination*, San Francisco, CA: Jossey-Bass.

Halifax, J. (1999), 'Learning as initiation: Not-knowing, bearing witness, and healing', in S. Glazer (ed.), *The Heart of Learning: Spirituality in Education*, New York, NY: Jeremy P. Tarcher/Putnam.

Halprin, A. (1995), *Moving toward Life: Five Decades of Transformational Dance*, Hanover, NH: Wesleyan University Press.

—— (2000), *Dance as a Healing Art: Returning to Health with Movement and Imagery*, Mendocino, CA: LifeRhythm.

Hawkins, A. (1991), *Moving from Within: A New Method for Dancemaking*, Pennington, NJ: A Capella Books.

Irwin, R. L. and de Cosson, A. (eds) (2004), *A/R/Tography: Rendering Self through Arts-Based Living Inquiry*, Vancouver, BC: Pacific Educational Press.

Knowles, G. and Cole, A. (eds) (2008), *The Handbook of the Arts in Qualitative Inquiry: Perspectives, Methodologies, Examples, and Issues*, New York, NY: Sage.

Leavy, P. (2008), *Method Meets Art: Arts-Based Research Practice*, New York, NY: Guilford Press.

Leggo, C. (2001), 'Research as poetic rumination: Twenty-six ways of listening to light', in L. Neilsen, A. L. Cole, and J. G. Knowles (eds), *The Art of Writing Inquiry*, Halifax, NS: Backalong Books, pp. 173–195.

L'Engle, M. (1980), *Walking on Water: Reflections on Art and Faith*, Wheaton, IL: Harold Shaw.

Levy, F. (1988), *Dance Movement Therapy: A Healing Art*, Reston, VA: American Alliance for Health, Physical Education, Recreation, and Dance.

Neilsen, L., Cole, A. L. and Knowles, J. G. (eds) (2001), *The Art of Writing Inquiry*, Halifax, NS: Backalong Books, pp. 173–95.

Pendergast, M., Leggo, C. and Sameshima, P. (eds) (2009), *Poetic Inquiry: Vibrant Voices in the Social Sciences*, Netherlands: Sense.

Richmond, S. and Snowber, C. (2009, 2011), *Landscapes in Aesthetic Education*, Newcastle, UK: Cambridge Scholars Publishing.

Snowber, C. (2002), 'Bodydance: Enfleshing soulful inquiry through improvisation', in C. Bagley and M. B. Cancienne (eds), *Dancing the Data*, New York, NY: Peter Lang, pp. 20–23.

—— (2004, 1995), *Embodied Prayer: Towards Wholeness Body Mind and Soul*, Kelowna, BC: Northstone.

—— (2005), 'The eros of teaching', in J. Miller, S. Karsten, D. Denton, D. Orr and I. C. Kates (eds), *Holistic Learning: Breaking New Ground*, New York, NY: SUNY, pp. 215–21.

—— (2007), 'The soul moves: Dance and spirituality in educative practice', in L. Bresler (ed.), *International Handbook for Research in the Arts and Education*, Dordrecht, UK: Springer, pp. 1449–55.

Snowber, C. (2011), 'Let the body out: A love letter to the academy from the body', in E. Malewski and N. Jaramillo (eds), *Epistemologies of Ignorance in Education*, Charlotte, NC: Information Age Publishing, pp. 187–198.

Notes

1   For more information on this performance, please see http://vimeo.com/29713167.
2   See www.bodypsalms.com.

Chapter 6

'Can They Dance?': Towards a Philosophy of Bodily Becoming[1]

Kimerer L. LaMothe

I live on a farm—96 acres of rolling hills and hay fields, meadows, woods, ponds and a stream. I live here with a rooster, two cats, two steers, two milking cows, four heifers, eleven laying hens, my life partner, our five children and a horse named Marvin.

I moved with my family to the farm in July of 2005, armed with a dream and a mission. The dream, which hatched in the early years of a marriage, was of writing and dancing in closer proximity to the natural world. The mission took shape during years spent teaching, writing, and dancing in the academy. I wanted to live a life that would enable me to think thoughts that expressed and honoured the wisdom and intelligence of human bodily selves. The opportunity arose. We moved.

In the past five years, the dancing and writing, living and loving I have been doing on the farm have been affecting me in ways that I wanted and never imagined. Life as a farm family is strengthening my conviction that we, as a culture, need a local, living philosophy that privileges bodily movement as the source and *telos* of human life—what I call a philosophy of bodily becoming. We need to dance—to think about dance, to study dance, and to practise dancing—for the sake of our well-being as creatures on this planet.

It is from this place that I engage four interlocutors, authors of three texts, all of whom propose to offer earth-friendly accounts of the modern subject. Gilles Deleuze and Felix Guattari in *One Thousand Plateaus*, Jane Bennett in *Vibrant Matter*, and David Abram in *Becoming Animal* all set out to dismantle mind over body logics that justify the pursuit of spiritual values at the expense of the earth and its inhabitants. They all seek to situate reason in a nexus of sensory, affective, bodily relations, and thus extend our perceptions of intelligence and agency to include the material, 'nonhuman,' or 'more than human world.' These are projects whose sympathies and concerns I, as a philosopher, dancer, farmer and mother, share.

Moreover, each text approaches this task of embodying reason and enlivening our sensory perception by developing a non-dualistic concept of materiality: Deleuze and Guattari describe a 'Body without Organs' (BwO), Bennett introduces the idea of 'vibrant matter,' and Abram evokes our 'animal body.' These authors coin these three concepts with the intention of changing how we think about bodies and how we experience bodies—our bodies and those in the world around us. Each of these concepts, moreover, shares a defining character: *movement*. In each text, the movement of this matter is a movement of *relating* and a movement of *becoming*. And in all three accounts, a person's ability to conceive and perceive this movement of relating and becoming is critical to imagining values and practices that reverse the current human programme of environmental death.

Figure 1: Mover: Kimerer LaMothe. Photographer: Geoffrey Gee.

To these three concepts of materiality I pose a question borrowed from Nietzsche: 'Can they *dance*?' (1974: BK 5, #366, p. 322). Can these ideas help us along in affirming and participating consciously in the rhythms of bodily becoming?

In the process of investigating each concept, I flesh out how and why a local, lived philosophy of bodily becoming can move us further along the path these writers tread towards an appreciation of dance as a practice and resource for earth-friendly ways of thinking and believing.

Can They Dance?

What on earth did Nietzsche mean? In his words:

Faced with a scholarly book. We do not belong to those who have ideas only among books, when stimulated by books. It is our habit to think outdoors—walking, leaping, climbing, dancing, preferably on lonely mountains or near the sea where even the trails become thoughtful. Our first questions about the value of a book, of a human being, or a musical composition are: Can they walk? Even more, can they dance?

(Nietzsche 1974: BK 5, #366, p. 322)

'Dance' is one of those words whose meaning we think we already know, or so it seems. The word appears regularly in so many works of contemporary theory without comment or explanation—including, as we shall see, in those by Bennett, Abram and Deleuze and Guattari. It appears more often than not as a *metaphor* used to describe something else, whether a natural phenomenon, the terms of a relationship, or a patterned movement. Yet the content of 'dance' that is carried over is rarely, if ever, acknowledged. *What is dance?*

Nietzsche is an exception. In his corpus, he uses the word to evoke a specific lived experience of bodily movement, whose pivotal significance he develops along with his project of revaluing values.[2] Briefly visiting his work will shed light on what is at stake when I ask of my interlocutors' concepts of materiality: can they dance?

With Nietzsche and dance, the place to begin is at the beginning, with his first book (and doctoral dissertation), *The Birth of Tragedy* (1967). In this book, as readers commonly recognize, Nietzsche celebrates the Attic tragedy of fifth century Greece for catalysing in spectators a radical *affirmation of life* in all its bodily, sensory, aesthetic aspects. What is seldom recognized, however, is the critical role that *dancing* plays in effecting that affirmation. Dancing secures a visceral bond between the spectators and the action of the play, such that they are able to experience what would otherwise be a horrifying indictment of their highest ideals as an occasion to participate all the more whole-heartedly in the ongoing creation of themselves and their worlds.

Dancing here is not a metaphor. It is what the chorus does. The anonymous members of the chorus move their bodily selves in rhythmic unity. This dancing, Nietzsche explains, affects spectators: it stirs a visceral response that bonds the spectator to the chorus in a surge of recognition or identification. So connected, spectators feel in their sensory awareness what the chorus embodies: the power and joy of participating in the forces of nature. Spectators feel compelled to express this feeling of visceral identification with the 'entire symbolism' of the body, in dance. So moved to dance, they experience themselves as god-like, as themselves gods, creating and becoming who they are by virtue of the movements they are making (LaMothe 2006: 19–108).

For Nietzsche, this dance-enabled visceral connection is the key to the success of the tragedy in catalysing an affirmation of life. It effects what Nietzsche calls a 'magic transformation,' such that the spectator, confronted with the downfall of a hero or the death of a god, welcomes the event as an occasion to celebrate the ongoing, irresistible power of life that they are feeling in their bodily movement. They know themselves, viscerally, as participating in the larger work of creation of which this death is but one moment. When this magic transformation occurs, Nietzsche avers, participants' joy overflows in a powerful yes to life, all of it.

As Nietzsche's philosophy matures, he uses dance again and again to evoke the practice and the fruit of affirming life.[3] To dance is to love life. To dance is to overcome the ascetic ideal that he identifies in his genealogy of Christian values. The ascetic ideal is one that guides us to deny our sensory selves in pursuit of spiritual or scientific truth. To dance is to overcome the ascetic ideal at the place where it attaches—in our lived, living experience of our bodily selves. To dance is to participate consciously, with the entire symbolism of bodily movement, in creating values that, in the words of Zarathustra, the dancer, 'remain faithful to the earth' (Nietzsche 1954: 125).

When Nietzsche asks of a scholarly book or idea, then—can it dance?—he has something specific in mind. He is asking whether it: (1) communicates *participation,* (2) in the *bodily* act of, (3) creating *values,* (4) that express and encourage a *love* of earthly life. He is asking whether it serves to move readers towards a bodily spirituality that honours the movement of life.

Bennett, Abram and Deleuze and Guattari, writing in Nietzsche's wake, all aspire to remember the affective, bodily sources of our thinking and being that our allegiance to ascetic ideals has denied. But can their concepts of materiality dance? Can they catalyse affirmation of our ongoing bodily participation in the creation of life-enabling value?

Essentially Movement

I begin as I always do, on the floor, on my back, knees grasped gently to my belly. I breathe down my spine, letting the mass of my bodily self sink through the rug, through the wood floor, down into the earth below.

I am in the one room of our house that—aside from the land—let us know within minutes of our arrival that the farm was ours. The room is 18 by 27 feet, a large exposed shell of the original 1840s timber frame. Its hand-hewn, dark-stained bents, assembled from an assortment of local trees, arc above my head like giant ribs. Out the front windows, I can see the roof of our pole barn, topped by a neighbour's hay fields and a forest-covered hill a half-mile beyond.

I place myself in the centre of the room, align my ribs with its, and let my thinking self fall into my sensory awareness. I yield to the rhythms of breathing that are happening in me, as me. This movement of my bodily self is always making me.

A belly-breaching diaphragm contracts upward, forcing air out, and then releases downward to allow its return. Exhaling again, vertebrae begin to drop, one by one, popping along an emerging sense of spine, as so many beads on a string.

Sensation begins to gather in familiar patterns. Energy stirs. A beating heart breaks into view, its textured rhythms tapping time. Blood flows through limbs, bathing every cell. I extend my left leg below me and stretch out through my left fingers and toes, and then repeat to the right, opening, exploring.

All at once, my experience shifts. I am behind my eyes, feeling what I am feeling. The pinch in my knee from chasing cows through the snow. The cramp in my shoulder from carrying buckets of water to the steers. The ache in my neck from sitting at the computer. I let go.

Tired sensations give way to fresh ones. Impulses to move appear. I receive them, yield to them, allow them to organize and align me. I arc and crest, bend and lunge, spin and spiral, discovering what I can do. Who I am. It happens every time and never the same way twice: moving, I am moved. The movements I make make me who I am.

I fall into the unfathomable mystery of a bodily becoming. I dance.

Body without organs. Vibrant matter. Animal body. Can these concepts of materiality dance? Can they guide us in appreciating the body of earth and our bodies of earth in such a way that we change our ways of acting? In what follows, I argue that each account of materiality takes us some distance in exposing our concepts of the modern rational individual as bad for bodies. Each notion embraces *movement*, *relationship* and *becoming* as integral to our existence as human selves. However, within each work, there are moments where the ascetic ideal creeps in, arresting the project's liberative potential. Tracking these moments offers a clear picture of what more is needed to advance our understanding of dance as a radical, generative act. In short, missing from their accounts of materiality is a viscerally enlivening account of how our *bodily movement* as humans can and does make us.

Body without Organs

In *One Thousand Plateaus*, Deleuze and Guattari succinctly state their plan: 'overthrow ontology, do away with foundations, nullify endings and beginnings' (1987: 25). This author duo writes to discredit as oppressive whatever values, ideals, and practices encourage humans to believe in themselves as rational, self-made, meaning-making individuals. As they intone, 'No significance, no subjectification' (1987: 22).

The concept of materiality they introduce to smooth their path is the 'body without organs,' or BwO.[4] The BwO, as they define it, is the 'ontological unity of substance' (1987: 154). It is a plane of possibility or field of immanence that extends through all things as an enabling condition of their existence.

Despite the static connotation of 'plane,' however, Deleuze and Guattari are clear. The BwO is 'the absolute state of movement' (1987: 267). It is nothing but movement, nothing other than 'relations of movement and rest' (1987: 265). It is desire (1987: 165), nature (1987: 258) and earth. And every 'thing' that appears on the plane, as an expression of the plane, by virtue of the plane, is again only movement, characterized by speed and slowness, by relations of movement and rest.

Moreover, as this absolute movement, the BwO not only enables each thing to exist, it also *relates* things to one another as expressions of itself. These relationships, mediated as they are by the BwO, are not determined by genetics or evolution, sequence or structure.

They are better conceived as 'assemblages' or 'rhizomes'—that is, multiplicities of heterogeneous things.

Further, it is because of these BwO-enabled alliances, Deleuze and Guattari affirm, that any particular thing *becomes* what it is. *Becoming* is what happens as alliances form and reform on the plane of infinite possibility. Every thing becomes what it is by becoming something else—becoming animal, becoming woman, becoming child. A favourite example of theirs is the orchid and the wasp, two things unrelated by genes or structure that nevertheless form an alliance, becoming morphologically like one another, in order to realize their respective potentials for living.

In Deleuze and Guattari's project, it is this character of the BwO as a *movement* of *relating* and *becoming* that grants it efficacy in deforming the subject. The BwO functions to dissolve all apparent individualities or dualities into a common field of assembling and reassembling forces. As Deleuze writes, 'The body without organs is an affective, intensive, anarchist body that consists solely of poles, zones, thresholds and gradients. It is traversed by a powerful nonorganic vitality' (1998: 131). Readers, Deleuze and Guattari hope, by adopting the concept of the BwO, will recognize the folly of trying to establish an individual identity over and against other bodies, including our own. We will realize that bodies are, 'nothing but affects and local movements, differential speeds' (1987: 260), thresholds across which gradients and intensities pass. We will be free to cultivate our receptivity to the movements of relating and becoming that are making us.

Here I pose the question: can the BwO dance? Does it catalyse in readers a visceral awareness of their own relating, becoming materiality? Does it communicate participation in the creation of values that remain faithful to the body of earth and our bodies of earth?

As I was reading along, admittedly repelled by the imagery of masochists, sadists, drug addicts and otherwise mad individuals, I stumbled on the following line. Confessing to their cast of dreary characters, Deleuze and Guattari protest, 'the BwO is also full of gaiety and ecstasy and *dance*' (1987: 150, my emphasis). They promptly return to their motley crew. Later Deleuze and Guattari assert, 'there is a pure plane of immanence, univocality, composition, upon which everything is given, upon which unformed elements and materials *dance* that are distinguished from one another only by their speed and that enter into this or that individuated assemblage depending on their connections, their relations of movement' (1987: 255, my emphasis). These quotations suggest that Deleuze and Guattari at least intend for the BwO to enable and include dancing.

Or do they? Who is dancing? Unformed elements and materials. Of what does their 'dancing' consist? Entering into assemblages. It is true: Deleuze and Guattari are appealing to a lived human experience of bodily movement (dance) to illuminate the moving, relating, becoming nature of 'things.' However, they do so while denying that same power of materiality to human bodies. How so?

First, as suggested above, the movement of the BwO, as a movement of relating and becoming, functions in relation to a human self as a force that dissolves its specific subject-oriented organization, and it does so by dissolving the organ-ization of the body. The body is without organs. This dissolution of a bodily form or norm is intended to liberate the subject from being judged (by God) on the basis of its ability to master its own body. If there is no body to master, the subject cannot fail. The form of a human body appears as one more constraint or 'strata' imposed upon the movement of the BwO—a constraint that the concept of the BwO is designed to help us escape. This liberation, then, is effectively a freedom from the body, from being a body.

Second, by allowing a dissolved body to stand for a human body, Deleuze and Guattari effectively deny the becoming, relating movement specific to the 'assemblage' or rhizomic range of materiality that takes shape in and as a human person. At best, in relation to the BwO, a human body appears as a site across and through which 'we' can invite and allow movement, so as to keep our sense of self flexible and malleable.

Third, without any ability to conceive of the movement specific to a human bodily form, Deleuze and Guattari leave intact a mental sense of self as the sole source and seat of subjectivity—one they begrudgingly admit is necessary. It is to this self that the authors appeal. As a result, they have few resources for discussing a responsibility for the earth that does not hang on the very rational, agentic subject they intend to (un)fix. The individual mind, humbled and sobered perhaps, is still left to identify the destruction it has wrought and come up with new solutions.[5]

Missing from the BwO, then, is action: an account of how the movement of our bodily selves—in relating and becoming other—might serve as an alternative source and ground for an emergent sense of self. What is missing is the most basic becoming of all: *becoming body*.

The form of a human body is not constraining in the same way that the concept of an individual subject is. Every limb and lobe, every nerve and vessel is itself an infinite capacity for making movement, unfolded over years of evolutionary history, developing in concert and cooperation with local forces, elements and other emerging forms. Every shape of a body's evolution represents a potential for reaching and running, for carrying and throwing, for singing and speaking and dancing—for following the rhythms of the breath and receiving impulses to move. (In my room, on my back, beneath the ribs.)

Nor does the form of a human body moving deny its heterogeneity, its impulse to connect, or its endless becoming. Only subject-driven concepts of it do. We humans are born as bodies that are always moving, always becoming; our task as subjects is to grow as, into and through the changing bodily selves that we are.

In sum, the BwO, because it does not help us conceptually or practically in cultivating a sensory awareness of how our own bodily movement is making, relating and becoming us, does not dance as Nietzsche describes. As a concept, it continues to deny what the notion of the rational subject was itself repressing: the creative potency of bodily movement. It remains a clever, abstract thought, guiding us in patterns of self-reflection that promise freedom from the finite materiality of our bodily selves.

Vibrant Matter

My shoulders roll to the left. My right leg stretches across my body. A tight ache flares across my lower back, revealing a fist of tension clenched around my sacroiliac joint. The pain focuses my attention. I sense the block. There is a place in me that is not moving in line with the rest—a place that my movement is revealing as stuck.

I respond as I have learned to—by *breathing* I discover what I always do: I am not breathing as expansively as I can. My vertical range of inhaling and exhaling is narrow, its wave banked on either side by muscular habits set while sitting, standing and sleeping. The pain is telling me this. There is more movement here to make, more me to be made, a potential for pleasure that has yet to unfold.

I gather in an exhalation, pressing air out, and then more, until a circular squeeze empties me. With its release, the edge of tension around the joint ebbs, a bit. The pain softens and spreads out from its centre, quieting down. Sensation appears in a place that was moments ago senseless. I am on the right track.

Over the next half hour, I follow the pain. It guides my breathing down, around, out and through. I wander into new sensory realms, inviting and welcoming new movements—patterns of sensing and responding that organize me differently than those that built the sense-blocking, pain-producing block.

Finally, I stand, different and differently. The movements I am making are making me—light. Released. My breathing is soft and easy. My pelvis swings and settles gently on the hinges of my hips, a rocking centre of gravity, cradle of intention, pleasure and desire. My sense of self dissolves by virtue of movements I am making—movements that swell and crest in the shape of an awakened sensory awareness. Quick and slow, smooth and staccato, splayed and gathered, tipped and ajar, 'I' move with a joy-stirring precision and grace I would not have found were it not for the pain—or for my breathing-enabled response to it. I catch currents of life, making movements that express my attention, my work, my faith in dance. *I am the movement that is making me.*

Jane Bennett (2010), building on the work of Deleuze and Guattari, goes farther than they do in the effort to grant agency to material bodies, or what she calls 'actants'. Her concern, from the outset, is to cultivate an 'ecological sensibility' in herself and others that will lead to changes in attitudes, values and behaviour. For Bennett, the key to such change is dislodging the ubiquitous, assumed notion that matter is inert. Such a concept, she claims, lures humans into believing that we are the only subjects, the only beings worthy of rights and respect. It thus actively impedes 'the emergence of more ecological and more materially sustainable modes of production and consumption' (Bennett 2010: ix).

In response, Bennett introduces the concept of vibrant matter to help us detect the animate nature of nonhuman beings, and acknowledge our ultimate dependence on such nonhuman actors and factors for those qualities we count as definitively human. She wants us to develop 'a cultivated patient, sensory attentiveness to nonhuman forces operating outside and inside the human body' (2010: xiv), in other words, to 'the presence of impersonal affect' (2010: xv).

In Bennett's concept of vibrant matter, as with the BwO, *movement* is key. As Bennett writes: 'there is no point of stillness, no indivisible atom that is not itself aquiver with vital force' (2010: 57). While we may perceive things as stable, she explains, that appearance is merely a function of our sensory range. Speeds that are slow 'compared to the duration and velocity of the human bodies participating in and perceiving them' (Bennett 2010: 58) appear to us as objects. Others do not.

This movement of matter, moreover, is what Bennett calls, with allusions to Spinoza, *associative*. All bodies are constantly affecting and being affected by others (Bennett 2010: 21), establishing alliances between them. What emerges from these affective relationships are instances of power or efficacy along a trajectory that is without any governing, intellectual intention or goal (cf. Deleuze and Guattari's [1987] 'lines of flight'). Things happen, and they happen as expressions of these relationships, enacting what Bennett calls 'confederate agency' (2010: 36). Her analysis of an electrical blackout and its proximate causes, for example, includes: weather patterns, government laws, the nature of electricity, the geographic dispersion of power plants and the pressures of the bottom line. For Bennett, agency is always distributed across a wide range of human and nonhuman factors.

Further, as with the BwO, the pulsing, connecting movement of vibrant matter is also an engine of becoming. It is through such relational effects of power, Bennett insists, that things and people become the material bodies that they appear to be. 'All bodies [… are] temporary congealments of a materiality that is a process of becoming' (Bennett 2010: 49).

When we learn to conceive of matter in these ways as animate, associative and ever-becoming—that is, vibrant—Bennett hopes, we will become 'vital materialists,' willing and able to 'engage strategically with a trenchant materiality that is us as it vies with us in agentic assemblages' (2010: 111). Describing such persons, she writes that they, 'are selves who live as earth, who are more alert to the capacities and limitations [...] of the various materials they are' (2010: 111). They are more willing to perceive relations across human and nonhuman entities as horizontal; they are more able to appreciate nature as emergent and not linear or determinative, and they are better able to 'capture the alien quality' of their own flesh (2010: 112). In support of her vision, Bennett cites the passage from Deleuze and Guattari quoted above: nature is a 'pure plane of immanence … upon which unformed elements and materials dance' (Deleuze and Guattari 1987: 255, as cited in Bennett 2010: 117).

Can vibrant matter dance?

Bennett is clear. She wants us to take this concept into ourselves and perceive the world through it. She wants to change our experience of the world at a visceral level, so as to reshape our habits of thinking, feeling and acting towards ourselves and others. As she queries, 'How can I start to feel myself as not only human?' (Bennett 2010: 116). So far so good.

Figure 2: Mover: Kimerer LaMothe. Photographer: Geoffrey Gee.

However, her ability to move readers in this direction, like that of Deleuze and Guattari, is limited by the fact that she does not discuss the agentic powers of the relating, becoming movement that occurs on the scale and span of a human form.

Bennett does go farther than Deleuze and Guattari in acknowledging the generative potency of form itself, human or nonhuman, and its role in the process of becoming. She writes, for example, 'human and nonhuman bodies re-corporealize in response to each other; both exercise formative power and both offer themselves as matter to be acted on' (2010: 49). So too, she admirably documents the formative power of nonhuman bodies, giving detailed accounts of how germs, laws, fats, dead rats, climate changes and other nonhuman actants affect human behaviour. Yet when it comes to the formative power of a moving, relating, becoming human body, she is curiously silent.

What, then, is the formative power of a *human vibrant materiality*? How does it operate? What are its affects? Are its formative powers simply a function of our ability to generate concepts that shape our perception of the world? A power of abstraction alone?

At times, Bennett gestures towards answers, when she refers, for example, to the ability of practices to increase our capacity to be moved by the movement of matter. She observes that the careful attention of a craftsman or scientist to her material can yield an appreciation for the agency of the materials with which she works, enabling her to learn from them what they have the capacity to be. However, Bennett does not analyse how the moving materiality of these persons' own bodily selves—their bodily movements—are making them capable of being so moved by other matters.

This lack of attention to the vibrant materiality of bodily movement is especially telling, because Bennett uses dance as a metaphor for the mutually formative relationship of human and nonhuman—writing, for example, that, 'Humanity and nonhumanity have always performed an intricate dance with one another' (2010: 31). Humans are dancing here. But, again, of what does this human dancing—its formative power—consist?

Ironically enough, dance offers answers that could further Bennett's project. Dance is, among other things, a practice of attending to the materiality of a bodily self as a source of agency and intelligence, knowledge and novelty. A dancer, through careful attention to her bodily movement, learns to discern impulses to move, as received and amplified by the ever-evolving sensory shapes of her bodily self. A dancer is willing to honour her bodily self, its pains and its pleasures, as actants, enabling and even guiding her how to move, how to become who she is.

Finally, when Bennett does call upon readers to cultivate a sensory awareness of their vibrant materiality, she, as noted, urges us to appreciate how alien our bodily selves are—how shot through with the hosts of nonhuman populations that enable us to be at all. While our bodies are indeed 'alien' in this sense, Bennett's call hides a more fundamental ignorance: we do not know our bodily selves in the first place. We have learned, through years of training ourselves to read and write and think, to ignore what our bodily selves are feeling, and how our movements are making us. We have only known 'the body' that our concept of the subject has allowed us to perceive.

As Bennett clearly demonstrates, the movements of our bodily selves are not the only movements making us. Even so, if we are serious about appreciating the vibrancy of matter, we need to grant to the scope and scale of our bodily materiality the same relating, becoming, agentic power we grant to the bacteria or oxygen particles or food substances that pass through us.

Further, we need to do so not simply for the sake of logical consistency, but in order to cultivate the 'ecological sensibility' Bennett recommends. A sensibility requires that we sense. We need to sense the pain and pleasure of the earth in our own bodily selves as our pain and our pleasure. We do and we can precisely because our bodies are the relating, becoming, open and unfinished movement that is making us. However, we will be limited in our capacity to do so unless we actively cultivate a sensory awareness of our bodily materiality as vibrant. As Bennett admits, after affirming the need for such practice, 'I am, for now, at the end of my rope' (2010: 122).

Animal Body

As I move through a series of reaches, an impulse appears: do the cycle of breaths. This cycle of four breaths is something I invented. Or rather, it swam into my awareness one day, pulled by the strokes of my own splashing through a glorious stretch of mountain lake.

Each breath of the cycle honours an element: earth, air, fire and water. With each breath, I cultivate a sensory awareness of that element in me, as me, relating to me.

Earth: I breathe and drop my weight into the upward pressing presence of earth, surrendering to the gravity that holds my earth body close to the earth's body. *Air:* I inhale each blast of white gas into my lungs, and sense it seeping out through my pores, dissolving depths and surfaces of skin into light. *Fire:* the punch of an emptying exhale strikes a spark in my belly, cradle of heat, centre of gravity, whose light beams outward to meet the rays of the sun. *Water:* breathing in and through, currents of fluid energy, ground-given, open and warm, flow out through my limbs, moving me powerfully through space.

It is nothing. A game I play. Yet, my movement pulled this cycle into thought. I chose to notice, to move with it, to repeat it. It has become me. Every time I submit to its form, the cycle of breaths gives me a visceral experience of a fact that I can think: every movement I make creates in me a pattern of sensation and response that connects me with the forces and elements that enable my life. Moving through the four breaths gives me a visceral experience of the rhythms of bodily becoming in which I am always participating, consciously or not. Moving through the cycle of breaths, I consciously create patterns of sensing and responding to my own bodily self that allow the intelligence of my own bodily movement to organize thoughts and limbs in response to challenges and opportunities at hand. I am this ability to create and become patterns of sensation and response that relate me to what is. Born to connect, to honour, to love.

Abram, the last of my interlocutors, is as passionate as Bennett, Deleuze and Guattari about generating a concept of materiality capable of dislodging the claims to human superiority that continue to justify the human destruction of the earth.

With a nod in his choice of titles to Deleuze and Guattari, Abram begins *Becoming Animal*: 'This is a book about becoming a two-legged animal, entirely a part of the animate world whose life swells within and unfolds all around us' (2010: 3). To become animal, for Abram, is to embrace our bodily, sensory participation in a cosmos, 'the creaturely world directly encountered by our animal senses,' of which we are but one intelligent and creative moment (2010: 9).

What our animal bodies perceive, according to Abram, as the reality of which they are a part, is a universe characterized by *movement*. It is a movement that is, once again, a movement of relating and becoming, enlivening a vast interdependent matrix of human and more-than-human elements. In calling us to become our animal bodies, then, Abram seeks for us a 'visceral experience of a world' that is 'in continual metamorphosis' (2010: 288, 296).

Further, this ongoing, shape-shifting movement, for Abram, as for Deleuze, Guattari and Bennett, finds expression in relationships that are not necessarily governed by genetic, evolutionary or structural relationships. Abram, too, reaches for a wider and more diverse plane of connectivity, affirming that,

There is a subtle entanglement and confusion between all beings of the earth, a consequence not only of our common ancestry, and the cellular similarities of our make up, but also of our subjection to variant aspects of the same whirling world.

(2010: 192)

Because of this common subjection, our animal bodies are related to heterogeneous others as fellow participants in the ongoing creation of what is. Together with the trees, birds, mammals and rocks, for example, we create an atmosphere on whose peculiar mix of oxygen, carbon dioxide, nitrogen and more our existence depends. An animal body, Abram writes, is an 'open unfinished entity utterly entwined with the soils, waters and winds that move through it—a wild creature whose life is contingent upon the multiple other lives that surround it, and the shifting flows that surge through it' (2010: 110). Earth. Air. Fire. Water.

As for Deleuze, Guattari and Bennett, this movement that is relating as an animal body is also a movement of becoming—the movement by which we become who we are. For Abram, we become the animal bodies that we are when we open our senses to perceive our kinship with the more-than-human world. Abram describes in vibrant detail his own encounters with sea lions, deer bucks and flying birds. With prose that is lush and vivid, rollicking with pleasure and keyed to every sense, Abram prepares us for the possibility of having such experiences ourselves. He sensitizes us to appreciate the significance of so doing. For Abram, when we become animal, we have the will, desire and experience we need to create ways of thinking, feeling and acting that honour what we know, in our sensory selves, to be true: our relatedness with all that is.

Does Abram's animal body dance?

Abram's book goes farther than our other texts in affirming the sensory re-education required by any intent to displace the modern subject. According to Abram, we need not only to think about our participation in a moving cosmos; we need to submit our sensory selves to the rhythms and cycles, the challenges and chills, of its relating, becoming movement. Such immersion quickens our animal senses.

At the same time, however, Abram's encouragement that we seek out such sensory experience is limited in its efficacy by a similar move to that we have seen in Deleuze and Guattari and Bennett. In the attempt to dismantle the subject, he dissolves the human body into its sense-able environments, effectively denying to the form of a human body the same qualities of animate intelligence he calls us to acknowledge in the relating, becoming movement of the material around us.

Abram does spin long, evocative passages describing the movement of individual senses. He describes, for example, how hours at the computer screen retrain our eye muscles not to perceive depth. The screen flattens the plane of perception for us, focusing everything to the same distance (2010: 89–90). Yet the senses, more often than not, are treated in isolation from the overall movement of a bodily self.

Abram also talks at length about the magicians and shamans who actively study the behaviour of animals in order to become them. Such persons, Abram notes are able to expand their sensory range in life-enabling ways. As he writes:

> Traditional, tribal magicians or medicine persons [...] seek to augment the limitations of their specifically human senses by binding their attention to the ways of another animal. [...] The more studiously an apprentice magician watches the other creature from a stance of humility, learning to mimic its cries and to dance it various movements, the more thoroughly his nervous system is joined to another set of senses—thereby gaining a kind of stereoscopic access to the world.
>
> (2010: 217)

Here, humans dance.

Nevertheless, lodged in this quotation are large questions that Abram has yet to explore. How is it that a human nervous system 'joins' to another set of senses? What is involved in learning to mimic or dance the movements of another? Is dance a matter of imitation? How and why are the bodily movements that a shaman makes effective? Why isn't it enough simply to think about becoming animal? And, in what sense are human senses 'limited' if they are capable of such transformation?

From the perspective of bodily becoming, the shaman's dancing—the practice and act of making bodily movements—is critical. With every movement we make, we create a pattern of sensation and response that resides within us as a kinetic image—a possibility for making further movements that animate a similar coordination of mind and muscle. As a result, when we move in response to a movement that appears to us—whether leaping animal, wind-waved tree, or air-born bird—the process is never simply one of 'imitation.' It requires that a person perceive a movement pattern and be moved by it; that she feel in herself the possibility of animating a similar pattern, and follow the impulses to move that arise within her. It is a practice that demands patient attentiveness to the other, combined with an acute sensory awareness of one's own bodily movement.

The 'dance' that results is not an act of becoming other, but of *becoming body*, a *human* body, capable of participating consciously in the process of creating and becoming patterns of sensation and response that relate us to whatever elements and individuals appear to us as life-enabling. Humans—born with immature brains and unspecified instincts, wholly dependent on others for our care—are capable, perhaps uniquely so, of participating consciously in the rhythms of our bodily becoming.

In short, in order to sustain the earth-friendly cosmology Abram desires, we need to affirm our ability to *dance*. We need to become *human* bodies capable of participating consciously in the movements of relating and becoming that are always already rustling and crackling, breaching and cresting, around and through our beating, breathing selves.[6]

This commitment lies at the core of a philosophy of bodily becoming.

We do not have or inhabit bodies; we are bodies. The bodies that we are are not things that move; they are themselves movement. The movement that we/bodies are is not formless or random; it is the movement that is making us. And the movement that we are that is making us is a rhythmic, open-ended, ever-ongoing action of creating and becoming the patterns of sensation and response that relate us to whatever and whomever support our participation in the ongoing rhythms of our bodily becoming. From this perspective, it is our responsibility as humans, uniquely perhaps, to ensure the health and well-being of every web of life by whose movements we are capable of being moved.

My time is over. Sons Kai and Leif, ages five and one, run in, skipping rings around me. A well of patience rests in my belly; opened sensitivities hum. I am in touch with my freedom. I have resources for finding new moves to make in response to whatever pain I am willing to feel in any realm of life. It is love.

I hear Geoff in the kitchen, getting breakfasts, making lunches and washing buckets. The older three kids are coming in from milking the cows. My mind is teeming with thoughts pulled by organs, bones, muscles and skin from currents of air and electricity, water and warmth, plans and memories passing through me. When I take pen in hand, I will want to hold what I am thinking and writing accountable to this practice of remaining faithful to the body of earth and this body of earth. I scoop up Leif in my arms, take Kai's hand and leave the space.

Conclusion

In order to create mutually enabling relationships with the more-than-human world, in order to name and bring into being earth-friendly values, gods and practices, thinking the loss of our subjectivity is not enough. We need to cultivate a sensory awareness of the movements making us that will guide us in creating and becoming patterns of sensation and response that honour the sources of our living.

We don't need a freedom from the body; we need the freedom to become body. We need the freedom to participate consciously in the rhythms of our bodily becoming. It is the freedom—as Nietzsche describes it—to do what we must for our great health.

This freedom is not something that can be given to us, although it is only given to us. It is not something our minds can claim for us; it is a strength and sensitivity our bodily selves *receive* when our thinking bends to attend to the movements we are making and to how they are making us. Finding the patterns of pain, we learn from them how to make movements in our lives that will not recreate them.

With this freedom and health, we have a moral compass for creating life-affirming values and practices that remain faithful to the earth in us and around us.

If we intend our work to be about human *life* (and not just human thought), if we are concerned with what makes a life worth living (and not just worth reading about), we need to use our thinking to access the intelligence that is being generated anew, every instant, in the rhythmic becoming of our bodily selves. We need philosophies—and philosophers—who dance.

References

Abram, D. (2010), *Becoming Animal: An Earthly Cosmology*, New York, NY: Pantheon Books.

Bennett, J. (2010), *Vibrant Matter: A Political Ecology of Things*, Durham, NC: Duke University Press.

Deleuze, G. (1998), *Essays Critical and Clinical*, Paris: Verso.

Deleuze, G. and Guattari, F. (1987), *One Thousand Plateaus: Capitalism and Schizophrenia* (trans. B. Massumi), Minneapolis, MN: University of Minnesota Press.

LaMothe, K. (2006), *Nietzsche's Dancers: Isadora Duncan, Martha Graham, and the Revaluation of Christian Values*, New York, NY: Palgrave Macmillan.

Nietzsche, F. (1954), *The Portable Nietzsche*, Walter Kaufmann (ed.), New York, NY: Penguin.

—— (1967), *The Birth of Tragedy and The Case of Wagner* (trans. and ed. W. Kaufmann), New York, NY: Vintage Press.

—— (1974), *The Gay Science with a Prelude in Rhymes and an Appendix of Songs*, New York, NY: Vintage Press.

—— (1984), *Human, All Too Human: A Book for Free Spirits* (trans. M. Faber and S. Lehmann), Lincoln, NE: University of Nebraska Press.

Notes

1   Many thanks to the students and faculty at Syracuse University's Humanities Center who invited me to present this paper as a keynote address for their symposium on 'The Anatomy of Affect,' April 2011.

2   The first half of *Nietzsche's Dancers* (LaMothe 2006) systematically examines all appearances of 'dance' in Nietzsche's major published works, from *Birth of Tragedy* to *Will to Power*, and assesses their significance in his developing project of revaluing values.

3   For example, in *Human All Too Human*, dance appears as the paradigmatic art, awakening and educating our senses to their inherent creative potential. In *Zarathustra* and *Gay Science*, dancing is the act of engaging those sensory selves to create values, ideals, and gods that remain faithful to the earth. To dance is to overcome oneself. In works from 1886 to 1988, dancing appears as a spiritual-physical practice that serves to stir our energy, discipline our desires, and refine our instincts, so that we are willing and able to take responsibility for what we are creating. See *Nietzsche's Dancers* (LaMothe 2006), chapters 1–3.

4   The term 'BwO' is one that Deleuze and Guattari borrow from Antonin Artaud, who used the term in an unbroadcast radio show 'To Have Done with Justice.' As Deleuze explains, for Artaud, the BwO is something that God has stolen from us 'in order to palm off an organized body without which his judgement could not be exercised' (Deleuze 1998: 131).

5   For example, in one place where they describe a 'practice' of becoming a subject, Deleuze and Guattari write: 'Lodge yourself on a stratum, experiment with the opportunities it offers, find an advantageous place on it, find potential movements of deterritorialization, possible lines of flight, experience them, produce flow conjunctions here and there, try out continuums of intensities segment by segment, have a small plot of new land at all times'

(1987: 161). Their advice is to 'connect, conjugate, continue: a whole "diagram" as opposed to a still signifying and subjective programme' (161). The agent in these programmes remains the solo thinking self.

6   In his concluding chapters, Abram does set out a programme for re-educating our sensory selves: he calls for a rejuvenation of oral traditions to recall us 'to our bodily participation in the metamorphic depths of the sensuous' (2010: 298). However, such practices will not go far enough in awakening our sensory awareness of how our *bodily movement* makes us.

Part II

Reflections on the Intersections of Spiritualities and Pedagogy

Sarah Whatley

We know Spirit is continuously creating each person and each person is a perfect portal to Spirit. This is the Big Dance.

(River & Melin, this volume: 339)

This section includes nine chapters that together provide interesting insights about the intersection of spiritualities and pedagogy. All of the writers have an established teaching practice and are significant authorities within their own field, which they draw on to reflect on their experience of spirituality. While each takes a different approach, there are recurrent themes, albeit expressed quite differently by each writer. Each, for example, reveals some hesitancy about the term 'spirituality' due to its popular association with religious expressions. They argue that, unlike some religious teachings, somatic movement practices are not concerned with transcending embodied experience, but advocate for a reconnection with the biological body as a means of worldly integration. So if somatic practices encourage an integrated body rather than a fragmented one—a sense of wholeness rather than thinking of the person as a series of parts (particularly the spirit being distinct from the mind)—then we can understand why the writers are troubled by views that spirituality (or spirit) might endorse what Schwartz describes as a separation or fragmentation of being. But as Yvan Joly points out in Sylvie Fortin's chapter, if spirituality refers to our interconnectedness with the world beyond, with environment and others, then it has more meaning within the context of somatic practices and Somatic Movement Education. A common theme is therefore a serious consideration about whether the spiritual is something within all of us, a condition to be discovered and found from within ourselves, or whether it is actually about reaching outside and going beyond ourselves, beyond our own distinct, single entities.

The proposition of a *spiritual journey* also recurs as writers reflect upon their own practice or the practice of others. A sense of personal awakening, or as Glenna Batson puts it, a 'personal epiphany' (this volume: 223) in finding a new philosophy or purpose in life underpins much of the writing. However, several authors also discuss their ambivalence about writing from their own subjective experience of spirituality, or at least the challenges that they encountered when writing from that place, and this confrontation becomes the focus for discussion in the early part of each chapter. Consequently, a feature of this part is the debate that each writer has with her/himself about the approach to take in the writing, and how to access thoughts about spirituality when the self is a primary source. Using the self as a resource in this way can run the risk of lacking criticality and privileging an ego-centric view of the world, but such is the power of this humanistic examination and excavation of a personal practice that readers will no doubt find resonances with their own search for meaning and understanding of how we relate to ourselves and others in the world. This recurring discussion is particularly interesting because it reflects and makes clear the specificity of the topic (spirituality) and is at the same time rooted in the authors' desire to transmit through an appropriate written form the particular nature of their practice. We therefore find out how different pedagogical approaches influence and shape perspectives on spirituality and also how each teaching method spawns a particular writing style. What emerges is writing that is playful and insightful, experimental yet rigorous, reflecting the wisdom that is embodied and embedded in the histories, practices and experiences of the authors. Simultaneously, we are also reminded that there is a paucity of pre-existing scholarship in the field of spirituality as it relates to Somatic Movement Education.

Many of the authors in this volume are women, and this reflects the strong connection between feminist thought and somatically-informed movement practice, which find an easy relationship in modes of bodily inscription, image forming and textual writing. Authored by women, the first five chapters provide deeply reflective accounts of journeys through moving, somatic practice, performance and the consideration of spirituality. The opening chapter, 'Reflections on the Spiritual Dimensions of Somatic Movement Dance Education' by Martha Eddy, Amanda Williamson and Rebecca Weber sets the scene for this part and something of a context for the book as a whole. Drawing on their collective wisdom and extensive knowledge, these authors pool their experiences as somatic practitioners, teachers and writers to provide a comprehensive review of the literature that contributes to our understanding of the roots of spiritualities and the role played by spiritualities within contemporary and New Age societies. They situate spiritualities within political, cultural and sociological frameworks and discuss what they see as connections in thought and practice between Somatic Movement Dance Education and religious teachings. For anyone wanting an introduction to the major themes and issues that help to illuminate the somewhat elusive and mysterious concept of spiritualities and its role within somatic practices, this far-reaching chapter provides a stimulating itinerary and orientation.

Jill Green's chapter, 'Postmodern Spirituality? A Personal Narrative' points to the partial and personal nature of spirituality. She sets out the inevitable tensions that occur if a holistic view of the sacred and spirituality is attempted, pointing out the contradictions inherent in such an endeavour, claiming that, 'there are no easy conceptualizations that deal with spirituality, Somatics and postmodernism as cohesive components of a holistic construction of thought. Rather, there are tensions between and among these ways of thinking' (this volume: 204). Reflecting on her own long career, she describes how such a private journey is made more tangible through the various encounters with Somatic Movement educators and theorists. She discusses the impact of postmodernism on how she made sense of her prior knowledge and experience, eventually arguing for a postmodern perspective on spirituality. At the heart of the chapter is an interesting analysis of how our experience of the soma and our sense of whom we are in the world changes through time because of broader social, political and cultural phenomena.

Helen Poynor's chapter unfolds as a reflection on what is, as with any other writer in this anthology, a hugely influential career as a movement practitioner. Poynor writes about the spiritual and cultural influences on her work as teacher, artist and dance movement therapist, and she describes the context of what she describes as a non-stylized and environmental practice. Based in the UK, Poynor writes persuasively about her affinity with the outdoors and how she is drawn to poetry, and specifically that of Rumi, to provide a textual framing for her practice 'as it challenges duality of body and spirit, affirms a different way of knowing and celebrates the beauty of the natural world' (this volume: 214).

Teacher, performer and somatic practitioner Glenna Batson similarly begins by tracing her own journey, this time through encounters with different religions in her quest for understanding. In her chapter, 'Intimate to Ultimate: The Meta-Kinesthetic Flow of Embodied Engagement,' she describes how she recognized the centrality of the body as a means to make sense of what she considers 'spiritual' and simultaneously how the body is 'largely suppressed as a source of spiritual insight' (this volume: 226). She looks to different modes of thought to argue for a discourse to support an embodied spirituality. Thereafter she introduces a discussion on meta-kinesthesis in the context of spirituality, which she describes as, 'that phenomenon which brings us into intimate contact with ourselves, with others and ultimately with the spiritual realm' (this volume: 226). She argues for the importance of kinesthetic consciousness in how we sense movement and how spirituality connects with a harmony of the self.

Sondra Fraleigh's chapter 'Permission and the Making of Consciousness' offers a reflective writing in two parts. The first provides an engaging insight to her very long and influential career as a somatic educator. She reminds us of the importance of language in how we teach and communicate with students in work that is rooted in somatic values. For anyone who has followed Fraleigh's teachings and writing over the years, this is a very honest and personal account of her journey through dance and movement, and her encounters with and considerations of different religious practices. She sets out twelve key principles that underpin her teaching, all of which emanate from her core idea; 'verbs of permission'. The second part begins with a more philosophical perspective on her work with Somatics, interwoven with references back to her own experiences. As with other writing in this collection, Fraleigh emphasises the importance of connection as a fundamental aspect of spirituality. Read together, Fraleigh's writing is an important touchstone for Somatic Movement educators and students alike.

The chapters that follow are all conversational in nature. Sylvie Fortin begins with a six-way conversation about spirituality in her chapter 'Conversations About the Somatic Basis of Spiritual Experiences.' In Chapter 13, Kathleen Debenham and Pat Debenham make the case for conversations of connection as a ground for spirituality. By contrast, Ray Schwartz offers a conversation with himself as a novel way of thinking through his relationship to spirituality in his chapter 'This Indivisible Moment: A Meditation on Language, Spirit, Magic and Somatic Practice.' By mirroring his own divided self, he considers how spirituality is both a conduit for arriving at wholeness, and a means to (or process of) division of the individual between body and spirit. His dichotomous debate skilfully demonstrates (and documents) the inevitable tensions and questions that continue to vex those involved in Somatic Movement Education. Finally, Suzanne River, in conversation with Kathleen Melin, provides a very different perspective in their chapter, 'Global Somatics™ Process: A Contemporary Shamanic Approach', which offers a vibrant and colourful dialogue that is rooted in shamanism and its connections with Global Somatics Movement Education (GSME).

Prompted by her experience of supporting a dying friend and recognizing something ineffable in their relationship, Sylvie Fortin offers in Chapter 12 what she describes as a 'collage' of interviews with mature somatic movement educators to explore the place of spirituality within their professional lives. Each respondent is situated within a different somatic practice (the Feldenkrais method, Body-Mind Centering®, Continuum, Alexander Technique and Ideokinesis) and the discussion reveals the interesting connections and areas of divergence in their practices and philosophies of movement. As in other chapters, they raise questions about the relationship between spirituality and religion. Fortin draws the conversation to a close by reflecting on the ways in which spirituality is embedded within Somatic Movement Education rather than being an explicit aspect of the work, which is illustrated well in Linda Rabin's comment about her practice of Continuum, where she states, 'I feel it is a movement and somatic practice that is like a spiritual practice, or at least it's a practice that lets me feel my spirituality while being in my body in movement, with breath and sound, and in a resonant field with others. It's all woven in' (Rabin, in Fortin, this volume: 268).

Kathleen Debenham and Pat Debenham also reflect on their own teaching experiences in their chapter 'Inner Dance–Spirituality and Somatic Practice in Dance Technique, Choreography and Performance'. Like Fraleigh, they emphasise the importance of 'connection' as a principle that underpins all their teaching and similarly offer a series of guiding concepts for their pedagogy. Grounded in the somatic practice of Bartenieff Fundamentals and informed by the theoretical constructs of Laban Movement Analysis, they examine how dance education can illuminate the sacred dimensions of each individual's embodied personal narrative, and provide lots of examples drawn from their teaching practice, which they call a 'pedagogy of embodiment'. They weave in comments by their students to illustrate another pillar of their teaching practice, which they describe as a 'constructivist pedagogy', which encourages students to construct their own knowledge by bringing prior knowledge together with current experience. They conclude their chapter with a statement that could equally apply to so many of these chapters; 'Through somatic pedagogies, we lay the foundation for connection, empathy and compassion, the ground for spirituality' (this volume: 302).

In Chapter 14 Schwartz's dialogic writing finds an imaginative form to skilfully illustrate some of the inevitable tensions in attempting to create a discourse for spirituality in relation to Somatic Movement Education, which avoids fixing or concretizing the idea of spirituality. He debates with himself what 'spirit' means and whether he can himself connect with the idea of spirit. Early on, he offers a radical proposition that there might be an association between Somatics and magic, arguing that both are concerned with 'connection, consciousness and experience', suggesting that the way in which people connect with the world can feel 'magical' (this volume: 311). The spirit, he suggests, 'lives between actions' and is perhaps 'simply the relationship between things' (this volume: 322). And spirit, he tells us, is connected with the immaterial, which is accessed through breath; 'the work I do with breath reinforces my sense of the integration of body, mind and emotion, and it causes me to question and reimagine spirit' (this volume: 322). But he concludes by questioning his own argument about the role of Somatics, experience, magic, embodiment and integration, acknowledging the impossibility in seeking definitions of the spiritual.

The final chapter of Part II reverts to a more conventional conversational mode between Suzanne River and Kathleen Melin. They provide important insights to non-Western sacred practice by focusing on River's work with shamanism, describing what shamanism offers and how shamanism is viewed by Western cultures. They document their dialogue about how they see spirituality and spirit in their work, claiming that 'the soma is a portal to spirit' and how in their practices of creating sacred space they go beyond themselves 'to reach a spiritual level' (this volume: 331, 335). Both writers are experienced GSME practitioners, which they describe as a contemporary shamanic approach. Their view about spirituality seems to connect with Schwartz's argument that spirit exists in the relationship between people, things and actions. But they also introduce the idea of 'aura', which is referred to as the 'spirit body' (as one of several namings) in shamanic studies (this volume: 337).

Collectively, the nine chapters in this part provide a fascinating insight into the ways in which experienced teachers of Somatic Movement practices explore and integrate ideas of spirituality in their work. They show how spirituality or 'spirit' draws attention to the core concerns of Somatics: the existence of the corporeal body, the necessity for individual agency and self awareness as well as the possibilities for deeper relationships with others, and above all, a healthy realignment of mind, body and spirit. As with most chapters in this volume, personal subjective experience and reflection is prioritized and emphasized in order to reveal more about how spirituality is a fundamental if unarticulated (or even an incomprehensible) thread in the work of movement practitioners, teachers, artists and scholars.

Chapter 7

Reflections on the Spiritual Dimensions of Somatic Movement Dance Education

Martha Eddy, Amanda Williamson and Rebecca Weber

This chapter is divided into two wide-ranging parts. Part One reflects on the intersection of Somatic Movement Dance Education with spiritualities, and further examines the field's affinity with themes associated with feminist spirituality and those associated with the growth of New Age spirituality. Part Two addresses an in-depth inventory of Somatic Movement Dance Education, and particularly the central precept of connectivity, which is so integral to practice and also reflective of the New Age spirituality paradigm. Part Two also acknowledges non-Western influences, which have in turn impacted and shaped the growth of connective practices. Additionally, Part Two explores how *pedagogies of connectivity* emerged from experiences of isolation and bodily disruption. Connective pedagogies which were developed through deep-body listening, imagery, somatic meditation, gravity and grounding, intuitive slowing and resting, and the space and the environment are discussed.

Within this chapter, we use the term "Somatic Movement Dance Education" (SMDE) to encapsulate a wide-ranging and varied international field. SMDE can be broadly defined as the educative field that applies either fundamental shared somatic principles or definable techniques from the wider fields of Somatics and Somatic Movement Education (SME) to the art and practice of dancing. Within university contexts, one can observe distinctive areas of application, such as—but not limited to—the following[1]:

The application and integration of a particular somatic technique, such as Ideokinesis, Body-Mind Centering®, Laban/Bartenieff Studies, Skinner Releasing Technique, Feldenkrais, and The Alexander Technique (Brodie and Lobel 2004, 2006; Fortin and Girard 2005; Batson and Schwartz 2007).

(Williamson 2010: 43)

The application of somatic principles to dance and movement within the realms of expressive arts, movement therapies and transpersonal psychologies.

(Williamson 2010: 45)

Five core somatic movement processes identified by Eddy in studying the first generation of somatic pioneers: slowing down to feel, breath and relaxation, releasing into gravity, three-dimensional use of space, and new coordinations/awareness (inclusive of how one initiates movement).

(Eddy 2002a; Eddy 2006; Eddy 2009; Eddy in press 2014)

The application of shared somatic principles to free improvisational movement strategies, such as the above, and in addition: 'deep-body listening,' 'attentive connection with

Figure 1: Mover: Rebecca Weber. Photographer: Weston Aenchbacher.

body-self,' 'attentive connections to others,' 'depth-support-in-movement,' 'sensory comfort and pleasure,' and 'attentive connection to the imagination.'

(Williamson 2009)

The application of the 'open framework' or 'semi-structured framework' (somatic models which rely on more autonomy in movement response lying with the client or student in studio-based dance techniques), where multiple principles are experimented with, derived from different disciplines.

(Weber 2010)

Part One: Broad Reflections and Observations

There is a 'growing wave of dancers/practitioners who sense spiritual nourishment in the dancing body,' and new somatically-oriented dance research frequently reveals that spirituality is an important (often *sensed, felt* and *vibrant*) dimension of moving experience (Williamson and Hayes 2012: 3–8; LaMothe 2012; Sargent-Wishart 2012; Roseman 2012; Kraus 2012).

However, setting out to study 'spirituality' is always a challenging venture, because as Stanczak notes, 'spirituality is very often discussed as a "search for the sacred"' (2006: 3). This very broad understanding encompasses 'a diverse spectrum of practices, rituals, beliefs, and social contextual influences through which individuals negotiate a personal connection' (Stanczak ibid: 3–4). Consequently, discussions of spirituality may necessitate tackling both secular and theistic understandings of the sacred; require negotiating individuality, plurality and diversity; and ideally acknowledge the wider socio-cultural contexts/influences in which religious/spiritual practices are produced.[2]

> Spirituality and its variant expressions are reflective and indicative of the wider changing socio-cultural and economic landscape (i.e. that the substantive/functional content of the sacred/spiritual is highly malleable and open to numerous constructions and creative expressions). As such, personal spiritual truths and faiths are instrumentally shaped by the wider socio-cultural landscape.
>
> (Williamson 2010: 40)

Historical and cultural context is an important component in the study and reflection on spirituality. As noted by Sheldrake, 'Spiritual traditions do not exist on some ideal plane above and beyond history. The origins and development of spiritual traditions reflect the circumstances of time and place' (2007: 5). The idea that socio-historic forces play a central role in the production and expression of spirituality is a difficult notion that may cause argument and debate. A spirituality which is held dear or perceived as 'truth' is potentially undermined when socio-historical context is discussed in relation to the material production of spiritualities. As Sheldrake posits, 'Spirituality is never pure in form. "Context" is not "something" that may be added to or subtracted from spiritual experiences or traditions but is the very element within which these find expression' (2007: 6). When considering spirituality within the field of Somatic Movement Dance Education (SMDE), it is beneficial to pay attention to broader shifts in religiosity and spirituality and contemporary socio-historic context—for the field does not grow in isolation, but rather co-creatively and interactively with the wider socio-spiritual landscape.

Spirituality is 'one of the most enchanting, yet elusive elements of pedagogical practice'; it is so 'fraught with definitional, conceptual, and methodological problems,' that the subject is often avoided in academic discourse (Williamson and Hayes 2012: 4; Williamson 2010). Yet the question of whether, and in what ways, spirituality in SMDE reflects and engages with the wider contemporary socio-spiritual landscape frequently calls our attention because the field shares so many features in common with current definitions and expressions of spirituality. For example:

1. 'Contemporary understandings of spirituality capture the dynamic, transformative quality of spirituality as lived experience, an experience linked to our bodies, to nature, to our relationships with others and society' (King 2009: 4).

2. 'Spirituality has come to represent individuals' efforts at reaching a variety of sacred or existential goals in life, such as finding meaning, wholeness, inner potential, and interconnections with others' (Paloutzian and Park 2005: 24–25).

3. Searching for wholeness, health, vitality, integration, balance and connection is simultaneously championed within the holistic spirituality paradigm, as well as within the field of SMDE (see Debenham and Debenham 2008; Eddy 2005).

4. SMDE shares some tangential similarities and characteristics with New Age spirituality, such as the disruption of meta-religious authority and an emphasis on self-authority, subjective spirituality and self-spirituality (Heelas 1999; Heelas and Woodhead 2005).

5. SMDE shares common ground with feminist spirituality, in raising the status of body, flesh, self and nature as sites of spiritual resource and sustenance, standing in stark contrast to dualistic male-centred religion that served to marginalize women and sacred immanental bodied experience (Daly 1973; Christ and Plaskow 1992).

6. The key components found in contemporary definitions of spirituality—such as the focus on personal experience, the journey of searching for the sacred, and connection (Kraus 2009; Paloutzian and Park 2005)—are akin to underlying themes in SMDE pedagogies.

7. The field shares a similar, if not, at times, identical, generic language with meditative and mystical traditions—for example, the field is shaped by meditative movement practices that focus on introspection, silent-sensing, reflection and contemplation (Williamson 2010: 47; Williamson 2009; Eddy 2005; Sellers-Young 2009).

Plurality and controversy

Stephen Wright notes spirituality is sourced from,

> a wide continuum of views, from those whose Source is strictly God-centred to those for whom there is only this human reality and nothing else; from those who experience, know or believe in something ineffable, numinous and 'supernatural' to those who find consideration of anything other than the rational, biopsychosocial experience abhorrent or irrelevant.
>
> (2005: xiii–xiv)

Significantly, people are not uniform in their spirituality; as Ursula King points out, 'Like all other human experiences, spirituality exists primarily in the plural. It is thus much more appropriate to speak of "spiritualities" rather than spirituality in the singular' (2009: 4, *original emphasis*). Within educational contexts alone, a wide range of spiritualities may be voiced and expressed:

Student groups, for instance, may consist of theists from various denominations, people of interfaith and multi-faith orientations, humanists, agnostics, atheists and not least postmodern spiritual wanderers—those exploring numerous and sometimes theologically contradictory spiritual territories. Therefore, within any given group there will be much difference in terms of how spirituality is valued, understood and experienced. For some, spirituality may be shaped through a theistic lens, yet for others it may be shaped through a more humanistic lens, perhaps devoid of the non-ordinary and transcendent. In short, perspectives from different faith orientations and various secular dispositions shape how spirituality is defined, *felt* and experienced. For many, spirituality may be shaped through a number of personal eclectic and hybrid sacred formations (syncretistic sacred narratives).

(Williamson 2010: 52, *original emphasis*)

Furthermore, this range of spiritual perspectives precipitates a broad range of responses to discussing spirituality by students involved in SMDE (Eddy 2005; Sellers-Young 2009):

The word 'spirituality' elicits a range of response in the studio and lecture theatre—from those who celebrate and embrace the word with enthusiasm and curiosity, to those who are highly skeptical and critical. In academic contexts, the word can provoke joy and interest, as well as acute discomfort. Recognizing the word is problematic and controversial is an essential ingredient and perhaps the best starting place in academic study. Most notably, the word is rooted in the traditional, yet proliferates widely in the non-traditional. On the one hand, 'spirituality' is an inclusive word, contemporarily encompassing a wide variety of religious practices and secular activities cross-culturally (King 2009). On the other hand, the word is largely Christian in origin.

(Williamson and Hayes 2012: 4)

In addition, fear of religious fundamentalism and/or religious hegemony may cause unrest in SMDE, putting many people off engaging in significant discussions. David Tacey notes, 'The confusion of spirituality and religious fundamentalism causes many reasonable people to reject both, in the belief that humanity is better off without the sacred, since it seems to be at the heart of contemporary conflicts' (2004: 12). Tacey provides a useful distinction between the two, noting that,

Spirituality and fundamentalism are at opposite ends of the cultural spectrum. Spirituality seeks a sensitive, contemplative, transformative relationship with the sacred, and is able to sustain levels of uncertainty in its quest because respect for mystery is paramount. Fundamentalism seeks certainty, fixed answers and absolutism, as a fearful response to the complexity of the world.

(ibid 2004: 11)

Defining Spirituality Beyond Theistic Territories

The word 'spirituality' is Christian in origin, and 'derives from the Latin '*spiritus*', breath, from '*spirare*', to blow, to breathe' (Roof 2003: 138). Dictionary definitions tend towards the other-worldly, non-material, ethereal and ephemeral. Such understandings of spirituality owe much of their legacy to dualistic and polarized conceptualizations of spirituality and materiality, which are largely Christian in origin. For example, King notes, 'The "spiritual" is often mentioned when we want to name a reality greater than ourselves, a power or presence that goes beyond the individual person' (King 2009: 4). In addition, McGuire points out, 'Many of us were brought up thinking that the spiritual realm is completely apart from the mundane material realm [and indeed spirit from body]—perhaps even opposed to it' (2008: 97). She further comments, 'Western societies, in recent centuries, have tended to frame spirituality and materiality as dichotomous, in tidy binary opposition' (ibid). Indeed, the term 'spirituality' is used 'frequently in express or implied distinction to *bodily, corporal* or *temporal*', and frequently-used 'definitions clearly point to the inherent polarity that is traditionally so often associated with spirituality—it is seen as opposite to the physical' (King 2009: 7). Naturally, a transcendental spirituality distinct from the body is severely at odds with SMDE, and hence it is not surprising the word 'spirituality' often causes tension. However, in contrast to a disembodied spirituality, new forms of spirituality emerging beyond the limitations and dualisms of traditional religion 'bring spirit and body, sacredness and sexuality, together in a redemptive experience of the totality and mystery of life' (Tacey 2004: 36). Immanental (embodied/bodied) orientated spiritualities have infiltrated and gained significant creative agency within the field of SMDE (Williamson and Hayes 2012).

Definitions of 'spirituality' are notoriously complicated because spirituality is difficult to measure and quantify. Depending on the field of study, the subject of spirituality may suffer academic depreciation, particularly because of its ephemeral, fleeting and elusive nature. However, applying contemporary definitions (with a sociological orientation) may serve to de-mystify spirituality by bringing the immaterial *down to earth*—positing that spirituality is creatively produced, generated and constitutionally shaped by people and in the material world (Williamson 2010). Such definitions provide a grounded, rather than ephemeral understanding of spirituality. In addition, contemporary definitions are wide-ranging, serving to include activities from both the sacred and secular landscape. The following full explanation by Kraus is one multifaceted example of an extensive, inclusive working definition—one that transverses theistic and non-theistic orientations, is agreed on in much scholarly discourse, and illuminates key components and dimensions of spirituality:

> Spirituality is primarily an individual phenomenon. Each person's relationship with the sacred is somewhat unique. [...] Second spirituality includes the sacred. The sacred is something perceived as exalted, above and beyond the ordinary, worthy of reverence, or set apart for a special purpose. It is isolated from those things that are considered everyday or commonplace. [...] Virtually anything can become sacred if people view it

as such. God can be considered sacred, but so can community, finding meaning, and in personal relationships. When people infuse objects, situations, or relationships with a sacred character, they may be more cautious with, take better care of, and consider these things a more core part of their lives, than if they did not view them as sacred. […] Third, spirituality is a journey to discover something larger than ordinary life. It is a dynamic, ongoing process, which sometimes includes negotiating one's understanding of and experience with the sacred. A spiritual journey can occur within religious institutions or outside these organizations in a variety of small groups, nature, or in one's home. […] A final component of spirituality is connection. People may attempt to commune with a Higher Power, such as God. In addition, they may try to become more aware of and tap into their deeper, and more authentic selves, or bond with other humans.

(Kraus 2009: 52)

What Do We Know About the Somatic Movement Dance Education Field Generally?

SMDE is on the whole an egalitarian, humanistic, democratic educational practice, and therefore not aligned with any one specific mystical, spiritual, psycho-spiritual or religious tradition. Spirituality is therefore democratically structured, and free from the imposition of fixed sacred narratives, of external and intellectually abstracted religious and spiritual ideals, and therefore an inclusive pedagogy, widely accessible to all.

(Williamson 2010: 46)

While institutional religion readily addresses issues of morality and ethical decision-making, SMDE, with its secular orientation, approaches morality by raising somatic awareness (Eddy 2005; Myers 2010). Thus, somatic awareness does have a role in affecting morality and decision-making but without being part of institutionalized religion. Listening within and contemplation are key. Moral and spiritual connections arise through attending to subjective sensation, following the heart or being led by gut feelings. The moving, dancing body thus becomes a resource for sensing what feels good, what feels right personally and what needs changing—and consequently can potentially offer choices to act in the world in ways that feel healthy and wholesome.

Because of this, SMDE pedagogies broadly reflect wider paradigm shifts in religiosity and spirituality, and particularly those forms of spirituality that directly challenge patriarchal monotheism by focusing on self-authority and self-spirituality (Heelas 1999; Heelas and Woodhead 2005). SMDE tends to reject metaphysical ideas that position spiritual authority as above and beyond an individual, or external to the material body and material life. As such, Christianity, and monotheism in general, is not popular in Somatics literature.[3] Monotheistic religion, particularly Christianity, is generally viewed as too authoritarian in texts, guilty of metaphysical violence—that of separating and distancing people from their own spiritual resources, their spiritual power, located in body, in sense perception and personal interpretations about the world (Johnson 1987, 1992; Williamson 2010). Exploring 'the wisdom of material reality' and the innate intelligence within the body is a clear theme in Somatics literature; that is, the body's internal sensory landscape and the life force *felt* moving within is sacralized as a site of spirit (life and luminosity) and spiritual sensitivity (Johnson 1995: xvii). The following are examples of central themes that shape SMDE pedagogies, which celebrate the *living-moving-breathing body*, and are drawn from the wider field of Somatic Movement Education:

- Self-regulation: in its broadest sense, self-regulation tends to mean the ability to sense imbalance within the organism and to move towards balance through conscious awareness and embodied action. Furthermore, it tends to mean listening to the self-regulatory intelligence of the body and following the body's desire for easeful functioning.
- 'Hedonic, self-regulatory behaviours': this means contacting and utilizing the organic bodily instinct to move towards pleasurable functioning and 'useful, live-preserving or life-enhancing, [...] enjoyable and adaptive' activities (Juhan 2002: 29, 31).
- Self-authority: this represents 'the active and intelligent engagement of the individual in the shaping of a vibrant and productive life' (Juhan 2002: 5).
- The re-validation of subjective experience: this repositions the body as an omnipresent source of wisdom and intellect, our quintessential intelligence: the body as 'the matrix for our ideas, values, emotions, and spiritual commitments' (Johnson 1997: 5).
- Inspirited anatomies: this signifies a living, breathing experience of anatomy (an inspirited body).
- The re-validation of sensual experience: this includes trusting the sensual experience of the body—sensing into personal and unique movement requirements in order to move towards healthy functioning.
- The re-validation of play: improvisational play stimulates and ignites the playful dexterity, fluidity, elasticity and resilience inherent within skeletal muscular system, and educators utilize improvisational play in order to support high degrees of adaptive skilfulness, easeful functioning and release of body tension.
- Slow-time and contemplation: this involves improvisational practices underpinned by somatic awareness, structured within variants of the following categories: resting, settling, sensing, perceiving, deep-body listening, conscious and creative embodied action, digestion, reflection, contemplation, assimilation and movement integration (see Johnson 2006: 47–58; Johnson 2000).

(Williamson 2010: 44)

Don Hanlon Johnson's work draws attention to the idea that the Somatics movement radically destabilizes authoritarian religious discourse (abstract theological narratives and external sources of power). Somatic literature tends to expound a subjectively centred, incarnate (bodied) earth-centred spirituality—the highly subjective emphasis and focus on the sensing body and personal decision-making processes can potentially disrupt theological discourses that emphasize higher, external, transcendent realms and supra-self divine orders of reality (Williamson 2010). As Johnson notes, the 'body in our work, is looked to as a source of, not the impediment to, basic human values. Knowledge, freedom and love are to be developed not by distancing ourselves from it, but by descending into it with the task of refining its sensations and movements' (1987: 31). Given this standpoint, spirituality within the field could be largely conceptualized as 'existential rather than "creedal"'—meaning that spirituality 'grows out of the individual person from an inward source, is intensively intimate and transformative, and is not imposed upon the person from an outside authority or force' (Tacey 2004: 8). The field, as it is primarily located within Western educational cultures, thus reflects the West's liberalized and thoroughly pluralized socio-spiritual landscape, and the democratization of spirituality, where 'personal autonomy and experimentation' render spirituality a deeply privatized and liberal terrain—and where the sacred narrative has been constitutively severed and liberated from the rhetoric of organized religion (ibid: 4).

As such, SMDE particularly reflects and engages with political underpinnings and central aspects of contemporary Western spiritualities, such as feminist spirituality (Plaskow and Christ 1989; Christ and Plaskow 1992; Daly 1973), New Age and holistic spirituality, (Heelas 1999; Heelas and Woodhead 2005; Tacey 2001, 2004) and progressive spirituality (Lynch 2007), which have grown following criticisms of patriarchal religion. Criticisms have in turn supported the growth of new forms of spirituality—directly challenging dominance, masculinity, transcendence, dualism and hierarchy, with a new found emphasis on democracy; freedom; feminine symbolizations of the divine; and the sacralization of the body, nature and immanent experience (see Lynch 2007; Heelas 1999; and Tacey 2001, 2004). As Williamson and Hayes (2012: 4) point out, 'Even though dualistic gendered religious symbols are somewhat entrenched in our shared Western consciousness, it is also clear that spirituality (within SMDE) has gained much cultural currency beyond patriarchal orders of the divine.' Put so well by Tacey, new forms of spirituality, such as New Age, 'compensates our established religious traditions by forcing us to attend to what has been repressed or ignored by Western religion: the sacred feminine, the Earth Mother, the Goddess, the body, nature, instincts, ecstasy and mysticism' (2001: preface).

Affinity with Feminist Spirituality

Partly because of the androcentric associations with the term 'spirituality,' academic and somatic movement/dance discourses have heretofore mostly refrained from explicitly studying or addressing spirituality. Williamson and Hayes note,

> Whilst loosened from its patriarchal construction and framework quite considerably, the word 'spirituality' is nonetheless historically associated with a male-centred,

heterosexist and imperialist religion (Plaskow and Christ 1989; Christ and Plaskow 1992; Daly 1973). Even though the word contemporarily extends beyond the boundaries of institutionalized Christianity, its male-centred roots and accompanying dualisms, which denigrate the body, flesh, nature, women and immanence, persistently cause tension and disquiet in the lecture theatre—and particularly in Dance Studies—a subject often dedicated to the body as a site of sacrality and intelligence, and in some genres, redemptive mystery. To use Mary Daly's words, the 'patriarchal possession' of the body may put people off engaging in the subject of spirituality, significantly and with ease (ibid). Notably, these patriarchal associations are particularly uncomfortable after the arrival of feminist spirituality, which advanced postpatriarchal and metapatriarchal socio-spiritual values—a word historically associated with violations, such as the exclusion and subordination of women, is naturally subject to scrutiny and suspicion in a field where women's voices are strong, and where the fleshy body is so visible and central in academic discourse.

(Williamson and Hayes 2012: 4–5)

In its broad and inclusive view of spirituality, SMDE reflects aspects of feminist spirituality. Feminists explicitly decried religion as 'sexist,' 'racist,' 'imperialist,' 'ethnocentric' and 'heterosexist' (Plaskow and Christ 1989: 2). Many questioned, and subsequently discarded, patriarchal religious symbols, identifying and naming agendas of political control and subjugation. Within this climate of change, a renewed appreciation of the Goddess strengthened and revitalized women's spirituality. The denigration of the female body in patriarchal religion and culture was challenged using symbols that respect the female body and natural bodily processes (Christ 1997; Sjöö and Mor 1991). These (and other) feminist spirituality cultures tend towards subscribing to theologies of freedom, of natural elemental force (elemental potency) and of embodied intimacy with the sacred (Daly 1973; Eller 1993). SMDE can be aligned with feminist spirituality and considered, in part, a post-patriarchal field of study that works to transcend and challenge phallocentric societal structures, i.e. value systems underpinned and produced by patriarchy (see Daly 1973).

Somatic movement/dance training methods potentially disrupt patriarchy and patriarchal symbols by repositioning the body as a locus of spiritual authority, and, in addition, using Johnson's language here, by advocating for the senses as a reliable source of spiritual wisdom (1992). In contrast, negative polarities traditionally associated with women, such as body, nature and flesh, occupy an elevated and revered position in Somatics literature and practices—[a vibrant and animated] sensual engagement with body and nature [are foundational in pedagogies].

(Williamson 2010)

Thus, despite presenting a very different viewpoint, the field of SMDE is naturally in conversation with patriarchal domination and all that serves to denigrate the body, nature, women, 'other' indigenous earth-centred cultures and a sensuous experiential engagement with the world. Like feminist spirituality, SMDE challenges patriarchal values, symbolism and dualism but presents an embodied, nature-based spirituality as an alternative, often supporting the development of an ecoliterate community (either explicitly or implicitly). Furthermore, it has been the emergence of female leadership that makes up the 'second generation of somatic pioneers' (Eddy 2009), who birthed the many practices of Somatic Movement Dance Education—practices that name and deepen emotional and spiritual connections within self and with nature as part of somatic exploration (Eddy 2002a; Eddy in press, 2014).

Related to the above, the field of SMDE is chiefly marked by the loss of metaphysical transcendence (the loss of monotheistic, hierarchal divine supraorders and transcendent symbolic universes) and a newly found focus on immanence (all that dwells within and on earth), creatively explored through pedagogies of 'deep immanence', 'elemental resonance' and 'inspirited anatomy', which engage deep-body listening and are thus often based on the following themes:

- Practices of deep descent into the *prima materia* of body-self (cellular and fluid resonating)
- Body-earth elemental movement explorations (breath flow, fluid flow, sensing into bone, skeletal-muscular release and flow)
- Participation and connection with the life force (rhythm, sound, motion, vibration work)
- An attentive focus on the life force *felt* within (sensing breath and fluid flow)
- Engaging and connecting with the existential nature of the moving universe—micro/macro movement resonance.

(Williamson 2010: 46)

Affinity with New Age Spirituality

The emergence and prevalence of new types of spiritualities is thought to be directly related to increased secularization, as evidenced by the 'decline in orthodox Christian beliefs and practices in most parts of the West', and the 'general decline in the power of religious institutions' (Gorski 2003: 111). Even though there is much scholarly controversy surrounding the exact nature and extent of secularization in the West (ibid), many scholars are exploring the 'spiritual revolution claim: that traditional forms of religion, particularly Christianity, are giving way to holistic spirituality, sometimes still called "New Age"' (Heelas and Woodhead 2005: x). These types of spiritualities are theologically characterized by a number of orientations, such as repositioning the self as the locus of spiritual authority, bodied unions with the divine, and the exploration and appropriation of a vast array of Eastern/non-Western spiritualities (Heelas 1999; Tacey 2001). The field of

Somatics growing out of this contemporary society shares some historical underpinnings with the New Age, such as the search for holism, some roots in Eastern spirituality, Jungian excursions into the imagination, the disruption of authority through an emphasis on self-authority, subjective spirituality, self-spirituality, the search for inner wisdom (bodied and incarnate), and the spiritualization/sacralization of nature and community (Heelas 1999).[4] As Williamson states, some strands of SMDE can be aligned thematically with spiritualities associated with the growth of the New Age, such as: strands of practice that spiritualize or sacralize nature through sensory participatory movement resonance, use spiritual symbols within practice pertaining to non-Western cultures; seek greater sensory union and communication with the inspirited life force *felt moving within*; seek deeper sensory connective unification with others, nature and the cosmos; and sacralize the inner self as a site of inspired intelligence—a valid, close, intimate source of knowledge (2010). Notably, the similarity is one of general themes, rather than fixed absolutes. The list of similarities below has been created through practice-observation and a literature review of Don Hanlon Johnson's work (1987, 1992, 1995, 1997, 2006) and leading theorists in the fields of New Age spirituality and contemporary spirituality, such as Paul Heelas (1996, 1998, 1999), Heelas and Linda Woodhead (2005), Gordon Lynch (2007) and David Tacey (2004).

- Self-spirituality: One listens to one's bodied self in order to discern what feels right (morals, ethics and spiritual values are discerned from within).
- Self-authority: Body-self senses what is spiritually authentic and true.
- Deep immanence: One seeks bodied corporal spiritual experience—repositioning the divine as part of, and within, the human body (omnipresent).
- The sacralization of the body: The material body is positioned as the locus of spiritual authority—body/flesh/nature are sacralized as sites of divine intelligence.
- Secular spirituality: Practitioners explore and integrate the secular-cum-spiritual realms of body-therapies, transpersonal psychologies and humanistic psycho-spiritual territories into dance and movement.
- Syncretistic spirituality: Practitioners appreciate the formation of deeply personal sacred narratives, fostered through what feels right and engendered from within.
- Eclectic spirituality: Mixing and blending sacred narratives from diverse sources is prevalent.
- Holism and connectivity: Practitioners experience connection to a deeper self, others, the community, the earth and the cosmos.

(Williamson 2010: 54–55)

Spirituality associated with the growth of the New Age has received criticism from various academic sources. For example, Steve Bruce observes the eclectic narcissistic nature of the New Age (Bruce 1996: 198–229). Marked by expressive individualism and consumerism, the narcissistic nature of the New Age has come under considerable scrutiny. However, with these criticisms in mind, spiritualities associated with the growth of the New Age are also characterized by many theological positives, such as: self-authority and self-expression, "bodied" spiritualities (inclusive of the senses), spiritualities inclusive of women and feminine religious symbolism, spiritual autonomy and creative freedom—these inclusive positives infiltrate international practice within the field of SMDE.

Part Two: In-Depth Observations on the Spiritual Dimensions of Somatic Movement Dance Pedagogy

Researchers such as Heelas (1999), Bruce (1996), and Tacey (2001), observe connectivity and inter-connectedness is a central characteristic of the New Age. Thus, in this second half of the chapter, we look in-depth at the scope of SDME, and in particular, at the concept of connectivity—a shared tenet which is integral to practice and reflects themes within the New Age spirituality paradigm. Here, we acknowledge non-Western influences which have impacted the development of connective practices to self, other,

Figure 2: Movers: Martha Eddy & Global Water Dancers. Photo Credit: Lesley Powell.

and the environment, and explore how *pedagogies of connectivity* were developed through experiences of isolation and bodily disruption. Lastly, an overview of other aspects of somatic spirituality is given, featuring deep-body listening, imagery, somatic meditation, gravity and grounding, intuitive slowing and resting, and connecting to space and the environment.

Experiences of Disruption and the Origination of Somatic Education

People readily turn to spirituality in times of distress or disruption (McGuire 2008, 2003). Traditionally, however, these are thought of as existing in realms beyond the material. But is a spiritual resolution of disruption necessarily metaphysical, and thus disembodied? The field of somatic education emerged from experiences of disruption (Eddy 2009); disruptions of community, bonds with family, or even connection with one's own bodily capabilities have served as leverage points for somatic investigation (Eddy 2012; Eddy in press, 2014). The choice to re-embody through somatic processes is a choice to be 'grounded in the body' and ideally integrates body-mind-spirit in present circumstances. In some cases, the somatic process has opened up spiritual awareness as well. Specific links with spirituality can be traced through the field's origination during periods of disruption in the lives of somatic education pioneers. It is evident in their concurrent senses of separation and isolation due to the challenges of dislocation, injury, illness, 'other'ness, World War II, and difference resulting in aloneness (Eddy 2009). Somatic Movement also interfaces with entering a crossroads and discovering newly the concept of the liminal. In the disruption of the habitual (a core principle of) and in dynamical systems (Thelan 1995), we open to newness. In the state of newness, we can enter the 'beginners mind' (a Buddhist concept) or perceive of the world as if we were a baby (e.g. opening to innocence; of Christ consciousness). Of course, responses to upsetting circumstances, especially trauma, can result in disassociation, a form of disembodiment (Knaster 1996; Levine 2010). Difficult circumstances can lead to trauma, PTSD, disassociation, lack of grounding and spiritual bypassing (Eddy 2011; Masters 2010; Orbach 2009). However, 'while the somatic leaders and their stories could lead to iconic institutions, their successes were not steeped in domination but rather in mindfulness, caring, and consideration' (Eddy in press, 2014). The somatic movement pioneers found wholeness, grounding, health and, in some cases, discovered the transcendent through their bodily investigations. Based on their commonalities (Bainbridge Cohen 2001; Conrad 2002; Eddy 2002, 2005, in press 2014; Fraleigh 2003; Halprin 2003; Summers 2003) the following pedagogical constructs were developed and are common across somatic movement training programmes:

1. Somaticization (contemplation of physical self in relative stillness) (Bainbridge Cohen 1993)

2. Breath awareness
3. Moments of silence
4. Contemplation while lying, sitting, standing, walking (Arrien 1993; Whitacre, the four dignities)
5. Contemplative movement in nature (Eddy 2005)
6. Movement of the unconscious and experiences of challenge and joy, both alone and with others
7. Rituals (especially movement attuning self with external or 'spatial' forces)
8. Dance and themes that emerge from the quiet of the unconscious

The Search

Disruption is frequently the impetus of searching for wholeness and the transcendent as a means of resolving the disruption. 'Searching' is a central 'feature of both religiousness and spirituality' (Paloutzian and Park 2005: 33), and it echoes the omnipresent explorative process of somatic movement/dance inquiry (Eddy in press, 2014). Like somatic explorations, the term 'search' indicates that spirituality is continuous, dynamic and creative—'the search for significance—discovery, conversation and transformation,' which 'unfolds throughout a lifespan' (Paloutzian and Park 2005: 34). Again, the search may be oriented through theistic or non-theistic activities—and is thus another inclusive feature of contemporary spirituality. Notably, 'searching' is an activity; spirituality is not a static concept, but rather possesses movement and dynamism. Thus, a very important aspect of spirituality is its creative, active and productive (ever-changing) component. Stanczak's definition outlined below is very useful for the SMDE field, because it renders spirituality unlimited in its expression, which is individual and collective, resourceful, active, pragmatic, creative, emotive and affective.

First, spirituality is *transcendent*, or at least somehow directed toward communicating with something subjectively perceived to be sacred.

Second, spirituality is an *active* and *ongoing* process that not only seeks out the sacred but also maintains and even changes in one's life.

Third, spirituality is *multidimensional*—traditional and/or creative, individual and/or collective.

Fourth, spirituality is *unlimited* in its experience and is bound neither to time nor place nor objects, but rather is accessible in all aspects of life.

Fifth, spirituality is *pragmatic*. It is both a resource and is resourceful, and as such it can be honed and utilized through active practice by individuals throughout their lives.

Finally, spirituality is *emotional*, connecting individuals to their lived environments in deeply affective ways.

(Stanczak 2006: 5, *original emphasis*)

Here, in his second stipulation, Stanczak reflects that the search is central to spirituality. In many ways, SMDE parallels this and other aspects of Stanczak's multidimensional components of spirituality, for it is emotional (Eddy 1990, 2002; Buckroyd 2000), pragmatic (a personal and collective resource for healing and efficiency), unlimited in its expression (the connections between cells and points of consciousness within the body and extending into the world are endless), an ongoing seeking (many somatic systems express themselves as explorations of philosophies of life) and, potentially, transcendent.

Process of Life in a Body

As some of the historical roots of SMDE illustrate, disruption may lead to a search or journey for the spiritual, which Somatics movement pioneers traversed through their lived bodily experiences. Through their life process, we know the embodied, lived journey can become sacralized. From conception to death, we are in a process of life in a body—a constant becoming. The lifespan development concepts engaged in by Alexander, Bartenieff, Body-Mind Centering®, Continuum and Feldenkrais® support preparedness for action on two levels: as a literal strengthening for individuals who stand up for integrity and as a metaphor for organizational development (Eddy 1998; Eddy 2011). As mentioned earlier, SMDE's orientation towards somatic awareness and self-authority has implications for individual ethics and decision-making elements of SMDE that are aligned with feminist and New Age spiritualities. In building an organization or establishing an individual activist perspective, it helps to see socio-political consciousness as an unfolding of different developmental stages. SMDE pedagogy can support this understanding as it aims to facilitate lived experiences of growth and development towards holism. As humans, we grow from the unicellular (having needs and desires because we are alive and breathing), to taking a stance (standing up for beliefs), to being able to shape complex rhythms and expressions (Eddy 1998). This is a progression from undifferentiated wholeness to differentiated parts, ideally connected to the whole. This is both a political and a lived experience, which can be sacralized or reflected in our individualized expressions of spirituality.

Suffering and Healing

A component of the somatic process is the development of empathy and compassion, often initiated by witnessing the experience of physical pain in self and others (which can also be an experience of disruption). Empathy and compassion exist as core strands of many religions; they can also provide the basis for tolerance of differences (Eddy 1998)—a shared philosophical tenet of Somatics perspectives. Somatic practices of embodiment that result in pain reduction generally also illuminate the shared humanistic experience of living in a body filled with sensation. The sensate soma can heal from pain during its self-regulation process; this process can also feel sacred (Eddy in press, 2014). Additionally, empathy is increased through experiencing new movement patterns, shared by others, and is accessed in accepting that which is perceived as unable to be changed (Eddy 1998, 2002b).

Connectivity

Connection is a key component in definitions of spirituality, and is a foundational aspect of SMDE pedagogy internationally (Williamson 2009). This 'connected space' that can be considered the spiritual nature of Somatics is perceptible throughout many somatic practices at various times. It can be gleaned from quotes about studying with F. M. Alexander (Johnson 1995), to hearing Sondra Fraleigh speak about the roots of her work (Fraleigh 2003), or in witnessing the natural movement of babies breathing (Bainbridge Cohen 1993). Attentive connection with body-self, to others, and to the imagination often shape practice (Williamson 2009). On social levels, SMDE connects us to others through touch and verbal/nonverbal modes of expression—we strengthen connection through skin, eyes, bones, hands, hips, and so on. We come to know each other through the nonverbal, thus playfully deepening our relationship to one another. On an existential level, moving with somatic awareness connects us to the movement that underpins all life; thus, we connect to something primary—something deeply intrinsic and core to our lived and shared experience. Deep connection is a central tenet of SMDE pedagogy, as Williamson notes:

> Re-inhabiting and reconnecting to the body is a central feature of community practice; in essence, practices of connectivity orientate the field internationally. Words such as 'interconnection,' 'connectivity,' 'matrix,' and 'reconnection' contribute to a shared discourse, which seeks to support and offer alternatives to feelings of disconnection and alienation. Advancing the health benefits of *depth-connection* to body through a felt dialogue with the blood, breath, heart, fluids, bone, and tissue are important processes that deepen connection with body and materiality. Furthermore, perceptual feelings of disembodiment and fragmentation are often remedied through practice which explores the integration of body with community, earth, and/or the inter-dependence of life.
>
> (2009: 40–41, original emphasis)

Evidencing this central connectivity, common descriptions relevant to the Somatics movement may include: an experience of oneness with all of humanity (Eddy 2009), the immanent experience of God (Wink 2002), connection to a higher purpose or somato-spiritual process (Dellagrotte 2012; Georghiou 2012), universal energy and a religious connection to an icon or deity. Informed by a somatic perspective, spirituality can be framed as a state of open-mindedness and reconnection with wonder that comes from embodying consciousness (Debenham and Debenham 2008). From a neurological perspective, spirituality can be thought of as entering a particular state of consciousness; this can be the experience of being guided fully by the 'right side of the brain' (Taylor 2006), or rather, allowing the right and left sides of the brain to coexist respectfully in all decisions.

During the somatic process of listening to the body, we can learn profound, extra-ordinary truths—that is, those that do not ordinarily manifest in daily life. We see, feel, hear and imagine truths for ourselves and attune with ourselves and others. Somatic tools are akin to meditation in that they involve contemplation through deep-body listening. These tools can awaken an experience of being part of 'all-humanity' or oneness (Walsch 2011). Spirituality can be defined as a loving sense of wonder and connectedness to the universal. Living life somatically can help to cultivate joy, ease, connectedness and even awe (of the miracles of the body, or the wonder of the gift of breath), giving birth to a spiritual existence (Eddy 2005). Another view of spirituality could be the shift of consciousness away from the strivings and worry of ego to the unbounded acceptance of support and goodness in life. Deep-body listening, as cultivated through somatic awareness, can lend itself to spiritual 'awakenings' and experiences of greatness from within if one chooses to listen and observe soma closely.

Through practices of deep-body listening, SMDE is a profound tool for eliciting the imagination and creativity and can become a sacred time for inviting spirit in (Summers 2003). Somatic education supports a notion of creating and connecting to an internal space that allows each person to be at home with her or himself, including children.[4] All investigations of the body can support this inquiry of connection, especially if the body is celebrated as sacred. Elaine Summers, originator of Kinetic Awareness, and Sondra Fraleigh, director of East/West Somatics, both address this in their teaching and writing: Fraleigh reports dancing as a young girl and feeling her spirit, while Summers talks about 'serendipity,' referring to the synchronicity of coincidences that bring us together, with the implication that the divine is intervening (Fraleigh 2003; Summers 2003). Furthermore, Somatic work can strengthen boundaries or minimize perception of boundaries and may even dissolve the physical boundary at times (Aposhyan 2004; Hartley 1995; Shafir 2011). Boundary-softening can be affined to a dissipated ego structure, for better or for worse. Similarly, somatic work can reinforce a clear sense of self, or serve to foster connectivity through adjoining selves to a transcendent whole of oneness. As the experiences of Jill Bolte Taylor (2009) demonstrate, various neuroscientific causes are linked with separation or merging. Logical-analytical personalities, traditionally identified as 'left brain' dominant, can lead to clear separation while creative, open-minded 'right brain' stimulus begs for the experience of shared connection to the universe. References by somatic teachers who facilitate connection, such as instruction to 'expand into space,' can be another neuromotor access route to move mind and body beyond limitation and into that which is larger-than-self; this can lead to transcendent experiences. Just as Emily Carr (1940) found transcendence in painting the wondrousness of nature or Thoreau in walking around Walden Pond (Vancouver 2013; Block 2001), somatic movement guided by a desire to be connected—either to self, to other or to the 'great beyond'—can open us to spiritual experience.

Connectivity to Self through Deep-Body Listening

Engaging and connecting with awareness of the existential nature of the moving body is an entry point to the numinous. This newly found focus on immanence can be attributed, in part, to the fact 'the field has been, and continues to be, shaped by a renewed interest in Eastern spirituality and non-Western concepts of the sacred' (Williamson 2010: 47; see also Eddy 2002). A central tenet is that paying attention to sensation is a key to spiritual awareness (Moore, as cited in Debenham and Debenham 2008: 46). Bartenieff, Feldenkrais, Rolf and Selver had teachers from Eastern traditions (Eddy, 2009) guiding them to pay attention to the present moment, look within and 'open up to the flow of breath and energy' (Eddy in press, 2014). However, none of the somatic pioneers (and no somatic leaders to date) have explicitly aligned with a religion or specific philosophic tradition as part of their pedagogy. Their practices parallel the discipline and outcomes of Eastern spiritual practices, but each has established her or his own philosophy integrating Eastern and Western principles with their personal lived experiences—reflective of the eclectic nature of syncretistic spirituality.

For example, Irmgard Bartenieff sought out a Chi Kung teacher during her annual visits to Hawaii. She was enamoured by the circular movements alive in Chinese traditions, especially in contrast to the lack of an observable 'rotary factor' in Eastern culture (Bartenieff and Lewis 1980). Her somatic system, Bartenieff Fundamentals, emphasizes the rotary factor in the scapula-humeral and ilio-femoral rhythm. An extrapolation of the importance of rotation draws upon the supporting Laban Movement Analysis principle that, 'function is an aspect of expression' (Bartenieff 1979)—the expressive intent of circular movement allows for self-awareness, a reaching outward and a balanced turning inward (versus unidirectional outwardly directed linear movement). The completion of this process can result in immanence through movement (Eddy 2006). Through circular movement, experienced with awareness from within, it may be possible to move outward to experience that which is larger than self, and back towards self, in one action. Furthermore, when supported by breath, the life force is contacted through this extension of circular movement out and in. Similar emphasis on circular movement appears in other Eastern systems, including (but not limited to) Judo, TaiChi, Kung fu, Jujitsu and the newer discipline of Aikido.

Several other influential somatic pioneers also had connections with Eastern spiritualities. First, Ida Rolf had an active yoga practice that influenced her thinking and beliefs (Johnson 1995); together with her husband, she brilliantly applied mindfulness to the art and act of living and to the living movement process. Furthermore, Moshe Feldenkrais was among the first Europeans to master the Eastern art-form of Judo (Reese 2012). As a black belt, he was exposed to circular movement, varying qualities of movement dynamics and the importance of movement intention for self-defence. Whether or not this led to any spiritual epiphanies for him is not evident in the literature, but may still be emergent. Additionally, F. M. Alexander has been referred to as the 'most religious person, in the real sense' for the concepts he portrayed (Barlow in Johnson 1995: 88). Physically allowing for emergent movement (as is typical in somatic movement explorations) and moving into width, circularity and expansiveness (modelled from Eastern movement forms), can potentially contribute to moving beyond egoistic, idealized (Green 1999) or goal-oriented movement into movement that supports compassionate connection with all (Eddy in press, 2014).

While this is only a small sampling of the somatic pioneers' intersections with non-Western traditions, the concepts engendered in these Eastern influences are clearly reflected in the Somatics modalities that the pioneers developed (Eddy 2002a). Though SMDE is unquestionably not a direct experience of the Eastern religious practices or spiritual worship, elements derived from these influences are pervasive in the field as a whole. The circularity, meditative qualities, connection to the life force and emphasizing inner and outer movement experiences all reflect the field's central tenets of deep immanence, mindful listening into oneself and connecting compassionately to that which is beyond oneself (community, nature, 'oneness'). Through connecting deeply to the self, aided by these techniques, somatic movement pedagogy can open avenues for spirituality to enter into one's practice.

Connectivity Beyond Self to Other

As evidenced by the influence of Eastern spiritual practices on Western somatic modalities, the field is pervaded by socially active spiritualities—spiritualities that extend beyond the individual, the private and internal. As Flory and Miller point out, particularly since the 1960s, 'private, individualistic, and non-institutionalized form[s] of spiritual fulfillment' have been dominant in the United States (2007: 202–203). However, other studies have revealed that spirituality is not quite so individualistic, but rather linked to social action (ibid: 203). When studying spirituality, it is vital to acknowledge the underlying socio-cultural implications. The intersection between SMDE and social change becomes apparent when one acknowledges that Somatics investigation affects morality (through elements such as the focus on individual authority and attention to somatic cues to support decision-making). Accordingly, it is important to acknowledge both the deeply internal/personal (individual), and the external/social (collective) dimensions of spirituality, which may extend beyond the individual in society and impact social change. Through the long history of community dance with visionaries such as Halprin, Laban, and Thornton (Bradley 2009; Reisel 2002) we have seen numerous socially active agendas advance, especially in the arenas of health, education, environmental sustainability, deep ecology and the arts (see chart below). Within SMDE modalities, while there is an intense focus on personal internal experience, there is also a central balancing principle of inner-outer balance. This principle connects the individual to the external and the collective—a connection which further supports self-authority and trust in incarnate wisdom and spirituality and also advances movers towards holism within themselves and in their communities. Self-acceptance and release of ego can be further supported by experiences of feeling loved and connected to other—whether other is human or universal, extending to compassionate action (Eddy, MR, 1982).

Models of Community Engagement and Socially Active Agendas
(One Perspective from NYC—Martha Eddy)

FORM Somatic Intention*	Community Dance	Dance and Somatic Leadership	Educational Activism	Community Organizing
Grounding	Body-Mind Dancing© and other somatic dance training systems	Somatic training programmes steeped in dance	Somatic training that includes early childhood and adolescent education	Bodily envisioning: Urban Bush Women; UN Decade on Sustainability: Youth Division
Expression	Somatic dance as activator Movement choirs	Expression of conflict and conflict transformation Swann and Eddy	John Dewey Grace Dodge Teachers College Columbia University	Spiritual Coordination New York Theological Seminary
Finding Integrity and Healing	Anna Halprin's dance rituals MovingForLife.org	Moving on Center's progression from personal Somatics to community activism	POST 9/11 Project renewal	Biblical Storytelling on streets of East Harlem (Eddy, M R 1982)
Subset of healing: Trauma and abuse	One Billion Rising Moving For Life DanceExercise for Health*	Relational peace	Inner resilience-educator retreats: Talent night to gentle movement	Transforming drug abuse to a medical condition
Communication	Dances of Universal Peace	Conflict Resolution through Movement and Dance (DEL at 92Y)	Transforming conflict through somatic skills (Moving on Center at EarthDance)	Global Water Dances: Invoking spirit at onset of performance
Subset of communication: Planetary awareness	Halprin's Planetary Dances GlobalWater Dances.org	SEEDS festival at EarthDance	El Puente School for Peace and Justice— EcoWalks CKE—EcoMoves for Kids©	"Eco-somatics" (Bauer 2008; Eddy 2006; Enghauser 2007) "Embedment" (Burns 2012) Ecopsychology

*The somatic intentions exemplified in this chart are the building blocks of the Dynamic Embodiment™: process—Waking Up to Self©, a model steeped in somatic approaches to anti-violence. Grounding, Expressing and Finding Integrity are what Eddy has identified as a progression of self-care and relating that supports improved inter-personal and inter-group exchange.

Connectivity to Space and the Environment

The experience of space as sacred is another inroad to spiritual support. Somatic lessons provide guideposts for physically relating to space, to our environment. By being aware of the cardinal dimensions and planes that intersect in the body, such as the patterns of movement in space and their relationship to the body that have been developed fully by Steiner's Eurhythmie and Laban's Choreutics (Bradley 2009), we can balance spiritual energies. Another approach is to physically align the body with the spiritual forces of nature. To feel and attune with the up and down rhythm of rain, to breathe into empathetic width with the horizon, to experience the sagittal ease of receiving light into the retina. Relationship to space is often best expressed by our 'shaping process.' We can see how we feel about a situation by assessing our postural attitude and movement and use this awareness to better accommodate to different situations. Laban/Bartenieff work and Spatial Dynamics™ infuse somatic awareness into elegant spatial sequences with an awareness of self and the surrounding world (Laban 1966, McMillan 2012). This spatial attunement to the environmental context can be brought into our awareness at all times. It is the basis of Alexander's teaching on 'use,' how we use the body in any instance. If the use of the body is focused on non-egoistic pursuits and attunes with bodily needs for harmony and a healthy environment, then this can intersect with the above-mentioned motivation for activism. As one example, in Dynamic Embodiment™, one aligns the body using a clear understanding of embodied anatomy within spatial forms (Eddy in press, 2014). For instance, one can sensitize to each of the glands through movement, sound and touch, as well as with an awareness of how the body moves within specific spatial forms. Then movement can be practised to heighten alignment, not only in static forms but while moving in space—indeed, new research reveals that shifts in alignment, when practised in dynamic movement, may affect more lasting change towards efficiency than those practised in static postures (Franklin 2012). This has implications for being able to be 'open to spirit' while walking down the street, dancing, or in contemplative action—thus enacting the holistic and constantly searching aspects of contemporary spirituality, the sacralization of the everyday (Kraus 2009: 52) and the ongoing, unlimited aspects of spiritualization of daily life (Stanczak 2006: 4–5).

Other Aspects of Somatic Spirituality

In addition to connectivity pathways, there are numerous somatic entry points in which a sensory experience can lead to a spiritual awakening. Many somatic practices begin with breath and easily move into places of rest and recuperation that lead to the contemplative (Eddy 2012; Sellers-Young 2009). The somatic processes of listening and observing in open compassion can often be interpreted as intuition. As somatic movement experts, we observe movement with such care that to the lay person it may seem that somatic movers are highly intuitive. Indeed, the opening to the flow of humanity supports being open to the right side of the brain—the undifferentiated, the numinous. This is then balanced with left brain awareness of patterns of movement and habits (some from early childhood neuro-maturational movement) (Eddy 2007), body alignment and its relationship to space (finding our own crystalline energy in the form of the body), as well as opening to the heart (and other energy systems of the body), which can feel as spiritual as prayer and gospel singing.

While teaching spirituality is rarely an explicit goal of a somatic movement training programme, there are numerous ways that the development of spirituality is supported. What specific topics within Somatics studies link to spiritual growth? All topics can be linked to the experience of 'oneness,' but what are the concrete physical activities that we can engage in that literally shift consciousness away from the secular and mundane and into an experience of the sacred and expansiveness in the body?

Cross-case analysis of thirty different somatic movement systems revealed four common themes in somatic movement programmes (Eddy 2006, 2012; Eddy in press, 2014) found to be consistent even if not described using the same language:

1. Slowing down to feel the body (to pay attention to bodily cues)
2. Releasing into gravity with breath support
3. Becoming aware of how to live and move in three-dimensional space
4. Discovering new patterns of coordination.

Somatic education in each of these four areas can introduce or deepen spiritual practice. For example, slowing down and breathing are quintessential features of meditation; to 'feel' is a celebration of the body, which can be a sacred act, and is reflective of Heelas' (1999) concept of deep immanence in New Age spiritualities. Additionally, letting go of bodily tension makes palpable the maxim 'let go and let God,' allowing release into an easeful, expansive state. Furthermore, connecting 'to the universe,' or to universal energy, can occur through the somatic experience of carefully aligning the body with three-dimensional space. And lastly, living from a philosophy that includes neuro-developmental principles of motor coordination connect all humans and animals to each other.

These and other elements of Somatics pedagogy can facilitate experiences of spirituality in somatic practices. Again, these elements appear commonly across a variety of SMDE practices that support spiritual experiences and include intuitive slowing and resting, giving into gravity or grounding, focusing on neuro-muscular maturation and development, somatic meditation, and the use of nature imagery to foster dance that is integral (Eddy 1995).

Intuitive Slowing and Resting

Being somatically aware and in touch with our own inner voice may help access the self-authority that is a central aspect in New Age spiritualities (Heelas 1999). As Heelas states,

Figure 3: Mover: Amanda Williamson. Photo Credit: Scott Closson.

'The "individual" serves as his or her own source of guidance [...] what lies within—experienced by way of "intuition," "alignment" or an "inner voice"—serves to inform the judgments, decisions and choices required for everyday life' (Heelas 1999: 23). A large percentage of what we 'intuit' in human interactions is actually based on observation—the nuanced movement and posture that is occurring at all times. Movement observation can be systematic; by far the most sophisticated somatic systems for movement observation are those based in Laban/Bartenieff Movement Analysis. They have been found to be reliable tools for human research (Davis 1973; Sossin 1987). Other scientific features of somatic movement that underlie the intuitive side of decision-making and preparing for action include neuromotor patterning and the expressive aspect of different physiological rhythms (Kestenberg-Amighi et al. 1999; Eddy 1990).

Quiet listening within to that which is working and easy (cellular activity, breath, etc.) and/or contemplating our connections to 'other' (be it people, community, nature, earth, cosmos, or beyond) are also deeply nourishing for the physical body. They restore the nervous system to ease and homeostasis. They are central in rebalancing from stress, resolving traumatic incidents or disruptions in life (Eddy 2006). Within the Laban model, this recuperation is going on during activity as well as a balancing response to it, and is an active and alive movement process. Indeed, rest has been a central pedagogical tool in many somatic movement disciplines, including Sweigard's Ideokinesis, Conrad's Continuum, Alexander Technique, the Feldenkrais Method and Bainbridge Cohen's Body-Mind Centering® among others (Eddy 2012). Furthermore, research demonstrates that embodied rest is an essential element in rebalancing and reorganizing the body (Batson and Schwartz 2007). It is central to Moving For Life for Health® that supports the recovery from cancer (Albert and Rosen 2013).

Giving into Gravity and Grounding

Grounding is a physical act of being more securely attached to the earth. Placing an emphasis on the numinous level brings us to acceptance of being incarnate, as spiritual beings living on earth. These experiences can awaken deeper caring about 'our mother, the earth' (Halprin 2003). As Ashkin highlights, somatic practitioners, as in African or African-American traditions, view dancing a 'weighted relationship to gravity as "honoring" the earth' (Ashkin 2011: 117). Much of the typical somatic movement lesson focuses on grounding—releasing into gravity, finding ease, making friends with the floor. From the floor, released as much as possible from the constraints of gravity, movers are able to more keenly attune to felt sensations and contact their life force. By using supine experiences to emphasize sensing the felt life force as incarnate, bodied and grounded, the somatic leader can contact the transcendent, larger-than-oneself and bring focus to the importance of our planet's health in supporting these processes.

Somatic Meditation

Somaticization and meditation are the content of somatic inquiry. The choice to take moments of silence to focus learning is a practice that has trickled down from Eastern and Native American influences and from existentialist educational practices (Block 2001). The use of the Four Dignities (Whitacre 1986), lying, sitting, standing and walking (Arrien 1993), is a natural link to meditation to somatic approaches used in the classroom for adults and children alike (Chiate et al. 2013; Eddy 2011). For example, in the Inner Resilience programme post 9/11, teachers or students are instructed to find rest and meditate comfortably in any of these positions before going for a walk outside and repeating the meditation by 'listening to nature.' At Moving On Center, the first Participatory Arts assignment is to spend time in nature in stillness and then in movement and to listen-feel-see what emerges as meaningful (Eddy 2005; Eddy with Swann 2011). This process is intensified by the teaching and practice of Authentic Movement, where individual authority and listening is strengthened in a supportive communal environment (Starks Whitehouse 1987; Adler 2002; Stromsted 2012). Somatic pedagogies such as this may facilitate connections within the community towards a new level of understanding, connection and problem-solving, and can facilitate the shift from contemplation to getting moving and taking action—again enacting and reflecting the inner ethical or moral authority emphasized in contemporary spiritualities (Heelas 1999, Rouhiainen 2008).

Somatic education highlights the experience that we have bodies—indeed, living bodies with natural intelligence (somas)—and it is this global human experience that links us all. Slowing down to feel our bodies is a form of meditation. In certain types of meditation, the mind is directed to make spiritual connections; the body is more prepared to stay with this process when the person has the somatic skill of physical mindfulness. The abilities to observe, to let go of tension and to breathe deeply serve these purposes. Indeed, paying attention to the breath is a classic meditation. The baseline for both somatic awareness and contemplation is listening. As Muktananda pointed out in his teachings, the key spiritual question is, 'What are you choosing to listen to?' (1981). You can direct your mind anywhere. In a somatic sense, you can attend to pain, or you can choose to attend to finding sensation that is calm and peaceful. The uncontrolled, easy observation of breath is one inroad (Benson and Proctor 2010). You can also listen to any other part of the body and be open to its potential for self-regulation towards healing. This force can be considered as a spiritual force or as a physiological given. Either is useful.

Imagery

The strong use of imagery within embodiment (sometimes referred to as 'somaticization') is another area of inquiry in the intersection of Somatics and spirituality. Indeed, it may be the focus on one's imagery and intent that shifts somatic movement or dance from the vernacular to the spiritual. In particular, the conscious or unconscious choice of one's imagery can open one to the sacred, something larger than ordinary life, or a connection to universality (a higher entity). To what extent is the religious experience or spiritual experience a result of images held, beliefs kindled? Kinesthetic imagery begs more specific questions. Imagery that is of embodiment brings us back to the body. As recent research shows, people thinking about exercise do not get the same benefit as the people actively feeling (embodying) the movement within their imaging process in their brains (Froud 2012). Fully embodying movement, sensing through kinesthesia, is a type of mind-map (and therefore mind-state) that includes the whole body and mind. In this way, it may in fact deepen the spiritual experience by making it more multidimensional. Furthermore, opening to the unknown helps access the spiritual; somatic inquiry is largely a guided exploration into the unknown aspects of the present moment (Eddy 2006). As posited before, neuroscience research may indeed conclude that spiritual experiences are correlated with entering into certain parts of our brains, including the right cortical hemisphere (Taylor 2006). Somatic Movement Dance Education provides one entry to these domains.

Neuromotor Maturation and Development

Somatic awareness allows us to revisit and re-pattern early developmental experiences (Eddy 2013). Our developmental roots link us to other animals and living beings. As Somatics pedagogy strives to connect us to our natural, incarnate selves as well as to the numinous beyond, many somatic modalities, such as that of Alexander, Bartenieff, Body-Mind Centering®, Continuum and Feldenkrais, use the neuro-developmental foundation in order to lead into explorations of connection to self and others (Eddy 2006, 2012). A neuro-developmental perspective can also inform actions about specific concerns, and as mentioned earlier, can have political, moral, or ethical ramifications in the way one lives in one's own lifetime of development (Myers 2003). Areas that may be affected by this perspective include the politics of conception, pregnancy health, childbirth practices, childrearing, educational trends, ageism, death/dying and euthanasia (Eddy 2012). Somatic engagement informs our own maturation or aging process. Somatic movement pedagogy could be applied to help develop stronger communities through embodied approaches to education, from sex education (Brook 2005) to hospice (Buss et al. 2010). The field of Somatic Movement Education and Therapy provides non-judgemental supportive frameworks that aid in childbirth, parenting, early childhood, adult identity and aging. When using the kinesthetic sense within a developmental model, movers gain appreciation of self as babies, within families, and as a species sharing the planet with other life forms (Eddy in press, 2014). The somatic culture commands respect for all ages. The somatic movement process is a starting place of appreciation of self and can also be a profound tool in the appreciation of 'other'; in all of these areas, spiritual somatic engagement, through attentive listening and self-authority, can help guide us through all aspects of life—sacred and secular.

Conclusion

Somatic Movement Dance Education shares tenets with contemporary spiritualities, both reflecting Western political shifts towards authority of the self and individualized practice and experience of the sacred. SMDE shares areas of common ground with feminist spiritualities and with New Age spiritualities (particularly the tenets of self-authority, the embodied spiritualization of the inner realm, secular and syncretistic spirituality, and holism). Somatic movement pedagogy, while born from pioneers' experiences of disruption and resulting in embodied holistic resolution of that disruption (Eddy 2009), has not yet been explicit in addressing the spiritual dimensions of somatic movement practices. This is particularly because 'spirituality' is such a complex and value-laden term. However, when viewed through a broad and inclusive definition of spirituality (such as Kraus 2009: 52), it is evident that somatic practices may encompass or contribute to individuals' experiences of their own spirituality: SMDE opens individualized avenues to the sacred in an ongoing journey of embodied investigation. Basic somatic principles can contribute to an experience of the numinous. These include attentive connectivity (to self, other, and beyond) and deep-body listening; active searching of the unknown; rest and recuperation through meditation and imagery; and the psycho-social attunement that evolves from consciously moving with sensation of being alive on planet earth and awareness of our multifaceted evolution through ongoing neuro-cellular development. Because it centres around individually sensing, honouring and deeply connecting to the lived body and its deep, authentic connections to community and beyond, there are inherently spiritual dimensions to Somatic Movement Dance Education pedagogy.

References

Adler, J. (2002), *Offering from the Conscious Body*, Rochester, VT: Inner Traditions.

Albert, J., Eddy, M. and Rosen, A. (2013), Moving for Life: Dance to Recovery, New York, NY: Dance to Recovery DVD, www.movingforlife.org.

Aposhyan, P. (2004), *Body-Mind Psychotherapy Principles, Techniques, and Practical Applications*, New York, NY: WW Norton & Company.

Arrien, A. (1993), *The Four-Fold Way: Walking the Paths of the Warrior, Teacher, Healer and Visionary*, New York, NY: HarperCollins.

Ashkin, S. (2011), 'Full body, free body: Somatic cultural praxis in United States dance forms', BA thesis, Middletown CT: Wesleyan University.

Bainbridge Cohen, B. (1993), *Sensing, Feeling and Action*, Northampton, MA: Contact Editions.

Bainbridge Cohen, B. and Cohen, L. (2001), Interview with Martha Eddy, Amherst, MA, 22 October.

Batson, G. and Schwartz, R. (2007), 'Revisiting the value of somatic education in dance training through an inquiry into practice schedules', *Journal of Dance Education*, 7:2, pp. 47–56.

Bauer, S. (2008), 'Body and earth as one: Strengthening our connection to the natural source with ecosomatics', *Conscious Dancer*, Spring, pp. 8–9.

Bartenieff, I. (1979), Class notes of Martha Eddy. Laban Certification Program. 10, Oct. 1979.

Bartenieff, I. and Lewis, D. (1980), *Body Movement: Coping with the Environment, Amsterdam*, Amsterdam: Gordon and Breach.

Benson, H. and Proctor, W. (2010), *Relaxation Revolution: Enhancing Your Health through the Science and Genetics of Mind-Body Healing*, London, UK: Scribner Books.

Block, A. (2001), *I'm Only Bleeding: Education as the Practice of Social Violence Against Children*, New York, NY: Oxford.

Bradley, K. (2009), *Rudolf Laban*, New York, NY: Routledge.

Brook, A. (2005), *Sexuality and the Sacred*, Boulder, CO: Annie Brook. Online book.

Brodie, J. and Lobel, E. (2004), 'Integrating Fundamental Principles Underlying Somatic Practices into Dance Technique Class', *Journal of Dance Education*, 4:3, pp. 80–7.

Brodie, J. and Lobel, E. (2006), 'Somatics in Dance—Dance in Somatics', *Journal of Dance Education*, 6:3, pp. 69–71.

Bruce, S. (1996), *Religion in the Modern World: From Cathedrals to Cults*, New York, NY: Oxford University Press.

Bruce, S. (2002), *God is Dead: Secularization in the West*, Oxford: Blackwell.

Buckroyd J. (2000), *The Student Dancer: Emotional Aspects of the Teaching and Learning of Dance*, London, UK: Dance Books.

Burns, C. (2012), 'Embodiment and embedment: integrating dance/movement therapy, body psychotherapy, and ecopsychology', *Body, Movement and Dance in Psychotherapy: An International Journal for Theory, Research and Practice*, 7: 1, http://www.tandfonline.com/doi/pdf/10.1080/17432979.2011.618513. Accessed 12 July 2012.

Buss, T., Walden-Galszko, K., Modlinska, A., Osowicka, M., Lichodsierjewska-Niemierko, M., Janiszewska, J. (2010), 'Kinesitherapy alleviates fatigue in terminal hospice cancer patients- an experimental, controlled study', *SupportCare Cancer*, 18:6, pp. 743–749.

Chiate, B., Eddy, M. and Suggs, J. (2013), *Eyes Openers DVD*, New York, NY: Suggs Media. www.EyesOpenMinds.com.

Christ, C. and Plaskow, J. (1992), *Womenspirit Rising: A Feminist Reader in Religion*, New York, NY: HarperCollins.

Christ, C. (1997), *Rebirth of the Goddess: Finding Meaning in Feminist Spirituality*, New York, Routledge.

Conrad, E. (2002), Interview with Martha Eddy. New York, NY, 25 October.

Daly, M. (1973), *Beyond God the Father: Towards a Philosophy of Women's Liberation*, Boston, MA: Beakon Press.

Davis, M. (1973), *Towards Understanding the Intrinsic in Body Movement*, New York, NY: Arno.

Debenham, P. and Debenham, K. (2008), 'Experiencing the sacred in dance education', *Wonder, Compassion, Wisdom and Wholeness in the Classroom*, 8:2, pp. 44–55.

Dellagrotte. J. (2001–12), 'The Feldenkrais Method with Yoga and Tai Chi', http://www.feldenkrais.com/method/article/the_feldenkrais_method_with_yoga_and_tai_chi/. Accessed 8 August 2012.

Eddy, M. (1990), 'Body mind dancing', in S. Loman and R. Brandt (eds), *Body Mind Connections in Human Movement Communication*, Keene, NH: Antioch NE Graduate School.

Eddy, M. (1998), 'The role of physical activity in educational violence prevention programmes for youth', Doctoral dissertation, Ann Arbor, MI: UMI Press.

Eddy, M. (2002a), 'Somatic practices and dance: Global influences', *Dance Research Journal*, 34:2, pp. 46–62.

Eddy, M. (2002b), 'Body cues and conflict: LMA-derived approaches to educational violence prevention', http://www.wellnesscke.net/downloadables/Body-Cues-Conflict.pdf. Accessed 8 August 2012.

Eddy, M. (2005 [1996]), 'Spirituality at school', *Somatics Magazine—Journal of the Bodily Arts and Sciences*, pp. 22-24, http://www.wellnesscke.net/downloadables/Spirituality-at-School. pdf. Accessed 25 August 2013.

Eddy, M. (2006), *Introduction to Somatic Movement: History and Principles*, Course Materials Dynamic Embodiment, New York, NY: Moving On Center.

Eddy, M. (2007), 'A balanced brain equals a balanced person: Somatic education', *SPINS Newzine*, 3:1.

Eddy, M. (2009), 'A brief history of somatic practices and dance: Historical development of the field of somatic education and its relationship to dance', *Journal of Dance & Somatic Practices*, 1:1, pp. 5–27.

Eddy, M. (2011–12), 'Contemporary movement choirs—Dance in public spaces connecting people, place, and sometimes "issues"', *Current: A Journal of the Body-Mind Centering® Association*, Winter, pp. 20–25.

Eddy, M. (2011), 'The role of the arts in community building: A post 9/11 review', in G. W. Miller, P. Etheridge and K. Tarlow Morgan (eds), *Exploring Body-Mind Centering: An Anthology of Experience and Method*, Berkeley, CA: North Atlantic Press.

Eddy, M. (2013), 'Past Beginnings Revisited', *Journal of Laban Movement Studies*, 3:1, pp. 54–79.

Eddy, M. (in press, 2014), *Somatic Movement Awareness & Dance*, Urbana, IL: Human Kinetics.

Eddy, M. with Swann, C. (2011), 'Tapping inner wisdom: What is somatics and how does it relate to conscious dancing', *Conscious Dancer Magazine*, May, 13, http://issuu.com/consciousdancer/docs/issue15. Accessed July 15, 2012.

Eddy, M. R. (1982), 'Life giving methods of bible study: The training of laity for leadership in ecumenical inner city community', Doctoral dissertation, New York, NY: New York Theological Seminary.

Enghauser, R. (2007), 'The quest for an ecosomatic approach to dance pedagogy', *Journal of Dance Education*, 7:3, pp. 80–90.

Eller, C. (1993), *Living in the Lap of the Goddess: The Feminist Spirituality Movement in America*, New York, NY: Crossroad Publishing.

Flory, R. and Miller, D. (2007), 'The embodied spirituality of the post-boomer generations', in K. Flanagan and C. Jupp (eds), *A Sociology of Spirituality*, Aldershot, UK: Ashgate Publishing.

Fortin, S. and Ginard, F. (2005), 'Dancer's Application of the Alexander Technique', *Journal of Dance Education*, 5:4, pp. 125–31.

Fraleigh, S. (2003), Interview with Martha Eddy, Personal telecommunication, 3 July.

Froud, K. (2012), 'Neuroscience of language and learning', Personal communication, New York, NY: Columbia University, 5 June.

Franklin, E. (2012), *Dynamic Alignment through Imagery*, 2nd ed., Champaign, IL: Human Kinetics.

Georghiou, D. (2012), 'Continuum movement meditation', http://www.continuummovement.com/, July 15, 2012.

Gorski, P. (2003), 'Historicizing the secularization debate', in M. Dillon (ed.), *Handbook of the Sociology of Religion*, Cambridge, UK: Cambridge University Press.

Green, J. (1999), 'Somatic authority and the myth of the ideal body in dance education', *Dance Research Journal*, 31:2, pp. 91–92.

Halprin, A. (2003), Interview with Martha Eddy, Kentfield, CA, 3 November.

Hartley, L. (1995), *Wisdom of the Body Moving*, Berkeley, CA: North Atlantic Books.

Heelas, P. (1999), *The New Age Movement*, London, UK: Blackwell.

Heelas, P. and Woodhead, L. (2005), *The Spiritual Revolution: Why Religion is Giving Way to Spirituality*, Oxford, UK: Blackwell.

Heelas, P. (ed.) (1996), *Detraditionalization*, Oxford: Blackwell.

Heelas, P, and Martin, D. (1998), *Religion, Modernity and Postmodernity*, United Kingdom: Blackwell.

Johnson, D. (1987), 'Body work and being: The deeper significance of somatics', *New Realities*, September/October, pp. 20–23.

Johnson, D. (1992), *Body: Recovering Our Sensual Wisdom*, Berkeley, CA: North Atlantic Books.

Johnson, D. (1995), *Bone, Breath, and Gesture*, Berkeley, CA: North Atlantic Books.

Johnson, D. (1997), *Groundworks: Narratives of Embodiment*, Berkeley, CA: North Atlantic Books.

Johnson, D. (2006), *Everyday Hopes, Utopian Dreams: Reflections on American Culture*, Berkeley, CA: North Atlantic Books.

Johnson, R. (2002), *Elemental Movement: A Somatic Approach to Movement Education*, www. USA: Dissertation/library/1121326a.htm.com.

Juhan, D. (2002), *The Physical, Psychological, & Spiritual Powers of Bodywork: Touched by the Goddess*, New York, NY: Barrytown/Station Hill Press.

Kestenberg-Amighi, J., Loman, S., Lewis, P. and Sossin, K. M. (eds) (1999), *The Meaning of Movement: Developmental and Clinical Perspectives of the Kestenberg Movement Profile*, New York, NY: Brunner-Routledge.

Knaster, M. (1996), *Discovering the Body's Wisdom*, New York, NY: Bantam Books.

King, U. (2009), *The Search for Spirituality: Our Global Quest for Meaning and Fulfilment*, London, UK: Canterbury Press.

Kraus, R. (2009), *The Many Faces of Spirituality: A Conceptual Framework Considering Belly Dance*, London, UK: Equinox Publishing Ltd.

Kraus, R. (2012), 'Spiritual origins and belly dance', *Journal of Dance & Somatic Practices*, 4:1, pp. 97–107.

LaMothe, K. L. (2012), '"Can they Dance": Towards a philosophy of bodily becoming', *Journal of Dance & Somatic Practices*, 4:1, pp. 97–107.

Laban, R. (1960), *The Mastery of Movement*, 2nd ed., London, UK: MacDonald and Evans.

Laban, R. (1966), *The Language of Movement: A Guidebook to Choreutics*, Boston, MA: Plays, Inc.

Levine, P. (2010), *Toward an Unspoken Voice. How the Body Releases Trauma and Restores Goodness*, Berkeley, CA: North Atlantic Books.

Lynch, G. (2007), *The New Spirituality: An Introduction to Progressive Belief in the Twenty-First Century*, New York, NY: I.B. Tauris.

Masters, R. (2010), *Spiritual Bypassing: When Spirituality Disconnects Us from What Really Matters*, Berkeley, CA: North Atlantic Books.

McGuire, M. (2003), 'Why bodies matter: A sociological reflection on spirituality and materiality', *Spiritus*, 3, pp. 1–18.

McGuire, M. (2008), *Lived Religion: Faith and Practice in Everyday Life*, Oxford, UK: Oxford University Press.

McMillan, J. (2012), 'Spatial dynamics', http://www.youtube.com/watch?v=xFEsjGZ5TGg. Accessed July 23.

Muktananda, S. (1981), 'The play of consciousness', talk given at Siddha Yoga Ashram, Catskills, NY, 30 October.

Myers, M. (2003), Interview with Martha Eddy, New London, CT, 30 July.

Myers, T. (2010), 'Morality is a somatic experience', in M. Keogh (ed.), *Hope Beneath Our Feet: Restoring Our Place in the Natural World*, Berkeley, CA: North Atlantic Books.

Orbach, S. (2009), *Bodies*, New York, NY: Picador Press.

Paloutzian, F. and Park, C. (2005), *Handbook of the Psychology of Religion and Spirituality*, New York, NY: Gilford Press.

Peck, S. (1993), *Further Along The Road Less Travelled: The Unending Journey towards Spiritual Growth*, London: Simon & Schuster.

Plaskow, J. and Christ, C. (1989), *Weaving the Vision: New Patterns in Feminist Spirituality*, New York, NY: Harper & Row Publishers.

Reese, M. (2012), 'A biography of Moshe Feldenkrais', http://www.feldenkrais.com/method/a_biography_of_moshe_feldenkrais/. Accessed 10 August 2012.

Reisel, M. (2002), *Laban's Legacy*, Lee, MA: Kinesphere Studio. DVD.

Roof, W. (2003), 'Religion and Spirituality: Toward an Integrated Analysis', in M. Dillon (ed.), *Handbook of the Sociology of Religion*, Cambridge, UK: Cambridge Press.

Roseman, J. L. (2012), 'Unlikely companions: Grief, dance and mysticism', *Journal of Dance & Somatic Practices*, 4:1, pp. 97–107.

Rouhiainen, L. (2008), 'Somatic dance as a means of cultivating ethically embodied subjects', *Research in Dance Education*, 9:3, pp. 241–56.

Sellers-Young, B. (2009), 'Contemplation, consciousness and pedagogy', in *Dance, Consciousness and Performance Across the Threshold Conference*, Durham, NC: Duke University.

Sargent-Wishart, K. (2012), 'Embodying the dynamics of the five elements', *Journal of Dance & Somatic Practices*, 4:1, pp. 97–107.

Shafir, T. (2011), 'My work is my play—the journey from survival to creativity', http://www.en234.com/Self_Improvement/Creativity/13803.html. Accessed 28 December 2011.

Sheldrake, P. (2007), *A Brief History of Spirituality*, Oxford, UK: Blackwell.

Sjöö, M. and Mor, B. (1991), *The Great Cosmic Mother: Rediscovering the Religion of the Earth*, New York, NY: HarperCollins.

Sossin, K. M. (1987), 'Reliability of the Kestenberg Movement profile in movement studies', *Journal of the Laban Bartenieff Institute for Movement Studies*, 2, pp. 22–28.

Stanczak, G. (2006), *Engaged Spirituality: Social Change and American Religion*, Piscataway, NJ: Rutgers University Press.

Starks Whitehouse, M. (1987), 'Physical movement and personality', *Contact Quarterly*, Winter.

Stromstead, T. (2012), Personal communication, San Francisco, CA, 12 January.

Summers, E. (2003), Interview with Martha Eddy, New York, NY, 8 November.

Tacey, D. (2001), *Jung and the New Age*, East Sussex, UK: Brunner-Routledge.

Tacey, D. (2004), *The Spirituality Revolution: The Emergence of Contemporary Spirituality*, East Sussex, UK: Routledge.

Taylor, J. (2006), *My Stroke of Insight*, New York, NY: Viking Press.

Thelan, E. (1995), 'Motor development', *American Psychologist*, 30:2, pp. 79–95.

Vancouver Art Museum (2012), 'Emily Carr and the Theatre of Transcendence', http://www.vanartgallery.bc.ca/the_exhibitions/exhibit_carr_theatre_transcendence.html.Accessed 8 August 2012.

Walsch, N. D. (2011), *The Storm Before the Calm*, Asland, OR: Emnin Books.

Weber, R. (2010), 'Integrating semi-structured somatic practices and contemporary dance technique training', *Journal of Dance & Somatic Practices*, 1:2, pp. 237–254.

Whitacre, J. (1986), 'The Four Dignities', *Currents*, Northampton, MA: BMCA.

Williamson, A. (2009), 'Formative support and connection: Somatic movement dance education in community and client practice', *Journal of Dance & Somatic Practices*, 1:1, pp. 29–45.

Williamson, A. (2010), 'Reflections and theoretical approaches to the study of spiritualities within the field of somatic movement dance education', *Journal of Dance & Somatic Practices*, 2:1, pp. 35–61.

Williamson, A. and Hayes, J. (2012), 'Dance, movement and spiritualities', *Journal of Dance & Somatic Practices*, 4.1, pp. 3–10.

Wink, W. (2002), *The Human Being: Jesus and the Enigma of the Son of the Man*, Minneapolis, MN: Augsburg Fortress.

Wright, S. (2005), *Reflections on Spirituality and Health*, London, UK: Whurr Publishers.

Notes

1   In this chapter, we use interrelated terms. The following definitions may serve to illuminate our choice of terms in specific places:

   Somatic movement is the process of exploring movement using the conscious awareness that emerges from paying attention to body sensations and feeling (Eddy in press, 2014).

   Somatic Movement Disciplines, Systems and Modalities are the particular pedagogies developed by the pioneers and their protégés, also referred to as Body Therapies (Myers 2003).

   The field of Somatic Movement Education & Therapy encompasses all somatic movement disciplines and their practices. It has a scope of practice and ethical standards as provided by www.ISMETA.com (Eddy 2009).

   When SME&T is applied to dance it is called Somatic Movement Dance Education (SMDE).

2   Discussing the full ramification or effect of various socio-cultural influences and their production in a multitude of religious contexts on the field of SMDE is outside the limitations of this chapter; however, we bring this point up precisely because of the importance of considering the socio-cultural contexts and recommend it as a fruitful and important avenue for further investigation in the spiritual aspects of somatic movement/dance practices. For some of the socio-cultural traditions that have influenced the development of the Somatics

field outside of its Western (Euro-American) roots, please see Eddy 2002, Williamson 2010.

3   The field of Somatics and SMDE are not informed by monotheistic patriarchal conceptions of the divine; however, it is an error to assume that all participants dismiss monotheistic conceptions of the divine as important expressive dimensions of experience.

4   In working with children, a basic process is 'palming' when combined with somatic imagery as explored in EyeOpeners of Dynamic Embodiment™ (Chiate et al. 2013).

Chapter 8

Postmodern Spirituality? A Personal Narrative

Jill Green

When I was asked to write a chapter of a book about dance, spirituality and Somatics, I felt a sense of anxiety deep in my gut. I have been immersed in postpositivist research and thinking for over 25 years, yet I have struggled to reconcile my affinities for postmodernism and spirituality in dance. I published many articles and chapters about a postmodern and critical theory approach to Somatics and dance (Green 1993, 1996a, 1996b, 1996c, 1999, 2000, 2001a, 2001b, 2002–03, 2004a, 2004b, 2007, 2008) while my scholarly interests shifted and changed. I moved to a more postmodern view, one that was reflected in my research methodology and belief that experience is socially, culturally and politically constructed.

Nevertheless, the area of spirituality is one that I have avoided—not because I do not feel spiritual, but rather that there were so many tensions between spiritual and postmodern ontologies and epistemologies. However unsettling this may be, I find the writing of this chapter to be an opportunity to struggle with the issues, delve into research in the area and investigate the connections between dance, Somatics, spirituality and postmodernism. First, I tell my personal story of how I came upon this dilemma. Next, I make an effort to define and describe terms such as 'spirituality' and 'postmodernism.' Lastly, I delve into the relationships and tensions between these paradigmatic standings in the world and place myself within these often-conflicting bodies of literature.

The key methodology of this chapter is a development of theory through a personal narrative or autoethnography. Narrative and autoethnography are key methodological tools used in postpositivist research. Although I am not using this self-reflexive tool to study myself in the field, through this approach, I may be able to understand how my own narrative may explore questions about the social construction of knowledge. Thus, I will be my own subject/participant in an investigation into the construction of beliefs about spirituality, Somatics, dance and life.

The Struggle: A Personal Narrative

When I was a little girl, I distinctly remember a number of times when I felt a deep connection to the world as I experienced a sense of heightened existence. I cannot easily articulate this experience because it filled my soma in a way that cannot be reproduced with words. It was a Zen-like sense of oneness and attunement. I found this same kind of experience when I

Figure 1: Jill Green doing Kinetic Awareness. Photo by Talani Torres.

began dancing and found a love of the art form. Dancing, for me, was always about a sense of engagement and connection to something that seemed real and alive.

Interestingly, my father was agnostic and my mother gave up her religious identity when she married my father. I did not know where this feeling came from. I was brought up in a secular Jewish environment.

When I was in my twenties and married to my ex-husband (his parents were Unitarian), we decided to try to search for our Jewish roots and attempted to find a synagogue that would meet our needs. When I was introduced to religion, I had an immediate resistance to the religious texts because, as I interpreted them, they required that women give up their lives to their husbands and because they seemed to instill a sense of fear in God that did not make sense to me. I had a difficult time understanding the stories as 'real' and found myself disconnected from all organized religion. I saw religion as a patriarchal institution with the intent to keep its citizens in line and subservient to the particular religious system.

During the ensuing years, after an injury and while at New York University where I was doing my master's degree, I began to find Somatics when I studied with Elaine Summers in Kinetic Awareness®.[1] Once again, I felt a deep sense of joy and connection doing the work. I entered the doctoral programme at Ohio State University with the intention to study Somatics as a humanistic and self-affirming area of study. I felt that Somatics could offer students a sense of wholeness and harmony, as I felt while working with dance and Kinetic Awareness®.

However, I found my sense of the world shaken and the rug (everything I thought I knew) taken out from under me when I began to study with Patti Lather, a postmodern educational theorist, and found out about another world of thought, postmodernism.[2] I say the rug was taken out from under me, because I began to question what I knew and how I knew it. Postmodernism questions foundationalism, individualism, essence, experience, truth and even the idea of holism. It points to a plurality of truths and acknowledges difference and fragmentation. It investigates partial truths and reveals 'grand narratives' written by a dominant political authority.

In other words, I began to understand that my knowledge and experience are socially, culturally and politically constructed. I found that I valued a necessary change in thinking in such a multidimensional and growing diverse milieu. I came to believe that we cannot assume everyone experiences the world in the same way. In addition, I found postmodernism as a creative venture—there was not always a black and white answer to the world or to presenting or performing ideas. I was attuned to a world of complexity and juxtapositions of viewpoints and epistemologies.

When I was hired to teach in the Department of Dance at the University of North Carolina at Greensboro, I taught dance education and Somatics. From the start of my career after my doctoral work, I used a postpositivist lens to see the world. Yet, while adhering to this approach, I found this sense of connection once again, when I found myself in North Carolina, remarried, and living on a fifteen-acre plot of land in the country. As a New York City native, I never quite experienced the trees, flora and fauna in such a connected and deeply felt way. I believed in a postmodern viewpoint but felt connected to the earth and life in a profound way.

This postmodern turn left me in a difficult position. I was moved by postmodern thought and felt it was a way to celebrate difference and acknowledge those who may be disfranchised. Yet I did not want to give up on the idea of experience, because it served me well in life and connected me to the world. It is the experiential and relational aspects of life that I did not seem willing to diminish. In addition, my work in Somatics kept me grounded in this experiential aspect of being. I began to reframe Somatics and see it through a postpositivist lens, cognizant of postmodern issues, yet open to experience (see Green 1993, 1996a, 1996b, 1996c, 1999, 2000, 2002–03, 2004a, 2004b, 2007, 2008).

Within this world of conflicting positionalities, I asked, 'How could I negotiate the value of a Somatics epistemology based in the world of experience and holism when I was recognizing the fragmentation of knowledge and the ways ideas of "truth" bumped up against each other?' I began doing this by questioning assumptions that tend to guide the field of Somatics, such as 'universal experience,' 'holism' and the necessary goodness of somatic practice.

So it is from this position that I delve into research in the area of spirituality, Somatics and postmodernism, hoping to find ways that make sense of these assumed oppositional viewpoints and find places where these views may overlap.

So What Is Spirituality?

According to the New Shorter Oxford English Dictionary, the word 'spiritual' is defined in the following ways:

1. Of, pertaining to, or affecting the spirit or soul, esp. from a religious aspect [...]
2. Of, pertaining to, or concerned with sacred or religious things, holy, divine, prayerful; of or pertaining to the church or the clergy, ecclesiastical [...]
3. Pertaining to or have consisting of spirit, immaterial [...]
4. Of or pertaining to the intellect; intellectual [...] (Brown 1972: 2990)

These definitions do not connect to Somatics, particularly numbers three and four. They do not pertain because they are not related to experiencing the soma, the living body. In addition, the religious or fundamentalist aspect of numbers one and two do not adhere to postmodern thought. Moreover, none of these definitions describe my past experiences. Does this mean that what I experienced was not spiritual? Amanda Williamson suggests that the definition may be more complicated:

> Spirituality is a scholarly subject that causes lively debate and sometimes a lot of aggravation. For some people, spirituality is profoundly meaningful—for others, it is deeply ambiguous and of far less interest. It is a highly contentious and controversial subject, open to criticism if pursued in public sector education.
>
> (2010: 36)

Williamson addresses Ursula King's diverse scholarly sense of spirituality that is 'invoked with great praise, even a sense of longing, so that it appears as a highly desirable ideal. On other occasions its very mention can meet with criticism, resistance, even rejection' (King, as cited in Williamson 2010: 36). King also suggests that the word is spoken of in so many different aspects of life that it may seem ambivalent. Yet, Williamson suggests,

> For other people, the word has potency, substance, depth, and vitality. Such a range of feeling reflects an era marked by choice, freedom and plurality. Steven Wright reminds us that in relation to this subject, '[t]here is a wide continuum of views, from those whose source is strictly God-centered to those for who[m] there is only this human reality and nothing else; from those who experience, know or believe in something ineffable, numinous and 'supernatural' to those who find consideration of anything other than the rational, biophysical experience abhorrent or irrelevant.'
>
> (Wright, as cited in Williamson 2010: 36–37)

Other writers have addressed the open quality of the term as well. Sutherland et al. (2003) suggest that spirituality means different things to people from different generations. While the parents of baby boomers in the West tend to conceptualize spirituality in a more religious context (religiosity), baby boomers (of which I am one) tend to relate spirituality to positive health perceptions. The authors cite psychological, medical and sociological literatures that point to a sense of personal awareness, and include meanings such as 'transcendence,' 'unity and meaning' and 'wholeness' and take people beyond self-interested concerns into the social world. They point to a move away from religiosity to one of life satisfaction and purpose as well as improved health (2003: 317). In addition, they claim that this move leads to a more non-objectified viewpoint. Further, since many baby boomers became known as countercultural figures, there was a move to challenge modern institutions and bring their ideas into an ideal that included political, social and spiritual synthesis. In this sense, there was a shift to a more 'experiential spirituality' (2003: 325).[3]

Some feminists have also brought the idea of the spiritual together with cultural/social/political agendas. For example, Eugenie Gatens-Robinson (1994) takes the idea of spirituality to mean a connection to the earth through the growing idea of an ecofeminism. According to Gatens-Robinson,

> From an ecofeminist perspective, the idea that we solve environmental problems without first profoundly changing our experiential relationship to nature is incoherent. Those who think seriously about these issues have come to realize that simply doing the things that environmental scientists tell us are necessary, even if that action is taken to serve out enlightened species' interest, is not a powerful enough response. The problem is not at base one of mismanagement, but a problem of impoverished experience.
>
> (1994: 208–09)

Gatens-Robinson cites Susan Griffin:

> If religion told us that the earth was a corrupt place, that our true home was heaven, that sensual feeling was not to be trusted and could lead us to hell and damnation, science did not in essence contradict that doctrine. For science told us too not to trust our senses, that matter is deceptive and that we are alien to our surroundings. […] In both systems, not only are we alienated from the world that is described as deceiving us; we are also alienated from our own capacity to see and hear and taste and touch, to know and describe our own experience.
>
> (cited in Gatens-Robinson, 1994: 208)

This movement towards a somatic/experience position opens the definition of spiritual to include a relationship to the earth, and additionally moves the intention to a socio-political focus.[4]

So here there is a move to a less dualistic, less authoritarian vision of spirituality based on connection and experience. This idea has connections to my prior experience and affinities. However, some of these authors represent views that are not yet postmodern because they may embrace individualism, foundationalism and experience—and may do so in a relational way. Yet this more fluid set of descriptions may move this thinking towards a more postmodern conceptualization of the term.

Postmodernism: Social, Cultural and Political Conceptualizations

How does one imagine the idea of a changed sense of spirituality within a postmodern world steeped in diversity and difference? A number of scholars have approached this query. Some writers attempt to open the idea culturally. For example, Kelly Besecke sees spirituality as a cultural language that 'incorporates simultaneous commitments to modern rationality and to the value of transcendent meaning. Reflective spirituality is thus a cultural resource that modern Americans are using to create guiding transcendent meanings for a rationalized society' (2001: 356). Besecke sees Wade Clark Roof's idea of a reflexive spirituality as 'a way individuals relate to religious symbols and practices in their efforts to gain personal meaning from religion' (Roof, as cited in Besecke 2001: 366). She further takes the idea towards spiritually as a cultural resource, shared in groups for people to talk with each other about meaning (2001: 336). She emphasizes 'spirituality's public, interactional, cultural dimension' and sees it as a method of social critique (2001: 367). In this way, the definition of 'spirituality' moves from individualism to the group and attempts to look at the plurality of the idea.

Alexander Tristan Riley suggests that modernism was an era where religion was dismissed and that postmodernism can bring back spirituality through the renovation of the sacred (2002: 243). Through a discussion about Durkheim and Bergson, he argues that postmodern theory can actually create a turn to the sacred. He does this by tracing two realms of scholarly thought: he suggests that although Durkheim (a sociologist) and Bergson, (a philosopher), have views that have been seen as opposing, that they both contributed to postmodern thinking. For example, Riley asserts,

The gist of both Durkheiman and Bergsonian thought is a profound criticism of the various kind of materialism that were the ascendant in French intellectual culture in the Third Republic, at least partially as a direct result of the very constitution of the Republic, in the concept of a deep anxiety that the existing, traditional forms of the sacred could and would not sufficiently answer to the dilemmas of the modern world, if indeed they even survived intact. The materialisms opposed by both Durkheimianism and Bergonianism included Marxism in some early forms but were more typically derived from other social sources indigenous to France. The ultimate thrust of both positions is toward recognition of the gravity of the secularization crisis and the need for an effort to reconfigure, rather than simply eliminate, the sacred.

(2002: 248)

Thus, Riley believes that there was a rejection of spirituality in modern times and that precursors of postmodernism sought a reconstruction of the sacred as a way to bring spirituality back to the world through postmodern thought. He did this by suggesting that a social analysis of spirituality reveals a socio-political aspect of sacredness and by opening the definition of the term 'sacred.' He includes postmodernist thinkers such as Deleuze and Guattari in a definition that expands the sacred to mean a kind of intensity of experience:

> Not in isolation but socially [...] they emerge in situations in which the individual disappears completely into the social form Deleuze and Guattari named the 'body without organs': Where psychoanalysis says 'Stop, find your self again,' we should say instead, 'Let's go further still, we haven't found our BwO [body without organs] yet, we haven't sufficiently dismantled our self.' More, the body without organs and the process of 'becoming-intense' [...] that it involves are tied in the molar, repressive social and moral order of capitalist relations to experiences that are the precise sort of transgressive, extreme experiences we find in the impure sacred, especially in the work of Georges Baraille, who is a key node of intellectual influence uniting the Durkeimians and the postmodernists.
>
> (Riley 2002: 253)

Thus, Riley is making the argument that there is a direct connection between postmodernism and the sacred. In this sense, he rejects the materialistic side of somatic experience, or holistic experience. His work is postmodern in that it recognizes the body as an energy field in a fluid form rather than as a material object.

Arnold Vento (2000) also makes direct reference to postmodernism through a discussion of the sacred, and speaks of a more nonlinear definition. Vento seeks,

> A redefinition of the sacred beyond the institutional and secularization of the metaphysical and transcendental idea of Divinity. The latter cannot assume the current structure of society worldwide; it must be seen within an evolutionary path that anticipates a cyclical end and beginning. If there is one area that all philosophers and scientists have agreed on, it is that everything changes, nothing remains the same. The age of linear thinking and materialistic progress is coming to an end. Many great thinkers, from Alfred North Whitehead to Octavio Paz have dealt with this idea.
>
> (2000: 184)

Vento points out a number of other postmodern ideas. He says, '"Sacred," in a functional definition, refers to consecrated or holy, usually for the worship of the divine. What is sacred in one culture or religion may be different for another' (2000: 193). He says there are alternative ways of knowing and suggests new directions for a revised sense of spirituality:

> The leading figures in movements such as feminism, cultural studies, critical theory, discourse analysis and deconstruction have begun to reopen negotiations with the religious. Currently, it represents not going back to traditional faith systems, but rather to work out some kind of synthesis between the secular and sacred ways of seeing. Some

theorists have begun to look at religion as 'the other,' while others seek to take account of 'the extraordinary cultural and ideological vitality which religion has given to certain popular social movements.'

(Edward Said 1983 as cited in Vento 2000: 194)

Thus Vento seeks a more postmodern definition in that it is nonlinear and reaches to community and connection, while acknowledging the significance of a focus on difference and who is disenfranchised via spiritual practice.

These postmodern writers present a pluralistic spirituality that connects to community, allows for divergent experiences and meaning and bases the spiritual on a constructed self and reality.

Of course, all of the aforementioned views of spirituality do not always resonate with each other and may bump up against each other. For example, an ecofeminist perspective that embraces experiential knowing may be problematized by postmodernists who do not believe in the experiential knowing and view it as a paradigm that does not take into account the social construction of spirituality. There are no easy conceptualizations that deal with spirituality, Somatics and postmodernism as cohesive components of a holistic construction of thought. Rather, there are tensions between and among these ways of thinking.

So Where Am I?

Thinking back to my experiences and viewpoints about spirituality in relationship to Somatics and postmodernism, I find some crossover areas. These definitions of 'spirituality,' including somatic, Eastern-oriented and postmodern ideas, tend to move away from an authoritative sense and move towards a more pluralistic definition. As Williamson suggests, 'personal spiritual truths and faiths are instrumentally shaped by the wider socio-cultural landscape' and move away from religion as an institution (2010: 40). Thus, definitions of spirituality can be malleable. As Somatics tends to embrace a more personal and subjective relationship to the world, postmodernism also recognizes that the world is not objective.

However, there still exists a tension between somatic/experiential definitions, and postmodern conceptualizations in these bodies of literature. While somatic and experiential descriptions tend to provide a relational experience to the world and value essence, truth and holism, it cannot be denied that postmodernism questions individualism and materialism, while acknowledging fragmentation, difference and partial truths.

But my larger question is, 'Is there a way to be able to negotiate these differences and still embrace parts of opposing worldviews?' Perhaps we can if we are aware of these tensions and differences—and if we do not avoid the divergent epistemologies from which they arise.

Postmodernism not only provides another way of viewing spirituality, but also addresses the state of the world. For example, in a world of difference, one that is getting smaller with constantly moving cultures, postmodernism acknowledges a certain juxtaposition of voices and viewpoints. Perhaps to see a postmodern world is to see that different and opposing worldviews can exist together. In this sense, one may be able to value aspects of one position while finding an affinity with an opposing worldview. In this spirit of postmodernism, I may be able to acknowledge the plurality of postmodernism and the acknowledgement of partial truths while holding on to a connection to experience. However, I believe that I must acknowledge that, for instance, Somatics may not bring all the answers and, like everything, is value driven—that there is no knowledge that is value-neutral (see Johnson 1992). As suggested in former articles (Green 2000, 2001a, 2001b, 2002–03, 2004a, 2004b), Somatics— and now for that matter spirituality—should not be romanticized or seen as a panacea for all the world's ills but as a tool that may help us connect to the world and make key problems and issues visible. Without questioning our motives through a self-reflexive process, we may be repeating the grand narratives and partial truths we attempt to challenge.

In other words, from a postmodern perspective, I see that experience is constructed. I can value experience but realize that my experiences contain partial truths, assumptions, and biases that may not apply to disenfranchised groups or others. I may find that my experiences are spiritual in the sense that they connect me to the world, but within a construction of spirituality that is partial and not the same for everyone. Others may have other constructions of spirituality.

Thus for me, a postmodern spirituality is one that deconstructs reality, truth and knowledge, yet allows me to embrace experience and connection. In this postmodern sense, I can acknowledge different epistemologies yet be aware that there are tensions between these schools of thought. This may seem to be an easy and useful conclusion to this discussion, but the concept is one I can employ to speak honestly about how views often bump up against each other.

I will end this discussion with another story about a question and answer. A couple of years ago, I was moderating a panel during a scholarly dance conference. One panel member presented a paper about ecosomatics and addressed the experiential and relational aspect of her work, without acknowledging culture or difference. When she finished her paper, one audience member asked a question. He said that her work is not valid because relational scholarship has been repudiated. He asked her how she can respond to this fact. The poor woman hemmed and hawed and was totally stunned by the critique of her work.

After the session, I thought about how I would have answered the question. I believe that I would have answered by saying, 'Yes, culture is important, and partial truths can be damaging. But I am not willing to give up experience and reconnection to the world even while questioning that relationship.'

For me, this may be applied to spirituality as well. I embrace postmodern thought yet believe we construct knowledge through experience as well as culture and history. Similarly, a postmodern spirituality may exist to some extent, but I may be unwilling to dismiss the idea and feeling of connection. I can see myself with one foot in Somatics and another in postmodernism, living with a spirituality that embraces experience but also acknowledges its limitations.

References

Besecke, K. (2001), 'Speaking of meaning in modernity: Reflexive spirituality as a cultural resource', *Sociology of Religion*, 62:3, pp. 365–381.

Brown, L. (ed.) (1972), *New Shorter Oxford English Dictionary*, Oxford: Clarendon Press.

Gatens-Robinson, E. (1994), 'Finding our feminist ways in natural philosophy and religious thought', *Hypatia*, 9:4, pp. 207–28.

Green, J. (1993), 'Fostering creativity through movement and body awareness practices: A postpositivist investigation into the relationship between somatics and the creative process', Unpublished Ph.D. thesis, Columbus, OH: Ohio State University.

—— (1996a), 'Choreographing a postmodern turn: The creative process and somatics', *Impulse*, 4:4, pp. 267–75.

—— (1996b), 'Moving through and against multiple paradigms: Postpositivist research in somatics and creativity—Part I', *Journal of Interdisciplinary Research in Physical Education*, 1:1, pp. 43–54.

—— (1996c), 'Moving through and against multiple paradigms: Postpositivist research in somatics and creativity—Part II', *Journal of Interdisciplinary Research in Physical Education*, 1:2, pp. 73–86.

—— (1999), 'Somatic authority and the myth of the ideal body in dance education', *Dance Research Journal*, 31:2, pp. 80–100.

—— (2000), 'Power, service, and reflexivity in a community dance project', *Research in Dance Education*, 1:1, pp. 53–67.

—— (2001a), 'Emancipatory pedagogy?: Women's bodies and the creative process in dance', *Frontiers*, 21:3, pp. 124–40.

—— (2001b), 'Socially constructed bodies in American dance classrooms', *Research in Dance Education*, 2:2, pp. 155–73.

—— (2002–03), 'Foucault and the training of docile bodies in dance education', *Arts and Learning*, 19:1, pp. 99–126.

—— (2004a), 'The body politic: Constructions of health and healing in dance education', in *National Dance Education Conference Proceedings*, National Dance Education Organization, Michigan State University, East Lansing, MI.

—— (2004b), 'The politics and ethics of health in dance education in the United States', in E. Anttila, S. Hamalainen and L. Rouhiainen (eds), *The Same Difference? Ethics and Politics Embodied in Dance*, Helsinki, Finland: Theatre Academy of Finland, pp. 65–76.

—— (2007), 'American body pedagogies: Somatics and the cultural construction of bodies', in *Congress on Research in Dance CORD Conference Proceedings*, Congress on Research in Dance, New York, NY.

—— (2008), 'Les Politiques et Èthiques de la Santé en Èducation de la Danse au Etats-Unis', in S. Fortin (ed.), *Les Politiques et Èthiques de la Santé en Èducation de la Danse au Etats-Unis*, Montreal, Canada: Presses de l'Université du Québec à Montréal, pp. 169–80.

Johnson, D. (1992), *Body: Recovering Our Sensual Wisdom*, Berkeley, CA: North Atlantic Books and Somatic Resources.

Lather, P. (2011), 'Biography', http://people.ehe.ohio-state.edu/plather/. Accessed 10 December 2011.

Riley, A. T. (2002), 'Durkheim contra Bergson? The hidden roots of postmodern theory and the postmodern "return" of the sacred', *Sociological Perspectives*, 45:3, pp. 243–65.

Roof, W. C. (1993), 'Toward the year 2000: Reconstructions of religious space', *Annals of the American Academy of Political and Social Science*, May issue, pp. 155–70.

Sutherland, J. A., Poloma, M. M. and Pendelton, B. F. (2003), 'Religion, spirituality, and alternative health practices: The baby boomer and the cold war cohorts', *Journal of Religion and Health*, 42:4, pp. 315–38.

Vento, A. C. (2000), 'Rediscovering the sacred: From the secular to a postmodern sense of the sacred', *Wicazo Sa Review*, 15:1, pp. 183–205.

Williamson, A. (2010), 'Reflections and theoretical approaches to the study of spiritualities within the field of somatic movement dance education', *Journal of Dance & Somatic Practices*, 2:1, pp. 35–61.

Notes

1   Kinetic Awareness® is 'one approach to somatic education that provides an opportunity to explore movement potential and develop movement possibilities. This system of body-mind re-education, developed by Elaine Summers, focuses on increased movement efficacy and ease through heightened awareness of automatic and conscious movement. It enhances the understanding the body uses to communicate with ourselves' (Green 1992: 61). Because this system uses graduated rubber balls to enhance body awareness and release excess muscular tension, Kinetic Awareness® is often referred to as 'the ball work.' Balls, placed under various parts of the body, provide contact with inner sensations, bringing to awareness inefficient patterns and psychophysical processes.

2   Patti Lather is a well-known postmodern and poststructural scholar in the field of educational research and methodology. According to her website,

> Patti Lather, School of Educational Policy and Leadership, has taught qualitative research, feminist methodology and gender and education at Ohio State University since 1988. She is the author of three books, *Getting Smart: Feminist Research and Pedagogy With/in the Postmodern* (1991 Critics' Choice Award), *Troubling the Angels: Women Living with HIV/AIDS*, co-authored with Chris Smithies (1998 CHOICE Outstanding Academic Title) and *Getting Lost: Feminist Efforts Toward a Double (d) Science* (2008 Critics' Choice Award). Her in-process book, *Engaging (Social) Science: Policy from the Side of the Messy*, is under contract with Peter Lang.
>
> Dr. Lather has lectured widely in international and national contexts and held a number of distinguished visiting lectureships. Her work examines various (post)critical, feminist and poststructural theories, most recently with a focus on the implications for qualitative inquiry of the call for scientifically-based research in education. She has

held visiting positions at the University of British Columbia, Goteborg University, York University, and the Danish Pedagogy Institute as well as a 1995 sabbatical appointment, Humanities Research Institute, University of California-Irvine seminar on feminist research methodology. She was the recipient of a 1989 Fulbright to New Zealand. She is a 2009 inductee of the AERA Fellows.

Dr. Lather received her BA in English from South Dakota State University (1970), her MA in American Studies from Purdue (1972), and her Ph.D. in Curriculum and Instruction from Indiana University (1983). Prior to OSU, she taught in Women's Studies at Mankato State University.

(Lather 2011)

I was so changed by Patti Lather's work that I took three research classes with her during my doctoral work.

3   Many of these ideas are grounded in the writing of Wade Clark Roof. Roof (1993) was one of the first thinkers who used the change in the baby boomer generation to reframe spirituality through a more postmodern lens. His ideal was to move into a more culturally sensitive place with the idea of pluralism as its base. He used the term 'reconstruction' as an approach that is

> in keeping with a newer sociology-of-religion paradigm gradually emerging that is more historically informed and that privileges themes of voluntarism and innovation, the continuing vitality of American religious culture, and simple-side, rather than exclusively demand-side explanations of change. It presupposes the viability of religion as an energizing force despite changing forms rather than secular assumptions of shrinking plausibilities.
>
> (1993: 157)

Thus, these ideas question traditional conceptualizations of spirituality and open the meaning through a less religious, more fluid, and more socially driven idea to work with. They offer a socio-political definition, one that reaches to the outside world and one that aligns with postmodernism. In other words, this more open, moving definition may allow for connections to a social somatic theory and practice.

4   Like Wade Clark Roof, Gatens-Robinson's ideas prompted a newer, more postmodern way of envisioning spirituality. Gatens-Robinson's ideas provided an impetus for the more recent developing area of ecofeminism as an experiential process.

Chapter 9

Working Like a Farmer: Towards an Embodied Spirituality

Helen Poynor

An underlying relationship to spirituality is threaded through my work as a movement practitioner—a relationship that is implied, but rarely articulated. Contributing to this anthology feels like an invitation to put my cards on the table.

I find myself reluctant to talk about spirituality in the context of my practice, although it is inherent. I believe our belief systems, whether secular or spiritual, are inevitably and rightly reflected and expressed in what we teach (and hopefully in our ways of being in the world). However, I am reticent because I am a movement practitioner rather than a spiritual teacher, and I am acutely aware of the pitfalls of my point of view being mistakenly interpreted from this perspective. My own spiritual understanding is gradually evolving. Having been exposed to various belief systems and spiritual practices, I believe that each of us holds fragments of truth, but that the whole picture can perhaps only be discerned when these slivers are brought together. In the meantime, I take the pragmatic position that any belief system that supports an individual to more fully realize their potential as a human being serves both them and the evolution of the human race. Spiritual belief is, in many respects, a personal matter.

There have been a number of different spiritual and cultural influences in my life and training. I appreciate having been raised in a Catholic family where spiritual beliefs and practices were an integral part of daily life; however, I have little patience with religious institutions. In my case, the interweaving of ritual, symbolism, poetic language and beauty as an affirmation of the pervasive presence of spirit, combined with an engagement with morality, outweighs any encumbrances from such an upbringing. The two primary influences in my movement training come from different cultural and spiritual backgrounds. Anna Halprin is Jewish and developed her work in the cultural environment of California. Suprapto Suryodarmo is a Buddhist whose work is imbued with Javanese cultural influences, including Sumarah meditation. I am deeply indebted to both of them. I have lived for several years in Australia, with some exposure to indigenous culture there. I have also been influenced by the spiritual awareness of a healer who has worked with, and supported, me for many years.

I understand life as an embodied spiritual journey. I believe that the experience of manifesting in a physical body in a material world is part of our spiritual evolution and that embodiment and engagement with the world around us serves our spiritual purpose. I do not believe that we are here to transcend the body and materiality; on the contrary, I believe that it is through embodiment that we can fulfil our purpose—or to put it another way, it is by arriving in our body on the planet that we can begin to accomplish that for which

Figure 1: 'Incubation.' Mover: Helen Poynor. Photographer: Annie Pfingst.

we came here. From this perspective, movement and work in the natural environment take on a different meaning. Many people attracted to movement work have issues around embodiment. Embodiment is not simply a physical process, but a process that integrates physicality, consciousness and feeling and which has the potential to both deepen our sense of self and to affirm our place in the world. Embodiment can be seen as a spiritual process that takes longer for some of us than others and which is beset by potential setbacks or interruptions. Assaults on the self can cause us to flee the body to escape the physical and emotional pain which is being experienced. Re-entering the body can entail re-encountering these emotions. Frequently, this path is not chosen until sufficient personal strength has been built, a safe holding environment is offered and/or the original survival strategy is no longer effective.

In order to further contextualize my perspective, I would like to briefly introduce my practice. My approach is rooted in non-stylised and environmental movement practice. I run the *Walk of Life Workshop and Training Programme*, working with members of the general public, movement practitioners and artists of all disciplines. I also work with individuals along a continuum which encompasses dance movement therapy, personal development and performance. As an independent movement artist, I work artistically as a performer and director.

I use the term *non-stylised* loosely to indicate that my approach is located outside movement/ dance styles that work with prescribed movement vocabularies, forms or techniques or with specific body types. The basis of my work is the structure of the body. I use simple movement scores to explore fundamental principles, such as the relationship to the ground or moving at different levels. The intention of the scores is to liberate movement potential and to heighten awareness of the body and of the self, of habitual patterns and preferences, and of space, the environment and other people. I work with process rather than form, except the form inherent in the structure of the body. The use of the word *practice* indicates the sense of a process that is ongoing, never closed down into a final outcome. It is not my intention to change an individual's body, but to work with what they bring—to offer possibilities and avenues of exploration. Over time, an individual's personal movement 'style' emerges, but rather than being static, it is in a process of continual evolution. This work incorporates kinesthetic experience, an individual's emotional and imaginative landscape and the environment in which they are moving—which includes other people and the wider landscape.

I live and work among the tidal landscapes of the Jurassic Coast World Heritage Site in East Devon/West Dorset, UK, and the surrounding hills and woodland. These rich natural environments are not merely inspiring backdrops for the work but an essential component of it. My approach facilitates a kinesthetic encounter with the natural environment: the moving human being is engaged with it in a responsive exchange. This is an encounter between the physicality of the body and the materiality of the landscape: a meeting of rock, earth, water and wind with bone, muscle, blood and breath. The environment becomes the teacher, different elements and changing weather elicit different experiences of the body and different movement qualities. I use the term 'natural' to indicate an environment in which elements such as cliffs, sea, rock, earth and trees predominate rather than man-made structures, while acknowledging that such elements are frequently subject to human influence.

I have little inclination to approach the theme of somatic experience and spirituality through the lens of academic theory. It appears to me that there is an inherent paradox in such an attempt, or at least a danger of the topic becoming progressively more elusive. I am strengthened in this belief by the references I find in Rumi concerning the difference between intellectual endeavour and spiritual understanding.[1] Perhaps it would be wiser to leave any attempt to articulate such matters to mystics and poets, although Rumi's writings appear to suggest that even such attempts inevitably fall short.[2] Nevertheless Rumi's writing provides a key, across time and cultural difference, to an understanding of the integration of body and spirit which is less evident in many spiritual traditions including Christianity and Buddhism.

If you have a body, where is the spirit?
If you are spirit, what is the body?

This is not our problem to worry about.
Both are both.
...

Invisible, visible, the world
does not work without both.

(Rumi in Barks 2006: 267)

I am more comfortable engaging with the material world than I am grappling with abstractions—more comfortable dealing with muscles, bones, earth, rock and trees than metaphysics. To attempt to express the ineffable in language is surely a contradiction in terms. I have written elsewhere about the difficulties of writing about kinesthetic experience (Poynor 1998: 7–33). How much more acute the difficulty when attempting to impose logical thought and language on an area of knowledge and experience that—by its very nature—transcends the limitations of such frameworks, where 'knowing' itself is of a different ilk. Working with feet moving over rocks, I feel no need to examine the nature of this reality—the fruits of the experience itself are enough. I want to elude 'the knot of intellectual discussion' (Rumi in Barks 2006: 208) and go out into the sunshine, with my feet in the water and the breeze on my skin. I resist lingering in windowless rooms discussing, for it depletes and disorients me, draining my vitality, my contact with myself and my faith in life. Instead, I call on poets and mystics who speak directly to me, reflecting my experience, deepening my understanding and supporting me to continue on my path. I am particularly drawn to Rumi's poetry as it challenges duality of body and spirit, affirms a different way of knowing and celebrates the beauty of the natural world.

Nevertheless I recognize the need to attempt to articulate our experiences and knowledge—not only through embodied presence and movement, but also in language—and wish to share some experiences and reflections from my practice working with others and from my artistic work. Before embarking on this endeavour, I want to acknowledge that there is no direct equivalence between these different modes of being and communicating—one does not, in fact, translate the other. Rumi's writings suggest that it is language that we need to liberate ourselves from, rather than the body, in order to deepen our spiritual experience and understanding:

Close the language-door
and open the love-window.

The moon won't use the door,
only the window.

(Rumi in Barks 2006: 80)

I am primarily a movement practitioner, a term which encompasses my work as a movement teacher, artist and therapist. I am interested in movement itself rather than movement as a vehicle to teach something else. I am interested in individuals and how they move, how they express and experience themselves through movement and in how this reflects their life. Training with Anna Halprin in the early 1980s, her approach to movement emphasized body, feelings, mind and spirit as equally important aspects of personal and artistic process (Halprin 1995: 15). By the early 2000s, when interviewing her for a book about her work, spirit/spirituality was no longer separated from the other aspects of her practice but seen as innate within all of them. This attitude of integrating the numinous with the other aspects of our humanity, rather than focusing on it as something special or separate from the mundane and the material world, makes sense to me. I am more at home with the notion of an immanent rather than a transcendent spirituality. From this perspective, movement practice may serve, at times and for some people, as a spiritual practice or it may sit alongside other spiritual practices which inform it or which it in turn informs. Movement practice supports me to be present, physically awake, attentive, and receptive to both myself and my surroundings. Movement can bring me to a place of quietness and stillness, interrupting the stream of mental chatter, letting emotional reverberations and physical restlessness settle, allowing another experience of myself and of the world around me.

Michael Mayne in *This Sunrise of Wonder* (1995), a collection of spiritual 'Letters for the Journey,' draws on a wide selection of poets and spiritual writers to attest to the relationship between really 'seeing' the wonder of the world and a spiritual awareness. For him, 'Spirit can only speak through matter' (Mayne 1995: 71). He claims that the starting point of our spiritual journey 'is not a striving after another world, but a deepening awareness of the true nature of this world and our place within it' (Mayne 1995: 70).

I spoke many years ago to Suprapto about a personal unease around the Western attraction to shamanic practices—which, in the Javanese cultural context in which we were studying, appeared to me at times to border on Orientalism. In response, he advised me to work like a farmer in the land. This has served me well, supporting a well-grounded, matter-of-fact approach to movement which suits me. This image also speaks to me of work that requires an intimate knowledge of the environment, respect for the forces of nature and for our place among them and the ability to work in harmony with them to bring forth sustenance for others. When I now work with practitioners whose orientation is more shamanic than my own, rather than attempting to travel with them, I support them to become fully grounded in their body, which I believe serves to anchor them, strengthening their psychic safety when journeying in other realms.

For some people who I work with individually, spirituality is explicitly or implicitly embedded close to the core of their life and movement work and needs to be engaged with directly. Similarly, in some group situations, it can become clear that not acknowledging the spiritual reverberations/dimension of the work constitutes an omission that could hinder understanding or the development of the work. Clearly, since I can only perceive what is happening from my point of view, it is important that there is enough spaciousness for participants to locate their experience within their own belief systems rather being unduly influenced by mine. For some, the spiritual resonance of the work is central and needs to be acknowledged, while for others it may be irrelevant or even a hindrance.

On several occasions, I have worked with clients with strong spiritual inclinations whose feet seem reluctant to touch the ground, whose upper body, arms, chest, eyes and head are drawn to the sky, embodying the Western dichotomy between body/earth and spirit. My work has been to help them land, to literally bring their feet into fuller contact with the earth, to support the connection between their upper and lower body, to encourage them to see what is before them and to bring them into relationship with the horizontal plane, not in order to contradict their spiritual yearning, but to support them to embody it more fully in their lives.

Working with non-stylised movement in the natural (rather than built) environment offers the opportunity for participants both to connect more deeply with themselves and to experience themselves in relationship to a wider environment. This fosters both a sense of interrelationship between their body and the earth and a sense of the place of human beings in a gestalt which encompasses both the minutiae of the life in a rock-pool and the magnificence of the coastal cliffs. Mayne's (1995) emphasis on the importance of opening ourselves to 'see' the natural world brings to mind the delight of an artist, who has worked with me for many years, on seeing for the first time the normally imperceptible movement of a limpet twirling on a rock. It was for her a pivotal moment. It is not a question of merging with other life-forms or the elements but rather of perceiving them as fully as possible and being aware of the distinctness of their presence. Mayne also stresses this sense of both receptivity and differentiation (1995). The added dimension when working with movement in the environment is that all the senses are opened: sight is not prioritized, and kinesthetic awareness is heightened, facilitating a more deeply embodied encounter with the natural world.

Such experiences may be, at times, overwhelming or challenging, but can also be sustaining and inspiring, affirming one's 'place in the family of things' (Oliver 1992: 110). For many, these experiences are imbued with spiritual significance. Mary Oliver's poetic writing suggests a link between our ability to be fully present in, and open to, the beauty of the world around us and spiritual experience. Her acute and passionate observation of the natural world and her embodied relationship to it, which is brought vibrantly to life in her writing, includes questioning the relationship between these experiences and a sense of prayer or holiness. In 'The Summer Day', she suggests that paying full attention to the exquisite detail of a particular grasshopper and time spent 'idle and blessed' in the fields is, for her, the equivalent of prayer (Oliver 1992: 94).

Personally, I feel a sense of wholeness, of being in balance, when I am in nature. I am more in touch with my internal landscape while simultaneously touched by the beauty of the world; this brings with it a sense of perspective. I am more receptive and more able to surrender, both fundamental to Sumarah meditation. I taste (momentarily, but paradoxically with an experience of timelessness) T. S. Eliot's 'condition of complete simplicity' and know that 'all shall be well' (Eliot 1983: 222–23). At times I am aware of a sense of the numinous.

In 'Duino Elegies', Rainer Maria Rilke suggests an urgent reciprocity in our relationship to the forces of nature:

Yes—the springtimes needed you. There were stars
waiting to be seen by you. A wave rolled

to your feet in the past [...]
… All this was your mission.
But were you up to it? Weren't you more often
distracted by anticipation ...

(Rilke 2006: 17)

It is as if human beings are called to bear witness to the natural world: for Rilke, this happens through language. In movement practice, this exchange—where we offer as well as receive—happens through the medium of the body, through an attentive and responsive presence.

Working in the studio, guiding others in movement or creating a performance, I have differing but related experiences of 'receiving.' What am I receiving, and from where? The experiences are clear, but describing them feels both challenging and open to misinterpretation. When I am sitting quietly witnessing someone move, and I have an impulse to say something that I do not fully understand, I 'check' the impulse, and—depending on the response—I say it and find that it often resonates in an unexpected way for the mover. I may have a similar impulse to use an unlikely phrase or instruction when guiding a group in movement, or to ask an individual a spontaneous question. I also have experiences of being 'guided' when making decisions about a site or a movement score.

Is this the 'still small voice of calm' of my upbringing, the inner teacher of Sumarah, channelling or my intuition? Does it matter? To me, how I name it does not seem crucial and may indeed depend on the context. The name is nothing more than a flag to indicate something intangible which is beyond my conscious ken which I experience as given and received rather than thought out or mentally constructed. Sometimes it is loud and clear, sometimes a fleeting glimpse which is easily missed in the busyness of daily life or the chattering of my mind. It may come in language, images or kinesthetic impulses/bodily sensations. It is often surprising, perhaps something I did not know I knew: it may contradict my rational thinking.

At times when I am working with an individual in a one-on-one session or in a group, I find myself thinking something and without communicating overtly with the mover, and without them seeing me, they appear to have 'received' it. Sometimes, I shift my internal attitude, and what I am witnessing in the room transforms. It is not simply that my perspective changes and therefore I 'see' the space and the movers differently; this internal shift appears to facilitate something different being embodied in the space. I am reticent about such elusive experiences, partly because I do not currently have a coherent frame of reference for them, and partly because I both sense their significance and know how easily they could be dismissed.

When creating performances, I tend not to start from an idea but from movement. As I move in the studio, characters may become manifest, apparently appearing directly in my body rather than passing through my imagination and being translated into movement. They 'arrive.' I get an inkling, a glimpse of 'who' they are, and as I 'follow' the movement, I find myself embodying them more fully. Similarly, while spending time moving in a site, an image, character or movement quality may emerge which becomes the basis of a piece—later, I discover that it reflects aspects of the history of the site or other stories of which I was

Figure 2: 'Crow-ne.' Mover: Helen Poynor. Photographer: Annie Pfingst.

unaware. I think of this way of working as 'kinesthetic research.' In the process of moving I 'receive' something—something that I have not constructed. My job is to give it 'house-room' to allow it to express itself as fully as possible. This is not an experience of possession but has clear kinship with processes that other artists, especially sculptors and writers, including Rilke, describe. The difference here is that my body is the medium. I am temporarily physically changed by what is received; there is no separation between body and inspiration. This is not a transcendent experience where I leave my body to travel in other realms, but rather one in which my moving body both experiences and expresses something other than my daily or conscious reality. The body, rather than being an obstacle to spiritual experience, becomes a conduit for it. Rumi's poetic writing offers insight into this apparent paradox.

> You are in your body
> like a plant is solid in the ground,
> yet you are wind.

(Rumi in Barks 2006: 113)

References

Barks, C. (2006), *A Year with Rumi: Daily Readings*, New York, NY: HarperOne.

Eliot, T. S. (1983), 'Little Gidding', *Collected Poems 1909–1962*, London, UK: Faber and Faber.

Halprin, A. (1995), *Moving toward Life*, Hanover, NH: Wesleyan University Press.

Mayne, M. (1995), *This Sunrise of Wonder*, London, UK: HarperCollins.

Oliver, M. (1992), 'The Summer Day' and 'Wild Geese', *New and Selected Poems*, Boston, MA: Beacon Press.

Poynor, H. (1998), 'Women-body-movement, non-stylised movement practice as a process of personal development, empowerment and expression for women', Unpublished MA thesis, Bristol: University of Bristol.

Rilke, R. M. (2006), 'The first elegy', *Duino Elegies* (trans. M. Crucefix), London, UK: Enitharmon.

Notes

1 This difference between intellectual endeavour and spiritual understanding can be found in 'Two Kinds of Intelligence' (Coleman Barks 2006: 43).

2 See, for example, 'A Dumb Experiment' (Coleman Barks 2006: 42).

Chapter 10

Intimate to Ultimate: The Meta-Kinesthetic Flow
of Embodied Engagement

Glenna Batson

You cannot love what you do not know, and so I ask you to study the theology of the body.

(LeJeune 2010, xii)

Prelude—A Personal Epiphany

I am a religious hybrid, the product of an Italian Catholic mystic and a Southern fundamentalist Baptist. My mother danced with American modern dance pioneer, Ruth St. Denis (1879–1968), herself a devotee of esoteric philosopher Rudolph Steiner (1861–1925). Mother was, in essence, a closet Hindu, worshipping animistic deities and believing in transmigration of souls to transcend the scourges of her impoverished origins and the banality of pedestrian life. My father was raised in the rural South, where the Baptist church held a firm rein on behaviour, corseting bodily urges to shape a soul fit enough to enter heaven after a life of unrelenting pragmatism. Despite their ideological harnesses, both religious traditions ironically fuelled the capacity for intensely passionate expressions of faith. Nonetheless, this passion evaded me for many years. I was baptized (into the Baptist faith) at age 12, married a Jew and converted to Judaism, divorced, underwent confirmation as an Episcopalian and married again to a lapsed Irish Catholic priest-turned Unitarian convert. Coming of age in the 1960s, and comfortably ensconced in leftist politics, postmodern dance and Somatics, situating myself in any religious niche was met with reticence, and even derision by my atheistic, existentialist circle of colleagues and friends. Despite this, I still sought spiritual outlets, but my journey to find 'home' in any conservative religious ethic often led to disappointment and despair rather than a sense of identification and belonging. I 'church shopped' for decades, trying on various 'costumes,' both contemplative and expressive. In the end, no cloth proved substantial enough to be my spiritual integument. My fragmented attempts to bond with the faithful were pockmarked by rebelliousness and meaningless dead ends. In 2000, in an attempt to revive a floundering relationship, I enrolled with my husband in a non-denominational spiritual direction programme. The programme met on extended weekends for two years of Jungian dream work and spiritual readings from various traditions. The programme was a call to spiritual service through abundant acceptance and contemplative prayer. I was hoping this experience would be revelatory, healing my own personal breach of body, mind and spirit. At one point in our training, a guest Episcopal theologian challenged us with the question: 'What is your covenant with God?' As each person shared, I listened for resonance, a sign that would reveal (to myself)

Figure 1: Mover: Anonymous. Photographer: Steve Clarke.

the crux of my own covenant. Many in the group described God's covenant with personified, anthropomorphic imagery—the 'father,' 'punisher,' 'absolver,' the all-knowing 'witness' or the compassionate (predominantly male) deity, who demanded good, moral behaviour to be among the righteous. All descriptions were familiar certainly, but did not feel authentic. I lapsed into cluelessness, and my anxiety mounted as my turn got closer. Then, suddenly, I heard a sound—a strange, unidentifiable sound that came from deep within the bowels of my being, and a deep torque seized my body. My spiritual covenant surfaced in a rapid flurry of images. Ecstatic visions flooded my brain of naked ancient Indian *devadasis* (temple dancers and servants of the gods) dancing before Shiva. I realized that my covenant with God could only happen through my body, through dancing. Expressive movement lay at the heart of my spirituality—the sensate body, moving in intimate communion with mythos and Eros.

While this epiphany reassured me of the validity of my checkered spiritual path, at the same time, I was overwhelmed by recognition of the source of the breach: my language of spirit was of the body and through the body—existential and phenomenal, not cognitive and mental. In answering this question when my turn came, I could not conjure up one logically coherent sentence to explain my innermost experience. While my behaviour was outwardly conforming (talking head, body seated upright and still), inwardly, I could feel the ruminations and rumblings that were the essence of this spiritual epiphany. This language spoke only in strange utterances, unidentifiable sounds, primitive sketches, not-yet-surfaced images and gestural riddles. I realized my spirituality could not be—and need not be— 'religious' in any formal sense of the word (Dewsbury and Cloke 2009; Janis 2008). I feebly explained that my body was 'my temple,' but this temple was fluid, evanescent, changing with fleeting episodes whose imprint lasted only moments in the ocean of experience. Feelings of sacredness, wonder, compassion and wisdom mingled with bodily feelings that I could only call 'spiritual.' To translate this experience into words seemed impossible. I needed my body as conduit. At that point, in silence, I got up and danced, much to the embarrassment, amazement and befuddlement of the group.

Introduction

Since the beginning of human kind, spirituality has been expressed through body-based rituals and dance (Clemente 2008). Yet, the language of body-based spirituality has been long forgotten, broken or dismissed in the history of Western (predominantly Caucasian) Judeo-Christian tradition. Because I could never communicate my experience of faith through any acceptable storyline within Western Christian faith (or within Eastern traditions, for that matter), I had always felt a deep sense of alienation and loneliness. This kind of alienation is an unspoken theme among many believers, who struggle to have their experience validated by the church (Mount-Schoop 2010). My story is an example of the circuitous path of knowing in and through the body. Looking back at my 'creation story,' I see at the core a crisis of my own faith—that is, the understanding of how to articulate, as well as the strength and confidence to follow, this inner guidance. Dance, Somatics and human movement science (the studies that have been the bedrock of my work) have opened many doors to this continually evolving mystery that still seeks a voice.

This chapter affords me yet one more way of understanding more deeply my own connection to spirituality as well as to further the scholarship of spirituality within dance. Here, I speak from my own voice, focusing on my own religious knowledge and experience that finds its roots in (predominantly Caucasian) Judeo-Christian religion and the more orthodox traditions of Catholicism and Protestantism. The focus is on 'meta- kinesthesis' as that phenomenon which brings us into intimate contact with ourselves, with others and ultimately with the spiritual realm. Beginning with a brief history of the Western orthodox Christian religious tradition where the body largely was suppressed as a source of spiritual insight, I go on to highlight the legacy of dance and Somatics, which celebrated bodily freedom and knowledge through movement awareness. Note that I have not included African-American religious and other cultural traditions, since these are foreign to me, personally. Perhaps bodily expression as a way to worship may be more readily acceptable or included in some of these cultures (see Kerr-Berry 2008, as an example). Instead, I draw from the work of somatic pioneers and contemporary dance scholars in the field of phenomenological embodiment. The second part of the chapter addresses the (still radical) perspective on meta-kinesthetic awareness as a way of knowing the material body as well as the route through the physical to the meta-physical and spiritual. The aim is to show that kinesthesia is not just the sensations of body movement as defined by science, but rather is an act of creative consciousness. Conscious awareness of sensory data issuing from the moving body is the alchemy that transforms ordinary experience (non-conscious, habitual, oblivious) into extraordinary relational depth. This sense-ability is 'meta-kinesthetic', creative in its functional and transfiguring roles. As such, it lies at the very centre of our moving, animate being and is the very source of relational depth that gives birth to, and transcends, relationships of self-to-self, self-to-world and self-to-spirit.

I define 'meta-kinesthesia' explicitly within the context of the pursuit of the self to find self-actualization through relational depth and transcendence. Spirituality can be defined simply as the experience of one's own personal relationship with 'the divine' (Janis 2009: 12). In this chapter, though, spirituality is defined as the deepening of relationships in life that enables a person to transcend the ego/self-focused existence towards more meaningful, blended bonding with humanity and other powers of expanding consciousness (Buber 1996). I have chosen the term relational depth as a shorthand way to describe the process that—through movement and its meta-kinesthetic dynamics and affinities—reveals the potential for spiritual transcendence. I borrow this term (merely descriptively) from depth psychology (Wyatt 2010: 5). In depth psychology, relational depth connotes Rogers' six therapeutic conditions that foster moments of intense contact and enduring experiences of connectedness (between therapist and client) (Rogers 1957). Here, conscious awareness of the meta-kinesthetic phenomena is the means through which movement brings us into contact with the body's possibilities of connection and transformation. Meta-kinesthetic awareness of the moving body (*soma*) then, as distinct from verbal dialogue alone, is the process and the potential that brings about self-actualization and deeper inter-subjectivity of presence.

The West's Legacy of Body and Spirit

The scope of religion and spirituality has been notoriously difficult to capture. Simply put, 'religion is the shell, while spirituality is the kernel within that shell. Religion is the map; spirituality is the territory' (Janis 2008, front piece). Schneiders explains the difference as, 'What seems to mark religions is that they are cultural systems for dealing with ultimate reality, whether or not that ultimate reality is God, and they are institutionalized in patterns of creed, code and cult. In some way, religion is about the human relationship to the sacred, the ultimate, the transcendent, the divine. These are not strictly equivalent terms but religion is basically a system for dealing with that which transcends the individual or even the social entity' (1999: 4–5). This quote expresses that behavioural conformity, 'right' conduct, is a prerequisite to being in relationship with god (the spirit), and implies control by hierarchical (and potentially oppressive) power structures. Spirituality, on the other hand, implies more phenomenally existential qualities, that is, representing 'something personal, positive and liberating' (Schneiders 1999: 1). This suggests transcendence of the human person through the practice of freedom and embracing the fullness of human experience in body and earth (Ferrar 2011). According to Janis, 'You don't have to do anything in particular to be spiritual. Spirituality doesn't require a list of specific actions. In fact, anything can be a spiritual practice, depending on your attitude, and a sense of service' (2008, front piece).

Although both religion and spirituality would claim to embrace the fullness of human experience, the history of Western orthodox Christianity contains within it the case for the disembodied body. Arguably, this is not because the body was completely ignored in practice, but rather because it was not given a chance to develop an articulate language, nor considered a legitimate source for attaining spiritual insights, realization and liberation (Ferrar 2011). Current definitions of spirituality claim the purpose is to 'go beyond self, to discover, enjoy, take pleasure in the range of flavors of human existence, to learn the boundaries of self control, to invite change, to be true to yourself' (Janis 2008: 59). But this pathway has not always been explicitly through the body. When Christianity became the official religion under Constantine during the imperial Roman Empire, Western culture lost its roots of Middle Eastern mysticism and therefore the experiential body of mystical, feminine and visionary hermeneutics (Douglas-Klotz 2001). Aramaic language gave way to Greek; the flesh of Jesus and his incarnate wisdom gave way to the divine Christ. For nearly 2000 years, Western culture developed a split between 'inner psychic' and 'outer normative consciousness,' as well as splits between cosmology and psychology, body and soul, and humanity and the natural environment. […] Western culture [evolved] without a language or worldview that [could] conceptualize expanded states of consciousness in a healthy way (Douglas-Klotz 2001: 1–2). Western Christian orthodoxy suppressed the body in pursuit of a clean, body-less transcendent spirit. This loss of the body, of bodily experience, was a crisis of birthright and a loss of deep intimacy—a loss of the merging of the self with its transcendent powers that enable ecstatic union with the ultimate. The body became separated from the conscious vitality of the mind and heart; these entities no longer were valued as embodied sources of spiritual insight and transformation.

'Sublimation, not integration, of the body, became religion's spiritual goal' (Ferrar 2011). Pope John Paul II has evolved a theology of the body (2008). On the cover of his book of the same name, the 'body' is represented by a plaster cast of two hands poised delicately upward in supplicating prayer. He states: 'the body, and it alone, is capable of making visible what is invisible' (2008: 3). With sublimation of the body as the ultimate goal, 'undesirable' instincts and urges (both in the eyes of society and God) must be transformed (through religious practices) into more acceptable behaviour. 'Because of its divine creation and redemption, the body is worthy of honor. At the same time, this body belongs to sinful men and women. When Paul [Jesus' disciple] writes of its "unpresentable [sic] parts," we remember the shame experienced by the first human beings as a result of sin. The sexual parts of the body are not unpresentable because of any dishonor. They are only unpresentable because of shame and lust—the fruits of sin' (John Paul II 2008: 115).

By the 20th century, a unique phenomenon arises: the concept of the 'self,' especially one that is reflective, self-involved, and liberatory. Postmodernism brought about a societal obsession with the body (Green 2007) and its 'technologies' (Foucault 1988: 18), a body which not only was the means of production, but also was 'the production itself' (Orbach 2009: 17). Everything about 'body' was worthy of investigation—simply being a body, my body, the lived body experience—embedded in a socio-cultural context (Zaner 1981), explicit, explicated and sexual. The concept of the lived and living body became a grande idée in intellectual circles (Bresler 2004: 4). Within academia, we see the evolution of the field of embodiment, a confluence of academic disciplines, including religion (Pederson 2010). This intellectual discourse coincided with the proliferation of body-mind (somatic) practices (Varela and Shear 1999) within humanistic psychology, the holistic health movement, and other movements (Eddy 2009).

Concurrently, the 20th century saw the emergence of modern dance, one counter-thrust to Cartesian dualism and the primacy of mind over body (Eddy 2009; Sheets-Johnstone 2011a), as well as liberation from Puritanism's historical suppression of bodily (sexual and otherwise) drives (Berman 1989). Early modern dance pioneers, such as Isadora Duncan (1877–1927), Doris Humphrey (1985–58), Rudolf Laban (1879–1958), and Mary Wigman (1886–1973), as well as the proponents of dance therapy, paved the way for liberation of the body (Hamalainen 2007). These pioneers and their descendants evolved a sensate language for the moving body. Although the body was conceived as a 'vehicle,' it was the 'vehicle for feeling' (Hawkins 1991: 13), through which one could practice 'freedom,' a consciously aware, autonomous self, acting from choice within reflexive movement practice (Anttila 2007: 19).

228

Likewise, Somatics advocated the practice of freedom through a plethora of body-based movement practices. Somatics offered a radical departure from the reign of the mental intellect (Eddy 2009), privileging first person experience (Green 2007), as well as giving permission to rejoice in the sensual (Johnson 1992). Philosopher and Feldenkrais practitioner, Thomas Hanna reminded us that our birthright was the physical, fleshy body, and our 'sarcality,' the 'fleshy' sphere of consciousness, the meat of incarnate perception (2007). Somatics gave us back holistic existence (Greene 1997–98: 50), full of vulnerability and potential, always in its process of expanding, accommodating, adapting and assimilating (Hanna 1990–91). Shifting the focus away from the objectified, mechanized body (Eddy 2009), Somatics reminded us of the physicalized right to occupy space, to acknowledge potential for freedom and expansiveness, have dimensionality, feel, know oneself, be the agent of one's own actions and to form bonds with self, others and realize realms beyond self (i.e. spiritual).

The dialogue between Somatics and (primarily postmodern) dance was well underway throughout the last four decades of the 20th century (Eddy 2009). Somatic education contributed to dance a potent means of investigation into pragmatic 'thereness' in relation to dance-making and performance. The idea of the sensate bodily self as having the inherent ability to create new events from itself (and through itself), helped forge a radical shift in dance training (Depraz 2008: 243; Batson 1990). Of the hundreds of psychophysical practices that proliferated throughout the 20th (and into the 21st) century, Somatics spawned many spiritual movements such as nature worship (eco-spirituality), contemplative traditions and ethnic/tribal rituals (Dewsbury and Cloke 2009). The initial somatic movement largely was secular in tone; however, advocating the practice of autonomy, which implied freedom from all dogma, including religious. While many bodily expressions of spirit flourished, discussion of Western religious traditions was avoided in somatic intellectual discourse. Among the array of pragmatic body and movement-based practices considered 'privileged mediators of change,'—'education, learning, sports training, and psychotherapy,'—religion is neither listed nor implied (Varela and Shear 1999: 4). Thomas Hanna argued for Somatics as science ('somatology') (Hanna 1973) in which the soma's first person perspective, realized through movement, was the source of individuation and unity and the foundation of thought, language, action and all conscious and non-conscious functions (Hanna 2007). Hanna spoke of the distinction between moral philosophy and natural philosophy (the latter of which evolved into 'science') (Hanna 2007: 4), purporting that the goal of philosophy was not the 'trans-human goal of eternal abstract trust, but the human goal of temporal, ongoing experiential freedom' (Hanna 2007: 8). Hanna recognized the basic elements of kinesthetic feeling as the groundwork of somatic (lived and living) experience. Somatics was 'the way of wisdom; it is a way of being wise, the obvious way of living wisely. To live in wisdom is to live in freedom, the authentic freedom gained through self-knowledge and self-control' (Hanna 2007: 6). He stated,

> The concern [of Somatics] to bring about a transformed and enhanced human being was formerly the more or less exclusive bailiwick of Christian and other evangelistic

groups in the US. [...] It is a concern that is not theologically motivated but, instead, is practically motivated toward reshaping the texture of human experience so as to make one more fluidly adaptable to the unique possibilities of living within a technologized society.

(Hanna 1973: 4)

Despite 350 years of critique of the Cartesian legacy, dance and somatic scientists and scholars still are evolving a movement-centred scholarship that moves beyond dualism (Sheets-Johnstone 2009). Much of the work on kinesthesia and embodiment outside of science has been grounded in the existential, ontological plane. Embodied spirituality still begs a place within this discourse (Clemente 2008). The language of embodied spirituality—and of human consciousness, in general (Brown 2002)—still remains limited (Douglas-Klotz 2001: 4). The burgeoning growth of the field of embodiment, while promising, falls short of capturing and articulating the impact and scope of movement and its transcendent values (Sheets-Johnstone 2011). Neither do constructivist nor affect-centred theories of body agency have much to say about kinesthesia and its role in motor intentionality in effecting change (Nolan 2009: 4). Scholarship exists, certainly, relating kinesthetic expressions to spirituality within select anthropological dance contexts (Szeto 2010). Yet, the interrelationship between kinesthesia and spirituality within dance merits deeper investigation and articulation, as is addressed in this volume.

Kinesthesia—Sensory Modality to State of Consciousness

One way to bridge the gap between kinesthetic embodiment and the spiritual is to view kinesthesia as having 'meta' capabilities. The prefix 'meta' implies the ability to 'transcend', 'go beyond' or evolve to 'one level of description higher,' than the ordinary usage of the word connotes (*Oxford English Dictionary* 1989). The etymological root of the word 'kinesthesia' derives from the Greek 'kinesis,' meaning motion, and 'aisthesis,' meaning feeling or perception—not only from the senses, but also from the intellect (cognition) (*Oxford English Dictionary* 1989). Science defines the word 'kinesthesia' as the sense of position and motion resulting from the afferent neural signals sent to the brain and spinal cord from the skin, fascia, muscles, tendons, joints, ligaments and other tissues, particularly of the limbs and trunk (Proske and Gandevia 2009: 4139). Sometimes the word 'proprioception' is used synonymously with 'kinesthesia,' but more often in science, 'proprioception' specifically relates to joint- or muscle-sense, per se, whereas 'kinesthesia' adds the dimension of the body's position and movement in space (Stillman 2002). Kinesthesia also has been referred to as a 'sixth sense,' differentiating it from the five basic sensory modalities of science: smell, taste, sight, hearing and touch (Garlick 1990). This term can easily become muddied with a layman's concept of extrasensory perception and thus is not considered a technical term within science. But kinesthesia is not just a 'mechanism' by which sensing occurs, nor a modality through which our body registers its place in space. A scientific lens is necessary, but not sufficient (Batson 2009; Sheets-Johnstone 2011a). Such reductionist interpretations ignore kinesthesia's meta-dimensionality: the affective, motivating dimension in movement (Sheets-Johnstone 2011b) and, by association, its transcendent dimension. Quite simply, our *modus vivendi* is not that we have a body with sense organs that connect to muscles that execute movement. Rather, kinesthesia is a 'meta-system' (Behnke 2008), a form of 'kinesthetic consciousness' (Sheets-Johnstone 1999: 130), by which we both generate and make sense of our experience. Kinesthetic consciousness not only is of the sensate moving body, but also is phenomenal in itself—both integral to movement generation as well as reflective of its actions. This consciousness is rooted in our human motility (Sheets-Johnstone 1999; Behnke 2008). It is the living expression of 'I can' (Behnke 2008)—of our self-actualizing potential. We do not have to make sense of our hands to make them move. As examples of prehensile, situated embodiment, they just 'know' what to do—antecedent to our conscious intentions and actions (Kielhofner 2005).

In bringing movement to consciousness, we enter a world of complexity—potentially transformational and transcendental. Statements such as 'I think,' 'I feel,' 'I know' and 'I believe' all have their roots in a felt sense of the moving body and are readily transformed into potential. Out of this kinesthetic consciousness, we are constantly 'making a body' (Behnke 1997: 186), whether within our active awareness or not, as we encounter gravity, inertia, friction, velocity, acceleration, timing, direction and so on. This body-making is not passive, but motivating, explicating, adaptive and world constituting (Kielhofner 1995). This kinesthesia, as a movement system, 'is constitutive of, not tangential to, the process of individuation' (Nolan 2009: 10). Enfolded into reality, kinesthesia enables us to evolve a distinctive, yet fluid, set of movement dynamics (and relationships), expressing through our three-dimensionality, verticality and space-time-effort values. In addition to Rudolph Laban's pioneering work in examining work habits and evolving Effort-Shape and Choreutics, other somatic scholars have sought to systematize movement dynamics beyond space, time and effort, as other states of consciousness, affective qualities or as phylogenetic and cosmic. For example, see Body-Mind Centering's® concept of 'mind' (Bainbridge-Cohen 1993), dance phenomenology's affective dynamics—tensional, linear, areal and projectional (Sheets-Johnstone 2009)—and Continuum Movement's wave forms (Conrad 2007).

In essence, without kinesthetic consciousness, we have no sense of movement (at least in the intact nervous system). Without movement, we have no sense of temporal and force dynamics and their affective qualities. As such, we may not be able to move at all, feel our existence in space, our movement potential or our empathic resonance. Note, however, that is it possible to move without kinesthetic sensation and that such movement may even appear 'normal,' albeit requiring an unfathomable amount of cognitive and visual attention to control the simplest of actions. Readers can learn about the case of Ian Waterman, who at 19, lost all sensation from the neck down due to a virus, and was able to regain functional movement through years of re-education (Cole 1995). Further, movement often happens with or without knowledge of itself. Lack of awareness of self-movement habitually occurs in the everyday automatic, non-conscious movement of life, a state Moshe Feldenkrais referred to as the 'elusive obvious' (Feldenkrais 2002). We can bring kinesthetic awareness to consciousness in immediate experience, or we can reflect on our movement experience. As Nolan states, 'kinesthesia designates sensory stimulation produced for the self, and as such, it opens up a field of reflexivity in which the subject becomes an object (as body) of her own awareness' (2009: 10). 'Such present-moment awareness is characterized by trust, spontaneity of feeling and freedom to be one's self, autonomous and free' (Greene 1997–98: 51).

Meta-Kinesthesis?

Meta-kinesthesis is of the body-in-the-world, and at the same time, of the spirit. Bodily expression is meta-corporeal (Sheets-Johnstone 1999: 59) and meta-kinesthetic, suggesting several vantage points—one that is within the experience itself (first person intersubjective) and away (outside first person experience, or third person perspective). Through meta-corporeal consciousness and meta-kinesthetic awareness, I can perceive myself from within, view myself from outside of myself, and resonate (empathize) with others through nonverbal, kinesthetic empathy (Reason and Reynolds 2010). Meta-kinesthesia, by its very nature as well as its spectrum of feeling states, functions to bring us into relationship with self and the world. Higher-level somatic processes than those of simple body awareness, these are hallmarks of our situatedness and embeddedness in life (Shalin 1971). Meta-kinesthesia allows the soma to 'make sense,' literally and figuratively, of the shape-shifting reality of its experience. Out of the simplicity of sensations through moving relationships come a range of complex emotions, attitudes and beliefs and experiences themselves (Gold 1992–93). Relationships as such are living, moving things. They are not fixed—rather in constant flux, evolving, expressing changing dynamic qualities—with ourselves, our material world, our fellow human beings and ultimately with any transcendent power we call 'spirit.' Meta-kinesthesia helps us remember the body, 'attuning us to complexity, creativity and possibility' (Mount-Shoop 2010: 21). Theologian Mount-Shoop equates feeling with more fundamental sensate experience, more evolutionarily fundamental and integral to life itself—forming earlier in development than emotion or sensory modalities. This use of the word 'feeling' resonates with meta-kinesthesis in its immediacy, its fullness of pure experience, and its relationship to our animate life (Sheets-Johnstone 2011). This expression of life experience can be compromised, for example, if the body is hurt, damaged or otherwise traumatized. Mount-Shoop states:

> Feeling is formal, primal and all encompassing. [...] It is not emotion, not thought, not sensation, but instead the most primary and most embodied mode through which we

navigate all experience. [...] Feeling is not simply experience; rather it is a physical mode of experience that grounds, conditions, and gives life to all our experience. Feeling is primary, embodied knowing [...] and itself is movement.

(2010: 18, 12)

Meta-kinesthesis immediately communicates what is needed to go from here to there, what is needed next, how to navigate. It is a fluid, affective, ongoing shaping of the body's movement in space that may or may not be goal-directed. Meta-kinesthesis is 'thinking in movement [...] a perpetual dissolution and dilation, even a mutability, of here-now movements and a moving present' (Sheets-Johnstone 2009: 34). We don't need an image of the 'what' or 'how' of movement, nor require a series of complex neurological processes that provide us with the known output of our experience. We do not need a symbol to mediate between experience and understanding (Sheets-Johnstone 2009: 35). The act of seeing does not require neuro-computation in which a series of little black boxes in the brain or imagistic schemata stand between experience and the retina. We resonate and are resonant. The layering of kinesthetic states enables us to locate ourselves at various points of relational depth within our world-making. We can be deeply immersed in ourselves and/or others, reflective and analytical of our experience, engaged socially and ultimately transcendental/transcendent. Through meta-kinesthesis, we are empathic, resonating with other actions we observe, empathizing with others, acting as if we could walk in their shoes, as well as inferring the next action before it comes (Reason and Reynolds 2010).

'Meta' also expresses a higher order of cognition—not in terms of class or categorical value, but rather in terms of the ability to capture more elusive or more abstract qualities of engagement. Meta-kinesthesia weaves together elements basic to somatic consciousness, facilitating a through-line between apprehension, awareness, apperception, perception, attention and intention. These acts of consciousness help 'direct the organs of sensation to keep a chosen experience within sensing range,' awakening movement impulses and giving them somewhere to go (Gold 1992–93: 35). Our 'knowing' is not due primarily to the kinesthetic and proprioceptive senses alone, but rather to the nameless, physical 'sense of the intricacy of our situations' (Gendlin 1992: 346). Feelings arise spontaneously out of the implicitness of our situation. Feelings 'just come' (Gendlin 2009: 335). From the spiritual perspective, this knowing, these feelings that 'just come' are those feelings that psychologist Gendlin says also can take on transcendental value. Mount-Shoop states:

Feeling is the element of experience from which piety comes (not from knowing and doing). [...] Feeling re-members the body by tuning us into its complexity, creativity, and possibility. [...] It is the mechanism of our living into the promise of redemption. [...] In a real sense, it is our imago Dei, God's image in us [...] the capacity to be spiritual, vital and capable of far more than that of which we are conscious.

(Mount-Shoop 2010: 12, 13, 21)

Grace—The Soma's Right Relationship

Finally, meta-kinesthesis promises a state of grace. From the Western Christian perspective, grace is 'unmerited pardon' (Hohertz 2002), an act of redemption and forgiveness of sins. The word 'sin' derives from the Greek, meaning, 'missing the mark,' as in an archer missing the target. The root of the word does not imply badness, wrongdoing or wickedness, but rather the loss of connection with one's higher spiritual nature (Borg 2004: 164–71). The somatic perspective on the interrelationship between grace, sin and redemption takes on a more secular tone, yet incorporates transcendent values. In Somatics, the 'sin' (or fall from grace) is the loss of kinesthetic connection with self. Meta-kinesthetic sensitivity 'lies at the heart of our redemption, whether as goal, birthright, or myth […] Somatics states our birthright as: the right to occupy (live into) our length, width, depth and symmetry, to manipulate our world, and to live rhythmically, according to context, but we need to align bodily feelings with intentions,' a function of conscious kinesthetic awareness (Gold 1992/93: 34, 35). Somatic grace implies a kind of right relationship as an alignment of body-mind-spirit with a meta-physical and meta-kinesthetic harmony of the self. This feeling of meta-kinesthetic harmony has a feeling of 'effortless agency,' the realization of our somatic potential (Fraleigh 1999: 17). To move gracefully is to move without interfering tensions, without compulsion, with awareness and freedom of choice in action—or, as Fraleigh states, 'the freedom we feel in those actions we perform in harmony with nature, those which become second nature to us, having passed through effort to release us from it' (1999: 16).

We can fall from grace in the somatic sense, suggesting a sense of a loss of kinesthetic awareness (consciousness). Following this biological imperative, Thomas Hanna described 'four dimensions of the soma'—standing, facing, handling and timing (Hanna 1979). Hanna left us with an eloquent description of 'somatic amnesia,' how the soma can lose the integrity of its basic physical expression in the world (Hanna 1988: 1). Somatically speaking, the alignment of our basic functions of attention and intention can become 'misdirected' (Gold 1992–93: 38), and our basic somatic patterns can become distorted, in a state of dis-ease. Our fall from grace can result from the dulling of our meta-kinesthetic senses secondary to familiarity, habit and trauma and unplanned, and un-sensed destruction of the body can insidiously ensue (Hanna 1979: 35). With misappropriated tensions, restrictions and other distortions, we stop moving, our tissue atrophies, becomes damaged or dies. As a result of physical and functional loss, more evolved somatic processes of intimacy, emotion and autonomy also become compromised. The path to redemption can begin when we bring our attention to focus on meta-kinesthetic awareness, but it is not complete. 'In order to restore our grace, the subliminal soma can be coaxed to awareness through attention, but it is more automatically lived through the totality of our body-mind' (Fraleigh 1999: 17). Bringing this body-mind into the spiritual world (whether formalized as religion or not) is to stand (and move) in wonder of its sacred mysteries, which are everywhere and 'saturated with being' (Eliade 1959: 12). We experience this sacred relatedness through our meta-kinesthetic consciousness in every waking and dreaming moment. Thus, our lives are suffused with the sacred, like 'the veins that flow with life' (McKenna 1971: 3). Restoration of meta-kinesthetic awareness brings us into 'thereness', into the life of grace that makes us holy. As Sheets-Johnstone reminds us:

> To re-enter the world of the living body is to recover a world of mysterious possibilities […] because the living body is a source of mystery, yet at the same time is utterly transparent; it is guileless, without pretensions it hides nothing. […] Freshness, unexpectedness, fortuity non-controllability, these are the ways in which mysterious possibilities are encoded. It is in these mysterious possibilities that the redemptive powers of the body are discovered. The world that is too much with us is forgotten.
>
> (2009: 21–22)

Conclusion

This chapter has addressed the concept of meta-kinesthesis as something that allows us entry into our corporeal nature as a means of transcendence. The living, moving, kinesthetically resonant body enacts spirituality. While the world of the spirit is described as imbued with sacredness, wonder, awe and mystery (Debenham and Debenham 2008), these characteristics are of the incarnate body. Ritualized, somatically-aware movement harnesses these mysteries, transforming the ordinary into the extraordinary and the physical into the meta-physical.

References

Anttila, E. (2004), 'Dance learning as practice of freedom', in L. Rouhiainen, E. Anttila, S. Hamalainen and T. Loytonen (eds), *The Same Difference? Ethical and Political Perspectives on Dance*, Acta Scenica 17, Helsinki, Finland: Theatre Academy, pp. 19–62.

Bainbridge Cohen, B. (1993), *Sensing, Feeling, and Action: The Experimental Anatomy of Body-Mind Centering*, Northampton, MA: Contact Editions.

Batson, G. (1990), 'Dancing fully, safely, and expressively: The role of the body therapies in dance training', *Journal of Physical Education, Recreation, and Dance*, 61:9, pp. 28–31.

—— (2009), 'Update on proprioception', *Journal of Dance Medicine & Science*, 13:2, pp. 35–41.

Behnke, E. (2008), 'The human science of somatics and transcendental phenomenology', http://www.donhanlonjohnson.com/syllabi/behnkesciofsom.htm. Accessed 26 May 2011.

Berman, M. (1989), *Coming to Our Senses: Body and Spirit in the Modern History of the West*, Seattle, WA: Seattle Writers' Guild.

Borg, M. J. (2004), *The Heart of Christianity: Rediscovering a Life of Faith*, San Francisco, CA: Harper.

Bresler, L. (2004), *Moving Bodies, Moving Minds: Towards Embodied Teaching and Learning*, Boston, MA: Kluwer Academic Publishers.

Brown, J. W. (2002), *The Self-Embodying Mind: Process, Brain Dynamics and the Conscious Present*, Station Hill, NY: Barrytown.

Bruzina, R. (2004), 'Phenomenology and cognitive science: Moving beyond the paradigms', *Phenomenology and the Cognitive Sciences*, 20, pp. 43–48.

Buber, M. (1996), *I and Thou*, New York, NY: Charles Scribner's Sons.

Clemente, K. (2008), 'Dance as sacred expression', *Journal of Dance Education*, 8:2, pp. 37–38.

Cole, J. O. (1995), *Pride and the Daily Marathon*, Cambridge, MA: MIT Press.

Conrad, E. (2007), *Life on Land: The Story of Continuum*, Berkeley, CA: North Atlantic Books.

Damasio, R. (1999), *The Feeling of What Happens: Body, Emotion and the Making of Consciousness*, New York, NY: Harcourt Brace & Company.

Debenham, P. and Debenham, K. (2008), 'Experiencing the sacred in dance education: Wonder, compassion, wisdom, and wholeness in the classroom', *Journal of Dance Education*, 8:2, pp. 44–55.

Depraz, N. (2008), 'The rainbow of emotions: At the crossroads of neurobiology and phenomenology', *Continental Philosophical Review*, 41, pp. 237–59.

Dewsbury, J. D. and Cloke, P. (2009), 'Spiritual landscapes: Existence, performance and immanence', *Social and Cultural Geography*, 10:6, pp. 695–711.

Douglas-Klotz, N. (2001), 'Missing stories: Psychosis, spirituality and the development of western religious hermeneutics', in I. Clarke (ed.), *Psychosis and Spirituality: Exploring the New Frontier*, London, UK: Whurr Publishers.

Eddy, M. (2009), 'A brief history of somatic practices and dance: Historical development of the field of somatic education and its relationship to dance', *Journal of Dance & Somatic Practices*, 1:1, pp. 5–27.

Eliade, M. (1959), *The Sacred and the Profane: The Nature of Religion*, Orlando, FL: Harcourt, Brace and World, Inc.

Feldenkrais, M. (2002), *The Elusive Obvious*, Cupertino, CA: Meta Publications.

Ferrar, H. N. 'Embodied spirituality, now and then', https://www.integralworld.net/ferrar2.html. Accessed 26 May 2011.

Foucault, M. (1988), 'Technologies of the self', in L. H. Martin, H. Gutman and P. H. Hutton (eds), *Technologies of the Self*, Amherst, MA: University of Massachusetts Press, p. 18.

Fraleigh, S. (1999), 'Freedom, gravity, and grace', *Somatics: Journal of Body/Mind Arts and Science*, 12:2, pp. 14–18.

Garlick, D. (1990), *The Lost Sixth Sense—A Medical Scientist Looks at the Alexander Technique*, New South Wales, Australia.

Gendlin, E. (2009), 'What first & third person processes really are', in C. Petitmengin (ed.), *Ten Years of Viewing from Within*, Exeter, UK: Imprint-Academic, pp. 332–62.

——— (1992), 'The primacy of the body, not the primacy of perception', *Man and World*, 25:3–4, pp. 341–53.

Gold, L. (1992–93), 'Gaining grace: A somatic perspective', originally published in *Somatics Magazine: Journal of the Bodily Arts and Sciences*, 9:1, pp. 34–39, http://www.somatics.com/page5.htm. Accessed 3 June 2011.

Green, J. (2007), 'Student bodies: Dance pedagogy and the soma', in L. Bresler (ed.), *International Handbook of Research in Arts Education*, Netherlands: Springer, pp. 1119–32.

Greene, D. (1997–98), 'Assumptions of somatics, Part II', *Somatics Magazine: Journal of the Bodily Arts and Sciences*, 11:3, pp. 50–55.

Hamalainen, S. (2004), 'The meaning of bodily knowledge in a creative dance-making process', in L. Rouhiainen, E. Anttila, S. Hamalainen and T. Loytonen (eds), *Ways of Knowing*, Acta Scenica 17, Helsinki, Finland: Theatre Academy, pp. 56–78.

Hanna, T. (1973), 'The project of Somatology', *Journal of Humanistic Psychology*, 13:3, pp. 3–14.

—— (1979), *The Body of Life: Creating New Pathways for Sensory Awareness and Fluid Movement*, Rochester, VT: Healing Arts Press.

—— (1988), *Somatics: Reawakening the Mind's Control of Movement, Flexibility, and Health*, Cambridge, MA: Da Capo Books.

—— (1990/91), 'Clinical somatic education: A new discipline in the field of health care', originally published in *Somatics Magazine: Journal of the Bodily Arts and Sciences,* 8:1, http://www.somatics.com/hannart.htm. Accessed 31 May 2011.

—— (2007), 'Somatology: An introduction to somatic philosophy and psychology, Part I', *Somatics Magazine: Journal of the Bodily Arts and Sciences*, 15:2, pp. 4–11.

Hawkins, A. (1991), *Moving from Within: A New Method for Dance Making*, Chicago, IL: A Cappella Books.

Hohertz, L. (2002), 'What is the meaning of grace?', http://www.servantsnews.com/sn0211/grace.htm. Accessed 21 January 2012.

Janis, S. (2008), *Spirituality for Dummies*, 2nd ed., Hoboken, NJ: Wiley Publishing, Inc.

John Paul II. (2008), *Theology of the Body in Simple Language*, Rome, IT: Philokalia Books.

Johnson, D. H. (1992), *Body: Recovering Our Sensual Wisdom*, Berkeley, CA: North Atlantic Books.

Kerr-Berry, J. (2008), 'Praise dance in community: An interview with Reverend Dr. Albirda Rose-Eberhardt', *Journal of Dance Education*, 8:2, pp. 56–61.

Kielhofner, G. (1995), 'A meditation on the use of hands', *Scandinavian Journal of Occupational Therapy*, 2, pp. 153–66.

LeJeune, M. (2010), *Set Free to Love: Lives Changed by the Theology of the Body*, Cincinnati, OH: Servant Books.

McKenna, B. (1971), *The Power of the Sacraments,* Cincinnati, OH: Servant Books.

Mount-Shoop, M. (2010), *Let the Bones Dance: Embodiment and the Body of Christ*, Louisville, KY: Westminster John Knox Press.

Nolan C. (2009), *Agency and Embodiment: Performing Gestures/Producing Culture*, Cambridge, MA: Harvard University Press.

Oxford English Dictionary (1989), Kinesthesia entry, Simpson, J. and Weiner, E. (eds), New York, NY: Oxford University Press.

Orbach, S. (2009), *Bodies*, New York, NY: MacMillan.

Pedersen, A. M. (2010), 'The nature of embodiment: Religion and science in dialogue', *Zygon: Journal of Religion and Science*, 45:1, pp. 264–272.

Proske, U. and Gandevia, S. C. (2009), 'The kinesthetic senses', *Journal of Physiology*, 587, pp. 4139–46.

Reason, M. and Reynolds, D. (2010), 'Kinesthesia, empathy, and related pleasures: An inquiry into audience experiences of watching dance', *Dance Research Journal*, 42:2, pp. 49–75.

Rogers, C. R. (1957), 'The necessary and sufficient conditions of therapeutic personality change', *Journal of Consulting Psychology*, 21, 95–103.

Roy, J. M., Petitot, J., Pachoud, B. and Varela, F. J. (1993), 'Introduction to naturalizing phenomenology', in J. Petitot, F. J. Varela, B. Pachoud and J. M. Roy (eds), *Naturalizing Phenomenology: Issues in Contemporary Phenomenology and Cognitive Science*, Stanford, CA: Stanford University Press, pp. 1–80.

Schneiders, S. (1999), *Spirituality, Religion, Theology: Mapping the Terrain*, IHM Theological Education Project, Cycle III, Mahwah, NJ: Paulist Press.

Shalin, D. N. (2007), 'Signing in the flesh: Notes on pragmatist hermeneutics', *Sociological Theory*, 25:3, pp. 193–224.

Sheets-Johnstone, M. (1992), *Giving the Body its Due*, Brockport, NY: State University of New York Press.

—— (1999), *The Primacy of Movement*, Amsterdam, NL: John Benjamins Publishing Company.

—— (2009), *The Corporeal Turn: An Interdisciplinary Reader*, London, UK: Imprint Academic.

—— (2011a), 'From movement to dance', *Phenomenology and the Cognitive Sciences*, 2, pp. 1–19.

—— (2011b), *The Primacy of Movement*, expanded 2nd ed., Amsterdam, NL: John Benjamins Publishing Company.

Sixth Sense, http://c2.com/cgi/wiki?SixthSense. Accessed 20 August 2011.

Stillman, B. C. (2002), 'Making sense of proprioception: The meaning of proprioception, kinesthesia and related terms', *Physiotherapy*, 88:11, pp. 667–76.

Szeto, K. Y. (2010), 'Calligraphic kinesthesia in the dancescape: Lin Hwai-min's cosmopolitical consciousness in the cursive trilogy', *Dance Chronicle*, 33:2, pp. 414–41.

Varela, F. M. and Shear, J. (1999), 'First person accounts—why, what, how?', *Journal of Consciousness Studies*, 6:2/3, pp. 1–21.

Wyatt, G. (2010), 'Relational depth: A window into an interconnected world', *Self and Society*, 38:2, pp. 5–24.

Zaner, R. (1981), *The Concept of Self*, Athens, OH: Ohio University Press.

Chapter 11

Permission and the Making of Consciousness

Sondra Fraleigh

This chapter is in two parts. Part One, Verbs of Permission, concerns issues of language and teaching in Somatics, and is also a personal account of some of my experiences with spirituality and religion in relation to dance, Somatics and yoga. Part Two, After Xenophanes, is philosophical. It examines Somatics through phenomenology, touches upon problems of body/mind dualism, and explains why phenomenology is of value to Somatics as a field of body-based practices and intellect.

Part One: Verbs of Permission

This short manifesto has guided my teaching at Eastwest Somatics Institute since its founding in 1990:

> We develop verbs of permission, life-enhancing words that sink into the watery soma of the body. Strength lives in spontaneous moments of dancing when flesh finds its own expression, and the bones are so tuned to gravity that they stand by themselves. Then we are in the flowing space of nature where spirit moves freely.

As I deconstruct my manifesto, I find a spiritual orientation towards nature, the natural tendency of the body towards source: flesh, bones, attunement to gravity and a faith in tensegrity—the tensional integrity, floating compression and structural wholeness of the body that allows it to stand, and—for the most part—not to fall down, except by accident or dint of will. Unification, coherence, oneness and spontaneity echo in the manifesto. The words 'spirit' and 'freedom' appear together. Consequently, I believe that the use of language makes a difference to life-enhancement and learning. All of these connections will reappear in terms of my institute and pedagogy at the end of this section, but first, what about our topic of religion and Somatics?

What about Religion?

I left the practice of religion behind when I left Mormonism and began my studies in mythology with Joseph Campbell, listening to his astounding presentations of the creation stories of many related cultures and his critique of Christianity, Islam and Judaism as 'warrior

Figure 1: Sondra Fraleigh's Plant Us Butoh event at the Kayenta Labyrinth in 2010, Kayenta Utah, Sondra Fraleigh in the foreground.

god religions.' He taught that these male-oriented religions stop us at a wall of judgement and don't allow passage, being based on rituals of conformity rather than love. On the other hand, his expositions of 'The Classical Mysteries of the Great Goddess,' at the Theater of the Open Eye in New York inspired my journey in eco-feminism and appreciation of the feminine divine (Studies with Campbell in 1973–75). The goddess is a 'myth to live by,' to use the title of Campbell's book (1972). She is not a judge; she is a goddess who dances in holistic spirals, and her love is unconditional. My goddess journey unfolds scholastically in *Dance and the Lived Body* (1987: 141–58), and later from various perspectives throughout *Dancing Identity: Metaphysics in Motion* (2004, especially Chapter 7: 151–93).

The other stream related to religion, and to dance and Somatics, that has been important to me is Buddhism. My book *Dancing into Darkness: Butoh, Zen, and Japan* (1999) looks at butoh through the lens of Buddhism. My Buddhist teachers say that Buddhism is not a religion; rather, it is the practice of peace, compassion and meditation. I see Buddhism as a practice with psychological moorings that are helpful in everyday living. It teaches one how to live through adversity with an eye towards acceptance and transformation, as does Buddhist teacher Pima Chodron's book, *When Things Fall Apart* (2000). Such transformative potentials are also important in butoh. Metamorphosis, or bodily transformation, is important in my approach to dance and somatic studies; although I do not claim to be Buddhist, except in the very real sense that everything is pervaded by the Buddha mind. Looking into the shadows and admitting pain and suffering is central to Buddhism, to butoh, and in all of my work.

Butoh, the form of dance coming out of Japan after World War II and oriented towards performance and healing, explores spirit from a point of view akin to Zen Buddhism. In butoh as in Zen meditation, images can morph. In their 'suchness,' they are what they are, admitting darkness, earth and flesh. In her 'suchness' (as she is), the butoh dancer empties her face as she turns towards light, and waits for form on the verge: nothing special, everything special, as in Zen. Images in butoh are set in motion through non-rational surrealist methods, and in the morphic manner of Carl Jung, whose psychology explained the shadowy unconscious as a rich resource to be acknowledged. Jung might well have appreciated the spiritual darkness of butoh, had he lived to see it.

Of India, Constancy, and Land to Water Yoga

I began my study of yoga in my twenties with Hatha Yoga (physical yoga) and Kundalini Yoga (the yoga of awareness). These preceded my practice of Sidda Yoga (the yoga of devotion) and Integral Yoga (Aurobindo's yoga of consciousness and action). If I do the math, I see a yogic path lasting about 50 years. Since the year 2000, I have been developing a somatic form of yoga that I call 'Land to Water Yoga,' which originated through my travels in India in the year 2000, and was elaborated on through my study of the principle of constancy in human development—the unconditional love of the mother. I went to India to choreograph at the University of Baroda and to speak at the Indira Gandhi Cultural Center in New Delhi.

I also wanted to visit Mahatma Gandhi's ashram. During my travels, I discovered Integral Yoga at the ashrams of Sri Aurobindo and The Mother.

Gandhi's philosophy of non-cooperation with oppression had its precedent in the political activism of Sri Aurobindo, whose ashram still stands in Baroda in Gujarat where he first established his spiritual ministry after returning from his studies at Cambridge. Later in Pondicherry near Chennai (formerly Madras), Aurobindo founded an ashram that became famous with seekers from around the globe as a sanctuary for active meditation—his project of bringing peace and higher intelligence into the world that constitutes Integral Yoga. He taught that 'transformation does not come by contemplation alone; works are necessary, yoga in action is indispensable' (Aurobindo 1995: 527).

I became acquainted with Aurobindo through my frequent visits to his modest Ashram in Baroda. He was dead by this time, but in his spiritual and historical presence, I felt renewed, if only for the time being, in the breath of meditation and quiet sense of place at his ashram, set back from the clutter of the busy street of Sursagar. Principles of spiritual and social revolution took seed in the life of Sri Aurobindo, as they later manifest in the world through Gandhi and Ahimsa as nonviolent resistance to exploitation (Gandhi 1927).

Sri Aurobindo's meditations and writings on consciousness are augmented immeasurably by his spiritual complement, the French woman who sat by his side throughout her life and was known simply as 'The Mother.' As spiritual teachers, she and Aurobindo developed a philosophy of consciousness in practical paths of moral action, surrender of self and grace. They referred to God simply as 'The Divine,' a vision not personified or given particular form.

The Mother stands for the mother of all and bestows love equally, allowing everyone to experience unconditional love as constancy, the confident feeling that we can be whole and happy. Constancy through the comfort of the mother prompts the courage we find to explore, because it offers us safety. It is fitting that The Mother, who sat beside Sri Aurobindo, is not Indian by birth. In transcending culture, she becomes an even more transparent servant of the loving feminine divine.

The Mother was born in 1878 as Mirra Alfassa in Paris, daughter of Maurice Alfassa (born in Adrianople, Turkey, in 1843) and Mathilde Ismaloun (born in Alexandria, Egypt, in 1857). From a young age, she recognized a longing for the divine and an interest in transcendent spirit. Between the ages of eleven and thirteen, she recounts that she had a series of psychic and spiritual experiences, and she later had the direct intuition of going to India to meet the immanent divine that she had witnessed:

Not only the existence of God but also man's possibility of uniting with Him, of realizing Him integrally in consciousness and action, of manifesting Him upon earth in a life divine. This, along with a practical discipline for its fulfillment, was given to me during my body's sleep by several teachers, some of whom I met afterwards on the physical plane.

(The Mother 1998: 34)

My creation of Shin Somatics® Land to Water Yoga, and my book, *Land to Water Yoga* (Fraleigh 2009), had its beginnings in Baroda at Sri Aurobindo's ashram, as I contemplated the empty sandals of Sri Aurobindo and The Mother. I also practised physical yoga there for two months with a small group of acolytes who were all Indian. Daily, I sat with Indian devotees at the ashram; later I travelled to Gandhi's ashram, situated on the bank of the Sabarmati River just outside Ahmedabad in Gujarat, not far from Baroda.

My somatic version of yoga continued to evolve for ten years after that, growing episodically as I gained more perspectives on infant movement development and included the flow of dance and the meditative/metamorphic essence of butoh. My work continues to evolve, now with human development from infant to individual as one of the narratives. None of us had a perfect infancy or a perfect mother, but we can fill in the gaps, especially through moving consciously in somatic processes. Yoga, meaning, 'yoke', is a way of practising the unconditional love of the ideal mother: constancy, forgiveness and oneness.

By now it should be evident that my definition of spirituality is wide, that I admit transcendent possibilities, but that oneness forms the root of my understanding. We are each on our own perfect path, even if it is not always clear to us. At the same time, we are not alone. We are not separate from one another or from nature. Whatever we do to nature, we do to ourselves. Wherever we are is sacred space if we connect to it that way, and the earth we walk on is sanctified. 'Shin', the word that guides our work at Eastwest, gives us several related ways into the concept of oneness, as I elaborate next.

Shin Somatics

Shin Shin Ichi Jo: Body and Mind are One. 'Shin' is a multifaceted Japanese and Chinese word that guides our work at Eastwest. 'Shin' is also a Zen concept that has implication for a non-dualistic understanding of body. The body/mind identity problem that Western philosophy has tried to articulate is cleverly solved in Zen with two strokes that become one. I first encountered shin in Tokyo through my Zen teacher Shodo Akane's calligraphy. He created brush stroke calligraphy to capture the essence of my work in a word and symbol, and he told me that my work in the world was to 'bring beings together in learning.' He also gave me my Zen name, 'Bright Road Friend.' I'm not sure he understands the field of Somatics, so his charge to me was general. His did ask me to dance, though. When I hesitated, he said, 'Empty yourself, and dance.' So I did! (Fraleigh 1999: 166–70).

He explained his calligraphy to me this way: the strokes are 'Shin Shin Ichi Jo,' and they mean shin (body) and shin (mind) are one. He asked me to notice the top two symbols or words, to see how the word for 'body' and 'mind' are both 'shin,' even though they look different. I still ponder the significance of a single word that means both body and mind, and how the words also represent differences that merge into one. 'Shin' has many related meanings, which my friends in Japan tell me are open to poetic interpretation and point towards a malleable, morphic centre. As concerns our study here, 'shin' also means 'spirit.' I make conscious use of several meanings of 'shin' in Somatics, as will become more apparent in Part Two of this chapter.

In Shin Somatics®, we work with bodily responsiveness through movement and imagery. We are not integrating the body with the mind. They are already one. When people are not stressed and able to move consciously, their movement can assimilate control and spontaneity at once. Such movement has power, but not wilfulness. It also has grace, balance, ease and poise. It can breathe. The mover integrates these attributes and makes them shine. Her movement can stop, start and shift into retrograde as well as go ahead. It exhibits choice. When it has ebb and flow, it is boundless—as in shin. Somatic therapists work consciously with movement to bring about integrative qualities, which are improved from and function in the person as a whole. When people improve, they upgrade their lives.

Verbs of Permission at Eastwest

At Eastwest Somatics Institute, we consciously cultivate verbs of permission to facilitate basic movement patterns, somatic yoga, non-interfering touch, musical flow and intrinsic dance. The development of 'verbs of permission' is a unique and important aspect of our somatic outlook, although the germ of this concept can be found in the non-judgemental focus of the Feldenkrais Method®. Butoh, the postmodern dance of Japan included in our work, remembers body as spirit and respects beauty in awkwardness, pain and humour. We call our butoh-influenced dance processes 'metamorphic dance.'

Eastwest lessons in somatic kinesiology, integrative bodywork, and depth-movement dance excavate body memories and possible-selves. Our work is objective, also recognizing the existence of interdependent energy fields of great potential and light. We understand the importance of ma ('the space between' in Japanese, Zen, and butoh) and respect the space between ourselves and others as a pregnant pause, or perhaps a chasm, in which wisdom and transformation can appear. Compassionate connections are waiting to happen, alive in each moment of awareness, each person's complex, mindful movement and beautiful body. When a student in the Eastwest Japan Program in 2006 asked me to define the guiding principle of my work, I replied without hesitation, 'To encourage the natural being of each person to shine.' To me, all beings are beautiful: they demonstrate this potential, and are at their most beautiful in moments of surrender and learning.

Since Eastwest is a teaching institute, we make a concerted effort to study teaching methods that support our somatic practice. Students often ask me to clarify what is important to me in my own teaching, especially as they add their own ideas, and we work together. In order to summarize some key elements, I wrote the following letter:

Dear Students,

Here are some thoughts on what is important to me in my somatic teaching methods. I hope my letter piques your curiosity and our further discussion.

1. Cultivating verbs of permission in language and teaching concepts: verbs like *allow*, *attend to*, *permit*, *create*, *play with*, *find*, *try without trying*, *trust*, *rest* and *let go*. Dance itself is a verb of permission when it encourages spontaneity and freedom. Relative to permission is accident and forgiveness with verbs like *trip*, *fall*, *surrender* and *fail*. Yes, I encourage you to fail. Failure is part of *risk*, which is another great verb of permission.

2. Teaching with questions and not with commands. For example: 'What would it be like if you tucked your arm under you as you rolled over from front lying to back lying? What parts of your body need to soften or accommodate to allow this to happen?' You can insert questions a lot to keep the learning exploratory and keep the students curious. Command teaching can make people tense and goal oriented. If I demonstrate how to put the arm under the back and then say, 'do it this way,' I have wedded a model to a command. I can do this, and I do on occasion, but I should know when I'm doing this and have a good reason.

3. Simple imperatives stated in an exploratory context also work. Then they don't sound like commands. 'Lift your arm when you decide to move your leg,' would be an example of this. Student teachers often slip into a 'we' form of teaching, thinking that it is less demanding and more inclusive. However, it has the effect over time of infantilizing the class. An occasional inclusive 'we' is great, but overuse cloys. I encourage people in my pedagogy classes to strive for a variety of approaches in the way they introduce movement to a class.

4. Describing movement: not demonstrating the intended movement in becoming the role model. Avoid goal setting and the achievement of standards. Help! Don't we want people to excel and do well? Of course we do, and sometimes we need goals and standards, but we also need an inclusive way of learning that allows open-ended situations to develop. These are discovery modes of learning, and not oriented toward achievement. Babies, children, scientists and artists learn through discovery. Recognition of achievement comes later, and matters less than the learning.

5. Cultivating problem-solving in the classroom, or as I would rather call it 'framing potentials' to challenge learning or promote healing through dance and movement. I like the use of the word 'potentials.' Does everything have to be a problem?

6. In the spirit of all of the above, paying attention to what emerges as meaningful for individuals and the group, rather than imposing meaning from the teacher's point of view. This is actually fun for me, to see what I learn from the students—especially as they express what is happening for them in the movement, what changes in their bodies or what they experience and value as movers and dancers in response to others.

7. Holding Presence: Be present to the stories of your students and clients. Remember how to listen in the present, accepting outcomes you may not have envisioned. Remember

how we apply this in group relationships, and also how we use 'holding presence' as a concept in movement explorations and hands-on bodywork. One of the ways we learn how to hold presence without expectation or judgement is through the practice of meditation: sitting as a conduit between earth and heaven, attending to the breath and humming vibrations through the body to let go of any concerns or worries.

8. I favor teaching people to start from what is at hand, and to learn from there. If someone can't do what I'm asking, I need to adapt it so they can. In this, I have to give up imitation of form as a dominant way of teaching. But what about classicism? There are forms to be learned in dance classes of all kinds, and patterns to be replicated in Somatics. Yes, but do we need to begin there? When form emerges from emptiness, we see emergence as part of the form, as Taoists and Buddhists will tell you. There is nothing so beautiful as form on the verge, even in classical dance. The challenge is in how we internalize form. Skillful movement acquired through training and challenge does not depend on willful domination of ourselves (mind over movement), but discovery of efforts in harmony with intent. When we rid ourselves of willful mastery, the dance shines through.

9. Respecting individuality. Not advising, but rather exploring options with students, and encouraging them toward their own individual solutions. But isn't giving advice part of teaching? No, it isn't. Providing situations and space for learning is. Create 'ma' in your teaching; learning lies in the space between you and your students.

10. Not fixing: Focus on what is working well rather than on what needs fixing. This implies not judging, and not developing co-dependence.

11. One of the meanings of 'Shin' (a Japanese and Zen word that guides our work) involves patience and waiting. Wait when you don't know the answer, not needing to know. Better answers often come from the group or someone else, not the teacher. Be ready to step in with your thoughts when you feel strongly about them. Offer them as part of the whole, not the only answer. As for me, I would rather offer a poem than solve a problem for others. I like to solve my own problems, but just when I think I have things in hand, another mountain appears.

12. In group work, practice being part of the circle of learning yourself. Offer your expertise while knowing your role as a facilitator, ready to set boundaries. The latter means keeping the learning environment safe by teaching people to respect each other. Teachers often want to be loved, or at least liked. I would say respect is more important. This is where power and love meet with objectivity. Distance is a factor in allowing others to be who they are. We dance together and apart. Not needing to lean, we can lean, and we can also support. I hope this is helpful.

Addendum: I remember being terrified the first time I taught a dance class in my twenties. Be patient as you internalize your own teaching style and sense of freedom. It won't come overnight—but it will come—unbidden and riding a golden horse.
My best to all, Sondra

Figure 2: Plant Us Butoh at the Desert Rose Labyrinth in Kayenta, Utah. Dance arranged by Sondra Fraleigh for a public performance in 2010. Dancers are bottom to top, Meredith Haggerty, Chicago, and Kayoko Arakawa, Tokyo, Japan. Photographer: Teri Koenig.

Part Two: After Xenophanes

> Feelings are the expression of human flourishing or human distress as they occur in the mind and body [...] Life being a high wire act, most feelings are an expression of the struggle for balance, ideas of exquisite adjustments and corrections, without which, one mistake too many, the whole act collapses.
>
> (Damasio 2003: 6–7)

Somatics fascinates me as a field that embraces practices of embodiment, with conscious designs for benefiting human development through movement and psyche. Movement, body and soma (bodily affect in feeling and action, or the body as perceived by the self) are deeply embedded in philosophy, often hidden in discussions of nature and God. The ancient Greeks exhibit this deep embedding in their unification of body/mind/spirit in the tripartite psyche (sometimes called 'soul'). With the advent of phenomenology and neuroscience in the twentieth century, consciousness and perception take centre stage along with concerns for identity: self and other, individuality and community. The body-self as socially, culturally and historically constructed is a newer concern for sociology and philosophy, but personal identity, or self, is not constructed apart from genetic inheritance and environmental interactions. New technologies also interest philosophers as factors in transforming bodily awareness and the conventions reflecting the values of any individual or group. My question is: how can we glance the whole?

I narrow this question by looking back historically and by keeping to my somatic project. Here, I look briefly into the pre-Socratic backgrounds of philosophies of the body, and then move quickly towards the philosophy of Spinoza, an important foundation for unified views of body, movement and mind. Finally, I fast-forward through history to explain how phenomenology offers value for themes of embodiment in Somatics. Definitions of 'Somatics' and 'spirit' are developed within the narrative, for how can we know what we are talking about, if we haven't defined it? I endeavour to define simply, since this is not a volume on philosophy. However, I remember that in the unified doctrines of the East, philosophy and religion are one.

Xenophanes: Motionless, Unchangeable God

'Xenophanes' is not a name for nose drops. He is a pre-Socratic Greek philosopher and poet who lived in the latter fifth and early sixth century BC, postulating a poetic theology of a motionless god who was not like humans or other natural forms. Xenophanes, unlike the Greeks who followed, did not anthropomorphize God (Lesher 1992)—or should we say 'the gods', since the gods of Homeric and classical fame were many, and—very like humans—committed sins of adultery, theft, jealously and even murder. They were human in soma (the Greek word for a living body) but in greatly magnified proportions, perhaps in order that we might learn to appreciate the importance of feelings and emotions, and forgive our foibles.

The pre-Socratic philosophers of early Western cosmology posited movement as arising from a vacillation between opposites. Xenophanes envisioned a point of stillness in the centre. Our present day work in somatic studies has come a long way since Xenophanes; it is based on the premise of change, not stasis. We have come to appreciate the plasticity of the brain and soma through the work of science, art and education in the 21st century. Neurobiologists, such as Antonio Damasio (as quoted in the heading), are leading the way in science, while somatic movement practices provide laboratories in art, therapy and education.

Spinoza: God in Nature, Enabling Movement

Nature, a key term in my somatic manifesto, is central to the philosophy of Spinoza. Nature, for Spinoza, is an expression of God, of everything that is or can be—and humans are part of this oneness. Through Descartes, we inherit duality, the thinking soul and extended body, substantively different. The body/mind split, of which Descartes is accused, is actually a body/soul split, the latter being the seat of thought for him. As a contemporary of Descartes, Spinoza was deeply familiar with and contradicted his views. Countering the philosophy of Descartes, Spinoza theorizes substance as one and not two. Spinoza's identification of God with nature is at the heart of his metaphysics. He often uses the term 'Dues, sive Natura'— 'God, or Nature' (Audi 1995: 763).

Spinoza has influenced the history of biblical criticism, literature and such diverse 20th-century thinkers as Freud, Einstein and Damasio. Contemporary physicists have seen in his monism an anticipation of 20th-century metaphysics. The Dictionary of Philosophy cites him as a leading forebear of 20th-century mind-body identity theory (Audi 1995: 763). As with somatic studies, Spinoza identifies mind and body as one, and the emotions as part of the whole. The propositions of Part III of his Ethics (1958) are followed by 48 definitions of the emotions: desire, pleasure, pain, love, hatred, fear, hope, joy, sorrow, disappointment, humility, anger, pride, shame and more. Human feeling (soma in yet another of its guises) is a dynamic, living part of the seamlessness of life for Spinoza.

Mind and body are one for Spinoza, and later on for phenomenology; in both views, there is no causal interaction between the mind and the body, rather they are relational attributes of humans and other beings as well. A phenomenologist might say that 'mind', 'body', 'soul' and 'spirit' are words that describe qualities of experience and consciousness. Consider this somatic question: is pain a physical or mental phenomenon? Isn't it both? We commonly describe pain through its physical manifestations, its felt, psychic affects, and also through ideation, or sense impressions. These are related aspects of pain, one is not of necessity the cause of the other; rather, they are interdependent.

Unity of Soma and Spirit: First Approximation at Definitions

As we consider spirituality more closely in the contexts of Somatics and dance, we turn first towards its semantic root. 'Spirit' is commonly assumed to be an ethereal quality or ghostly entity that releases us from flesh, something other than body. Correlates of the word 'spirit' are: strength, ghost, soul, fire, feeling, guts, will, fortitude, moral fibre, determination, and more. Let us bracket such common qualifiers of 'spirit' and set them aside for now.

The word 'Somatics' is very broad, but its root returns us to the ancient Greeks (remember Xenophanes) and their word 'soma': the body as perceived by the self, or the experience of body—the latter referring to the cellular, watery, precognitive self. At the precognitive level, soma provides the conditions for perception and self-perception, as these are somatically founded in bodily experience. Perception is a neurological process with a cellular background, but we know it does not end there. Perception is vast: it underlies powers of observation and interpretation, and is key to understanding Somatic Movement and its possible modes. This chapter takes Somatics as its central definitional project, narrowing the wide field of somatic practices with the word 'movement'. Dance is movement, and more than movement, because its many forms are aesthetically and culturally constructed. When dance is taught or practised from a somatic point of view, it takes on a set of values associated with perceptual knowledge and experience.

A Lean Definition

Advancing a phenomenological definition which goes beneath assumed views and moves towards intention, let us say that Somatic Movement is: (a) movement structured around perceptual phenomena, and (b) movement interpreted through perceptual phenomena. A phenomenon is a thing—anything solid at hand, an object of the mind, a visible movement, a self-moving kinesthetic sensation, the perceivable qualities of a dance, a feeling or an emotion. Perception is a sensory precursor to affective-motivational and cognitive insight. Presentational and reflective knowledge build from there, as does practical knowledge, including somatic practices and conceptual intellect. All are rooted in sensitivities of perception and awareness, and can be observed in the responsive processes of somatic education. Perception is preverbal, global and not linear; conception, on the other hand, depends on words and linear thinking.

Somatic Intention

We could rightly say that somatic qualities (perceptual qualities) can be discerned in any and all movement, but movement that is structured and interpreted somatically involves conscious, intentional use. Let me provide some examples: In terms of movement structured around perceptual phenomena, could we ask about the intentions of the person structuring the movement? In a classroom, does the teacher have students' powers of observation and awareness in mind, or is she simply providing movement for them to follow? The intention of translating dance and yoga processes in bodywork also makes the somatic difference in the Shin Somatics® work we develop at Eastwest. We use dance and somatic yoga processes intentionally—as structural guides for bodywork techniques, defining flow patterns, improvisations, and finally choreographic emergence of whole compositions.

Somatic Context

One could also ask about the context or narrative sustaining particular kinds of movement. In a dance class where the visual look and virtuosic execution of the movement are part of the structure, does the teacher provide options in the learning process? In performance where movement will be judged, does the teacher minimize judgemental elements, or teach students how not to take criticism personally? Such questions assume that context and intention influence perception in learning.

Perceptual phenomena are perceivable aspects of body and movement. For instance, pain and joy are both perceptual phenomena. We might well wonder how these feelings can be thought of as 'things in themselves' (phenomena), and as the structural matter of movement. Consider the treatment of pain in many yoga classes, where the teacher knows an asana will be painful for most participants, so she asks students to go just to the edge of pain and no further. Or she might ask students to 'make friends with the pain.' This suggestion then becomes part of the narrative structure of her class. In another instance, a teacher might point out the potential for pain in a particular movement, but instruct students how to move behind or around the pain, and not to invite it. The teacher might modify the intended movement making it doable without pain. Or a teacher might ask students to go into pain and endure it: 'no pain, no gain.' Dancers face the question of pain on several levels in classes and performance. Asking students to endure pain is not a good idea if their health and well-being matter. In many cases, pain, or the avoidance of it, is part of the structural understanding of the movement. Pain is a somatic issue.

When movement is consciously structured with somatic potentials in mind, it is possible to work subjectively and productively with the paradigm of pain. One can learn how to transform through pain: how to listen to it and not be trapped in it. The potential for joy might be an intended part of movement structure also, as in a back arch with an upward lift of the chest. Process and intention are key elements of structured somatic movement explorations. Somatic designs for teaching movement encourage students to work and play through processes at their own pace and with their own bodily potential, learning as they go. Moving without expectations can, however, pose a delicate balance in educational settings. This brings us to the second half of the original definition above: movement interpreted through perceptual phenomena.

In terms of this, students might ask, 'How do I experience the movement?,' 'What happens to me in the movement?' or 'What do I understand or know about my relationship to the environment and others through the movement?' These would be subjective questions of perception, and particularly of somatic interpretation. As individuals, people will answer quite differently, even as they often find perceptual similarities. We observe and tender these varied matters of perception daily in somatic studies, as people describe their experiences or show them nonverbally in movement and dance explorations.

In summary, we see that a major purpose of somatic practice is the structure and interpretation of movement experience. Of course, we know that improvement through movement is also a purpose. Do I feel better? What has changed in my sense of self, in my body or in my relation to others? Do I feel stuck, or can I step forward with a purpose? Am I ready to accept unpredictable outcomes? Can I improvise with results as in a dance, or am I attached to guarantees? These would be subjective, interpretive and self-reflective questions. How can I maintain forward momentum without slipping back? How others judge the movement or the dance is a less important question in somatic contexts.

Movement and Awareness

If movement is designated as somatic, it already has a stated context. We could rightly say that all movement is somatic because it is felt in the personal body. As a phenomenon (something that appears to consciousness), movement is both kinematic study and kinesthetic orientation. We can study it conceptually, but we know it first through sense perception and soma. Movement does not really exist as a singular phenomenon. It includes sight—seeing where we are going—and all of the senses interactively. Movement and feeling belong to each other. Awareness, an influential concept in somatic studies, builds upon such perceptual matters. To bring the dimension of awareness to movement is a conscious act. We do not automatically ask ourselves how our every movement feels, or what effect it is having on us.

Somatic Field

Somatic Movement, as such, designates a whole field of available movement modes with their accompanying states of awareness. Some modes that I understand are: (a) movement and dance designed for conscious learning, (b) re-patterning of dysfunctional movement, (c) explorations of self-awareness through movement, (d) methods to improve performance, (e) exercises in extending imagination, (f) sitting and moving meditations for self-development and well being, (g) informally presented dance events to promote community, (h) dance and movement experiences in relation to natural and architectural environments and on camera, (i) interaction with others through dance and movement and (j) integrative bodywork. Four general categories of movement emerge from this—aesthetic, educational, interactive and therapeutic.

Spirituality and Embodiment

Chasing

The reader may have noticed that we left spirit behind in an effort to say more about the broad field of Somatics. Pursuing spirit in its possible connections to somatic topics, especially the human body, Spinoza's philosophy can assist once more. Spinoza saw opposites as integrated, which got him into trouble with both the synagogue and the church. He regarded what many saw as the most other of others, namely God, as integrated with nature. This would be, then, an immanent God, and in Spinoza's day, this was heresy. He made claims like the one in the Fifth Part of his Ethics Proposition XXIV: 'The more we understand individual objects, the more we understand God' (Spinoza as cited in Wild 1958: 385). He further saw the human body as part of nature and eternity, quite a spiritual turn. In Ethics, Fifth Part, Proposition XXII, he also says: 'In God, nevertheless, there necessarily exists an idea which expresses the essence of this or that human body under the form of eternity' (Spinoza as cited in Wild 1958: 384). Thus, he attempts to integrate apparent dichotomies: God and Nature as well as human embodiment and eternity. Spinoza held a very unpopular notion for his day—that the human mind is the idea of the human body. Because of this, he is widely regarded as a philosopher of unity.

Embodiment of Mind and Spirit

Spinoza saw movement as a quality of nature and thus of humans, pointing towards today's discoveries of embodiment of mind in neurobiology. In the everyday practice of somatic work, I experience that mind is qualitatively expressed in movement, dance and bodywork, and that an understanding of mind as embodied is necessary for health and wholeness. We can identify realizations as embodied knowledge, as Karen Barbour shows in her book, *Dancing Across the Page: Narrative and Embodied Ways of Knowing* (2011). My question to students when we move together is often, 'What is available to you now?' This question presupposes an intrinsic connectivity of body, mind and spirit, as well as the power of choice. The Feldenkrais Method®, together with phenomenology, gives me this perspective.

Shin as Spirit

As I mentioned in Part One, 'shin' has several related meanings. *Body*, *mind*, *spirit*, *soul*, *heart*, *centre* and *tree trunk* are a few I identify with. These attributes are all parallel in shin. We have already seen in Part One that 'shin' is 'body and mind at once.' What we now see is that 'shin' is also 'spirit.' Differences can be expressed through words, signifying varieties of experience, but words do not change the essence of oneness when this is the truth of an experience. Through my work in Shin Somatics®, I bring attention to what is already one. My butoh mentor, Yoshito Ohno, son of Kazuo Ohno-sensei, inspired me with further meaning of 'shin' in a butoh workshop. He compared shin to a slow growing orchid representing 'the patience of not starting' (Fraleigh 2010: 218). In his classes, I follow every molecule of motion into stillness.

In Japan, I present my work through body as spirit. My Japanese students suggested the simple beauty of this phrase. Their language is pictorial and rich in imagination, even in script. If, as I learned in Japanese phenomenology, spirit is present as a quality of embodiment (Nagatomo 1992: 215–21), we can say that through embodiment, spirit also manifests in qualities of movement; any change or improvement of movement has the potential of enhancing spirit. It is obvious that we are never quite complete as bodies. We are creating the human qualities that we embody throughout our lives. We can twist our faces into the shapes of disgust everyday, or live with gratitude. Thoughts and movements shift soma. Quietude signals rest and momentary completion.

Looking West

I have noticed in my work with individuals that they often associate spirit with a depth of feeling that wells up in them, and with heartfelt emotions of tenderness and love. Wilfulness drops away at such times, and there is readiness to receive as well as to give. Because I am a phenomenologist, I believe we can and should describe 'spirit' as an aspect of consciousness, available to us through awareness. Philosophy is not much good if it doesn't inform how we think and live. The conceptual axis of phenomenology arose first in Europe through Husserl, who taught that consciousness is always consciousness of something. Can this 'something' be spiritual? Can we be conscious in a spiritual way? Can aspects we commonly think of as spiritual come to consciousness? Of course they can, and they do, every day, when we ready our bodies and become consciously aware of being in this state of openness to giving and receiving.

Closer to Experience: Embodied Relationships

Phenomenology in Action

When I work with my hands through the Shin Somatics® processes I have evolved in relation to Feldenkrais principles, yoga, intuitive dance and experiential anatomy, I experience time, space and expression in embodied relationships. I understand my relationship with the other who is not me; yet we are in touch in the moment of awareness. Something intangible exists in the space between us. I listen with my heart and hands, as I ground my feet through my root chakra. Sometimes I feel a lack of connectivity in the person I am working with or in myself. I do not make an effort to affect wholeness, however. Rather, I wait, trusting that there is an intrinsic integration that my body and the body of the other can find together. This is the dance. I regard myself as a catalyst. If healing or improvement is available, it will not come through me, but through healing tendencies of the body. The body-self seeks balance and integration. The ground of being is not chaos. As Einstein is often rumoured to say in addressing issues of quantum mechanics, 'God does not play dice with the universe.' Building trust in a friendly universe is highly beneficial for those who would be healers.

I also realize that people can unconsciously prevent improvement for many reasons. But I need to bracket that realization. I use gentle micro-movement techniques that invite and listen for developmental paths to become available. I am not doing anything to anyone; rather, I enter a process together with my client. I let go of doing, and enter the space between us. I am not just sending good wishes. Wishful thinking and divine provenance are not what I teach. I do not consider that I have any special healing powers, nor do I teach anything about higher powers or the soul. Whatever my own beliefs, it is not my role to teach in this capacity. I do believe that most anyone can learn how to be with others in a beneficial way, and that putting people at ease can be learned. Healing begins with feelings of ease rather than disease.

At Ease

In Shin Somatics® processes, we learn specific ways of communicating, both verbal and nonverbal, how to 'hold presence' with and for someone, how to move with the client and how to wait for releases through listening touch, with permission to move on. We work within structures, flow patterns and bodywork choreographies, but the body of the other shows the way to carry out the dance. Once set in motion, integrative bodywork is a kind of wonderful body talk—a conversation without words—an intuitive dance, intrinsic and responsive. Even so, words are very important in setting the tone of any interaction; thus, we study effective communication skills. Listening, not judging, not interpreting and not advising, we encourage options in thought processes and life situations. A woman I worked with recently said that through our lesson on the jaw and tongue, she understood that she had been holding her head up with her neck and causing stress, rounding her shoulders forward, which caused her chin to jut out. These were her discoveries. I taught her how to let her neck hang down from her jaw, high up from the temporomandibular joint (TMJ), and that she could at the same time allow the dome of her head (her lotus crown) to float upward. She said everything changed for her, physically and spiritually.

Somatics, Intuition and Phenomenology

First Person Voice

What if I say for the sake of discovery, 'I don't know what this thing (this phenomenon) is?' I could adopt this stance towards Somatics—as a term or a whole field of study—as I did earlier. Preceding such analysis, I might go intuitively, descriptively into the topic. I could save analysis for later. Such descriptive escapades have poetic value, and they also release what one knows or has experienced so that something new can emerge. The pedestrian aesthetic of American postmodern dance came out of such a venture, as its pioneers said 'no' to received notions of dance. Butoh, the postmodern dance of Japan, resulted from Hijikata Tatsumi's refusal to accept received definitions of dance, both Eastern and Western. The descriptive function of phenomenology is likewise associated with originative experience, creative impulse and first person intuitive voice. Phenomenological descriptions study experience in other words, as do somatic processes. One can take this in any direction, letting perception well up naively, as I do below, directing my attention somatically out towards nature and in towards home.

Third Eye Experience

Last night in Utah, I walked under the early October moon of Saint George, colours galore in sight of the fading cliffs and receding mountains. The malingering moon was first in my vision, then behind me. As I moved my position relative to its glow—an astonishing shift—I was amazed. Yes, I can imagine a giant eye seeing me from behind, as I had tried to imagine years ago in a butoh class with Ashikawa Yoko in Tokyo. But this time, it is an integral part of my experience in the moment, and the warm eye seeing me from behind is, in reality, the moon, silvery-peach, near and neutral. I fell in love with the world again—as the valley city disappeared through my third eye from behind and above me, stars of the darkening Southwest sky lifted my crown in gratitude. Home, at last.

Reflections on Experience

Somatic studies and phenomenology have the same central questions: How can we be with our experience? How can we listen to it and learn from it? How can we expand our experience? 'Love,' 'freedom' and 'illumination' might just be other words for spiritual experience, the kind that is always with us, as part of our nature not bound by the content of personality. This level of experience is available to all, and not just some. The paradox is in arriving there, because there is no place to go. I arrive through dance and walking at night. Meditation brings me there—as does teaching and moving consciously with others. We all have ways of arriving and know what they are.

Analysis Comes after Description in Phenomenology

Investigating Experience, A Brief History

Merleau-Ponty wedded experience with theory through his descriptions of embodiment and perception in *Phenomenology of Perception* (1962), and in his last work (which was never completed), *The Visible and the Invisible* (1968). He provided a way into critical discourse on arts and the body that is still foundational. What was new for philosophy through the phenomenology of Merleau-Ponty, Heidegger and Simone de Beauvoir? They sought a more concrete experiential voice, the first person, expanded finally through theoretical analysis. Merleau-Ponty developed an aesthetic and psychological voice. Beauvoir, the heroine of my book *Dancing Identity* (2004), lent phenomenology a female voice, both feminist and ethical in *The Second Sex* (1957). Susan Kozel's work is a recent addition. I appreciate her investigations in *Closer*, a book on phenomenology and computer technology, with dance forming the bedrock of her investigations (2007).

I can't copy any of my mentors: I have had to find a dancer's way through the thicket of phenomenology. My lifelong learning has expanded through reading and travel, and by living in American and Indian ashrams with shorter stays at Zen centres in Japan. I was introduced to depth movement processes at the Mary Wigman School in Berlin in the 1960s. Thus in my twenties, I was already preparing a somatic focus. I don't know what all of this adds up to, but I have risked and really had fun. I hope I'm wiser than I was at twenty, but I'm not sure. I don't want to forget the past. I continue to learn from it.

I continue to seek understanding of how varied movement experiences become affective, and how feelings (the somata of consciousness) can flow from struggle towards balance in movement—the high wire act Damasio lays out in the quote at the beginning of this part of my chapter. I do not believe that all instances of dance and yoga promote joy, health and balance, but if they are conceived consciously through the charming medicine of care, they can. In healing the body, we heal our earthly home and recognize our oneness. We have learned a lot since Xenophanes.

References

Audi, R. (ed.) (1995), *The Cambridge Dictionary of Philosophy*, New York, NY: Cambridge University Press.

Aurobindo, S. (1995), *Letters on Yoga, Volume Two, Part II*, Pondicherry, India: Sri Aurobindo Press.

Beauvoir, S. de (1957), *The Second Sex* (trans. and ed. H. M. Parshley), New York, NY: Knopf.

Campbell, J. (1972), *Myths to Live By*, New York, NY: Viking Books.

Chodron, P. (2000), *When Things Fall Apart: Heart Advice for Difficult Times*, Boston, MA: Shambhala.

Damasio, A. (2003), *Looking for Spinoza: Joy, Sorrow and the Feeling Brain*, Orlando, FL: Harcourt, Inc.

Fraleigh, S. (1987), *Dance and the Lived Body: A Descriptive Aesthetics*, Pittsburgh, PA: University of Pittsburgh Press.

—— (1999), *Dancing into Darkness: Butoh, Zen, and Japan*, Pittsburgh, PA: University of Pittsburgh Press.

—— (2004), *Dancing Identity: Metaphysics in Motion*, Pittsburgh, PA: University of Pittsburgh Press.

—— (2009), *Land to Water Yoga: Shin Somatics Moving Way*, New York, NY: iUniverse Inc.

—— (2010), *Butoh: Metamorphic Dance and Global Alchemy*, Urbana, IL: University of Illinois Press.

Gandhi, M. K. (1927), *An Autobiography, or The Story of My Experiments with Truth* (trans. M. Desai), Ahmedabad, India: Nanajivan Publishing House.

Kozel, S. (2007), *Closer: Performance, Technologies, Phenomenology*, Cambridge, MA: The MIT Press.

Lesher, J. H. (1992), *Xenophanes of Colophon: Fragments: A Text and Translation with Commentary*, Toronto, Ont: University of Toronto Press.

Merleau-Ponty, M. (1962), *Phenomenology of Perception* (trans. C. Smith), London, UK: Routledge & Kegan Paul.

—— (1968), *The Visible and the Invisible* (trans. A. Lingis), Evanston, IL: Northwestern University Press.

Nagatomo, S. (1992), *Attunement through the Body*, Albany, NY: State University of New York Press.

Spinoza, B. (1958), 'Ethic', in J. Wild (ed.), *Spinoza: Selections*, New York, NY: Charles Scribner's Sons.

The Mother. (1998), *The Mother on Herself*, Pondicherry, India: Sri Aurobindo Ashram Press.

Chapter 12

Conversations about the Somatic Basis of Spiritual Experiences

Sylvie Fortin, Ninoska Gomez, Yvan Joly, Linda Rabin,
Odile Rouquet and Lawrence Smith

Prologue

At the time I received the invitation to participate in this book, I was with a friend of mine, Christine, who had a malignant brain tumour. Christine was an ex-dancer and university professor who had reoriented her career as a psychologist. In fact, I was one of three friends taking care of her. Michelle was responsible for all the legal matters. Louise supported Christine with all her medical appointments over three years, and I acted as a kind of witness to her spiritual journey, which included the promise to do my best to keep contact with her 16-year-old son after her death. As a Feldenkrais practitioner, I gave her some hands-on lessons in the last year of her life. I will always remember her reactions after the first few sessions. Completely astounded, she would say, 'She is still there … I am still here … there is still a Christine, not sick.' I could feel the deep connection between her and me, and could recognize our capacity to touch the 'core' of her, of me and of something very difficult to name, something ineffable and timeless. I remember once, in the spa on the terrace behind her house, Christine saying to me, 'Sylvie, on a larger scale, my life is nothing. Look at this leaf, it will live one season. It is its contribution. Me, I will have lived 50 something years. I am not really afraid of death … life is so beautiful.' In the last year of her life, she shared with me her quest in exploring different religions and spiritual meanings of life and death. It is maybe this context that made me accept the invitation to join the authors of this book, but at the same time alter their request slightly by suggesting a collage of individual interviews with friends who all happen to be experienced and internationally known somatic educators involved in the field of dance. To me, this was a way to pursue the journey Christine had launched. At the same time, what follows is also a tribute to Ninoska Gomez, Yvan Joly, Linda Rabin, Odile Rouquet and Lawrence Smith, the participants in this constructed group conversation, who nurtured my individual spiritual quest at different times in my life. I am deeply grateful to them.

Each of them teaches a specific method of somatic education: Somarhythms for Ninoska, Feldenkrais® for Yvan, Continuum and Body-Mind Centering® for Linda, Analysis of the Body in Danced Movement for Odile and the Alexander Technique for Lawrence.[1] Their narratives offer their own personal synthesis, informed by the specific methods they teach which, as is the case with other somatic methods in the larger field of somatic education, are not aligned with any one specific spiritual or religious tradition (Williamson 2010). All participants are over 50 years old and have taught, or are still teaching, in a variety of dance and/or somatic settings. They all come from different cultures (Québécois, French, Jewish, American, South

Figure 1: Name of the sculpure: A la mi-carême. Year: 2007. Artist: Nicole Cossette. Made of: Paper and acrylic. Photograph: Aïdan Trochon-Hanrahan.

American); however, I did not take this cultural diversity as a point from which to conduct comparative interviews. Inspired by feminist research (Ramazanoglu and Holland 2002), I allowed myself to follow the flow of a spontaneous conversation with each of them. After briefly explaining my project of a group conversation by creating a collage of individual responses, I asked them open-ended questions about the possible place of spirituality in their professional life. I did not have an original conversation guide. In feminist research, it is common to think that approaching a phenomenon with preconceived notions of what should be discussed can inhibit valuable underlying issues that could emerge. As Campbell and Salem put it, respondents 'must be in the driver's seat of research' (1999: 67). Thus, I let each of the somatic educators orient the conversation in ways that were meaningful to them. Since there is little 'methodological elitism' or agreement of 'methodological correctness' in feminist research (Reinharz 1992), when it came time to construct the final collage, I trusted my creativity in making links between what they had said individually. At the end of the process, I invited the interviewees to make changes if they desired, but I unavoidably left a personal mark on the final conversation by my choice of the specific excerpts. As a researcher who, in the past, has conducted studies in both positivist and postpositivist epistemological traditions, I felt at ease that such a postpositivist approach would provide a valuable contribution to an inquiry about spirituality. Revealing what these five somatic educators valued, when suggesting a conversation about spirituality to them, fills a gap in the literature. As it stands, the current literature on spirituality in the arts is in its very early stages and even more incipient when examining an area such as Somatic Movement Dance Education (SMDE). Consequently, the following fictitious gathering aims to widen our appreciation of possible spiritualities within the field of Somatics. As such, some echo a theological monotheistic conception of the divine, others embrace an atheist perspective, some emphasize the mysteries of the 'great beyond' and others attempt to reconnect science with somatic processes.

LAWRENCE:	It's weird that you are asking me for an interview about spirituality, because I'm an atheist; I don't like to proceed by belief and faith. I like to have an explanation for things.
NINOSKA:	We humans have always wanted to understand what is more complex than ourselves. For one system to be able to understand another system, the first has to be more complex. Thus, we face the contradiction that to understand ourselves, we would need to be more complex than ourselves. We understand our complexities as humans more and more, but it is difficult to think that one day we will understand everything. So spirituality is, for me, about life's mysteries.
LAWRENCE:	Actually, I prefer to talk of 'consciousness' rather than spirituality. 'Spirituality' implies that there is a 'spirit', but this term is so loaded with religious connotations. Usually, the spirit is thought of as

something that exists beyond the physical body and brain that might continue when the body dies. I don't believe that, but that is the foundation of most religious thought. I think what people seek from religion is assurance of the continuity of consciousness. Yet, looking for consciousness may be a bit like looking for the spirit, in that I don't believe that any neuro-researcher has yet come forward with a claim of seeing concrete evidence of consciousness of self as a specific brain pattern—we haven't yet seen evidence of a physical spirit. When people use the term 'spirit,' are they not referring to that part of themselves, real or imagined, that might be theoretically considered as apart from brain and body—that part of us that knows we are feeling and moving, but which has not yet been viewed by brain scans? Is that not the same thing as consciousness?

YVAN: There is more and more recognition of the scientific validity of the contribution of meditation and mindfulness in healing for the prevention of cancer and helping people deal with heart disease. So-called 'spiritual' issues are becoming the object of scientific interests. Somatic education—at least the Feldenkrais Method, which is the method I know—has a lot of virtues that can be transposed to a certain spiritual outlook, what I call 'a non-denominational spiritual path.' The problem is to determine what we mean by 'spirituality.' Originally, the word refers to 'the spirit,' which is in itself an oddity in somatic education, where we address the person as an embodied whole, not as a sum of separated parts—and surely not as a body animated by a spirit. Maybe there's such a thing as 'the spirit,' but in the context of somatic education, we are involved with incarnation and embodiment. So for me, whatever we put under the headline of 'spirituality' has nothing to do with the spirit, as separated from the mind, as separated from the emotions, as separated from the body and the sensations and all the usual partitions of the person. But if we mean by 'spirituality' a sense of connectedness to the world out there, the nurturing of a certain quality of harmony with ourselves, with others around us and with the environment, then we may have a conversation. To make an analogy, as many astronauts or astrophysicists report 'spiritual' insights in their exploration of the vast world 'out there,' somatic educators, in their exploration of the vast world 'in there' cannot *not* be affected in their perception of life itself.

ODILE: Indeed, defining 'spirituality' is not easy. I would say that being embodied is spiritual in a way. Actually, I also don't make categories such as physical, psychological or spiritual, because all these are interrelated. Spirituality is more about an attitude towards life, toward the world. Different attitudes are linked to different rules of conduct, different processes, different ethics. Embedded in somatic education is already an idea of respect towards other human beings, which is a spiritual attitude. Of course, there are different ways of talking about it. If I am within Zen religion, I will not have the same relationship with the environment than if I am a Christian, because Christianity is based on a person who was embodied. It provides a kind of model based on Trinity. God exists in three persons. It is a mystery, but that means that there is a dialogue or relationship between three perspectives, spaces or dimensions. It is not necessarily three persons but a concept of triangulation between three elements or components or anything. That means that most important is the interaction between rhythm, space and matter for a movement to be embodied or an open relationship between the teacher and the student to be giving birth to space. This is why I say that religion, or what we believe in, influences the way we teach and how we talk and relate to people.

YVAN: When I talk about spirituality, I don't refer to any kind of religion. That is a whole different topic, because religions are like ways to frame spirituality and enunciate values for morality, how we should behave and how to situate oneself in a tradition. In the context of the Feldenkrais method of somatic education, it's not at all an issue of helping people to find a way to live dictated by any kind of external principles. On the contrary, the project is to help people learn how to reestablish their inner authority.

ODILE: If we put the notion of God behind the spiritual attitude I am talking about, it will certainly not be an authoritarian God. In Catholicism, there is a person relating to another person: the Christ. It is a belief that there is another person, a loving person, with whom I can dialogue and get inspired. That gives a model for relationship, what I referred to earlier regarding a spiritual attitude towards people and towards the world. For example, in teaching I can't manipulate the dancer who is in front of me. I have to develop dialogue and not establish a rapport of authority/submission.

NINOSKA: I think the best way to live our spirituality is in the action, in the way we behave. As I have matured, I have been finding out what makes me grow and brings peacefulness. I feel I am a sort of 'tree,' that needs these weather conditions, and this water, and this and that. Rather than trying to grasp religion or spirituality as such,

I have come to understand my limits, my constraints as a form, and at the same time this form is a way to define my possibilities, which are enormous. So I view spiritual teachings as different points of view on how we can use our possibilities and have come to discriminate a spiritual teaching from a dogmatic teaching. Personally, somatic education allowed me to develop a context to understand that we are a whole, we are one. And that is a mystery— there are so many things I can't explain, we can't explain. It helped me to understand that all the religions, no matter what they are, are perspectives that have developed in a given social context for diverse reasons. People explain things in a certain manner, different forces interact with each other, wars happen, there are different ways to defend the essential principles of life. But do we need a master who tells us what to do? I have also come to understand that all religions are saying, in one way or another, that God is in you. The supreme force is in you. The mysteries of life are within us. To me, 'spirituality' is to tame that, it is to refine my being, to become more aware of this power.

LINDA: There's the whole big question about religion and the impact it's had on us and our view of spirituality. In my younger years, spirituality was associated with religion, and that meant with the Judeo-Christian tradition. Growing up female in a patriarchal environment, a Jewish home in a Catholic province, I felt, 'Okay, I've got to say "stop" to this; this is affecting my development as a woman in many ways.' Or at least, that's what it was like in those days. And then, when the sixties came, with the hippie revolution, there was so much liberation and freedom. Everybody was in search of spirituality, and we went to the East and we found Hinduism and certainly Buddhism. And then, in the seventies and eighties, what evolved out of that was the New Age. For me, personally, I don't feel that I'm practising in a formal way of any kind. I'm not practising a spiritual practice, but I feel that there is a spiritual quality in the way I live my life. I'm interested in what is beyond the evident, how everything in life is connected. And that always feeds me. With Continuum, I feel it is a movement and somatic practice that is like a spiritual practice, or at least it's a practice that lets me feel my spirituality while being in my body in movement, with breath and sound, and in a resonant field with others. It's all woven in.

YVAN: For me, spirituality is a certain sense, a feeling of being connected to more than just the inner or outer surface of our skin, what is sometimes referred to as 'Greater than Thou.' In the context of somatic education, it's a very common misunderstanding to think that when you go inside, you stay stuck inside. Jokingly, I call this excess an internal bellybutton gazing or navel contemplation. On the contrary, diving deep down inside is actually a spring board to connect to the world around us, the environment, other beings and life itself.

LAWRENCE: Zen monks show simultaneous high activity in extrinsic and intrinsic neural networks, one involved in exteroception, the other in interoception (Lioa 2011). This is not seen in the brains of other subjects tested. Interestingly, it is just this simultaneous activity, a melding of proprioception with perception of the surrounding environment, which is sought in the Alexander Technique.

ODILE: When somatic work is too focused on a narcissistic exploration of one self, I am not interested, because it is a dead end to me: it is not anymore about movement, about relationships, about an internal intent and an external intent. It is difficult to name it exactly, but I see clearly when we are at a level of life, giving birth to movement, or when we are at a lethal level.

YVAN: In a certain way, for some people, that might be how it starts. It's like you turn your attention inside and you interiorize yourself. There's nothing 'outside' that is not connected to something inside of us. So, whenever we help anyone to have a better sense of themselves, I think we affect their sense of connectedness to themselves, yes, but we also affect the continuity between each person and all the environment. So, if I talk about spirituality, it is with this caveat: it has paradoxically nothing to do with the spirit in itself. What I experience of myself is an embodied phenomenon; it's a neurological and biological phenomenon. When we address spirituality, people still have such a strong commitment to think that they 'have' a mind, and that their mind can influence their body and their body can influence their mind or their spirit, for that matter. This is such a deeply engrained historical philosophical error. I think that the functional integration of our own person is still something to be discovered, including in places that have so much sophistication in the process of awareness and consciousness. I hear this body-mind split, including in the domain of mindfulness and within many meditational practices, where people still make such a fuss about 'the mind,' as if it were existing in itself. Somatic integration of the person still has a long way to go, including within the field of consciousness studies.

LAWRENCE: Recently, I had a discussion on meditation with a Hasidic Rabbi; yes, in an Alexander lesson. I was comparing the non-doing in Alexander Technique to that of certain kinds of meditation. He stated that the meditation of which I was speaking was different from what he considered meditation. In his, he was looking for God, whereas in mine, I was looking for my higher self. (Actually, I am just sitting observing my plain old lower self, but that is another discussion.) I replied that I do not think that one can know what he is looking for until he finds it. Alexander famously wondered why people believed that they could do something that they have never done. Perhaps these things, God and the higher self, are one and the same, and perhaps the tools used in the search are also similar.

NINOSKA: When I refine my sensations, I try to connect to the most intimate part of myself—a tiny place of me, and when I get there, it is incredible. All the explanations we have created are not enough to explain what we discover from our sensing. We discover more and more about sensing, body organization, the organization of the universe and all the analogies we find everywhere. So, somatic education helped me understand links. Spirituality, for me, is just a way to describe a facet of the whole, a name for those aspects of ourselves that we don't understand, a way by which we describe the forces that organize the universe beyond our control.

LINDA: Years ago, I had a very profound shift in my consciousness from one of my Alexander sessions. I was opening myself up to something that was beyond dance movement and day-to-day physical activities, from a muscle and bone perspective. I was thinking there must be something more and beyond that. The teacher was trying to get my pelvis into alignment, and I can't remember if it was that I was too tucked under and she wanted it more out, or it was too out and she wanted it more under. But whatever it was, it felt wrong to me, and I was resisting. Finally, she was able to get me there, meaning that my body and psyche accepted being there. When I left, I started to feel the knots in my brain unravel. That's the metaphor that came to me. It felt like when you have a knot and you tease out the threads. I got on the bus then looked at people in front of me, and it was if I had X-ray vision: I could see inside them. I could see how they were harmonious or not. I could see one part of their body was contracted. Another part was more flowing; or they were unhappy, but they were pretending not to be unhappy. I could see the mix and mess, or the confusion of messages in the body. I was seeing so clearly. It was as if I knew what to do to bring about more harmony and clarity. And I thought, 'Gee, I'm hallucinating. What's going on here?' Later, when I started teaching at the Batsheva Dance Company, I remember at the barre I was able to see how the dancers' bodies were flowing, or not, from head to toe. I was in my Alexander awareness. Clearly, something had expanded in my vision of what I saw in the body, as well as the space around the body. And when I worked with people choreographically, my relationship to space and the flesh, they weren't separate. There was a dialogue between the body and space; the body itself was made up of space. Sometimes, I would talk about how the body was like a sieve, or like cheesecloth, that the air could pass through the fibers, in and out—it was so receptive and responsive. And I relate that to perceiving something beyond just, 'Here's the body, here's the dance floor, here's choreography and here we express our material/matter selves.' It was about expressing ourselves with some kind of universal awareness as well.

ODILE: Dancers can easily be mystic. It is not only movement that attracted them to dance, because they could have chosen sport. They are looking for something else than movement—to express themselves on a deep level, and to get in touch with the universal laws of life.

LINDA: In my case, there was an interweaving of a search. That searching had to do with looking for what is of the essence, what is at the root, the source, what is the truth. But I was already curious about that at a young age. When I went into dance, those ideas got awakened further through different teachers I had. Not because it was brought out in any deliberate way, but because the way they 'languaged' their teaching struck a chord and continued to wake up that awareness in me. You know, it could even have been something as simple as when I was studying the Graham technique: all of the spiritual aspects of the energy rising through the spine and speaking about the contraction, of bowing to the earth, of our connection with earth and then towards the heavens and of man as in between. It's speaking a language that goes beyond the mundane, beyond day-to-day living. There were metaphors and images that were brought into the class that spoke about something larger than the self. I felt that with José Limón, through a more noble language, and also with Anna Sokolow. She was such a minimalist. You couldn't do anything extraneous—she wouldn't allow for it—so you had to tap into something very deep in yourself. So I would say that, already, in my early professional training, and probably before that, it was awakened in me, and it was cultivated further. At Julliard, I had classes with Lulu Sweigard in Ideokinesis. So already then, we were looking at freeing up the body, which, at that time, I only appreciated as a tool to help me with my dancing. In retrospect, I see it as a step that brought me along my path toward somatic practices, which is related to my spiritual path. But we have an expression in English: 'What came first, the chicken or the egg?' I can't say. Did it start because it really was something in me, from a very young age, or is it due to the encounters I had with different teachers from a young age? For example, my Hebrew education went from kindergarten through to the ninth grade. When we studied the Bible, the Torah, we were always given the understanding that whatever we were reading, there was always another message to be understood, another interpretation you could look for. So this search for what lies beneath the surface was already introduced to me then. An early education … I wonder if that's how it all began.

YVAN: Historically, for me, having a relationship to something greater than myself has been important through all my upbringing, but it was then a mixture of religion weaved with morality and rules of behavior. So at one point, I realized, 'This is really not working for me, and I'm being abused by a system dictating my behaviour.' It was a great disappointment to realize what religion was all about. And I threw away the baby with the bath water. I just pushed away these questions, and I oriented my life in a different way, eventually turning my attention inside in order to find meaning. Then I realized that with the work that I'm doing now, that there is a deep sense of connectedness to something greater than just myself. And it's not that I'm always in touch with that, but I feel that in my work, I nurture that. So there's a very strong root of religion— meaning, 'religare' in Latin, which just means 'feel that you are related, connected.' So that's one root of my current non-denominational path. The other important source is Moshe Feldenkrais, but he was always very, very aloof about these issues. A few times, when we caught him at the right time, when he felt like it, he would extrapolate on his description of his method. For example, he would say that giving Functional Integration lessons is a work of love. You have to love the person or to find a way to love the person, in the greater sense of the word. You need to have a relationship of mutual acceptance, deep compassion for the person, and from there you can interact and create a lesson for that person to improve their movement qualities and learn what they need to learn in order to do what they want. But he was also aware that if you say, 'Learn the embodied love process,' it's a little tricky in our society and in the circles of where Moshe Feldenkrais wanted to be recognized. It seems to me that he was well aware of all the dangers of misinterpretation of statements having to do with insights about love and connectedness. These were not his world of reference. Even to talk about consciousness and awareness is suspicious to some people and to some institutions. Much of the deeper values of somatic education practices are thus more implicit than explicit.

LAWRENCE: In the Alexander Technique, we are trying to improve consciousness of the body, and of the thoughts and unconscious impulses that move the body, in order to replace automatic response with consciously directed action. We don't know to what extent this is really possible, because there is very good, replicated research that shows that we prepare for an action before we decide to carry out that action. That is, the self prepares unconsciously for action slightly before we are aware of deciding to carry out that action. The goal in the Alexander Technique is to sense that preparation, inhibit the postural set, and attempt to replace the automatic preparation with conscious choice. I think that this is not unlike the goal of Zen meditation, in which one sits, alert and aware, eyes open, deciding not to respond to impulses—trying, as in the Alexander Technique, to open a window between stimulus and response, in which consciousness may act. Not just reflective or anticipatory consciousness, but consciousness in action. So it makes sense that if you teach people conscious choice of response, they feel calmer. But I don't find anything spiritual at all in that. I think the sense that one gets when one does hands-on somatic work is the sense of unity of the practitioner with the participant. The sense that you're not doing something *to* somebody, but that you're joining them. You're putting your two systems together to better understand each other. And that, to me, has that Buddhist, spiritual, 'we're all one' kind of aspect.

YVAN: Finding a way to align your skeleton, to be at a place of solidity and mobility, I think, is a deep spiritual experience—meaning a change in the way we feel about ourselves in the world and about the world 'out there.' Though some people have that kind of experience, and they would never call it spiritual. I'm convinced that when I'm in that state, myself, I relate very differently to people. I also have a very different sense of my 'ego,' by which I mean a greater sense of humility. I think it's all a deep spiritual experience. In Feldenkrais terms, we often talk about 'the proportional distribution of work' so that there's a uniform distribution of muscle tone. We talk about it as if it were an event of physics, which it is. But it's not only an event of physics in a living system being harmonized with gravity; it's actually changing your state of consciousness. If you change your state of consciousness, well, I think you're affecting your outlook on yourself and your perception of yourself in the world and the perception of the world itself. Is that spiritual or not? Does it matter to call it spiritual or not?

LINDA: At first, people may come to my class because there's some issue they want to work with, they're simply curious to discover what this work is about or they're interested in sound or exploring fluidity. There's some reason why they come in. And then, once they're in, if they get hooked, it's because there is this unspoken level that touches their heart and soul. Emilie Conrad always says, 'There's the A theme and the B theme in Continuum.' Many people come for the B theme, to fix this, or it's going to help with that. But Continuum is really about the A theme, the larger questions about life: What is it to be a human being? What's our reason for being here? What's our connection with this planet, with this universe? The practice opens you to a more universal consciousness. People often say about the practice, 'It feels like coming home.'

YVAN: When I teach Awareness Through Movement® I think I give a lot of hints to the connection that we have with space and the environment, to finding harmony, to not forcing, to listening, to respecting our own limits, to knowing ourselves and so on. To me, that's the somatic basis of spiritual experience. I often make comments which allude to the fact that it's our continuity and relationship, not only with the ambient air or the environment, but with other human beings and other species. To paraphrase Plato, if you want to know the human species, please know one person deeply. Start with yourself. So, if you want to know the species and appreciate life and the world out there, you go deeply inside yourself. Then, in the process, you prune out all the specifics of your own family upbringing and the culture, and you find something more deep. You find what is common to all the individuals of the human species—what I call 'human universals,' and then you find also that you are connected with other species and that there is a continuity between ourselves and the rest of the planet and the cosmos, for that matter. So, you could say, 'Is that spiritual?' In a certain way, yes, but is that ecological? Surely.

NINOSKA: Nature, for me, is the main master. Living full time in the tropical jungle of Costa Rica for the last twenty years has allowed me to experience deep states of wonder, of astonishment, of fear beyond words. I can appreciate beauty and energy in so many fantastic ways that I can't even figure it out; it goes beyond what we can imagine or visualize or think about. To be in wonderment about what surrounds us with a beginners' attitude is great, because when we are beginners, we don't have expectations. So, for me, spirituality has been to be in wonderment about the revelation of all the things that organize the world. We are now experiencing so many problems as a society. The advances in science and technology confront us with different kinds of issues—for example, global warming. So now we have cars and we have a lot of comfort. Then, we're having consequences that we could not foresee. So there is some kind of organization that makes the world go around, and that is beautiful. For me, spirituality is having a relationship with nature, with something greater than myself that is ever present. It is about humbleness.

YVAN: Awareness is a process done in the interaction that I have with my own movement and the rest of the world. So if I contribute to being more at ease and more at peace with myself, I just synthesize myself in a Functional Integration way. The relationship I have with other people is affected at the same time. Our own somatic education serves our relationships with our family and with other people.

LINDA: When I discovered Continuum, I saw in it a practice that was about movement and so directly related to this spiritual path that I was on, that I am on. When I saw a video that first inspired me to try Continuum—and then, because of what I experienced in my body, the innate movement of our tissues, the innate movement of the fluids that we are—it brought me right there. I felt that this body I am is a universal being, not only flesh nor separate from others, but rather a part of this 'all.'

ODILE: Students can take our teaching at different levels. Some students will say, 'if I do this or that, my pirouette will be better,' but others will think about what facilitates a process, what facilitates one's life.

Some will go further and question the source of life. To me, a source of my inspiration is the Christian mystics. At one point of my life, I could teach only if I had a kind of spiritual theme behind the concrete bodily notion I was teaching. If I didn't have this layer, I was missing a kind of dynamic; I was drying up, draining myself. It emptied me to talk only about muscles. This is why I stopped teaching anatomy. It wasn't vital to me.

YVAN: In any form of somatic education, it's about the relationship to gravity, to the ground and the reading of the connection between the head and the tail, and the heel, and so on and so forth. It's great stuff, but we can also help people to appreciate that their relationship to the way they put their foot on the ground has something to do with how they can look around them, and how they feel a relationship with the environment. In Awareness Through Movement®, sometimes everybody moves in unison and synchronizes with other people, and this creates a sense of community without a leader or without somebody yelling at them or whistling at them or without having to imitate someone or even follow a musical score. We are using Awareness Through Movement® to nurture certain ideas that resonate beyond our separated selves. I think that Awareness Through Movement® is a very potent way to do just that. But this will rely on the intent of the practitioner and the way the practitioner conceives of his own responsibility at work. For myself, connecting the pelvis to the head, I do not think it's interesting enough for thirty years of research and teaching. But finding how embodiment is actually the basis for my relationship to meaning in the world and to make a meaning of my own existence is interesting. In fact, these years, my work as a somatic educator is a form of applied cognitive science. And in that domain, spiritual practices and spiritual insights are part of the topics of interest.

NINOSKA: In my teaching, what I try to communicate is that everything is related, and, again, I see it so clearly in nature. Nature has so many manifestations, sometimes contradictory, but we can't reject anything that happens to us. If you have pain or anything else, it is for a reason. So you have to accept the organization of living processes and witness what happens. I say to the students, 'Accept everything that is there, observe it. It is then that you will learn.' Just by observation, we learn so much. That is important. We don't need to do one thousand things; we can keep quiet and contemplative, and let things happen and unravel by themselves.

LAWRENCE: To paraphrase Alexander, I would say that sometimes, if you don't do the wrong thing, the right thing does itself. So it's not about the conscious control of movement, it's about learning not to have certain kinds of learned automatic responses. My best analogy for the Alexander Technique is a very simple one. When my son was little and was riding a bike with training wheels, he came to me one day and said, 'How come I have training wheels and my friends don't?' I said, 'Well, let's take them off.' And I took him to the park, and I told him, 'I'll hold your bike, so you don't have to worry about falling.' And then, I didn't (laughs), and he rode the bike and he was fine. Basically, of course, I held it, but as soon as he wasn't thinking about trying to balance, I let go and he was fine—balance is not a 'doing.' And I kind of feel that way about the Alexander Technique. I don't feel you teach anybody anything, but you give them the context of an external authority. People sometimes need a voice outside themselves. Or, literally, someone to take their balance for them. So, sometimes we need someone external to us to say, 'It's okay, you can jump off the diving board.'

LINDA: It's not so much what I'm teaching, but I think it's more about who I am, and therefore how I express myself and how I perceive the students. So that when I propose exercises to do with breathing, for example, I give my students the practical tools, transmitting that information from the way I perceive. And I think that what is particular to how I teach is that I speak about how everything is connected and related within the body, between us and all things—something about what exists beyond the obvious. There's more to 'it' than just what I'm doing. Every act, every thought is infused with not only my personal life history; but there is a planetary history, there's a universal consciousness. I bring that in just by who I am, and not necessarily because I name it per se. How we work on ourselves is how we transmit what we teach. And when I hear certain students naming something related to that level, I think, 'Oh, yes! Thank you!' I feel touched by that, because then I know that the message has been received. Most probably, those individuals are the ones who are aware of that path in themselves or are awakening to that. They have it in them as well. So we're resonating on that level.

ODILE: It is important to focus on the experience in and of itself, and not on the theory of the experience or on a guru system or on religion, because there are definitely different ethics and philosophies in the somatic milieu. Religion is not fashionable right now. When I will be retired and out of institutional constraints, I will attempt to name further the Christian inspiration that supports my work. But concretely, to come back to what I teach, in 'Analysis of the Body in Danced Movement,' the manner we move is the manner we see the world. Taking into account the spiritual dimension means that there is always a space, an opening, a possibility for the student to relate to something other than the teacher. As a teacher, we are always in process. And we have to present it as a process, so that the student will not say, 'This is the truth.' The idea of Trinity in Catholicism that I talked about earlier leads to an opening, a perspective, a space for dialogue and empowerment of the student process.

YVAN: Whatever can be found in spiritual practices or philosophy, I try to find inside my own work as a Feldenkrais practitioner and trainer, so that I don't need to go elsewhere to find it. It's not easy—sometimes I feel I'm very isolated, very much alone in having that perspective, because not everyone in the Feldenkrais community is explicit about these dimensions. But, honestly, giving a good lesson to someone, for me, is an act of love. It's an act of compassion; it is a form of connectedness, and it leaves me with a better equanimity that means I can move here, there. I'm more neutral in my own joints, in my own breathing and in my own emotions and thoughts. So it does something great for me. And the question, then, is, 'How do I transpose that in the rest of life, when I play tennis, when I interact with my family, talk to the neighbours?' At this point, it's a little bit like I'm travelling without a map, with the Feldenkrais method as a guide for the process. And sometimes I wish I had a place to go that would really put it together. But you know what? Honestly, I don't think it really exists. I'm attempting to do that by myself—and I think that is an influence of Moshe Feldenkrais—but it's not a comfortable place. Sometimes, I would like an external authority to say, 'You are on the right track.' But then, what is 'the right track' anyway? It's maybe an issue of personality or arrogance to try to resolve it all by myself, but it's the choice I've made so far. Indeed, it can be a lonely place. But feeling isolated and cut off is the exact lack of the connectedness that spiritual practices tend to offer, thus my own need to develop more in my own non-denominational spiritual path.

Epilogue

Hopefully, this collage is a step to share our experiences and break the isolation. If I chose not to make a thematic analysis of the interviews I had with each person and only to link the ideas in a kind of conversational flow, it is because I trusted that this way would better reflect our meandering individual quests. In the above text, I purposely stayed absent from the conversation. Some readers could critique my authorial passivity. As a feminist poststructuralist researcher, I think rather that this choice provided an inclusive space to blur methodological boundaries where hierarchical positions and referential categorization are well defined. The unresolved, uncompleted, sometimes opposing voices of the constructed conversation also challenge the idea that our self/body/soma (no matter the preferred label) is monolithic. Instead, this constructed conversation explores the concept of a multiplicitous, shifting, and sometimes self-contradictory wording of our experiences. For Beringer, 'the self should not be a noun, but a process, *selfing*. [...] Selfing implies a dynamic process which is ongoing' (2001: 36). Certainly, our spiritual quest is an ongoing journey.

There can be no conclusion to such a chapter addressing the somatic basis of spiritual experiences. However, I will offer a final wrap-up to attempt to connect the narratives of the interviewees with some of the literature. In my early training in dance and Somatics, I often felt that spirituality was taboo, which goes with Martyne Tremblay's (2004) and Amanda Williamson's (2010) observations that spirituality is not at the forefront of our secular Western institutions. Although spirituality is not overtly present in official dance or somatic programmes, this group conversation constructed from individual interviews reveals how it is often elusively embedded in class material or ingrained in the way teachers present their content. Linda's narrative is particularly close to what has been coined by Jackson (1968) as the 'hidden curriculum'; that is, the values that are implicitly part of the teaching and learning process, but that are not openly acknowledged or articulated in the teacher's statements. To determine whether or not it would be beneficial to say to the students that spirituality might be a by-product of their involvement in Somatic Movement Dance Education classes goes beyond the scope of this chapter. Furthering this fundamental issue is a direction for much needed research to come.

Without being specifically asked, all the interviewees addressed the theme of religion. For them, spirituality is wider than religion. Odile, the most theologically oriented interviewee, made a point of saying that religion is not fashionable these days. In a rich review of literature on spirituality within the field of Somatic Movement Dance Education (SMDE), Williamson (2010) points out, referring to Thomas Hanna, that religion, monotheism and Christianity in particular, are not popular in the Somatics literature, partly because Somatics is rooted in Darwinism. She explains that the field at large has rejected higher, external and transcendental orders of reality in order to establish its foundation on the evolution of life itself, which is 'biological, observable and measurable' (2010: 45). Organized religion is thus often perceived as a site of dogma, authoritarianism and an external source of power, whereas spirituality, located in the body-earth interconnectivity, is viewed as a site of freedom, liberation and autonomy. For Don Johnson, she writes, spirituality and liberal forms of religion are not that incompatible. To him, the central theme of Somatics, which is the sensing body as a source of knowledge, destabilizes abstract theological discourses. Pursuing Williamson's investigation of how somatic pioneers came upon a stance toward religion and/or spirituality is another avenue of research worth taking.

Except for Lawrence, all the interviewees placed the sensing body/self/soma as the daily source of spiritual experiences and addressed the challenge to explicitly talk about them in Western secular teaching institutions. Among the interviewees, Lawrence is the one for whom spirituality was the most problematic. He preferred to talk about consciousness and to connect it to scientific knowledge, which is a theme of progressive spirituality. Quoting Lynch, Williamson explains that progressive spirituality is defined by a 'theology of oneness' and has been shaped by the following:

> The need for a credible religion for a modern age; the need for religion which is truly liberating and beneficial for women; the need to reconnect religion with scientific knowledge; and the need for a spirituality that can respond to the impeding ecological crisis.
>
> (Williamson 2010: 55)

Interestingly, these notions have all been addressed by the interviewees. Yvan, for example, gave examples of how deep sensory unification with oneself, with others and with the environment is actually an undisclosed spiritual dimension of Somatics. Linda said that her patriarchal environment constrained her from moving forward in her individual spiritual quest. Ninoska strongly affirmed how spirituality is a dimension of the larger ecosystem we live in.

Williamson appropriately points out these themes as possible research avenues for investigating spirituality in the field of SMDE. It is worth remembering that research on spirituality will always depend upon people capable of introspection and willing to uncover and share their personal life as Lawrence, Linda, Ninoska, Odile and Yvan have done here. But most importantly, such sharing of autobiographical journeys opens space for others to feel and reflect on their own spiritual journey.

References

Beringer, E. (2001), 'Self-imaging', *The Feldenkrais Journal*, 13, pp. 33–38.

Campbell, R. and Salem, D. A. (1999), 'Concept mapping as a feminist research method: Examining the community response to rape', *Psychology of Women Quarterly*, 23, pp. 65–89.

Gomez, N. (1992), 'Somarhythms: Developing somatic awareness with balls', *Somatics Magazine: Journal of the Arts and Science*, 8:4, pp. 12–18.

Greene, L. (2009), *Somatic Approaches to Movement*, DVD, www.rechercheenmouvement.org.

Jackson, P. (1968), *Life in Classrooms*, New York, NY: Holt, Rinehart & Winston.

Lioa, G. (2011), 'Brain scans of Buddhist monks show benefit of meditation', AsianScientist. com,http://www.asianscientist.com/health-medicine/buddhist-monks-meditation/. Accessed 8 June 2012.

Ramazanoglu, C. and Holland, J. (2002), *Feminist Methodology: Challenges and Choices*, London, UK: Sage.

Reinharz, S. (1992), *Feminist Methods in Social Research*, Oxford, UK: Oxford University Press.

Tremblay, M. (2004), 'La Spiritualité dans le Parcours Professionnel et Personnel de Danseurs Contemporains', Unpublished MA thesis, Montréal: Université du Québec à Montréal.

Williamson, A. (2010), 'Reflection and theoretical approaches to the study of spiritualities within the field of somatic movement dance education', *Journal of Dance & Somatic Practices*, 2:1, pp. 35–61.

Note

1   For further information about the Alexander Technique, Body Mind Centering®, Continuum and the Feldenkrais Method®, see the DVD *Somatic Approaches to Movement* (Green 2009). For information on Somarhythms, read Gomez (1992).

Chapter 13

Inner Dance—Spirituality and Somatic Practice in Dance Technique, Choreography and Performance[1]

Kathleen Debenham and Pat Debenham

Discovering the Dance Within

Deep inside each individual, there resides a dance—a unique and sacred personal narrative. Though no one can tell another how to find this dance, we believe that engaging in a constructivist pedagogy where value is placed on embodied knowing and meaning making leads dancers to access their own 'sacred' dance. Grounded in the somatic practice of Bartenieff Fundamentals (BF) and informed by the theoretical constructs of Laban Movement Analysis (LMA), this chapter examines how dance education can illuminate the sacred dimensions of each individual's embodied personal narrative. Our experience as teachers who have integrated somatic approaches into the teaching of technique, choreography and performance in university dance programmes bears witness to the positive effects of what we have come to call a 'pedagogy of embodiment.' We draw from the fields of contemplative education, somatic practices and psychology and consider ways in which the spiritual self can be nurtured in the development of technical virtuosity, personal voice in choreography and heightened expressiveness of performance.

The pedagogy presented herein values experiential learning and encourages students to peel away body armor in order to delve mindfully into sensation. This allows them to connect to the essential self that knows. In class and in rehearsals, students are guided through exercises in which sensory modalities and feelings are explored that encourage them to move and to create from a profound place of inner knowing as they access the spiritual power of their own movement voice. Time for reflection, personal processing and sharing—both verbally and nonverbally—support the students' efforts to make connections between body, mind and spirit; between self and other; between dance and life. Below, we offer our own—as well as the students'—perspectives, and the method through which body, mind and spirit become connected. We also share how the exploratory process is further integrated into technique and performance.

Spirituality and the Sacred

We believe that all human beings experience the sacred. We also believe it is essential, within the context of education, to acknowledge, address and discuss with our students the impact and relevance of such experiences. For this discussion to be appropriate in education,

Figure 1: *Where Light is Made to Travel* by Amy Margraff Jacobson. Contemporary Dance Theatre, Brigham Young University. On the path to discovering one's own sacred narrative, sensing inner intention with clarity and vulnerability are fundamental. Photographer: Mark Philbrick.

particularly in public education, spirituality must be supported by a definition that is broad and inclusive.

Our sense of what is 'spiritual' is guided by the overarching concept that we are connected to and illuminated by something beyond ourselves—that we have access, through means that may be 'mysterious' to us and others, to information that helps us see that we are part of a greater whole. This in no way negates or diminishes the inner voice that guides us. This inner voice too gives us information about our place in the world, connecting inner with outer by intuitive means.

Concepts grounded in our own spirituality that motivate and guide us as teachers in constructing learning environments that support spiritual sensibilities are as follows:

- Life is sacred.
- The body reveals to us, even through us, things that are sacred.
- Creation is a spiritual endeavour.
- A desire for a feeling of wholeness and unity in our lives is a key aspect of the spiritual quest.
- Awareness of the sacred journey moves us from the ordinary to the transcendent through focus on process.

- The spiritual quest engages us with the enduring questions of life.
- Knowing that we are part of a greater whole is the ground for developing spiritual qualities of relationship and connectedness.

Something Within and Beyond Self: The Numinous

Jungian psychologist Lionel Corbett (2007) in *Psyche and the Sacred: Spirituality beyond Religion* offers an expansive notion of 'the sacred,' one that is broad enough to include secular sensibilities of the sacred. In his first chapter, titled 'The Numinosum: Direct Experience of the Sacred,' he discusses how the spiritual, or the numinous (a sense that we have been addressed by something holy, supernatural, or divine) becomes apparent and available to us through informed somatic sensing. (Note: In our discussion of the sacred, 'numinous' and 'spiritual' are words that we use interchangeably.)

According to Corbett, this spirituality that emerges from direct experience comes from the deepest level of our being where, 'we are not separate from the experience—we *are* the experience' (2007: 35). In this light, connecting with the divine is not a concept that is derived from establishing a relationship with a 'wholly Other' outside of ourselves. It comes from a place deep within us that 'asks us to discover our own living story' (Corbett 2007: 32).

This concept of the divine being deep within is linked to an innate human capacity to conceive of and connect to something larger than ourselves. 'When we have a numinous experience, we feel as if we are being addressed by a consciousness that is different from our own' (Corbett 2007: 43). The experience transforms us and is at the heart of our capacity to wonder, to search for meaning, to be mindful, to be compassionate, to be engaged in the act of creation and to ask the big questions of life.

The numinous experience and the spiritual journey are extremely personal. Both are 'located deep within our subjectivity' (Corbett 2007: 15). This is an important point in relation to a somatically based, constructivist[2] pedagogy: we value the subjective nature of our students' experience. The emotional, the feeling-full, the intuitive, the trans-rational and the unconscious are all inroads to personal understanding and to the sacred. The feelings and emotions that 'accompany a numinous experience are important not simply because they help us to identify the experience as sacred. These emotions tell us that the experience has been embodied [...] we know an experience is numinous not only by its content but also by the way our bodies respond to it' (Corbett 2007: 17).

Corbett's focus on the embodied nature of the spiritual offers a valuable trans-disciplinary lens for connecting the spiritual with the physical. It is particularly illuminating when considering ways in which dance education can lead to deeper awareness and understanding of what it is to be human. Enlightenment can be mediated through the body by directing attention to connections between inner sensations and outward expression. Attending to inner information on a bodily level can indeed be numinous; we are enlightened, uplifted, given new information—in some way we see and move in the world in a new light.

Creativity and the Sacred

Fundamental to our pedagogy of embodiment is the belief that the act of creation is a spiritual endeavour. Embodiment through movement is an act of creation and itself 'embodies' the numinous. As such, it is an endeavour towards spirit, however defined. When addressed through a pedagogy that focuses on somatic practices, creative processes and products resonate with an authenticity that transcends craft. A somatic pedagogy where personal voice and meaning making are central creates a space for the numinous.

As a portal to the sacred, art making transforms the inward and abstract experience of spirituality into a visible object. To a significant degree, art making is 'a somatic act, one in which the physical body expresses what is known in those portions of the brain [and the body] that operate nonverbally' (London 1989: 97). It is from this nonverbal place that 'images and gesture convey their knowledge' (London 1989: 97).

Art making opens our awareness to fundamental archetypal themes. The memories and emotions imbued in what we create are often the embodiment of spiritual sensitivities that reveal our authentic selves more fully and with deeper meaning than every day activities. The images portrayed, having been created through our sensorimotor system, make the abstract more accessible, the imaginative more possible and when the 'imagination is allowed to move to deep places, the sacred is revealed' (Moore 1998: 286).

Linda Leonard states that, 'Creativity is an adventure of the soul in its quest for meaning' (Leonard 2009: 1). Meaning making, our innate drive to make sense of lived experience, is at the root of spirituality, creativity and educational endeavours. Acts of creation and spiritual journeys mirror each other in process and intent; both mine the inner self in reflective ways and grapple with questions about the meaning of life and the dimensions of existence.

Through consciously connecting the creative act and the sacred, students learn to trust their own inner guide. In doing so, they are transformed. They become deeply aware of their own uniqueness within a pluralistic interdependent universe and come to believe in the value of their original voice.

Pedagogy of Embodiment

A pedagogy of embodiment, informed by LMA and BF, supports transformative education. The experimental approach of Bartenieff Fundamentals invites students to explore patterning fundamental connections in the body according to principles of efficient movement; the goal is 'total body integration that encourages personal expression and full psychological involvement' (Hackney 1998). With a focus on dancing from the inside out rather than from the outside in, a pedagogy of embodiment guides students to access their inner, imaginative dance by means of evocative images and metaphors that lead them to heightened intention, sensation and awareness. It is a constructivist practice grounded in the belief that within the context of a community of learners, the individual participates in the creation of their own knowledge by integrating prior knowledge with present experience. The approach 'acts upon and acts with human beings in such a way as to transform their embodied consciousness, thereby producing meaning in the process' (Pryer 2004). A pedagogy of embodiment honours the individual experience and empowers students to construct meaning from their own knowing. It is then, by necessity, subjective. To 'know thyself' is at the heart of the embodied journey.

This approach is certainly not singular to us. During the last twenty years, at least in the United States, the inclusion of specific somatic classes and the use of somatic sensibilities in other courses within university dance curricula has increased. Our awareness and introduction to somatic practices came as a result of our LMA training. It radically shifted our sense of who we are as movers, teachers and creative agents. Prior to undertaking LMA certification, our pedagogy reflected our fairly traditional university training that emphasized the h'Doubler/Nikolais/Humphrey[3] approaches to technique, choreography and performance. The language of shape, space, time, energy and motion provided the general categories that we used to choreograph and to describe what was happening, whether in technique, composition or improvisation. For example, the design of the body emphasized what one looked like, not what it felt like to embody a particular shape. In choreography, it was important that everyone 'looked' the same; in technique, students visually replicated the teacher—was your arm at the correct angle and did you tilt your torso to the same degree as the teacher?

In the LMA certification programme, we experienced a very different pedagogy than that we had been using for more than 25 years. The following progression was foundational to the approach that our mentors Peggy Hackney, Janice Meaden, Pam Schick and Ed Groff used:

- First, we experience ourselves moving.
- Second, we perceive our physical involvement in a movement event; we notice and are aware of the sensation of moving, what it feels like.
- Third, we describe the sensations we feel. We name them, give voice to the sensation and create visual confirmations of the sensations.
- Fourth, through reflection we make meaning of what we have experienced. We give it a context, we make sense of it and we claim what we know and 'move' it into our lives.

This pedagogy is grounded in somatic practice that values individual experience, meaning making and personal voice.

Two Foundational Concepts

Two overarching concepts are foundational to the process and products that evolve from a pedagogy of embodiment. They are: (1) embodiment as a kinetic process, and (2) personal meaning making. We see these as the cornerstones of a pedagogy of embodiment.

Embodiment as a Kinetic Process

Embodiment is the ability to somatically 'read' what we are experiencing and to make it concrete and perceptible in an ongoing way. It is to incorporate and personify principles, concepts and values that we believe in and want to exemplify (Webster's 1963: 270). Rather than seeing this as an arrival or a destination, we find it more useful to consider embodiment as an ever-evolving process of 'be-coming.' This becoming takes on a special meaning when the moving body is the means of this transformation.

When we attune to our bodies and process our experiences through the soma, we begin to understand the subtle underlying physical, psychological, emotional and intellectual currents that are operative in our lives. 'The beauty of physical practice […] is that you do not have to know what you are doing in order to begin. You just begin, and the doing teaches you what you need to know' (Taylor 2010: 58). Processing through somatic sensing also touches us at a spiritual level as we begin to see that the micro is a model for the macro, that inner knowing allows us—perhaps requires us—to experience transcendence as a quality of being that is not reserved for transformational moments of illumination. The quotidian can become spiritual when experienced somatically. There is a certain reverence that comes from allowing ourselves to be and become through the felt experience.

> Our bodies tell our stories: Where we have been; what we have been encouraged to do and prevented from doing; what we have attended to or ignored in our daily lives; what we have learned directly through felt experience; and what we have acquired by way of education.
>
> (Pitt, as cited in Knaster 1996: 363)

Somatic attunement is not easy. It is transformational work that asks us to delve beneath the surface in order to enrich technical virtuosity, performance connectivity and choreographic resonance. Through it, we begin to understand and appreciate the richness of our being, not just our doing. By 'listening' somatically we begin to feel not only the 'connective tissue' of our bodies but the connective threads that weave the many aspects of our lives together. Embodied learning is truly integrative learning.

Personal Meaning Making

Meaning making through exploration of kinetic and kinesthetic movement material is inherent in LMA and BF. It serves to both close the learning loop—I experience, I perceive, I describe, I make meaning—and to re-initiate it in a recursive process. 'A man's body is his bridge to and model of the world; therefore, as a man is in his body so will he be in the world' (Keen 1990: 147–48). Meaning making takes information gleaned in preverbal sensory experience and translates it to language. In other words, thought and or language emanates from the body. 'We think and name in one world, we live and feel in another' (Proust, as cited in Lee 1994: 134). Language offers us a way in which to process felt experience. It also allows us to build connections and relationship to others as we share the lived experience.

Consider the young child who keeps asking 'Why?' to every reasonable answer you provide for a question they ask. The desire to create meaning in relationship is an inherent characteristic of the human species. Eventually, simple questions can lead to existential questions, to bigger questions about life; reflection leads us to hone in on what is core and essential for us. A desire to make sense of our experience opens the door to physical, emotional, cognitive and even spiritual impressions that teach us about relationship, connectivity and the notion that there is something larger than ourselves.

Moving Towards Embodiment and Meaning Making

How do we teach embodiment and meaning making to our students? It is through pedagogy grounded in the conceptual frameworks and the global concepts/foundational principles housed in LMA and BF. Through them, we direct our student's attention and awareness, opening up possibilities for them to process their experience in multidimensional ways. LMA and BF as interrelated bodies of knowledge spring from Laban's belief that movement and dance are manifestations of 'a poetic and spiritual emanation of man's body-mind' (Laban 1971: 64).

In this statement, originally written in 1939, Laban acknowledges the unity of the body and the mind, reinforces their interrelatedness through the hyphen and at the same time foregrounds the body as the vehicle by which we share who and what we are with others. 'Body-mind' foregrounds the intentionally moving body as the primary organizer and animator of our being.

Laban's writings, which are infused with references to connectivity, relationship and the spiritual essence of movement, reveal a belief that our essential self, (we would say our 'spirit-filled' self) is manifest in and through movement. While a specific somatic experience may not lead to transformative numinosity, over time, as we move towards meaning making, experiences of embodiment shape our perception and orientation. Cumulatively, through repeated experiences with meaning making, there is the potential for personal and spiritual growth that leads to integration and wholeness.

The Process

Our LMA/BF certification experience helped us recognize the potential power of a somatic approach in all aspects of dance. Because of it, our praxis over the last 15 years has become increasingly focused on using constructivist pedagogies and a pedagogy of embodiment to assist students in constructing embodied knowledge through a process of:

- acknowledging trust in being as the basis of inner knowing;
- in-dwelling to attune to inner sensation;

- moving from inner sensation which manifests itself in authentic outer expression;
- reflecting on the process, sharing awareness and increasing integration.

The belief that sensation coupled with awareness has the potential to lead to empathy and compassion, both of which are spiritual qualities, is fundamental to this process. Through directed exploration, dancers begin to understand the deep meaning that resides in their personal narrative and come to know the value of subjective experience over objective distancing. With this understanding, they strengthen their personal voice and bear witness to what they believe and know about the world.

Acknowledging Trust in Being as the Basis of Inner Knowing

In a society that rewards performance and productivity (and thus attention to the outward and external), our students need the time, the space and the strategies to access a trust in their own being. We believe the basis for this trust is breath, the first pattern of Total Body Connectivity (PTBC) in the Laban/Bartenieff work. It is not surprising that this foundational physical pattern is also the threshold through which many spiritual traditions access a sense of connection to self and to other, including that which is holy.

Breath provides students with a needed opportunity to experience and explore 'being.' In the fluid connectivity of breath, they begin to trust inner sensation as a place of knowing. As they experience the oneness of breath, they begin to sense themselves as whole, experiencing and trusting that the simplicity of this pattern as a place of mystery and potential. Though strange and unfamiliar at first, and sometimes disorienting because it does not have the sense of form our students are used to, breath eventually opens them to what Peter London calls 'the boundary between what is known and all that is yet to be known' (London 1989: 81). This is a place of humility, an opportunity to trust that each exhale is followed by an inhale which 'inspires' and sustains us both physically and metaphorically.

The prevailing objectivism of the day 'insists that we can know the world only by distancing ourselves from it' (Brady 2005: 1). Distancing ourselves from ourselves in such a way comes at a price. Consider Kate Dawson's experience: 'I had so little bodily awareness that I did not realize that by cutting off my breathing I was also cutting myself off from my sensations and feelings' (1994: 21).

It is our experience that once students understand the recuperative and even healing power of breath, they relish opportunities to 'be and not do.' Through breath, their cellular experience reveals to them the value of being. This new awareness provides an increased ability to access inner sensation, increased access to dynamic range, a sense of wholeness/oneness and a feeling of calm readiness for life's challenges.

In-Dwelling to Attune to Inner Sensation

As students become comfortable with inner sensation of breath, they are then invited to widen their sense of attunement to include other aspects of their being. In LMA and BF, this attending is often referred to as 'in-dwelling,' where one becomes aware of one's inner impulse to move and to manifest oneself in the world. In-dwelling creates an environment rich in feeling and sensation that enhances body mind spirit awareness and deepens the potential for change.

The sensibilities that Pryer (2004) and Driver (1998) express when they talk about ritual coming from a somatic place affirms that the body is a site for knowing and through awareness (in-dwelling) we clarify that knowing. Through 'sharpened attention' and awareness of the sensual, the tacit and nonverbal 'actions of material bodies,' we become aware of their connection to 'thought, feeling, imagination, dream and intuition.' They state that, 'the body that does is of no less importance than the mind that knows' (Driver 1998: 81). Indeed, one could say that 'the body that does, is the body that knows' (Pryer 2004: 9).

A final but powerful example comes to mind as we consider the idea of in-dwelling with attunement to prepare for outward expression. There is an ancient Hebrew term that refers to an instrument or object through which one can receive revelation. It was called a '*urim and thummim*.' By some interpretations, this instrument was a vehicle through which light and truth were revealed. In our experience, through in-dwelling with attunement, we experience corporeal light and truth. The body literally becomes a *urim and thummim* revealing the truth contained in our cells, muscles, sinews and bones. The body thus becomes a site for personal revelation.

Moving from Inner Sensation that Manifests Itself in Outer Expression

All movement is preceded by an inner impulse. This impulse manifests itself in many ways, through the shaping of the body, through our Effort life or through the way we interact with the space around us. By asking students to actively attend to their inner impulse, sense it, dwell in and with it and then notice what emerges in movement from that impulse, we help them access an authentic place of personal knowing. In a playful exploratory process and without judgement or expectation, students are asked to simply notice what appears, subsides and reappears as a consequence of that impulse. What results is a dyad between inner and outer, another of the major themes of the LMA system. Inner/outer is a lively dynamic lemniscate that weaves the inner/spiritual with outer action in the world.

We help students negotiate the dynamism of this lemniscate by engaging them in specific directed experiences that allow the inherent 'spiritual' nature of what's happening to become apparent. The following are examples of content, processes, structures and language that facilitate this.

Through dynamic exploration of the six patterns of Total Body Connectivity students come to understand how the body organizes itself. Inherent in each pattern are behavioural (spiritual) attitudes or patterns that can reveal connections to larger themes of life and living. For example, the core/distal pattern creates a lively sense of connection between centre and edge via the six limbs (two arms, two legs, head, tail). Through practising and playing with this pattern, the individual necessarily strengthens her core. The life connection here is finding what is core for you as an individual. What matters to you? What do you value and want to connect to? This in turn prepares you for grounding in relationship to an outside force, being willing to be in relationship with another, providing support for or relying on another.

Practice of Bartenieff Fundamentals is likewise sensual and somatic and affirms that the 'body that does, is the body that knows' (Pryer 2004: 9). However, what is experienced moves to the verbal when students are asked to share with one another their embodied experience. Movement experiences are designed to engage students in both preverbal and verbal ways of processing in order to connect the inner experience with the outward expression.

Rich evocative language invites students to fully engage sensation that reveals the body's kinesthetic wisdom. It also provides a feeling-full inroad to exploration. For example, to help students achieve greater stability through grounding, Kathleen uses verbal cueing such as:

Soften the soles of your feet so they yield to and embrace the heart of the earth; let the strength of the earth stream up through the starfish-like limbs of the lower body and swirl into your core. Can you sense the core of your body resonating with the core of the earth? Feel it enliven and warm T-12 (twelfth thoracic vertebrae) and then feel it stream upwards along the spine and out through the crown of the head into the heavens.

We also provide opportunities for students to create their own evocative imagery. It is not unusual for students to struggle at first in creating their own images. However, when given models and encouragement, what they create moves beyond the mundane to the exquisite. Recently one student shared the following images that supported her in dynamic liveliness and shaping of the entire body in performing parts of the A Scale, one of Laban's Space Harmony movement scales.

I paint the stars in the sky.
I skid my hand on the top of the water.
I am a great mystic whirlpool.
I long for my dreams to come true.
I am completely exposed and vulnerable.
I ride the roller coaster of life.

(Waite, J. Class presentation, 2011:1)

Empowered with the ability to create personal meaning from movement, students begin to see themselves and their world in new and significant ways. By manifesting sensation and feeling in outward expression that is supported by personally meaningful images, they gain enhanced ability to communicate through and about movement.

Reflecting on the Process, Sharing Awareness and Increasing Integration

Inherent in the notion that one reflects upon and then shares with others their embodied experience is the notion of listening deeply. Mary Rose O'Reilley writes:

> Attention: deep listening. People are dying in spirit for lack of it [...] Seldom is there a deep, openhearted, un-judging reception of the other [we would add self] [...]By contrast, if someone truly listens to me, my spirit begins to expand.
>
> (O'Reilley 1998: 19)

In an increasingly mechanized and secular world, attention that expands our spirit has the potential to move us beyond ourselves, lead to empathy and compassion and foster relationship self to self, self to other and self to world. Through relationship, meaning is created and confirmed as we discover connections to the global and to the cosmic.

One method through which students develop awareness is through sharing reflective writings. These might include, for example, an assignment to write a 'body story,' a reflective paper in which they describe their own sense of being in their bodies and what meaning might come from that sense. One student shared:

> I move because I see it as potentially the most universal language of all. I move because my spirit demands expression. I move because I can feel it wanting to achieve a unity with the flesh. My body is pushed toward that goal through the pursuit of movement, despite all the feelings of inadequacy I bottle up inside. It is an attempt to be honest with myself, pursue what I feel might help me communicate with the world, and find peace within my soul.
>
> (Ryzeczycka, A. Class response, 2011:1)

The following client reflection shared by a Certified Movement Analyst attests to the transformative power of the BF work. (This was shared with the client's permission on the CMA listserv). The young woman who had misaligned legs following a horrific car accident related:

> I marvel at the simplicity and deepness of the thigh lift exercise. Engaging my whole being fully to carry out the simplest and smallest movement, where every part [is] working together harmoniously toward one meaningful goal, is a wholesome, magical experience. In fact, the magic starts with the intention to commit myself fully to the task. In a way, we

can never fail, if we are clear about our intention. I find the quality of outcome is as good as that of intention.

(Bradley 2011)

Such heartfelt sharing is evidence of the way in which LMA/BF can connect body, mind and spirit. By working somatically, we enhance spiritual connectedness and integration; we learn empathy and compassion as we sense and appreciate the embodied experience of others.

In summary, these are the things we attended to when engaging in a pedagogy of embodiment:

- Construct guided experiences/improvisations that allow for focused exploration through movement, discussion, writing, drawing, et cetera.
- Direct students' attention to their own bodily sensations.
- Encourage non-judgemental attention and curiosity for the lived/felt experience.
- Ask open-ended questions about the student's sensory experience:

  ○ What does it feel like?
  ○ If you do _____, how does it change what you know or understand?
  ○ Where does that knowing reside in the body?
  ○ Might it be connected to anything larger than the immediate experience?

- Ask questions that encourage reflective responses that lead to the big pictures of life.
- Provide opportunities for the students to connect physical sensation to feeling and emotion through drawing, writing and the use of evocative language.

Embodied Personal Narrative that Leads to Transformation

It is vital to the process of spiritual embodiment within dance to extend what is gained in exploratory and experiential learning into technique, choreography and performance. The following brief examples demonstrate ways we have come to foreground the spiritual in teaching technique, choreography and performance. Principles of embodiment infuse the pedagogy in which constructivist processes invite students to weave their existing knowledge with new knowledge and make personal meaning of their moved experience. The examples reveal the somatic sensibility that knowing is based in the body. They are not exhaustive, but are illustrative of how students construct an embodied personal narrative that is rich in meaning when they experience dance by means of a pedagogy of embodiment.

Technique

As teachers, we want our dancers to manifest qualities of wholeness and connectivity, physically and feeling-fully connecting outer technical virtuosity with an inner sense of awareness. This moves beyond rote replication to an engaged sense of transcendent performative liveliness. Direct somatic experiences ignite a life force, a spiritual aliveness in the dancer as they dance with a creative power previously unknown to them.

Other than participating in a class specifically designed to address somatic principles, the dancer's technique class offers perhaps the most obvious opportunities to integrate somatic principles into a dance curriculum. Over many years of teaching beginning to advanced levels of contemporary dance technique, we have noted the tendency for dancers to seek visual rather than kinesthetic feedback. They tend to focus on the reflection of a shape in the mirror not the dynamic internal process of the body shaping; they see the lines of the body but do not internally sense the direction and influence of spatial pulls; they struggle on the surface of dynamic replication without understanding how Effort is the outward manifestation of an inner impulse to move. Because they have not been given a theoretical framework within which to experience, understand and perform movement, technique class has often been for them a series of rote replications of what the instructor is doing. It can appear that the students are 'just going through the motions.' This is not surprising, since they have not been asked to connect the inner to the outer or function to expression in holistic, integrative ways.

Following are two specific examples of how BF principles and body-based concepts can be integrated into dance technique classes. These examples reveal how somatic principles lead students to an expanded sense of their own sacred personal narrative.

The concept of breath is a somatic concept that is at the centre of dance training and spiritual practices alike. As already noted, it is one of the six patterns of Total Body Connectivity used in BF and is also found in the Body-Mind Centering® work of Bonnie Bainbridge Cohen. Breath animates the body, fills it with vitality and aliveness. It can free us from holding patterns, patterns that impede physical, emotional and spiritual growth. Dancers frequently unintentionally hold their breath when learning or performing new and unfamiliar motor patterns in technique class. Holding the breath restricts the flow of sensation hence information. Intentional breathing allows the body, the mind and the spirit to yield and soften, physically facilitating the cellular exchange of carbon dioxide (what we let go of because we no longer need it) and oxygen (what we need and take in to support us.) Where there is breath, there is the possibility for change.

Joseph Heller and William Henkin in *BODYWISE* illuminate this concept, stating, '*Inspiration [...]* denotes both the physical inhalation phase of the breathing cycle and the metaphysical taking in of spirit of life force [...] Freeing the body's breathing structures [...] expands a person's ability to feel and express high levels of energy' (Heller and Henkin 1991: 103–04).

Peggy Hackney (1998) furthers this notion of the physical being a 'ground' for the metaphysical and models a process for accessing multiple levels of awareness in her book *Making Connections*. Hackney directs the mover to find connections between the physical act of doing and the global/spiritual concept that is embodied in the doing. When she discusses 'connectivity,' an essential aspect of anyone's technical training regardless of genre or style, she moves from what she considers to be a fundamental physical principle, that the 'whole body is connected' with all parts and pieces moving in relationship, to connectivity as spiritual principle. She states that an individual is connected when they, 'move in harmonic relation to him/herself, other people, and/or the universe' (Hackney 1998: 234). In this sense connectivity is a spiritual principle. 'To sense connection is an essence of spirituality in most spiritual traditions' (Hackney 1998: 234).

Many students we encounter experience 'technique' as the place where they understand the body from a functional point of view. But our technical body, as a student in a Bartenieff Fundamentals class shared, is also a site that deepens our connection to self and others helping us negotiate our place in the world.

> Dancing has shaped my life and how I view the world. I find it very effective for me to feel a concept physically to truly understand it cognitively or philosophically—a few examples include trust falls to explore trusting others and releasing inhibitions, breathing with people and moving together to feel unity, or even weight sensing and lifts [… to explore] the idea of taking care of others while still taking care of yourself […]. Concepts such as these encourage me to connect my life experiences with dancing. This close relationship for me personally is why I think I dance the way I do—I dance like I live, I live like I dance.
>
> (McArthur, M., 7 September 2011, Student paper)

When students are encouraged to experience technique class in this way, their perceptions of themselves and others can transform their dancing.

Choreography

Choreography can be seen as an interior journey reflected in outward form. In and through the container of the body, thought, emotion, sensation and spirit are woven together creating an 'internal coherence.' Through the 'consciousness of the body' the inner is 'released into public symbolism, language [and] form' (Peat 2011: 16). As students 'quicken their senses' (London 1989: 97), respond to the eternal archetypes that resonate in the body and attend to the narrative of their own lives, the work they produce will reflect not only on the physical nature of their movement but of the heartsongs of their own souls.

'Our bodies tell our stories' (Knaster 1996: 363). Stories that emerge from a personal physical narrative differ from those that come from the mind. Movement that is cognitively-mapped can be clear in form yet devoid of personal voice. Movement that issues forth from cellular knowing is vibrant, authentic and demonstrates an organic sense of structure. In choreography, the body can be the guide leading the mind in the creation of transformative images and stories.

As previously noted, Peter London identifies the creative process as an act of somatic engagement. 'If we train ourselves to become cognizant of what our bodies already know and are expressing, we will have important and accurate information that can guide us along our way.' When we do so 'art can be understood as the externalization of interior states of mind and body' (London 1989: 99–100).

Laban clearly understood what London posits, 'Dance does not speak through the intellect to the heart as does the spoken word; it speaks directly to our heart, and afterwards perhaps also to the brain, to the intellect' (Laban 1975: 178). Laban and London both affirm that the soma is a primary source for knowledge and creativity.

In summer 2010, Pat presented a dance he collaboratively created with his students at the International Oral History Conference in Prague, Czech Republic. The work, *Fragile Presence,* drew its inspiration from oral history interviews his students conducted with individuals that had experienced the loss of a loved one. For the students the experience became a vehicle for transformative spiritual expression. Throughout the rehearsal process and in performance all came to understand the potential that dance-making, accessed through somatic sensing, has to connect us to the numinous.

Inherent in the process was an investment in personal narrative and an attention to the kinesthetic/somatic cues present in the bodies of both the dancers and the interviewees. One story in particular became the heart centre of the work, a story of a young couple whose first-born child was stillborn. It was a solo from the husband's point of view. Beginning with kinetically charged phrases from the interview and gestures the student had observed during the interview, the dancer was asked to embody sequences that Pat created in his response to the interview. He was also directed to create his own phrases that reflected the inner movement 'voice' contained in their interviewees' story; back and forth—language, movement, teacher, student, inner sensation and outward expression all creating and shaping a unique and sacred personal narrative.

Each choreographer has a body story that can be explored to express their own divine individuality. Choreography that springs from a place of trust in eternal potential is intensely personal and unflinchingly authentic. Sadly, we find that students whose training has largely been focused on technical virtuosity and reproducing someone else's movement are strangers to their own creative impulse. Our challenge is to help them unveil that which is deep within themselves and provide support as they bravely give voice to it.

Performance

It's tremendously satisfying to see the transformation that happens when students delve into performance from a somatic perspective, especially as they connect via the spirit to what they are doing. Getting students to access sensation as 'inspiration' for performance, though, can be difficult. This is not surprising, since for the most part Western culture asks that they respond to the world cognitively and objectively—not from the subjective, intuitive and soulful place of the senses. In their educational experiences, they generally have not been asked to think, write or respond evocatively from a bodily perspective. Even in dance, a body-based discipline, they have not been asked to engage with the sensuous, learning 'the grammar of the gut, the syntax of the sinews, the language of the legs' (Lee 1994: xiv). To coach for mindfully authentic performance, we direct our students to the sensory stream that is just beneath the surface of their general awareness and then provide tools to enable them to express sensation and feeling through kinetically rich language and metaphor deeply rooted in the body.

It is clear in the current performance landscape that the technical/functional aspects of movement are essential and provide a foundation for physical virtuosity. But a technician without a connection to the soul or spirit of a work is just that, a technician. As Becker and Becker state, 'All the pirouettes in the world, all the spectacular feats cannot impress me as much as a simple movement that originates from a deep feeling of aliveness' (as cited in Knaster 1996: 267). As audience members, we want to be moved by that 'deep feeling of aliveness,' an attitude reflected in Laban's Effort work as well. Performers who do manifest this aliveness do so through Effort, or nuanced, qualitative action, action that is connected to an inner feeling, attitude or state of being. When in performance, 'We train ourselves to become cognizant of what our bodies already know and are expressing, we will have important and accurate information that can guide us along our way [...] art can be understood as the externalization of interior states of mind and body' (London 1989: 99–100).

A recent post by Catherine on the Segullah Blog provides a clear example of a performer who, through her embodied performance, invited the audience to participate in the choreographed, lived somatic journey of the dancer. Clearly, the writer felt the effects of the movement in/on her own body; she recognized that she had been moved beyond her own sensation to a compassionate and deeper understanding of her relationship with another human being:

> The way she moved looked weightier, more burdened than usual. [...] I noticed [...] the way she used every vertebrae, leapt bigger than big, and pulled inertia with her. [...] She danced from the inside out. [...] All the while spinning, folding, leaping, and stopping abruptly—feet wide—so close I could hear her breathe ... compulsive and deliberate ... a siege of determined abandon [...] she pulled [a shirt] rapidly over her head. She took off another, and another. [...] I twisted in my seat. I was sweating for her, feeling the bulk of her living with all those layers, wanting just as much as she did to throw them off. [...] Something caught in my throat the moment she peeled that last layer and I saw her move like I knew she could. [...] Jill was soaring. I hadn't expected to cry. But when I saw her [...] dancing without pretense, I pressed my hand to my chest, and swallowed against the tightness [...] watching her spin under the spotlight and fly against gravity made me think, I want that kind of freedom. I want to live that unburdened. That free. I want to live the layers that matter.
>
> (Catherine 2011: 1–5)

Guiding students to resonate with 'the layers that matter' by means of their own experience asks them to consider how they connect to the cosmic. This is rich with spiritual meaning.

If a choreographic work is narrative, as in the following example where explicit themes of relationship and connection feature prominently in the choreography, performers may find it easier to access emotional and spiritual connections. It is equally important in works that are not explicitly narrative for a performer to move beyond the surface level of the movement and access enduring themes, connecting the movement in meaningful ways through their own lived experience.

This past year a student of Pat's transformed her performance through accessing her own lived experience. She (Rachel) was to perform in a trio as the mother figure in a work where her two 'daughters' transgress familial codes through rebellion. During one particularly intense rehearsal Pat was trying to get her to move beyond the technical aspects of the dance and embody the role in an Effortful way. It was difficult going.

What was unknown to Pat at the time was that Rachel had, through her own mother, 'lived' the emotional trauma that was an inherent message of the dance. Pat could tell that Rachel related in a visceral way to what the 'mother' needed to express but that she was unable to access how to do so. Locked in her own tissue were memories, images and feelings that had the potential to inform her dancing but that she could not release.

Through Pat's coaching from an LMA Effort and Shape perspective and by Rachel giving herself permission to bring her own subjective experience to the performance, Rachel accessed the physical, emotional and spiritual essence of the dance and gained a sense of authenticity in performance that was riveting. What follows is an excerpt of Rachel's reflection on her experience:

> Our director had asked us to verbalize a section of the piece in which the two daughters clearly rebel against the mother. I did so half-heartedly, uncomfortable with the [...] potential of exposing deep inner feelings and thus embarrassing myself. At the end of the section, I sit in a chair in the center of the stage and stare straight ahead. I don't know what really happened, but in my perception of the memory both my director and the choreographer began closing in on me, pulling for those intense feelings that I was holding tight inside, demanding that I verbalize them with Strength and Directness. It was a moment [similar to] that of the [memorable] scene in the film *Dead Poet's Society* when Robin Williams is forcing his student to expose a place deep within himself in the creation of a poem about Walt Whitman.
>
> Physically at that moment, I felt beaten and exposed. [...] I felt like a bandage suddenly had been ripped off that had been hiding the wounds of heartache. I felt a new and intense wave of all the sadness, desperation, and anger overcome me. The most I could do to express what was inside of me was to cry.
>
> That was what it took for my outer expression to truly reflect my inner intention. I was then able to grapple with those experiences and emotions in a way far more productive than tears by bringing them into the open through dance. [...] I was able to dance with more Strength, because I accepted those powerful emotions that yearned for a Strong expression. I was more aware of my body attitudes, my Shaping, and how my Breath

could be used [...] not by forcing these technicalities upon the dance, but by simply living my experience [...] all that mattered was my own inner narrative [...] and poignant memories and emotions that were within me.

(Robinson, R. in Personal email, 2011)

In that moment and in subsequent performances, Rachel soared. Having liberated her body, mind and spirit she experienced the work in a numinous way and went on to generously share that with the audience.

Concluding Thoughts

'In all forms of art, informed somatic sensing of our experience leads us to an understanding of our own "living story" discovering that the divine [is] within us' (Corbett 2007: 32).

Experiencing dance technique, choreography and performance somatically, like living somatically, leads us to new truths and confirms already known intuitive truths about ourselves and the world we live in. The pedagogy of embodiment that we have presented invites dance educators to create learning environments wherein the numinous is encouraged and valued. Through somatic pedagogies, we lay the foundation for connection, empathy and compassion, the ground for spirituality.

As dance educators who value and seek embodied life in and beyond the studio, we affirm the primacy and sacred nature of body-based knowing. 'The body always leads us home [...] if we can simply learn to trust sensation and stay with it long enough for it to reveal appropriate action, movement, insight or feeling' (Ogden as cited in Knaster 1996: 369). As members of a spiritual community that views the physical body as sacred and necessary to learning and eternal progression, we celebrate the gift of bodily wisdom and encourage our community to explore ways for our students to claim their inner knowing and to discover and embody their inner sacred dances.

Acknowledgements

Permission was granted via written correspondence to reference student names, coursework assignments and rehearsal description.

References

Bradley, K. (2010), e-mail to listserve CMA, cmalist@denison.edu, 29 September.
Brady, R. (2005), *Spirituality in Higher Education Newsletter*, 2:2, p. 1.

Catherine, A. (2011), 'Layers', *Segullah*, 9 November, http://segullah.org/daily-special/layer/# comment-193106. Accessed 7 July 2012.

Corbett, L. (2007), *Psyche and the Sacred: Spirituality Beyond Religion*, New Orleans, LA: Spring Journal Books.

Dawson, K. (1994), 'Leaving my father's house', in J. Lee, *Writing from the Body*, New York, NY: St. Martin's Press.

Driver, T. (1998), *Liberating Rites: Understanding the Transformative Power of Ritual*, , in A. Pryer (2004), 'Marking and making the (earth's) body: On ritual, relationship, place and pedagogy', *Educational Insights*, 9:1, http://www.ccfi.educ.ubc.ca/publication/insights/v09n01/articles/pryer.html. Accessed 25 November 2011.

Hackney, P. (1998), *Making Connections: Total Body Integration through Bartenieff Fundamentals*, Amsterdam: Gordon and Breach.

Heller, J. and Henkin, W. (1991), *Bodywise*, Oakland, CA: Wingbow Press.

Keen, S. (1990), *To a Dancing God—Notes of a Spiritual Traveler*, San Francisco, CA: Harper.

Knaster, M. (1996), *Discovering the Body's Wisdom*, New York, NY: Bantam Books.

Laban, R. (1939), 'Dance in general', in L. Ulmann (ed.) (1971), *Rudolf Laban Speaks about Movement and Dance*, Addlestone, UK: Laban Art of Movement Centre.

Laban, R. (1975 [1935]), *A Life For Dance* (trans. L. Ullmann), London, UK: MacDonald & Evans.

Lee, J. (1994), *Writing from the Body*, New York, NY: St. Martin's Press.

Leonard, L. S. (2009), *The Call to Create: Listening to the Muse in Art and Everyday Life*, New Orleans, LA: Spring Journal Books.

London, P. (1989), *No More Second Hand Art*, Boston, MA: Shambhala.

Moore, T. (1998), *Care of the Soul*, New York, NY: HarperCollins.

O'Reilley, M. R. (1998), *Radical Presence—Teaching as Contemplative Practice*, Portsmouth, NH: Boynton/Cook Publishers, Inc.

Peat, D. (2011), 'The alchemy of creativity: Art, consciousness and embodiment', http://www.fdavidpeat.com/bibliography/essays/embody.htm. Accessed 8 July 2012.

Pryer, A. (2004), 'Marking and making the (earth's) body: On ritual, relationship, place and pedagogy', *Educational Insights*, 9:1, http://www.ccfi.educ.ubc.ca/publication/insights/v09n01/articles/pryer.html. Accessed 25 November 2011.

Taylor, B. B. (2010), *A Geography of Faith: An Altar in the World*, New York, NY: HarperOne.

Webster's Seventh New Collegiate Dictionary (1963), Springfield, MA: G. & C. Merriam Company.

Notes

1 In this chapter 'dance' refers to modern and contemporary dance forms of the 20th and 21st centuries.

2 Constructivist theory encapsulates the belief that all knowledge must be actively and subjectively constructed and that the meaning-making process takes place in environments

where personal discovery and reflection are valued. This meaning-making process is heightened through constructivist practices such as kinesthetic learning, visual and auditory modalities and dialogue that encourages deeply personal connections to the subject matter being presented.

3   Margaret h'Doubler, Alwin Nikolais and Doris Humphrey developed pedagogies that became the scaffolding for dance curricula and programmes in higher education in the United States in the first half of the 20th century.

Chapter 14

This Indivisible Moment: A Meditation on Language, Spirit, Magic, and Somatic Practice

Ray Schwartz

A Body-Mind Centering® teacher of mine once suggested that, 'Matter is the universe's way of making love with itself'.

(Bruhn 1997)

Note on the Format of the Chapter

It took me a while to arrive at the structure of this chapter. Many drafts were initially written in a more traditional manner, one that presupposed a narrator speaking to an unknown reader. The further I went into my research, the more I realized that this was not an accurate or representative model of the process by which I was engaging with the issues. As I built the chapter, I would spend days reading and writing, and then on my 'down time', I would find myself asking questions and talking to myself in order to try and make sense of very complex subtleties. What became clear over time was that questions of spirituality, for me, lay in the space of relational action—and that for me the best model to discuss this was by modelling a dialogue. In the following pages, I present a conversational meditation on various aspects of spirit and somatic practice, because I wish to illustrate the cognitive/reflective/dialogic process that I went through in considering the themes of this book. It is my hope that rather than presenting a fractured, fragmented, or dualistic self, I am able to reveal the complex intellectual back and forth that arises for me when trying to negotiate territories of experience that are seemingly both concrete and ephemeral.

Could you tell me a little bit about yourself?

Sure, my pleasure. I am a dancer, a choreographer, a somatic movement educator, bodyworker and arts activist. I believe in the body. I am interested in how attentive embodied practice leads one towards a treasure trove of innate wisdom and fundamental function that guides one into the mysteries and profundities of life. I love movement. I love sensation. I love to pay attention to the multitudes of possibilities that arise for expression and artistry when one engages with the self in an embodied way.

Well, that's a mouthful. How did you come to be such a fan of the body and embodiment?

I used to run and play soccer and swim as a child, but there was not a whole lot of embodied energy in my home. We used words a lot, and did not always use them effectively to

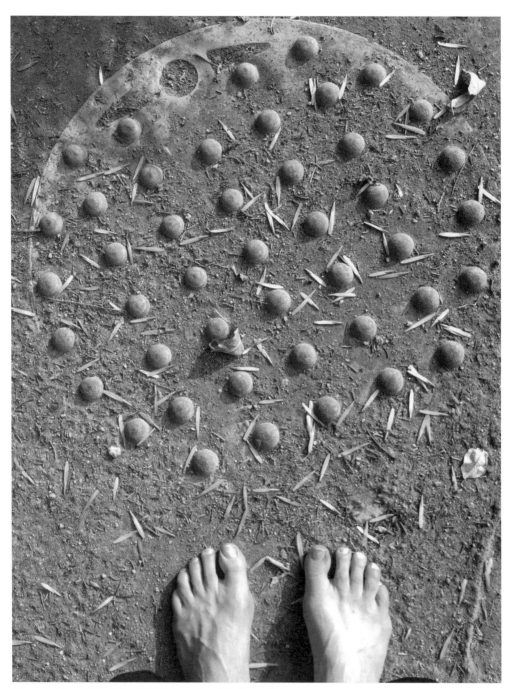

Figure 1: Mover: Julie Rothschild. Photographer: Julie Rothschild.

communicate emotionally. I remember that I carried a lot of anger and I felt a strong sense of injustice in the world. I am sure I had a lot of other feelings as well, and I did not have as many models for expressing them as I might have wanted. As I grew up, I started to find myself attracted to theatre and eventually dance. The combination of expressive and aesthetic opportunity, integrated with a practice of physical discipline and rigor, seemed to both offer me more models for expression and to give me direction for a way to be in the world.

I understand how artistic practice could have given you all of that. How did you end up becoming interested in Somatics?

I began my serious dance training at a conservatory, the North Carolina School of the Arts (NCSA). My initial training there focused on classical modern dance. Graham, Nikolais and Horton techniques formed the foundation of my dance education. While the education I received was valuable, it came saddled with what some might call an 'old school' approach. In this model, it was the teacher's job to break you down and build you back up in the image considered most effective for success.

The methods used to achieve this often took the form of verbal abuse, psychological manipulation, fear-based pedagogy and an absolute demarcation between student submission and faculty authority. What many of the faculty who were teaching there at that time saw in us, I suppose, was the raw material for their own imprimatur rather than a person with his/her own values who might be guided into conversation and development. We were led to value the outside eye more than our own internal sensations; we were encouraged to work towards the teacher's approval at the expense of our own interests or desires, and we were often reprimanded or berated as way of motivating us to work even harder.

As a young artist trying to navigate the terrain of a novel and alien form such as modern dance, this proved very confusing. I was, on the one hand, being invited into a history of Western theatrical dance that valued experimentation and personal expression, while at the same time being told that to stray outside the lines of external approval and design was unacceptable. While I am sure that there were good intentions behind all of these methods, it was hard to see them at the time.

Seems like a heavy place.

It was, in its way, but it also helped me in many ways. I gained an experiential appreciation for the history and legacy of modern dance from NCSA. Understanding who preceded me in this field, what they were responding to and how they planted the seeds of this unique tradition has helped me to understand my own place within its lineage. Many aspects of the technical foundation I received from my training there still live in my body today. Additionally, I have heard that the school has changed a lot since those years, and that some of those changes began when teachers who had an interest in Somatic Movement Education started to add their voices to the pedagogy.

Okay, so where did you go after your conservatory training?

After I left NCSA, I transferred to a university dance programme in Virginia. In contrast to my early conservatory experiences, my college years offered a model upon which a democracy of learning could be built. Studies at Virginia Commonwealth University (VCU) exposed me to a range of technical and creative synthesis that helped me see ways for integrating my past into a dance practice that was more expressive of myself. For someone who was attracted to the arts because of their expressive potential and their ability to effect social justice, I was relieved to find other models of education available.

While there, I enjoyed an environment of profound support for the creative process and experimentation. I learned to value the principles of creative research, intense questioning, rigorous discipline, personal freedom and a dance that speaks of its time. I also learned that there were other ways to frame a life of the body.

And when did Somatics come into the picture?

At VCU, I had my first experiences with Somatic Movement Education, being introduced to the work of Laban Movement Analysis, Body-Mind Centering® (BMC) and the Feldenkrais Method. I am now certified as a practitioner of Body-Mind Centering® and the Feldenkrais Method.

And how does this somatic practice inform your work as a dancer now?

Somatics, while in many ways consistent with values implicit in some dance, differs from a dance framework that is concerned with external modelling, quantitative analysis of body positioning and objectification of the body for the purposes of creating a functioning instrument as opposed to an expressive person. As Sondra Fraleigh once told me:

> If you come through the professional world of dance, you will have various experiences with the choreographers who are producing their work, and they are often, but not always, more interested in the work they are producing, and the dancers are their tools—and are, unfortunately, treated that way. In more classical and dualistic definitions of dance they are material. The body is the instrument, and the medium is movement. This instrumental idea of the body, that you are just playing an instrument—that these are tools—kind of objectified the person. To believe that the medium of dance is really the human being is a little bit different than viewing the body as an instrument.
>
> (2005)

I think my work with Somatics has guided me away from this instrumental notion of dance and towards a more humanistic and phenomenological engagement with dance practice. I assume it is this 25-year odyssey of working with dance and somatic practice that afforded me the invitation to be a part of this book.

Yes, I think the editors were interested in what people with a history of embodied practice may have to say about spirit.

I must admit, when I was first approached about contributing to this book, I was hesitant.

Why?

Mostly because I would never have suggested that I am terribly concerned with questions of spirit in my work as a somatic practitioner. As a somatic practitioner, I spend a lot of time pursuing and advocating for an integrated self, and the word 'spirit' tends to bring up images of separation and fragmentation of my being.

Well, I propose a challenge. What if you agreed to wrestle with your own preconceptions and see if there might be something missing?

You mean like a thought experiment? A game of ideas, if you will?

Yes. Is there a way in which we could investigate your prejudices in order to reclaim a relationship to spirit that doesn't feel so alienating and uncomfortable? Is there some way to construct a conversation that allows you to get closer to a definition of 'spirit' that coheres to the work one does as a somatic practitioner? How might this lead us to a place of better clarity and appreciation of spirit?

Okay. I can give it a try. But in order to do that, I think I need to expand the argument to include more than just Somatics and spirit. I need to discuss magic.

Magic? What is your argument?

What if the premise was the following: Somatics is like magic. Magic and Somatics concern themselves with connection, consciousness and experience. When one engages in magical or somatic practice, one activates spirit in the world, and this can be a very powerful thing. This activated spirit is not the spirit of moral and religious association, neither a fundamental presence that transcends life, nor a second self that lives parallel—rather it is a consequence of living in relation to the world.

What would be necessary in order to accept that argument? How would you build it?

First I would have to examine the links between Somatics and magic, then I would have to discuss the ways in which the concepts implicit in the word 'spirit' have been cut away from embodiment, and finally I could propose to reframe the idea of spirit as a moment of activated engagement—a definition that feels embraceable to me as a somatic practitioner.

So you would reframe and reclaim the concepts embedded in the word 'spirit,' and in doing so, present a way of approaching spirit that might be useful for other somatic practitioners?

That is what I hope to do, but it seems a complex proposition. Maybe my own intellectual journey here will provide some food for thought for people who have similar struggles, and maybe, in the end, it will allow the concept of 'spirit' to come out from the shadows of somatic work and take a place at the table, where it need not be ashamed. If I am successful in my intention, I will have begun to free spirit from its restrictive notions, to release it from the imposition that having to represent a pure and untainted separateness has afforded it.

If I understand you, by taking this thought journey, you hope to move a step or two closer to repositioning the concept of 'spirit' as one of connection and exchange. Perhaps you can let spirit be not a thing, but a moment, a moment of action that is manifested when consciousness relates.

Exactly. But in order to do that I would need to establish what I mean by 'consciousness' and 'relation.' I have found that turning to magic seems to give me a way in. Let us begin with a quote:

> If there is a single thing that life teaches us, it's that wishing doesn't make it so. Words and thoughts do not change anything. Language and reality are kept strictly apart—reality is tough and unyielding and it doesn't care what you think or feel or say about it. Or it should not. You deal with it and you get on with your life. Little children do not know that. Magical thinking: that's what Freud called it. Once we learn otherwise we cease to be children. The separation of word and thing are the essential facts on which our adult lives are founded. But somewhere in the heart of Magic that boundary between word and thing ruptures. It cracks, and the one flows back into the other, and the two melt together and fuse. Language gets tangled up with the world it describes.
>
> (Grossman 2009: 216)

What I like about this quote is that it puts the world together again. It lets us understand that magic is about the way things relate, not the way they differentiate. And this is an important idea for me.

When you mention magic, the first things that come to mind are wizards, fireballs and realms of fantasy and hocus-pocus.

In the age of Harry Potter, many people find themselves enchanted but deeply misinformed about the world of magic. Susan Greenwood notes:

> It [Magic] comprises a 'holistic' alternative way of seeing the world, one that is frequently rooted in an awareness of the spirituality of the everyday, the earth, the body with all its attendant thoughts, feelings and emotions, and a sense of the interconnectedness of it all.
>
> (2005: Xi)

I have sometimes heard what we do in Somatics described as magic.

When I was teaching Body-Mind Centering® (BMC) for dance at the Bates Dance Festival in the summer of 2002, the students began to devise alternative definitions for the abbreviation BMC. One such title was 'Big Magic Crackers.'

Why do you think they used those words?

I think they chose this term because the group that year was particularly connected. The level of exploration, intimacy, movement exploration and expression was quite profound, and the experience felt a little unbelievable, as if we were subject to magic.

So magic is mysterious, impossible to explain?

I don't really think so, but perhaps they did. I will admit that for some people, the effects of somatic practice are difficult to explain. We feel it, but something about the experience seems to transcend the logical mind. The depths of sensation, the unearthing of images and memories, the emotional connections, the altered states of consciousness, the involuntary movements that sometimes arise from somatic exploration—all of these can seem like sorcery.

But I personally don't think it is sorcery. Eugene Subbotsky recently wrote an intriguing book about magical reality. In it he argues for a re-consideration of magic as not something impossible or fantastic but rather a logical system that can be articulated and described. Of most interest to our discussion, though, is the following: 'In contrast to natural forces (such as gravity and electromagnetic fields), which operate in a predictable way and are devoid of any consciousness, magical forces assume implicit communication between a person and the world' (2010: 9).

So this implicit communication, where does it fit into Somatics?

Communication between conscious entities is a necessary starting point for any somatic intervention. Let us look at where the concept of Somatics comes from. The term 'Somatics,' drew from 'soma,' 'the Greek word which since the time of Hesiod has stood for the living body' (Joly 2004: 3). Thomas Hanna, responsible for organizing various methodologies under the name 'Somatics' described the field in the following way: 'The field which studies the soma: namely the body as perceived from within by first person perception' (1986: 4).

Don Hanlon Johnson, a former Jesuit priest and a leading force in theorizing the diverse practices associated with Somatics, spoke to the history of Hanna's word choice:

He was inspired in that definition by the phenomenologist Edmund Husserl, who at the turn of the century set out an agenda for what he called a 'somatology,' a study of the relationships between knowledge derived from direct bodily experience and scientific studies of the body. These phrases originate in the classical Greek contrast between the dead body, necros, and the enspirited person, soma. That 'somatology' would stand as a corrective to what might be called a 'necrology', the body of medical science whose fundamental ideas about body parts and their structures have been derived from the dissection and analysis of corpses.

(1997: 10)

Interesting. Johnson mentions soma as an 'enspirited' person. Are we getting closer to something here?

I think it would be useful to ask Johnson what he means by 'spirit' here. As a former Jesuit priest, he may have some relationship to spirit that is aligned with religious perspective—an animating force that gives more meaning to the body than a collection of tissues or a mass of flesh.

Is that what spirit is for you?

I don't think so. But perhaps we need to travel a bit more deeply into Somatics and magic before we get there. For my purposes, I note that Somatics focuses on body and mind as an integrated process, respects subjective experience as a priority and places this subjectivity within a dialogic model. That definition of Somatics seems like it may offer some points of connection with Subbotsky's ideas of magical practice. Unlike hard science, which seeks to remove subjective experience from the experiment, Somatics and magic embrace the personal and relational in the equation. Or as Greenwood says when describing magical consciousness,

> Magical consciousness, as an aspect of human cognition, may be equated with what Lévy-Bruhl has termed 'the law of participation.' Lévy-Bruhl saw participation as a psychic unity, a fundamental state of mind, that included individuals, society and the living as well as the dead; he described it as a type of thinking that created relationships between things through unseen forces and influences.

(2005: 89)

Could it be that, drawing on this analogy with magic, the somatic approach is that tissues, which are sometimes viewed in science as solely objects, are in fact objects with consciousness?

I remember something Bonnie Bainbridge Cohen wrote once about BMC: 'The essence of BMC is the embodiment process. This is the act of awakening and enlivening the consciousness of our whole being, in all the cells of our body' (2009).

By working with these tissues, are we working with consciousness?

Personally, I think that is what we are doing in Somatics, but it is important to note what we mean by consciousness. The type of consciousness we are discussing could perhaps better be described as 'vibration.' The velocity, frequency and tone of these vibrations differ from object to object. By perceiving consciousness as vibration, and employing techniques of resonance, communication with and among the natural world becomes possible.

Communication towards what end?

Towards living a more complete life, one in which there is a balance between internal and external authority, and an honest communion with our inner nature and the world that we inhabit.

This reading of Somatics is different from the typical stance in which bodywork and somatic education have attempted to embrace and expand scientific knowledge in order to address issues of functional and mechanical use, as well as deepen access to efficient movement patterns and ease.

While that is certainly one application of somatic practice, it is not the whole picture. Within the framework of a Western, individualistic and anti-intellectual culture—concerned with pragmatism—the therapeutic aspects of somatic work have overshadowed its phenomenological roots. Given this precedent, it is not surprising that more practical aspects of the work have come to the foreground, while ignoring or even advocating against the implications inherent in a method which questions authority and recalibrates assumptions about where knowledge lies. Somatic education may foster a richer sense of authority and agency in a person. Personal agency is something to value, not fear; and agency achieved through embodiment can contribute to a state of living in respectful harmony with one another and the world we are a part of.

Somatics has a radical posture towards the world.

And therein lies the potential problem. The somatic approach places the knowing of the student in an important place in the rubric of who is an expert and who holds power in a situation. Agency can be perceived as a threat to systems that wish to exert their dominance on social and cultural contexts.

What is agency?

Agency is the ability to act within the world from a place of self-definition. Let me tell you a story that might help explain it:

When I was about 7 years old, a family friend took me along with his wife and kids, to eat at a cafeteria. In the cafeteria, you basically went along the line choosing different foods that you wanted and then paid for the food, found a table and ate. My eyes had obviously been tantalized by more than my stomach could manage. So after a while, I was full, yet still had food left on my plate. The family friend made it very clear to me that we were not going to leave the restaurant until I had finished every single thing on my tray. And through my tears and pleading, he remained a stern and stoic figure who would not budge in his authority that I must learn that I needed to complete the proposal that I started. If I said I wanted that much food to eat, then by golly, I would eat that much food.

I am not trying to demonize him. There are millions of versions of my story. From the 'do not waste your food because people somewhere do not have the luxury to eat even a small portion of what you have,' to 'if we paid for that much food, then you need to understand the value of money, and so you will consume what we paid for,' etc. All of which, on a certain level, have some sort of moral value in considering, and he was not trying to be evil in his efforts to teach me what he felt was an important lesson.

Years later, though, when this story came up in a somatic training in which I was participating, another interpretation of the situation was presented to me. While it was true that my empty stomach and my hunger had inspired me to choose a variety of dishes before I sat down to eat, during the meal, my senses and perceptions were communicating to me that I was full. My internal authority said stop eating, but the external authority of a surrogate parental figure who apparently had the right to tell me what to do, made it clear that I should not trust my own internal authority but rather submit to his. In a sense—while I do not think this overtly affected my future relationship to food—I was being trained not to trust myself. It was a moment that could have had serious repercussions. It could have been the beginning of an eating disorder.

In my case, while I do not think the experience contributed to a problem, the point is to note that from an early age I remember being told not to trust somatic information. I was being taught that there was a more important authority with which I should align myself. The same message came through again and again in schools, through religious training, via the media and advertising. In some way or another, I was being taught how to be in the world. How to be was not related to how I felt, but rather to how I should behave, regardless of what my corporeal impulses told me.

So you are saying that Somatics contributes to agency by providing tools for knowing ourselves in an experiential way and encourages us to value the sensations, images, thoughts and emotions that arise from connecting to our embodiment?

Yes, as a sailor may value his compass when deep in the dark sea on a night without stars.

Connecting magic back into the conversation. How does magic embrace agency?

By acknowledging 'the assumption that physical objects at the receptive end of a communicative process have some kind of consciousness' (Subbotsky 2010: 9). This agency is the prime actor in the drama of our lives, and all too often cultural pressures to conform or to obey can dampen the vital light within this aspect of our character.

To limit somatic practices to the mechanical is to limit the true function of the work.

The function of Somatics—and I would add, magic—is one of art and philosophy, not one of science. While informed by scientific knowledge and tendencies, the central questions are concerned with action and experience.

Phenomenology argues that, 'although philosophical proofs for the independent existence of objects perceived through the senses are impossibly difficult to establish, human beings nevertheless experience the external world as objects of consciousness, regardless of the ultimate ontological status of these things' (Auslander and Deal 2008: 137).

The existence, or not, of an objective reality is not important because it cannot be proven. What we should be focusing on is, instead, experience of these objects that engage our attention.

Or as Subbotsky says, 'Both art and magic imply a fusion between mind and nature. They aim at a different goal from that of science; whereas the ultimate goal of science is product, the ultimate goal of art and magic is meaning' (2010: x).

Exactly. Can magical thinking help us to free spirit from the political and cultural cage we find it in? Could magic's supposition that the world is embodied and that there is consciousness in everything aid us in knowing sprit?

I would like to think so. But let's look at how language has created problems for us in our quest to know spirit. Merleau-Ponty said, 'Our own body is in the world as the heart is in the organism' (1986: 205). Through language, he was able to transmit the primacy of being that formed the foundation of his phenomenological argument.

And yet language can also confuse or obfuscate.

So much language has been employed in the service of manipulation, confusion and misdirection as to make us distrustful and perhaps shy of embracing it as somatic practitioners. As a result, we sometimes herald experience and sensation as being more important than intellect, analysis and clarity of thought.

Isn't this a necessary approach if we are to attempt to reclaim our lives and agency from a reality that can seem predetermined and inflexible?

Well, yes, but it should not deny the fact that language is a part of us, born from this same experience and capable of shaping the future of our embodiment.

Structuralists attempted to use language to describe an inflexible and absolute reality. Reality, though, is tendency.

To paraphrase Bergson and Andison (1965), when we use concepts from language, we are trying to fix these tendencies, thus our descriptors can only be a fragment of reality, but not reality itself.

Language defines and divides. It captures ideas and places them inside conceptual containers thus allowing us to handle them with a sense of clarity and distinction, but language can also destroy wholeness by compartmentalizing the world into pieces.

It seems to be a Faustian bargain. Here, on the one hand, is a tool for communicating about the world, but in order to have this communication, the world must surrender its experiential integrity and be subject to the differentiating power of words. Language, while being intimately linked to experience, often seems to be a finger pointing at the moon rather than the feeling of bathing in a lunar glow. So how do you deal with this problem?

When I began my Feldenkrais training, I was struck by the way words were used in such a precise way. As part of the methodology of 'Awareness through Movement™', the teacher does not demonstrate the movements contained in the lesson. Rather, he describes them with precise and specific language. A good teacher can be very exacting in his descriptions and the students are able to find their own relationship to the instructions. In this way, the students are not modelling the actions of something outside of themselves but are invited to engage with their own patterns and habits as a way of knowing themselves better. In learning this method, I became fascinated with the subtext implied in the words chosen to describe things. To say 'move your body', or 'lift your arm' was to emphasize the body as an object, something passive, without its own intelligence, that we controlled and which was subject to the whims of a separate entity in the pilot's seat.

Master teachers in the training often made statements like 'feel the contact with the floor', 'observe the self rising and falling', or 'lift the arm' rather than 'lift your arm'. As subtle a difference as it is, these language choices seemed to me to be an attempt to amend the Cartesian split, to reunify body, mind and spirit in to a single integer—a self—which could describe the integrated whole that we are energetically activating when we enter into somatic processes. In my own work, I often use the term 'self' rather than 'body'. I find it slightly more expansive and thus slightly more available to contain the wholeness with which I wish to engage.

I like that, because it seems that when we use the concept of 'self', we are focusing on the fact that our work is with individuals, unique persons who cannot be treated mechanically. They are integrated, not separated. This supports the idea that we are working with consciousness.

Yes. I am often uncomfortable with terms like body, mind, soul, spirit and so on to describe aspects of a consciousness that is really, for me, a continuous whole. My exposure to Christian, Hindu and other traditions that assume a separate and eternal self—one which transcends biological life as we know it, and contributes to a feeling apart from embodied experience—confuses me. It flies in the face of my convictions that spirit is something else—not related to life and afterlife, but rather related to engagement, relation and connection within this life.

What is important for me in considering the themes of this book is the idea that by linguistically identifying something as spirit, we may err on the side of assuming that this spirit is something with the quality of concreteness.

What I wish to argue is that spirit is pure experience. It does not exist apart from its relationship to other things and cannot be identified purely as a discrete object. To have devoted a word to this experiential moment undercuts the power of its presence by subjecting it to the isolation and containment that language gives to phenomena.

Given all these challenges with language, it is perhaps more easily understood that something about Somatics distances itself from the spirit. Maybe spirituality is not often discussed directly in the world of Somatics because the traditional notion of 'spirit,' or perhaps religiously postulated 'spirit,' suggests something apart from the corporeal, and Somatics views the self as an expression of an integrated corporeal reality. This division and its resulting conflicts may be one reason why somatic practitioners have heretofore refrained from embracing it as a primary focus in the development of the field.

This is certainly true for me. I find myself so in awe of the subtleties of movement and texture, and the intelligence that lives in tissue that I wonder if I even need concern myself with understanding immateriality when there is such richness to be found in the flesh.

You seem puzzled by the idea that there is soul, sprit or eternal self, separate from bodily life.

It is not how I feel intuitively. Intuitively, I feel that mind and body and spirit and soul are not separate entities, but rather different expressions of vibrational frequencies through which the universe manifests itself. Perhaps contributing to my confusion is that I grew up in a world in which there was so much media information available. As an avid reader, and a watcher of movies, a committed consumer of music and song, and as someone who loves the visual, I have been inundated with images, ideas and expressions of sprit from around the world, born of today or archived through human history. A lot of this information supports the notion of a transcendent separate spirit. Having grown up in the 1970s and 1980s in the United States, my adolescence coincided with the birth of the New Age movement in which bodies of light, supra-physical meditation practices, create-your-own-reality seminars, energy work and non-denominational grab-bags of spiritual tendencies were marketed as do-it-yourself, instant inner lives.

Growing up in the U.S., Hollywood's apparent obsession with depicting the life force as an image of coloured light escaping the body at the moment of death was coupled with countless images of Christian ideology in which bodily suffering, as the price Jesus paid to save our eternal non-earthly souls, was articulated as an inspiration to adopt a set of values and beliefs that would award spiritual peace and a promise of everlasting life in a heaven beyond this world. Soaring melodies and sustained notes in song were meant to inspire my higher perceptual faculties and relate these feelings to spirit. Poetry and language sought to lift me from my baser instincts and guide me upwards into refined expressions of mind.

If spirit is not separate, then how can we re-frame our relationship to it so as to counteract the above-mentioned cultural influences?

One way is to move away from what Don Hanlon Johnson, in his book *Body, Spirit and Democracy*, calls 'vertical enlightenment' (1994: 101–07), and look down into the substance of body, sensations, feelings, vibration and movement. Rather than seeking to submit myself to an awesome disembodied power above me, I can connect to the ecological support systems within which I actually live. For me, working with embodiment gives me the assurance

I need to survive life's existential doubts. Within the body, in all of its gristle and pulse, is my necessary truth.

So the body has all you need to know?

In my years as a somatic practitioner, I have found myself marvelling at how much there is to notice, to feel, learn from, activate and engage with in my bodily life. Must there be anything else? Let me tell you another story. In the summer of 1990, I was studying in an intensive language course in Bahasa Indonesia at Cornell University. I lived in a co-op, the Stuart Little House, with a mix of students. One of my housemates was an Indian physicist working on his Ph.D. One evening, we began to talk about his research. He told me he was working on reincarnation. In college I minored in Religious Studies, with a focus on Asian traditions. In the late 1970s, much of the cutting edge research in theoretical physics was often hard to distinguish from Vedic philosophy. Theories like quantum physics, string theory, etc., resonate with theories of multiple planes of reality or the vibrational tone of Om as the fundamental structure of the universe.

When my housemate mentioned that he was studying the physics of reincarnation, it was both intriguing and also not difficult to imagine. I remember his work as the following: If it is true that the law of conservation of mass is true and that nothing escapes the universe, then it might also be true that the constituent mass of our selves follow some sort of predictable algorithm when we die that determines how this mass might disintegrate from us and re-integrate into the world. In other words, are there principles that govern the re-distribution of me into the surrounding biosphere either throughout life or after death?

I began to see that my notions of reincarnation had been influenced by a Christian notion of an eternal spirit that lives separate from its vessel and changes houses, as it were, in the process of reincarnation. This soul/spirit/personality would leave one earthly body and enter another in a continuous cycle of death and rebirth. I realized that reincarnation could exist without the need for an eternal personality. When I let go of my own cultural background about the meaning of the term, it ended up looking a lot more like recycling, and for me this notion of a non-personal yet interdependent reality seemed like a much more morally and ecologically satisfying way to imagine my responsibility to the world and my agency within it.

Life is temporary, or at least as far as we can tell, it begins and ends. The need to imagine ourselves beyond the time we have has given rise to certain impulses that give us permanence.

And that permanence has become the subject of moral and religious focus by powerful parties with interests both honest and prurient. As battles for control are waged between religious and scientific visions of the universe, we can sometimes see the limits of the debate. Both sides work with extremes. Spirit is or it isn't.

There doesn't seem to be any effort to listen and/or dialogue about what we might really be talking about. There seems to be little room for working together to generate new forms of knowledge.

The heritage of language has made the struggle to reconcile religious notions of purity and morality with the often obtuse and mysterious temporality of embodied life very challenging indeed. In his book, *After Death*, author Darryl Reanny (1995) suggests that post-biological permanence, rather than being an ordained truth delivered by an omniscient god, is an assumption that humans have developed because of the conflicts presented by a biologically programmed need to survive, mixed with a consciousness of mortality. In his theory, once we know that we must die, it is fundamentally necessary to generate some kind of belief system that allows us to believe that there is something approximating a life after death because without this belief our cognitive systems would determine that there is no reason to live and we would lose initiative or purpose and essentially die from depression and inertia.

The notion of an eternal spirit is perhaps a psychological survival mechanism for a species that knows too much?

I do not deal well with the idea of something after death. My biggest problem with religious ideas that depend on the purity or cleansing of a soul or spirit is that it seems to me that we are outsourcing responsibility in this life for one that will come after. It seems that the impulse to treat each other well during our time on this planet is based on what kind of reward you will get after you die rather than on the simple fact that life is more pleasant when we treat each other with kindness.

So here we are, in this body in this life, trying to find a connection to the world. Trying to be here now, as it were. How does one do it?

For starters, I work with breath a lot. It is fundamental to almost all movement practice and has a lot do with the interface between pure concrete physicality and emotional work as well. Also, as defined by Michele Dillon, 'spirituality derives from the Latin *spiritus*, [or] breath, from *spirare*, to blow, to breathe' (2003: 138). Breath … so undeniably fundamental to the act of being has been separated in many notions of spirituality, from its root in the somatic self, signifying for many, it seems, an essence apart from corporeal life. Spirit, a moment of engagement, when reconnected to breath is an animating energy: a life force. A force that awakens in matter a feeling of aliveness.

How do you work with breath?

I do a variety of things with breath. Allow me to share two ways in which I think breath is important in my work. When I work with young dance students, I often ask them why they want to dance. Often times they report that they wish to express themselves. They want to perform so that the public can feel what they feel. This is all well and good, except for the fact that the students have very little understanding of what it means to analyse and reproduce the variables implicit in emotional expression within a theatrical context. They assume that if they just 'feel,' it will be enough. One of the exercises I use to help them understand that expression is a bodily activity, and that our bodies and minds are deeply integrated, is to teach them to explore breath. We look at the depth, velocity, rhythm, force and weight of the breath in order to understand the body's participation in feelings like anxiety, happiness, anger, desire, etc.

After a while of working with these techniques, it seems like you can begin to understand that we are not separate, and that by going into somatic practice, one can access the emotional and feeling body as well as the fleshy one.

Another thing I do, when I am working privately with clients in bodywork, is to use powerful tactile interventions that can bring up intense sensation. In certain contexts, clients will come to a point of crisis in which their ability to sustain presence in the face of bodily sensation is challenged. Oftentimes, the client will retract. The remedy to these moments of escape is breath. It is through consciously connecting to breath that people are able to reconnect to the present moment and to remain rooted in the here and now. Clients have reported that by learning to breathe through crisis, they were better able to relate to challenges that the world presents.

And how do these breath practices relate to spirit?

When we consider that spirit is associated with the immaterial, it is interesting to note that one can access the supposedly immaterial through breath. Are we contacting spirit? Perhaps, but for me, the work I do with breath reinforces my sense of the integration of body, mind and emotion and it causes me to question and reimagine spirit.

Okay. So here we come to the crux of this discussion. We have discussed Somatics, magic, connection, consciousness and experience. We have noted that relational consciousness is a common theme and that both Somatics and magic are concerned with valuing the agency that exists within and arises from respecting this consciousness. You have suggested that when one engages in magical or somatic practice, one activates spirit in the world, and this can be a very powerful thing. But what is this spirit that you are activating if it is not a spirit apart, out of time and space?

Good question. Spirit is, perhaps, a frequency of vibration that occurs when two or more sources resonate. This resonance need not be consonant or dissonant, but rather exists in states of tension or release and is dependent for its expression on where it arises from and how it transforms into the next moment. Spirit lives between actions. It manifests in particular ways only through the fact that there are antecedents and responses. It cannot exist apart from time and does not remain stable and permanent once it has come into expression. Rather, its expression forms the conditions for further possibilities of interchange and dynamic action. Viewed in this way, spirit does not need to be an eternal personality that lives beyond death; it does not need to dress itself in white light and float about on clouds. Perhaps it is simply the relationship between things.

Umm…sorry to interrupt, but I am getting little bit lost. What concerns me is that a moment ago it seemed that you had this idea about spirit being embodied and now it seems like you are changing your perspective. It seems you were trying to say that spirit was a part of body, not something separate. Now it seems like you are saying something else entirely.

Not really. I do think spirit is a part of body, in that it requires a body to manifest itself, but as well, it does live apart, but it is not eternal and does not manifest as a permanent self. It lives in relation to experience. It is a result of relationship, and relationship is a result of being embodied and capable of engaging in the world. Agency, if you will.

Okay, I can go with you there. Spirit is sort of ephemeral; it is here and not here. Sort of like trying to catch air with open fingers. It passes through.

No, not exactly, because that would assume a permanence. The air is there but you cannot touch it or contain it exactly. What I am saying is that spirit is only present when there is relation. When I connect to you, or you connect to a tree or a dog connects to another dog, this is when spirit is manifested. It requires action. Without this relation, spirit is not present. Spirit is the movement in a relationship.

That is good. Somatics is deeply concerned with movement. So are you saying that when Somatics works with movement, it is working with spirit?

I might be. I think the movement has to be relational, though. If the movement that occurs when your consciousness is resonating with yourself or with another aspect of the world and, in particular, is embracing the consciousness or vibration of that other aspect—then we may be working with spirit. When I am simply touching a stone but not the stone-ness of the stone, so to speak, then perhaps I am not working with spirit.

I am thinking of a zero balancing teacher who told me that there is 'moving the bones and then there is the movement in the bone' (Smith). Could that be what you mean by stone-ness?

Yes, exactly. We can touch the object, but that is just objectifying something. Magic, for example, doesn't happen in that kind of relationship. When you touch the essence of something or create a resonance with that essence, then magic occurs. We seek resonance. We want to interface with the movement in the bones more than the movement of the bones.

Ok, so you are interested in magic.

Well yes, if magic is defined as I have mentioned above, then I am interested in reconnecting to what moves us in the world. If magic is a practice that can aid in that reconnection, then I am certainly interested in it.

So you want to cast spells on people when they are coming to work with you in your somatic practice.

No, I am not interested in that. I want to help people to reclaim something. A sense of being able to trust themselves, to feel that their internal authority is respected and that the choices they make are informed by an organismic intelligence. To quote a friend, who after reading a draft of this chapter wrote:

> Yes, Somatics is Magic. Engaging with the material world in a transformative way expands our sense of self, and that allows for the kind of awareness and intention in relationships and interactions that can continue to connect us to something larger than ourselves, the web of life.
>
> (Beadle 2011)

I guess you could say I want to help people to feel like they have access to their own personal magic in living their lives.

And that by becoming fluent in this magic, they can connect to spirit?

If by becoming able to practise embodied magic, spirit is accessible, yes. And when spirit is accessible, life is richer.

Perhaps what we call 'spirit' is a consequence of living, not a fundamental truth that transcends it. And by accepting that, we can knit the spirit back in to the world of somatic practice. Spirit becomes something we experience, not something we are. It is the moment of quickening in the world when an incantation is voiced. It is the vibration between my attention and that which I am attending to. It is the movement between the tissues I touch and myself, the communion between the consciousness of the world and my own intentions.

Or perhaps spirit actually is magic. The union of word and world, where language is dissolved and fragmentation reverses. Perhaps spirit is trusting experience, and by grounding oneself in the phenomenology of the experience, we can access the consistently renewing present in which, what linguistically we mark as mind, body and spirit, all unify into *this* indivisible moment.

References

Auslander, P. and Deal, W. E. (2008), *Theory for Performance Studies: A Student's Guide*, London, UK: Routledge, p. 137.

Beadle, D. (2011), 'Feedback on draft of chapter', Personal communication, 2 October.

Bergson, H. and Andison, M. L. C. (1965), *An Introduction to Metaphysics*, Totowa, NJ: Littlefield Adams.

Bruhn, M. (1997), 'Class on the endocrine system', Lecture delivered at the School for Body Mind Centering Practitioner Certification, Amsterdam, the Netherlands.

Cohen, B. B. (2009), *A Body-Mind Centering® Approach to Yoga* (brochure), El Sobrante, CA: The School for Body-Mind Centering.

Dillon, M. (2003), *Handbook of the Sociology of Religion*, Cambridge, UK: Cambridge Press.

Fraleigh, S. (2005), 'Discussion of Somatics and dance', Personal communication, 13 November.

Greenwood, S. (2005), *The Nature of Magic: An Anthropology of Consciousness*, Oxford, UK: Berg.

Grossman, L. (2009), *The Magicians: A Novel*, New York, NY: Viking.

Hanna, T. (1986), 'What is Somatics?', *Somatics Magazine: Journal of the Bodily Arts and Sciences*, 4, pp. 4–8.

Johnson, D. H. (1994), *Body, Spirit, and Democracy*, Berkeley, CA: North Atlantic Books.

——— (1997), *Groundworks: Narratives of Embodiment*, Berkeley, CA: North Atlantic Books.

Joly, Y. (2004), 'The experience of being embodied: Qualitative research and somatic education: A perspective based on the Feldenkrais Method', *The Feldenkrais Research Journal*, 1, pp. 1–19.

Merleau-Ponty, M. (1986), *Phenomenology of Perception*, London, UK: Routledge & Kegan Paul.

Reanney, D. C. (1995), *After Death: A New Future for Human Consciousness*, New York, NY: William Morrow.

Smith, S. I. (1997), 'Discussions of bodywork methodology and observations while giving me a session', Personal communication.

Subbotsky, E. V. (2010), *Magic and the Mind: Mechanisms, Functions, and Development of Magical Thinking and Behavior*, New York, NY: Oxford University Press.

Chapter 15

Global Somatics™ Process: A Contemporary Shamanic Approach

Suzanne River, interviewed by Kathleen Melin

Introduction

Suzanne River developed the Global Somatics™ Process (GSP), an embodiment modality which weaves the physical soma and subtle energy body. In 1982, Suzanne founded her school, Green River Dance for Global Somatics (GRDGS), in Minneapolis, Minnesota, United States. GRDGS offers professional training, continuing education, therapy and research in Somatic Movement Education and Therapy, bodywork and energy medicine.

Suzanne practises as a Somatic Shamanic Practitioner and Global Somatics Teacher/Practitioner. She is certified as a Body-Mind Centering® teacher/practitioner, registered Somatic Movement Therapist, cranio-sacral therapist, Reiki master and Reconnective Therapy practitioner. She attributes her energetic capacity to ongoing personal transformation, direct connection with spirit, recognition of the essence of each person and the ability to connect subtle frequencies into the cellular, molecular and subatomic structures of the body.

Kathleen Melin is the author of *By Heart: A Mother's Story of Children and Learning at Home* (2008), a memoir of progressive education. Her creative work has appeared in *Dust and Fire*, *Feminist Parenting*, and *A Woman's Place*.

Our dialogues took place in Spring 2011. Sitting on the earth, encircled with bird song and green blossoms, we communicated at a level that embraced the magic of words and the spirit from which they spring.

SUZANNE:	Kathleen, Thank you for helping me to articulate how the Global Somatics™ Process (GSP) serves as a contemporary shamanic approach.
KATHLEEN:	In 1993, while I was a graduate student in Creative Writing at the University of Minnesota, you were ten years into developing your pioneering work, named in 2003 as the Global Somatics™ Process. I am delighted you are contributing your voice to *Dance, Somatics and Spiritualities: Contemporary Sacred Narratives*, an academic mosaic of viewpoints about how spiritual authority lives in the moving body.
SUZANNE:	The Global Somatics curriculum and pedagogy provide a conceptual framework for the somatic mapping of spiritual experience. For us, spirituality entails the embodiment of the whole

Figure 1: Mover: Suzanne River. Photographer: Jesse River.

self. The soma is a portal to spirit. My perspective on shamanism may help clarify the influence of non-Western sacred experience.

Most people enter shamanic states through experiencing native practices and using shamanic tools of various cultures, like plant medicines, power objects, chanting and various rituals. I call this the 'outside-in' method. Global Somatics™ Process (GSP) teaches the 'inside–out' method to shamanic experience. We directly educate the body to function like a shaman's body. The primary tool of shamanism is the *natural body* of the shaman—the shaman's bodily or somatic experience.

KATHLEEN: I have personally experienced your teaching and healing. I am curious about your understanding of shamanism and how it relates to GSP.

SUZANNE: For me, GSP and shamanism function as open-ended systems of inquiry into the nature of reality and the evolution of conscious perception. The Global Somatics keystones correlate beautifully with certain shamanic principles. My current response to that inquiry is: *Shamanism and GSP are acts of embodying the natural body that lead to enhanced perception in molding the world around us.*

KATHLEEN: I was expecting something less abstract and more magical.

SUZANNE: For me, to abstract means to make myself available to the spirit by being aware of it. Magic references the art of changing consciousness at will.

KATHLEEN: We will unfold your definition. Do you consider yourself a shaman?

SUZANNE: I identify with contemporary wisdom keepers who are called by spirit to serve the needs of their community, though they may be long separated culturally from their original shamanic roots. I call myself a somatic shamanic practitioner, rather than a shaman, out of respect for my indigenous shaman teachers and in-depth awareness of the shamanic range. Through my study, however, I see that I was born with certain 'birthmarks' that match the traditional shamanic calling. These include early near death experience, easy contact with invisible realms, clear listening to a silent knowledge, unusual abilities, and intimacy with nature. From youth, I practised blessing and healing as well as teaching and perceiving group energy. Through my somatic dance experience, I awakened my native bloodlines (Mohawk and Cherokee).

KATHLEEN: In looking at our lives as children, we often see a predisposition to our later calling. Tell me about your shamanic development.

SUZANNE: Nature, spirit and life are my primary teachers. I have practised Celtic Shamanism since I was 30. During my forties, I studied many Native American traditions, especially Iroquois, Apache, Hopi and Lakota. In my fifties, I worked with Toltec shamanic practices. For my 60th birthday, I gifted myself with an intensive two-year programme in shamanic studies facilitated by Jose and Lena Stevens of the Power Path in Santa Fe, New Mexico. I expanded my understanding of eclectic shamanic philosophy. I worked with indigenous shamans in Mexico, the Andes and the Amazon of Peru, South America. Through this programme, I clarified how the GSP acts as a contemporary shamanic approach.

I currently learn from the Shipibo (Amazon), Huichol and Toltec (Mexican), Q'ero (Andes) and Native North American traditions. While the skills to be learned in shamanic training may vary, they 'usually include diagnosis and treatment of illness, contacting and working with benevolent spirit entities, appeasing or fighting malevolent spirit entities, supervising sacred rituals, interpreting dreams, assimilating herbal knowledge, predicting the weather and mastering their self-regulation of bodily functions and attentional states' (Krippner 2002: 2).

KATHLEEN: Tell me about a time when your way of working was recognized and affirmed by an indigenous shaman.

SUZANNE: I am recognized in my totality by my indigenous teachers. When I was in the Amazon jungle in 2009, the lead female Shipibo shaman asked me for a healing. I did what I usually do—attune to the whole person and then follow spirit using touch, sound and movement on and off the body. Within the first five minutes, she exclaimed that I was doing shamanic healing—that I had it! She proceeded to direct me to work on different areas of her body by pointing and saying: '*Trabajo aqui*' ('Work here'). When we completed the session, she said, 'Now tonight I can sing in ceremony again. If I had known you were a healer, I would have had you help me every day since you came.' I worked with her the next day and was amazed at how much her body had integrated—at lightning speed—more than anyone else I have ever touched. I remember her every day.

KATHLEEN: This experience validated how you have practised your authenticity in following the voice of the unknown. Perhaps what is new is not what you're doing, but your recognition of what you're doing as shamanic.

SUZANNE: In this lifetime, I am focusing on the basics of energy and of the body. My research of shamanism, mythology, physics and body-mind medicine partially explains how I can do what I do.

My study inspires me to live well. It offers reference points and language so I can share it with others.

Shamanic Context and Question of Political Correctness

KATHLEEN: The definition of 'shamanism' is profoundly contested. It is entangled with our white postcolonial projections of the 'exotic other.' Many Native Americans, for example, object strongly to having their traditional healers called shamans, because it is a term imposed by the dominant culture.

SUZANNE: I find that many people are more attracted to the 'exotic other' than the mystery and power that lives right within their very own bodies. I understand the 'other' to include those people outside of dominant culture. We tend to project disowned or shadow aspects of ourselves onto the 'other.' I am sensitive to acts of imposition or appropriation. Strangely, *neo shamanism* has become almost faddish in the West even as indigenous tribes and their shamans are endangered. Every culture that disappears diminishes a possibility of life for all of us.

I want to heal the native in me who communes with nature along with the white consumer who feels entitled to everything in the world. Personal embodiment might help us appreciate diversity from the inside out. During the embodiment process, one often reconciles a mixed bag of DNA. Sensing the movement of the soma inspires presence. Meeting others with this presence dissolves separation and yet honours uniqueness. Today, there are no boundaries, and maybe the only true shamanism is that of the planet itself and the shared common tool—the inner body.

KATHLEEN: Hence the name 'Global Somatics'—attending to the world of the body while attending to the body of the world. I see many people with a hunger for true being, the intuitive and wild nature in us. Maybe the term 'shamanic' awakens this sense.

SUZANNE: I want to clarify what it means for me to use the term 'shamanism' in association with the work I do.

Shamanic experience lives in the DNA, in the fluids and in the morphogenetic field of every person and of the planet. Stanley Krippner, a well-known American psychologist and consciousness pioneer, states that, '*shamanism* can be described as a body of techniques and activities that supposedly enable its practitioners to access information that is not ordinarily attainable by members of the social group that gave them privileged status. These practitioners use this information in attempts to meet the needs of this group and its members' (Krippner 2002).

By speaking of the GSP as a contemporary shamanic approach, I gratefully respect our ancestors and contemporary shamans and honour where I am planted. If I lived in the Andes, I would heal using sacred stones and coca leaves, because that would be my culture. If I were a Plains Native, I would use the Sacred Pipe and tobacco and participate in ceremonies brought by White Buffalo Calf Woman. If I were in the Amazon jungles, surrounded by the power of plants and the rain forest, I would sing songs and honour the holy anaconda and work with plant medicines because that would be my culture. Each of these cultures expresses universal motifs in a particular way grown in a certain society and a bound field. I am living in America and serve by contributing to the medicine of body-mind consciousness, embodiment and connection to nature.

Like all human endeavors, shamanism evolves through the work of its practitioners. GSP contributes to the evolution of shamanism. I want to awaken that inner power and capacity so individuals share their gifts with love.

KATHLEEN: If shamanism is a group of activities and experiences shared by shamans in cultures around the world, what are some of its fundamental elements?

SUZANNE: For me, the most fundamental elements are how shamans experience reality, the central purpose of shamanic activity and how shamans use their bodies.

KATHLEEN: How do shamans—or you, as a shamanic practitioner—experience reality?

SUZANNE: I feel reality as a moving energy fabric with many folds. Each fold is a world or a different dimension. One can move into and out of these dimensions by shifting perception. Reality is an interconnected web of energy that is held together by an agglutinating vibratory force. This force can be witnessed and felt. It has many names—spirit, Wakan Tanka, Tao, infinity, power, force, nagual, Spider Woman. Consciousness flows as a continuum between energy and form or matter. Essentially, every form, whether it is a molecule, tree, person or angel, is a living configuration of energy and arises from the same source. The shamanic worldview values respect for diversity, empathy for other humans and concern for other life forms.

KATHLEEN: What is the purpose of shamanism?

SUZANNE: The essential activity of shamanism is to shift perception and transform or channel energy. Confusion arises, I think, because shamanism is often associated with its tools rather than the activity for which the tools are designed. The tools focus attention and help expand the parameters of perception. They are the specific cultural ways or practices used to do the work. Every tool—communal dancing, singing, incantations, drumming, use of plant medicines and power objects—facilitates a perceptual shift.

KATHLEEN: It seems to me that these practices of creating sacred space—incense, liturgy, eternal flames, gathering as a community, sung repetitions—help us go beyond ourselves to reach a spiritual level.

SUZANNE: Tools work because of the energy of the person using them. The primary tool of shamanism is the natural body of the shaman—the shaman's bodily or somatic experience.

KATHLEEN: This is a significant point. How does a shaman use her body?

SUZANNE: A shaman experiences her body as a confluence of energy fields. She willingly uses her body as a highly sensitized conduit for energy. The body acts like a high-powered radio capable of receiving and transmitting frequencies by tuning in to different channels. Through my body, I access alternative states of consciousness. My somatic attention moves between internal and external foci while I maintain awareness of human relations and the natural world. I am able to recall what has happened through enhanced perception.

KATHLEEN: I have witnessed how you invoke an additional aspect of yourself that transforms the experience into something extra special.

SUZANNE: At Green River Dance, we train people in the medicine of movement, touch, voice and energy. Students are empowered to fulfill their soul's task, whether as a healer, movement therapist, activist, artist, or teacher. Shamans were the first physicians, diagnosticians, psychotherapists, religious functionaries, magicians, performing artists, and storytellers (Krippner 2002). These professionals work in voluntary, ecstatic trance states, which alter consciousness so that they can travel to the realms of the invisible worlds.

    It is important to realize that shamans do not choose to enter these heightened states solely for personal enlightenment, release from the world or ecstatic experience. Their ability to gain information and make changes in the invisible realms is dependent upon the working relationships they develop with 'spirits' there. They use this information, knowledge and power to help and to heal members of their community, as well as the community as a whole. In this sense, shamanism is a relationship-based practice of making changes in invisible realms to impact healing, of individuals or communities, in the realm of ordinary reality.

KATHLEEN: That sounds like the vision, mission and environment of Green River Dance. You do seem to attract change agents!

Definition and Keystones

KATHLEEN: Let's return to your definition: *Shamanism and GSP are acts of embodying the natural body that lead to enhanced perception in molding the world around us.* As we amplify the meaning of these words, we can anchor them with your list of keystones. What are the 'keystones?'

SUZANNE: Keystones are the primary practices and underlying principles that build the energetic capacity of a GS practitioner. Seven keystones hallmark a Global Somatics session or class.

- *Mapping* refers to the cognitive system used to interpret reality.
- *The big dance* recognizes each being as an entrance to spirit.
- *Vibrational aspects* addresses the personality and subtle energy bodies.
- *Realconnect* establishes an energetic connection.
- *Cellular consciousness* honours the intelligence of the cell.
- *Learning wheel* explains stages of perception.
- *Trauma holding and healing* explains how unresolved trauma is held and healed in the body-mind.

KATHLEEN: What do you mean by 'embodying?'

SUZANNE: 'Embodying' means to fully inhabit or live in the body. It involves learning from direct experience and being able to own or use again what I have learned—to literally have it 'in my body.'

KATHLEEN: I've heard you use the term 'Natural Body'. What does that signify?

SUZANNE: 'Natural Body' is my name for the matrix of primordial creativity that manifests as the tapestry of the self—the unity and interplay of the physical soma and the spirit body. GSP is unique among somatic and energy medicine approaches because it works with embodying the spirit body. The Global Somatics™ Process empowers individuals to activate channels between the physical soma and energy field for self-realization, authentic healing and conscious evolution. We use kinesthetic perception to embody the subtle energy body and this directly links our work to shamanic activity.

KATHLEEN: How so?

SUZANNE: From my study of various shamanic approaches, duality is ascribed not to the physical body–mind dichotomy, as in our Western culture. Instead, the body-mind is addressed as a unit. In shamanic understanding, the duality is between the body-mind and the subtle energy body.

KATHLEEN: Are you referring to what some call the 'aura?'

SUZANNE: Yes. In many esoteric traditions it is called the 'subtle energy body,' and in shamanic studies, it is referred to as the 'spirit body,' the 'other,' the 'double' and the 'dream body.' These two aspects of the self begin in unity; then, through life experience, one part turns outward to become the physical body and the other turns inward to become the energy body or soma. Global Somatics explores our ability to shift our 'hard' awareness of the solid physical body to the 'fluid' awareness of the soft inner body. The invisible counterpart of the soft inner body is the spirit body, which permeates the physical body and radiates from it.

KATHLEEN: Is there a traditional shamanic philosophy that matches your schema?

SUZANNE: The Toltec tradition of Mexico describes the totality of self as the 'tonal' and the 'nagual.' The tonal includes everything known in our world, everything we can talk about—our bodies, feelings, concepts of the divine, etc. The tonal is to be respected and cared for. GSP serves to boost the tonal by transforming somatic patterns. When the tonal reaches a state of healthy integrity, personal power increases and this allows the nagual to safely emerge.

KATHLEEN: What is the nagual?

SUZANNE: The nagual represents the unknowable—the mystery whose effects we can behold but which we can never pin down. We experience the nagual through inner silence and through the spirit body. Toltecs call this the 'second attention.' The second attention opens us to another way of understanding. We see and communicate directly with energy without the limitations of a particular cognitive programme. We feel and relate to the very essence of different types of beings—the essence of tree, of bone, of another person.

KATHLEEN: So this is what you mean by 'enhanced perception?'

SUZANNE: Perception, for me, is the capacity to apprehend selected fields of energy with the senses. *Shaman* comes from Tungusic *saman* from the Siberian culture and translates as 'seer.' From my understanding, when shamans speak of 'seeing' it is not merely with the vision but with the whole body as an eye—with a kinesthetic sensing of energy or the essence of something. Global Somatics considers the natural body as an instrument of perception. 'Seeing' is a complete 'being with' experience. We can only see or perceive what we know ourselves to be. If I experience myself as a moving configuration of energy fields, I can directly perceive energy as it flows through the mysterious universe.

KATHLEEN: As children, our senses are open, and we experience the wonder of life without interpretation. Many children have what might be called paranormal experiences (seeing fairies, hearing voices, knowing the future, feeling energies of the past, communicating with animals) before they learn to shut down certain senses.

SUZANNE: However, we are encultured to perceive reality a certain way by how we are raised. Attention is so powerful. It is our ability to focus our awareness. I was taught to have the physical certainty that the world is made up of concrete objects. Toltecs refer to that as our 'first attention.' From this social base, I have been energetically conditioned to perceive this world of objects as the only world there is. I look at a tree and call it a tree. I am building an inventory of descriptions and interpretations, a cognitive system, if you will. This cognition can block the direct meeting of energy—in this case, perceiving the essence of a tree.

Movement and touch are the first senses to develop, the first portals to directly receive information and make interpretation and are therefore, I feel, the most innocent of pre-conception. Movement is the first language of energy! Movement is direct energetic perception.

KATHLEEN: So movement is medicine?

SUZANNE: Yes. Dance is an ancient means of feeling the flow of spirit and communicating through moving energy. Kinesthetic memory and movement serve to quiet the talking mind—the reason—through which we keep our self-important stories alive. This allows us to shift to other states of awareness and eventually into a deep silence and the silent knowing that resides there.

In trance, ancient shamans experienced their bodies moving automatically and spontaneously through a vibratory force. These movements were later choreographed to restore the wellbeing experienced in such altered states. We know some of these memorized movement forms as yoga, Qiqong, Tai Chi, magical passes or martial arts. In GSP, we tap directly into the primordial flow of energy. The body dances from there. Dance is a way of discovering new dimensions while still remaining in touch with our bodies.

KATHLEEN: The natural body itself is an instrument of perception. GSP teaches people they have this resource so they shift perceptions. Do you return to your child body so to speak?

SUZANNE: What a beautiful way to see it! In Global Somatics, we practise beginning from a felt perception of acceptance and dynamic wholeness. We know spirit is continuously creating each person, and each person is a perfect portal to spirit. This is the Big Dance. I attune with the Realconnect to all the person is—every aspect of her as a manifestation of spirit.

KATHLEEN: I remember the class experience of first learning the keystone of Realconnect. We worked with a partner with a brightly colored stretchable fabric between us. The fabric was symbolic of our relationship, our connection. When the scarf was loose, we each experienced our individuality but couldn't feel our connection. When the scarf was tight, we became fused and the relationship had no movement.

SUZANNE: I loved how we danced, finally growing into following the intention of the scarf itself or spirit! Realconnect is a dynamic realization of energy exchange and reciprocity from all aspects of the self to another. The Q'ero of the Andes refer to it as *ayni*—energetic reciprocity! Realconnect can be made within the body, with other people, with stars, plants and so on.

When I am directed to use power objects, such as tobacco or feathers, I make Realconnect with the essence of that object. For example, in using tobacco, I connect with the morphogenetic field of tobacco that includes all of its ceremonial uses. I pray into the tobacco with my breath and song. I then introduce the client to tobacco, making a Realconnect between them. Then tobacco and I work as a team to help the person by following spirit's guidance from within them. That is very much like energetic trio work.

KATHLEEN: What do you mean by mapping?

SUZANNE: In introducing this keystone, I remind students 'the map is not the territory.' In mapping the territory of the natural body, we explore initiating from the first language of the body. Some people talk to the body with words but the native language of the body is non-verbal and includes vibration, breath, movement, touch, sound and psychophysical process. I ask students to journey into the natural body by creatively exploring each of these attentions—to be with patterns of energy, to be with breath, to sound, to move and finally to be with emotions, thoughts or metaphor. After our embodiment, each person draws a map of her journey. We share our work by choosing one part of our map and guiding the group to have a direct personal experience.

KATHLEEN: I can imagine that if I acted from each of these alone or in combination, it would take me into a state of multidimensional consciousness and feel somewhat like a shamanic journey.

SUZANNE: Every class and private session invokes these capacities. For example, while I cognitively know I have organs, and can name, locate and speak about their function, I may not feel them as a part of me. I claim them as myself through the embodiment process of directly communing with them through breath, vibration, sound, movement and touch. They in turn communicate with me through sharing stored emotions, memories and beliefs and, finally, pure energy.

KATHLEEN: How do you map the spirit body?

SUZANNE: Using the Vibrational Aspects™ System, we research the spirit body in four distinct ways. First, we experience that every atom, molecule, cell and system of the body has a morphogenetic field that it creates through its movement. These multitudes of fields or mini auras culminate in the spirit body. We can sense in the physical body everything that is in the body. I can work non-locally with someone in Korea and sense their fluid system, bones, organs et cetera as if I were giving them an in-person bodywork session.

Secondly, we embody the chakra system, not through clairvoyance, but with movement, touch, breath and sound. We know from the inside out what physical tissues are contributing to the vitality of the chakra and resonate with these.

Third, we recognize the natural body to be a dance of seven bodies—physical, etheric, emotional, mental, the soul, spirit, and creatrix. As abstract as it sounds, each of these bodies is actively experienced and sensed within the physical body and in the space around the body. Using kinesthetic perception, we are able to feel the fluid and membrane of each subtle body. The creatrix—furthest out—body can be sensed up to a block from the physical body.

Finally, we do something called 'weaving the field' which works with the body as a constellation of luminous fibers. 'Weaving the field' integrates, clears and balances all of these bodies.

KATHLEEN: Do you consider yourself unique in your ability to sense the energy field?

SUZANNE: I think all humans directly perceive energy—it's just that some of us know we do. I recently evaluated the Vibrational Aspect skills of a student who began our two-year training highly skeptical of subtle energy work. In her competency demonstration, she worked with a client's heart chakra to support the perceptions held in a cluster of lung cells. She kinesthetically sensed an affinity between the client's mental subtle body and those physical cells. The client shared that she didn't believe she had the right to breathe in her family of origin. The student listened with unconditional acceptance and supported the cellular respiration of those cells.

She was able to accomplish this through developing her skills for direct energetic perception. Through awareness of her habits of ego or false personality, she has freed personal energy. As she uses her perception humbly and with love, she strengthens her direct link to spirit.

KATHLEEN: I like that she renewed her relationship to spirit. It seems like clearing ourselves of ego is the work of a lifetime. How does your work support those tasks?

SUZANNE: Global Somatics^{TM} Process, like shamanic initiation, requires self-transformation. This involves dying to the idea of self or certain self-limiting identities. We are each born with a certain amount of basic energy to perceive, learn and act. GSP helps us recover energy that is locked in the tissues of the body and energy field. We are cleaning the island of the tonal. As students naturally clear physical holdings, memories, outworn beliefs and emotional habits, they regain their authentic energy. More energy is freed or distributed for greater perceptual shifts.

The Q'ero have a beautiful way of perceiving energy. They see two kinds of energy—disharmonious energy—*hucha*—and the light energy that is the purest essence of the universe—*sami*. *Hucha* is not evil but simply the leftover from learning in the body—the mistakes or energy that just doesn't resonate with a person's essence. The simple practice involves exhaling *hucha* through the pelvic floor into the earth and inhaling *sami* though the top of the head.

KATHLEEN: Lovely. Say more about the keystone of Cellular Consciousness.

SUZANNE: I am using the term 'consciousness' to describe an organism's patterns of moving, feeling, thinking and perceiving. We feel the cells moving and breathing. We experience the cells as assemblage points of perception. The cellular membrane is a perceptual gate filled with dynamic receptors that actually shape-shift to inhibit or draw neurotransmitters or hormones into the cells. We balance the membranes of the cells. Each cell has a spirit body through which it instantaneously communicates with all other cells and the energy field.

The cells hold ancestral software in the fluids and in the DNA. Our genes convey all the information about every past life, every lesson learned, every agreement kept. The entire history and future of the human race is found in our gene pool. Yet in the nuclear fluid, there are molecules that can shift the DNA if they are incorporated into it.

In *The Cosmic Serpent: DNA and the Origins of Knowledge*, Narby makes a connection between the research of DNA and the serpents that instruct Amazonian shamans during ceremonies with the plant medicine ayahuasca: 'By considering shamanism and biology at the same time, stereoscopically, I saw DNA snakes. They were alive' (Narby 1988: 157). When Narby explained his understanding to his indigenous shamanic teacher, his teacher queried, 'What took you so long?' (1988: 152).

KATHLEEN: Hence your tag line—'Changing the world one cell at a time.'

SUZANNE: For us, the cells are 'learning wheels,' another keystone. The learning wheel happens on multiple levels—the nervous system, the cellular membrane and the spirit body. I accept that my body-mind is a pre-conception from which I filter sensory information. I receive what I expect to let in. Then I creatively interpret that information, giving it a personal meaning. Based on my interpretation, I plan and take action. From the feedback of my actions, I make further interpretations that then feed into my pre-conception. The learning wheel allows for repetitive patterns of perception and corresponding behavior and habits. It also offers awareness to moments when I can shift my consciousness. I can sense-interpret-act in a new way.

KATHLEEN: The past conditions the present and the future. And the power is in the present moment.

SUZANNE: My body soma holds the perceptions I created about past circumstances.

KATHLEEN: What is a memorable moment in your healing work?

SUZANNE: In 1998, I worked with a woman who was experiencing terrible migraines and pain in her eyes. As I followed the unwinding of her brain, I perceived that her whole head was held in a rusty vice or iron mask. Her body curled up tight. She said she was in a small box and that she felt like she was drowning. After that resolved, I changed the tape in my recorder intuitively to one with bird songs. On hearing the bird caws, she cried out 'The crows are eating my eyes!' I turned off the tape and felt in her energy field for where her 'eyes' had been taken and brought them back to her physical body. Then a crow appeared on the branch outside the window and began to caw. The woman experienced profound calm and the headaches went away. This is an example of a 'soul retrieval,' which included a resolution between the woman and crow.

Years later, I was researching witches in Salem and I learned that some women were punished by having to wear iron masks and being drowned in small wooden crates; their bodies were then thrown by the road side, and the crows ate them.

KATHLEEN: How do you explain all that?

SUZANNE: I don't. It is a many-layered mystery. Some people may say it was a past life recapitulation. Our keystone Trauma Holding and Healing applies here. Trauma Holding and Healing explains the physiology of shock through the nervous system.

Think of swimming the breaststroke. This movement demonstrates how the central nervous system functions through receiving sensory information into the back of the spinal cord. In the center of the spinal cord that information is interpreted by the interneurons. Then the motor nerves flow out the front of the spinal cord. The healthy cycle is 'Receive in the back, interpret in the center and act out the front.'

However, when information is overwhelming or traumatic, it attempts to enter the back as usual but after some initial perception is made, it reverses its flow and goes out the back. The information is carried to a personally subjective constellation of cells that keep this perception in the body and in corresponding aspects of the spirit body. The information is then returned to the spinal cord through the front of the body—again a reversal of normal flow—and then flows out the back. The acting out the back results in habits of behaviour and mind based on the unprocessed trauma. In shamanism, they are referred to as *sustos,* or habit patterns of fear that include how I perceive myself, treat myself and others and blocks in the physical body.

KATHLEEN: So perceptions created from trauma are held in the body and energy field. Doesn't life then keep bringing similar situations to us in an effort to work out this original wound, so to speak?

SUZANNE: Yes. The whole thing stays frozen in the pre-conception of the natural body, so we are molding the universe or world around us by attracting what is both familiar and what we need to resolve. Recapitulation happens layer by layer when there is enough support, readiness and will. Our work with the cells, movement and energy field facilitates this beautifully. In a shamanic sense, we are clearing ancestral imprinting or extracting disharmonious energy patterns. Ongoing embodiment celebrates the return to the wholeness and illumination that is always present.

KATHLEEN: So the woman you spoke of was resolving a trauma from a past life, parallel universe or an interpretation of a childhood trauma using that story?

SUZANNE: Maybe all of it. I remember, how when asked about the causes of disease and how she worked with them, one beautiful female Paco (Andean shaman) smiled patiently and said, 'People asked to be healed, and we heal them.'

What matters to me is that her natural body experienced more health and harmony. Anything held in the spirit body will eventually show up in the physical body unless it is shifted. So our work is preventative. Likewise, if changes are made in the physical body without the correlation with the subtle body, they will just move to a different area in the body. Somatic Shamanic healing is about perceiving the body in wholeness and carefully clearing the field and body of disharmonious energy. The roots of disease are most often in the mind, emotions and energy body. These roots are stored trauma from our lives and the lives of our ancestors.

KATHLEEN: So this is what you mean when you say GSP helps authentic healing?

SUZANNE: Healing involves the accurate diagnosis of the seen and unseen energies at the root of the problem and carrying out the specific choreography of energies needed to resolve the problem. For me, healing depends on first the client, then on the practitioner, not on any specific body of knowledge, whether it be Western or non-Western medicine. Healing is not a formalized discipline. Rather, it happens when the perception of the person shifts, or we may say, the body-mind 'dreams' itself into new possibilities. Someone who helps to restore health can help alter the body's basic feelings about itself and its link to the world. This entails breaking down the habitual mold to which the body-mind has learned to conform. Other dimensions of awareness become accessible and the body-mind can crystallize new meanings.

KATHLEEN: So we are now at the point in our definition where you address '*molding the world around us!*'

SUZANNE: Maybe the world is whatever we perceive in any manner we may choose to perceive. Our personal embodied vibration influences the world around us. I speak of the Global Somatics™ Process as an initiation in to the intimate mystery of the natural body.

KATHLEEN: The word 'initiation' makes this sound like an esoteric spiritual event.

SUZANNE: For me, 'initiation' means to awaken something dormant within oneself and also requires commitment, discipline and work. The Q'ero tradition from the Andes recognizes initiation as an opportunity for intense personal experience, not a secretive ritual. 'Intimate mystery' refers to the personal embodiment quest of an individual. The spirituality with which I am concerned begins with the self and is readily available to everyone. The Huichol Indians of Mexico consider each person to be like a flower. Spirituality for them helps each person blossom into full potentiality.

KATHLEEN: How is all of this fleshed out in your classes?

SUZANNE: My shamanic practice profoundly affects how I teach. I treat every person and class as a sacred ceremony. As a teacher, I weave energy—transmitting, raising, shifting and grounding power. I encourage active participation and use power objects and simple ritual where appropriate.

We enter altered states of consciousness through dancing, singing and healing in community. Every guided somatization is an inner journey into the sacred ground of inner nature—the invisible microcosm. Direct energetic perception grows through the experience of every system of the body as an intelligent consciousness.

In 2008, shamanic principles became an explicit part of our somatic training programme. We begin each five-day intensive by creating a sacred space by invoking the seven directions and setting stone guardians around the space. We learn ways of using breath to clear disharmonious energy and fill ourselves with positive life force. I integrate practices and theory from various shamanic traditions to clarify and support our embodiment work. Students are introduced to traditional practice called shamanic journeying where, assisted by drumming, they can journey within to get answers. During the Moving Perceptions Course, we give ourselves permission to use scents, foods, and power objects to shift perceptions.

Ceremony is an integral part of the curriculum, whether we are holding hands in silence; creating a sacred container by invoking the directions, Mother Earth and Father Sky; or doing an honouring dance of our ancestors in the skeletal course! Besides being an instrument of perception, the body is a direct conduit to Nature through the wind, fire, water, earth and ether that live inside us. We are Nature. When I reach out to Father Sky, it is not an intellectual pretense but a deep resonance from the space I experience between the atoms in myself. I relate to the power of water from intimate knowing of myself as a fluid being. When I experience myself as a cellular being—a universe—I commune with all biological life on the planet. I know plants, animals and others as relatives.

The energy medicine curriculum teaches how to embody the spirit body. Post graduation, I offer Vibrational Aspects IV that transmits shamanic techniques and tools for those students who respect and are drawn to this way of working. These GS Practitioners offer somatic shamanic healings that demonstrate integration of the keystones. They effectively and creatively follow spirit through the physical and energetic bodies of their clients.

KATHLEEN: I better understand of your idea of how the Global Somatics™ Process and shamanism relate—*Shamanism and GSP are acts of embodying the natural body that lead to enhanced perception in molding the world around us.*

SUZANNE: For me, it is important not to fly away and get lost in the glamour of the unknown but to live a sane, sober, impeccable life of wonder, service and love. I practise living in 'the third attention!' This means perceiving both the form and the energy at the same time, bridging visible and invisible worlds. I experience it when I feel connected to 'All That Is' and interdependent with what is happening in the moment.

Real power arises from a great love that demands reciprocity. I can still see David's glittering black eyes and the quick urgent movement of his hands. David is a thirty-some year old Shipibo shaman known for his singing, healing and psychic ability.

He sought me out in my last hour in the jungle, bringing a translator with him.

'I want you to listen to me. You must understand this. The plants love the people. The shamans feel this great love. And with this love, we sing our songs. With this love, we heal. It is the love, not the things, that comes first.'

I remember standing alone under the night skies of a sacred desert in Mexico. The clouds were moving frames and within the frames, liquid white stars spun constellations. 'I need no miracle, just show me the truth.' The clouds stopped moving. The stars balanced in stillness. And I felt that there is no single equilibrium anywhere. In the realm of infinite atoms and light years, all dancers lean upon one another, holding, touching, re-enforcing the whole that is love.

References

Bear, H. and Larkin, M. (1996), *The Wind is My Mother: The Life and Teachings of a Native American Shaman*, New York, NY: Berkley Books.

Bentov, I. (1977), *Stalking the Wild Pendulum: On the Mechanics of Consciousness*, Rochester, NY: Destiny Books.

Campbell, J. and Moyers, B. (1988), *The Power of Myth*, New York, NY: Doubleday.

Capra, F. (1991), *The Tao of Physics*, 3rd ed., Boston, MA: Shambhala.

Castenada, C. (1969), *The Teachings of Don Juan: A Yaqui Way of Knowledge*, Los Angelos, CA: Regents of the University of California.

—— (1971), *A Separate Reality*, New York, NY: Washington Square Press.

—— (1972), *Journey to Ixtlan*, New York, NY: Washington Square Press.

—— (1974), *Tales of Power*, New York, NY: Washington Square Press.

—— (1977), *The Second Ring of Power*, New York, NY: Washington Square Press.

—— (1981), *The Eagle's Gift*, New York, NY: Washington Square Press.

—— (1984), *The Fire from Within*, New York, NY: Washington Square Press.

—— (1987), *The Power of Silence*, New York, NY: Washington Square Press.

—— (1993), *The Art of Dreaming*, New York, NY: HarperCollins.

—— (1998), *Magical Passes*, New York, NY: HarperCollins.

—— (1998), *The Active Side of Infinity*, New York, NY: HarperCollins.

Davis, W. (2009), *The Wayfinders: Why Ancient Wisdom Matters in the Modern World*, Toronto, ON: House of Anansi Press.

Deloria, V. (1973), *God is Red: A Native View of Religion*, Golden, CO: Fulcrum Publishing.

Diamond, I. and Orenstein, G. (eds) (1990), *Reweaving the World: The Emergence of Ecofeminism*, San Francisco, CA: Sierra Club Books.

Eliade, M. (1964), *Shamanism: Archaic Techniques of Ecstasy*, Princeton, NJ: Princeton University Press.

Harmer, T. (2003), *What I have Always Known: Living in Full Awareness of the Earth*, New York, NY: Harmony Books.

Harner, M. (1980), *The Way of the Shaman*, New York, NY: Harper & Row.

Krippner, S. (2002), 'Conflicting perspectives on shamans and shamanism: Points and counterpoints', http://stanleykrippner.weebly.com/index.html. Accessed 27 August 2002.

Mehl-Madrona, L. (1998), *Coyote Medicine: Lessons from Native American Healing*, New York, NY: Simon & Schuster.

Melin, K. (2008), *By Heart: A Mother's Story of Children and Learning at Home*, Duluth, MN: Clover Valley Press.

Nichol, L. (ed.) (2003), *The Essential David Bohm*, London, UK: Routledge.

Ouspensky (1949), *In Search of the Miraculous*, San Diego, CA: Harper.

—— (1971), *The Fourth Way*, New York, NY: Vintage Books.

Perkins, J. (1994), *The World as You Dream It: Shamanic Teachings from the Amazon and Andes*, Rochester, VT: Destiny Books.

Rock, A. and Krippner, S. (2011), *Demystifying Shamans and Their World: An Interdisciplinary Study*, Exeter, UK: Imprint Academic.

Ruiz, D. (1997), *The Four Agreements*, San Rafael, CA: Amber-Allen Publishing.

Ruiz, D. and Nelson, M. (1997), *Beyond Fear: A Toltec Guide to Freedom and Joy*, Tulsa, OK: Council Oak Books.

Sheldrake, R. (1995), *The Presence of the Past: Morphic Resonance and the Habits of Nature*, Rochester, NY: Park Street Press.

Starhawk (1979), *The Spiral Dance: A Rebirth of the Ancient Religion of the Great Goddess*, San Francisco, CA: Harper.

Stevens, J. and Stevens, L. (1988), *Secrets of Shamanism: Tapping the Spirit Power Within You*, New York, NY: Avon Books.

St. Pierre, M. and Long Soldier, T. (1995), *Walking in the Sacred Manner: Healers, Dreamers and Pipe Carriers—Medicine Women of the Plains Indians*, New York, NY: Simon & Schuster.

Talbot, M. (1991), *The Holographic Universe*, New York, NY: Harper Perennial.

Whitaker, K. (1991), *The Reluctant Shaman: A Woman's First Encounters with the Unseen Spirits of the Earth*, San Francisco, CA: Harper.

Wilcox, J. (1999), *Masters of Living Energy: The Mystical World of the Q'ero of Peru*, Rochester, NY: Inner Traditions.

Part III

Cultural Immersions and Performance Excursions

Glenna Batson

When we attempt to study what is deemed 'spirited,' 'sanctified' or 'sacred,' we need to sidestep getting entangled by dualisms of body versus mind, emotion versus thought, improvisation versus scripted choreography or healing versus performance; otherwise, scholarly accounts will lean toward reductionist interpretations and an unending regress of narrative commentary, all disconnected from the subject matter. In other words, our study of dance, especially spirited dance, becomes easily distanced from the bodies that enact it and the ineffable essence that serves to inspire its production.

(Hillary and Bradford Keeney, this volume: 359)

This section of the book offers the perspective on transcendent consciousness through dance. Every culture in the world strives to find words for the experience of transcendent consciousness. Most likely, the dances (ritual forms) of these cultures express it best. Many terms come to mind that suggest the transcendent and altered states of consciousness that bring us closer towards presence, heightened sensitivity, deepening inter-subjectivity and the far reaches of liberatory expression. Vitality, life force, healing, higher power, spirit ... these terms afford insight into our inherent capability to transcend the here and now—to reunite with the wholeness within ourselves and with the universe. Through performing dance we readily tap into this agency, expanding our relationship through the body to the meta-worlds. The word 'perform' means simply to carry out a promise, to carry out an effect, fulfil completely, discharge. The moving body, in its ritual performative context, frees the mind from rationality and its interfering and distancing modes of analysis, interpretation and representation as well as the insistent need to understand.

In this text, the authors strive to express the inexpressible. Based on their experience with the dance/rituals of selected cultures, these authors pay homage to what can only be called the experience of amazement—something that defies analysis and interpretation. This section begins to tackle the overall question: How can we, as scholars, get a glimpse of a moment of a dance (perhaps steeped in thousands of years of history) and begin to grasp the essence? How can we describe these experiences—necessarily separated from their contexts—without minimizing, delimiting, misrepresenting or otherwise contaminating the purity of the experience?

Dance anthropologists Hillary Keeney and Bradford Keeney, in 'Dancing *N/om*,' address these and other questions in their description of the ancient *n/om* dance of the Kalahari Bushmen. They handle the subject sensitively, reflecting on their own role as witness to the dance and the dancers. *N/om* is essentially a dance of 'healing,' although there is no delineation, method, or series of 'moves' that are designated or intended as such. They describe the essential ingredients of a dance within a culture that knows how play and laughter within a shared, loving community 'softens' the mind-body, opening a gateway to channeling spirit. Although movements emerge that appear choreographed, they appear more as patterns of biologically endowed entrainment, rather than willed movements. At this point in the long period of dancing *n/om*, the dancer and the dance are one. They state, 'This movement—neither willed nor shaped by a performer—dances anyone, with or without training, who becomes its vehicle for expression. When the body is tuned and made ready for its movement, the beauty of dance is realized in a way that inspires even its witnesses to feel more alive. The universe then owns the dancer, as the dancer owns the universe' (this volume: 372). This is reminiscent of William Butler Yeats' quotation: 'How can we know the dancer from the dance?' Their experience of the Bushman culture has left them with a deep sense of affection and reverence not only for their dance, but also for dance in general. They conclude, 'Perhaps the word "dance" should be reserved as a name for that which honours movement that is inspired and infused by the highly charged ineffable, whether it is called n/om, duende or life force… There is nothing to understand, but everything can be danced' (this volume: 365).

Dance educator and somatic practitioner Susan Bauer's life changed when she entered the graduate programme in Dance and Movement Studies at Wesleyan University in the late 1980s. In studying Dance Anthropology, she learned of the Balinese *Legong* dance and its origins in *Sangyhang Dedari*, the trance dance enacted to heal the village. She states, 'Sharing a similar instinctual belief in the healing power of dance, I decided to go to Bali to learn the Legong dance and, perhaps, also understand more about my earlier choreographic experience' (this volume: 377).

As one of 17,000 islands of Indonesia, Bali embodies centuries of understanding of spiritual dimensions steeped in the framework of Balinese Hinduism. Here, the body is seen as a vehicle for embodying the Divine. Dances often involve trance in order to welcome the 'unseen' (ancestral and animal worship, for example) or channel the powers of reincarnation. According to Bauer, 'the mark of a truly great dancer traditionally was one who possessed *taksu*, a "spiritual charisma"' that corresponds not only to a heightened state of perceptual awareness and consciousness, but also the ability to captivate an audience (Bauer, this volume: 381). Bauer invites us into the implicit and explicit training of dancers in Balinese villages, offering rich description of the customs and processes of a deeply tactile and kinesthetic culture.

Centuries of appropriation, colonization and acculturation have affected Balinese culture such that the ancient culture that gave birth to Balinese has become separated from the spirit of the dance. With Western contact during the 1960s and the opening to the modern world, village-based ceremonial dance shifted from the sacred form toward a more secular art form. Bauer relates how these forces led to the standardization of dance within the university system in Bali. Bauer explores the relationship of modernization and consumerist culture to the ancient traditional expression of embodied spirituality, reflecting upon the role of dance education in American culture and in Westernized institutions of dance education. Using her own teaching of Balinese dance within the academy as a case study, Bauer outlines in depth her culturally-sensitive process in teaching about Balinese dance. She draws from her own work in Somatics as well as from other postmodern dancers whose work has paved the way for a process that helps us behold the essence and integrity of something sacred.

In Chapter 18, Sandra Reeve tackles the problem of ecological dynamics—the co-creative complexity of dancing body and environment when creating contemporary dance within ancient temple sites/traditions. Her work of the past two years has been in creating movement practices and performances in both historically significant and sacred sites in the UK, Ireland, Java and Bali. For her, then, the word 'sacred' suggests ecological and spatial embeddedness. By attuning to a temple site and creating contemporary performance/ ritual art at designated sacred ground, Reeve creates a site-responsive performance destined to re-awaken the perception of sacred purpose for other visitors by revealing a non-habitual way of moving within that particular site. Reeve embraces the concept of spirit broadly as a co-creation and mutual interdependence between an individual's movement and their environment. Through rich discussion, Reeve elaborates on this 'sacred narrative' in which co-creation between mover/dancer and site transforms both the place and the person. In her *Move into Life* programme, Reeve embodies in her teaching the use of 'non-stylized movement, environmental movement and—more recently—ecological movement' (this volume: 420). She describes, substantiates and gives examples of these differences in ways that differentiate their orientation, perceptual attunement, quality of movement, mutual influence on performer and witness and other aspects of the dynamic spectrum. These movement dynamics and functions are cross-culturally accessible. The practice forms a framework for dialogue, reflexivity and unity of the individual within the confines, liberties and paradoxes of the individual within the environment. Using herself as a case study, Reeve ends her chapter with a description of *Threshold*, an improvised performance for the annual inter-cultural Srawung Seni Candi (Temple Art Festival) in the Javanese-Hindu temple of Candi Sukuh, Central Java. The festival is initiated by Suprapto Suryodarmo, founder of the Padepokan Lemah Putih, an interdisciplinary movement-based arts institute in Solo, Java. The site for the performance is a 15th century Javanese-Hindu fertility temple on the slopes of Mt. Lawu above Solo, Central Java. Mt. Lawu is considered a sacred mountain for the worship of ancestors and nature spirits. Offering us both the view from within (her own experience as performer) and without (the audience's transformation), Reeve shows a way into continuity of participation in a very ancient history.

Sarah Whatley with Naomi Lefebvre Sell, in 'Dancing and Flourishing: Mindful Meditation in Dance-Making and Performing,' explore the role of mindfulness through Zen meditation within dance practice and performance. Both authors have extensive experience in applying somatic practices to dance pedagogy. Drawing from this ancient-turned-contemporary tradition of meditation, the authors narrow the spectrum to a form of meditation that enhances a 'lived-body state' as a method for preparing mind and body for performance (Whatley and Lefebvre Sell: 441). The chapter is replete with substantiation of the role of the choreographer as researcher in examining the effects of a spiritual practice on dance learning and performance. Lefebvre's deep engagement with meditation led to designing a study in which both choreographer and dance artists could build and reflect on their relationship to themselves, a choreographic work and the world. Through both an objective instructor-led and subjective self-led meditation practice, the creative process achieved a unique level of embodiment and transmission of an aesthetic. The authors offer an account of the reflections of four contemporary modern dancers who spend nearly one year practising meditation in coordination with preparing for the performance of Lefebvre's work, *dharmakaya*. The dancers recount their challenges in maintaining postural stillness, working towards a state of 'nothingness', being and presence, acceptance and release of ego (this volume: 447). What emerges is a near-achievement of stillness in which a transformative state towards a shared language, understanding and practice grounds the choreographic experience. In documenting the experiences of the dancers, Lefebvre Sell constructs a series of 'tales', incorporating the dancers' own spoken and written reflections on how the Zen teachings were assimilated (this volume: 445). Expressions of spirituality emerged from the written (as well as observed) spiritual narratives that guided and supported them, both within and beyond the dance studio. Significantly, the dancers noticed a change in their capacity for understanding their relationships to others, both in personal and dance contexts, and they were able to register emotional responses to others more clearly. For the dancers, the meditation practice directly had a positive impact on the embodied state of readiness for collaboration and learning within choreography. For the choreographer, the process of mind-embodiment unity opened the stage for a unique level of mutual support and sharing.

Jayne Stevens, in "What You Cannot Imagine": Spirituality in Akram Khan's *Vertical Road*, takes a more contemporary approach to defining 'spirituality'—one emphasizing the contemporary, embodied foundation of human nature within spiritual practices, rather than one that favours attempts to transcend worldly existence. Heralding the work of Lynch, Stevens adheres to the idea that contemporary forms of spirituality advocate active engagement with the environment and society whilst, at the same time, resisting the secularization brought about by, for example, technology and consumerism. A spiritual journey, therefore, is not only for the purpose of searching for something entirely outside of oneself but also for finding the sacred within the self and others. Underlying this theme is embodiment and connectedness as basic human values. By necessity, then, this form of embodied spirituality embraces religious diversity. Diversity of expression renders collaboration and exchange between different religious beliefs and spiritual practices not only possible, but also desirable. With this broad ethos of progressive spirituality in mind, Stevens considers the work of Kathak and modern dancer Akram Khan's *Vertical Road*. As choreographer and director, Khan draws directly from the dancers' life experience (of personhood, family, culture, etc.). Khan appears drawn to the spiritual through things both mystical and visceral. Khan arguably negotiates between Indian and Western movement ideologies, utilizing a hybrid movement vocabulary, movement quality and aesthetics. This alleged 'confusion' of movement vocabularies only appears to heighten the ambiguity, dichotomies and paradoxes in cross-cultural dance, which in the end, are spiritual statements (Stevens, this volume: 466). Stevens suggests that *Vertical Road* is a negotiation of cultural values and world views, especially in relation to aspects of Eastern (Islamic) and Western (Christian) spiritual traditions. Less about religion and more about the spiritual, the piece calls for reverence as well as reflection on the material and immaterial, life and death, past and present, self and others.

Collectively, this last section beckons the reader to reflect on these authors' concepts of spirituality in light of world hybridization, (mis)appropriation, and global sharing of dance. How do these uniquely synthetic practices give way to transformative experience? How are these embodied movement experiences translucently spiritual? What is their purpose? How do they tie the threads of history into a weave that meets the challenges in our world today?

Chapter 16

Dancing *N/om*

Hillary Keeney and Bradford Keeney

We dance for many reasons. We dance because it is fun. We also dance because it makes us feel better about each other. It fills our hearts with happiness and takes away any bad feelings we might have for another person. Dancing keeps us healthy—our sickness may be taken away and our life revitalized. In the dance, special experiences can happen for the doctor. He or she may even see the Big God. This is why the dance is our greatest treasury and mystery.

(Told by a Bushman doctor, as cited in Keeney 2003: 29)

For many cultures throughout the world, no transformative performance—whether held in a healing ceremony, wisdom teaching, or celebratory holy event—occurs without the presence of spirited dance. When we attempt to study what is deemed 'spirited,' 'sanctified' or 'sacred,' we need to sidestep getting entangled by dualisms of body versus mind, emotion versus thought, improvisation versus scripted choreography or healing versus performance; otherwise, scholarly accounts will lean towards reductionist interpretations and an unending regress of narrative commentary, all disconnected from the subject matter. In other words, our study of dance, especially spirited dance, becomes easily distanced from the bodies that enact it and the ineffable essence that serves to inspire its production.

We call for a discourse concerning transformative dance that evokes what is essential in its spirited performance. Here we will turn to the oldest living culture, the Ju/'hoan Bushmen, whose dancing tradition has served to entertain, inspire, transform and heal for thousands of years. We do so with full recognition that the contemporary study and practice of dance have also entered therapeutic and healing modalities, taking it outside its typical performance venues. Here somatic psychology, dance therapy and various forms of movement healing workshops flourish and spawn new modes of transformative engagement. However, we do not wish to separate or dichotomize healing versus performance dance. We regard this separation as isomorphic of the way Western epistemology perpetuates the very dualisms (e.g. body/mind, feeling/thought, spiritual/intellectual) that inhibit the heartfelt presence of that which both healing and performance seek to embody.

What is it that makes dance heal and soar, whether in a clinic or on stage? For the Spanish flamenco dance tradition, the word *duende* refers to the unexplainable essence that underlies a dance that is fully awakened, spirited and full of the universal life force. This strong, passionate force is said to possess a flamenco singer or dancer or even a bullfighter when they are at the height of their best performance. It has been likened to 'an inexplicable

Figure 1: Ju/'hoan Bushman Dancers. Photographer: Patrick Hill.

power of attraction, on rare occasions, to send waves of emotion through those watching and listening to them' (Lorca and Maurer, 1955/1998: ix).

For the Bushman healing dancers, the word most similar to duende, or life force, is *n/om* (Keeney 1999, 2003). It is also arguably equivalent to kundalini, chi or holy spirit. One could say it is related to the unnamable thing that gives jazz its swing and blues its soul. Though often depicted as 'energy,' n/om is regarded by Bushmen as the amplified emotion that arises from a heart awakening (Keeney 1999, 2003). It may be inspired by a sacred relationship, the longing for present or past loved ones or a felt intimacy with the biological world in general, including its trees, animals and honeybees. As a Bushman n/om-kxao (healer) is filled with n/om, it not only makes them dance, it excites them to ecstatically tremble and shake, touching others with fluttering hands and vibrant hugs. When a Kalahari healing dance performance is filled with the spirited or soulful expression of deep passion, those present are touched by it as well.

N/om or duende is said to reside inside those who possess it and sometimes for those who witness another's expression. All may weep and cry out with joy. Finally, and perhaps most importantly for our concerns, is that once a dancer, musician or healer has experienced n/om, they will seek or hunt it forever. It becomes the most important experience in life. Now dance is a form that only comes to life when n/om fills its form. The dancer who dances with n/om, duende, life force and spirit, is both a dancer and a healer, whether giving a performance or a therapeutic intervention.

For the Bushmen, n/om is activated and shared inside their healing dance. In their culture, which is less organized by body-mind dualisms (Keeney 2007), heightened emotion is naturally connected to ecstatic expression of the body. But n/om is not defined by the presence or absence of a particular kind of movement or physical display. While it has an inseparable relationship to dance and ecstatic movement, it is not dance or movement itself.

The Bushmen say that it is impossible to describe and explain n/om with words. It must be witnessed, experienced and felt. The same is often said of dance. This chapter organizes a discussion about the relationship of n/om to the Bushman dance, and dance in general, that is written so it follows the typical flow of a Bushman healing dance as it moves from gathering around a fire, initiating songs and clapping hands in syncopated rhythms, readying oneself to receive n/om, to the ecstatic crescendo of becoming filled with n/om and sharing it with others. This form of presentation is less concerned with an analysis of the Bushman dance, but instead utilizes its forms, movements and choreography as metaphors and inspiration for discussions on how to awaken and work with the mystery that gives rise to the dance itself.

When discussing n/om and their dance, Bushman dancers and healers emphasize what they call becoming 'soft' (Keeney 2010: 13), a way of underscoring an openness to experience that involves relational sensitivity, heightened affection and ecstatic expression, all done without any importance given to construed understanding, persistent questioning, and the endless interpretive meaning making of a rational mind. In contrast to the now popular meditative and contemplative means of minimizing the latter, they emphasize the importance of playful absurdity, teasing and raucous laughter.

N/om also requires more non-purposeful engagement inside the dance and its context of transformation. Though the Bushman dance does have a particular structure and form, it appears more like an improvisational performance, guided by the experience of feeling and sharing n/om. The openness and uncertainty fostered by improvisation helps us become more available to unexpected movement and the aesthetics inspired by a presumed interaction with mystery, whether the latter is named or not. However, n/om takes us past improvisation as it is typically understood in dance contexts. Bushmen propose that they are danced by n/om. Here the dancer is not improvising, but is improvised by n/om. This depiction invites us to expand our understanding of both improvisation and choreography in the context of awakening a spirited dance performance.

Bushman n/om-kxaosi are the ones who become an 'owner' of n/om (here 'own' means 'to own the feeling for it'), and it is they who share it with others, sending what they call 'arrows' of transmitted n/om ('arrows' refer to the assumed deliverance, impact, and reception of ecstatic experience) into those who need healing (Keeney 2003: 33). This is done through movement and interaction without words. Though the Bushmen were arguably studied more than any other culture in anthropology, their healing dance epistemology has evaded scholars' attempts to pin it down. They have been a culture without written texts and, more surprisingly, they have not given any particular importance to oral culture (Keeney 2003). Their most valued form of experience, knowledge and teaching is somatically held. More specifically, the movements and sensations of their body in relationship and interaction with others constitute their way of knowing and being. They are a dancing culture. They know through dance and what they dance includes their arms and legs, as well as their ideas, emotions and laughter. Their world moves, like the changing seasons, and they move with it, valuing the constant movement and change more than any particular frozen moment (Keeney, 2003).

We will conclude with a fictional conversation between two voices, a salsera (woman salsa dancer) and a Kalahari Bushman *n/om kao* (healing dancer) in order to help illustrate the way a Kalahari inspired improvisation can dance words and meanings. The 'metalogue,' advanced by cybernetic systems thinker Gregory Bateson (1972: 1), is a written form that

Figure 2: Ju/'hoan Bushman Dancers. Kunta Boo (male) and Texae ≠oma (foreground). Photographer: Patrick Hill.

itself dances the exchange of ideas; it is meant to be a performance of that which it discusses. Because n/om arises from and is held inside relationship, a metalogue serves the elaboration of its conveyance, transmission and dance between two people.

This chapter serves to highlight n/om and its vital role in inspiring dances that heal. We aim to contribute to a more complex way of holding and examining the relationship between dance, movement and embodied interactivity across performance and therapeutic contexts. It is ironic that we situate our discussion inside a healing dancing culture, the Kalahari Bushmen, in which the kinds of distinctions with which we sometimes struggle—between stillness, ecstatic expression, dance, spirituality and other experiential domains—for them require no theoretical or intellectual reconciliation. Might one ask whether Bushman culture is more expressively advanced when it comes to embodying the circularities of performance and life that hold a more spirited way of bringing themselves forth? We invite the reader to dance with the unspeakable nature of n/om, doing so with an openhearted softness and availability to ever-changing movement. In this way may your passion for dance become that which most inspires, organizes, and dances your dancing body.

Gathering for a Dance

Bushman healing dancers tremble and shake when filled with n/om, but it is not the shaking that brings n/om forth. It is the arousal of heightened feelings that inspires ecstatic dance, shaking and any free-form movement. Remembering the longings of love inspires music, rhythm and dance, and this in turn feeds the felt presence of love's longings. It is a circularity, a virtuous feedback circle where music inspires dance as dance inspires music, while heightened emotion inspires ecstatic expression as ecstasy amplifies even more emotional intensity.

We are cautious about being too specific or limiting in the way we talk about when, where, how and for whom n/om can arise. This binds it too tightly to the particulars of form, practice, place or even culture. It is also not useful, however, to speak too generally about n/om and simply equate it with any kind of ecstatic feeling, spirited dance or aroused expression. Its presence has little or nothing to do with wilful intention. N/om is not a 'thing,' but a way of indicating how something mysterious in life and dance can be felt, something that words delimit and short-circuit. Hence the Bushmen have no treatise on it. If one must say anything about it at all, it is far better to sing about it, but to do so with the fewest words. Bushman song lyrics involve only one word or a few words at most, usually the name of the animal that inspires their affection, sung over and over in ways that improvise around a general melodic line.

Let us assume we have said enough about n/om. Otherwise we risk getting tangled inside too much conjecture and assumption that lead us astray from the inspiration it points towards. The Bushmen are familiar with how discourse can become a trap leading us away from the very thing we are trying to experience. They regard language as the invention of 'trickster'—it is the narrating and interpreting mind that likes to name, categorize, know and explain (Keeney 2010: 81). Trickster discourse is utilized in certain practical matters, but it is not allowed to interfere with matters of dance and n/om.

Getting Soft: Teasing the Mind, Waking Up the Heart

Well-being includes increasing our capacity to creatively participate in ongoing, unpredictable change (the latter of course being an unavoidable fact of living). Just as dancers train to increase flexibility because this serves a more varied and complex repertoire and ease of movement, loosening the stranglehold of thoughts, theories and narratives can make us more available to be danced inside the changing contexts of our everyday.

Therefore, when we cultivate a transformative context in the domain of talk, including discourse about spirited dance, we should give more importance to the degree to which our performance embodies creativity, flexibility and responsiveness to change than we do to the presence or absence of a particular idea, way of speaking, method, behaviour or ideological position. This is similar to the way a Zen master is usually more on the lookout for her student's capacity to play inside paradox and contradiction than her ability to recite any kind of Buddhist doctrine or view (Suzuki 2006).

All of this is another roundabout way of saying that the presence of n/om does not require any particular way of thinking, 'state of consciousness', explanatory schema, map, model, interpretation, analysis, understanding or even understanding about not understanding. When the Bushmen talk about 'getting soft', they mean that the mind and its artillery of thoughts and ideas must get out of the way and drop its defences so that the heart can be made more available to receive arrows of n/om (Keeney 2010). We become soft when the deep feelings of the heart become stronger, bigger and more encompassing than what the mind can make sense of. Rather than battle the mind, we can love it into submission. Better to play with it, tease it and humour it, than try to control its productions.

'For the Bushmen, the great mysteries of spirituality are delivered through two mediums—love and laughter' (Keeney 2010: xx). Though nowadays, meditation and contemplative practices have become popular means for 'quieting' the mind, the Bushmen offer an even older way of bringing it down to size: playful absurdity, teasing and nonsense help shake, rattle and roll any stuck or rigid knowing.

The Bushman dance begins with a barrage of laughter and playful teasing. This is not done in a highly structured or purposeful way. It takes place naturally, similar to the way family and friends gather for a birthday party where there is spontaneous laughing, chatting and joking around. The Bushmen do not have play therapy or 'laughing yoga;' they simply embrace teasing and humour as essential parts of family life, community and spiritual communion with the mystery of dance.

In the beginning of a dance, the dancing is simply for fun. But there is a serious lesson contained inside this kind of play. Unlike the solemnity and seriousness that mark so many other kinds of spiritual rituals, the Bushmen know that laughter literally is a kind of medicine. At least it is a necessary ingredient in helping us soften and awaken the heart, giving less importance to the interpreting and constraining mind. Any overly serious attempt to manage our thoughts, feed our narratives or adopt a preferable way of understanding maintains an allegiance to the mind's productions. On the other hand, nonsense, absurdity and teasing help relax the grip of rational, purposive mind, freeing one to be organized more easily by spontaneity and improvisation.

We suggest that all manner of interaction and performance, including conversations about these concerns, can incorporate this same spirit of play. Though it is sometimes implied that dance or movement itself provides the antidote to any overemphasis on rationality and disembodied thought (Pallaro 2007), dance alone is likely not enough to weaken our tendency to continuously narrate, interpret, or analyse our felt experiences. This is particularly true when dance therapists encourage clients to perform certain movements based on a particular therapeutic rationale or to reflect upon or interpret their embodied experiences during or after a dance. These forms of exploration may have their value, but they have little to do with awakening the life force or n/om so it may inspire a more spirited embodiment of dance.

There are other ways to conversationally dance inside an interaction that bring movement to any rigidity of thought or stuck pattern of behaviour. One example of this can be found in the use of Zen Buddhist koans, or records of unusual, often paradoxical exchanges mostly between teacher and student dating back several hundred years in China and Japan (Loori 2006). In some schools of Zen Buddhism koans are used as live, interactive teaching tools between student and Zen master. Though often associated with flashes of deep insight and ancient wisdom, koans are also playful (Roshi Egyoku Nakao, personal communication). Often nonsensical and absurd, they contain no answer to be unlocked, and it has been said they have no inherent meaning at all (Yamada 2004). When face-to-face with a Zen teacher, one must present the koan right there, on the spot. Consider for a moment that a student finds herself in a little room with incense and a candle burning. Suddenly a Zen master demands, 'Pour me a cup of tea made of no' (Roshi Egyoku Nakao, personal communication). Or maybe she asks, 'Why has the Western barbarian no beard?' (Yamada 2004: 17). There is no habituated answer that will help. What the teacher never says is that the answer is not found in any answer, but in how a student spontaneously dances with the whole question-answering interaction. This conversational form echoes the way Bushman n/om-kxaosi talk about their dance and the way they relate discourse to n/om. There is nothing to understand, but everything can be danced.

Performing koans with a Zen teacher is more like verbal contact improvisation than the spiritual discourse of pedagogies that presume they are handling specialized knowledge. Koan interactions mirror the absurdity of anyone thinking they can understand, know, control, fix or cure life's challenges. Transformative work of any kind can benefit from practices that reveal the absurdity of life, including dance, healing and spirituality. Koans provide a skilful means for shaking up our habituated ways of relating to the everyday, doing so while silently and loudly hinting a deep truth about the nonsensical, funny and absurd nature of all narrated experience.

Contemplative practices, with their emphasis on stillness and 'mindfulness,' have become more popular in the West in both spiritual and secular contexts, including therapy and higher education. Various forms of contemplative dance are now in existence both inside and outside academic programmes. But in the spirit of keeping ourselves soft for the arrows of n/om, the Bushman practice of 'insulting the meat' (Keeney 2010: 85) reminds us to caringly tease all forms, methods and theories, especially if they have become an accepted part of our pedagogical or therapeutic routines. Perhaps it is time to dance with koan-infused conversation and Bushman teasing and playfully announce a new M.F.A. concentration in 'Koanic Salsa,' or start a new somatic healing workshop dedicated to 'Contemplative Bushman Teasing.'

Therapists, traditional healers and dancers do not always need to present their clients, students and audiences with koans, nor do they need to begin each session by cracking jokes—unless the moment calls for it. However, one can be on the lookout for any opportunity to welcome the absurd in order to bring forth the spirit of improvised play. Do so knowing that

Figure 3: Ju/'hoan Bushman Dancers. Gwanta Komsta (foreground). Photographer: Patrick Hill.

it is difficult to wake up n/om inside talk, dance therapy or inspired movement performance whenever anyone follows a routine that relies too heavily on habituated ways of moving.

N/om is never present when we are not inspired. We need a kick-start to get ourselves ready for its vital breath. A tidal wave of deep feeling must build, stir, and advance inside us. This typically arises from constantly changing feelings and contradictions, whether recognized as laughter, sorrow, love, frustration, hope or longing. Like stretching an exercise spring, when both sides of a duality or distinction are held and then stretched, the whole relationship trembles. In the holding, tension and trembling of difference, n/om is felt as it naturally produces and releases energetic motion. Here, spirited dance is born.

Danced by N/om

As the Bushman dance progresses, the singing and clapping around the fire become louder as more people gather in a circle. Everyday talk and laughter give way to enthusiastic singing as the n/om-kxaosi become filled with n/om. When the men doctors dance, n/om makes them shake and bend forward, stomping their feet in the sand. The women n/om-kxaosi stand and sway, trembling intensely like trees. When this begins, n/om takes over and guides the doctors' movements. Without purpose or conscious thought they may be led to lay their trembling hands on someone sitting near the fire, thereby providing healing or revitalization.

There is a 'choreography' involved with this dance, but it is unlike that found on any ballroom floor or theatrical stage. Nor is it like an ecstatic dance gathering where people experiment with movement or improvisation. The Bushman dance arguably is not about dance at all. Nor is it purposefully about shaking or ecstatic expression, although these take place. The Bushman dance is about awakening, serving and sharing n/om. The same can be said for the flamenco dancer who lives for duende. Here dance—always with spirited song— is the expressive vessel for the life force which, in turn, is inseparable from a sacred love for life, creation, relationship and all that is danced.

Sometimes improvisation is viewed among contemporary dancers as a more viable vehicle for bringing forth spirited experience (Banes 2003; Pallant 2006). But the Bushman dancers are not solely improvisational. Although they improvise within constraints of form in both song and movement, it is neither choreography nor improvisation (or the relationship between them) that matter in the Kalahari. It is n/om, and the arrival of the latter carries us beyond both conceptual and pragmatic distinctions between purposeful and improvisational modes of interaction.

Whereas the distinction between scripted choreography and improvisation implies forms of movement that may be chosen by the performer, spirited dance acknowledges a more complex situation where the inhabited body has no choice other than to surrender to a mystery that never stops moving. When this occurs, dance becomes more about the feeling and expression of the ineffable than an intellectual study of its various methods and techniques. This view, however, has also been expressed among contemporary dancers. Recall this statement by Martha Graham:

> There is a vitality, a life force, an energy, a quickening that is translated through you into action, and because there is only one of you in all of time, this expression is unique [...] It is not your business to determine how good it is nor how valuable nor how it compares with other expressions [...] You do not even have to believe in yourself or your work. You have to keep yourself open and aware to the urges that motivate you. Keep the channel open [...] No artist is pleased. [There is] no satisfaction whatever at any time. There is only a queer divine dissatisfaction, a blessed unrest that keeps us marching and makes us more alive than the others.
>
> (as cited in DeMille 1991: 264)

Whether we call it a 'blessed unrest' or the hunt for n/om or duende, a re-emphasis on these vital aspects of dance is essential in any discourse wishing to make clear the relationship between dance performance, healing and spirited expression.

The Bushmen have a beautifully complex way of working with n/om that has developed over tens of thousands of years, and it is not possible to tease it apart and extract particular elements for transplantation into other contexts with the expectation of bringing forth a similar experience. Yet there is something to be learned from a culture that knows how to go past discourse and even past improvisation to instead be organized and guided principally by the awakening and presence of n/om—of that which dances dance. Though we may never experience n/om inside any workshop, classroom or clinic the way it is experienced in the Kalahari, we can learn to give less importance to whatever we think we know about transformation, dance improvisation or ecstatic movement and instead be moved by whatever feels alive, amplifies our emotions and initiates movements that arise spontaneously.

Metalogue: Danced Inside a Kalahari Embrace

The following metalogue further explores the relationship between dance and n/om by speaking creatively in the voices of two dancers, a *salsera* and a Bushman n/om-kxao. We write in these voices based in part on personal experience—Hillary is a long time salsa dancer and Brad, recognized by the Bushmen as one of their n/om-kxao, has been dancing in the Kalahari for over twenty years. Note that we cannot, nor do we intend to, speak for or represent either salsa dancers or the Bushmen. In the spirit of both salsa and the Bushman healing dance, here we play with metaphors, use creative expression, and take poetic license to authentically perform the feeling of being danced by n/om, whether in the Kalahari sands or on the salsa dance floor.

SALSERA: Please, can you tell me something about n/om?

N/OM-KXAO: You are a dancer. I bet you already know something about n/om.

SALSERA: I'm not sure it is the same when I dance as when the Bushmen dance. I love to dance because it makes me feel alive in a way that I can't describe. But your dance is about healing, while I dance just for fun.

N/OM-KXAO: It makes me very happy to hear that you have fun and feel alive when you dance. That's good. You should keep dancing. That's why we dance too.

SALSERA: Yes, I will always keep dancing as long as I can! It feeds my heart and soul. But from what I have read about n/om, it is more than the 'high' and release that I feel sometimes when I dance. However, I believe that dancing salsa is sacred because it makes my body and heart happy. Is n/om something more than that?

N/OM-KXAO: N/om may visit salsa as readily as it comes to the Kalahari dance. We dance for fun and to heal and to feel close to God. But we know what all dancers who talk like you know: that we may be danced at any time by the dance. When that happens, it feels like we are puppets for the gods or the life force. Then we are the vessels for spontaneous movement to express itself. Here the Tao of dance removes any separation from dance, dancer, choreography, dance tradition, muse and the gods. Here everything dances, is danced, and is dance. This is n/om. When you fully surrender to it, you shape-shift. You become the dance. Then you may become the choreographer or at least the inspiration they had when they created the movements. And finally you can step inside God's dancing shoes. This is the ultimate experience of life.

SALSERA: Yes, I confess, that I have sometimes felt like I was danced by the gods of salsa. This is why some of us danced every night we could. But it is impossible to explain.

N/OM-KXAO: Exactly. This is why it's wise to have a word like *n/om* that is not easily definable, and to use that word whenever this topic arises in a conversation. If we gave too much definition to it, its mystery would disappear. Our understanding would then behave as if it conquered and domesticated the non-understandable. This would take the n/om out of n/om.

SALSERA: When you get n/om, you start healing. I just keep on dancing. Should we start healing one another in the salsa clubs?

N/OM-KXAO: Actually, we never stop dancing. When our trembling hands touch another person, we are dancing them with a vibration that helps carry n/om into their body. It helps them catch the dance in a more deeply felt way. Perhaps you do that with your dance partner when you stare into his eyes or grip his hand more firmly.

SALSERA:	That does happen. Do you stare into the eyes of others when you heal?
N/OM-KXAO:	Yes, that is one way we send the n/om. We can sing it into you, stare it into you or vibrate it into you by touch.
SALSERA:	Is there n/om without music?
N/OM-KXAO:	Is there a dance without music?
SALSERA:	Music is in the dance. If you dance, you hear the music, with or without a band.
N/OM-KXAO:	Yes, there is always music. When you are a n/om-kxao, you always have music inside of you. It feels like you are dancing with everything in life, even when you are sitting still or lying down. The world vibrates, moves, changes and dances in each and every moment. This is what it means to be an owner of n/om.
SALSERA:	I think that is what it means to really be a dancer.
N/OM-KXAO:	Perhaps that's why we call our healers our special dancers and our healing a dance. Perhaps you should call your salsa clubs a healing temple.
SALSERA:	I might call it a 'n/om club.' That way no one would know what it means, and thereby it would be less likely that understanding would short circuit anyone's receiving n/om.
N/OM-KXAO:	Now you are talking like a n/om-kxao. Perhaps you should come to my club. It has the highest ceiling in the world and it not only dances with those who have their feet on the ground, we also dance with the stars.
SALSERA:	I think dancing with a star would be a lot more fun than dancing with the stars on television. Seriously, I would be delighted to dance with you. You are welcome to come dance salsa in Los Angeles as well.
N/OM-KXAO:	Thank you very much. I would love to have some salsa n/om. Maybe it's better than giraffe n/om.
SALSERA:	What's giraffe n/om?
N/OM-KXAO:	When we dance to the giraffe song, we try to catch the feeling of love we have for the giraffes. Then we dance the giraffe dance. Isn't that what you do? Don't you try to catch your love for salsa so it can dance you? What kind of animal is a salsa?
SALSERA:	Salsa is music. It is inspired by a passion for life with all its possibilities for love and joy.
N/OM-KXAO:	That is the same as n/om. I will tell my friends that there is a flavour of n/om called salsa.

SALSERA:	Can you have n/om with my salsa music?
N/OM-KXAO:	I don't know. It depends upon whether salsa music opens my heart. I need a song that can wake up my heart, break my heart, open my heart and make me empty enough so the universe can enter and dance itself to the end of time.
SALSERA:	Even Jesus danced and supposedly said, according to the Gnostics, 'To the universe belongs the dancer.'
N/OM-KXAO:	I like to say that I own the universe. I own the feeling for it.
SALSERA:	You mean that you love the universe and its dancing?
N/OM-KXAO:	I own the way I said it, but I am attracted to what you said. It might help me dance tonight.
SALSERA:	Have you ever met a flamenco dancer?
N/OM-KXAO:	Do they dance the flamingo? That would be very nice.
SALSERA:	They do stand tall (laughing) and I guess that is close enough. They have their duende and it seems similar to your n/om.
N/OM-KXAO:	Excellent! Three flavours are better than one. Salsa, duende, and n/om. Now we have three ways of getting cooked in the dance. You see, n/om cooks us. That's why we dance. We dance to get cooked by n/om—which is another way of saying that we get cooked by the gods.
SALSERA:	I think I want to get cooked by salsa and n/om. Actually I just want the gods to cook me.
N/OM-KXAO:	That I can help you with. Once you are cooked, you will have an inner band that never stops playing and singing. The dancing will never stop. You will feel it all the time. This is what it means to own the dance, the music and the gods. To the dancer belongs the universe!
SALSERA:	Do you dance in your dreams?
N/OM-KXAO:	Yes, those are the best dances of all. Perhaps that is why we dance—in order to get readied for the dream dancing. Or that is why we dream of dancing—to bring the dancing gods back to earth.
SALSERA:	The dances of dream and everyday must dance.
N/OM-KXAO:	That is the dance of n/om.
SALSERA:	And the salsa bird that dances with a giraffe!
N/OM-KXAO:	You are a Bushman dancer! Thank you for dancing your n/om with me. I will feel your salsa when I see a giraffe. I hope you will feel my giraffes when you are clubbing.
SALSERA:	Yes, I will always feel you dancing in my heart. Thank you, my dear friend.

Final Thoughts

Is dance ever not spirited? Or would such a performance be nothing more than uninspired movement? Perhaps the word 'dance' should be reserved as a name for that which honours movement that is inspired and infused by the highly charged ineffable, whether it is called n/om, duende or life force. This movement—neither willed nor shaped by a performer—dances anyone, with or without training, who becomes its vehicle for expression. When the body is tuned and made ready for its movement, the beauty of dance is realized in a way that inspires even its witnesses to feel more alive. The universe then owns the dancer, as the dancer owns the universe.

Should anything more be said about spirited dance? Let us not ask nor reply with words, but submit our inquiry to the movements of those who own the feeling for dance, allowing them to have the last embodied expression.

References

Banes, S. (2003), 'Spontaneous combustion: Notes on dance improvisation from the sixties to the nineties', in A. C. Albright and D. Gere (eds), *Taken by Surprise: A Dance Improvisation Reader*, Middletown, CT: Wesleyan University Press, pp. 77–85.

Bateson, G. (1972), *Steps to an Ecology of Mind*, Chicago, IL: University of Chicago Press.

Keeney, B. (1999), *Kalahari Bushmen Healers*, Philadelphia, PA: Ringing Rocks Press.

——— (2003), *Ropes to God: Experiencing the Bushman Spiritual Universe*, Philadelphia, PA: Ringing Rocks Press.

——— (2007), 'Batesonian epistemology, Bushman N/om-kxaosi, and rock art', *Kybernetes*, 36:7/8, pp. 884–904.

——— (2010), *The Bushman Way of Tracking God*, New York, NY: Atria Books.

Loori, J. D. (2006), *Sitting with Koans: Essential Writings on Zen Koan Introspection*, Somerville, MA: Wisdom Publications.

Lorca, H. de F. G. and Maurer, C. (1998 [1955]), *In Search of Duende*, New York, NY: New Directions Publishing.

Mille, A. de (1991), *Martha: The Life and Work of Martha Graham*, New York, NY: Random House.

Pallant, C. (2007), *Contact Improvisation: An Introduction to a Vitalizing Dance Form*, Jefferson, NC: McFarland & Company, Inc.

Pallaro, P. (ed.) (2006), *Authentic Movement: Moving the Body, Moving the Self, Being Moved*, London, UK: Jessica Kingsley Publishers.

Suzuki, S. (2006), *Zen Mind, Beginner's Mind*, Boston, MA: Shambhala.

Yamada, K. (2004), *The Gateless Gate: The Classic Book of Zen Koans*, Somerville, MA: Wisdom Publications.

Chapter 17

Dancing with the Divine: Dance Education and the Embodiment of Spirit, from Bali to America

Susan Bauer

This chapter is divided into two parts, with an introductory prologue that serves to frame this discussion of the dancing body as a vehicle for embodying the divine.

Part One presents ancient paradigms from Balinese Hinduism regarding the body and dance in order to explore the nature of dance training geared towards transcendent experience. Then, by tracing the evolution of dance training in Bali from a primarily village setting to that of an institution of higher education, Part One also explores the relationship of standardization, modernization and consumerist culture to the expression of embodied spirituality.

Part Two draws upon this case study from Bali, along with the author's experience as a dance educator, performer, and somatic movement educator, to define and suggest ten specific practices that encourage an expanded state of embodied consciousness for the dancer. This section further reflects upon the role of dance education in American culture and its educational institutions, using examples from the work of various prominent educators and artists. Part Two concludes with implications and recommendations for curriculum development in the field at large as a means to expand the paradigm of dance education.

Prologue: Three Anecdotes and Chapter Overview

Sanghyang Dedari

The Balinese *Sanghyang Dedari* ceremony, in which the classical *Legong* dance has its roots, involves two young pre-pubescent girls who are put into trance by a priest, then generally placed on the shoulders of the largest village men and, to the sound of Balinese chanting, become possessed by celestial nymphs. They then begin dancing—in perfect unison, having never studied the dance, with eyes closed. After the dance, the priest sprinkles the girls with holy water to take them out of trance. (Literally, '*sanghyang*' means trance ritual, while '*dedari*' means celestial nymph, and thus indicates this particular type of possession.) This purification ritual has been performed for centuries to ward off epidemics or other disturbances of village life.

When I was living in Bali for a year while on a Fulbright grant, a *Sanghyang Dedari* ceremony was called for in response to a problem in a village in northeastern Bali.

Preparations were made, and on the given day the village gathered in the *banjar*, or meeting hall. Though usually held in the temple, because of a previously scheduled ceremony, it was moved to the *banjar*—a less sacred space, but deemed sacred enough in a pinch. After hours of waiting, the young girls did not go into trance; the spirits did not descend. The waiting continued all day long, but still nothing happened. Eventually, the ceremony was deemed a failure, and all went home. As this only rarely occurs, in the days to follow everyone tried to figure out what had gone wrong. Apparently, after many hours and impatient with waiting, some of the village boys had brought a TV to the *banjar*, and began to watch it as they were awaiting the start of the ceremony. Others got out their cell phones, while others scooted off on their motorbikes for a quick meal at the *warang*. These were quite new 'additions' to the ceremony, which was generally held in the inner temple where such activities would not occur. Most Balinese I spoke with agreed that it had been these modern 'distractions,' (and not the move to the *banjar)* that had interrupted the ceremony, and they soon began to consult the Balinese priest for the next auspicious day to make another attempt to hold the ceremony properly, and thus, heal the village—which was successfully accomplished in the temple shortly thereafter (Bali, Indonesia; 2001).

Early Insights

In my freshman year in college, I was asked to choreograph a dance as part of my first modern dance class. I had no idea of what this meant, in the modern dance sense (as a jazz dancer from New Jersey) and I was quite petrified at this challenge. I went into a studio, and basically sat down and prayed for guidance. After a long time of stillness, I felt this intense movement 'leap' out of me, like something was moving my body from within and 'dancing' me for quite a while. I did not know what had happened, but I did my best to remember some of the movement, and I made this into my 'dance,' which I showed for class the next day; it was so enthusiastically received that later I developed it into my first choreographed piece that I performed in the college dance concert that semester.

About a year later in New York City, I was sitting on a park bench in Central Park when I happened to meet a woman who was an anthropology student at New York University; she invited me to her class that day to see some films about dance. The films turned out to be by Maya Deren and were about trance dances in Haiti, documented in the 1940s.[1] In one section of a film, the narrator explained that the woman dancing was possessed by a certain deity, as evident by the movements that are characteristic of that particular deity. Then on the screen, I saw about a one-minute section of 'my' dance. I never spoke to anyone about this (or about how I had made that first dance for that matter), but I began to believe there was more to dance than what I was studying in my 'dance education.'

Years later, I entered the graduate programme in Dance and Movement Studies at Wesleyan University and began to study, among other things, Dance Anthropology. This is where I first learned of the Balinese *Legong* dance and its origins in *Sangyhang Dedari*, the trance

Figure 1: Sang Ayu Ketut Muklen and Susan Bauer, dance lesson, Ubud, Bali, 2001. Photographer: Bonnie Simoa.

dance enacted to heal the village. Sharing a similar instinctual belief in the healing power of dance, I decided to go to Bali to learn the *Legong* dance and, perhaps, also understand more about my earlier choreographic experience (Vermont, USA, 1985; New York, USA, 1986; Connecticut, USA, 1990).

Performing Legong

In Bali, the popular *Legong* dance has many village versions and is performed for religious ceremonies and tourist performances alike. Back from my second trip to Bali, I performed the solo role of the *chondong* from the *Legong* dance I had studied with my teacher Sang Ayu Ketut Muklen, who, at 71, was believed to be the eldest living teacher of *Legong* on the island. This first performance was for a student dance concert at the private high school in New England at which I was dance faculty. Before the performance, I enacted all the necessary rituals I had been taught, such as a blessing ceremony for my headdress. When the music began and I took the stage, I had a very unusual experience.

First, I became instantly aware that a certain friend I had hoped would attend the concert was there in the audience, and that a certain student's father, whom she had very much

Figure 2: The headdress is considered one of the most sacred parts of the dancer's costume, and is kept in a special basket in a high place in the home and blessed with holy water before being used in performance. Photo of Susan Bauer in *Legong* costume, performance in a Balinese family temple in Klungklung, Bali, 2000. Photographer unknown.

wanted to come, was not. (Later I learned that both of these were true.) I was aware there would be a corresponding sense of happiness that my friend came, and a sense of sadness for the student whose father had not made it, but I did not actually experience those feelings. Next, I realized as I began dancing that I had a newfound confidence; it was as if there was an energy present in my body that definitely knew the dance. Perhaps most notable, as I continued dancing I began to feel a subtle force from outside my body 'directing' my movements, somewhat like the Balinese dance teacher does as she moulds the pupil's body from behind in the initial stages of learning the dance. For instance, in the *ngregseg*, a combination of small stepping movements done in a semi-circle first to the right and then to the left, as I was still completing the movement to the right side, I could already feel my body being 'pushed' to the left. I realized it was impossible to make a mistake in the choreography and could simply relax and enjoy the dancing. Third, unlike my usual state of semi self-consciousness, I had no concern for what others might think of my dancing. Rather, all that mattered was that the dance be performed as an offering. I did not think myself into this altruistic state—it just occurred as a shift of attitude within me. Finally, after I finished dancing and left the stage, I felt very expanded and energized, and also had an incredible urge to receive the holy water I had made and brought with me to bless my headdress before the dance. I went directly to the dressing room and sprinkled myself with the water.

Months later, when I talked to a Balinese friend about this experience, none of this surprised him at all; he recognized each of these shifts in perception and sensations as aspects of the experience of *taksu*, the Balinese term referring to divine inspiration in one's dancing (Massachusetts, USA; 1997).

Cultural Framework

Unifying these stories is the relationship of the dancer to the unseen, that realm of being or experience that many cultures call 'spiritual.' A wide range of experiences can be considered to be involved with such a spiritual dimension, often referred to as 'spirit' or 'the divine.' These terms can be used to refer to both the spirit or divine within, as well as to a larger universal energy—one that is omnipresent and of which we are also a part. There also clearly exists a multiplicity of cultural paradigms worldwide for perceiving this complex interrelationship between the material and spiritual realms. In the American culture in which I grew up and attended school, I found that little emphasis was placed on spirit, or its relationship to my human life. Likewise, in our educational systems, we are often left secularized and our bodies objectified—our lives and our dancing often void of spiritual power and divine grace. Yet as these stories suggest, such a connection to, or experience of, a spiritual dimension is not necessarily bound by place, culture or religion. These experiences may occur in the inner temple in Bali, during a community ritual in Haiti, in the privacy of a dance studio in Vermont or on stage at a high school in Massachusetts. What is it to 'connect to the divine,' or to 'experience a spiritual dimension?' How might these experiences be of value and positively impact us, both personally and collectively? Further, how can this connection be cultivated through dance and our moving bodies? And finally, how can we maintain and foster a spiritual connection in our arts and systems of dance education—even within our modern day culture? These are questions that have captivated me over the past 25 years.

Many cultures have centuries of understanding of spiritual dimensions and, as such, have developed specific language and paradigms for discussing these domains. Of these, I am most familiar with the framework of Balinese Hinduism, which I have found offers many specific perspectives that help to frame a discussion of the dancing body as a vehicle for embodying the divine. In this chapter, I first draw on ancient paradigms from Balinese Hinduism regarding the body and dance in order to explore the nature of dance training geared towards transcendent experience. Then, by discussing such topics as the standardization of dance within the university system in Bali, and its relevance to the 'failed' *Sanghyang Dedari* ceremony mentioned in the previous anecdote, I explore the relationship of modernization and consumerist culture to the expression of embodied spirituality. Finally, using this case study from Bali, along with my experience as a dance educator and somatic practitioner, I suggest specific practices that encourage an expanded state of embodied consciousness for the dancer, as well as reflect upon the role of dance education in American culture and its educational institutions.

Though just one of over 17,000 islands that make up the archipelago of Indonesia, Bali has clearly become the 'centrepiece' of Indonesia, with its international image having been carefully captivated and cultivated over the years by the influence of foreign visitors, Dutch colonial occupation, and its own Indonesian government (Bauer 2010). Bali's history and its arts are therefore inextricably interwoven with many socio-political and economic realities, some of which are briefly alluded to here in the context of both religious ritual and arts education, though beyond the scope of this chapter to address in depth. A plethora of sources exist on Balinese culture, particularly its often-romanticized religion and arts. However, in addition to my own primary research, I have chosen to rely mainly on sources with a Balinese author or co-author to avoid potential misinterpretations of the Balinese-Hindu belief system. While minimal sources of this type exist, one particularly relevant work, *Balinese Dance, Drama and Music* (2004) by I Wayan Dibia and Rucina Ballinger, serves as a guiding source for this chapter. A second text, *Nadi: Trance in the Balinese Arts* (2000), published by a group of Balinese artists and scholars through the Taksu Foundation, is also a main reference.

Finally, though I have been studying in Bali since 1995 and teach university courses in Balinese dance and culture, I often feel that the more I learn about Balinese Hinduism, the less I know. The same could be said for my connection with spirituality in general, or with the human body for that matter. In all of these cases, the complexity and mystery are just so great. For instance, when living in Bali, I attended an international arts conference that included a discussion on *taksu* with many of the artistic leaders in the Balinese community.[2] Yet while the discussion lasted nearly three hours, I began to notice that more questions were being asked than answered. Clearly topics such as *taksu* or connection with the divine within our human bodies remain complex and negotiable, in this case even among Balinese themselves. Nevertheless, we can aspire to explore the mystery as part of the learning process and, thereby, expand our perception—and enliven our experience—of what it means to be human.

Part One: Balinese Hinduism and the Evolution of Dance Training in Bali

Embodying the Divine—Balinese Hinduism and the Concepts of *Sekala* and *Niskala*

Balinese Hinduism, with its combination of ancestor worship, Hinduism, Buddhism and animism (the worship of spirit in certain elements of nature and animals), is unique to the island of Bali. In Balinese-Hindu cosmology, the worlds of *sekala* (that which is seen, or the material realm) and the world of *niskala* (the unseen, or the spiritual realm of ancestral spirits, deities, and demons) are specifically identified and seen as equally important and inextricably interwoven. Balinese describe shifting from one world to another with ease and communicating with spirit in a variety of ways, such as creating a special shrine in the rice field to worship *Dewi Sri* (the rice goddess), or visiting a local *balian* (a trance medium or healer) to request the correct remedy for a particular illness (Dibia and Ballinger 2004: 12, et al).

Further, within the Balinese-Hindu belief in reincarnation, the human body is seen as a vehicle for the spirit, such that infants are considered to be still in to the realm of the gods and, therefore, are not allowed to crawl on the ground 'like animals' until their six-month birthday ceremony; at this time the child's feet symbolically touch the ground for the first time and they are considered fully human. Once human, one's body is still seen as a reflection of the larger spiritual dimension, as reflected in the Balinese use of the Sanskrit word '*bhuana*' that describes both one's body and the universe. *Buana alit,* or small body, refers to one's physical body, while *buana agung,* or the great body, refers to the cosmos. In this way, one's body is seen as the microcosm of the larger universe or macrocosm (Eisman 1990: 6; personal communication). As children and adults, Balinese likewise have a deeply embodied connection with nature. For instance, no matter where they live on the island, most Balinese sleep with their head towards the sacred Mount Agung in northeastern Bali, or in the *kaja* direction (vs. *kelod,* towards the sea). So deeply engrained is this directional sense that it is a commonly known anecdote that after spinning around with eyes closed and then stopping, most Balinese still always know which direction is *kaja.* Nature, humans, spirit and the cosmos are thus distinct, yet intimately interwoven, aspects of life.

Yet according to Balinese Hinduism it is the enactment of ritual performance that allows the individual to move through the liminal space of what is referred to as the *langse* (or curtain between the two worlds), such that the dancer bridges the worlds of *sekala* and *niskala* and beings in the spiritual realm can more fully enter into the material world (Dibia and Ballinger 2004: 12–13). Masks are considered particularly *tenget* (or spiritually powerful) vessels and, when properly carved and sanctified by a priest, can become empowered by the presence of a deity. When worn during a ritual dance performance, then, the mask and dancer transform into a protective guardian with magical and healing powers (Dibia and Ballinger 2004: 12; Slattum 2003: 13; personal communications). In Balinese ceremonies, the spiritual, artistic and social elements intermingle to create an event that is considered truly '*ramai*,' or colourful and busy, to enhance the human and spiritual realms alike.

This concept—of the dancer as a vehicle for the divine, with associated healing powers that impact the community—is a common perception for Balinese, such that the mark of a truly great dancer was traditionally one who possessed *taksu,* an inner power or 'spiritual charisma […] the pinnacle of energy which every Balinese performer strives for to mesmerize both the human and divine audience' (Dibia and Ballinger 2004: 8). While we in the West may refer to this as 'stage presence,' *taksu* goes quite beyond that:

Having *taksu* is possessing the ability to hold and bind your audience, to become magnetic and enchanting [...] on stage. In the West, some might call this stage presence but it is much more than that as there is a definite connection with divine forces.

(Dibia and Ballinger 2004: 11)

For the dancer possessing *taksu*, there are corresponding shifts in consciousness that create a heightened state of awareness or perception:

... the dancer becomes not necessarily a specific personage, but the essence of the character. His or her own ego is forgotten. Many performers can tell of the exhilaration of doing a role well, of pleasing not only the human audience but the divine as well.

(Dibia and Ballinger, 2004: 13)

Similarly, other Balinese artists have told me that *taksu* is experienced like an 'inner sun shining within,' or simply as the joy of 'being one with one's activity' (Berata 2012).[3] In my experience, this state of *taksu* allows for a merging with the divine in which one's consciousness expands and one becomes more fully present. Often in these instances, more information is intuitively available and a 'knowing' may arise that is understood as imagery or thought, but is beyond intellectual knowledge—as in the earlier anecdote in which I became aware of the presence of particular audience members. One may also experience a certain detachment from one's emotions, as also noted in the previous anecdote. This type of shift in consciousness is often similarly referred to as 'transcending one's ego' in various meditation practices, from Hindu and Buddhist traditions alike. Considered achievable through meditation and spiritual practice, this egolessness is seen in such religions as an essential aspect of attaining enhanced spiritual awareness.[4] Likewise, *taksu* cannot merely be sought after; it arrives under the right conditions when one is properly aligned within oneself. Thus, the dancing itself becomes a spiritual practice—expanding one's embodied awareness of the realms of both *sekala* and *niskala*. Javanese dance shares a similar concept in the term '*rasa*,' which refers to an inner feeling and associated expanded spiritual capacity, such that the embodied Javanese self is best understood as a field of forces and potentials, some of which are more bound to the body than others, rather than as an individual entity (Hughes-Freeland 2008: 80). In Balinese Hinduism, in fact, the arts are believed to be one of three vehicles, along with meditation and prayer, through which to achieve enlightenment or *moksa* (Eisman 1990: 24).

While *taksu* is aspired towards in performance, it is distinctly different from, though related to, the concept of trance in Balinese Hinduism, which is equally accepted and cultivated:

The Balinese accept trance as an ordinary occurrence, a way of communicating with the gods, spirits and ancestors. [...] Trance may occur in performance as well as in religious rituals. It is a sign that the deities have truly descended.

(Dibia and Ballinger 2004: 13)

Between these two extremes are a range of states of 'embodied spirituality' that are categorized roughly as slight *taksu*, medium *taksu*, strong *taksu* and light trance, medium trance and full trance (personal communication). A full trance implies that an ancestor, deity or demon has temporarily possessed one's body, such as in the earlier description of the *Sanghyang Dedari* dancers inhabited by celestial nymphs. Further, the *Sanghyang Dedari* dancer who is considered to be in full trance is also considered to possess *taksu*, while a dancer who is not in trance may also possess *taksu* (Sugriwa 2000: 27). But above all, it is this quality of *taksu*—an experience and expression of the divine embodied that transcends one's individual physicality—that is the pinnacle of what is considered exceptional in both ritual and non-ritual performance. If this quality of *taksu* is so essential, how does a dancer 'qualify' to receive *taksu*? More simply put: how do Balinese dancers connect with the divine in their dancing bodies?

Balinese Village Styles—Training the Dancer

In the traditional Balinese dance training, several aspects contribute to a dancer's ability to receive *taksu* that include the nature of one's training and the completion of specific personal and community ceremonies. First, an essential component of dance training is physical transmission, which occurs as the master teacher is physically touching and moulding the pupil's body. Here, in addition to reinforcing the movements through rigorous physical training, the teacher is transmitting the 'energy' of the dance, through touch, phrasing and quality of movement, from his or her body and its cellular memory to that of the pupil. In this way, '*taksu* can be passed down from a parent to a child or from a teacher to a pupil' (Dibia and Ballinger 2004: 11). Rather than merely mimicking the physical form of the dance, or striving to add to or interpret the form through one's own individual creativity, the dancer thus begins to embody the actual character of the dance form itself.

Secondly, a serious dance student also has many specific rituals to participate in before their performance, including blessing ceremonies for the mask or headdress, along with three levels of ceremonies to further assist the dancer to become one with the blessed objects. Such ceremonies are important because an object such as a mask may also posses *taksu*—and thus assist the dancer in helping it to 'come alive' during performance (Dibia and Ballinger 2004: 11, personal communications). Further, on the day of the performance, the dancer makes certain prayers and offerings for the object(s), asks for permission to perform in the particular temple, engages a priest to bless the stage area and the music ensemble which will accompany the dance and prays for *taksu* at their home temple (Sugriwa 2000: 17, 18; Dibia and Ballinger 2004: 16). For certain roles considered more magically dangerous, performers may abide by certain rules before the performance, such as abstaining from specific foods and/or from sexual relations (Dibia and Ballinger 2004: 17). In this way, the dancer's own behaviour and interaction with the community and performance space itself are part of the preparation for dancing.

Figures 3 and 4: In teaching Balinese dance, the teacher often moulds the student's body, transmitting the 'energy' of the dance through touch, phrasing, and quality of movement. Figure 3 here: Sang Ayu Ketut Muklen and Susan Bauer, dance lesson, Ubud, Bali, 1997. Photographer unknown. See also Figure 4 on next page.

Other aspects which assist the dancer in acquiring *taksu* are classified into three categories based on the Balinese-Hindu triad of *bayu* (energy), *sabda* (inner voice) and *idep* (thought) that are inherent in each individual. These three aspects must be aligned and in balance: 'A dancer [...] must have energy in order to move, his or her inner voice or convictions must be present in order to perform well and there must be clarity in one's thought process' (Dibia and Ballinger 2004: 11). To attain such clarity of thought, one must first create a one-pointed focus, which assists in connecting with the spiritual realm:

When a dancer obtains *taksu,* he or she can be called *nadi*. Then he/she is considered mature. [...] *Nadi* begins with a stimulus. The stimulus makes the dancer focus his mind and when his focus is narrowed on a single thing only, the dancer is in the *nadi* state. At this stage there will be a taking over of bodily control by other powers, both from within and from without the dancer's body. Soon after this he will dance beautifully and amazingly.

(Sugriwa 2000: 22, 58)

Figure 4: Students at University of San Francisco with Professor Susan Bauer, dance lesson, Balinese Dance and Culture course, January, 2013. Photographer: Cristian Polanco.

The single-pointed focus of the *nadi* state is represented in the Balinese dancer's makeup by the *cundang*, a white dot applied between the eyebrows 'symbolizing the Third Eye of strength and concentration'; dancers thus often say a mantra and ask for *taksu* when applying this sacred symbol (Dibia and Ballinger 2004: 20). Many other cultures also describe the Third Eye—one of the seven energy centres in the body, called chakras—as the focal point of spiritual connection or 'God' perception.

The more stable the dancer becomes in his or her inner development, such that the three realms of body (*bayu* or energy), mind (*idep* or thought) and spirit (*sabda* or inner voice) are in balance with consistency, the more likely one is to receive *taksu* more consistently as

Figure 5: In preparing for a dance performance, dancers apply the *cundang* make-up, a white dot to represent the Third Eye of strength and concentration that is considered necessary for performing well; Susan Bauer, Klungkung, Bali, 2000. Photographer: I Kadek Sukadanah Preharta.

well—and thereby to make contact with the divine forces.[5] The gift of *taksu* is thus granted based on one's inner character and state of being, rather than purely upon one's technical prowess. While we may be familiar with technical precision and even mental focus as a requirement for dance training, we are likely less familiar with the idea that one's internal character or right motivation can affect one's dancing or performance. Yet for the Balinese performer, who is considered to be enacting his or her duty of *ngayah* (or ritual devotion to the gods) as service to the community, such inner motivation is seen as essential to the success of the performance (Dibia and Ballinger 2004: 108; Sugriwa 2000: 18). In fact, in the Balinese language there is no word for 'art' or 'artist'; rather the Balinese words—such as '*pragina*,' used to identify a dancer or actor and meaning 'one who beautifies' the ritual (Dibia and Ballinger 2004: 8)—thus point towards this sense of ritual devotion or offering. The experience of *taksu*, therefore, goes beyond a state of presence of the dancer, to become an offering to and experience for the community as well, as the energy of *taksu* is emanated to both those in the human world and the spiritual realm.[6] With this in mind, what type of school or curriculum might be developed to support such a dancer, who aspires to achieve technical skill and spiritual maturity of character enough to impact the human and divine audience alike? To address this question, we can examine the evolution of dance training in Bali from its village origins to the more recent creation of its arts institutions in the 1960s to see what can be learned about the relationship of its sacred arts within modernized society.

The Institutionalization of Dance in Higher Education in Bali and the Impact of Modernization

While traditional village teaching methods include a rich combination of touch and ceremonial preparation as described previously, with the opening of both an arts high school and an arts university, administrators began to develop a distinct training geared towards the dancer's more secular roles, such as at tourist performances or official functions.[7] Yet such a shift in focus further emphasized a distinction between art, performance and ritual that is

Figure 6: The Balinese *Legong*, with roots in the sacred *Sanghyang Dedari*, has transformed over time through many various 'incarnations'—including from a court dance (*Legong Keraton*) to this tourist performance in the Ubud Palace. Balinese *Legong* dance, *Chondong* dancer, name unknown, Ubud Palace, 1995. Photographer: Susan Bauer.

actually quite contrary to Balinese-Hindu beliefs. Due to the influence of tourism, however, this Western construct has become an element with which the Balinese have inevitably had to contend (Picard 1996: 134). It was not until 1971, in fact, that the Balinese Arts Council produced the now commonly accepted separation of dances into three categories in an attempt to protect their sacred dances from commercialization.[8] Drawing upon the essential Balinese Hindu triad of *desa* (place), *kala* (time) and *patra* (occasion), they created categories based on the place and purpose of the dance: *wali* ('offering'), which are sacred ritual dances performed generally in the inner temple; *bebali*, ceremonial dances generally performed in the middle temple; and *bali-balihan* ('that which is watched'), dances performed in the outer temple or outside the temple grounds altogether (such as at tourist venues) and considered secular dances (Dibia and Ballinger 2004: 10; Picard 1996: 153–156). Despite these theoretical distinctions, however, in practice the lines between these categories often become blurred in response to the Balinese community's desire to take appropriate ritual steps to invoke *taksu*, regardless of the context, to ensure a good performance (Picard 1996: 160; Dibia and Ballinger 2004: 11; personal communications). In such a way, whether for tourists or temples, most Balinese artists simply refused to 'disenchant' their performances.[9]

Yet as noted by scholar Rucina Ballinger (1985) in an article titled 'Dance in Bali: the Passing on of a Tradition,' in order to teach these more secular dances, the arts institutions began to adopt many Western approaches that were often in direct opposition to those used in villages. Curricular changes included an introduction of the Western idea of 'warm-up' exercises rather than simply learning the dance itself, and a tendency to teach several styles of dance to a single dancer (rather than insist on specialization), as well as specifics in the way the dances themselves were taught. This included using the terms left and right to replace the Balinese directional sense of East and West, taped music instead of live gamelan music and the use of mirrors to accommodate larger numbers of students (Ballinger 1985). Moreover, though not noted by Ballinger, the shift from a village setting to a studio also initiated a change from an outdoor setting to an indoor one. A seemingly simple evolution, when combined with the reliance on studio mirrors versus physical contact transforms a once primarily sensual, kinesthetic and tactile learning experience into a more external one—and thus initiates a major change in the experience for both the dancer and the teacher. Further, using taped music rather than working directly with musicians separates the dancer from the larger community and segregates the arts into separate disciplines. As I have observed, many of these curricular methodologies were initiated by Balinese who had pursed advanced degrees in music and/or dance at U.S. universities, and later went on to become the major teachers and administrators at Bali's arts institutes (Bauer 2002).

While the traditional Balinese concept of a professional performer had been reserved for those with the spiritual maturity to possess *taksu*, such Balinese artists with degrees from the U.S. brought a new idea of professionalism, as implied here by I Made Bandem, a former director of the arts university, and one of the first Balinese performers to attain a graduate degree in the United States:

> The motivations for the performing arts, so far, have been religious ones. But now, we cannot isolate ourselves from globalization anymore … We have to live with overseas and domestic tourists. Therefore, now is the time for our artists to conduct themselves like professionals.
>
> (Bandem, 1991, in Picard 1996: 171)

The motive of Balinese administrators for adopting Western teaching methodologies thus relates to the desire to create 'arts professionals' based on this more Western model of one who makes a living as a performer. Complicating matters further are the increasing demands of tourism, village opinion, and more recently, the interest of some Balinese artists to diverge from classical tradition in the name of artistic innovation (Dibia and Ballinger 2004: 98). This seems to be particularly the case at the arts institutions where standardized dances, both newly created dances and shortened versions of traditional forms, now prevail over more traditional village styles:

> The original goal […] was to create teachers as well as to preserve traditional forms and develop new ones. Graduates brought back to their village what they had learned, and local versions were neglected and eventually forgotten. Students at both schools [Bali's arts high school and arts university] are extremely well-trained in a variety of art forms with a myriad of teachers so they no longer follow one teacher's style, but have the 'school style.'
>
> (Dibia and Ballinger 2004: 16)

Many of these standardized dances taught at the university were first mandated by the Indonesian government, through its provincial agencies in Bali, to feed the tourist circuit (Picard 1996: 171); thus, institutionalization of the arts, tourism, and professionalization evolved simultaneously. Moreover, with the establishment of 'professional' dancers from the university who performed at tourist venues and in temple ceremonies alike, a certain hierarchy developed over time that caused many village girls and women to feel uncomfortable performing their village styles for temple ceremonies, further deteriorating such village styles (personal communications).

While some Balinese support the presence of arts institutions, maintaining that it helps Balinese dance to gain prestige and world acclaim by training 'professional dancers,' for all these reasons, many other Balinese complain that the new teaching methods are undermining the quality of dance in Bali. In fact, the professional dancers from the university are often the ones most specifically criticized by Balinese audiences for lacking *taksu* in their dancing (personal communications). For example, I recently saw a performance by a group from the Balinese arts university on tour in California. While the dancers were highly skilled technically, my own sense as a dancer was that many of the performers seemed to lack a dynamic connection to the movement, which I have experienced as central to an expanded state of consciousness, such that I actually felt more like I was watching an aerobics or exercise class. This again reminded me of the difference between dancing that appears mechanical, and that which feels—both for performer and audience—transcendent. It is quite intriguing, then, that when the presence of *taksu* remains the highest standard of judgement for dance quality among so many Balinese, that the arts institutes would have adopted methodologies taken from American culture and its educational system which, as I learned in my own college dance experience, often has so little direct concern with the spiritual dimensions of dance. Further, how these more modern teaching methods—such as indoor studios, taped music, and a reliance on mirrors rather than touch—relate to the cultivation of *taksu*—or lack thereof, is an interesting question, not unrelated perhaps to how cell phones, televisions and motorbikes effect the cultivation of trance, as in the earlier story of the failed *Sanghyang Dedari* ceremony. Do the Western dance teaching methods and elements of modernization, in fact, undermine the cultivation of *taksu* or connection with the divine? (Bauer 2002).

Some Balinese note that modern life may, in fact, be seen as a contributing factor, as bemoaned here by I Wayan Dibia, Ph.D., one of the arts institute's past directors:

> Even though the number of performers has increased greatly over the last century, those with *taksu* have decreased. Modernization and globalization are partly responsible for this. The attention span is shorter and concentration less strong than it was in the past. [...] Dancers have reasons other than solely devotion (money and fame among them) for performing at a temple ceremony. Just a generation ago, children in a village would get so excited about performing at the next temple festival [... with] all their neighbors and relatives watching. Today there are after-school activities, video games and, of course, television. All of this has an impact on the arts.
>
> (Dibia and Ballinger 2004: 11)

Clearly our cultural conditioning affects our perceptions of and relationship to tradition and modernity. For today's Balinese dancers who attend the arts university, their arts education is a prime factor impacting such perceptions. For example, while I was living in Bali, my teacher, Sang Ayu Muklen, was proud to have gained two new Balinese dance students from the arts university. She soon found, however, that they studied just enough to learn the first short section of the nearly hour-long *Legong* dance—which she later discovered was all they needed to fulfil their requirement to perform twenty minutes of a village style for their final exam. Yet, while interest in the village styles may be waning among the younger generation, as mentioned performances of the more prevalent and shorter modern versions they prefer to perform are often seen within the Balinese community itself to be lacking in *taksu* or spiritual charisma.

At the arts university, the shift away from the more holistic focus on the three elements of *bayu* (energy), *sabda* (inner voice) and *idep* (thought) to a more narrow focus on the development of dance technique alone can clearly be seen as a contributing factor. Most significantly, the Balinese authors of *Nadi: Trance in the Balinese Arts* note that students in the university who learn through Western methods are not being taught about the single-pointed focus of the *nadi* state—the opening of the Third Eye of spiritual perception, as previously discussed—which would assist the dancers in being more creative and fully concentrated in their dancing (Sugriwa 1998: 59). As noted in the previous quotation, they also have reasons other than devotion to perform. The failed *Sanghyang Dedari* ceremony could likewise be seen to relate to the dissipated intentionality of the participants and the subsequent breakdown of a community focus on the divine, rather than to the introduction of material objects—in this case, cell phones and televisions—themselves.

In fact, Balinese have long been notorious for appropriating modern day elements into their art and ritual settings as meets their needs. For example, I once saw an elderly woman participating in a *wali* ceremony in the inner temple who was dancing holding a Coke® bottle; eager to join the group of dancing women holding the traditional bowl of flowers and incense, she had fashioned her 'offering bowl' out of the empty bottle, into which she had placed a piece of lighted incense. While that would seem sacrilegious to some, from a Balinese perspective this method of adaptation simply allowed her to participate in religious worship. Further, Balinese note that occasionally even a non-consecrated mask may become '*tenget*' or spiritually charged (personal communication), while in a particularly powerful ceremonial ritual, such as the *Calonarong*, even audience members have been known to fall into a trance (Dibia and Ballinger 2004: 11). Thus it is not necessarily the object, nor the traditional or contemporary dance form itself, that is 'sacred' or 'secular,' but the fuller context, along with one's inner intention—or in Balinese terms, the context of *desa* (place), *kala* (time) and *patra* (occasion)—that influences the level of interaction between the worlds of *sekala* (seen) and *niskala* (unseen), and, thus, the spiritual impact.

What can be learned from these observations on the institutionalization of dance in Bali and the relationship of its sacred arts within modernized society? In addition to the obvious commentary on the potential distractions caused by our modern technology and over-industrialized lives, there would seem to be a correlation here, particularly in relation to the shift in teaching methods discussed earlier, between the degree of attention to the personal dimensions of body, mind and spirit and the potential for experiencing the type of expanded consciousness associated with *taksu* or connecting with the divine. In fact, within the Balinese arts community itself this issue of the impact of arts education on *taksu* may finally be coming to the forefront. Administrators of the Bali Arts Festival, held on the campus of the arts university each year, recently took *taksu* as its umbrella theme, having recognized that 'the idea of *taksu* has been ignored for too long in any public discourse on Balinese culture' (Dibia 2013).

How does this relate to my own American education, and to the role of dance education? What type of contemporary dance curriculum might be created to engage the lived experience of the dancer in a fuller, more holistic sense—one that supports dancers to experience their bodies or *buana alit* (inner cosmos) as part of the *buana agung* or larger cosmos? From this perspective, the term 'soma,' in reference to one's living body or lived experience in one's body,[10] can thus include such a spiritual dimension as well. Perhaps one could even say that the further we stray from our soma, the further we stray from the divine; thus the closer we live in alignment with our soma, the closer we may come to experiencing our body as a vehicle for the divine within us and without. How might we create a context to invite this expanded somatic experience into our dancing, our education—and even our lives—in our modernized society and within our contemporary dance forms?

Part Two: Recommendations—A New Vision of Dance Education

Introduction

Drawing from the Balinese-Hindu paradigm, particular elements of the village teaching methods can be distilled to create a specific approach to dance education that is inclusive of the three realms of body (*bayu* or energy), mind (*idep* or thought) and spirit (*sabda* or inner voice) as previously discussed. This approach would help dancers to develop the kind of inner power associated with *taksu*, and thus serves to integrate the worlds of *sekala* and *niskala*—even in our contemporary educational systems. For while some aspects of the traditional Balinese dance training process are unique to Balinese culture, other aspects can be seen to be more universal—and thus applicable to other contemporary styles as well. For example, while the use of touch by the teacher to invoke the energetic transmission of a particular Balinese dance character and pass it from one generation to the next is specific to Balinese culture, the use of touch to facilitate proprioceptive awareness in the dancer's body is a specific, yet less culturally bound, principle more easily applicable to contemporary dance education.

Framing a discussion in these Balinese terms can be helpful, as one aspect that is so refreshing about the Balinese-Hindu perspectives is the specificity with which spiritual terms are defined and applied to the traditional process of training the dancer. In the case of ritual performances, clarity also exists in the ways that rituals are created, and success or failure of the ritual itself is evaluated by the community. In my own American culture, which lacks a common religious or spiritual paradigm, 'spirituality' is generally a vague and elusive concept. Therefore, in creating such contemporary approaches or 'formulas,' an inherent danger exists of either superficial New Ageism or rational intellectualism, both of which may lack depth and clarity. To address these many challenges, I focus on certain principles and methods that people from many cultures and spiritual perspectives can relate to, such as the use of touch as previously described, or the concept of dedication or the development of concentration. Thus we can employ such simple principles, while remaining aware of the particular context—that of *desa* (place), *kala* (time) and *patra* (occasion)—of our own teaching situation, in order to choose appropriate methods. Whether or not they are presented within an expressly 'spiritual' context, such principles can assist in expanding the dancer's state of embodied consciousness—and thus enliven our human experience, both individually and collectively.

Elements that support such conscious and embodied awareness, drawn from my own experience and the paradigm of the village teaching methods in Balinese Hinduism previously discussed, include the following:

1. Invocation/preparation
2. Clear intention/dedication/offering
3. Sense of contribution/community
4. Focus and concentration/meditation
5. Open receptivity
6. Expanding our perceptual base/embodiment
7. Connecting to nature
8. Creating a clear container
9. Closure/dedication/clearing the space
10. Integration/re-entry

Because many of these categories I have defined in fact overlap, it becomes difficult to speak about them separately; I will therefore interweave these various themes in this next section and suggest some possible ways to integrate these elements into existing dance curricula. I ground this discussion in specific examples from my own teaching and experience as a dance educator and somatic movement practitioner that I have found to be helpful, along with examples from the work of several contemporary colleagues. As such, I aspire to both demonstrate the practical application of these principles, as well as to highlight a dynamic generation of educators, somatic practitioners, and artists who I feel share a similar vision.

Ten Transformative Principles for Contemporary Dance/Movement Education

Invocation, Clear Intention, Dedication, Offering, Sense of Contribution/Community (1, 2 and 3)
As in the Balinese-Hindu concept of *ngayah* (devotional activity) mentioned earlier, the simple act of sincere dedication can be incorporated into dance teaching to encourage the idea of making a meaningful contribution, to invoke a sense of devotion and well-intentioned motivation and to reinforce the idea of being part of a larger community. Such dedications

Figure 7: Students at University of San Francisco rehearse outdoors as part of the Balinese Dance and Culture course, January 2013. Photographer: Cristian Polanco.

can clarify and strengthen the aspect of *sabda*, or the inner voice or conviction, of the dancer as referred to in the traditional village model of Balinese dance training. Buddhism shares a similar practice of dedication such as practiced by the *Bodhisattva*, a Sanskrit term meaning 'enlightened being,' that refers to those who are motivated by compassion and seek enlightenment not only for themselves, but also for all beings. In Tibetan Buddhism, those who take the vow of the Bodhisattva are taught to dedicate their practice or actions for the benefit of all beings both at the beginning and end of an activity, which is believed to expand the benefit of the actions themselves. Yet in a more general sense, dedications need not be related to any particular religious views or even to any particular notion of spirituality to inspire a deeper motivation and fuller participation in one's activity.

In my Balinese Dance and Culture course, students are invited to dedicate their dancing before beginning a class or performance, as well as to dedicate their efforts afterward. In this process, students silently make their dedication to whatever is important to them—whether for themselves or others. Dedications can include healing from an illness; dedications for others, such as friends, relatives, or pets; or dedications for world situations, such as to recent hurricane victims or the concept of peace. Students are generally very enthusiastic about the dedications and will even remind me if I have forgotten to initiate them. Some

Figure 8: Susan Bauer performing *Touching Peace*, at the International Bali Arts Festival, 2000.
Photographer: I Ketut Rina.

who are dance majors have also told me they incorporate dedications into their performing 'ritual' before the semester dance concerts as well, regardless of the dance style they perform. Dedications can also be performed as a group. Before a recent outdoor performance of Balinese dance, the students formed a circle and took a moment together to dedicate their performance to those who had suffered from a volcano that had occurred in Indonesia just days before which had killed hundreds of people. Though only one of them was Indonesian and the rest had never been to Indonesia, just from spending that semester learning about the culture of the people of Bali and Java, and engaging in their arts, a caring and concern had developed that came forth in their decision to dedicate the dance to that particular event.

Sharing the dedication with the audience is also another level of creating community, as I experienced when performing at an annual conference of Indonesian Fulbright associates called 'Making Democracy Work' that was being held in Bali.[11] That year, I had created a contemporary masked-dance solo, called *Touching Peace*, that I had recently performed in the International Bali Arts Festival and which I agreed to perform for the conference. In considering how to make a meaningful contribution, I decided to dedicate my performance to a peaceful transition in the upcoming presidential election in Jakarta, where in the recent months many riots had broken out in response to the deteriorating political situation. The

Figure 9: Dedications can be done individually or as a group, such as in Anna Halprin's *Planetary Dance*, shown here in California, dedicated to a variety of topics such as global peace and healing. *Planetary Dance* with Anna Halprin (centre), Santos Meadow, Mt. Tamalpais State Park, California.
Photographer: © Marguerite Lorimer.

host announced this in Indonesian and invited the audience to join in a prayer for peace during a particular section of the dance. A hush surrounded the opening of the dance, and later in that section, as I glanced out the very thin slits of my mask before closing my eyes in prayer, I saw that many in the audience had joined me in the traditional Balinese-Hindu position of placing the palms together and raising both hands to one's forehead. This sincere moment of invocation developed a palpable sense of community and caring among us. Perhaps, one could hope, we even assisted in some small way in the outcome of a future event—the peaceful election which was held the following month. On a larger scale, events such as Anna Halprin's *Planetary Dance*, in which hundreds of people join to engage in a group ritual dedicated to a particular cause, also serve a similar purpose. In this dance ritual which I attended in California—and which is similarly done in countries throughout the world—participants call out their dedication before entering into the concentric circles of what is called the Earth Run, walking or running to the common pulse of drummers in the centre. By having a clear purpose and calling upon a higher power to join in the human prayers, *Planetary Dance*[12] is a contemporary example of an inspiring community dance of invocation and dedication that aims to serve the well-being of the community.

Finally, through methods such as dedications, we invoke a sense of dance as an offering and a contribution to one's community, in contrast to the sense of presentation or competition that often exists in our dance programmes. As generally approached, competition often contributes to the stress level of the individual and creates tension in the community, thwarting the potential of both the individual and the group. Within a necessarily competitive environment, such as dance auditions for department concerts, we can encourage students to compete to do their best, rather than compete to do better than others. They can even dedicate their efforts at the audition itself. This type of healthy competition—focused on one's own growth and learning—can actually inspire one's creativity and encourage individual potential, while maintaining a sense of community participation.

Focus and Concentration/Meditation, Open Receptivity and Embodiment (4, 5 and 6)

Many methods can be used to develop focus and concentration, a state of open receptivity, and physical presence or dynamic embodiment—such as meditation, mindful movement, somatic movement practices and forms of martial arts. To begin with, meditation can stimulate clarity of thought or the *idep* of the dancer, such as the one-pointed focus present in the *nadi* state, while practices that support embodiment strengthen the *bayu*, or physical energy, producing a more powerful state of presence within the dancer. Since becoming aware of the *nadi* state, for instance, I have taught my dancers a particular method I learned to attain a one-pointed focus—by visually focusing on a specific point or by bringing one's energy up to the centre of the forehead (Tadd 2010)—that we integrate into our rehearsals and performances.[13] Not only are the dancers more dynamic, focused and less apt to experience stage fright when using this technique, but many audience members have commented that the dancers appear more deeply centred in themselves. As another example, a close friend of mine from college once travelled to New York City to audition for Sankai Juku, a renowned Japanese dance company with roots in butoh dance. She was among over a hundred dancers who had travelled from around the country, and at the audition found that they were simply asked to walk slowly forward in lines of 10 across; most were then eliminated, except perhaps for one or two from each line. This infuriated many of the dancers, who had studied for so many years to perfect their various dance techniques. Yet, as they discovered, what was actually required was rather a certain level of presence. In addition to her dance training, my friend had studied Tai Chi and meditation for many years, and in the end was one of the few dancers chosen to join the company for this particular performance. Similarly, many contemporary somatic practitioners and artists have been deeply influenced by certain forms of martial arts, as is the case with Bonnie Bainbridge Cohen's study of Aikido and Tai Chi[14] or Simone Forti's lifelong practice of Tai Chi.[15] Clearly there are many perspectives of what it means to be skilled in movement or dance; as dance educators, we can help our students expand their view of what that might mean.

Indonesian choreographer Sardono Kusumo, for example, used quite unorthodox teaching methods for a university setting in a graduate course I took with him during his residency at UCLA. Upon entering the studio for the first day of class, we found Sardono chanting and dancing in quite an internal state and seemingly oblivious to our presence. When he finally opened his eyes, Sardono invited us to join him. He first taught us exercises to centre ourselves, align with our breathing, and prepare our bodies to receive our more subtle impulses for movement. Part of this training was a simple phrase of breathing and movement that we would repeat for nearly half an hour, first in repetition and then with certain improvisational freedom in relation to the order and timing of the movements, which I referred to as our 'emptying phrase.' On other occasions, he had us bring a bowl of rice or noodles with spicy sauce, which we ate in slow motion for over an hour to invoke our sensory perceptions; or rehearse until long after midnight, to experience different times of day and night in our bodies and increase our concentration level. At the end of our course, we incorporated the emptying phrase into our performance event, starting it a full half hour before the audience arrived. Not only did this initiate a shift in our internal state, but as Sardono explained, it also created a powerful energetic field into which to invite our audience.[16] Whether sitting in stillness or moving with mindfulness, meditative awareness brings a quality of depth that is reflected within the individual—and is present in the transmission that we offer through our bodies.

Various other practices can be engaged in to develop such subtle states of embodied presence and open awareness. For instance, specific somatic movement disciplines that encourage a more internal, sensory or parasympathetic nervous system focus—such as Bartenieff Fundamentals, Body-Mind Centering® and Ideokinesis, for example—can be included in dance curricula to balance the often more external, sympathetic nervous system focus of many dance styles and techniques. Methods of touch and hands-on re-patterning often included in such disciplines also increase one's proprioceptive awareness and develop further embodiment. Somatic movement practices are increasingly being integrated into the teaching of dance and movement by dance educators trained in specific somatic disciplines. In fact, while the use of mirrors has been prevalent in university dance programmes for years and may be supportive for certain styles where adherence to outer form is particularly important, many dance departments across the country have begun to fashion curtains to draw across the mirrors for specific dance classes, such as modern dance and Contact Improvisation, to further encourage such inner sensing. Somatic movement practices help dancers to slow down and listen to their bodies, as well as to begin to align the aspects of *bayu* (energy), *sabda* (inner voice) and *idep* (thought).

Figure 10: Methods of movement, touch and re-patterning used in Embodiment in Education, a training for dance/movement educators: Top photo: (left to right): cognitive and experiential study of anatomy; touch with self and other (partner work; self-touch); movement exploration. Photographer unknown. Bottom photo: Movement session exploring organ support and expression with Guest faculty Bonnie Bainbridge Cohen. Berkeley, CA, 2013. Photographer: Susan Bauer.

Figure 11: Moving in nature enlivens dancers' perceptions and invokes a sense of spiritual connection. Photo of Maru Matthaei, Susan Bauer, and Prapto Suryadarmo, waterfalls, Bali, Indonesia, 2000. Photographer unknown.

Thus, while not all somatic disciplines have a defined spiritual focus, the type of inner sensory and kinesthetic perception they develop can be seen as training towards a more receptive state of embodied awareness, one that is conducive to an expanded spiritual capacity.

Likewise, in addition to the somatic practices previously mentioned, Authentic Movement is perhaps the most powerful training I have had for developing what I would call a state of open receptivity. While beyond the scope of this chapter to discuss in depth, the form itself is profound and simple, and involves a 'mover' and a 'witness.' In Authentic Movement, movers follow their inner impulses for movement, with eyes closed, in the presence of a skilled witness, and then discuss the movement experience with the witness afterward. This discipline has been known as a vehicle for opening to the movement impulses in one's body as a resource for accessing aspects of the personal unconscious and the collective unconscious (Adler 1987: 142), as well as various spiritual dimensions, since its beginnings in the work of founder Mary Whitehouse, and its subsequent development into a particular discipline by such teachers as Janet Adler. As Adler describes, 'with an increasing capacity to concentrate, to listen to impulse, the mover learns to recognize the channel within which the creative or authentic energy flows' (Adler 1987: 156). Further, the concept in Authentic

Movement of 'being moved' can be seen as related to the concept of *taksu* in the sense of becoming fully present, surrendering, and invoking an energetic experience of the realm of *niskala*, or the unseen dimension, through movement. In retrospect, I see that my practice of Authentic Movement gave me an expanded experiential understanding of my body that served to prepare me for the masked dancing and other styles that I was to engage in later in Bali. In more advanced trainings or programmes Authentic Movement can be an avenue for developing a state of open receptivity and for exploring such realms.[17]

Connection to Nature (7)

Another essential element of developing fuller embodiment is expanding our perception to include our interconnection with the natural world. For many, being in nature invokes our sense of spiritual connection and invites enlivened sensory perception. Like many Balinese, who can sense the direction of their sacred Mount Agung in their own bodies, we can begin to open to the energies of the natural world around us—thus opening to the *taksu* of the land itself. For although this chapter has focused mainly on the concept of *taksu* related to the spiritual charisma of the individual, from a Balinese-Hindu perspective, places can also possess *taksu*. We may be most familiar with this idea in the delineation of certain places around the world as 'sacred sites'. Yet in most dance education settings, dancers spend most of their time indoors. How might we invite outdoor experiences in our dance education training or performance? In my Balinese dance course, we often rehearse the dances outdoors when possible, and have included one outdoor performance each year. Likewise, in a workshop in Authentic Movement as Spiritual Practice that I lead in California, we spend part of the time outdoors on the coast as part of our practice, as we respond to the energy of place and specific elements of nature.

Other movement artists, such as Javanese dancer Suprapto Suryadarmo (Prapto), conduct their sessions almost entirely outdoors. Prapto developed an improvisational movement practice that he calls *Joged Amerta*, which was influenced by his dance and meditation studies and integrates movement in nature within a context of sacred space and cultural exchange. In studying and performing with Prapto in Bali and the United States, we danced at temples, by the ocean and in open parks and fields—connecting with the dynamic energy of the elements and with specific aspects of nature through movement.[18] Many other contemporary resources can be also drawn upon that similarly provide specificity and depth to such practices. For example, Anna Halprin's outdoor dance deck studio in California has been a site for movement and sensory investigation for over half a century, while Jamie McHugh, a somatic practitioner and faculty member with Halprin at Tamalpa Institute, creates workshops on the California coast to explore the relationship between the inner and outer ecosystems through a process he calls Somatic Expression.[19] Emilie Conrad, founder of Continuum, engages movers in their 'fluid body', which she sees as related to our emerging as primordial beings from the waters of the planet.[20] In performance, dancers such as Eiko and Koma often engage with the natural world as a subject matter (such as *Tree*) or as an environment in which to perform (such as *River* and *Water*). By doing so, they investigate their moving bodies as part of the natural landscape. As Eiko reminds us, wherever we are, 'in every breath we take and in every birth and death, we are a part of the natural world.'[21]

Approaches that allow us to move and dance in nature expand our experience of our bodies to remind us of this intimate interdependence with the earth—and also serve to inspire greater stewardship of the planet as we reconnect to the vitality and power of the land itself. As is true in many places around the world, however, in Bali there is growing concern about increasing land development, pollution and other environmental threats to the island, prompting Balinese arts administrators to suggest that 'in-depth public discourse on *taksu* is now relevant with the current situation in Bali [,] where many places, land, historical and sacred sites are now losing their *taksu*' (Dibia 2013). The same may be true for many places on our planet. More than just a concept to aspire towards, the development of a conscious and embodied awareness of our place in the whole is becoming essential to our very survival.

Creating a Clear Container and Clearing the Space (8 & 9)

As we have seen in the Balinese-Hindu tradition, a variety of steps may be taken to create a clear container or a sacred space that involve both the individual and the community. While on some level all spaces are sacred, attention to the performance space or practice location itself, as well as to the participation of the people involved can heighten this sense, such as noted in the Balinese practice of engaging a priest to bless the stage space, or the many rituals the Balinese village dancer must undergo before a performance. Methods that help to create a strong container include setting a clear intention and pure motivation—as discussed in the previous section on dedications—along with establishing clear boundaries. A first step in creating clear boundaries is framing an activity with a defined beginning and ending, sometimes referred to as opening and closing the space. This helps to provide participants with a sense of clarity at the beginning and of closure at the end of an activity. We can draw from our own experience in creating simple rituals that will help in this process.

One method often used in the discipline of Authentic Movement is to begin and end by sitting together in a circle, while the movement session itself may begin and end with a bell to clearly delineate the opening and closing of the movement time. In my Authentic Movement groups and private sessions, I have also added a period of silent meditation to the opening and closing circles. Another method draws on what Janet Adler calls 'sprouting,' used with a circle of witnesses as a means to create a clear container for the movers in the centre. As the witnesses 'sprout' their arms by opening them to the sides, they make eye contact with one another, further strengthening the container. I often use this 'sprouting' ritual in both Authentic Movement groups and in other group contexts to create a clear beginning and ending, as well as at certain times during a session when working with an individual client. As I have found, when this gesture is used between two or more people it serves to frame the moment, allowing us to first 'harvest' what has been experienced and then to bring completion to that moment, such that we become ready to open to the next

Figure 12: The 'sprouting' gesture helps to create a clear container of focus and attention. Susan Bauer leads students at Moving on Center School in using 'sprouting' to create group focus before a movement session; Oakland, CA, 2008. Photographer unknown.

moment or activity. It is like taking a pause to breathe after someone has spoken, to each really hear and experience what has been said before continuing the conversation.

Another method of opening and closing the space is a simple bow phrase used at Naropa University and taught by Barbara Dilley, a founding dance faculty member there who teaches a form of mindful movement she calls Contemplative Dance. Done in a circle by the group at the beginning and end of a class, the bow has three stages based on the concepts of 'hold,' 'feel' and finally, 'give,' which is said while bowing down.[22] In addition to providing a clear opening and closing activity, this movement process also invokes the aspects of presence and contribution previously mentioned. While the methods for opening and closing the space discussed thus far are quite meditative, a favourite and more dynamic closing ritual is to have participants stand in a circle and clap together loudly three times and then throw their arms up towards the sky while shouting '*Ho!*,' a Native American word meaning 'blessings.' As in the Balinese-Hindu concept of *desa* (place), *kala* (time) and *patra* (occasion), we can

Figure 13: When used between two people, the 'sprouting' gesture serves to frame the moment and allows us to become fully present to what has been shared. Susan Bauer and client, California, 2013. Photographer: Babak Gholamhossein.

choose opening and closing rituals that best suit the particular moment, along with the situation and group with whom we are working. In fact, after experiencing several of these methods, groups often become quite resourceful, spontaneously choosing the one that feels most appropriate to them in the moment.

Finally, depending upon the context, it may be important for the teacher or facilitator to clear the energy of the space either before and / or after a class or session. When done at the end, this process serves to leave the space refreshed for the next activity; it can also be combined with a final dedication as well. In Balinese rituals the space will generally be cleared both before and after a ceremony, such as by sprinkling holy water or spreading burning incense smoke around the space. Many other cultural traditions similarly acknowledge the need to attend to this energetic aspect of physical spaces.[23] For instance, I use various methods for preparing and clearing the space that I learned from certain Balinese artists and priests and from my Tibetan Buddhist teachers. As educators and practitioners, we can more skilfully facilitate our classes and sessions within a strong container when we bring clarity to the way we begin and end the movement time, as well as when this level of awareness of the energetic space is taken into consideration. While this may sound superfluous or esoteric to some, I have found these methods serve to invite a deeper experience for the participants and provide an enhanced atmosphere of clarity and safety.

This is especially important in work with masks, which under certain circumstances can be particularly *tenget* or spiritually charged. For example, in working with the international masked dance troupe Tuju Taksu, founded by the American director Maru Matthaei,[24] I found that we engaged in many practices related to this energetic level of the space. Based on her experience in Western dance/theatre and her deep knowledge of Balinese culture, Maru's rehearsal process likewise integrated many of the other training methods previously discussed (in numbers 1–9), such as the use of dedications, rituals to open and close the space, and movement meditations. Of course, particular care must be taken not to appropriate specific cultural rituals when one does not have an understanding of the culture from which they come. Yet when this type of container is honoured and created appropriately and with respect, such as in this case, the spirit of the masks are thought more likely to 'descend' and influence one's dancing—as in the literal translation of *tuju taksu*, which means aiming towards *taksu*.[25]

In my own rehearsals for a particular dance/theatre piece using masks of my own design that I had made in Bali, inspired by my work with Tuju Taksu, I drew upon many of Maru's training methods. Along with the emptying phrase I had learned from Sardono, which helped to prepare for dancing with the masks, I found these practices essential in inviting the more powerful presence associated with *taksu* from both the dancers and the masks themselves. Interestingly, this proved equally true for both the main dancers who wore the sacred, wooden carved masks I had made in Bali,[26] as well as for the chorus of dancers who wore plain white plastic masks I had purchased; in fact many audience members adamantly believed the white masks were moulds based on each dancer's face, when in actuality all of these masks were identical. Similarly, Balinese dance teachers are known to be able to perceive the expression of the dancer's face beneath the mask. In training for embodying a specific character, then, the teacher will often coach the dancer on both physical movements as well as on facial expressions. In rehearsals in Bali with Prapto for a solo masked dance performance, he similarly commented on the expression of my face beneath the mask, suggesting subtle shifts in my internal emotional state based on what he perceived in the mask itself.[27] Whether in mask dancing or in other forms of dance, creating a clear container supports such interaction between the material realm of *sekala* and the many subtle aspects of the spiritual realm of *niskala*.

Figure 14: Balinese teachers will often comment on the dancer's expression behind the mask, to ensure that the feeling of the character is properly embodied by the dancer. Susan Bauer performing with her 'Grace' mask in The Nature of InterdepenDance, MFA concert, UCLA, 1999. Photographer: © Carol Peterson.

Integration/Re-entry (10)

After completing a dance or movement practice, especially one in which one's physical body has been energetically expanded, such as through somatic movement practices or performance, it is important to find a means to physically integrate one's experience. For example, a more active motor activity like brisk walking or dancing can be included after exploring certain somatic movement practices that may be slower paced or more inner-directed. This supports participants to integrate the previous parasympathetic nervous system activities, re-orient to their outer environment and be prepared to move on to the next activity after a class or session. In larger group activities, such as in my experience of Balinese performance rituals, participants will often leave the ritual performance space and then gather together to rest, eat, drink, talk with others and slowly enter what would be considered everyday activities. Likewise, after Anna Halprin's *Planetary Dance* described earlier, participants left the open field and then socialized over a potluck lunch for several hours. Rather than being tangential, this 'food-sharing ritual,' based on Native American pow-wows, was intentionally included[28] and clearly provided a necessary avenue for integrating our experience and re-grouping as a community.

With both my students and individual clients, I emphasize the importance of taking the time for integration and give suggestions for such activities, such as taking a walk in nature, sitting in meditation, or drawing or writing about one's experience. Particular means of self-care, such as sleeping or napping, can help one's body to rest and integrate one's experiences; bathing can also be used to cleanse one's energy. Thus it is important to consider how to provide an appropriate vehicle for integration at the end of an activity, as well as to offer suggestions for continued personal self-care.

Implications

As we acknowledge these more subtle spiritual dimensions of our human existence, we invite a broader context for dance and performance—one that necessitates a broader educational training process. Just as in Buddhism there are many paths to follow in order to meet the needs of a variety of different individual natures—such as the scholarly path of scripture study, the devotional path of deity visualization, or the Bodhisattva path of compassion for self and others, similarly there is a need for many paths to dance and dance education to accommodate the variety of different natures of human beings. Although dance in higher education in America was clearly influenced by many Western artists and educators who did refer to spiritual inspiration, such as many of the pioneers of modern dance, nevertheless the dance curriculum in our educational institutions has become strongly secularized. Currently, degrees in dance in the United States at the BA, MA and MFA levels largely focus on the Western notion of dance as a performing art form, with training in specific dance techniques and/or choreography as the main focus. Following suit, the National Dance Standards also are largely centred on the concept of dance as an art form, and even most U.S. granting agencies, private and public, are set up to fund dance performances and art-related projects. There also exist Ph.D. programmes in dance that primarily emphasize scholarly study and intellectual critique, and MA programmes in Dance Therapy that emphasize therapeutic application, often in clinical settings.

Yet in the culture at large, many contemporary examples exist of a growing yearning to experience our dancing bodies as an avenue to cultivate deeper awareness and expanded consciousness, both personally and collectively. These approaches to dance may or may not fall within the conventionally defined contexts of art-making, scholarly study, or therapy. In the past half century, individual dancers such as many of those mentioned here—Mary Whitehouse, Janet Adler, Bonnie Bainbridge Cohen, Anna Halprin, Barbara Dilley and Emilie Conrad—have reached beyond their traditional dance training to create new paradigms for dance and movement that have expanded our experience of our bodies, our perceptions and our consciousness. The uprising of national and international trainings in a multitude of alternative dance forms, such as Gabrielle Roth's 5 Rhythms® practice (even referred to as 'sweating your prayers'[29]), and also in various somatic movement certification programmes, seems likewise to be a testament to this need in our contemporary culture for broader training focused on movement as community ritual and/or embodied personal growth. With the ever-evolving wealth of experiential inquiry now being offered and developed in the broader field of dance and Somatics, we can draw on existing resources to expand the paradigm of dance education within the university system. As such, to meet the expanding needs of the 21st century, dance curricula could include practices like meditation, mindful or contemplative movement, somatic movement disciplines, martial arts, masked dance, or even movement practices in nature.

While certain dance programmes may be beginning to move in this direction, clearly this is still an area for further development nationally. University dance programmes could engage professionals with experience in these areas and expand to offer degrees and graduate programmes in such topics as Dance in Community, Dance as Ritual Immersion, Dance and Somatics, or Embodied Movement Practices, for instance. While some educators may wonder how dancers with such degrees will create a livelihood, I believe that as we open up the idea of dance, we forge new careers. Who would have thought, for instance, that Anna Halprin could make a career as an artist and teacher when she first ventured outside the indoor dance studio or the proscenium theatre? Or Bonnie Bainbridge Cohen when she left her dance training or her work as an occupational therapist in hospital settings? Yet it is this expanding of the paradigm of movement and dance—in fact of our human potential—that calls forth a larger context for individual and group dance experiences than is currently encompassed in the Western perspective of dance in higher education. The image I have is that of the shape of an hourglass, with the base representing the breadth and depth of the perspective of dance in many indigenous cultures, and the middle the narrowing of that perspective through the objectification of our bodies and the secularization and commodification of dance; yet the top of the hourglass is inevitably opening up—representing the welcome calling of the times to expand our perspective once again and reclaim our more embodied spiritual identity.

As we broaden our perception of movement and dance, whether within the community or within an institution of higher education, specific principles can be drawn upon to expand our consciousness and develop our human potential. To summarize, a sampling of these elements could include the following concepts as discussed previously:

- *Invocation/preparation*—opening and closing rituals to help focus one's intention and invoke spiritual connection.
- *Clear intention/dedication/offering*—dedications to inspire a sense of compassion, whether it be towards oneself or others, and to create relevance for our offering within a particular context or community.
- *Sense of contribution/community*—to remind us of dance within the context of contribution versus competition, and to develop a clear motivation and awareness of one's larger community.
- *Focus and concentration/meditation/mindful movement*—to develop the skills of focus and concentration, to open the Third Eye of spiritual perception, to allow for fuller expression of our own creative selves, and to develop our physical presence.
- *Open receptivity*—emptying, to bring us into the present moment, as well as to create a more receptive state of being.

- *Expanding our perceptual base, embodiment*—touch and/or somatic movement practices to support a more embodied, dynamic awareness of our living beings.
- *Connecting to nature*—to invoke a sense of heightened sensory perception and an enlivened awareness of our interdependence with the natural world.
- *Creating a clear container*—to create an atmosphere of clarity and safety that invites a deeper experience for participants.
- *Closure/dedication/clearing the space*—to provide closure for participants and then to disperse the energy of the activity and leave the space refreshed for the next activity.
- *Integration/re-entry*—to ground in our bodies and prepare to enter more everyday activities.

Including such principles can serve to expand our dance pedagogy and curriculum development. As dance educators, there are many resources that can be drawn upon to develop our skill in each of these areas. Most importantly, expanding our own perceptual base will thus translate into our individual embodied presence and into the curriculum we teach.

Resources

Many professional development opportunities exist worldwide for gaining such experience and for expanding dance curricula to include various approaches mentioned in this chapter, such as trainings in meditation, mindfulness, Somatics, Somatic Movement Education, contemplative dance, Authentic Movement, masked dance and martial arts. While this realm is incredibly vast, in addition to those resources previously discussed here, I will mention just a few further sources from my own work and that of others with which I am most familiar. As a major resource, the organization of ISMETA, International Somatic Movement Education and Therapy Association, lists over 25 various trainings in the United States and abroad through which to take workshops and/or to become certified in specific somatic movement disciplines. Furthermore, books such as Andrea Olsen and Caryn McHose's text, *BodyStories: A Guide to Experiential Anatomy*, provide a concrete approach structured as a semester course at the university level. My own curriculum in experiential anatomy, documented in *A Body-Mind Approach to Movement Education*, is designed for teens and young adults. This curriculum forms the basis of my training programme, 'Embodiment in Education: Professional Development for Dance/Movement Educators,' which offers specific pedagogical approaches to experiential anatomy and somatic movement education. The developing field of ecosomatics includes approaches based on a view of the body as one with nature and movement as a natural expression of our bodies.[30] In this realm, we can draw on innovative curricular guides such as Andrea Olsen's *Body and Earth*, which bridges the study of experiential anatomy with environmental education, and Caryn McHose and Kevin Frank's co-authored book, *How Life Moves, Explorations in Meaning and Body Awareness*, which focuses on perception and our evolutionary roots though movement.

In exploring meditation and mindful movement, methods such as the Mindfulness Based Stress Reduction techniques of Dr. Jon Kabit Zinn—renditions of which are currently being taught in schools and hospitals across the country—can provide examples for including meditation in a purely secular context. Similarly, the Integrated Amritra Meditation Technique® is a simple combination of yoga and meditation that has been taught internationally through free trainings for individuals, organizations and companies. Retreats and trainings in more spiritually based practices are also available—such as Vipassana meditation from the Theravada Buddhist tradition, or the Zen Buddhist approach to mindful living as offered by such teachers as the Zen monk Thict Nat Hahn. In the realm of Authentic Movement, Janet Adler's book *Offering from the Conscious Body* serves as a primary resource, along with two volumes of essays compiled by Patricia Pallero, while the Authentic Movement Community website offers a full listing of international resources for teachers, programmes and publications in this practice. Additionally, the journal 'Contact Quarterly' includes articles and resources for and about contemporary dance and movement programmes internationally. Some further resources in many of these areas are listed at the end of this chapter in the references section.

Conclusions

As we have seen, whether in a university or community setting, to aspire towards and invite *taksu* or connection with the divine in our dancing necessitates reaching beyond mere technical prowess to include focus on one's personal growth, such that the areas of *bayu* (energy), *sabda* (inner voice) and *idep* (thought), are aligned and equally well developed. This includes learning to focus and concentrate, maintain a positive motivation, and cultivate an attitude of contribution to the larger community. It also entails increasing our proprioceptive awareness and embodied presence, as well as reclaiming our internal connection to the natural world around us. All of these methods help us to be more present and to become one with our actions. Therefore, as educators, even in instances in which it may not feel appropriate to directly discuss spirituality, techniques such as those described in this chapter can be used to facilitate the type of inner power and quality of consciousness often associated with such an expanded spiritual capacity. It should be noted, however, that while spirit always exists within and without, as in the concepts of *bhuana alit* (small body or inner cosmos) and *buana agung* (great cosmos), it comes to the forefront when focused upon. Thus, actually acknowledging and honouring the spiritual dimension of life can be a further key to facilitating such a process, as noted by one of my spiritual teachers, Sri Mata Amritanandamayi Devi, often referred to simply as Amma: 'We should eliminate the egoistic notion that our life will become fruitful through human effort alone. *We should bow down. Only then will the power supporting the cosmos flow into us*' (Amritanandamayi 2010: 29, emphasis added).

Connecting with the divine through awareness of the spiritual dimension thus allows the power of the 'cosmos' to flow into us. Similarly, '*taksu*' is one word from a Balinese-Hindu paradigm that refers to an energy that can 'flow into us' and can be conceptualized as spiritual, in the sense of connecting with the unseen, or *niskala*. This inspiring and energizing quality is experienced in many cultures through various types of spiritual and artistic practices when engaged in by sincere, focused practitioners. *Taksu* need not be sought after, but can emerge naturally—like the inner sun shining within—from one's focused intention, concentration and skills. Activities that are undertaken with this quality, such as dancing, contribute to the well-being of both the individual and the community. While no one educational system or method will be appropriate cross-culturally, I offer this chapter as inspiration for the envisioning of future curricula that expands our notion of both dance education and of our human potential. The creation of this book on dance, spirituality and Somatics, in fact, is a testament to the growing interest among dance, movement and somatic professionals to engage in such a dialogue worldwide. I would like to dedicate this chapter to all those working towards this goal, as well as to the benefit of all beings. May this book lead us towards a new and inspired vision of dance, artistic expression, and dance and Somatic Movement Education.

Afterword

In our quest for proof of Spirit, we all want to see a miracle, such as the bird that swims or the fish that flies. Yet in actuality, it is the bird flying and the fish swimming that is the true miracle.[31] Likewise, while the Balinese celestial nymph dancing in a human body draws our attention, it is no less miraculous to dance the divine within us. We are so fascinated by the extraordinary, yet the miracle is truly here—in ourselves, each other, the earth, the universe—and our enlivened dancing bodies.

Acknowledgements

For their generous support in reading sections of this chapter, I would like to thank Janet Adler, Marc Choyt, Bonnie Bainbridge Cohen, Barbara Dilley, Eiko and Koma, Sean Feit, Simone Forti, Judy Gantz, Anna Halprin, Maru Matthaei, Caryn McHose, Jamie McHugh, Regina Marler, I Made Moja, Andrea Olsen, Ellen Tadd, and Jacques Talbot. And my most special thanks to my Balinese teachers Sang Ayu Muklen, I Ketut Kantor, and Ida Bagus Oka.

References

Adler, Janet (1987), 'Who is the Witness', in P. Pallero (ed), *Authentic Movement, A Collection of Essays*, London and New York: Jessica Kingsley Publications, pp. 141–159.

—— (2002), *Offering from the Conscious Body, The Discipline of Authentic Movement*, Vermont: Inner Traditions.

Amritanandamayi Devi, Sri Mata (2010), *Cultivating Strength and Vitality, An Address by Sri Mata Amritanandamayi Devi*, India: Mata Amritanandamayi Mission Trust.

—— (2005), *Being with Amma, A Collection of Sayings*, San Ramon, CA: Mata Amritanandamayi Center.

Authentic Movement Community website, http://www.authenticmovementcommunity.org.

Bainbridge Cohen, Bonnie (1993), *Sensing, Feeling, and Action, The Experiential Anatomy of Body-Mind Centering*, Northampton, MA: Contact Editions.

Ballinger, Rucina (1985), 'Dance in Bali: the Passing on of a Tradition,' in B. T. Jones (ed.), *Dance as Cultural Heritage: Volume Two*, NY: CORD 1985 Dance Research Annual XV.

Bauer, Susan (2010), 'Bali Takes Center Stage', San Francisco, CA: *In Dance Journal*, pp. 4, 11.

—— (2008), 'Body and Earth as One: Strengthening our Connection to the Natural Source with EcoSomatics', *Conscious Dancer*, 1: 3, pp. 8–9.

—— (2007), '"Welcome to City of Nice People": Cross Cultural Dialogues on Authentic Movement in Thailand', *Contact Quarterly*, Massachusetts: Contact Editions, pp. 48–55.

—— (2007), 'Oracles, Authentic Movement and the *I Ching*', in P. Pallero (ed.), *Authentic Movement, Moving the Body, Moving the Self, Being Moved, A Collection of Essays, Volume Two*, London and Philadelphia: Jessica Kingsley Publications, pp. 364–367.

—— (2005), 'Finding the Bone in the Wind: A Journey with Prapto Suryadarmo in Bali, Indonesia', *A Moving Journal*, 12: 3, Fall Winter, pp. 14–20.

—— (2002), 'Antique Legong: Perceptions on the Evolution of Dance in Contemporary Bali', unpublished manuscript, presented at Popular Culture Association/American Culture Association Conference, March, Toronto: Canada; and (2005) at the Association of Asian Performance Conference, July, San Francisco: CA.

—— (2000), 'Must to the Mountain: A Journey with Sardono Kusumo at UCLA', *Contact Quarterly*, MA: Contact Editions, pp. 21–37.

—— (1999, privately published 2008), 'A Body-Mind Approach to Movement Education for Adolescents', MA Thesis, Connecticut: Wesleyan University.

Buckwalter, Melinda (2010), *Composing While Dancing, An Improviser's Companion*, Wisconsin: University of Wisconsin Press.

Candell, Arianna (2008), 'Beyond the Great Indoors', *Conscious Dancer*, 1: 3, p. 10.

Contact Collaborations, Inc and Contact Quarterly, website, http://www.contactquarterly.com/index.php.

Cook, Vern (trans. and ed.) (1998), *Bali Behind the Seen: Recent Fiction from Bali*, Australia: Darma Printing.

Dibia, I Wayan and Ballinger, Rucina (2004), *Dance, Drama, and Music: A Guide to the Performing Arts of Bali*, Singapore: Periplus Editions.

Dibia, I Wayan (2013), as quoted in 'Cultural Blueprint on the Table Soon', by Luh De Suriyani, Jakarta Post, Bali Daily, edition 5 July 2013, http://www.thejakartapost.com/bali-daily/2013-07-05/cultural-blueprint-tablesoon.htm.

Earthdance Thinktank (2008), 'Radical improv', *Conscious Dancer*, 1: 3, pp. 11–12.

Eiseman, Fred B. Jr (1990), *Bali, Sekala and Niskala, Volume 1: Essays on Religion, Ritual, and Art*, Singapore: Periplus Editions.

Enghauser, Rebecca (2007), 'The Quest for an Ecosomatic Approach to Dance Pedagogy', *Journal of Dance Education*, 7: 3, pp. 80–90.

Hughes-Freeland, Felicia (2008), *Embodied Communities: Dance Traditions and Change in Java*, New York and Oxford: Berghahn Books.

International Somatic Movement Education and Therapy Association website, http://www.ismeta.org.

Integrated Amrita Meditation Technique®, as taught by Sri Mata Amritanandamayi Devi (Amma), website, http://www.iam-meditation.org.

Juhan, Deane (2002), *Touched by the Goddess, The Physical, Psychological, and Spiritual Powers of Bodywork*, Barrytown, NY: Station Hill Press.

Kingston, Karen (1997), *Creating Sacred Space with Feng Shui*, New York: Broadway Books.

McHose, Caryn and Frank, Kevin (2006), *How Life Moves, Explorations in Meaning and Body Awareness*, Berkeley, California: North Atlantic Books.

McHugh, Jamie (2008), 'Embodying Nature, Becoming Ourselves', *Conscious Dancer*, 1: 3, p. 11.

Mindfulness Based Stress Reduction Technique website, http://www.mindfullivingprograms.com/index.php.

Mindful Schools: Integrating Mindfulness into Education website, http://www.mindfulschools.org.

Nhat Hahn, Thich (1991), *Peace is Every Step: The Path of Mindfulness in Everyday Life*, New York, New York: Bantam Books.

Olsen, Andrea (2002), *Body and Earth*, New Hampshire: University Press of New England.

—— and McHose, Caryn (1991), *BodyStories: A Guide to Experiential Anatomy*, New York: Station Hill Openings, Barrytown, Limited.

Padepokan Lemah Putih, directed by Suprapto Suryadarmo, website, http://www.lemahputih.com.

Pallero, Patricia (ed.) (2007), *Authentic Movement, Moving the Body, Moving the Self, Being Moved, A Collection of Essays, Volume Two*, London and Philadelphia: Jessica Kingsley Publications.

—— (1999), *Authentic Movement, Essays by Mary Starks Whitehouse, Janet Adler, and Joan Chadorow*, London and New York: Jessica Kingsley Publications.

Picard, Michel (1996), *Bali: Cultural Tourism and Touristic Culture*, Singapore: Archipelago Press.

Ramseyer, Urs and Tisna, I Gusti Raka Panji (eds), *Bali, Living in Two Worlds, A Critical Self-portrait*, Museum der Kulturen, Basel, Switzerland: Schwabe & Co. AG Verlag Basel.

Reichle, Natasha (ed.) (2010), *Bali: Art, Ritual, Performance, Asian Art Museum Catalogue*, San Francisco: Asian Art Museum.

Ricard, Matthieu (2003), *Monk Dancers of Tibet*, Boston and London: Shambhala.

Slattum, Judy (2003), *Balinese Masks, Spirits of an Ancient Drama*, Singapore: Periplus Editions.

Spirit Rock Insight Meditation Center website, http://www.spiritrock.org.

Sugriwa, Drs. IGB. Sudhyatmaka (ed.) (1998), *Nadi: Trance in the Balinese Arts*, Denpasar, Bali: Taksu Foundation.

Tadd, Ellen (2010), *Wisdom of the Chakras, Tools for Navigating the Complexity of Life*. Brooklyn, New York: Lantern Books.

Vickers, Adrian (1989), *Bali: A Paradise Created*, Singapore: Periplus Editions.

Notes

1 See *Divine Horsemen: The Living Gods of Haiti*, 1985. [video] Directed by Maya Deren. USA: Mystic Fire Video.

2 This discussion occurred during a presentation by Balinese artists at the Sharing Art and Religiosity conference held in Samuan Tiga, Bali in January, 2001. For more information see: Butler, D. C., 2011. *Religiosity in Art inspired by Samuan Tiga and Tejakula, Bali: Unity in Diversity*. Ph.D. University Udayana, Bali. (Abstract and summary published online) http://ejournal.unud.ac.id/abstrak/e-journal_diane_carol_butler.pdf.

3 Personal communication, I Dewa Putu Berata, musician and director of Cudamani, the world-renowned dance and music group from Pengosakan, Bali; 2012, California.

4 In Buddhism this state of egolessness is called *anatman* and is considered fundamental to be achieved in order to reach enlightenment.

5 Other cultural paradigms support this perspective as well, such as the requirements for dancers of the sacred *cham* dances, or 'dancing meditations' of Tibetan Buddhism, in which the dancer must apply three essential points: physical clarity of expression of the dance form, perfect concentration and right motivation (the wish to benefit all beings) (Ricard 2003: 50).

6 Some Balinese believe that the presence of *taksu* has even occasionally been seen or captured in photographs as waves or balls of light; when such an unknown object or phenomenon appears in real life or on film it is referred to as *penampakan*, an Indonesian word indicating that which is unknown, or related to the spiritual realm of *niskala* (personal communication, Ni Ketut Arini, 2013).

7 The High School of Performing Arts, *Sekolah Menengah Karawitan Indonesia* (SMKI) was formed in 1960. The Indonesian Dance Academy, or *Akademi Seni Tari Indonesia* (ASTI) Denpasar was founded in 1967, then transformed into an undergraduate programme and renamed the College of Indonesian Arts, *Sekolah Tinggi Seni Indonesia* (STSI). Finally, in 2003 the institution became formally established by the Indonesian Government as an Indonesian Arts Institute and renamed *Institute Seni Indonesia* (ISI), Denpasar, the name by which it is known today.

8 The Balinese Arts Council was first called upon by the cultural authorities of the province to hold a seminar on 'sacred' and 'profane' to determine the degree of sacredness of a dance as a means to prevent the appropriation of its most sacred dances for the benefit of the growing tourist population. Because this conceptual distinction was completely unknown in Balinese cosmology, however, the committee's first response was to misinterpret the task and to produce a single list of 'sacred and profane dances', tellingly missing the point, before producing these three categories in their second round of discussion (see Picard 1996: 152, 153).

9 For more information on this discussion of the disenchantment of Balinese dance and the commercialization of dance in Balinese culture see Michel Picard's 1996 text, *Bali: Cultural Tourism and Touristic Culture*.

10 Thomas Hanna, founder of Hanna Somatics, first used the word 'soma' to distinguish between the 'soma' (lived experience of one's body) and the physical 'body'. Hanna thus used the term 'somatics' to name a field of study that had developed in the early part of

the 20th century in Europe and the United States. Although the term somatics refers to disciplines developed primarily in Europe and the United States, many somatic principles are acknowledged to have roots in indigenous wisdom (Bauer 2011).

11 This one-day conference was sponsored by a branch of the Fulbright Association, the American Indonesian Exchange Foundation (AMINEF), on 25 May, 2001 held at the Putri Bali hotel in Nusa Dua, Bali.

12 See Anna Halprin's website www.annahalprin.com for further description of the intent and enactment of the Planetary Dance.

13 This specific method to attain the one-pointed focus associated with opening the Third Eye referred to here can be found in Ellen Tadd's book, *The Wisdom of the Chakras: Tools for Navigating the Complexity of Life* (2010), pp. 21–25. (This section also includes specific reference to the benefit of this type of focus for artists and performers). I have studied with Ellen since 1989, and have found these techniques to be highly effective with students and clients alike, and adaptable to a secular context.

14 Personal communication with Bonnie B. Cohen, 2012, California.

15 Personal communication with Simone Forti, 1999, California.

16 For further description of Sardono's teaching methods and an interview with him on this process see Bauer, Susan (2000), 'Must to the Mountain: A Journey with Sardono Kusumo at UCLA' , *Contact Quarterly*.

17 While Authentic Movement has been included in some undergraduate dance programmes there is some controversy about the appropriateness of including Authentic Movement in an academic setting, given the deep level of material that may emerge in one's movement along with the power dynamic of the teacher/student relationship. Therefore, I would recommend this discipline be included mainly in graduate programmes and other professional trainings where there is a further level of independence and maturity to negotiate this complex terrain.

18 For further description of Prapto's teaching methods see Bauer, Susan (2005), 'Finding the Bone in the Wind: A Journey with Prapto Suryadarmo in Bali, Indonesia.' Also see Buckwater, Melinda (2010), 'Composing While Dancing, An Improviser's Companion' pp. 53–55.

19 For more information on Anna Halprin's work see www.annahalprin.org; for more information on Jamie McHugh's Somatic Expression see www.somaticexpression.com.

20 For more information on Continuum see www.continuummovement.com.

21 Personal email communication with the author, 2012. For more information on Eiko and Koma and the dances mentioned see *Time in Not Even, Space Is Not Empty,* by Eiko and Koma (2011) or see www.eikoandkoma.org.

22 This bow is from the Shambhala Buddhist tradition as taught by Chogyam Trungpa Rinpoche. (Personal email communication, Barbara Dilley, 2012.)

23 A resource for simple space-clearing techniques that can also be used in a secular context can be found in Karen Kingston's book *Creating Sacred Space with Feng Shui* (1997), in which she describes methods learned from her studies with Balinese priests and shaman.

24 Maru works with masks of her own design, often based on specific archetypes, which she had made in collaboration with a Balinese mask carver, Ida Bagus Oka. All these masks have been blessed in a Balinese ceremony to render them sacred performing masks. For more information see www.tujutaksu.com.

25 Over many years of dancing with these same masks, in fact, Maru and many of her dancers have seen that the improvisation of the dancers generally takes on a similar quality and a quite specific movement vocabulary with each mask, such as I have experienced when performing with certain masks one year and later watching other dancers begin the rehearsal process with the same masks.

26 These masks were based on my own designs and made in collaboration with a Balinese mask carver, Ida Bagus Oka, and blessed in a Balinese ceremony to render them sacred performing masks. The dance/theatre piece referred to in which these masks were used was titled *The Nature of InterdepenDance*, and was performed at UCLA; MFA concert, 1999.

27 Bauer, Susan (2005), 'Finding the Bone in the Wind: A Journey with Prapto Suryadarmo in Bali, Indonesia'; see this article for further description of Prapto's teaching methods.

28 Personal communication, Jamie McHugh, 2012, California.

29 Gabrielle Roth's practices are outlined in her book, *Sweat Your Prayers: Movement as Spiritual Practice*.

30 See articles by Bauer 2008; McHugh 2008; Candell 2008; Earthdance Thinktank 2008; Enghauser 2007.

31 This conceptual metaphor is expressed by Sri Mata Amritanandamayi Devi in *Being with Amma: a Collection of Photos and Sayings*, published by the Mata Amritanandamayi Center, April 2005, San Ramon, CA. Used by permission.

Chapter 18

The Sacrum and the Sacred: Mutual Transformation of Performer and Site through Ecological Movement in a Sacred Site

Sandra Reeve

Think, for instance, of the difference between a football pitch with and without a game taking place on it. The presence of moving bodies is not only a physical transformation of the pitch: it also alters the imaginative, affective, sonic and social qualities of this space.

(McCormack 2008: 1828)

The notion of a 'sacred narrative' interests me—a co-creation between mover/dancer and site, a narrative that transforms both the place and the person. I have chosen the title of 'the sacrum and the sacred,' because the sacrum is the fulcrum of support for the human torso (Stross 2007: 2), and I like it as an image of the body in movement within a sacred space. Movement practice and performance in both historically significant and sacred sites has been an important aspect of my work for the past 25 years, in the United Kingdom, Ireland, Java and Bali. It is this particular thread of my work that I want to examine within this chapter.[1]

By creating contemporary performance/ritual art at a temple site, I suggest that movement artists re-enliven sites that have become deadened by their predominant perceived identity as tourist or heritage attractions. In turn, the performers can themselves be re-enlivened by 'incorporating' (Ingold 2000: 194) themselves within a sacred site, rather than using the site as a backdrop. These site-responsive performances may also re-awaken the perception of sacred purpose for other visitors by revealing a non-habitual way of moving within that particular site.

What interests me in terms of a sacred narrative is developing an attitude of embodied respect for the sacred and cultivating my own sense of being one part of this sacred world by moving through life as an involved witness rather than an external observer. I experience the sacred as being manifest in the mystery of the unknown and the unknowable in life; at the same time, I can learn to respect all other sentient and non-sentient living beings as part of the sacred, too. An attitude of 'being among' rather than 'at the centre of' the world, of respect for the unknown and of humility are, for me, key aspects of a sacred narrative.

As part of my introduction, I feel the need to admit that I have chosen to avoid the word 'spiritual.' It is often either rife with potential misunderstandings or lost in translation, especially if used within an intercultural context. 'Spiritual,' or 'of the spirit(s)' can be translated as shamanic practice, as mystical practice, as occult practice, as a form of healing practice or as New Age practice, to name but a few. The word 'spiritual' can also be used to avoid the words religion, religiosity or God. For me, it is a word that inevitably has 'no-body'

Figure 1: *Threshold*: an improvised performance at Srawung Seni Candi, December 2010. Candi Sukuh, Java. Performer: Sandra Reeve.

and which emphasises a relationship with that which is 'of the spirit.' As a movement artist, I am aware that the danger of a body/spirit split suddenly looms large, a split which positions the body as a vehicle for the spirit, a notion which is utterly out of date. By contrast, for me the word 'sacred' refers to a quality that is usually conceived of spatially, for example, the area immediately surrounding the temple. This environmental emphasis supports a more biocentric approach to life, in which the human being can be incorporated as just one part of the sacred.

In the first part of this chapter, I shall examine the experience of ecological movement in sacred sites as a transformative practice for the performer, for the site, and ultimately for the audience.

My embodied understanding of the co-creation and mutual interdependence between an individual's movement and their environment is reflected in the module titles in my Move into Life programme: non-stylized movement, environmental movement and—more recently—ecological movement. Here, I will use these same titles as a framework for this examination of movement practice. Their subtexts include a demonstration of what is meant by non-stylized movement, and how it can cultivate in the performer an attitude of liminal awareness between the moving self and the changing environment as a first step towards transformative practice.

Next, I would like to propose a definition of environmental movement, examining notions of an affective inter-dependence between mover and environment relevant to site-specific or site-sensitive performance. Within this, I shall offer an introduction to the praxis of ecological movement, which proposes four key movement dynamics as tools for the potential transformation of autobiographical material through environmentally aware movement. This approach defines transformation as inherent to the process of 'becoming,' rather than as a disruption or challenge to a fixed sense of being. It also proposes the idea that transformation can be seen as a release from conditionings—a release that allows fresh choices to replace compulsive behaviours.

Finally, I shall draw on James Gibson's (1979) theory of ecological perception and his concept of affordances to facilitate an analysis of how—through an awareness of embodied movement—both the 'being-in-movement' and, in this case, the sacred environment, are engaged in a process of mutual transformation. This is my understanding of a contemporary sacred narrative.

The second half of the chapter offers as a case study an improvised performance for the annual inter-cultural Srawung Seni Candi (Temple Art Festival) in the Javanese-Hindu temple of Candi Sukuh, Central Java.

Non-Stylized Movement

Kinesthetic awareness of context or environment has always been fundamental to my research and my movement practice, as it challenges my conditioned experience of myself as being both in control of, and fundamentally separate from, the cyclical life of my environment. The cultivation of environmental awareness through movement serves as a way of being simultaneously involved and self-reflexive within the presently changing moment.

The source of 'non-stylized' movement is daily life; movement practice supports the emergence of an individual's movement vocabulary, which is informed and given form by their particular body. For a performer, the relevance of the practice lies in the exploration of 'mundane' movement:

> Dance seems to separate itself from non–dance by its atypicality, its non-normal, non-mundane character. Dance acquires its meaning by referring us back always to the world of mundane actions, to what these performers would be doing, were they doing anything but dance.
>
> (Gell and Hirsch 1999: 143)

Movement is primary to human expression. It precedes and underpins cognition, language and creative art. Movement may be seen as the skill of skills and one that adapts to the environment. How we move is as distinctive as how we speak and lies at the root of how we dance. Our movement has its own accents and vocabulary, but we seldom notice them. Ultimately, non-stylized movement practitioners develop their own unmistakable 'signature' style of movement which reflects their actual experience of moving rather than their capacity to achieve a predetermined technique. If movement is the skill of skills, through which we act in the world, and are acted upon, then a study of movement should reveal the process of my unique 'becoming-being-becoming'[2] in the world.

Non-stylized movement is inclusive and non-judgemental. Non-stylized movement develops a shifting awareness of soma,[3] body, environment and others in the environment, giving equal value to each. In this context, a dancer, performer, visual artist, psychotherapist and architect can work side by side without either censoring any of their previous performance or dance/movement experience, or leaving behind their experience of the relevance of embodiment in their particular profession. It is a useful forum for inter-cultural exploration and dialogue as the task-based style of work is broad enough to encompass different approaches and interpretations. In movement workshops, the dialogue between people from different disciplines, both verbal and nonverbal, stimulates and enhances the process of learning by offering a wide variety of perspectives and passions.

Once participants have an awareness of both structure and space through movement, they practise embodying responses to their inner process and to their external environment as they move. This may be seen as an adaptation of the skill of Bare Attention, a traditional meditative tool within the Buddhist practice of Satipatthāna, or Way of Mindfulness, which cultivates endogenous and exogenous attention to being-in-the-environment in the present moment. 'Bare Attention is the clear and single-minded awareness of what actually happens to us and in us, at the successive moments of perception' (Nyanaponika 1983: 30).

I call this skill liminal because it implies a condition of literal and metaphorical 'shifting balance' within the changing moment, without either searching inside for some essentialist idea of deeper authenticity or becoming totally conditioned by the external activity of the environment.

Environmental Movement

Environmental movement takes non-stylized movement out of doors to play within environmental systems. Here, the co-creative relationship between the moving body and the changing environment is perhaps more immediately apparent than in the studio, as the terrain is less familiar. New environments can stimulate entirely new ways of moving. New ways of moving can call forth entirely new relationships with the environment. Either can afford new perceptions of a changing self.

In nature, practice often starts from movement tasks or moving with no fixed intention and allows associations, feelings, images and, ultimately, meaning to emerge from the constantly shifting context. Through working in an outdoor environment, the dialogue between movement and site often produces a theme relevant to autobiographical material.

This corresponds with Gibson's theory of affordances—that is, how we pick up information appropriate to our needs directly from our surroundings (1979: 128). Environmental movement creates the psychophysical conditions for individuals to experience themselves as situated in their bodies and embedded in the presence of the environment. This requires being present each moment to the changing of person and place.

The Santiago theory of cognition was developed by biologists Humberto Maturana and Francisco Varela (1987) and offers a more explicit understanding of environmental movement. Speaking of interactions between organism (or autopoietic unity)[4] and environment, they state that, 'the structure of the environment only triggers structural changes in the autopoietic unities (it does not specify or direct them) and vice versa for the environment […] there will be a structural coupling' (Maturana and Varela 1987: 75). This indicates a mutually dependent co-creation of any moment between the organism and its environment. Through recurrent interaction, a particular kind of terrain may trigger a certain kind of walk because of its physical and potential dangers, e.g. sharp rocks and the possibility of snakes (Gell and Hirsch 1999: 146). Changes are triggered at a structural level, but the organism is able to choose which triggers to respond to, at least initially. As Maturana and Varela propose, 'A way of seeing cognition not as a representation of the world "out there," but rather as an ongoing bringing forth of a world through the process of living itself' (Maturana and Varela 1987: 11).

However, when an organism responds to a particular trigger in the environment, I would argue that affect precedes cognition in conditioning that choice. New movements, which challenge habits and change perception are 'disruptive' and open up new feelings, which in turn trigger a change in understanding. I interpret the interactions of an organism with its environment as primarily kinesthetic and affective, operating initially through a felt sense, rather than through cognition.

Imagine an individual's body structure and how that has developed over time, influenced by genetic disposition and environmental factors. Imagine how that body engages with its environment, which it does through movement, in many different ways—this is what I am calling a body practice. Practice implies repetition until a particular pattern is integrated into the organism and into the environment. Such patterns may be unconsciously integrated or deliberately cultivated. They become 'incorporated' habits (Connerton 1989: 75). Connerton claims that:

Habits are more than technical abilities […] All habits are affective dispositions […] a predisposition, formed through the frequent repetition of a number of specific acts, is an intimate and fundamental part of ourselves. Postures and movements which are habit memories become sedimented into bodily conformation […] Habit is not just a 'sign.' Habit is a knowledge and a remembering in the hands and in the body; and in the cultivation of habit it is our body which 'understands.'

(Connerton 1989: 93)

Here, Connerton suggests that a habit is an affective disposition ('disposition' means a 'natural tendency' or 'inclination' and is the term that I would like to use in this context), which may explain, for example, the power of addiction over rational intention. It may be that what specifies our response to triggers in the environment is our limbic brain, that is our affective life, rather than cognition, which would relate to the cortical brain. As we saw above, interaction with terrain may produce a particular style of walk which becomes incorporated as a habit. The practical function of the walk is forgotten, and it becomes a walk across any terrain, unless a new terrain is extreme enough to interrupt the habit and to allow the possibility of a new physical and affective response to the environment.

Moving in environments in ways that engage the whole body, such as crawling and rolling on stone or grass, both opens up fresh perceptions of that place and challenges our habits, calling forth adaptability, flexibility and creativity. In order to develop skilfulness in movement, which would include the possibility of stepping outside of ingrained habits, it is necessary to cultivate an awareness of how a moment is co-created between the body and a particular environment. This develops contextual awareness and makes sense of types of embodiment. Otherwise, if 'I' concentrate on training 'my body' as an isolated individual, not only am I training the body out of context and thus reinforcing an invalid belief in my own autonomy, but also the influence of context—which could enable a greater sense of freedom (from compulsion, for example) or stimulate possibilities of transformation—is always missing from my awareness.

With the Santiago theory, I reach the threshold of the ecological body, which goes beyond the environmental body. I define the ecological body as a co-creating, immanent body, a body constantly becoming within a changing environment, where body and the spaces in between bodies are considered as equally dynamic. Body and environment, I suggest, co-create each other through mutual influence and interactional shaping. The body-in-movement, as a relational body, sets up different practices through habit according to its intentions, perceptual life, experiences and cultural preferences.

The Ecological Body

The intelligence of the body-in-movement is a basic premise in ecological movement. The body is not placed in duality with mind or seen as a medium for expressing psychological realities; it is—and expresses—the very fabric of our being. Tim Ingold, a cultural anthropologist, refers to a similar experience of self: 'when you yell in anger, the yell is your anger, it is not a vehicle that carries your anger […] the echoes of the yell are the reverberations of your own being as it pours forth into the environment' (2000: 24). Similarly, I see that each person's movement is who they are, it is not a vehicle that carries who they are. I describe an ecological body as a 'body in movement in a changing environment.' It is this emphasis on viewing the world through a lens of transition or flux, from an experience of movement and constant change that distinguishes ecological movement in my mind from environmental movement, which is often viewed through a static lens.[5] The ecological body lives within movement itself and as a system dancing within systems, rather than as an isolated unit.

The ecological body is aware of the effect that its movement is having on others and on the environment itself, and how they, in turn, are conditioning its movement. Habitual characteristics and tendencies become apparent in its movement patterns: they are the movements which repeat themselves through changing environments. An ecological body is situated in flux, participation and change. The changing body/soma experienced through movement as part of the changing environment challenges any fixed and determined notion of self and stimulates a different sense of self-as-process, participating in the movement of life.

This perceptual transformation from 'self' as a discrete entity to 'self' as constantly becoming-in-the-environment and as present within the changing moment stimulates a participatory, fluid, incorporated and transient experience of 'self' which may, in turn, condition future attitudes, communication, behaviour and performative acts.

Ecological Movement: The Four Dynamics

Over time I have identified a series of movement dynamics, which, in my experience, facilitate the capacity to create ecological movement, which means movement embedded in (rather than superimposed on) its context or environment. These are the dynamics of active and passive; proportion; transition/position; and point, line and angle.

As we shall see though Gibson's description of ecological perception, the very same dynamics exist in the environment, so this selection immediately creates a bridge between an individual as a dynamic system and their environment. These four dynamics are outlined below.

First, the active/passive dynamic is taught in pairs as a way of recognising characteristic movement patterns:

a. How I am influenced by the other to initiate an action.
b. The quality of action/movement that I initiate (e.g. how strong or how weak, how direct or how indirect).
c. The consequences of that action for the other in the environment.
d. How that influences them to respond to me.
e. The imprint of the exchange between each pair on the wider situation.[6]

By recognizing my part in the cycle, I can at the very least practise initiating actions that produce a positive response for the other in their situation, and I can practise initiating through choice rather than through the compulsion of habit. Active/passive can also offer a way of analysing and being comfortable with the extremes of 'doing' and 'being' within a given environment.

The second dynamic, proportion, may help movers to experience their changing selves as part of the changing composition of the landscape. Proportion only exists in a relational world. The length of an arm may be laid along a fallen tree trunk, while the mover reaches up towards the sky with the other hand. If the mover pays close attention to their physical proportion as part of a wider composition, then they may experience themselves in a relational world. Equally, the mover may enter a consideration of how much, how often, how visible or how slow, in terms of an affective, proportionate, movement response to either another person or to the environment. This in turn could influence attitudes to consumerism, for example, cultivating a sense of how much I need in relation to the context around me. An embodied and embedded proportional response gives any movement both volume and presence.

A key feature of ecological movement is that movement is studied from its most literal, physical manifestation, through an understanding of the attitude embodied in that movement, to its broadest implication in society. For example, transition/position, the third dynamic, gives a structure for exploring 'travelling and staying' as different modes of being. Motivations, desires and perceptions of place change according to which mode one is operating within. As a result, different values can often lead to misunderstandings between 'dwellers' and 'travellers,' for example, or between indigenous peoples and tourists. At a broader level, these preferences connect with inter-cultural issues of territory, invasion, colonialism and the flux of emigration and immigration. The structure of transition/position in movement may help us to perceive cultural attitudes that we may not have challenged within ourselves—for example, qualities of directness or circumspection and tact. Applying cultural lenses to different movement dynamics, such as active/passive, transition/position, proportion and point, line and angle may reveal the somatic origins and heritage of other habitual cultural mechanisms.

By becoming aware of how our behaviour and societal practices are still influenced by these incorporated patterns, we may eventually create a conceptual and physical 'gap,' so that we have the capacity to adapt and to be flexible enough to create a third possibility, between going and staying, which seems necessary for a fluid, intercultural society. I see this as a co-creation of a complex environment which values diversity, proportionate activity and personal transience. Such an environment was created temporarily for the Temple Art Festival described in my case study.

The practice of the fourth dynamic—point, line and angle—stimulates us through movement to develop a movement vocabulary without assumptions or expectations. This vocabulary emerges in direct relationship to point, line and angle in the environment.

In his definition of 'ecological perception,' Gibson maintains that we relate to the environment through our senses, including the kinesthetic sense: we exist in an environmental scale of proportion; we perceive changes, processes and sequences rather than the abstract of time (Gibson 1979: 11). The environment, according to Gibson, is both static and improvised, consisting of substances, mediums and surfaces. Surfaces are where substance and medium meet, and the layout of adjoining surfaces can be perceived at corners, edges and angles. He states: 'The fundamental way in which surfaces are laid out has an intrinsic meaning for behaviour unlike the abstract, formal, intellectual concepts of mathematical space' (Gibson 1979: 11).

This aspect of ecological perception offers a perceptual explanation for the significance of studying point, line and angle through movement. Not only does this encourage movers to engage with their own patterns of movement in a fresh way, relatively free from judgement, but it also connects them directly to the pattern of other surfaces and substances in the environment. An awareness of point, line and angle through the senses in movement offers a new perception of familiar objects and environments as a part of ever-changing patterns, which tangibly alter according to one's own position. Momentarily released from the habit of verbal labels, there is a glimpse of an unnamed underlying geometry of surfaces, particularly at the borders where substances and mediums meet. This jolts our habit and permits new and often unpredictable pathways of connection through the world.

As relatively neutral tools, these dynamics allow performers to observe sensations arising in the moment rather than to anticipate or assume any particular affective stance. This kind of living geometry encourages us to incorporate ourselves in the actual environment, rather than to move in our description or associative interpretation of the environment. For example, in practice, we become aware of the distinction between relating to the actual stone of the temple or relating to the associations that arise when we see the stone.

Crucially, ecological perception is based on the notion of a moving body rather than on the scientific study of sight from a static position. Human beings are either creating pathways through locomotion, moving through a medium from one point of observation to another (transition), or else setting up barriers to locomotion, creating sequences of exits and entrances to and from dwelling places (position). The available paths of locomotion in a medium constitute the set of all possible points of observation. Any individual can stand in all places, and all individuals can stand in the same place at different times. In this sense, the environment surrounds all observers in the same way that it surrounds a single observer (Gibson 1979: 11). From this description, transition and position—as movement dynamics which can be practised—seem to create the moving matrix which supports the process of perception.

Additionally, where I am standing allows me to perceive the environment in a certain way, but it also informs the environment about me. These two processes are inseparable and lead to Gibson's theory of affordances: that is, how we pick up information appropriate to our needs directly from the environment. An affordance is equally a fact of the environment and a fact of behaviour. It is both physical and psychical, yet neither. An affordance points both ways, to the environment and to the observer (Gibson 1979: 129). The emphasis here is on the fact that we are active participants in this process—the universe is not communicating to us; we are picking up features relevant to us from the environment.

Through the four dynamics, ecological movement can reawaken awareness of the mutual influences that exist between our movement and our changing environment. Movement is created by the being moving and its relationship with the place it is moving in. At the same time, the environment is changed by the mover's activity. Both of these traces invite us to look at a changing pattern of our preferred ways of being and doing in the world and the effect that we have on our surroundings. Our embodied movement may result in a perceptual shift: enabling us to see ourselves as part of the environment.

Finally, the movement dynamics are accessible cross-culturally, as a framework for movement dialogue, but also illuminate different approaches to the same dynamics; they stimulate a tangible way to be self-reflexive about intentions, actions and the effect of those actions in the world. Movement dynamics support the individual to learn to see movement from transience, rather than from a static position—a dynamic is the 'movement' of movement itself. As Ingold posits, 'The polarised debates between "nature" and "nurture" and between intra- and interpersonal dynamics are made redundant through the practice of ecological perception, which encourages an undivided approach to "organism-in-the-environment"' (Ingold 2000: 170).

Case Study

So far, I have explored how individuals transform themselves through movement; simultaneously their movement 'taskscape'[7] transforms their environment. Equally, the environment conditions how they choose to move and the associations that arise from their movements. The skill in ecological movement is to remember and to embody both sides of this equation.

As a case study, I shall take the evolution of my own movement piece at Candi Sukuh to indicate how ecological movement practice led to an improvised transformative performance called *Threshold*. During the performance, a new aspect of the temple was revealed that resonated with the theme of my performance and with elements of my own autobiography. The performance allowed me to disrupt the audience's stereotypical image of Western tourists visiting heritage sites and, if just for a moment, to offer respect to this sacred site.

Performances at Srawung Seni Candi

This was the seventh Srawung Seni Candi, or Temple Art Festival, to take place at Candi Sukuh, a 15th century Javanese-Hindu fertility temple on the slopes of Mt Lawu above Solo, Central Java. Mt. Lawu is considered a sacred mountain for the worship of ancestors and nature spirits.

Returning for a moment to my choice of title, in fact, the words 'sacrum' and 'sacred' share a common etymology from the Latin adjective 'sacer, sacra, sacrum' which means 'sacred or pertaining to the gods.' Particularly in the Mesoamerican cultures, the sacrum was believed to be a 'holy' bone because it protected the reproductive organs, which seems apt for Candi

Sukuh as a fertility temple. It was also the bone that was believed to be a 'resurrection' bone, from where a person was reborn (possibly because it is the last bone to disintegrate) as well as a cosmic portal to other levels of reality (Stross 2007: 5). All these qualities echo the theme of transformation which was present at Srawung Seni Candi through the various movement–based rituals and performances.

The festivals are initiated by Suprapto Suryodarmo, founder of the Padepokan Lemah Putih, an interdisciplinary movement-based arts institute in Solo. His intention is to gather together and to share traditional and contemporary performance inspired by temples or sacred sites around the world. Through sharing practice and performance over the years, he is creating a network of 'temple art practitioners.' A couple of hours dedicated to theoretical and academic papers during the festival also stimulated discussions around the nature of culture and heritage, archive, memory and movement art.

Suryodarmo himself has practised Joged Amerta,[8] his own movement practice, in Candi Sukuh for over 40 years, first alone and then with international groups of students as well as with local artists. Suryodarmo's stated intention in his practice is, 'to lessen the sense of identification through the practice of movement arts. Hence, it is more than an approach to improvisation; Joged Amerta is a practice cultivating an attitude towards life' (Suryodarmo 2010).

Figure 2: Candi Sukuh Temple, Java.

This inclusive approach to movement art was reflected in the wide variety of work presented by an inter-cultural and inter-generational group of performers and ritual artists.

For two days, this atmospheric, misty temple was filled with new sounds, songs, movements, ideas, processions, colours, words and conversations between practitioners from all around the world. From dawn until dusk, performers and both international and local audiences mingled freely, witnessing different pieces of work in every corner of the temple, sharing food and drink. Local children and families received gifts of clothes and young trees to celebrate the occasion. They delighted in a traditional Reog 'lion' dance as well as witnessing open-mouthed a wide range of site-responsive contemporary performances from around the world, specifically evoking the history, myths, spirit and/or the architecture of the temple.

The performances in celebration of the temple—some improvised, some choreographed and some scored—took place through sun, mist, wind and torrential monsoon rain. Performers and audience alike remained relatively unperturbed through the changing situations, creating a mood of joyful goodwill, curiosity and celebration.

Ingold elaborates on Gibson's notion of changes, sequences and processes as 'practical' time, by introducing the notion of a taskscape (Ingold 2000). This is the visible sign of relational activities in the environment, through time. The landscape is the taskscape in its embodied form, just like the body is the lifecycle in its embodied form. Landscape and body (being) manifest the functional aspects of environment and organism (doing), respectively, but they are simply different aspects of the same process. Seen in this way, the cycles of relational activity in both organism and environment are constantly in flux and 'in-form' each other (Ingold 2000: 19–20).

For two days, the taskscape of the temple was transformed from its normal state of windswept quietness, punctuated by occasional tourist groups, local visitors with picnics, the ice cream vendor's insistent tune and the eager call to buy *Sate! sate! sate!*[9] The temple was not a backdrop for the various performances: it was incorporated into the acts, actions and activity of performers and public alike and transformed moment by moment for the audience, according to the particular lenses that the performers had chosen for their response to the site.

I shall analyse my own performance, *Threshold*, with reference to the ecological dynamics and as an example of performer, environment and audience in a condition of mutual transformation.

I chose the role of a tourist wandering through the temple with headphones listening to Moroccan[10] pop music (transition/position). The music was suddenly broadcast for all to hear, as I amplified my movements (proportion), marking myself out as the performer. At the same moment, my attention was drawn by one particular relief of a blacksmith forging metal for the traditional *keris,*[11] in the presence of Ganapahit, the Elephant Head God. This relief stands at a side entrance to the temple. I stopped, removed my cap and headphones, lit some incense and began to move in front of the scene, imitating, absorbing and receiving the full impact of the relief. I moved with it, 'reading' where it sits in relation to the rest of the temple through proportion and point, line and angle; 'reading' the movement of the audience around me through transition and position, active and passive; responding to the wind, the light and the sounds; and re-membering[12] images of the powerful traditional *keris* purification ritual which had taken place at that site the day before. All of these elements informed my improvised movement.

As I kinesthetically received the relief in context, without a particular score in mind, I was struck by the mouth of a drainpipe, which stuck out of the old stone wall just to the left of the blacksmith relief. I imagined that once Candi Sukuh would have had a complex system of water canals running through it as part of an irrigation system. Now they were dry. In that moment the temple felt parched, wizened and dried up to me, no longer fertile, despite the frequent rains. As I continued to move, embodying these internal responses, the pipe became a symbol for me of how the all-consuming tourist eye can deaden and dry out the juice of a sacred site, in the name of heritage. I felt the distinction between knowing about a place, but not knowing it, affectively, at all. I found myself kneeling by the pipe and sprinkling on it some water, that was lying in a puddle near by, left over from the last rainfall. I sprinkled the water with a prayer that water may return to Candi Sukuh and that it may

Figure 3: *Threshold*: an improvised performance at Srawung Seni Candi, December 2010. Candi Sukuh, Java. Mover: Sandra Reeve.

continue to be a place of fertility, purification and irrigation for all those who visit. I was a guest there. It was the prayer of a guest.

I believe this kind of experience to be what has been described as 'an event-full' space by Derek McCormack, a human geographer, in his analysis of 'corporeally precipitated' memories:

> In effect what happens is this: the affective relations between these lines of movement somehow cross a threshold of consistency in such a way as to produce an event-full space through which memory emerges without recollection, a space in which the actuality of the present is charged with the enlivening potential of the virtual, that 'pressing crowd of incipiencies and tendencies', a 'realm of potential [...] where futurity combines, unmediated, with pastness.'
>
> (McCormack 2005: 121)

According to Buddhist philosophy, the person present in any given moment is, in fact, the only one that there is to receive. This statement does not ignore the reality of repetition, habits and characteristic tendencies in each person, which gives the impression of a fixed self, but it bears witness to constantly evolving beings from a position of infinite choice and potential transformation within the present moment. Just as the environment is as it is at any given moment, containing both traces of the past and seeds of the future within its present 'presencing', so the present movement of each person is as it is, embodying past conditionings within present circumstances. How each movement evolves in the present moment will condition each person's possible futures. It is this attitude to the moving 'organism-in-the-environment' that informed my performance. Transformation as an ongoing process is implicit within this view.

In performance, I can develop the capacity to become aware of how the context is both influencing and being influenced by my movement. I become aware of my familiar, recurrent interests in the environment. I become aware of the shifts taking place in me in response to different situations as a set of preferences rather than seeing myself as having a fixed character, which no longer has any choices to behave differently. Transformation is the capacity to embody different stories about a changing self from within the changing moment. As I perform from the notion of no fixed or determined sense of self, I am free to change character mode whenever I like, similar to in a dream life.

I bowed, put on my cap and headphones and moved off down the path, once again returning to my role of the casual tourist.

Through different movement responses to my environment, I moved from tourist to temple dancer and back again, inviting the audience to journey through the different strata of the temple with me. This was an improvised performance, but the idea had evolved from my movement practice among tourists at Avebury Stone Circle in the United Kingdom, and I had brought elements of the costume and the soundtrack with me. I selected the site before witnessing the *keris* ceremony, but that ritual had served to deepen my cultural understanding of the significance of the relief.

Sharing the sacred site of Candi Sukuh as the primary source for our performance material meant that we could appreciate different responses to the same site. Martin Jackson points out that undertaking a practical task in another culture can often convey an embodied sense of that activity. The worker is doing the same thing as other bodies, but they are doing it in their own way. This, he says, is a creative technique which reveals both consonance and individual meaning. He sees this as a way of 'opening up dialogue between people from different cultures or traditions, ways of bringing into being modes of understanding which effectively go beyond the intellectual conventions and political ideologies that circumscribe us all' (Jackson 1989: 3).

Undertaking physical tasks, whether based in daily life activity, in non-stylized movement or in performance seems to be an important, non-hierarchical way of giving presence to other-than-verbal (I prefer this to nonverbal, as I try to avoid making 'verbal' the defining term) experiences of each other's beings-in-the-environment, as a way of promoting 'holarchy,' a recently coined term to indicate a human system, each element of which displays both self-assertive and integrative tendencies (Leicester and O'Hara 2007). Jackson argues that 'persons actively body-forth the world; their bodies are not passively shaped by or made to fit the world's purposes' (1989: 136). He does not see bodily behaviour as symbolizing ideas conceived independently of it. Environment and culture, in this approach, are inextricably linked and are both present in the articulations of the moving body.

Ecological movement reconnects the performer with a corporeal, embodied sense of themselves as part of the environment. This process takes time, and embodied time is slower than cognitive time—but from the position of no fixed sense of self, transformation is seen as a natural process. The performers are invigorated by the process of exploring different ways of moving in, and relating to, the temple. The site itself comes alive in a whole new way.

Audience in Transformation

We have seen that both the performers and the temple were involved in a process of transformation throughout the festival. What conditions might be necessary to offer the audience the possibility of transformative experiences at this international gathering?

As in most outdoor performances in Java, including *wayang kulit*,[13] people were immersed in the atmosphere and able to move around and to choose what they watched. In terms of the ecological dynamics, this means that they are active in creating their own pathways, positions and viewpoints throughout the festival, and that they selected their own proportion—i.e. how near, how far?—as based on personal need. They came and went as they liked, which seems important as an obligatory atmosphere of immersion can invite its opposite: alienation. They followed their preferences, which gave them information about themselves as well as about the performance. In Gibson's terms, they might have become more aware of their selection of 'affordances,' as they made their choices, and might have seen that they were indeed co-creating the event through their own particular perceptions. They had the opportunity to shape their own pathways throughout the festival while being offered new experiential lenses through which to gaze at their familiar temple.

The case study also indicates that the audience's view of a tourist may have been disrupted momentarily by my own, and other, site-responsive performances. I felt that the integrated role of the audience as active participants from a passive position, who were themselves moving through the sites, was helpful in creating a shared ecology of 'being in performance,' where each participant was clear about their changing role during the event.

On my return to England a few months later, while writing this chapter, I came across a description of the water systems of Candi Sukuh:

> An examination of the surroundings of the Candi indicates a system of water ducts, leading down from the hillside beyond the pyramid, where a spring or a catchment were located. One arm of the ducts led to the Candi to fill into the holy pond, where rites of oblation were performed and to supply water for other ceremonials and rituals that were performed by the priests and Rsis at various altars and shrines at Sukuh.
>
> (Fic 2003: 47)

These words validated my affective kinesthetic response to a previously unnoticed drainpipe, at a time when I felt 'incorporated' in the temple. The archaeological facts were unknown to me, but movement 'reading'—in this case a kind of somatic excavation— revealed the almost invisible water world of the temple and a sense of its spiritual significance.

The affordance of the drainpipe perceived in movement connected me to personal associations within my own autobiography as well as to the cultural significance of the site. Moving in a way that connected organism to the environment, a new ritual took place. Such ritual art—which does not repeat past practices, but where the intention is to respond to a place as sacred rather than as an archive for visitors—creates a new sacred narrative in performance.

Threshold was a skilled improvised movement offering to the 'intangible heritage of the temple' (Brusaferro 2006: 1). I created the conditions for transformation not only of myself and the site (when my embodied understanding of the site stimulated me to make an offering of water to the temple) but also of the visitors' perception of how a tourist might participate in the contemporary life of the temple.

The embodied process of mutual transformation of both site and participants through the application of liminal awareness, environmental perception and ecological movement skills created a contemporary site-specific sacred narrative in Candi Sukuh.

References

Brusaferro, P. (2005), 'Heritage management and artisan skill as "Invisible Heritage"', UNESCO University and Heritage 10th International Seminar, Cultural Landscapes in the 21st Century, Newcastle-upon-Tyne, UK, 11–16 April.

Connerton, P. (1989), *How Societies Remember*, Cambridge, UK: Cambridge University Press.

Fic, V. M. (2003), *From Majapahit and Sukuh to Megawati Sukarnoputri: Continuity and Change in Pluralism of Religion, Culture and Politics of Indonesia from the XV to the XXI*, New Delhi, India: Shakti Malik Abhinav Publications.

Gell, A. and Hirsch, E. (1999), *The Art of Anthropology*, London, UK: Athlone Press.

Gibson, J. (1979), *The Ecological Approach to Visual Perception*, Boston, MA: Houghton Mifflin Company.

Leicester, G. and O'Hara, M. (2007), *Ten Things to do in a Conceptual Emergency*, St. Andrews, UK: IFF Publications.

Ingold, T. (2000), *The Perception of the Environment*, London, UK: Routledge.

Jackson, M. (1989), *Path towards a Clearing: Radical Empiricism and Ethnographic Enquiry*, Bloomington, IN: Indiana University Press.

Legrand, D. (2007), 'Pre-reflective self-consciousness: On being bodily in the world', *Janus Head*, 9:2, pp. 493–519.

Maturana, H. and Varela, F. (1987), *The Tree of Knowledge: The Biological Roots of Human Understanding*, Boston, MA: Shambhala.

McCormack, D. P. (2005), 'Diagramming practice and performance', *Environment and Planning D: Society and Space*, 23, pp. 119–147.

—— (2008), 'Geographies for moving bodies: Thinking, dancing, spaces', *Geography Compass*, 2:6, pp. 1822–1836.

Nyanaponika Thera, N. (1983), *The Heart of Buddhist Meditation*, London, UK: Rider.

Stross, B. (2007), 'The mesoamerican sacrum bone: Doorway to the otherworld', http://research.famsi.org/aztlan/uploads/papers/stross-sacrum.pdf/. Accessed May 2011.

Suryodarmo, S. (2010), 'Joged Amerta: Art in Joged Amerta programme 2010–2011', http://www.lemahputih.com/. Accessed July 2010.

Notes

1 Full details of my practice, Move into Life, can be found at www.moveintolife.com.

2 I use this term as a reminder of the notion of 'self' as a process rather than a fixed and determined state of being.

3 An inner or subjective experience of the body.

4 Autopoiesis, a term used by Maturana and Varela, is the system that makes living beings autonomous systems. An 'autopoietic unity' is a single living organism. It is their self organisation that defines them as unities (Maturana and Varela, 1987).

5　In my readings of the 'situated' body (which may be seen as an environmental body) although change, movement and process are referenced throughout, I feel that this same distinction holds true: the primary lens through which the body is viewed remains static, as indicated by the choice of word 'situated' (Ingar Brinck, 2007; Dorothée Legrand, 2007; Shaun Gallagher 2007).

6　The practical exercise comes from Joged Amerta, the somatic practice of Suprapto Suryodarmo, Javanese movement artist. Here, I outline my interpretation of it.

7　Tim Ingold's notion of taskscape is defined elsewhere in this case study.

8　Literal translation: The moving-dancing nectar of life.

9　Meat or chicken on skewers.

10　This was a syncretic choice, alongside the natural sounds and the Hindu-Buddhist architecture at the temple.

11　The *keris* or *kris* is an asymmetrical knife/dagger, which is said to be created by merging metal with spiritual or magical properties. They are often handed down through the generations and certain rituals are performed to maintain their sacred power.

12　Embodying my memories through movement.

13　*Wayang kulit* is the Javanese term for shadow puppets.

Chapter 19

Dancing and Flourishing: Mindful Meditation in Dance-Making and Performing

Sarah Whatley and Naomi Lefebvre Sell

Part One

Introduction

This chapter will explore the role of meditation within dance practice and consider how its integration within dance training might influence prevailing pedagogical approaches within the dance studio. It will discuss a choreographic project, which introduced meditation as a fundamental part of the dance-making process to show how meditation can both have a profound influence on a dancer and foster a different kind of bodily awareness and sense of embodiment. What follows is therefore an account of the dancers' encounters with meditation and how expressions of spirituality emerged from this practice, exposing the (unspoken) spiritual narratives that guided and supported them, both within and beyond the dance studio. The aim will thus be to illustrate how meditation can expand Somatic Movement Education and extend understanding of spiritual experiences in dance, influencing thought about teaching and research within a professional dance training environment. As co-authors, we hope to provide a perspective on this work that is simultaneously inside and outside the project that is the principal focus for discussion. As an 'outsider,' my etic approach will seek to offer a broad framework for the discussion, provided in Parts One and Three, before introducing Naomi Lefebvre Sell's 'insider' or emic experience as project leader,[1] which is the focus for Part Two.

What spirituality means in a dance context, or indeed in any context, is not easily defined. As Williamson points out in a detailed overview of the spiritual tradition in relationship with somatic movement practices (2010), spirituality is a contentious proposition, being neither well understood nor comprehensively theorized. She offers that in somatic movement practice 'you can ascertain through textual discourse that the body is theoretically positioned as the locus of spiritual authority; the body is viewed as a fundamental "resource" (a sensory guide) in decision-making processes' (2010: 46) but that 'there is no one singular sacred narrative or spiritual tradition orientating the field [of Somatics]' (2010: 47). Many dance practitioners may refer either directly or by inference to a spiritual or existential experience; an episode which takes them 'out of themselves' and prompts them into a new state of being, which seems to connect them more fully to their own presence, offering a deeper awareness of their physicality. But uncertainty about the connection between this intangible stage of receptivity and spirituality remains.

For some dancers who are not so used to working somatically, meditation can be a valuable way to encourage a highly disciplined, yet quieter and more self-reflective approach

Figure 1: Mover: Daisy (with Lucille). Photographer: Naomi Lefebvre Sell.

to moving and movement-making. What emerges through the project discussed here, and what we hope to demonstrate, is that choreographers and dancers who participate in meditation describe their dance/movement experiences in a more 'holistic', authentic way, and are able to talk about what they experience in relationship with their own intentions and desires. In contemplating the connections between these experiences and spirituality, we do not intend to offer any resolved definition of spirituality, but hopefully at least some contribution to thought about spirituality in relation to dance.

Keen to explore the relationship between her choreographic practice and her experience of meditation, Naomi led a group of four second year students at Trinity Laban[2] on the BA (Hons) Dance Theatre course through a rehearsal process beginning in September 2007, leading to the creation of a dance work, *dharmakaya*,[3] and its performance in London in March 2008 and in Giessen, Germany as part of the TanzArt Festival in May 2008. Naomi describes her process of creating the work and her thoughts on how meditation influenced her own method of working collaboratively with her dancers.[4] Reciprocally, comments drawn from the dancers reporting on their experience of being offered meditation as a different kind of preparation for making and rehearsing movement material are included. Naomi's aim was to identify practical methods for dance artists and choreographers to apply meditation teachings and principles to choreographic and performance situations to enhance the overall process and final outcome. Central to Naomi's enquiry was a study into the dancers' and her own understanding and experience of embodiment. How might meditation access a different or deeper awareness of embodiment? What bodily awareness might meditation, as a practice for preparing the mind for moving, offer the dancers as they move, talk and write? Would meditation enable the dancers to feel that they were embodying movement differently and be able to articulate a 'felt-sense' of moving from meditation? Importantly, while the project focused on the process of making the work, it did not concern itself with the performance itself, other than what the dancers reported to Naomi and the inevitable influence the performance had on Naomi's reflections post-performance. Consequently, the focus here is not on the performance and its reception, but on the process leading up to it and the impact that it had on thinking about how dancers are supported through that experience; and how expressions of spirituality are manifest within that process.

The institutional context for a project such as this is particularly relevant. Traditional approaches to dance training and technique acquisition, which tend to still be prevalent within leading dance institutions, take the body of the dancer for granted and construct the 'dancing body'; and choreography takes this dancing body and moulds it in a creative process for display. The emphasis is on the development of a highly trained, responsive and technically proficient body. Students at Trinity Laban have some experience of different somatic practices, which encourage students to be more inquisitive about their approaches to moving and making dance, but meditation does not routinely form part of their learning. Though not designed as an action research project to test out a particular approach to teaching and learning within a conservatory context, the findings nonetheless suggest that meditation, and particularly the principles that underpin meditation (taking time, attending to breath, connecting with self, understanding the place of judgement) could support a broader somatic education programme, influencing and rethinking traditional pedagogic approaches to the training of dancers and thus be a valuable process in empowering dancers and helping them to sustain their practice.

Meditation as, or Meeting, Somatic Movement Practice

Meditation is a discipline where the emphasis lies in the practice of accessing a present place. To potentially increase the dancers' ability to be in the present, and to access a phenomenological or 'lived-body' state, the dancers were trained in mindfulness through Zen meditation. Zen meditation, though not a somatic modality, shares some of the principles of somatic traditions, such as the concern with accessing a quiet and still place from which to begin moving, and a focus on attending to the body's own inherent wisdom through encouraging a state where a 'beginner's body' is the source for moving. To date, there is little research into the relationship between meditation and an in-studio creative dance process. But a number of performance practitioners and theorists have identified positive connections between meditation and accessing an enhanced state of creativity (for example, Zarrilli 2002; Yoo 2007; Fraleigh 1999), indicating the likely positive impact of meditation on dance. Beyond the dance and Somatics community, Tierney, who writes on holistic healthcare practices, suggests that the practice of meditation seeks 'a sense of peacefully living in the moment,' which can 'stimulate creative, intuitive and problem-solving capabilities [...] it can increase self-acceptance, self knowledge, and confidence by focusing inward' (2007: 169). Similarly, Kabat-Zinn, who is a leading proponent of the benefits of meditation in reducing stress and improving health in general, provides an illuminating description of the emphasis placed on being in the present state in mindfulness meditation, saying that, 'meditation is really non-doing [...] it is the only human endeavour I know of that does not involve trying to get somewhere else but, rather, emphasizes being where you already are' (1990: 60).

As with many somatic movement practices, meditation is not a training system to achieve an end goal and requires the practitioner to commit to an ongoing attitude and/ or life philosophy. According to Zen master, Shunryu Suzuki (1993), the practice of Zen meditation, in relation to creative practice, is integrated as a lifelong practice where the practitioner is encouraged to keep his/her beginner's mind, stating that, 'all self-centred thoughts limit our vast mind [...] when we have no thought of achievement, no thought of self, we are true beginners [...] then we can really learn something' (Suzuki 1993: 228). A similar respect for 'being in process' is shared by many somatic movement practitioners. Thomas Hanna, who introduced the term 'somatics,' offers that the concept of soma 'is a process' which is a further reason 'for holding to the word "soma" rather than the word "body"' (1980: 6). For Hanna, 'body' suggests something that is static and solid, whereas a soma is neither 'static nor solid; it is changeable and supple and is constantly adapting to its environment' (1980: 6). In keeping with Zen philosophy, Hanna states that, 'in the same way that a soma is not a "body," it is equally not a "mind," "spirit," "soul" or any other such human projection' (1980: 7). Many somatic practitioners similarly embrace a more Eastern, holistic conception of body and mind.

There are also documented links between meditation and the reduction of performance anxiety, as reported by, for example, choreographer Meredith Monk, who shifted her rehearsal process after being introduced to the teachings of the Buddhist meditation master, Chogyam Trungpa, in the mid-1970s (Alfaro 2006). Monk stated that she was able to see clearly that fear is something many dancers have in common, and that it creates a lot of conflict and anxiety. Since practising the teachings of Trungpa, Monk felt that she developed patience, respect and compassion towards the people she worked with, especially when dealing with her dancers' stage fright. In relation to creativity, Monk links this directly back to meditation, where 'staying present' throughout the process is key (2004).

Dance artists may well practice meditation as a method for preparing the mind and body, but Naomi's project is the first sustained study of the impact of meditation on a rehearsal process within a teaching environment, on the dancers involved in the process, and which captures the dancers' own reflections on their experiences. By designing the study to move from rehearsal to performance and analysis, Naomi focused on how dancers approached the idea of presence and mindfulness in a context of dance-making, the impact that had on their experience of embodiment and the relationship between meditation and theories of creativity. What was challenging, therefore, was constructing a methodology and programme of research that would keep her focus firmly on investigating the impact of meditation on the dancers' process of making and rehearsing, but which would enable her to produce a performable dance work. This produced an interesting tension between attending to the immediacy of the individual dancer's and her own experience, and working towards a performance, which—although not the principal focus of her research—might be seen as a validation of the particular approach that she was taking.

What follows is a distillation of the extensive documentation and observations collected by Naomi during the project. Writing together, we therefore offer a meta-reflection on the dancers' experience with meditation. By looking back on Naomi's empirical study of how dancers incorporated meditation within the dance-making process, and the stories that emerged, we consider the role of presence and mindfulness in enhancing the experience of embodiment and the relationship between embodied presence and spirituality.

Part Two

The Project—Naomi Lefebvre Sell

My project did not sit neatly within one particular methodological paradigm. By creating a contemporary choreographic work, and involving the dancers in a rehearsal process that offered them a deep engagement with the principles and practices of meditation, I was able to test out the impact this had on my own creative practice. This is quite unlike other studies that have offered insights into how somatic or meditation practices influence creativity (such as those by Green [1993] and McPherson [1974][5]) but which did not involve the creation of a full choreographic work to be performed in a theatre before a live audience.

My research had two foci: first, the artists' relationship with themselves, engaging with their own general world, within both instructor-led and self-led meditation practice; and second, the rehearsal/creative process, with meditation drawn upon as a choreographic tool for bodily creation in which the intent is both embodied and transmitted.

Embodiment and Mindfulness

While I led the choreographic process, the meditation sessions were led by a certified Yoga and meditation teacher, which allowed me to enter the activity as a participant-observer. These sessions were taken weekly throughout the project, consisting of Zen sitting meditation (mindful moving and Yoga Nidra for deep relaxation) followed by Dharma talks (the teachings of the Buddha). The sessions followed the traditional meditation training process by including two separate but complementary disciplines: mindfulness meditation, which develops the ability to let go of the surface level mind chatter; and the practice of deep relaxation, which permits the free flow of ideas and images from the unconscious mind. However, we acknowledged in the sessions that the practice of meditation is inevitably subjective because the experiences take place purely within the participants' minds—any teachings or instructions can only be offered by the teacher's own subjective experiences of the practice.

The sitting Zen meditation was taught as a way to achieve a greater experience of the self; a reflective practice where the participant becomes an observer of herself. The practitioner is just 'being', staying and returning to the breath, doing nothing, with no thought of right or wrong, while also refraining from thoughts of judgement. Taught as a practice of mental discipline, we started the meditation practice by sitting for five minutes and then progressed to sitting for thirty minutes at each session. As beginning meditators, the challenge of this demanding sitting practice was eased by practising Yoga Nidra, or Yogic sleep, commonly referred to as deep relaxation at the end of the teacher-led meditation sessions. Deep relaxation allows the body to release and free the mind and has the potential for recognizing different mental states. During the practice, we were encouraged to stay connected to our breath in order to not fall asleep, while remaining conscious of ourselves relaxing.

Exercising the same discipline as in the Zen sitting, the practice of mindful moving is a process in which the meditator remains mindful in the present state while exploring movement. In a traditional meditation setting, a basic walking exercise is practised where attention is on the movement of the feet and legs. Mangalo (1993) explains how the walker would note to themselves 'lifting', as the right foot begins to rise from the floor; 'moving' as they begin to move forward; and 'placing' as they place the foot again on the ground. All distracting thoughts, images or sensations should be noted in the appropriate manner: 'looking' should be immediately registered before reverting to the mindful movement or walking. Looking at objects or thinking distracting thoughts is considered lustful for the eyes and is contrary to the practice. 'Mindfulness' links to the notion of 'presentness' or 'being present', so mindfulness also provided grounding for the dancers' physical understanding of embodiment. In reaching a state of being mindful, the hope was that the dancers would be able to relate their decision-making to the changing nature of their sense of presence within varying environments (Edinborough 2011: 23), which it was anticipated would play a significant role in shaping the choreographic process and eventual performance of *dharmakaya*.

Supporting Texts

We were given four readings that supported our process as beginner meditators: *Zen Mind, Beginner's Mind* by Shunryu Suzuki (1993), *The Practice of Recollection* by Bhikkhu Mangalo (1993), *To Forget the Self* by Dogen Zenji (1993) and *The Sutra of the Heart of*

Transcendent Knowledge translated by The Nalanda Translation Committee (1993), which is one of the most important of the Buddhist sutras. The central theme of this sutra is the Buddhist concept of emptiness, which refers to the perception that all phenomena are empty of inherent existence. We were encouraged to continue with our own personal meditation practice and it began to emerge that we all attempted to bring mindfulness into our daily lives, in particular within interpersonal situations.[6]

Since integrating a meditation practice into my choreographic process was new to both the dancers and to me, I recommended that we always began each rehearsal with a group discussion and reflection on how our personal meditation practice was going, whether we had any new creative thoughts that emerged from the sittings as well as recapping where we left off from the last rehearsal. It was important to create a situation where the dancers could reflect and speak about their experiences to allow the sitting meditation sessions and the dharma teachings to have an impact on the creative process. We decided that the dancers would always start the physical portion of the rehearsals with ten to fifteen minutes of mindful moving,[7] to allow them to tap into their place of mindfulness and become present for the creative/movement tasks. Consequently, the practice of mindful moving, which was first experienced in the meditation sessions, was brought directly into the rehearsal process early on, influencing how I approached the rehearsals, and which in turn encouraged the dancers to utilize the meditation experiences to feed into the creation of *dharmakaya*.[8] Moreover, mindful moving was something that remained as a useful and integrated practice even until the final performance.

Choreographer-as-Researcher

In the role of what I named 'choreographer-as-researcher,' I utilised ethnographic principles to extensively observe and videotape the work in progress in rehearsals, record my own rehearsal notes, interview the dancers and direct them to document their experiences in a personal journal (which was subsequently shared with me). Interview questions dealt with the dancers' changing concept of embodiment or lived experience through using meditation as a preparatory activity in rehearsals. The written journals were used to triangulate my own observations and the individual and group interviews, all of which together formed the entirety of the data. The practical data-gathering period concluded with the performance of *dharmakaya*. The performances were followed by a lengthy period of analysis of all that had been collected; from the choreographic rehearsals, performances and meditation sessions throughout the 30 weeks of the practical activity. I drew on van Maanen's (1988) categorization of ethnographic writing styles to write up the data as a number of 'tales,' to give voice to the dancers and to discover more about my own engagement with the research. The first of these were 'realist tales,' which provide a direct, straightforward picture of the subject studied with little concern for how the fieldworker produced such a portrait. The most prevalent and familiar form of ethnographic writing, realist tales allow the narrator to adopt the device of permitting various informants to 'speak for themselves.' Realist tales are not multi-vocal narratives and do not display multiple views; an 'author typically narrates the realist tale in a dispassionate, third-person voice [...] the result is an author-proclaimed description' (van Maanen 1988: 45). In a realist tale, 'only what members of the studied culture say and do and, presumably, think are visible in the text. The fieldworker, having finished the job of collecting the data, simply vanishes behind a steady descriptive narrative [...] taking the "I" (the observer) out of the ethnographic report' (van Maanen 1988: 45). I wrote realist tales for each of the four dancers (Daisy, Katy, Lucille, Tara)[9] in order to allow for their view of the story, an account of their journeys through the creative process, to be told. Writing these tales revealed how differently the dancers communicate their experiences. Daisy, for example, was comfortable in expressing herself verbally, whereas Lucille talked about how she often struggled to 'find the words' in order to communicate her findings, questions and her experiences in an honest way.

In contrast to realist tales, confessional tales are written from the perspective of the researcher and often include self-reflection. According to van Maanen, the confessional tale attempts to 'demystify fieldwork or participant-observation by showing how the technique is practised in the field' (1988: 73). These tales are written from a more personal standpoint by the author/researcher and typically coincide with realist tales and are elaborations on the formal descriptions (van Maanen, 1988: 74). The confessional tale is particularly appropriate for this type of study as it attempts to represent the 'fieldworker's participated presence in the studied scene, the fieldworker's rapport and sensitive contact with others in the world described [...] it is necessarily a blurred account, combining a partial description of the culture alongside an equally partial description of the fieldwork experience itself' (van Maanen 1988: 91). I wrote three confessional tales, one that discussed my experience in the field in the role of choreographer-as-researcher, one focusing on the dance-making process in the studio, and the third considering the field of the live performance.

Impressionist tales, on the other hand, are personalized accounts of the fieldwork, and may have multiple interpretations or uncertain meanings and carry elements of both realist and confessional writing (van Maanen 1988). Impressionist tales are about what rarely happens; not about what usually happens. These are memorable moments within the fieldwork experience and are reconstructed in dramatic form; they are periods the author regards as especially notable and hence reportable (van Maanen 1988: 102). I wrote a final narrative tale based on the impressionist tale principles to discuss the period leading up to the final choreographic work.

This combined approach to telling the tales allowed me to bring several writing styles into the documentation, which variously privilege personal, poetic and objective positions through the narrative tales. The writing of the tales and a subsequent period of reflection on the stories that emerged from the tale-writing allowed me to identify recurrent themes, which provided a structure within which I could examine the impact of the project on my work as choreographer and on the dancers' experience of rehearsing and performing dance supported by meditation sessions. The themes I identified were 'understanding the effects of *judgement*,' 'the importance of *honesty*,' and the practice of 'being present through the understanding and integration of *mindfulness.*' These themes also provided a lens through which the dancers' own comments could be analysed further, which then led, iteratively, to new insights about my own choreographic practice and the particular character of the role of choreographer-as-researcher, when traditional approaches to dance-making are inflected by meditation principles. Notwithstanding the challenges that this qualitative research process generated, I found that engaging with the meditation principles unveiled for me a new and unfamiliar choreographic and performance perspective. The aim therefore was not to prove the value of a practice or to generate a series of truths, but to privilege my own experience and those of the dancers—as shared with me through their verbal reporting and journaling, and as I witnessed in their dancing—to argue for the benefit of meditation practices in a dancer's training and rehearsal process.[10]

Some Observations, Revelations and Reflections on the Research

The dancers shared their views of how, at times, they found the sitting meditation sessions[11] very challenging, both physically and emotionally. We discussed that it is one thing to learn about meditation and another thing to apply it. In the beginning stages of our meditation practice, just holding the posture was enough to 'hold our minds.' In working towards a state of 'nothingness' while simultaneously becoming more bodily aware, through noticing breathing or discomfort through the sitting practice, the emphasis shifted from a discipline of the mind to a heightened somatic awareness. We were encouraged to try the meditation sittings with a little Buddha smile, by lifting up the corners of the mouth. We were taught that the secret of the Buddha smiling is the moment of realization that he spent years searching for something that he already had. In rehearsal, I observed that the use of the Buddha smile became a useful tool, as it encouraged the dancers, while moving, to return to the beneficial principles learned through the sitting practice. The use of the Buddha smile therefore became a valuable element of the performance itself as it encouraged a relaxed focus within the dancers.

Continuing the theme of just 'being' was non-doing—a process of continually returning to the sitting and breathing in that moment. But engaging with the concept of non-doing actually encouraged a great amount of 'doing,' and this came in the form of creative ideas stimulated through the practice of patience. Hence, as we discovered, the state of mind 'cultivated by sitting practice' has the ability to strengthen and deepen the creative process of art-making (Rockwell 1989: 187).

The concept of 'being' allowed for the dancers to find a new effective way of sharing and 'recalling' choreographed movement material, which would maintain the essences of their experiences and honour the dancers' lived experience in its creation. The dancers learned the material without watching directly to copy, but by listening, sensing and by responding to a set of imagery-based instructions. This was quite unlike the 'drilling' experienced by the dancers in much of their other training, when, according to Foster, 'the aim is nothing less than "creating the body"' and that 'with repetition, the images used to describe the body and its actions *become* the body' (1997: 239, emphasis in original). Although the devising period for this research project did not take on the characteristics of a traditional technique 'drill,' it did use repetition as a means to embody metaphors. The images were not just a language for the dancers to talk about their bodies but were a way of experiencing embodiment and a method of creating material. So by contrast, in this choreographic process, the images and intentions of the dancers were at the forefront, and therefore became embodied simultaneously when creating the choreographed movement; so there was no 'drilling.'

The dual processes of image-based discovery and repetition seems to align with the views of both Trevor Leggett (1978), a teacher of yoga and philosophy and James Austin (1999), a clinical professor of neurology, who have discussed the 'ri' principle in meditation practice, as the inspiration or spirit and the 'ji' principle as the formal technique. Austin states that 'ri' means to be 'so in contact with the true, universal nature of the situation that one expresses its beauty and power both naturally and efficiently [...] ri is inspired by our innate creative wellsprings within [...] it cannot be taught or imitated' (1999: 669). However, the 'ji' principle can be taught and observed, having been handed down from some other person's concept of 'ri.' Perhaps the dancers' original inspirations of 'ri' were handed down to each other through this new found way of sharing choreographed material, prompted by the particular teachings offered by meditation. The introduction of meditation into the embodied space of the dance studio, and the collective process of making movement, seemed to shift the group towards a more spiritual engagement, where each dancer experienced greater ease in the body and a sense of wholeness and unity, corresponding with awakening the 'ri' principle in their moving.

Reconciling Presence and Practice, and the Place of Ego

We discussed within the group what the difference was between being mindful and mindless, as this was at times becoming blurred for the dancers. Trungpa's writings helped clarify this by explaining that, 'there has to be a certain discipline so that we are neither totally lost in daydream nor missing the freshness and openness that come from not holding our attention too tightly [...] this balance is a state of wakefulness, mindfulness' (1976: 33). The dancers often noted that when they became reflective while moving, they were no longer present, and the feelings they had been experiencing were lost. As an example, Daisy said in interview she would like to reach a state of being where she is so acutely aware in her body that her body always takes over. She said that she did practise with 'putting her mind into parts of her body' and that this was the closest she had felt to true embodiment.

It was also challenging for the dancers to realize that there is no 'right' and 'wrong' in the practice of mindfulness—the aim is to 'be' in the moment. This is very different from their traditional dance training where there is often a right or wrong way of executing movement, so for the dancers it took some time for them to understand the practice of mindfulness; this was not only in how they practised it bodily but also in how they reflected upon it. The dancers experienced a sense of freedom in being in the present/mindful place, allowing them to be present in the movement and to experience it more fully. Consequently, the dancers came to a physical and conceptual understanding of the practice of mindful moving, the core values of which are in establishing a present state and letting go of judgement. Once established, the mindful moving practice became the access point for gaining a deeper understanding of embodiment. The discovery and understanding of mindfulness was most valuable when the dancers' intention and commitment to the truthfulness of an experience was maintained.

The dancers also quickly established that practising mindful moving was the most productive way to begin each rehearsal, to prepare them for the creative process and to find authenticity in the movement explorations. Many other areas of practice or concerns then revealed themselves—namely the unnecessary, in this context, tradition of 'polishing' or 'cleaning' of a choreographic work.

Owning the process was often a challenge for me, since my sense of authorship shifted significantly, when as a group we engaged with the concept of letting go—particularly letting go of ego. The challenge was to let go of the sense of ego while analysing the benefit of losing the ego. In allowing the dancers to 'own' their experiences, I tried not to lose my anchoring in the analyses of the work.

In one of our final meditation sessions, our teacher spoke of how it is not possible to transcend the individual self—the ego-based self—until we stop building the ego. When we stop doing that, very quickly the ego begins to crumble and deconstruct itself. When that happens, it can be a very frightening process; it is like a death and no one willingly destroys herself. According to Rockwell, the ego 'builds itself up to protect itself, creating biases in experience. Art created from this state of mind remains narrow and confused,' whereas 'egolessness, or openness to one's existence free from territorial biases, means that one is unencumbered and works freely and dynamically with energy, space and one's existence free environment' (Rockwell 1989: 189). The dancers also found that in engaging with 'egolessness,' they were able to be more present. The teachings and engagement of 'egolessness' created further understanding of the meditation principles and had a positive impact on the creative process.

Understanding Judgement and Honesty

I consciously set out to create a choreographic work in a way that would enable me to understand my habitual choreographic methods through a process of non-doing. In allowing these choreographic techniques to surface in my consciousness, I was able to observe them and make decisions about their relevance and applicability, rather than rely on them as givens. I was interested in what embodiment meant in this context. I was not seeking to make the dancers 'more' or 'less' embodied; rather, I wanted to see if the attention to embodiment provided either insights to, or a different kind of, experience of creativity in relation to choreography. The experience of judgement initially appeared as a strong challenge for the dancers and the process itself, but as we progressed, this concept had a positive impact on the creation of the work and remained as a continual checking-in point and place of growth.

Daw Thynn Thynn, a medical doctor and dharma teacher, stresses that 'letting go of beliefs, doctrines, gurus, ideals and judgements is extremely difficult, because one holds them very dear to oneself,' and that 'they become one's possessions, like material wealth and power, and then one is not free and does not proceed further' (1995: para. 3). Thynn Thynn states that achieving freedom within the self requires only two things: 'a silent mind and an open heart' (1995: para. 6). Through the experiences of the meditation practice, the dancers began to find this openness from letting go, which in turn encouraged a greater sense of embodiment and was one of the most valuable themes discovered from the research process.

The meditation teacher also spoke of Satori, which is a realization that is small or great, a flash of insight, something that stops you and brings you to stillness. When experiencing moments of clarity, when suddenly we understand something that we have been struggling with, something changes. This often comes from a moment of stillness, and something arises from the self, which is this Satori or realization. The difficulty is allowing these moments of insight to take hold, allowing them to change us. We were encouraged to remember that whatever comes up in meditation or elsewhere, if we do not sit with it, and allow ourselves to stop and look at it, then it does not have the power to change us. This is the benefit of the power of any kind of stillness practice. The more that we can be still with some kind of realization, the more it has the ability to do something in our lives.

For the dancers, a sense of greater presence came from these moments of stillness. These realizations were first felt in the meditation experiences and were then transferred to movement. The practice of stillness also had an impact on the structure of the choreographed work; moments of stillness allowed for sections of the work to shift in energy or dynamic. We also utilized stillness to allow for moments of 'group listening' or to have time to have the impact of a previous section of the work to settle.

Learning to judge less was a significant development in the process and had an impact on the dancers' ways of working. In one rehearsal, Tara spoke of how they were all worried about judging each other and said that she had a real sense of self-doubt. Tara also discussed in her first interview how the notion of right and wrong comes into play a lot for her in creative processes and how it would create freedom if she had less judgement. Tara reflected on her early meditation experiences in her journal:

An inundation of distractions—a shock to realise how full my mind is of things which cannot be dealt with at that point in time. My body was resistant to the procedure at first … itches, pains … but I managed to focus my mind on accepting those distractions and resisting the urge to do anything about them. Nevertheless, the mind often was concerned about 'doing the task' correctly. Am I sitting right? How should I be thinking about my distractions?

Katy also expressed that she hoped she would become less judgemental as she was always comparing herself to others, rather than reflecting on whether what she was doing was valid. Katy noted this in her journal:

> The start of rehearsal was very open, and I was improvising with quite a carefree manner about 'coming back to centre.'[12] Once we had to set material though, I felt as though my brain went into shut down. I couldn't move away from the most basic notion that thoughts draw you away and bring you back and all I was doing was reaching away from my body and bringing arms into my chest. Then I just started panicking, so I was at a loss. It brought up a lot of things. Firstly, should we be judging ourselves when we create movement if it is coming from a truthful response to the exploration? What it looks like should not necessarily be part of the equation, as it usually would be. I need to try and retain as much as possible that anything I do and put together is 'right' in the same way that there is no right or wrong way to do the sitting. Currently, I'm being too judgemental of myself in relation to what the others are creating, when this really doesn't matter and will only stifle my natural responses. It is not about doing it right; it is about accepting what is there.

Honesty in the movement explorations was very important to the dancers throughout the creative process and was a concept that continued to grow. The dancers felt they had to be truer to the investigations in this process than they would be in another project.

Tara questioned in one rehearsal, 'How can this "magic" and truth of improvisation be kept when creating something and refining it ... [when] the elements of judgement/right and wrong start to enter—contradictory to values of meditative practice?' Katy likewise reflected in her journal by writing:

> It seems to be like a ritual, these [rehearsal] sessions. A precious space in which we explore, discuss, refine, similar to the way we do the sittings. There is definitely truthfulness to this process, an exploration that I haven't experienced in such depth before. We questioned how true we were being if we were trying to purposely make things happen between us, rather than letting them occur naturally. Can you ever escape personal judgement when setting material? Is it possible to entirely let go? The more you return to movement, does it become more truthful as you explore it, or does it lose something?

As the priority towards truth and sensing developed, so did the material. This concept developed into a checking-in point for the process, as a sense of knowing. And this checking-in point developed a sense of ritual as Katy mentioned, a way of always coming back to the posture, the breath and honesty of the movement explorations which continually supported their experiential understanding of embodiment.

Rethinking Myself in the Role of Choreographer-as-Researcher

As the choreographic process developed, I began to focus more intently on the dancers' engagement and their insights, and my personal progress became less important because the meditation teachings shifted my way of viewing and directing. I began to be less interested in myself and my ego and relinquished concern and the need to 'gain' something artistically from the process, although I maintained a focus from an artist/researcher point of view.

Drawing on elements of the realist and confessional tale writing styles, I wrote my own version of an impressionist tale, to provide a personal perspective of the performance of *dharmakaya* by drawing on the dancers' reflections and my own views of the work from the position of observer of both the live and recorded performance. Through the practices learned, they were able to articulate their impressions of performing the work. The dancers gained an ability to be embodied and mindful while executing the choreographed movement and most importantly maintained the ability to discuss it later. They talked of being aware of what came before in the work while remaining present, and of how listening to the space and to each other created a wholeness in the work. The dancers also spoke about their intention, that of 'being present.' After the final rehearsal and before the performance, the dancers reflected on how they viewed the work and the space. This discussion was important: the dancers were able to articulate how they experienced the work and to listen to each other's formed impressions:

Katy: There are times when the space clears and you see what is left behind, and there are other times when repeated patterns come back and you are resetting what the traces had left behind …

Lucille: That moment of listening, you take everything with you … when you run, you take the whole side of the room with you.

Daisy: It is like you grab it and pull it, like a curtain trailing behind you; you are the space.

Tara: There are moments when the space is intimidating [...] when I do the 'cutting,'[13] for example, [...] you see the space and think, 'how am I going to reach the end of that?' [...] It is an extraordinary feeling. The space is the fifth person in the work.

Daisy spoke about how, in the meditation sittings, she looked at one spot on the floor and she blurred that spot and opened her focus to the peripheral. For her, that was the experience of having people watching; she was still aware that they were there, while remaining present in herself. Daisy's thoughts have some continuity with Rockwell's thesis on meditation:

> There is a sense of a general vision rather than focused attention, yet the precision of the mindfulness is not lost […] someone costumed at a carnival, holding out in front of himself a teaspoon of water that he must not spill as he walks through the crowd. One is both mindful of the spoon and yet completely aware of the surrounding environment.
>
> (1989: 189)

An overall sense of heightened awareness gained from the meditation teachings and the application of them within the dance-making was experienced by the dancers in performance and by me in the role of the choreographer-as-researcher. What we came to realize was that the work was not about trying to replicate a state found in meditative practice, which is concerned with the noticing, and through this noticing the 'putting away' of unnecessary distracting thoughts (i.e. the attempt to clear the mind). Rather, it was about the practice running alongside the creation and performance of *dharmakaya*, as a means to support sharpness of focus on the physical task at hand and to improve clarity in sensing and understanding relations—to body, to space and to others. It was not about 'clearing the mind,' but rather allowing relevant information to flourish in the mind and the imagination—therefore, this information could become clearly present in the body. The dancers identified that they could become more 'present' as a closer connection between mind and body developed. They noticed a growth in their personal sense of embodiment within other work, and believed this supported a clearer sense of personal physical expression. I had hoped the project would make me a better choreographer. What I have discovered is that meditation can be integrated with, and importantly, can enhance the choreographic process for both the dancers and choreographer. Consequently, it may have made me a 'better' choreographer or director, but not in the way that I had imagined. As Tusa states, 'Creative innovation is vital to the process of understanding ourselves, of seeing the world differently as it presents itself anew, of presenting novel propositions about the way we see, hear, look and conceptualize' (2004: 7). For me, this process has encouraged me to view my choreographic world from a different perspective, positively shifting my way of working. It was no longer relevant to 'fix' movement with arbitrary suggestions. I also had to let go of the need to build the 'ego.' I now know how to engage with the dancers and propose scenarios that encourage presence and creativity simultaneously.

The focus of the choreographic process was not only situated in the sharing of creative ideas, but was also located in the collective experiential exploration of presence. A deeper collaboration meant that the findings from the research study have been more transformative and have presented lasting change in those who participated.[14] Foundational values were established, leading to a shared understanding, which was manifested through language, practice and performance.

Part Three

Meditation, Dance and Spirituality

Naomi's project provided her and her dancers with a focused period of exploration into how meditation might influence the dance-making process. Situated within a dance training institution, the project addressed the interface between established dance pedagogy and meditation, and was designed to investigate the impact on the development of a performance in a traditional proscenium arch theatre. As with many projects that are ethnographic in orientation, her dialogic process meant that the work was bound to be unfinished; returning to the data continues to reveal more insights and opens up further lines of enquiry.

In documenting the experiences of the dancers, Naomi constructed a series of 'tales', incorporating the dancers' own spoken and written reflections. These tales revealed how the dancers assimilated the teachings of Zen meditation, influencing not only their dancing but also how they described their experiences in the studio and in performance. The dancers talked about a new sense of responsibility for their actions, a new found receptivity, and a deep trust in the process.

Lucille talked of the contrasting experiences of being both deeply embodied and in 'herself' while she simultaneously 'steps out completely of herself' as a way of opening her awareness and allowing herself to be vulnerable. Her journal entry reflected further on this:

> Being present, I think is a feeling that I had during the whole process, and because I identified it, I now can accentuate it during my dance practice. This is what the process brought to me overall. I think what we call 'mindful moving' is what I was taught to do and to engage with when I was taught contemporary dance [as a child]. Although I had never been able to put a word on that and to analyse it as clearly as I do now, this is what the process gave to me, which also allows me to now accentuate that presence and play with it, try to capture it somehow which is challenging, fascinating and enriching.

As they moved towards performance, the dancers reflected on the experience of taking the work into the theatrical space. Talking together, they were able to discuss and share their impressions of this part of the process. Daisy commented in discussion after the performance; 'it is about constantly finding. It is not about the movement but what the movement creates [...] and what we leave behind and find again and find for ourselves.' Lucille offered, 'when I stand, I listen to the space, listen to your steps, it makes me scan the space, the space is vast.'

Post-performance, the dancers reflected on their experiences of performing and commented on what the experience was for them. In her journal, Tara asked:

> Did we come *out* of our lived experience of the movement because of a desire or habit to 'perform' or project? My response would be no, I had enough internal stimuli for the movement (e.g. the colouring, the imprinting, the energy being created between

someone else/the group), that I could focus almost purely on these things without overly 'coming out of myself' (although of course there were fleeting moments of concern for aesthetic and audience opinion). The movement's starting points and lived motivations were ingrained and inherent within it, so for me it became practically impossible to lose these on the day.

Neither Naomi nor the dancers specifically discuss spirituality as part of their experience, but in dancing and working through challenges together, a sharing of thought and language began to emerge. The dancers were encouraged to articulate their experiences, not just within their dancing but also in the relationship between moving and speaking, and moving and writing. It is this connection between moving and reflecting through the written and spoken word that indicates a spiritual connection for the dancers in the work.

Significantly, the dancers noticed a change in their capacity for understanding their relationships to others, both in personal and dance contexts, and they were able to register emotional responses to others more clearly. The dancers discussed how they felt that it was very important to be a group of four, in order to be able to exchange and understand their individual processes through working together and also to witness how their own identities were established and embodied in relation to the practice.

None spoke about their participation as a 'personal search to connect with the sacred' (Kraus, 2009, as cited in Williamson 2010: 39), but the project promoted intense connections between them, and supported each individual dancer's deepening connection with their own lived experience as well as a heightened awareness of the context in which they were working and moving. As demonstrated by Tara's journal entry, the dancers did not so much seek for an experience that took them 'out of themselves,' but one which enabled them to attend to their dancing with great care, which then allowed them to articulate the lived moment more vividly. What was evident was a developing sense of wholeness, unity and inter-connection; which can be linked to spirituality (Williamson 2010: 49).

The project asked questions of how to integrate mindfulness into the training of dance artists and choreographers. The positive outcomes could argue for meditation training to be incorporated into contemporary dance training in order to augment performance presence and to generate stronger collaborative and choreographic works. Importantly, situated within an elite dance training institution, the project reveals how meditation can support mainstream practice by creating a bridge between didactic and somatic approaches to dance-making. Naomi's project has demonstrated how the practice of meditation can provide a unique and valuable understanding of embodiment through the integration of mindfulness, as well as providing a choreographic methodology that encourages reflection and analysis as an ongoing supportive process. Incorporating meditation, while not a somatic practice in itself, thereby offers a valuable support for somatic movement education by providing a preparation for the dancer, to be in a state of readiness, open and attuned to her own body/mind experience.

There are no immediate plans to repeat the project, but Naomi, as faculty member of Trinity Laban, believes that its outcomes have implications for the institution's curriculum and pedagogical methods. The dancers responded well to being introduced to a practice that provided space to question and reflect on their body-based practices, to access a different state of being, to focus on their own subjectivity and which they perceived as having longer-term benefits. This initial project might well stimulate discussion about the balance between different learning modalities, and bring more attention to transformative practices such as meditation, which could both enhance and support a broader somatic movement education and which help dancers to flourish. In time, it may have wider influence, drawing more attention to the role that meditation can play in helping to dissolve the dualisms of body and mind that tend to exclude mental disciplines from the dance studio. In this project, it was clear that meditation promotes a strong sense of embodiment and awakens the body to the mind—and the mind to the body—to offer new and productive connections for all those involved, and in doing so, new expressions of spirituality.

References

Alfaro, N. (2006), 'Mind your body: Meditation – How stillness improves performance skills', *Dance Magazine*, November, http://findarticles.com/p/articles/mi_m1083/is_1180/ai_n27032249/. Accessed 12 January 2011.

Austin, J. (1999), *Zen and the Brain: Toward an Understanding of Meditation and Consciousness*, Cambridge, MA: MIT Press.

Edinborough, C. (2011), 'Developing decision-making skills for performance through the practice of mindfulness in somatic training', *Theatre, Dance and Performance Training*, 2:1, pp. 18–33.

Foster, S. L. (1997), 'Dancing bodies', in J. C. Desmond (ed.), *Meaning in Motion: New Cultural Studies of Dance*, Durham, NC: Duke University, pp. 235–257.

Fraleigh, S. (1999), *Dancing into Darkness: Butoh, Zen, and Japan*, Pittsburgh, PA: University of Pittsburgh Press.

Green, J. (1993), 'Fostering creativity through movement and body awareness practices: A postpositivist investigation into the relationship between somatics and the creative process', Doctoral dissertation, Columbus, OH: Ohio State University. Available from Dissertation Abstracts International, UMI No. 9411953.

Hanna, T. (1980), *The Body of Life: Creating New Pathways for Sensory Awareness and Fluid Movement*, Rochester, VT: Healing Arts Press.

Kabat-Zinn, J. (1990), *Full Catastrophe Living: Using the Wisdom of Your Body and Mind to Face Stress, Pain, and Illness*, New York, NY: Dell Publishing.

Leggett, T. (1978), *Zen and the Ways*, Boulder, CO: Shambhala.

McPherson, T. (1974), *Philosophy and Religious Belief*, London: Hutchinson University Press.

Mangalo, B. (1993), 'The practice of recollection', in S. Bercholz and S. Chodzin Kohn (eds), *Entering the Stream: An Introduction to the Buddha and His Teachings*, Boston, MA: Shambhala, pp. 130–140.

Monk, M. (2004), 'The art of being present', http://www.thebuddhadharma.com/issues/2004/spring/forumintro.htm. Accessed 8 January 2011.

Nalanda Translation Committee (1993), 'The heart sutra', in S. Bercholz and S. Chodzin Kohn (eds), *Entering the Stream: An Introduction to the Buddha and His Teachings*, Boston, MA: Shambhala, pp. 153–156.

Rockwell, I. N. (1989), 'Dance: Creative process from a contemplative point of view', in L. Y. Overby and J. H. Humphrey (eds), *Dance: Current Selected Research*, vol. 1, New York, NY: AMS Press, pp. 187–198.

Suzuki, S. (1993), 'Zen mind, beginner's mind', in S. Bercholz and S. Chodzin Kohn (eds), *Entering the Stream: An Introduction to the Buddha and His Teachings*, Boston, MA: Shambhala, pp. 227–239.

Thynn Thynn, D. (1995), *Living Meditation, Living Insight: The Path of Mindfulness in Daily Life*, Barre, MA: Buddha Dharma Education Association.

Tierney, G. (2007), *Opportunities in Holistic Health Care Careers*, New York, NY: McGraw-Hill.

Trungpa, C. (1976), *The Foundations of Mindfulness*, vol. 5, Boulder, CO: Shambhala.

Tusa, J. (2004), *On Creativity*, London, UK: Methuen Publishing.

van Maanen, J. (1988), *Tales of the Field: On Writing Ethnography*, Chicago, IL: University of Chicago Press.

Williamson, A. (2010), 'Reflections and theoretical approaches to the study of spiritualities within the field of somatic movement dance education', *Journal of Dance & Somatic Practices*, 2:1, pp. 35–61.

Yoo, J. (2007), 'Moving ki in inner and outer space: A Korean perspective on acting process in the water station', *Contemporary Theatre*, 17:1, pp. 81–96.

Zarilli, P. (2002), *Acting (Re)Considered: A Theoretical and Practical Guide*, Worlds of Performance series, Abingdon, UK: Routledge.

Zenji, D. (1993), 'To forget the self', in S. Bercholz and S. Chodzin Kohn (eds), *Entering the Stream: An Introduction to the Buddha and His Teachings*, Boston, MA: Shambhala, pp. 205–210.

Notes

1 The project was the principal focus for Naomi Lefebvre Sell's practice-based Ph.D. Sarah Whatley was Naomi's external supervisor.

2 Trinity Laban Conservatoire of Music and Dance, London, UK.

3 *Dharmakaya* means the 'body of reality.'

4 The project formed part of Naomi's Ph.D. by Creative Practice (Dance) titled '*dharmakaya*: An investigation into the impact of mindful meditation on dancers' creative processes in a choreographic environment.'

5 This research study was part of a literature review conducted by Kanellakos, D. and Lukas, J. 1974, titled *The Psychobiology of Transcendental Meditation, A Literature Review*, California: W.A. Benjamin.

6   Although the project was not directly concerned with Buddhist teachings, the readings provided us with a broader understanding of the connections between Zen Buddhism and Zen meditation, to support a close attention on the ideas of rediscovery through meditation, and on our own inner wisdom.

7   In the mindful moving, the dancers were encouraged to spend time being mindful in the body, staying mindful in what their experience was and not getting led away with their thoughts. During this time, the dancers tended to spend time on the floor, would then move into walking and shifting in space to eventually exhibit more full-bodied dance movement. The dancers always spent this time on their own, yet still aware of the group. The mindful movement sessions never included contact movement or overt interaction between the dancers. The meditation teacher would clap his hands to signal that this portion of the meditation session had concluded.

8   As the dancers experienced a greater sense of embodiment, they effectively became 'co-authors' of the work: they continually questioned the intention and integrity of the choices being made and had a distinct 'willingness to trust hunches.' For example, the practice of stillness had an impact on the structure of the choreographed work. The dancers and I decided to include moments of stillness to allow for sections of the work to shift either in energy or dynamic. We also utilised stillness to allow for moments of 'group listening' or to have time to allow the impact of a previous section of the work to settle.

9   All four participants gave permission to use their real names throughout my study and related publications.

10 All comments were checked and agreed with the dancers before being included in the writing.

11 We removed the practice of Yoga Nidra (often referred to as 'corpse pose' or 'deep relaxation') half way through the study, as this is not a mindful practice. The practice is to come out of your body to such a degree during this pose that you are lying like a dead thing. It is helpful to let the body die and collapse fully and let go, particularly after an intense sitting, which initially was very helpful at the beginning of our practices.

12 A named movement section in *dharmakaya*.

13 A named section in *dharmakaya*.

14 Although not originally designed to be a longitudinal study, two years on from the completion of the choreographic process, I contacted the dancers as I was curious to see if the process had had longer-term effects on them, both within their dance practice and wider life experiences. All of the dancers reported that they have carried the experience with them in some way. I asked the dancers to write down their final reflections on the research process and I constructed these writings as a final set of realist tales, which point to an impact beyond the completion of the study. The dancers reported that the meditation concepts and principles have remained with them and that exploring movement freely and integrating the concept of non-judgement remains key in their practice. The dancers continue to use mindful moving in warm-ups as a preparation for coming to a place of 'presence' within creative processes, rather than reverting to more traditional ways of warming-up.

Chapter 20

'What You Cannot Imagine': Spirituality in Akram Khan's *Vertical Road*

Jayne Stevens

I died from minerality and became vegetable;
And from vegetativeness I died and became animal
I died from animality and became man.
Then why fear disappearance through death?
Next time I shall die
Bringing forth wings and feathers like angels;
After that, soaring higher than angels—
What you cannot imagine,
I shall be that.

(Rūmī, as cited in *Vertical Road* programme note)

This poem by the 13th century Islamic poet and mystic, Jalāl al-Dīn Rūmī, formed the main programme note accompanying performances of *Vertical Road*, a full-length ensemble work by the contemporary British choreographer, Akram Khan. *Vertical Road* premiered at Curve in Leicester in September 2010 and toured internationally until December 2012. This 27-month tour saw the work performed throughout Europe (including Russia), the Middle East and Asia, both North and South America and in Australia. It is a work that proved to have global—inter-national and inter-cultural—appeal. It is also a work, as Rūmī's poem signals, in which concerns about spirituality are central. This chapter investigates the nature of the spiritual enquiry embedded in and embodied by *Vertical Road*. It does so by examining *Vertical Road* within the context of Khan's work generally and considering it in relation to aspects of contemporary spirituality. Critical appreciation of Khan's work has tended to focus on its cross-cultural significance, primarily in relation to identity politics and hybrid performance practices. This book provides an apt and timely opportunity to consider his work as a reflection on and embodiment of inter-cultural ideas, values and practices concerning spirituality.

Amanda Williamson (2010) has mapped a territory for scholarly study of contemporary spirituality and dance. In doing so, she noted the relative under-representation of such study in current Dance Studies literature. Whereas recently, some academic and professional disciplines—notably heath care, social and youth work—have afforded spirituality greater significance in both the theory and practice of their work, dance has shown relatively little interest. The locus of what interest there has been is largely in relation to dance education and participation in dance for reasons of health and well-being. Williamson suggests that the impact of secularization on many Western cultures has been to render 'sacred and spiritual dance a thing of the past, or indeed a thing/object belonging to the non-Western' (2010: 51). That a successful, contemporary, British choreographer should concern himself with the sacred and the spiritual in a direct way seems to go 'against the grain,' and indeed, this aspect of Khan's work has been largely overlooked. In this chapter, I will show how *Vertical Road* reflects some key aspects of contemporary, progressive spirituality by embodying the multicultural experiences, values and practices of its artistic collaborators and performers.

There is no singular definition of spirituality. Indeed, many contemporary texts refer to 'spiritualities' and to the pluralized nature of 'postmodern spirituality,' acknowledging the frequently individualized, personal and transmutable meanings ascribed to spirituality (Erricker and Erricker 2001; Heelas 2008).[1] It is appropriate to identify some of the themes recurrent in the many definitions and variations that are in play and that relate to the examination of *Vertical Road* that follows later.

The term 'spirituality' derives from the Latin *spiritus*, generally translated as 'breath' or 'air.' It relates to spirit as 'the animating or vital principle in man' (OED 2011) and is often expressed as a search for purpose and meaning in life. Searching and journeying are common ways of describing spiritual pursuits and aspirations. Spirituality may be said to encompass the experiences, thoughts, feelings and behaviours that arise from the search for what is sacred in life (Larson et al. 1998). Many aspects of an individual's life may be sacred or 'sacralized' by virtue of the high value and special respect afforded them. 'Virtually anything can become sacred if people view it as such. God can be considered sacred, but so can community, finding meaning and personal relationships' (Kraus 2009 in Williamson 2010: 39). Life itself may be sacred (Heelas 2008: 43). If, as Williamson puts it, 'in contemporary contexts the sacred floats freely, finding expression in variant secular activities' (2010: 42), then it is clear that spirituality, the search for the sacred, is not confined to religion.

Spirituality extends beyond traditional forms of religion, which are viewed by some as inherently authoritarian and exclusive (Lynch 2007: 23). Spirituality may afford an individual more freedom in terms of the practices, identities, experiences and relationships it legitimizes (Lynch 2007: 41). So, though religion gives expression to spirituality, it does not have a monopoly on it. Other vehicles may allow more creative expressions of spirituality. Indeed, artists may be said to practise their spirituality through their art (Heelas 2008: 43; Cobussen 2008: 42), and not least through the art of movement and dance.

Traditionally and popularly, spirituality is conceived of as dealing more or less exclusively with other worldly, transcendent, immaterial phenomena and with the pursuit of perfection. Recently, however, more emphasis has been given to the grounded, embodied and essentially human nature of spiritual practices leading to 'a spirituality, which animates and activates human beings to cope with the world rather than to inwardly escape from it' (Teilhard de Chardin in Erricker and Erricker 2001: 6). Contemporary forms of spirituality, such as progressive spirituality, advocate active engagement with the environment and society while, at the same time, resisting the secularization brought about by, for example, technology and consumerism (Lynch 2007).

Williamson suggests that progressive spirituality provides a useful paradigm for identifying broad themes in contemporary spirituality (2010: 55) and makes a persuasive case for its relevance to current dance practice—in her case, Somatic Movement Dance Education. I suggest that some of the key themes of progressive spirituality (as summarized by Lynch 2007) provide a useful framework for examining *Vertical Road*—an example of current theatrical dance performance.

Lynch suggests that progressive spirituality is emerging as a spiritual ideology with identifiable values and beliefs and the potential to unite across and beyond religious traditions (2007: 20–21). In summarizing the key tenets of progressive spirituality, Lynch is at pains to point out that these are not simply abstract ideas but aspects of a lived ideology and part of spiritual and cultural practices (2007: 41). In fact, he advocates that, 'serious scholarship on changing patterns in religion and spirituality in the West can only really proceed on the basis of careful reading of cultural products—like books, websites, magazines' (Lynch 2007: 7–8), to which I would add—and dances.

Lynch sees the fundamental tenets of progressive spirituality as organized around common assumptions about the divine, nature, humanity and religious traditions (2007: 43). He suggests that amongst religious and spiritual progressives, the divine is held to be an ineffable unity that creates and sustains an unfolding cosmos, the evolution and workings of which may be understood through scientific enquiry (Lynch 2007: 44–46). The divine, however, is not outside of this creation but within the material form and energy of the universe. Drawing ideas from quantum physics of the cosmos as an energy field, the divine is sometimes referred to as energy (Lynch 2007: 47). In this view, the divine is 'that in which all things live and move and have their being' (Lynch 2007: 48) and not a separate, removed or distant entity. It follows that every living individual has the potential to experience and to know the divine through a variety of practices. The second key feature of progressive spirituality is a general concern that the natural order—those things outside of human cultural activity but influenced by it—should be respected and cared for and that humanity should recognize the responsibilities of its role within a complex ecosystem. Thirdly, progressive spirituality views humanity as an aspect of divine life: 'in contrast to religious views of the self as inherently flawed or sinful, progressive spirituality sees the self as another manifestation of the divine intelligence and energy' (Lynch 2007: 55). A spiritual journey, therefore, is not in search of something entirely outside of oneself but also for the sacred within the self and others. This view of spirituality emphasizes the underlying connectedness of humanity and values the complexities of embodied experience. Fourthly, progressive spirituality values a range of religious traditions in so far as they share its core assumptions about the divine, nature and humanity (Lynch 2007: 61). Religious diversity is welcomed and different practices and modes of expression freely drawn upon. So, as a common ideological framework, this makes collaboration and exchange between different cultures of religious belief and spiritual practice not only possible but also desirable. With this broad ethos of progressive spirituality in mind, let me now turn to a consideration of Akram Khan's *Vertical Road*.

Vertical Road is a 70 minute ensemble performance with a specially commissioned score by Khan's long-time collaborator, the composer Nitin Sawhney. The set, an opaque plastic backdrop stretched across the full height and width of the performance space, was designed by Jesper Kongshaug (who, with Fabiana Piccioli, also designed the lighting) and Kimie Nakano (who also designed the costumes). Ruth Little was dramaturge and Farooq Chaudhry was producer. The work was made for and with a cast of eight performers reflective of the culturally interactive nature of the company: Eulalia Ayguade Farro (Spain), Konstatina Efthymiadou (Greece), Salah El Brogy (Egypt), Ahmed Khemis (Algeria/Tunisia), Young Jin Kim (South Korea), Yen-Ching Lin (Taiwan), Andrej Petrovic (Slovakia) and Paul Zivkovich (Australia).[2]

These performers brought rich, embodied resources of cultural and performance capital to the devising process—a process which they describe as inclusive, improvisational and collaborative (Zivkovich in Mackrell 2010; Farro in Jennings 2010). Khan feels that it is only by exploring the personal stories that dancers carry with them that a narrative with universal relevance can be discovered and revealed (Khan in Katrak 2011: 215). As choreographer and director, Khan builds 'on the dancer's experiences of life, of dance, of walking, of family, of the past, of the weather' (Khan in Ellis 2004). A key example of this is the role created in *Vertical Road* for and with Salah El Brogy. In 2009, Khan saw El Brogy performing in Beirut, Lebanon.[3] Khan was struck because, as he states,

> The quality of his performance—even of steps that were of little interest—drew my attention. I asked him what he was thinking of onstage, and he replied that he was not thinking of anything, simply speaking to God. It was enough for me to hire him immediately.
>
> (Khan in Boccadoro 2011)

El Brogy's embodied understanding of Sufism and of Sufi dancing, folk dance and improvisation was the impetus for a powerful and distinctive performance at the core of *Vertical Road*.

El Brogy occupies a central role of a traveller, prophet or 'searcher for truth' (Crompton 2010). Seen by reviewers as mystical and other-worldly (Boccadoro 2011) he gives performances that are visceral, urgent and imbued with the rawness that so interests Khan (Khan in Machon 2009: 113). Fellow performer, Paul Zivkovich has said of him, 'the movement and the rhythm come from a different place for Salah, and it can be seen in the performance. His eyes close and he experiences exactly what he's in, in that moment' (in Mackrell 2010) (Figure 1). El Brogy has said that on stage it is his soul rather than his body that speaks (El Brogy 2010). El Brogy is a disciple of Sufism, that branch of Islam that emphasizes inner spirituality and unity with God. Movement and dance are significant spiritual practices in Sufism, perhaps most well known as part of the sama ceremony where dance is practised as a turning prayer or meditation.

Khan's own dance background is in contemporary dance and in Kathak. From the age of seven, Khan trained, and still continues his own daily practice, in Kathak. This classical

Figure 1: Salah El Brogy in *Vertical Road*. Photo: Laurent Ziegler.

dance form developed mostly in Northern India, where it incorporated elements of both Hindu mythology and Islamic philosophy (Iyer 1997). To learn Kathak means to learn 'the philosophies and heritage of India' (Anwara Khan, Khan's mother, in Smith 2008: 81) and requires an understanding of Indian spiritual and religious ideas. Indeed, for many dancers, Kathak is as much a spiritual as an artistic practice (see Shah 1998). Khan describes Kathak as a 'mental, physical and spiritual approach' in which 'the physical training of the body is the final necessity' (Khan in Haroon 2010).

Khan continues to perform Kathak as a solo artist but also explores the interface between contemporary dance and Kathak (Norridge 2010: 416) mostly in ensemble and collaborative works that are generally viewed as contemporary performance and which have contributed significantly to the development of British dance (Mitra 2009: 54). Khan has said, 'when I put my bells on there's a sense of spirituality, which is important to me. Classical is me in search of the spiritual, and contemporary is me searching for science, destroying and taking things apart' (Khan in Jaggi 2010). Increasingly these interests, in the spiritual and the scientific, are brought together in his contemporary work. For example, in *Kaash* (2002) Khan and his collaborators explored scientific ideas about the nature of the universe, including dark matter and black holes, by focusing on Shiva, the Hindu God of creation and destruction (Burt 2004a; Sanders 2004: 7). Burt argues that *Kaash* expressed 'superhuman divine imagery' not through traditional performative practices but in Khan's negotiation of 'Indian and Western movement ideologies' (Burt 2004b: 105). Such cross-cultural negotiation has been much discussed in connection with Khan's work, especially with regard to his movement vocabulary, movement quality and aesthetics—these being 'the unintended consequence of learning two physical systems which became overwritten in his muscles' (Sanders 2008: 60). *Vertical Road* also demonstrates elements of the hybrid movement language that Khan has developed from the 'confusion,' as he puts it (Perron 2008: 39), of contemporary and Kathak training: elements such as spins and twists, especially of the upper body; fluid use of arms and hands which spiral and carve space about the head and shoulders; complex rhythms with exact timing; sudden and statuesque stillness. I suggest, however, that more prominent in *Vertical Road* is a negotiation of cultural values and world views especially in relation to aspects of Eastern (Islamic) and Western (Christian) spiritual traditions. Khan has said, 'Classical to me is clarity where the boundaries are clear and visible. Contemporary is chaotic' (in Vasudevan 2002: 18). It is the chaos that contemporary dance affords that provides rich opportunities to explore the dichotomy and ambiguity to be found in, for example, the material and immaterial, life and death, past and present, self and others. This is what Khan seems interested to do in *Vertical Road*.

At the start of *Vertical Road* is a sort of prologue in which the figure of El Brogy is just visible behind the opaque backdrop (Figure 2). To sounds reminiscent of softly running water, he strikes the backdrop as if trying to arouse the seven figures sitting crossed-legged, heads bowed to the ground, in front of the scrim. El Brogy draws large, spiralling circles and writes in a cursive (perhaps Arabic) script on the scrim. As rumbling sounds build to a threatening crescendo, his attempts to communicate with those on the other side of the

Figure 2: *Vertical Road.* Photo: Laurent Ziegler.

scrim become increasingly urgent. Perhaps in frustration at the lack of response, he slams his head against the scrim and suddenly all is dark and silent. As the sound of wind whistles eerily and light returns, El Brogy is seen on the stage space where the seven dancers are now standing motionless. He gently examines them and the seven stone tablets which are standing on end at the front of the stage. As he tumbles the tablets, which clatter sequentially to the ground, a metronome begins to tick and the dancers jerk violently into action, clouds of dust rising from their hair and clothes (Figure 3).

This begins a long, mostly unison, ritualistic dance to Sawhney's driven, percussive score. The seven dancers feverishly wipe away the dust clinging to their clothes and bodies, strike the ground, twist their torsos and thrust out their arms as if struggling to free themselves from unseen bonds (Figure 4).

El Brogy is sometimes drawn into their insistent, martial-arts like movement, seeming to absorb its dynamic into his own throbbing, percussive action. At other times, he seems to pull the other dancers to him; a tall, commanding figure around which the often earth-bound dancers gather (Figure 5).

They crawl and scrabble, insect-like around his feet, beating their bodies causing dust to fly. At one point, in their midst, El Brogy begins to spin, one palm turned upwards while, with the fingers of his other hand, he beckons as if inviting an ethereal force into himself on

Figure 3: *Vertical Road.* Photo: Laurent Ziegler.

Figure 4: *Vertical Road.* Photo: Laurent Ziegler.

Figure 5: *Vertical Road.* Photo: Laurent Ziegler.

behalf of the group. Some critics have likened this to *The Rite of Spring* (Newman 2010; Gray 2010), and indeed the sense of a communal and powerful ritual is overwhelming. Having risen to life from the dry, dusty earth, the dancers seem to embody the notion of divinity as pure energy, coursing through individual bodies and holding them together in a vortex of movement (Figure 6).

This energy that both animates and connects is also apparent in the following section of *Vertical Road.* As the force, which seems to have driven the group, gradually ebbs away, the sound of wind howling through an empty landscape returns and the dancers are left standing quietly. El Brogy makes to leave. As he does so, the hem of his long gown is caught, and he is stopped by one of the female dancers, Konstatina Efthymiadou. The vignette created brings to mind the incident related in the gospel according to Matthew of a woman who, in a crowd of people, caught hold of the hem of Jesus' cloak in order to be healed (Matthew 9:20 RSV). In *Vertical Road*, this action initiates a trio in which El Brogy and Efthymiadou are joined by Paul Zivkovich and explore ways in which their actions, sometimes deliberately but often unwittingly, affect one another. The outcome is sometimes playful and mischievous but at other times manipulative and disturbing. So, a seemingly careless wave of El Brogy's hand sends a violent shudder through Zivkovich's body even though they are some way apart from each other. Khan seems to be expressing the essential connectedness of humanity, a concern he has voiced in interviews about

Figure 6: *Vertical Road*. Photo: Laurent Ziegler.

Vertical Road in which he has described the work as a 'search of what it might mean to be connected' (Newman 2010). He has posed himself the question, 'with the increased global communication that technology has given us, do we actually feel connected?' (Khan 2010). What connects El Brogy, Efthymiadou and Zivkovich is their awareness of and intention to animate each other. An unseen force appears to operate between them, making them inescapably part of each other's world.

Khan has also said that *Vertical Road* is about spirituality rather than religion (Watson 2010), and nowhere is this clearer than in a section in which two duets occupy the stage at the same time and so are juxtaposed. Two male dancers, El Brogy and Ahmed Khemis, are drawn to the stone tablets which might represent religious books; repositories of spiritual authority external to and existing independently of the performers. The dancers handle them carefully and reverently. They become increasingly fascinated by and fixated with the tablets. Khemis sits crossed-legged, cradling a tablet lovingly and rocking to and fro. At the same time a male and female dancer, Andrej Petrovic and Eulalia Ayguade Farro, begin a duet, at firstly courtly but then increasingly intimate, that takes them slowly around the edge of the stage space. They appear completely engrossed with one another, rolling in intricate and gentle embraces (Figure 7).

Figure 7: Andrej Petrovic and Eulalia Ayguade Farro in *Vertical Road.* Photo: Laurent Ziegler.

Khan describes this as a love duet and specifically as ghazal (Khan 2011b). Ghazal is a poetic form now found in many languages but originating in Arabic verse. Sufi poets, including Rūmī, composed ghazals. It became a popular form in Urdu (a language of Northern India), and so the concept of ghazal was incorporated into Kathak. The central theme of ghazal is love. The intended recipient of love may be divine or mortal; the love expressed may be spiritual or sexual. The two are often ambiguous. For Khan, the two meanings, one referring to a lover and one referring to God, were what interested him, that and 'by forming a physical, intimate relationship with another person, God existed' (Khan 2011b). As Petrovic and Farro's delicate love duet unfolds, the precious tablets appear to be exerting their own force upon El Brogy and Khemis. The two men now pass the tablets between them, each contact seeming to electrify the dancers, sending ripples through their bodies and throwing them into a complex series of spins and falls (Figure 8).

The men are now completely focused on the tablets, which perhaps encapsulate divine revelation, while Petrovic and Farro are entirely involved with each other, seeking the divine within themselves and each other. A beautiful, rhythmical melody with soaring Arabic voices envelops both duets. Khan seems to be suggesting parallel pathways to spiritual

Figure 8: Ahmed Khemis and Salah El Brogy in *Vertical Road*. Photo: Laurent Ziegler.

understanding: one through embodied, sensuous experience and one through engagement with disembodied revelation.

Both duets having reached a climax—the participants experiencing revelation in their different ways, darkness falls. Sounds reminiscent of rumbling thunder and the crackling of an electric storm are heard, and light flashes, illuminating the motionless dancers. Gradually, light floods the stage. To music that seems to emerge from sounds of gently babbling water, Yen-Ching Lin draws the dancers into a glorious section of continuous, fluid, harmonious movement. Together the dancers trace circles, spirals and waves within and around their bodies and through the space. They spin in ways distinctly referencing the turning meditations of Mevlevi *samazens*—head slightly tilted, arms out-stretched, right palm facing upwards to receive divine grace and left palm facing downwards to channel it to the earth. Their long, full skirts billow around them. The patterning of the spinning dancers is balanced and symmetrical, bringing to mind the orderly orbiting of celestial bodies. Both movement and music pulsate with the rhythmical ebb and flow of a life force in which the dancers now appear to be completely immersed—the dancers, that is, apart from El Brogy. He sits downstage, outside of this life-affirming dance, quietly examining the stone tablets. One by one, whirling and twisting, the dancers leave the stage as if spun out of view

472

Figure 9: *Vertical Road.* Photo: Laurent Ziegler.

by centrifugal force. El Brogy is left alone. Eventually he approaches the opaque backdrop through which the ghostly figures of the other dancers can be made out gradually fading into the distance. As El Brogy stands before the scrim, water begins to drip and then roll down it. When he reaches out to touch it, the scrim falls—revealing for a moment a dark void behind, then leaving the stage in darkness with only the sound of gently falling water (Figure 9).

The vision of spiritual journeying that *Vertical Road* opens up is not the straightforward stairway to heaven that some reviewers might have us believe. Instead, *Vertical Road* is a complex, eclectic and nuanced exploration of contemporary spirituality. There are no simple, spiritual certainties here. For example, the central character in *Vertical Road*, as portrayed by Salah El Brogy, is on a journey—but a journey that is not without its complications and interruptions. For much of the piece, his attention is wrested back and forth between his fellow dancers, the inanimate stone tablets and his own self-absorbed, idiosyncratic movement. He seems uncertain as to where salvation lies—in relationships with others, in intellectual study, deep within himself or beyond all of these. Even the start and end points of his journey are ambiguous. He seems to be the catalyst that pulls the other dancers from their dry, dusty resting place and propels them into action. Eventually, he is abandoned as these companions pass behind the plastic scrim and fade from sight. His final gesture seems to bring the world crashing down while at the same time releasing a downpour of water, symbolic of bringing new life to what was once parched earth.

At play in *Vertical Road* are some of the ideas characteristic of progressive spirituality that were identified earlier. A particular idea is the manifestation of the divine as energy that vitalizes the universe and all life within it and, as a consequence, the search for divinity in the complexities of embodied social and sensual experience. Khan has said that he is interested in how human beings access the spiritual and that whereas we usually look up to see God (Khan in Katrak 2011: 218) his own sense of the divine comes through his interactions with others (Khan in Swoboda 2012). The Rūmī poem, which forms the programme note for *Vertical Road*, speaks not only of transcendence and transformation but also of a cycle of earthy, material existence. Lynch puts it particularly well when he writes that progressive spirituality is 'not so much a striving towards a state as yet unachieved, as it is a process of learning to recognize the true spiritual condition in which we are already living' (2007: 59). This seems to me to epitomize *Vertical Road*.

The spiritual condition that *Vertical Road* seeks to understand is born of an increasingly interconnected world—a world that the Akram Khan Company, as a transnational organization, exemplifies. Thus, the creative team responsible for *Vertical Road* came from Europe, Asia and the Middle East. The production was sponsored by Colas, an international construction company based in France, and co-produced by cultural organizations in Abu Dhabi, Europe and Canada. In *Vertical Road*, Khan and his collaborators draw on practices and iconography from Islamic, Christian and secular worlds to explore the nature of spiritual aspiration in a globalized, technologically enhanced world. In tracing the origins of *Vertical Road*, Khan relates an incident in Sydney, Australia when he was elbowed aside in a queue for taxis. He explains,

> I got into another taxi and felt like hearing my father's voice so I telephoned him, something I never do on tour although we're close. As I hung up after a casual chat, in Bengali, the language we use at home, the taxi stopped and the driver asked, astonishingly in Bengali, whether my father was from Algichar, a small village in Bangladesh. Only 200 people in the world could know that and 195 of them live there, the other four being my parents, my sister and me, leaving the only one other person—a taxi driver at midnight on the other side of the world.
>
> (Khan in Boccadoro 2011)

The incident led Khan to reflect on whether this unlikely reunion was mere chance or an intervention by 'taxi-snatchers who were really angels in disguise' (Khan in Boccadoro 2011). It exemplifies Khan's concern with what inspires people to connect with each other. This concern is apparent throughout *Vertical Road* and it is fundamental to Khan's artistic endeavour and his practice. It underpins the creative collaborations that Khan acknowledges as integral to his journey as an artist (Khan 2011a). Speaking of collaboration in relation to his work generally and *Vertical Road* in particular, Khan describes a turning point in the process of making work when,

> There is just 'us', or 'we' left behind, a collection of artists, of different disciplines, different languages, different cultures, different education, but we are all in the same room, in silence, and all our passionate gestures and fierce negotiations, have come to a standstill, and with it, a sense that we all want a single 'truth', that this journey together has to end up giving birth to our creation [...] that somehow, we as individuals, are like small jigsaw pieces, but together, we form a single, but powerful and larger fuller picture.
>
> (Khan 2011a)

This eloquent description of the reality of a collective, artistic enterprise could equally be an iteration of the spiritual condition identified by contemporary spiritual progressives. It acknowledges the struggle involved in finding meaning but also celebrates the possibility of doing so through mutual identity based on shared concerns, responsibilities and aspirations.

Like the Rūmī verse that contributed to its inspiration, *Vertical Road* is a poetic and at times mystical reflection on our spiritual condition. Through a symbolic journey pursued in dance, it reveals the spirituality of seeking that questions current attitudes to self, others and the divine.

Acknowledgements

I am indebted to Akram Khan and members of the Akram Khan Company for the generous way in which they allowed me to interview them and observe rehearsals and for providing recordings of *Vertical Road*.

References

Boccadoro, P. (2011), 'Akram Khan: The making of Vertical Road', *Culturekiosque*, 6 April, http://www.culturekiosque.com/dance. Accessed 16 August 2011.

Burt, R. (2004a), 'Contemporary dance and the performance of multicultural identities', http://www.akramkhancompany.net/html/akram_essay.php?id=15. Accessed 2 November 2011.

—— (2004b), 'Kaash: Dance, sculpture and the visual', *Visual Culture in Britain*, 5:2, pp. 93–108.

Cobussen, M. (2008), *Thresholds: Rethinking Spirituality through Music*, Aldershot, UK: Ashgate Publishing.

Crompton, S. (2010), 'Vertical Road', *The Telegraph*, 7 October, http://www.telegraph.co.uk/culture/culturecritics/sarahcrompton. Accessed 8 October 2010.

El Brogy, S. (2010), 'International Dance Festival Birmingham Interview', http://www.youtube.com/watch?v=Db3EAJqcKGc. Accessed 25 October 2011.

Ellis, S. (2004), 'Dance was about breaking all the rules that were set in my body', *The Guardian*, 22 April, http://www.guardian.co.uk/culture/2004/apr/22/samanthaellis.guesteditors/print. Accessed 24 October 2011.

Erricker, C. and Erricker, J. (eds) (2001), *Contemporary Spiritualities: Social and Religious Contexts*, London, UK: Continuum.

Gray, J. (2010), 'Dance scene: United Kingdom: Vertical Road', *The Dancing Times*, 101:1203, p. 52.

Haroon, L. (2010), 'Rhythm of heritage', *Gulf News*, 19 February, http://gulfnews.com/arts-entertainment. Accessed 2 November 2011.

Heelas, P. (2008), *Spiritualities of Life: New Age Romanticism and Consumptive Capitalism*, Oxford, UK: Blackwell Publishing.

Iyer, A. (1997), 'South Asian dance: The traditional/classical idioms', *Choreography and Dance*, 4, pp. 5–17.

Jaggi, M. (2010), 'A life in dance: Akram Khan', *The Guardian*, 25 September, http://www.guardian.co.uk/culture/2010/sep/27/akram-khan-dance-life/print. Accessed 24 October 2011.

Jennings, L. (2010), 'Akram Khan: Despite the chaos, we're all connected', *The Guardian*, 12 September, http://www.guardian.co.uk/stage/2010/sep/12/akram-khan-vertical-road-jennings. Accessed 14 September 2010.

Katrak, K. (2011), *Contemporary Indian Dance: New Creative Choreography in India and the Diaspora*, Studies in International Performance series, Basingstoke, UK: Palgrave Macmillan.

Khan, A. (2010), Interview with Jayne Stevens, Curve Theatre, Leicester, 15 September.

—— (2011a), 'Keynote address: The art of collaboration', *Congress of The International Society for the Performing Arts*, Times Center, New York, 11 January, http://www.akramkhancompany.net/html/akram_essay.php?id=14. Accessed 2 November 2011.

—— (2011b), Interview with Jayne Stevens, Sadlers Wells Theatre, London, 1 November.

Larson, D., Swyers, J. P. and McCullough, M. E. (eds) (1998), *Scientific Research on Spirituality and Health: A Consensus Report*, Rockville, MD: National Institute for Healthcare Research.

Lynch, G. (2007), *The New Spirituality: An Introduction to Progressive Belief in the Twenty-First Century*, London, UK: I.B. Tauris.

Machon, J. (2009), 'Akram Khan: The mathematics of sensation: The body as site/sight/cite and source', in J. Machon (ed.), *(Syn)aesthetics: Redefining Visceral Performance*, Basingstoke, UK: Palgrave Macmillan.

Mackrell, F. (2010), 'Akram Khan's Vertical Road', *ArtsHub*, 29 September, http://www.artshub.com.au/au/newsPrint.asp?sId=182476. Accessed 1 October 2010.

Mitra, R. (2009), 'Dancing embodiment, theorising space: Exploring the "third space" in Akram Khan's Zero Degrees', in A. Lepecki and J. Joy (eds), *Planes of Composition: Dance, Theory and the Global*, London, UK: Seagull Books, pp. 40–63.

Newman, B. (2010), 'Reviews: Akram Khan company', *Dance Magazine*, 84:12, pp. 86–87.

Norridge, Z. (2010), 'Dancing the multicultural conversation? Critical responses to Akram Khan's work in the context of pluralist poetics', *Forum for Modern Language Studies*, 46:4, pp. 415–430.

OED (2011), Oxford English Dictionary, 3rd online edition, http://www.oed.com. Accessed 30 November 2011.

Perron, W. (2008), 'Global dance: East and West meet in the body of Akram Khan', *Dance Magazine*, 82:11, pp. 38–40.

Sanders, L. (2004), *Akram Khan's Rush: Creative Insights*, Alton, UK: Dance Books.

——— (2008), 'Akram Khan's Ma (2004): An essay in hybridisation and productive ambiguity', in J. Lansdale (ed.), *Decentring Dancing Texts: The Challenge of Interpreting Dances*, Basingstoke, UK: Palgrave Macmillan.

Shah, P. (1998), 'Transcending gender in the performance of kathak', *Dance Research Journal*, 30:2, pp. 2–17.

Smith, L. (2008), '"In-between spaces:" An investigation into the embodiment of culture in contemporary dance', *Research in Dance Education*, 9:1, pp. 79–96.

Swoboda, V. (2012), 'Troupe to travel Vertical Road without leader', *The Gazette*, 20 January, http://www.montrealgazette.com/entertainment/Troupe+travel+Vertical+Road+without+le ader/6028807/story.html. Accessed 21 January 2012.

Vasudevan, P. (2002), 'Clarity within chaos', *Dance Theatre Journal*, 18:1, pp. 16–19.

Watson, K. (2010), 'Akram Khan: Quest for a way to connect', *Metro*, 13 September, http://www.metro.co.uk/lifestyle/840797-akram-khan-quest for-a-way-to-connect. Accessed 15 September 2010.

Williamson, A. (2010), 'Reflections and theoretical approaches to the study of spiritualities within the field of somatic movement dance education', *Journal of Dance & Somatic Practices*, 2:1, pp. 35–61.

Notes

1   Williamson (2010) gives a concise overview of the current field.
2   Paul Zivkovich was later replaced by Elias Lazaridis (Greece).
3   Salah El Brogy and Ahmed Khemis both performed solos in the Arab Dance Platform as part of Beirut International Platform of Dance 23–26 April 2009.

Notes on Contributors

Glenna Batson (PT, ScD, MA) is professor emeritus of physiotherapy at Winston-Salem State University (USA) and a Fulbright Senior Specialist in dance education. For over three decades, she has correlated theories from contemporary dance, Somatics, human movement science and neuroscience, as educator/lecturer, practitioner, movement coach and performer. Currently an independent lecturer in dance science at Trinity Laban Conservatoire of Music and Dance (London, UK), Glenna was faculty of the American Dance Festival (1986–2013) and Hollins/ADF MFA programme (2004–2013), and remains an internationally recognized teacher in Alexander Technique (qualified 1989). A certified spiritual director (Haden Institute 2002), Glenna infuses her spiritual muse with somatically aware movement, evoking the mutable, transparent, textural and the transcendent.

Susan Bauer (MFA, MA, RSME/T) is a dance and Somatics educator who has taught in both college and community settings over the past 30 years, informed by her extensive background in dance, Authentic Movement, and Body-Mind Centering®, as well as dance anthropology and cultural studies. She serves as adjunct professor in performing arts at the University of San Francisco, and has a private practice in the San Francisco Bay area as a registered somatic movement educator/therapist. Susan is also a Fulbright Scholar to Bali, Indonesia, where she has studied Balinese dance, mask-making and ritual since 1995, and leads tours to Bali in Arts and Spirituality. Susan has been dedicated to the practice of Authentic Movement since 1984, has studied extensively with Janet Adler in California and facilitates Authentic Movement in the United States and Asia. Susan's articles on Authentic Movement and international teaching have appeared in several publications, including *Contact Quarterly* and in the book, *Essays on Authentic Movement*, Volume 2, 2007. She is also the author of *A BodyMind Approach to Movement Education*, which presents her unique curriculum in Experiential Anatomy for teens and young adults. Susan is the founder of Embodiment in Education, a professional training programme for dance/movement educators based on this curriculum; guest faculty have included Bonnie Bainbridge Cohen, Deane Juhan and Caryn McHose. She began her study of Body-Mind Centering® with founder Bonnie Bainbridge Cohen in 1984; other somatic disciplines she has studied include Ideokinesis (with Irene Dowd), Laban/Bartenieff Fundamentals and the Feldenkrais Method. She developed her own form of dance improvisation, called Moving-from-Within™, based on the philosophy of Authentic Movement, that she founded in 1987. Susan served as programme director and core faculty at Moving on Center School for Participatory Arts in California from 2004 to 2009. She has served on the Executive Board of Directors of ISMETA (International Somatic Movement Educators and Therapists Association) since 2012. She holds an MFA degree from the Department of World Arts and Cultures at UCLA, an MALS in Dance and Movement Studies from Wesleyan University, and a BA in Dance from Middlebury College.

Pat Debenham is a professor of contemporary dance and music theatre at Brigham Young University. He is a Certified Laban/Bartenieff Movement Analyst, has been a master teacher for the Utah Arts Council and for fifteen years co-directed Contemporary DanceWorks—a semi-professional modern dance company in Utah. As an artist/educator themes of his scholarship and creative life have focused on dance as a process of personal and cultural discovery, and meaningful embodiment. He is an active presenter in dance, theatre and humanities organizations—ATHE, NAHE, LIMS, CORD, daCi, NDEO and Motus Humanus, and has taught workshops and presented choreography regionally, nationally and internationally. He has published in *Research in Dance Education, NAHE Interdisciplinary Journal, Contact Quarterly, Journal of Dance Education* and most recently in *Dancing Dialogues: Conversations across Cultures, Artforms and Practices* on subjects such as pedagogy, Somatics, spirituality, history and choreography.

Kathleen Parsons Debenham is a professor of dance at Utah Valley University where she founded the Dance Department and has served as dean of the School of the Arts and as associate academic vice president. As a master artist-educator Kathie co-directed the Young DanceMakers at Brigham Young University for more than twenty years and conducted residencies throughout the state for the Utah Arts Council. She received her certification in Laban Movement Analysis from the University of Utah Integrated Movement Studies programme in 1997. Kathie has presented widely on dance education and somatic practices, as well as assessment in higher education. She has co-authored with her husband Pat articles on spirituality in dance and education and varied applications of Laban Movement Analysis. Currently Kathie is focusing on embodied leadership for women in higher education. She and Pat have enjoyed many years of collaboration with family-making at the heart of their dance-making.

Dr Martha Eddy (CMA, RSMT, EdD) is director of the Dynamic Embodiment Somatic Movement Therapy Training (DE-SMTT) affiliated with Moving On Center (www. MovingOnCenter.org) and in partnership with the State University of New York—Empire State College (www.ESC.edu/MALS), housed at the Center for Kinesthetic Education (www. WellnessCKE.net) in New York City. CKE provides somatic movement sessions to individuals of all ages and professional consulting to schools, hospitals and community centres in the use of movement and kinesthetic awareness in education, health and creative endeavours. Martha Eddy is a leading pioneer and authority in Somatics and dance education. Her somatic studies began in 1976 in Laban Movement Analysis and Body-Mind Centering® simultaneously. She quickly began teaching theories of neuro-developmental movement therapy together with Bonnie Bainbridge Cohen and Irmgard Bartenieff in their certification programmes (beginning in 1982). She also undertook a 500-hour training for healers led by minister and psychic Eva Graf. She weaves these diverse spiritual and somatic strands into her teaching as well as her work in communities, developing such diverse programmes as Peaceful Play Programming, Movement for Life dance programmes for people with chronic illnesses, Spiritual Coordination work at the New York Theological Seminary, BodyMind Dancing© and her own ISMETA-approved Dynamic Embodiment training for somatic movement educators and therapists that is affiliated with undergraduate and graduate degree programming.

Sylvie Fortin is full professor at the University of Québec at Montreal, Canada. Her field of specialization includes post-positivist research methods, somatic education, sociocultural study of the body in the domains of health, dance pedagogy and education in the arts. She has published more than one hundred papers in numerous scientific and professional journals. Her diverse research interests have led to further interdisciplinary collaborations notably within the interdisciplinary research centre on biology, health, society and the environment (CINBIOSE). In 2008 Sylvie was author and editor of the book *Danse et Santé: Du corps intime au corps social*, an international collection of authors addressing current issues in dance and health. In 2011, she co-edited a special issue of *Recherches Feminists*, a journal on social inequity in women's health. In 2013, she co-edited a special issue of *Journal of Dance and Somatic Pratices* on Somatics and cultural issues. In the last 10 years, she has received funding from Canadian and Québec research councils for a series of interdisciplinary research projects involving dancer and non-dancers with varying bodily issues. A certified teacher of the Feldenkrais Method of somatic education since 1996, Sylvie has recently been supervising three action research projects conducted with women suffering from eating disorders, fibromyalgia and depression. She is also currently involved in a three-year project founded by the Ministry of Education on embodiment in creative process in the arts in Québec, Canada.

Sondra Fraleigh is a renowned scholar and pioneer in the wider field of Dance Studies and within the historical development of the Somatics movement. For more than 30 years, Sondra has been a leader in the study of movement and dance. She is professor emeritus of the State University of New York, College at Brockport, where she chaired the Department of Dance. Her innovative choreography based in Somatics has been seen on tour in America, Germany, India and Japan. She served as president of the Congress on Research in Dance, and as a Faculty Exchange Scholar for the State University of New York. Her articles have been published in texts on dance and movement, philosophy and developmental psychology. She is the author of five books: *Hijikata Tatsumi & Ohno Kazuo* (2006), *Dancing Identity: Metaphysics in Motion* (2004), *Dancing into Darkness: Butoh, Zen and Japan* (1999),

Researching Dance (1999) and *Dance and the Lived Body* (1987). She has also published many articles and book chapters, including 'Freedom, Gravity, and Grace' in the *Somatics Magazine/Journal of the Mind/Body Arts and Sciences* 22/3 (Fall/Winter 1999/2000), and she received the 'Outstanding Service to Dance Research Award' from the Congress on Research in Dance (CORD) in 2003. She is currently writing a guide book for her unique somatic yoga: *Shin Somatics® Land to Water Yoga,* which will be available soon. Her recent book on butoh will be published by the University of Illinois Press and is now in press: *BUTOH: Metamorphic Dance and Global Alchemy.*

Ninoska Gomez, born in Venezuela, dancer, psychologist, PhD, doctorate in developmental psychology, has studied Body-Mind Centering® since 1982 which inspired her to create the Somarhythms approach for working with inflatable balls and other objects. She was associate professor and researcher at the Physical Education Department of the University of Montreal in Quebec, Canada for 17 years. In 1991 she founded the studio Los Almendros, a retreat centre, a tranquil natural setting dedicated to movement arts and sciences—www.studiolosalmendros—in Playa Cedros between Montezuma and Cabuya, on the southern tip of the Nicoya Peninsula, Costa Rica. There, Ninoska teaches all kinds of movers, professionals, students, educators, families and children and occasionally travels to teach elsewhere in Costa Rica and abroad.

Jill Green (PhD) is a professor of dance at The University of North Carolina at Greensboro. She is director of Graduate Studies, conducts research and teaches Somatics, body studies and pedagogy. In addition, she is a certified Kinetic Awareness® Master Teacher and directs a teaching programme at her studio. Her work is published in a number of journals and books. Dr Green is a Fulbright Scholar (Finland) and former co-editor of *Dance Research Journal.*

Daria Halprin (dancer, poet, teacher and author) is among the leading pioneers in the field of movement/dance and expressive arts education and therapy. Her work bridges the fields of somatic psychology, movement/dance therapy, expressive arts therapy, community-based arts and health education, organizational consultancy, leadership development, social change and performance. Bringing a life-long practice in the arts to her work, published writings include: *Coming Alive; The Expressive Body in Life, Art and Therapy;* contributing author *Expressive Arts Therapy: Principles and Practices, Poesis: Essays on the Future of the Field.* In 1978 Daria co-founded the Tamalpa Institute where she directs training programmes in movement/dance and expressive arts education, consultancy and therapy. She teaches in educational, health and art centres throughout the world.

Linda Hartley (MA, BMCA, SnrDMP, RSMT, CTP Dip Psych) works as a transpersonal and body psychotherapist, a somatic movement therapy trainer and a writer. Based in the United Kingdom, she is founding director of the Institute for Integrative Bodywork and Movement Therapy, through which she has run training programmes since 1990 in Germany, England and currently Lithuania and Russia. She has also taught and practised as a therapist in various settings in the United Kingdom and internationally. With an MA in Somatic Psychology, Linda is author of *Wisdom of the Body Moving, Servants of the Sacred Dream* and *Somatic Psychology*, and editor of *Contemporary Body Psychotherapy: The Chiron Approach*. Her studies in Authentic Movement with Janet Adler deeply inform all her work, and many years of practice in Buddhist meditation give support and inspiration.

Dr Jill Hayes is a researcher, senior accredited (ADMPUK) dance movement psychotherapist, teacher and writer, seeking to encourage the experience of the living imagining body in a variety of education, social and health settings. Jill has worked in residential community settings in Germany, the United States and England seeking to make environments that facilitate stillness and creativity through embodiment and the imagination. Her practice has been applied specifically in residential care for young people, people with life-threatening illness, people with addictions and people with dementia. As private practitioner Jill specializes in working with abuse and loss, entering a woven body/movement-based dialogue with clients to find restorative patterns through movement and image. Jill has taught in the Dance Department of the University of Chichester for 15 years, where she runs a BA Dance Foundation Year in Dance Movement Psychotherapy, coordinates the MA Dance and supervises PhD work. She is currently the co-editor of the journal: *Dance, Movement and Spiritualities*, Intellect Publishers.

Don Hanlon Johnson (PhD) is a professor of Somatics in the School of Professional Psychology and Health at the California Institute of Integral Studies in San Francisco. In 1983, he founded the first graduate degree studies programme in Somatics. He has written several books and journal articles focusing on the role of body practices in social and personal change.

Yvan Joly (MA Psychology) is a psychologist registered in Québec, Canada and practitioner-trainer and educational director of Feldenkrais Professional Training programmes, teaching worldwide. He received his master's in psychology in 1973 from l'Université de Montréal, with a speciality in cognitive science. In private practice since 1983, he applies his expertise in movement and body awareness to issues in the domains of health, sports, education and the arts. Yvan was the co-founder and first president of le Regroupement pour l'Èducation Somatique in Québec. For more than 25 years, he was a lecturer at the Dance Department of L'Université du Québec à Montréal (UQÀM) particularly in a Postgraduate Diploma in somatic education. Yvan Joly has written many articles, both for the community of somatic educators and for the public.

Bradford Keeney (PhD) has served distinguished careers as a pioneer of creative therapy, university professor, social cybernetician, anthropologist of cultural healing traditions, conversation analyst, improvisational performer and foundation vice president. The author of over 40 books, he has conducted fieldwork with the Kalahari Bushmen for nearly twenty years. A display honouring his breakthrough fieldwork and contributions to understanding the origin of human culture is permanently installed as an exhibition in the Origins Centre Museum, Johannesburg, South Africa. He is presently Professor and Hanna Spyker Eminent Scholars Chair, University of Louisiana. Brad is co-founder of The Keeney Center for Seiki Jutsu, dedicated to the teaching and practice of the art of the vital life force.

Hillary Keeney (PhD) is a distinguished scholar, author and practitioner of creative transformation and improvisational performance. Co-founder and director of The Keeney Center for Seiki Jutsu, she is presently Distinguished Visiting Professor in Psychology, Benemérita Universidad Autónoma de Puebla (BUAP), Mexico and Adjunct Faculty in the Creative Systemic Studies doctoral programme at the University of Louisiana. Her scholarship has made contributions to the study of interdisciplinary pedagogy, social cybernetics, creative therapeutic practice and training, ethnographic study of healing traditions, qualitative research of communication, and dance. Her most recent books include *Circular Therapeutics: Giving Therapy a Healing Heart* and *Creative Therapeutic Technique*, both published by Zeig, Tucker, and Theisen, Inc. Dancing since she was a child, Hillary is an avid tango and salsa dancer, having spent six years dancing nightly in the clubs of Los Angeles, California.

Kimerer LaMothe is a dancer, philosopher and scholar of religion, who writes and dances on a farm in upstate New York. After earning a doctorate in religion from Harvard University, teaching at Brown and then Harvard Universities, receiving fellowships for her work from the Radcliffe Institute for Advanced Study and the Center for the Study of World Religions, and writing two books, LaMothe moved with her partner and their children to the country, where she has found ample inspiration for her writing and dancing. She is currently at work on her fifth book, *Earth Within: Why Dancing is a Biological, Ethical, Spiritual, and Ecological Necessity*, and performs regularly in local venues. Her earlier titles include: *Between Dancing and Writing: The Practice of Religious Studies* (2004); *Nietzsche's Dancers: Isadora Duncan, Martha Graham, and the Revaluation of Christian Values* (2006); as well as her two farm books: *What a Body Knows: Finding Wisdom in Desire* (2009) and *Family Planting: A Farm-fed Philosophy of Human Relations* (2011).

Kathleen Melin is the author of *By Heart: A Mother's Story of Children and Learning at Home* (2008), a memoir of progressive education. Her creative work has appeared in *Dust and Fire*, *Feminist Parenting* and *A Woman's Place*.

Helen Poynor is an independent movement artist whose approach has evolved out of 30 years of professional practice. Helen established and runs the *Walk of Life Workshop and Training Programme in Non-stylised and Environmental Movement* based on the Jurassic

Coast World Heritage Site in East Devon/West Dorset UK. She specializes in movement in natural environments, site-specific, autobiographical and improvisatory performance and cross art-form collaborations combining movement with installation, film, text and the visual arts. An internationally recognized movement teacher, director and performer, Helen's early intensive training with Anna Halprin at the San Francisco Dancers' Workshop/ Tamalpa Institute and Suprapto Suryodarmo from Java served as the foundation for the development of her unique approach to non-stylized and environmental movement. She is recognized by Suprapto as a teacher and is a guest associate teacher for Tamalpa UK. Helen is a mentor for a number of established and emerging dancers, community dance practitioners and performers/artists and a visiting professor of performance at Coventry University. She is a registered dance movement therapist (ADMP) and a somatic movement therapist (ISMETA) working with individuals in private practice. Publications include: *Anna Halprin*, Routledge 2004 and 'Wrestling the Slippery Fish' in *Research Methods in Theatre Studies*, Helen Nicholson and Baz Kershaw (eds) Edinburgh University Press 2011 both co-authored with Libby Worth; 'Anna Halprin and the Sea Ranch Collective, an embodied engagement with place' in *Journal of Dance and Somatic Practices* Intellect Books, 1.1; 'Yes, But is it Dance?' in *An introduction to Community Dance Practice* (Diane Amans, ed. Palgrave Macmillan 2008) and 'Dance and Place-making' in *Dancers and Communities,* co-editor with Jacqui Simmonds (Ausdance NSW 1997).

Linda Rabin brings to Continuum more than 40 years of experience in the field of dance and movement education. As a teacher, Linda facilitates individuals and professional artists to realize their personal, creative and performance processes. She is a Canadian dance pioneer who has contributed to the emergence of several generations of dancers in this country. In 1981, Linda co-founded LADMMI (recently renamed École de Danse Contemporaine de Montréal), one of Canada's leading professional schools in contemporary dance training. She is also a certified practitioner of Body-Mind Centering®. An international Continuum workshop leader, Linda teaches in her native Montreal, Canada, Europe, Asia and Israel. She shares her life's passion with people from all walks of life—movement both as art and healing, as a way of life knowledge and spiritual practice.

Dr Sandra Reeve is a movement artist, facilitator and teacher who lives in West Dorset, UK. She teaches an annual programme of autobiographical and environmental movement workshops called Move into Life®, offering a practice in environmental embodiment for performers, community artists, teachers, psychotherapists, arts therapists and health professionals. Sandra is an Honorary Fellow at the University of Exeter, and has lectured in Performance and Ecology and Physical Theatre. She creates small-scale local ecological performances and events, as well as mentoring creative movement projects. She is a movement psychotherapist, offering therapy and supervision in private practice. Sandra first studied with Suprapto Suryodarmo in Java in 1988 and subsequently worked with him intensively for 10 years, based in Java from 1995 to 1998. Their practice together continues to evolve to this day through workshop collaborations in the United Kingdom and in Java. Her first book Reeve, S. (2011), *Nine Ways of Seeing a Body*, Axminster: Triarchy Press has been highly commended internationally as an invaluable resource for students of movement, dance, Somatics, psychology and performance.

Suzanne River is the founder and director of Green River Dance for Global Somatics; School for Somatic Movement Education/Therapy, Bodywork and Energy Medicine, Creator of the modalities—Global Somatics™ Process and Vibrational Aspects™ System. Green River Dance for Global Somatics (GRDGS) is a health resource centre recognized for innovative continuing education, professional trainings, research, therapeutic services and performance. Founded in 1982 by Suzanne River, creator of the Global Somatics™ Process and the Vibrational Aspects™ System, GRDGS is the only USA Midwest somatic school providing a comprehensive curriculum in experiential anatomy, developmental movement and embodiment of the energy field.

Odile Rouquet, dancer and choreographer, has been teaching 'Analysis of the Body in Danced Movement' since 1990 at the National Conservatory of Music and Dance of Paris. In 1977, she received a Fulbright scholarship to study at Columbia University's Teacher's College in New York, where she obtained a Master of Arts in Dance Education. While there, she worked under Irene Dowd who taught her 'Ideokinesis.' After returning to France, she published *Les Techniques d'Analyse du Mouvement et le Danseur* in 1985, followed by *La Tête aux Pieds* in 1991. She was a member of the Scientific Council for the *Larousse Dictionary of Dance*, published in 1999. She also published articles in various journals such as *Théâtre Public and Médecine des Arts*. She is author of *The Creative Gesture*, filmed by Marie-Hélène Rebois and co-produced by the National Conservatory of Music and Dance of Paris and the Ministry of Culture. Artistic director of Recherche En Mouvement, she is responsible for a DVD collection on somatic approaches and artistic creation. She has taught many workshops in France and abroad, working with professionals in as varied fields as dance, circus, marionette and the martial arts.

Ray Eliot Schwartz is coordinador de la Licenciatura en Danza, Universidad de Las Américas Puebla, Departamento de Artes. Co-director Performática: Foro Internacional de Danza Contemporánea y Artes de Movimiento. He is the co-founder of four contemporary dance projects in the southern United States: Sheep Army, The Zen Monkey Project, Steve's House Dance Collective and THEM. He has been guest artist for diverse student populations in communities, colleges and universities in the United States, Indonesia and México. Since 1999, he has represented the integration of somatic movement education and dance practice on multiple occasions as a member of the faculties of the American Dance Festival, Bates Dance Festival, MELT, the ZMP Summer Dance Intensive, the Colorado College Summer Dance Festival and SFADI, among others. Somatic studies include certifications in Body-Mind Centering and the

Feldenkrais Method. Additional studies include Zero-Balancing, Gross Anatomy, Cranio-Sacral Therapy and Traditional Thai Massage. He is a research associate at the Center for Mind Body Movement and has been a guest lecturer at the Institute of Kinesthetic Education. He currently serves as coordinator of the Bachelor of Dance, Universidad de las Américas Puebla, San Andrés Cholula, Puebla, México. He is certified practitioner of Body-Mind Centering, certified practitioner of the Feldenkrais Method, dancer, teacher, choreographer, and arts activist.

Naomi Lefebvre Sell is a senior lecturer at Trinity Laban Conservatoire of Music and Dance, UK. Within the Faculty of Dance, Naomi lectures in choreography, performance and research methods. Originally from Canada, Naomi has gained a Diploma in Dance from Grant MacEwan College; BFA Dance, Simon Fraser University; MA Choreography, Trinity Laban and has recently completed a PhD at Trinity Laban entitled *dharmakaya*: Choreographic process as a means to investigate mindful meditation and creativity. Naomi has performed with the Canadian dance companies Kokoro and Buntingdance and she has received numerous grants and commissions to have her choreographic work presented across Canada, England and in Germany.

Lawrence Smith, past president of the Canadian Society of Teachers of the Alexander Technique, began his study of the Alexander Technique in 1978, when he was an actor studying dance, and trained throughout the 1980s with some of the world's top practitioners of the Alexander Technique. He has taught the Alexander Technique full-time since 1989, directing the Manhattan Center for the Alexander Technique in New York City before moving to Montreal in 1998. Lawrence Smith has been invited by the Montreal Symphony Orchestra to teach for the OSM Standard Life Competition for strings and harp, and he often teaches dancers and musicians at UQÀM. He has twice been a presenter at the International Congress of the F. M. Alexander Technique in Lugano, Switzerland, and he was a presenter at the 2012 American Society for Teachers of the Alexander Technique AGM in New York City.

Celeste Snowber (PhD) is a dancer, poet and educator who is an associate professor in the Faculty of Education in the area of arts education at Simon Fraser University outside Vancouver, B.C., Canada. She has written extensively in the area of arts and embodiment and is author of *Embodied Prayer* and has co-written *Landscapes of Aesthetic Education*. A passionate mentor of graduate students, she focuses her work in the area of embodied ways of inquiry and arts-based research. Celeste continues to create site-specific performances in the natural world, which include dance and poetry in sites near the ocean and is working on a one-woman show entitled, 'Woman giving birth to a red pepper'. Celeste lives outside Vancouver, B.C., Canada and is the mother of three adult sons—all a tribe of artists. Her website can be found at www.celestesnowber.com and her bodypsalm blog can be found at www.bodypsalms.com.

Jayne Stevens is head of dance at De Montfort University, Leicester. In 2000 she was one of the first recipients of a National Teaching Fellowship awarded by the Higher Education Academy. From 2006 until 2010 she was head of pedagogic research for the Centre for Excellence in Performance Arts at DMU. She is currently working with the Akram Khan Company on the development of archival and educational resources.

Tina Stromsted (PhD, MFT, BC-DTR) is a Jungian Analyst and Board Certified Dance therapist with a private practice in San Francisco. Past co-founder and faculty of the Authentic Movement Institute in Berkeley, California, she was also a founding faculty member of the Women's Spirituality Programme at the California Institute of Integral studies (CIIS, in San Francisco), a long-time Core faculty member of the Somatics Programme (CIIS) and group leader at the Esalen Institute (Big Sur, California). Currently she teaches in the Analytic Training Programme at the C.G. Jung Institute of SF, and is Core Faculty in the Marion Woodman/BodySoul Rhythms Leadership Training Programme. She also teaches in the Somatics Doctoral Programmes at SBGI and Pacifica Graduate Institute, the Expressive Arts Therapy Programme at CIIS, the Body Psychotherapy Certificate Programme at ZIST (Penzburg, Germany), Art Therapy Italiana's graduate Dance/Art Psychotherapy Programme (Bologna, Italy), Zentrum fur Ausdruckstanz und Tanztherapie (Expressive Dance & Dance Therapy) in Graz, Austria, and at other universities, conferences and healing centres internationally. Tina's roots in dance and theatre give rise to her life's investigation of the creative process and embodied spirituality. With 35 years of clinical experience, her publications explore the integration of body, mind, psyche and soul in healing and transformation.

Rebecca Weber is an adjunct professor in dance at Richard Stockton College of New Jersey and at Temple University, where she earned an MFA in dance and a Teaching in Higher Education Certification. Rebecca holds an MA with distinction in Dance and Somatic Well-Being from the University of Central Lancashire, where she later served as associate lecturer. As director of Somanaut Dance, her choreography has been presented in Philadelphia, New York, Georgia, Delaware, Canada and the United Kingdom. She has performed for many independent choreographers in Philadelphia, including Eun Jung Choi, Colleen Hooper Performance Projects, Stone Depot Dance Lab, the Naked Stark and others, and is a performing collaborator for Alie and the Brigade. Her research has been published in the *Journal of Dance and Somatic Practices*. She is an associate editor for the *Journal of Dance, Movement, and Spiritualities*, and serves as co-communications director, social media manager, editor and dance critic for ThINKingDANCE.net. www.somanautdance.com.

Sarah Whatley is professor of dance and director of the Centre for Dance Research at Coventry University. Her research interests include dance and new technologies, dance analysis, somatic dance practice and pedagogy, and inclusive dance practices. She led the AHRC-funded Siobhan Davies digital archive project, RePlay, and is currently leading another AHRC-funded project that explores the relationship between dance, disability and the law. She is editor of the *Journal of Dance and Somatic Practices* and is on the Editorial Board of the *International Journal of Screendance*.

Amanda Williamson is Principal Editor of the *Journal of Dance, Movement and Spiritualities* (Intellect), a Visiting Professor at Coventry University and a Visiting Fellow at Chichester University. She founded MA Dance and Somatic Well-being: *Connections to the living body*, at UCLan/New York (approved programme of study by The International Somatic Movement Education and Therapy Association). She has written and developed undergraduate and postgraduate dance degree programmes in the United Kingdom and the United States. Her publications explore the intersections between religion, spirituality, Somatics and dance studies. She is currently heading international publication projects in areas such as: post-colonial discourse, spirituality and epistemologies.